D1191574

CIVIL LITIGATION IN COMPARATIVE CONTEXT

By

Oscar G. Chase
Russell D. Niles Professor of Law
New York University

Helen Hershkoff
Joel S. and Anne B. Ehrenkranz Professor of Law
New York University

Linda Silberman
Martin Lipton Professor of Law
New York University

Yasuhei Taniguchi
Professor Emeritus, Kyoto University Faculty of Law
Professor of Law, Senshu University
Member, Appellate Body, World Trade Organization

Vincenzo Varano
Professor of Comparative Law
Faculty of Law, University of Florence

Adrian Zuckerman
Professor of Civil Procedure
University of Oxford
Fellow of University College, Oxford

Oscar G. Chase and Helen Hershkoff
General Editors

AMERICAN CASEBOOK SERIES®

Mat #40294871

© 2007 Thomson/West
     610 Opperman Drive
     St. Paul, MN 55123
     1–800–328–9352

Printed in the United States of America

ISBN: 978–0–314–15596–2

 *TEXT IS PRINTED ON 10% POST CONSUMER RECYCLED PAPER*

Dedicated to

Understanding Across Boundaries

*

Preface

This book reflects a fortuitous collaboration among its authors. As a group, we teach and practice law on three different continents and have explored civil procedure from a comparative point of view in a number of venues over the past decades. When we realized—through our own teaching experience—that there was no accessible set of materials to support a course in comparative procedure, we decided to fill that gap through our collective effort. We have learned an enormous amount from each other during the ensuing period of discussion and correspondence, and we hope that the fruits of this collaboration resonate throughout the book.

We designed the book in the hope of presenting materials that expose students to the many fascinating varieties of process one encounters in the world's procedural systems. Professors who share our sense of the importance of the transnational study of law may wish to assign it as a supplement to a traditional casebook in an introductory procedure course. We also encourage proceduralists and comparatists to offer a comparative procedure course in the university in which they teach, wherever it may be located. We hope, too, that this book will serve as a brief but adequate guide to scholars, lawyers, and judges who are curious about "how others do it," i.e., how nations other than their own meet the challenge of disputing in the modern world.

Although the book was a collegial product it is important to acknowledge that each of the chapters had one or more primary authors, so we provide those attributions here for the edification of our readers.

Chapter 1: An Introduction and Overview
        Introduction (Oscar Chase and Helen Hershkoff)
          A. The Civil Law System (Vincenzo Varano)
          B. England (Adrian Zuckerman)
          C. The United States (Linda Silberman)
          D. Japan (Yasuhei Taniguchi)

Chapter 2: The Structure of the Legal Profession (Vincenzo Varano)

Chapter 3: Organization of the Courts (Vincenzo Varano)

Chapter 4: Initiating a Law Suit, Defining the Issues, Gathering the Evidence (Adrian Zuckerman)

Chapter 5: Resolving the Case in the First Instance Court: The Trial and Analogous Processes (Oscar Chase)

Chapter 6: Short-cuts to Judgment and Provisional Remedies (Helen Hershkoff)

Chapter 7: Appeals (Adrian Zuckerman)

Chapter 8:   Aggregation of Parties, Claims, and Actions (Helen Hershkoff)

Chapter 9:   Finality and Preclusion (Linda Silberman)

Chapter 10:   Enforcement of Judgments (Yasuhei Taniguchi)

Chapter 11:   Transnational Litigation (Linda Silberman)

Chapter 12:   Harmonization of Civil Procedure: Prospects and Perils (Oscar Chase)

In preparing these materials, we have benefited from our own teaching experience and from the ideas of colleagues throughout the world. Courses in comparative civil procedure have been offered at the New York University School of Law for over a decade and have been taught in a variety of iterations by Professors Chase, Silberman, Taniguchi, and Varano, along with our NYU colleague, Andreas Lowenfeld. Professor Zuckerman has for some years offered a similar seminar at Oxford University; Professor Varano, at the University of Florence; and Professor Taniguchi, at Kyoto University. During the same time period, Professors Hershkoff and Silberman designed and taught a course on American civil procedure to LL.M students from civil law countries—in itself an exercise in comparative procedure.

We also have been fortunate to participate in conferences and workshops on a range of issues involving comparative civil procedure. These include: the 1996 Symposium on Civil Procedure in Comparative Context, organized by New York University School of Law and the Institute of Judicial Administration at the Villa La Pietra; the 2003 conference on procedural reform in comparative perspective at the University of Florence; the 2004 and 2006 conferences and workshops of the American Association of Law School on integrating a transnational perspective into the law school curriculum; the 2006 McGeorge School of Law workshop on Globalizing the Law School and Curriculum; and the annual colloquia of the International Association of Procedural Law.

We all have benefited from the magisterial work of Professors Peter L. Murray and Rolf Stürner on German civil procedure, which enlightened us and served as a helpful model of comparative procedural scholarship. Likewise, in their role as Reporters for the ALI/UNIDROIT project that yielded the Principles of Transnational Procedure, Professors Geoffrey Hazard and Michele Taruffo stimulated much informative writing and discussion about civil procedure in a comparative light. Finally, like all comparativists, we owe an enormous intellectual debt to the late Sir Jack Jacob and Mauro Cappelletti, great scholars who paved the way for all contemporary comparative proceduralists.

We acknowledge the intellectual support of colleagues and friends Jerome Cohen, Norman Dorsen, Rochelle Dreyfuss, Samuel Estreicher, Stephen Loffredo, Andreas Lowenfeld, John Sexton, Marcel Storme, and Frank Upham, in addition to those already mentioned.

We offer thanks for the research assistance of José-Miguel Bello y Villarino, Karsten Behn, Jocelyn L. Burgos, Alexander Dmitrenko, Seth Endo, David Firestone, Susanna Greenberg, Matthew I. Haar, Aryeh Haselkorn, Kayla Gassmann, Jacob Karabell, Kathryn A. Rumsey, Ben Steinbruck, John Sorabji, Catharine Zurbrugg, Barbara Zylberg, and Clara Zylberg.

Radu Popa, Linda Ramsingh, and Mirela Roznovschi provided exemplary library assistance.

John Easterbrook, Richard Kelsey, and Ted Shuttleworth, as well as Yvette Bisono, Jennifer Bernucca, and Robert Gatto, provided essential assistance in preparing the manuscript for publication.

We also thank Louis Higgins of the West Publishing Company for his enthusiastic support of this book from its earliest stages, and Kathleen Vandergon, the West Group Production Editor, for her indispensable assistance.

Professors Chase, Hershkoff, and Silberman acknowledge financial support from the Filomen D'Agostino and Max E. Greenberg Research Fund in connection with this project.

June 12, 2007

*

Summary of Contents

*

Table of Contents

___

Table of Cases

The principal cases are in bold type. Cases cited or discussed in the text are roman type. References are to pages. Cases cited in principal cases and within other quoted materials are not included.

CIVIL LITIGATION IN COMPARATIVE CONTEXT

*

Chapter 1

AN INTRODUCTION
AND OVERVIEW

I. INTRODUCTION

A. WHY TAKE A GLOBAL APPROACH TO THE STUDY OF CIVIL PROCEDURE?

If civil procedure has been part of your law studies, you no doubt focused primarily on how courts resolve private disputes in your nation. We think it is desirable to put the subject into a still broader perspective by introducing you to the procedures used in other nations. As Professors Henry Hart and Albert Sacks famously explained a half century ago:

> [T]he possible variations in particular types of procedures are endless. So also are the variations in the relationships between each type of procedure and the system as a whole. * * * [N]o social question can be intelligently studied without a sensitive regard to the distinctive character of the institutional system within which the particular question arises.[1]

To this end, we have prepared materials that can be studied along with national rules that deal with a functionally similar stage of the litigation process. This brief introductory note will give you some background by sketching out the major differences among the various systems in use throughout the world. We begin by explaining why we think the global method—incorporating international, transnational, and comparative approaches—is useful and by noting a few of the problems that this method inevitably faces.

Good reasons favor taking a global approach to the study of civil procedure. For one, it highlights the reality that procedural systems are the product of choice; there is no universal consensus on how best to serve the values of accuracy, fairness, and efficiency, and even on whether these are the values that a procedural system ought to serve. Exposure to the choices made by some other systems will help you to

---

1. Henry M. Hart, Jr. and Albert M. Sacks, The Legal Process: Basic Problems in the Making and Application of Law 6 (William N. Eskridge, Jr. and Philip P. Frickey eds., 1994).

think critically about your own and will present alternatives to consider. Professor John Langbein, for example, has argued that the American procedural system leaves much to be desired when compared to that of Germany. His article, The German Advantage in Civil Procedure,[2] has prompted a great deal of discussion.[3] More fundamentally, because rules of procedure have political implications—affecting such issues as the enforcement of rights, the distribution of wealth, and the allocation of opportunity—it is important, as the late Professor Mauro Cappelletti argued, to consider a procedural rule's "ideological foundations, its philosophical background, its socio-political impact."[4] We suggest that you consider the consequences for different social sectors and interest groups of the key differences among the procedural systems that are presented.

Second, the study of other procedural systems will let you see more clearly the inter-connection of procedural rules. Professor Andreas Lowenfeld compares the development of a procedural system to the child's game of pick-up-sticks, in that it is very hard to move one piece without disturbing the whole board.[5] This is also what lawyers mean when they refer to procedural systems as a "seamless web." Whether or not a jury is used to decide issues of fact, for example, will affect the way in which the facts of a dispute are investigated and presented, as we will describe below.

Finally, and most obviously, there are pragmatic considerations to taking a global approach to civil procedure, stemming from the increasing internationalization of both the law and the legal profession. In the course of your careers, many of you will be called to represent clients whose interests and needs transcend the borders of your home nation. Whether this means litigating on behalf of human rights, representing a parent in a custody dispute with a spouse in another country, or negotiating a multi-national contract, it will be essential to have some sense of how current or future disputes would be handled in the relevant foreign legal system.[6] Moreover, as stewards of the legal system, you will bear the primary responsibility for making changes to today's procedural system that respond to the needs of a globalized economy. It will be up to you to construct methods for fair and efficient adjudication of disputes involving parties from many parts of the world. In sum, we hope that you find a global approach to the study of civil procedure to be both stimulating and informative.[7]

2.   52 U. Chi. L. Rev. 823 (1985).

3.   See, e.g., Oscar G. Chase, Legal Processes and National Culture, 5 Cardozo J. Int'l and Comp. L. 1 (1997); John C. Reitz, Why We Probably Cannot Adopt the German Advantage in Civil Procedure, 75 Iowa L. Rev. 987 (1990).

4.   Mauro Cappelletti, Social and Political Aspects of Civil Procedure—Reforms and Trends in Western and Eastern Europe, 69 Mich. L. Rev. 847, 882 (1971).

5.   Andreas F. Lowenfeld, Introduction: The Elements of Procedure: Are They Sepa-

rately Portable?, 45 Am. J. Comp. L. 649, 652 (1997).

6.   Those of you interested in human rights litigation might enjoy looking at Laurence Helfer, Forum Shopping for Human Rights, 148 U. Pa. L. Rev. 285 (1999), for a discussion of the impact of different procedural systems on the enforcement of international norms of justice.

7.   See Helen Hershkoff, Integrating Transnational Legal Perspectives Into the First Year Civil Procedure Curriculum, 56 J. Legal Educ. 479 (2006).

B. CATEGORIZING THE WORLD'S LEGAL SYSTEMS AND THEIR PROCEDURES

The world's modern legal systems are for convenience usually divided into two major groupings, the "common law" and the "civil law" countries.[8] The United States is a member of the common law family, like other nations with legal roots in England. Most other countries share the civil law tradition, which originated in the Roman Empire and then spread to Continental Europe. This may have been the result of prior colonialism (as with Latin America) or conscious adaptation from foreign systems (as with Japan and China). Although there are significant differences in the historical development and styles of legal reasoning between the common law and civil law systems, most important for your global appreciation of civil procedure are the differences in the rules that govern disputes in court.

(Please keep in mind the different uses of the word "civil." "Civil" procedure is the process used for typical private disputes such as tort or contract and is distinguished from the procedure used to prosecute crimes. The word "civil" has an entirely different meaning when used to differentiate between the "common law" and "civil law" families. In the latter situation, "civil" refers, as already noted, to the legal system originating in Continental Europe.)

Differences in the rules of civil procedure have led to the controversial division of procedural systems into "adversarial" and "inquisitorial." Commentators often refer to procedure in common law (Anglo–American) countries as "adversarial" because this system vests a good deal of control over the proceedings in the parties and their attorneys, which allows for a sharper clash of forensic skills in the courtroom. Under the civil law system, on the other hand, the process tends to reserve more authority over the law suit to the presiding judge, even including responsibility for questioning witnesses; this prompts the "inquisitorial" label. Many observers emphasize this differential allocation of authority between the parties and the judge as the defining distinction between common law and civil law procedural systems. However, the literature also sharply criticizes this terminology, in part because the categories are imperfect at best—differences between nations within a category can be considerable.[9] Thus, although the United States and England are both "common law" countries with "adversarial" procedural systems, one finds many differences between them.[10] Most notably, the availability of a jury in civil cases, which is common in the United States, has been virtually eliminated in England. In addition, one can point to an erosion of some of the differences between the common law and civil law systems.

---

8. For a discussion of this categorization and of its limitations, see Rudolph B. Schlesinger, Hans W. Baade, Peter E. Herzog, and Edward M. Wise Comparative Law 283–290 (6th ed. 1998) (hereinafter, "Schlesinger").

9. See Mirjan R. Damaška, The Faces of Justice and State Authority 3–6 (1986) (hereinafter, "Damaška").

10. Id. at 5.

Moreover, the words "adversarial" and "inquisitorial" are mischievous in this context in another way: many Continental lawyers deny, sometimes vehemently, that their system is "inquisitorial" in any pejorative sense. They reject any implication that their processes are similar to the infamous "Inquisition" of the medieval Church.[11] And it is certainly the case that the dispute resolution procedures of all modern states share such deep principles as the right to be heard and to present evidence, the right to representation by counsel, and the right to an impartial adjudicator.

Nonetheless, the labels serve as useful shorthand, so long as we recall their limitations. Even Professor Mirjan Damaška, who criticizes too simplistic a reliance on this division, agrees that "the core meaning of the opposition remains reasonably certain. The adversarial mode of proceeding takes its shape from a contest or a dispute: it unfolds as an engagement of two adversaries before a relatively passive decision maker whose principal duty is to reach a verdict. The nonadversarial mode is structured as an official inquiry."[12]

We now turn to brief descriptions of the systems represented by the authors of this book. We begin with an overview of the civil law system, follow that with two "common law" examples—England and the United States—and conclude with Japan, whose system combines elements of civil law and common law procedure. These will help you to better understand the chapters that follow, each of which deals with a different aspect of procedure emphasizing the functions to be served.

II. AN OVERVIEW OF DIFFERENT PROCEDURAL SYSTEMS

A. THE CIVIL LAW SYSTEM

1. *Introduction*

This section sketches the main features of the civil law model of procedure. However, some early warnings are appropriate. Unless we want to fall into stereotypes, it is not correct to let the reader assume that there is only one model of civil law procedure, and that such systems of procedure as, for example, the German and the Italian are just the same. There are as many differences among civil law systems as between the common law systems of England and the United States.

---

11. See id. at 4 (noting that "[t]o Anglo–Americans, * * * the two concepts are suffused with value judgments: the adversary system provides tropes of rhetoric extolling the virtues of liberal administration of justice in contrast to an antipodal authoritarian process").

12. Id. at 3.

The second warning concerns the differences between civil law and common law procedure. In a historical perspective, it may be easy to identify certain key differences between the two, which have contributed to the establishment of two models of procedure. As is well known, the jury trial has informed the common law tradition and explains the main features of that procedure. The concentration, orality, and immediacy of procedure, especially at the proof taking stage, are certainly related to the presence of the jury, as well as a passive role for the judge and the markedly adversarial nature of the proceeding. On the civil law side, no significant lay participation similar to the jury has ever been an important aspect of procedure. The fact finding process has always been entrusted to a professional judge, endowed also with initiative powers; the proceeding, in turn, has been characterized by a piecemeal unfolding, by the predominance of writing, and the lack of immediacy.[13]

If there have been, and there are still, differences, though less and less crucial, the other stereotype to be avoided (as already noted) is that between a common law "adversarial" model and a civil law "inquisitorial" model. By now, a general consensus has developed that the two models are less at odds than they have often been described; that they share the same fundamental principles (independence and impartiality of the adjudicator; right to be heard) and attribute the same purpose to civil procedure—the efficient and just dispatch of private disputes; and that they both stick to a private conception of procedure, based on the principle of party disposition in its various facets. The role of the judge can be more or less active; she can be vested with more or less penetrating powers (and she is certainly more active, and vested with broader powers in the Austrian or German model of procedure than in the Italian or in the common law model—though not in the post–1998 English model).

With the above warnings in mind, we shall try to identify the principal core elements of civil law procedure, especially in comparison with the common law model, through the lenses of German, French, and Italian procedure. Points deserving to be highlighted at this stage in the comparison are the organization of the courts, the judiciary, and the stages of the first instance proceeding, with particular reference to discovery and proof taking, summary and provisional remedies and their role, appeals, and enforcement of judgments. A more in depth treatment will be offered in later chapters.

2. *The Machinery of Justice: Courts and Judges in the Civil Law Tradition*

The machinery of justice in a civil law country reflects a distinctively different approach to the organization of the courts and the judiciary than its common law counterpart.

---

13. On the historical differences between common law and civil law procedure, see Mauro Cappelletti and Bryant G. Garth, Civil Procedure, Ch. 1, at 3–8, XVI International Encyclopedia of Comparative Law (1987).

Civil law systems organize courts based on a plurality of separate court hierarchies, as opposed to common law countries that organize courts on the principle of a single court hierarchy (albeit with some specialized trial courts, such as "family courts"). The "ordinary" courts in civil law countries deal only with civil and criminal matters. However, some civil law countries—Germany, for example—have as many as five court hierarchies: civil and criminal, administrative, labor, social, and financial courts,[14] each with its own trial and appellate courts. In addition, judicial review of legislation is entrusted to an ad hoc constitutional court. In some cases, such as that of France, review is considered to be more political than judicial, since it is vested in a body, the *Conseil constitutionnel*, which has the power to check the constitutionality of statutes prior to their promulgation.

Several reasons help to explain the civil law system's reliance on a plurality of court hierarchies, including a more rigid conception of separation of powers and the search for specialization. The use of a centralized court for constitutional judicial review is further explained by the plurality of supreme courts and the possibility of conflicts among them, the relative weakness of the precedential value of their decisions, and the fact that a career judiciary is not well trained to deal with policy oriented issues.[15] We focus in this section on the system of ordinary courts, which in a civil law country is typically based on the following pattern. The jurisdiction over first instance proceedings is usually distributed between two sets of courts. The jurisdiction of the lower set extends to relatively small claims, but may also cover certain subjects independently from the value at stake. In some countries, the judges vested with this jurisdiction are honorary lay judges, as in Italy since 1991 (*giudici di pace*); in others, such as France (*tribunaux d'instance*)[16] and Germany (*Amtsgerichte*) they are professional judges. Lower courts are distributed all over the country, close to their potential users. In turn, the higher courts of first instance—*Tribunaux de grande instance* in France, *Landgerichte* in Germany, *Tribunali* in Italy—are courts of general jurisdiction, and are generally located in major cities. The prevailing tradition in the civil law has been in favor of adjudicating panels, usually sitting with three judges, even in first instance courts of general jurisdiction. More recently, the trend towards single judge courts

---

14. On the organization of courts, see generally Schlesinger, supra note 8, at 405–413. For Germany, see Peter L. Murray and Rolf Stürner, German Civil Justice, especially Chapter 4 (2004); for Italy, see Vincenzo Varano, Machinery of Justice, in Introduction to Italian Law 99–124 (Jeffrey S. Lena and Ugo Mattei, eds., 2002); for France, see Jean Vincent, Serge Guinchard, Gabriel Montagnier, and André Varinard, Institutions Judiciaires (6th ed. 2001) (hereinafter "Vincent"); Loïc Cadiet, Civil

Justice Reform: Access, Cost, and Delay. The French Perspective, in Civil Justice in Crisis 291–346 (Adrian A.S. Zuckerman, ed., 1999).

15. For a comparative discussion of the different models of judicial review, see the seminal book by Mauro Cappelletti, Judicial Review in the Contemporary World (1971).

16. At first instance there are special civil courts which are staffed exclusively (*tribunaux de commerce:* commercial courts), or at least in part (labor courts:

seems to be taking foot, as in Italy, where the *Tribunali*, since 1998, sit as a three judge panel only in more serious or complicated cases.

There are two levels of appellate courts. The intermediate courts of appeal sit as three judge panels, and are generally distributed on a regional basis. Appeal normally involves a full review of the case and is not limited to questions of law. The supreme court sits, though not invariably, in the capital city, and reviews appellate judgments only for errors of law. Contrary to the common law idea of a supreme court, the highest courts in the civil law are large bodies divided into several divisions, civil and criminal, and staffed by several dozens of judges (140 in Italy, for example). More judges are attached to a division than are necessary to decide a case.

Turning to the judges themselves, the feature that makes the comparison with the common law particularly interesting is that judges in the civil law system are career judges. There may be variations from one country to the other—in France attendance of the *Ecole Nationale de la Magistrature* is required prior to seeking admission to the judiciary through competition; in Germany, a higher degree of university education has to be achieved through the second "Staatsexam"; in Italy, the national competition is open to law graduates—but the fundamental common principle is that the judiciary is one of the careers open to law graduates, who, once admitted, proceed toward the upper levels of the hierarchy on the basis of seniority as well as merits. Professional judges in a civil law country typically number several thousand (roughly 9,000 in Italy, 7,000 in France, and over 20,000 in Germany[17]). Interestingly enough, public prosecutors are part of the judiciary (and counted in those numbers, at least in France and Italy), even though the prevailing rule is that of a career separation between judges and prosecutors.[18] Judges in a civil law country are basically civil servants. Moreover, although civil law constitutions tend to provide for strong guarantees of judicial independence, these provisions do not inevitably apply, or apply to the same extent, to investigating judges and prosecutors, who in France and Germany are agents of the executive power.

3. *The Proceeding of First Instance*

The most significant feature of the traditional structure of the first instance proceeding ("trial" stage) is that it is not divided sharply into a pre-trial and trial stage, as is the case in the Anglo American model. Rather, the proceeding unfolds in a piecemeal fashion through an indefinite series of hearings without any "precisely defined boundaries between preliminary, evidentiary and plenary proceedings."[19] In these

conseils de prud'hommes; agricultural tribunals: *tribunaux paritaires des baux ruraux*; social security disputes: *tribunaux des affaires de sécurité sociale*) by lay judges representative of the opposing interests, according to a long standing tradition.

17. For Germany, Murray and Stürner, supra note 14, at 38, give the figure of 20,969 judges and add that "[I]n the entire world Germany is number one both in the

absolute number of professional judges employed as well as the number of judges per capita"; for Italy, see Varano, supra note 14, 113; for France, see Vincent, supra note 14, at 589.

18. The new Italian law on the judiciary makes it very difficult to move from the bench to the prosecution, and vice versa.

19. Murray and Stürner, supra note 14, at 14. For a short description of the tradi-

hearings, the case is "prepared," attempts at settlement are effected, evidence is offered, admitted and eventually presented, pleadings and briefs are exchanged, amended, and filed with the court. The judgment of the court will usually be rendered in written form, some time after all the evidence has been taken and the final briefs have been submitted.

However, a number of civil law countries show an important trend of reform towards adjudicative concentration, aimed at meeting a demand for the rationalization of litigation and the reduction of delay. This reform favors a two stage procedural model directed respectively to the preparation (and possibly the anticipated solution) of the case, and then to the proof taking and decision, concentrated, if possible, in one single main hearing. This assumes that there has been a sufficient clarification and narrowing of the issues in the preparation stage, which is increasingly being pursued by strengthening the role of the judge. Many procedural rules in the various countries have this goal in mind. Section 139 of the German Code of Civil Procedure vests with the judge the duty to clarify the issues, while sections 272–273 give her the power to order a series of activities in view of a carefully prepared main hearing. Under the French code, the court may ask clarifying questions from the parties pursuant to articles 8, 13, 442 of the Nouveau Code de procédure civile (NCPC); in turn, the code takes away from the parties the direction of the process, and transfers it to the judge who can mold it according to the difficulty of the particular case (arts. 3, 763–764 of the NCPC).[20]

Contrary to the American practice of notice pleading, the system of fact pleading prevails in the civil law model of procedure. This means *e.g.* that the initial statement of claim must illustrate the facts at issue, the legal arguments supporting the claim, and must include offers of evidence, oral and written, and the prayers for relief. The reliance on fact pleading diminishes the need for American-style discovery devices, which are largely absent from civil law procedural systems. However, the approach to discovery is changing in the civil law world, prompted by the search for concentration as well as the pursuit for justice on the merits. So, for instance, art. 10 of the French Civil Code, as amended in 1972, introduces a general duty of procedural disclosure, by providing that "each party must bring her contribution to the administration of justice in view of the ascertainment of the truth," and that the party who defaults without justification can be forced to fulfill her duty through the imposition of an *astreinte*.[21] In turn, art. 11 of the *dispositions liminaires*

tional system of litigation in Italy, which, although frequently modified in the 1990's has not solved the problem of delay seriously affecting the administration of justice, see Vincenzo Varano, Civil Procedure Reform in Italy, 45 Am. J. Comp. L. 657 (1997).

20. For France, see Frédérique Ferrand, The Respective Role of the Judge and the Parties in the Preparation of the Case in France; for Germany, see Gerhard Walter, The German Civil Procedure Reform Act

2002: Much Ado About Nothing?, both in The Reforms of Civil Procedure in Comparative Perspective 7, 67 (Nicolò Trocker and Vincenzo Varano, eds., 2005).

21. The *astreinte* is an order of the court to the judgment debtor to pay a monetary penalty to the creditor for failure to comply with the judgment. What is particularly interesting is that the remedy has been judicially created and developed, and that it has been recognized by the Law no.

of the NCPC reaffirms the duty of the parties to contribute to the proof-taking, and specifies that it will be sanctioned as far as the disclosure of documents is concerned. Even more interestingly, French courts have interpreted art. 145 of the NCPC so as to facilitate the securing of documents from the opponent or a third party before, and independently from, litigation, even beyond the need to conserve or establish facts upon which a solution of the dispute may depend.[22] A similar trend is evident in Germany, where the 2001 amendments of §§ 142 and 144 have granted the courts the power to order parties or third parties to disclose documents in their possession on the simple basis that they may be relevant to the issues raised for the decision—a nearly revolutionary reform with regard to the German tradition of procedural law.[23]

In some respects, the principle of party presentation dominates the civil law of evidence as much as it does the common law. Under civil law procedural codes, the judge does not conduct official investigation: the court, with limited exceptions, is confined to those proofs which have been offered by the parties.[24] Notwithstanding this crucial similarity, there are still significant differences between the civil law system's approach to evidence and that taken in common law systems.

First, the civil law of evidence historically has relied on the preponderance of written over oral evidence. Indeed, documents do not even need to be introduced as evidence: they prove their own existence unless they are specifically challenged. If they are drafted by a notary, they are defined as public acts and constitute legal proof, until and unless they are challenged by means of a very complicated procedure with criminal connotations. The importance of written evidence is further enhanced in some countries, such as France and Italy, which restrict, though with qualifications, oral proof of contracts involving more than a certain value.[25]

Secondly, the civil law of evidence is based on the principle of the free evaluation of evidence, which at least in theory should not leave much room to the exclusionary rules, so typical of the common law tradition of the jury. The principle, however, has its exceptions. We have already mentioned the strong evidentiary value of documents. We can

72–676 of July 5, 1972. See J. Bearsdley, Compelling Contract Performance in France, 1 Hastings Int'l and Comp. L. Rev. 93 (1977).

22. See Gerard Chabot, Remarques sur la finalité probatoire de l'art. 145 NCPC, Dalloz, 2000, at 256.

23. See Walter, supra note 20, at 75–77; Murray and Stürner, supra note 14 at 639–640.

24. See Michele Taruffo, Civil Procedure and the Path of a Civil Case, in Lena and Mattei, supra note 14, at 168. The author refers to Italy, but the statement

applies as well to the civil law. See Schlesinger, supra note 8, at 462. Under German law, the judge has more power, but she "will likely hear the evidence which the parties have designated with respect to any factual issues. Within the scope of the factual assertions by the parties the court has the power to order production of relevant documents and tangible things on its own motion * * *. The court is restricted to witnesses named at least by one of the parties." Murray and Stürner, supra note 14, at 14.

25. See generally Schlesinger, supra note 8, at 443–468.

now add the so called decisory oath (*giuramento decisorio*), an ancient and seldom-used relic still surviving in some jurisdictions (France and Italy among them) according to which if a party accepts the challenge of the opponent to swear to the truth of a favorable material fact under the threat of religious and moral sanctions in case of perjury, the oath will determine the outcome of the case.[26] Also to be mentioned is the rule that parties cannot be heard as witnesses though they can make probative statements by way of confessions and oaths. The disqualification of the parties is a firm, though criticized, principle of the civil law codes. In general, however, the parties can be examined by the judge, and their unsworn statements will be freely evaluated.[27] Thirdly, there are substantial differences concerning the examination of witnesses. The civil law does not provide for cross-examination. All the questions are asked by the judge. The parties are entitled to suggest further questions, but they will be actually addressed by the judge.[28]

A final difference concerns expert evidence. The prevailing rule in the civil law countries requires a court appointed expert, as compared to the partisan expert system of the common law jurisdiction. The parties, if the court decides to appoint an expert—who is considered an auxiliary of the court rather than a witness—may in turn appoint their own. The latter, however, are not considered a source of evidence.[29]

Once the proof taking stage is concluded, and the parties have had a final round of briefs and oral arguments, the court will render its decision. For common lawyers, it will be interesting to know that the judgment (i.e. the dispositive part of the decision) is invariably accompanied by the reasons for the decision—which are considered everywhere as a requirement of fairness. This requirement is in some countries enshrined in the Constitution.[30] The style of the decision varies significantly from one country to the other, but two features are common and noteworthy. First, even if the decision has been rendered by a panel, neither separate opinions, if any, nor the votes of individual judges are disclosed—and this can be probably explained by the status of the judge as a civil servant. Among the notable exceptions are the decisions of all Spanish courts, and those of the German Constitutional Court. Second, as compared to the common law, the emphasis is on law rather than on the facts, to the point that legal journals often omit the publication of the "facts" of the case—and this has to do with the deductive nature of the judicial process in the civil law.

4. Special Proceedings

The procedural codes of the civil law area provide for a number of special proceedings to be used in particular cases. In Italy, for instance,

---

26. See Taruffo, supra note 24, at 171, who adds that the oath may also be initiated by the court in two cases: "When there is some evidence of a fact but the court thinks that it should be supported by a sworn statement" (*giuramento suppletorio*), or when it may be useful to determine the value of something (*giuramento estimatorio*).

27. See the monumental two volume work by Mauro Cappelletti, La testimonian-

za della parte nel sistema dell oralità (1962).

28. See Schlesinger, supra note 8, at 457–460.

29. See Taruffo, supra note 24, at 172–173. The rule is the same throughout the civil law, with England coming close under the new Rules of Procedure.

30. See, e.g., the Italian Constitution, art. 111 para. 6.

labor disputes and landlord-tenant cases are handled through a stream-lined procedure aiming "at a quicker and more effective disposition of cases."[31]

Other types of special procedures are used very frequently for the collection of debts, whenever the claim is not likely to be seriously contested: the Italian *procedimento di ingiunzione* and the German *Mahnprozess*[32] are important examples of summary proceedings addressed to solve very quickly and effectively questions of that kind. If the debtor wishes to contest the order of payment issued summarily by the court, she will have to initiate an ordinary proceeding.

Provisional remedies aimed at preserving the status quo, and/or at assuring some kind of temporary relief until a final judgment is entered are available within the civil law as much as in common law jurisdictions. Prominent among them is the French *référé*. Traditionally, it is a provisional measure which can be granted by the judge in cases of urgency and in the absence of a serious question (NCPC, art. 808) in order to prevent irreparable harm, protect assets, etc. The code, however, as amended in 1985 and 1987, has introduced other forms of *référé*, authorizing the judge to grant an advance payment on a claim (*référé-provision*), or to order the performance of obligations (*référé-injonction*), as long as the claim is not seriously contested, while the requirement of urgency has been dropped. As a consequence, resort to *référé* procedure is used very frequently, and litigation is often discontinued once the order—which is subject to enforcement in the same way as a judgment—has been granted.[33] As Fréderique Ferrand has aptly pointed out, the *référé* has become a " 'safety valve' for a judicial system overloaded with many cases."[34]

5. Appeals

First instance judgments are subject to appeal as of right in most if not all jurisdictions, and in most cases. The right of appeal has no

---

31. Taruffo, supra note 24, at 161.

32. As to the Italian *procedimento di ingiunzione*, "[it] is available to the creditor with written proof of his or her right to monetary payment or to the delivery of movable goods. In such cases, the creditor may obtain from the court a decree *inaudita altera parte* * * *. If the debtor thinks that it has been wrongly issued, the order may be attacked in subsequent proceedings". Taruffo, supra note 24, at 161. Sergio Chiarloni, another noted Italian proceduralist, points out to the importance of the ingiunzione procedure: "Every year in Italy courts issue more ingiunzione decrees than judgments after ordinary proceedings (617,-179 injunctions as compared to 350,936 judgments in 1992)". See Sergio Chiarloni, Civil Justice and its Paradoxes: An Italian Perspective, in Zuckerman, supra note 14, at 272.

The *Mahnprozess*, or statutory warning procedure, "can be used to get prompt en-forcement of claims for the payment of money which are not likely to be in dispute. Using preprinted forms creditors can cause their debtors to be served with warning notices (*Mahnbescheide)* and notices of impending execution (*Vollstreckungsbescheide*) that will ultimately support executions if timely objections are not filed by the debtors." A simplified procedure also exists for claims based solely on documentary evidence, such as checks (*Urkundenprozess, Scheckprozess*)." See Murray and Stürner, supra note 14, at 18.

33. On the *référé* procedure, see generally Loïc Cadiet and Emmanuel Jeuland, Droit Judiciaire Privé 408–416 (5th ed. 2006). See also Wallace R. Baker and Patrick de Fontbressin, The French *Référé* Procedure—A Legal Miracle?, 2 Miami Y.B. Int'l L. 1 (1992).

34. See Ferrand, supra note 20, n. 2.

constitutional basis anywhere, but it is so deeply rooted in tradition as to be considered a part of the fundamental guarantee of a fair procedure. Appeal normally involves a full review of the case and is not limited to questions of law. The scope of appeal is traditionally very broad, and may extend to new facts not asserted below, new defenses and new evidence not introduced during the first instance proceeding. Though the scope of appeal has been limited in recent years,[35] the comment can still be made that it may be "considered as a continuation of the first instance proceedings rather than as a totally separate review",[36] i.e., a "second instance" proceeding.

According to tradition, appeals to the court of last resort may also be taken as of right. Review can be in the form of "cassation" or that of "revision." In any case, it is limited to errors of law. Under the "cassation" model, originating in France at the time of the Revolution, the Supreme Court (*Cour de Cassation* in France, *Corte di Cassazione* in Italy) either affirms the judgment from below, which then becomes final, or quashes it. In the latter case, the court cannot ordinarily render a judgment of its own, but must remand the case for a new decision to a different court on the same level as the court which rendered the judgment that has been quashed. Under the "revision" model, of German origin, the court is instead allowed to decide the case on the merits.

Although supreme courts have also the power and the duty to assure the uniformity in the interpretation and application of the law, they lack the discretionary case selection power which allows their common law counterparts to effectively perform that function. As a consequence, review tends to be considered simply another opportunity to present one's case, and thus a "third instance." This means, in turn, that thousands of appeals are brought every year to the supreme courts, and that they render thousands of decisions, which lack the precedential value attached to decisions of the House of Lords or the Supreme Court of the U.S. Only in recent years have some legal systems such as France, Germany, and Spain introduced filters aimed at reducing the caseload and backlog of their supreme courts, so that they can perform more properly their role.

Decisions of the highest courts are not subject to other appeals. In Germany, however, an appeal may lie to the Federal Constitutional Court against decisions which are alleged to violate a fundamental right protected by the Federal Constitution (*Bundesverfassungsbeschwerde*).[37]

The European Court of Justice and the European Court of Human Rights, often referred to as the "Strasbourg Court," have played increasingly important roles. The former has jurisdiction over the European Union; the latter concerns those countries which have signed the European Convention for the Protection of Fundamental Rights, and include

---

35. In Italy, for instance, the law of November 26, 1990, no. 353 has reformed significantly the intermediate appeal. First, it has provided that, as a rule, the first instance judgment is immediately enforceable. Secondly, the reform has somewhat limited the scope of the appeal, and prohib-ited the introduction on appeal of new defenses and new evidence: See Varano, supra note 19, at 671.

36. Murray and Stürner, supra note 14, at 16.

37. Id., at 408–417.

nearly all European countries including Russia and Turkey. Courts of the European Union countries may—or must, if they are the court "against whose decision there is no judicial remedy under national law"—refer issues concerning the interpretation of European Law to the European Court of Justice, whose decisions will be binding on national courts.[38] On the other hand, parties who allege violations of the European Convention may apply to the Strasbourg Court for relief against their own government, after having exhausted all available administrative or judicial appeals in the signatory state.[39]

6. *Enforcement of Judgments*

The general rule is that final judgments are automatically enforceable. Judgments subject to appeal are also immediately enforceable, though a security may have to be posted.[40] If the judgment is not complied with, the judgment creditor will seek compliance in court, opening an execution proceeding which is everywhere complicated, and somewhere—as in Italy—slow and ineffective.[41] Execution of money judgments is directed against the property (chattels, real estate, and intangible property) of the judgment debtor, which will be sold at the latter's expense in order to satisfy the judgment creditor. Enforcement of judgments not for money, and in particular decrees for specific performance, is supported by coercive measures in Germany and France, but not in Italy, where, as a consequence, it is very difficult to enforce them.[42] The difference between German and French law is that according to the former the fine imposed on the recalcitrant judgment debtor goes to the state (§ 890 ZPO), while the French *astreinte* accrues to the judgment creditor.[43]

7. *The Performance of the Civil Law Procedural Model: A Tentative Assessment*

Having sketched out the civil law model of procedure, we attempt here an assessment of its performance. We start from the premise made at the outset: just as there are differences among the various procedural systems that share the civil law model, so there are differences from the perspective of actual performance.

As to Germany, for instance, a recent authoritative treatise in English has statements of the following kind: "German civil justice appears to be working well at fulfilling its assigned role of vindicating private legal rights and applying the norms of law to resolve civil disputes. Some have even suggested that it is working too well, namely

---

38. See art. 234 (formerly art. 177) of the European Treaty.

39. The decision by the ECHR is binding on the petitioner, the government of the country against which the case has been taken, and the courts of that country. The Court may render a declaratory judgment to be implemented through national judicial relief or may grant damages.

40. See, e.g., Murray and Stürner, supra note 14, at 446 (Germany).

41. See Taruffo, supra note 24, at 177–179.

42. Ibid.

43. For an exhaustive comparative treatment, see Schlesinger, supra note 8, at 736–744, especially at 743.

that its relatively low cost and high efficiency are actually fostering litigation and causing citizens to resort too readily to the courts."[44] To the other extreme is Italy, whose procedure is characterized by such a pathological delay as to warrant the statement: "The Italian civil process is largely useless to citizens who ask for justice."[45]

Statistical data confirm the above statements. They indicate that in Italy an average of almost ten years is needed for the final determination of a civil dispute through first instance, appeal, and review by the *Corte di cassazione*. This figure explains the countless decisions rendered by the European Court of Human Rights against Italy for the violation of the right to a reasonable duration of proceedings (art. 6, para. 1 of the European Convention).[46] France and Germany fare incomparably better with regard to delay. In France, Frédérique Ferrand reports an average duration in 2001 of 9.1 months before the court of first instance of general jurisdiction; 17.7 months before the *Cour d'appel* and 24.8 months before the *Cour de Cassation*.[47] Even more impressively, in Germany, the average duration in 1998, of a first instance proceeding before the *Landgericht* was 6.7 months; of an appellate proceeding before the *Oberlandesgericht*, 8.5 months; while the *Bundesgerichtshof* disposed in "less than 6 months in 30% of the cases and less than a year in 70% of the cases."[48]

From the point of view of costs, the civil justice systems which we have briefly discussed can be commented upon favorably. Once again, a statement by Murray and Stürner may be quoted to illustrate the situation in Germany and to some extent in other countries as well: "* * * the German system offers parties access to justice at relatively modest cost. The division of labor between judge and lawyers and the effect of the statutory fee schedule and fee shifting regime combine to moderate the parties' overall costs to conduct litigation in German courts."[49] Furthermore, in Germany and to varying degrees in other civil law countries such as France and to a lesser extent, Italy, a rather sophisticated system of state funded legal aid contributes to attenuate the economic barriers to access to justice for its low income citizens. At the same time, legal cost insurance schemes are becoming rather common, which in general reimburse the policy-holder's costs for their attorney's fees as well as the opponent's legal costs in case of defeat.[50] Finally, we may ask how the civil law and common law processes compare with respect to producing judgments that accurately reflect the facts in dispute. On this score, the American reliance on lay juries whose verdicts are unsupported by any offering of supportive reasons is suspect in the minds of civil law jurists. Similarly criticized is the passivity of the

44. Murray and Stürner, supra note 14, at 19.

45. See Chiarloni, supra note 32, at 264.

46. See Varano, supra note 14, at 111–112.

47. See Ferrand, supra note 20, at note 30.

48. See Murray and Stürner, supra note 14, at 82–83.

49. Id., at 19.

50. For Germany, see id., at 116–125; for France, see Cadiet and Jeuland, supra note 33, at 43–44.

American judge, who rarely acts to remedy the inequality of "litigation arms" when one party enjoys enormously greater resources than another. On the other hand, common law jurists are uncomfortable with the relative passivity of the civil law attorney at the trial and the absence of vigorous cross-examination of witnesses. Moreover, the lack of probing, lawyer-driven pre-trial discovery in the civil law world may prevent the proverbial "smoking gun" from coming to light. Since the accuracy of any sui generis dispute can never be tested scientifically, we urge the reader to explore these arguments in the light of the detailed materials that follow.

B. THE COMMON LAW SYSTEM—ENGLAND

1. *Introduction*

Litigation in England is largely governed by the Civil Procedure Rules 1998 (the "CPR").[51] Practice Directions (PD) supplement the rules, which are intended to clarify and elaborate the rules or provide detailed directions for practitioners engaged in litigation. The rules must be interpreted and applied in accordance with the overriding objective of enabling the court to deal with cases justly (CPR 1.1). Dealing with a case justly includes ensuring that the parties are on an equal footing; saving expense; dealing with the case in ways which are proportionate to the amount of money involved, the complexity of the issues and the financial position of each party; ensuring that it is dealt with expeditiously and fairly; and allotting to it an appropriate share of the court's resources, while taking into account the need to allot resources to other cases.

2. *Outline of a Litigation in England*

a. **Pre-action Protocols**

Persons contemplating litigation are required to engage in a pre-action dialogue with their likely adversaries. This requirement is imposed by pre-action protocols, which are designed to help litigants appreciate the desirability of resolving disputes without litigation, to enable them to obtain the information they reasonably need in order to determine whether they have a case, and to lay the ground for expeditious conduct of proceedings. Different protocols are designed for particular types of actions. They set out codes of best practice, which the parties are expected to follow as soon as a dispute is likely to give rise to litigation.

---

51. The rules are statutory instrument, or delegated legislation. They are drafted by the Civil Procedure Rules Committee, in accordance with the authority conferred by the Civil Procedure Act 1997, §§ 1 and 2, on the Civil Procedure Rule Committee. The power to make rules "is to be exercised with a view to securing that the civil justice system is accessible, fair and efficient" (§ 1(3)). Section 4 of the 1997 Act empowers the Lord Chancellor "to amend, repeal or revoke any enactment to the extent he considers necessary or desirable in consequence of * * * section 1 or 2, or * * * [the] Civil Procedure Rules". Since 1999, the CPR apply to civil proceedings in both the County Courts and the higher courts.

The personal injuries pre-action protocol, which deals with one of the more common types of claims, includes the following provisions. A plaintiff who contemplates litigation must write a letter of claim to the defendant and to the defendant's insurer, in which sufficient information must be given to enable the defendant and his insurer to assess their potential risk. The letter must include details of the accident, a description of the nature of the injuries and an outline of financial loss. The defendant is required to acknowledge receipt within 21 days of the posting of the letter of claim. Thereafter, he has three months within which to investigate the claim and state his position. If the defendant denies liability, he must give reasons, including mention of any alleged contributory negligence, and accompany his response with material documents. The parties may require information from each other.

Before proceedings commence the court has no power to intervene if parties fail to comply with their pre-action duties, but the court has ample powers to deal with serious failures to comply once proceedings are under way. Failure to comply with protocols may be taken into account when giving case management directions or granting extensions of time. Most significantly, the court must take into account this factor when determining costs (CPR 44.3(4), (5)(a)). The fact that uncooperative conduct may have serious costs consequences provides a potent incentive for adopting reasonable attitudes. The pre-action protocols and the culture of co-operation to which they give tangible expression have changed the character of English litigation for the better.

b. Commencing the Proceeding

The bringing of legal proceedings normally involves two steps: (1) the issue of a claim form in an appropriate court, and (2) its service upon the defendant. These processes serve distinct functions. A process of commencement marks the formal start of the legal process, the precise time of which is important for a number of purposes. Principal amongst them is the need to determine whether the claim has met any relevant limitation period, beyond which the claim becomes time-barred. The commencement process must be capable of being carried out unilaterally, simply, and quickly. By contrast, notification requires communication to another party. Unlike commencement, it is not just a matter of formality. It is a fundamental requirement of justice that proceedings should be brought to the notice of the affected parties.

The main method of commencement is the CPR 7 claim form, which is applicable in the majority of claims. A claim form identifies the plaintiff and the defendant. It instructs the defendant to satisfy the plaintiff's claim or, alternatively, to acknowledge service of the claim form on an attached form and state whether he intends to contest the plaintiff's claim. The defendant is warned that unless he satisfies the claim or returns the acknowledgment stating that he intends to contest the claim, the plaintiff may obtain a default judgment without further notice to the defendant. The claim form must contain a concise statement of the nature of the claim and include a description of the remedy that the plaintiff seeks.

c. The Defendant's Response

The defendant need do nothing until he has received the particulars of the claim. Thereafter, the defendant has broadly speaking four options: to admit the claim, to contest the jurisdiction, to contest the claim on the merits, or to do absolutely nothing. If he does nothing, the plaintiff will in most instances be able to obtain a default judgment.

A defendant who wishes to defend all or part of a claim must file a defence. The particulars of the claim provide the reference point for the defence. The defendant's response has to address the points made in the particulars of the claim. Accordingly, the defendant must state which allegations in the particulars of claims he denies, which he admits and which he is unable to admit or deny but which he requires the plaintiff to prove. A defendant who fails to admit allegations that are plainly true may be penalized in costs. Where the defendant denies the plaintiff's allegations, he must state the reasons for his denial; and if he intends to advance a different version of events from those stated by the plaintiff, he must set out his own version. A defendant who fails to deal with an allegation is taken to admit that allegation.

The claim form, the particulars of claim, and the defence are known collectively as statements of case. In most cases, the exchange of particulars of claim and of defence should be sufficient to join the issues. But in some cases a reply to the defence may prove necessary, as where the defendant has gone beyond a denial of the plaintiff's grounds for the claim and has alleged new facts in support of his defence. A reply must be used only for dealing with matters that could not have been addressed in the particulars of claim. No statements of case may be served beyond the reply, without leave of the court. Such leave is unlikely to be given, save in exceptional circumstances.

Statements of case must be verified by a statement of truth (CPR 22.1). A statement of truth is an affirmation by the person making the statement that he believes that the facts stated in a document are true.

d. Disposal of the Case Without Trial

The vast majority of actions that are commenced are disposed of without trial. Most of these are settled by agreement between the parties while others are struck out or disposed by summary judgment. Only a tiny minority (under 2%) are decided by trial. The reasons for the high settlement levels are largely due to the high cost of litigation. Formal methods of disposal without trial are intended to ensure that the scarce resources of the courts are not wasted on disputes that do not require the employment of the complex and expensive trial procedures.

Default judgment. A plaintiff who has not received a response from the defendant may apply for a default judgment. A plaintiff applying for a default judgment must show that particulars of claim have been served on the defendant; that the defendant did not file an acknowledgment of service or a defence and that the time for doing so has expired; and that the defendant has neither satisfied the claim nor returned or filed an admission.

A defendant may apply to the court that entered a default judgment to have the judgment set aside. Setting aside is a matter of right where the default judgment was not properly entered, otherwise it is a matter of discretion. If the defendant applies promptly and demonstrates a real prospect of successfully defending the claim, the court would normally set aside the default judgment.

Striking out. Where a party advances a groundless claim or defence it would be wasteful to put the case through the trial process. The court has therefore the power to strike out a statement of case if the statement of case discloses no reasonable grounds for bringing or defending the claim. Unlike a default judgment, striking out under this rule is a decision on the merits. It may be challenged only by means of appeal.

Summary judgment. The summary judgment procedure enables litigants with a clear and unanswerable case to obtain judgment without having to negotiate the normal procedural hurdles. Summary judgment is available to defendants as well as plaintiffs. It may be given against a defendant or a plaintiff, if the court considers that the party has no real prospect of succeeding and there is no other compelling reason why the matter should be disposed of at a trial. Accordingly, the procedure is suitable for cases where it can be easily demonstrated that one or other of the parties has no seriously arguable case.

e.   Interim Remedies

An interim order is a measure ordered by the court before final determination of the dispute for the purpose of achieving some procedural end or regulating the parties' conduct pending litigation, without finally deciding the issues in dispute. An interim order may provide protection for rights pending litigation, such as an interim injunction to restrain a defendant from pulling down a building that is subject to dispute.

Whether the court grants or refuses an application for an interim injunction it inevitably runs a risk of harming rights. If the court grants a plaintiff an interim injunction and he fails to establish his claim at the trial, the defendant's rights will have been harmed in the meantime. Similarly, when a court refuses to grant an interim injunction and the plaintiff establishes her rights at the trial, the plaintiff's rights will have been harmed in the meantime. Given that both pre-trial interference and forbearance can result in harm to rights, the court should follow a course most likely to protect rights. The method adopted by English law to this end is known as the "balance of convenience," or the "balance of justice." The plaintiff's need for protection must be weighed against the corresponding need of the defendant to be protected against injury resulting from his having been prevented from exercising his own legal rights.

The balance of harm that lies at the heart of the interim injunction jurisdiction hinges on two factors: the likelihood of harm occurring and its magnitude. The court must assess the applicant's chances of establishing the alleged right (because if he has no right he can suffer no harm), the probability that this right will suffer irreparable harm, and the magnitude of such harm. The court must then assess the probability and magnitude of irreparable harm that the respondent would suffer if an injunction were granted and he goes on to obtain a favourable judgment at the trial. Lastly, the court must strike a just balance between the competing claims to protection from irreparable harm pending litigation.

A plaintiff applying for an interim injunction must give an undertaking to the court to pay any damages which the defendant may sustain and which the court considers that the applicant should pay. By giving an undertaking in damages the plaintiff accepts the responsibility for the respondent's losses as the quid pro quo for obtaining the interim injunction.

A party who wishes to obtain compensation must apply to court for the enforcement of the undertaking. If the court considers that there are good reasons for doing so, the court would order an enquiry as to damages, at which the party would have to prove the loss that he suffered as a consequence of the interim injunction.

Notice of an application for an interim injunction must normally be given to the defendant. However, a without notice application may be justified on grounds of unavoidable necessity. This may happen where there is urgency and no time for adequate notice, or where there is a risk that on receiving notice the defendant would take precipitate action designed to defeat the applicant's rights. An applicant for a without notice injunction must persuade the court both of an imminent threat to his interests and of the necessity to forego notice to the respondent. A without notice order will normally be of short duration, until a hearing can be held to reconsider the application in the presence of both parties. A person who applies for a without notice injunction is under an obligation to make full and frank disclosure of all material facts, including those that favor the opponent. Failure to discharge this duty is a very grave matter.

In England, there are no formal means of discovering in advance of judgment the defendants' creditworthiness. Therefore, plaintiffs run a risk that by the time they obtain judgment, the defendant would be left with no means of satisfying it, and the investment in litigation would have been wasted. However, plaintiffs may obtain some form of security in advance of proceedings, if they can establish that there is a real risk that the defendant will dissipate his assets in order to evade enforcement of judgment. The order is know as a freezing injunction. A freezing injunction restrains the defendant from removing his assets from the jurisdiction or from otherwise dealing his assets wherever they may be.

A freezing injunction does not affect the rights to the frozen assets and does not give the plaintiff any precedence over other creditors with respect to the frozen assets. Obedience to the order becomes obligatory as soon as the person concerned has been notified of the existence of the order. Disobedience of freezing injunction amounts to contempt of court. A defendant who is subject to a freezing injunction may apply to court for an order allowing him to use frozen funds for normal living expenses, paying pre-existing debts, and legal expenses. A plaintiff obtaining a freezing injunction must provide an undertaking in damages, which will enable the court to order compensation to the defendant in the event that the latter suffers undue harm as a result of the injunction.

The court may make an interim payment order directing a defendant to pay the plaintiff a sum of money on account of any damages, debt or other sum (except costs), which the court may award against the defendant in final judgment. The procedure seeks to ensure that a plaintiff with a clear right to a money judgment is not kept out of what is the money due to him by the necessity of quantifying the exact amount to which the defendant is liable. An early payment is particularly desirable where the plaintiff is in need of funds in order to obtain treatment or avoid hardship. An interim payment order may be made only where the defendant has already admitted liability, or been found liable in a court judgment, or the court is satisfied that, if the claim went to trial, the plaintiff would obtain judgment against the defendant from whom the interim payment is sought for a substantial sum of money.

f. Case Management

The court is endowed with management powers and compliance powers. The former are used to control the conduct of litigation by means such as setting timetables, directing the pre-trial preparations, and regulating the manner of the trial. Compliance powers enable the court to deal with party failure to comply with process requirements. In addition to the compliance powers contained in the CPR, the court has an inherent jurisdiction to protect its process from misuse and abuse. These powers are designed to deal with non-compliance with procedural requirements and can only impose procedural sanctions, such as the striking out of a case or forbidding a litigant from calling a witness. These powers must be exercised in accordance with the overriding objective. Lastly, the court has powers to enforce orders that impose obligations such as an order restraining a defendant from removing a disputed object or dissipating his assets. Such orders are enforceable by the sanctions for contempt of court, i.e., imprisonment of up to two years or unlimited fine.

Case management powers are used for matching process to dispute, i.e., to obtain a satisfactory correlation between the needs of individual cases and the process adopted for their resolution. Process matching is done at both the macro and micro level. At the macro level, there are three different procedural tracks for dealing with cases: the small claims track, the fast track, and the multi-track. The court determines allocation to the appropriate track. The small claims track, which is normally intended for money claims up to £5,000, is meant to provide a simple and cheap method for resolving run of the mill disputes. The fast track is designed for mid-range cases, of between £5,000 and £15,000, where the trial can be held within 30 weeks from commencement and can be concluded in one day. The multi-track procedure is reserved for the really serious or difficult cases, which require closer case management attention. At the micro level, the court has the power to give directions concerning the management of individual cases, which is used to ensure that the process employed is proportionate to the requirements of the case, regardless of the track.

CPR 1.4(2) states that the "court must further the overriding objectives by actively managing cases." It spells out the aims of active case management to include encouraging the parties to co-operate with each; identifying the issues at an early stage; deciding promptly which issues need full investigation and trial and accordingly disposing summarily of the others; deciding the order in which issues are to be resolved; fixing timetables; considering whether the likely benefits of taking a particular step justify the cost of taking it; and giving directions to ensure that the trial of a case proceeds quickly and efficiently.

The court has limited but important powers to control evidence. CPR 32.1 states that the court may control the evidence by giving directions as to the issues on which it requires evidence; the nature of the evidence which it requires; and the way in which the evidence is to be placed before the court. The court may exclude otherwise admissible evidence if it is disproportionately expensive or time-consuming.

g. Pre-trial Disclosure

Modern English procedure has embraced a "cards on the table approach," which seeks to ensure that parties to a dispute are able to find out as much as possible about each other's case and as early as possible, so that no party is taken by surprise and the court is appraised well before the trial of the evidence and arguments. A variety of measures exist for this purpose.

Parties have a right to obtain from each other documents that are directly relevant to the issues in the case. In many situations documentary disclosure may be obtained even before commencement of proceedings. Where there is a real prospect of litigation, potential parties may seek an order compelling potential adversaries to disclose directly relevant documents so as to enable them to assess the advisability of litigation. Relevant documents may also be obtained from non-parties in advance of proceedings. In the fast track and multi-track, disclosure directions are normally given at the allocation stage or as a result of a case management conference.

The process of disclosure is composed of two distinct steps. The first, disclosure, consists in simply providing a list of all the relevant documents in the party's possession. The second, inspection, involves allowing the party to whom a document has been disclosed an opportunity to inspect it. The court has discretion in determining the range of disclosure and may limit it to what it considers reasonable proportions. Reasonableness depends on factors such as the number of documents involved, the nature and complexity of the proceedings; the ease and expense of document retrieval; and the likely contribution that documents found as a result of search are likely to make to the determination of the issues.

The court has power to order the search and seizure of relevant documents that are in the hands of the defendant. A search order may be made without notice and before service of originating process on the defendant, but only if there is a risk that defendant would destroy evidence. A search order directs the defendant to permit authorized persons to enter the defendant's premises in order to search, inspect, or take away items described in the order. A search order does not authorize forcible entry. But a refusal to allow entry and to comply with the requirements of the order may amount to contempt of court.

Unlike in the United States, the parties cannot compel strangers to the litigation to provide oral information in advance of the trial. There are limited exceptions to this principle, such as disclosure of the identity of a tortfeasor, or the whereabouts of missing funds.

A party who wishes to call a witness at the trial must serve on all other parties a written statement by the witness, which contains the evidence that the witness will be invited to give at the trial. Witness statements normally stand in place of evidence in chief, so that at the trial the witness will not have to repeat his written statement but will only be subjected to cross-examination.

The parties may rely on expert reports only with the permission of the court. The court may limit the number of experts that a party may call. It may also require opposing experts to produce a joint report in which they identify the agreed issues and the disputed ones. The court may order that the parties submit an issue to a joint expert. All experts owe a duty to assist the court to get to the truth.

There are a number of matters that are excluded from the obligation of disclosure or, indeed, from the obligation to testify. One of the most important exceptions concerns matters covered by legal professional privilege. Thus, communication between lawyers and their clients for the purpose of obtaining legal advice or preparing for litigation are privileged, as are communications by the lawyer or the client with nonparties for the purpose of litigation. The privilege confers immunity from disclosure. A further prominent privilege is the privilege against self-incrimination. It entitles any person (party or witness) to refuse to provide information that may incriminate that person. Communications between the parties in the course of settlement negotiations are privileged, and may not be used in evidence. This privilege is known as the "without prejudice" rule.

h. Trial

The trial is the final and most visible stage of the litigation process. With few exceptions, trials are held before a judge sitting alone (without a jury). The trial is continuous: once it has started it will not normally be interrupted before its conclusion. At the trial, the parties present their evidence, probe the opponent's evidence, and present their arguments. This process is largely oral.

In the past, a sharp division existed between the pre-trial and the trial stages. The former consisted of a series of different procedural steps undertaken by the parties at various time intervals without much court interference. The materials gathered by the parties would be seen by the court for the first time at the trial. Today, the court will familiarize itself with the documents, witness statements, and parties' arguments before the trial hearing. There would be therefore no need to present these materials at the trial. Witnesses would not normally give evidence in chief, but will only be offered for cross-examination. Expert evidence would be limited to written reports and cross-examination. Much of the trial hearing is now devoted to the clarification of difficult points and to commenting on matters that the judge designates. It is therefore possible to say that the final adjudication process is already under way well before the trial hearing has opened.

i. Appeal

Subject to very few exceptions, there is no longer in England appeal as of right. An appeal is only by court permission. Permission may be sought from the court that delivers the judgment. If such an application has not been made, or if it has been rejected, the appellant is entitled to apply to the appeal court for permission. The application procedure is non-adversarial, in the sense that the respondent does not have to be involved. An appeal court will normally consider the application on the basis of written materials without a hearing. If permission is refused without a hearing, the appellant may renew his application at a hearing before the appeal court. A decision to grant or refuse permission to appeal is final and may not be appealed.

An appeal consists of a review of the judgment of the lower court. An appeal is confined to a scrutiny of the lower court's decision. The appeal court does not normally hear evidence or entertain points that were not raised before the lower court. As long as the lower court did not commit an obvious mistake of fact, or an error of principle, or follow a seriously defective procedure, the appeal court will not disturb its decision.

j. Costs

The various aspects of litigation costs occupy a central place in the English administration of civil justice. Disputes as to who should bear the costs or the calculation of the recoverable costs can give rise to litigation, which could be more extensive and costly than the litigation over the merits of the underlying dispute.

There are two general principles governing costs recovery. First, the award of costs is in the court's discretion. The court has therefore discretion whether to order costs and to determine the amount of recoverable litigation costs. Second, the court will normally order the unsuccessful party to pay the reasonable costs that the successful party incurred. However, in deciding whether to order costs recovery and how much to order the court will take into account not only success in the litigation but also the parties' conduct during the litigation and the extent to which they were helpful and cooperative with towards other parties and the court. The court may deny a successful litigant his costs, or even order him to pay the opponent's costs, if it considers that the litigant pursued litigation in an obstructive or oppressive manner or unnecessarily protracted or complicated it.

Litigation costs in England tend to be very high because lawyers are normally paid by the hour, without an upper limit and regardless of outcome. However, litigants may obtain some form of protection from costs by making a binding settlement offer. Two examples will illustrate how this works. A defendant who is sued for $100,000 may offer the plaintiff $60,000 in full settlement and pay this sum into court. If the plaintiff takes the money, the litigation is at an end and he is also entitled to his costs. If the plaintiff refuses but fails to recover more than $60,000, the plaintiff will have to pay the defendant's litigation costs from the time of the offer. A plaintiff who fails to beat a defendant's offer will therefore end up having to pay two lots of lawyers' fees, which could well wipe out his entire recovery. A plaintiff can also make an offer to settle. In our example the plaintiff may offer to accept $80,000. If the defendant declines and the plaintiff obtains more than that sum at the trial, the defendant will have to pay enhanced interest on the plaintiff's costs and on the sum awarded to the plaintiff. Offers to settle (also known as CPR 36 offers) figure prominently in any serious litigation.

Contingency fees U.S. style are not allowed, but instead a system of conditional fees is in operation. Under a conditional fee agreement (CFA) a lawyer agrees to charge the plaintiff nothing if the plaintiff is unsuccessful. But if the plaintiff is successful, the lawyer will be entitled to recover his normal hourly fees from the defendant plus a success fee of up to 100% of the hourly fees. The success fee is also recoverable from the defendant. When entering into the CFA, the plaintiff normally takes out an insurance policy against the risk of having to pay the defendant's costs. The premium of this policy is also recoverable from the unsuccessful defendant. In practice, lawyers offer representation on a CFA basis only where plaintiffs have a strong case, such as in claims for personal injuries arising from road accidents.

C. THE COMMON LAW SYSTEM—THE UNITED STATES

1. *Introduction*

When discussing "procedure" in the United States, one must keep in mind that the United States has a federal system of government in which power is shared between the fifty states of the union and the federal government. Each of the states and the federal government has its own system of courts. Typically there are three tiers—a trial court, an intermediate court of appeals, and a supreme court—although in some state systems there are only two tiers. In the federal system, the trial courts are called district courts and the intermediate courts (responsible for a geographic region known as a circuit) are called courts of appeals. The highest court is the Supreme Court of the United States. The Supreme Court functions as a final appellate authority not only over cases brought in the federal courts but also over cases brought in the state courts that raise issues of federal law. The state courts have plenary authority to hear cases involving any matter not exclusively reserved to the federal courts. Within a particular state system, there may be specialized courts, such as criminal courts or family courts as well as courts of general jurisdiction. The federal courts have limited authority, however, and can only hear cases where jurisdiction is expressly conferred by federal statute and falls within the judicial power of the United States as defined in the Constitution. In certain areas, such as bankruptcy and copyrights/patents, federal statutes have made the jurisdiction of the federal courts exclusive. But it is the state courts that hear most cases, and almost 98% of all civil litigation takes places in the state courts. An unusual feature of American courts, both state and federal, is that any trial judge or appellate court has the authority to review the constitutionality of a statute or of other governmental actions. Unlike many other systems there is no special constitutional court that has exclusive jurisdiction over such issues.

The Federal Rules of Civil Procedure set forth the procedure for cases brought in the federal courts. The state courts have their own set of procedures, although some states have either adopted the Federal Rules for cases in their courts or promulgated rules quite similar to the Federal Rules. In a few instances, there are some distinctive departures,[52] but it is nonetheless appropriate to discuss a general system of procedure that operates in courts in the United States.[53]

---

52. For example, California has successfully implemented a fast track system in its state courts, and Arizona has adopted fee shifting offers of judgment, judicial evaluation by litigants and use of pro-tem judges. See William W. Schwarzer, Comment on Burbank and Silberman, 45 Am. J. Comp. L. 705, 705–706 (1997).

53. For another overview, see Outline of a Lawsuit, in Linda Silberman, Allan Stein, and Tobias Wolff, Civil Procedure: Theory and Practice 1–12 (2d ed. 2006).

2. *Overview of a Lawsuit in the United States*

a. Investigation and Fee Arrangements

A client contemplating litigation will usually consult with an attorney. Unlike the English system, there are no formal pre-action protocols imposed on the lawyer, but a lawyer in the U.S. system does have a professional obligation under professional codes of conduct to ascertain that the client has in fact suffered a wrong that gives rise to a legal obligation capable of redress by a court. The attorney interviews the client to learn the client's version of the facts, and then conducts legal research to determine whether the client has a viable claim. In addition to the ethical rules of professional responsibility governing the conduct of lawyers, the procedural rules in federal courts[54] and in many state courts may impose a formal certification requirement upon an attorney to state that the lawyer has conducted an investigation into the facts and the law prior to filing suit.

The lawyer will make some arrangement with the client for payment of the fee. Unlike the "loser pays" rule typical in most other judicial systems, in the United States each side generally pays for its own attorneys' fees whether the party wins or loses.[55] In some cases, particular statutes may permit prevailing parties, often limited to plaintiffs, to recover their attorneys' fees from the other side. In addition, a "contingent fee" is a common method of financing litigation in the United States. Under this arrangement, a client agrees to pay the attorney a percentage of any recovery should the plaintiff win, but has no responsibility for payment should the plaintiff lose.

b. Choice of Court

Whether the plaintiff decides to sue in a state or federal court will be in part a function of the allocation of subject matter jurisdiction between the state and federal systems. In some circumstances, the plaintiff may have a choice between state or federal court, whereas in other situations, the matter may lie within the sole competence of one or the other. Also, if suit is brought in a state court, a defendant, in limited circumstances, may be able to move the case to federal court. In addition, in the United States, a plaintiff may have a choice as to the particular state of the United States in which to bring suit. Often, plaintiffs may desire to sue in their home state if they can obtain personal jurisdiction over the defendant, but other factors—including backlog and caseload, choice of law rules, or particular procedural rules, such as unanimous or non-unanimous jury verdicts—may influence a plaintiff's selection of the court.

---

54. See, e.g., Fed. R. Civ. Proc. 11.

55. One notable exception in the United States is Alaska, where there is a general two-way "loser pays" statute.

c. Commencing the Proceeding and Serving the Defendant

An action is usually commenced by the filing of a complaint or a summons. In some jurisdictions, the summons will be brief and reveal only that a lawsuit has been initiated; in others, the summons will be more elaborate and give a short synopsis of the type of claim that the plaintiff is asserting. In those jurisdictions where a complaint rather than just a summons is required to commence a lawsuit, the complaint will contain allegations of the plaintiff's claim against the defendant. Depending upon the particular jurisdiction, the complaint may be relatively sparse, merely stating the nature of the legal obligation and requesting relief[56]; alternatively, the complaint may provide a more detailed account of the events giving rise to the claim and specifying the nature of the damages or other relief.[57] In some circumstances, the plaintiff may be able to seek certain types of "interim" relief, such as a preliminary injunction or a temporary restraining order, if it appears that plaintiff will suffer imminent harm or that the defendant may remove assets during the proceedings. In extreme cases, such an order may even be granted *ex parte*.

Typically, either the summons, or the summons and complaint, will be served upon the defendant. Service can be made in a variety of ways. The traditional method is personal service, whereby a judicial official or private person authorized by law will personally deliver the summons and complaint to the defendant. Today, most judicial systems permit service to be made through the mail, requiring that the defendant return a signed receipt acknowledging that service has been made.

d. Defendant's Responses

Once the defendant has been notified of the lawsuit, the defendant has a number of possible responses. The defendant may attempt to have the case dismissed without taking a position on the facts by filing a dispositive motion to have the suit dismissed on either procedural or merits grounds. For example, the defendant may offer an objection to the particular court in which the action is filed by making a motion to dismiss for lack of personal or subject matter jurisdiction or venue; or defendant may believe that under the applicable law, no viable claim has been asserted and may move to dismiss the action for failure to state a claim. Alternatively, the defendant may choose to raise these objections as defenses to be included in the answer. In the answer, which serves as the defendant's response to the complaint, the defendant will either admit or deny the allegations of the complaint as well as raise any specific affirmative defenses that defendant has to the complaint. In

---

56. See, e.g., Fed. R. Civ. Proc. 8, requiring a statement of the court's jurisdiction, a "short and plain statement of the claim showing that the pleader is entitled to relief," and a demand for judgment for the relief sought.

57. The most common type of relief is a request for money damages. The plaintiff may also seek an injunction, which is an order by the court that the defendant either perform a particular act or refrain from engaging in certain conduct.

addition, the defendant may assert a counterclaim against the plaintiff, alleging claims that the defendant has against the plaintiff. In some jurisdictions, if the counterclaim is closely related to the plaintiff's claim it must be asserted or it will be waived.[58]

The pleading stage of an American lawsuit has a limited role to play in the ultimate framing of issues in the litigation. The later stages of the pretrial process, specifically case management in the context of discovery, do a more robust job in illuminating the nature of the dispute between the parties.

e. Case Management and Pretrial Discovery

Unlike civil law systems where civil litigation proceeds along a continuum, a lawsuit in the United States is bifurcated into pretrial and trial phases. The pretrial phase sets the stage for the trial and it includes not only the pleadings and motion practice discussed above but also case management and pretrial discovery. The pretrial phase of litigation is subject to judicial oversight and case management. Case management has become an important element of procedural reform in the United States[59] and includes a variety of devices, such as pretrial conferences, pretrial orders, and sanctions. In addition to certification requirements imposed upon lawyers with respect to pleadings and motions and discovery requests and objections, other procedural rules have sought to confirm the authority and underscore the responsibility of trial judges to actively manage the pretrial process. For example, a revision of Rule 16 of the Federal Rules of Civil Procedure dealing with pretrial conferences sends a message that judges should take command of the pretrial process to move cases along and to help effectuate settlement.[60] In addition to requiring an early pretrial scheduling order, the Rule identifies the specific issues that should be addressed by the court and the parties, including the formulation and simplification of issues, the control and scheduling of discovery, restrictions on expert testimony, and the possibility of settlement. Indeed, the vast majority of civil cases are settled before reaching a trial.

One of the significant features of the American legal system is the ability of a litigant to obtain relevant information and documents from the opposing party and from third persons. Traditionally, most discovery in courts in the United States was adversarial—that is, a party would produce information only in response to a request by the opposing party. More recent reforms in discovery practice, both in the federal courts[61]

---

58. See, e.g., Fed. R. Civ. Proc. 13(a).

59. See Stephen B. Burbank and Linda J. Silberman, Civil Procedure Reform in Comparative Context: The United States of America, 45 Am. J. Comp. L. 675, 678–683 (1997).

60. See David Shapiro, Federal Rule 16: A Look at the Theory and Practice of Rulemaking, 137 U. Pa. L. Rev. 1969 (1989).

61. For a discussion of the reforms under the Federal Rules, see Burbank and Silberman, supra note 59, at 678–683; Carl Tobias, Congress and the 2000 Federal Civil Rules Amendments, 22 Cardozo L. Rev. 75 (2000).

and in some state systems[62], have produced rules that impose obligations of mandatory initial disclosure upon the parties, whereby each party is required to produce certain types of information without a specific request by his adversary. The required disclosures encompass names of persons likely to have "information that the disclosing party may use to support its claims or defenses," copies of, or the location of, documents that the disclosing party may use to support its claims or defenses, computation of damages sought by the disclosing party, and any relevant insurance coverage.[63] Later in the pretrial process, other disclosures relating to expert testimony and other trial witnesses may be required.[64] In addition, other adversarial discovery devices may be used to supplement information obtained through the initial disclosures; these include interrogatories, depositions, requests for production of documents, medical examinations, and requests for admission. Certain of these devices—depositions and production of documents—may be used to obtain information from non-parties to the lawsuit when a subpoena is issued for attendance or production. The propriety and extent of these discovery devices is subject to the control of the court. Moreover, recent discovery reforms in both state[65] and federal courts[66] have imposed various limitations on the number and length of certain types of discovery. Also, in the federal system and some state systems, lawyers must certify that their discovery requests, responses, and objections are warranted and not unreasonable given the context of the particular case; and violators will be subject to sanctions.[67] Many of the discovery devices used in the United States, such as interrogatories and exchange of documents, are found in other common law systems. The oral deposition, however, is more unusual. In the United States, a deposition—an examination of a witness under oath—may usually be taken of "any person",[68] although a subpoena is required to compel the attendance of a nonparty.[69] That contrasts with the approach in other common law countries where depositions, if appropriate at all, are directed only to a party[70] or when

62. See, e.g., Alaska R. Civ. P. 26; Ariz. R. Civ. P. 26.1(a); Ill. S.Ct. R. 222(d); Utah R. Civ. P. 26(a) (1). For an excellent survey of discovery practice reforms in the state courts, see Seymour Moskowitz, Rediscovering Discovery: State Procedural Rules and the Level Playing Field, 54 Rutgers L. Rev. 595 (2002).

63. See, e.g., Fed. R. Civ. P. 26(a) (1).

64. For example, the Federal Rules require that within 90 days of the trial, a party must disclose to the other side the identity of any person who it will call as an expert, to be accompanied by the expert's report. See Fed. R. Civ. Proc. 26(a) (2); and within 30 days of the trial disclose the names of witnesses and identification of documents to be used at trial. See Fed. R. Civ. Proc. 26(a) (3).

65. See Moskowitz, supra note 62, at 613, 617–618.

66. In the federal courts, for example, leave of court is required if more than ten depositions are proposed (Fed. R. Civ. Proc. 30 (a)(2)(A)), or if more than 25 interrogatories are to be served (Fed. R. Civ. Proc. 33). Also, unless authorized by the court or stipulated by the parties, a deposition is limited to one day of seven hours (Fed. R. Civ. Proc. 30(d)(2)).

67. See, e.g., Fed. R. Civ. Proc. 26(g).

68. See Fed. R. Civ. Proc. 30.

69. See. Fed. R. Civ. Proc. 45.

70. In Canada, depositions are called "examinations for discovery." There is a right to examine each individual party and one representative of each corporate party. Non-parties can be examined in Canada only when it can be shown that the party seeking information cannot obtain it in another way and that it would be unfair to

that rule is relaxed, to a non-party in very limited circumstances.[71] In the United States, the deposition is primarily used to elicit information in preparation for trial, but deposition testimony may also be used at trial for limited purposes, such as to impeach a witness's trial testimony[72] or in special circumstances, such as if the witness is unavailable at trial.[73]

The scope of discovery in courts in the United States has, since the enactment of the Federal Rules of Civil Procedure, been very broad but in recent years the trend is toward a narrowing construction. A common formulation is that a party may seek information regarding any matter, not privileged, that is relevant to subject matter of the action.[74] Relevant information need not be admissible at the trial if the discovery appears reasonably calculated to lead to the discovery of admissible evidence.[75] The broad scope of discovery also allows each party to require other parties to allow inspection of any and all documents that meet the open-ended test of relevance as well as to obtain documents under that standard from non-parties to the lawsuit. Privileged information is protected from discovery. The important attorney-client privilege, for example, protects communications between attorney and client for the purpose of securing legal advice. Most courts in the United States also offer a more limited protection for materials produced by the lawyer as part of the legal preparation of the case. Thus there is a presumptive privilege for all materials "prepared in anticipation of litigation," and such material is discoverable only upon a showing that the party has substantial need of the information and cannot obtain it through alternative means.[76]

f.　Summary Judgment

One of the perceived advantages of broad discovery practice is to allow the parties to evaluate the strengths and weaknesses of their respective cases based on information that will be produced at trial, and ideally induce a settlement between the parties. Moreover, if, at the close of discovery, one of the parties does not have a sufficient evidentiary basis to support a verdict or judgment in its favor, it would be futile to proceed to trial. Accordingly, procedural systems in the United States provide for a method of "summary judgment" to dispose of a case without a full trial when it is determined that there is "no genuine issue

---

proceed to trial without this information. See Stephen N. Subrin, Discovery in Global Perspective: Are We Nuts? 52 De Paul L. Rev. 299, 306–307 (2002).

71.　For example, in Canada, if a witness is unlikely to be available for trial, a party may apply to the court for permission to take an oral deposition for use at trial. Id., at 306 n. 34. See also, in England, CPR 34.8.

72.　See Fed. R. Civ. Proc. 32(a)(1).

73.　See Fed. R. Civ. Proc. 32(a)(3).

74.　Fed. R. Civ. Proc. 26(b)(1) permits a party to obtain discovery of any matter, not privileged, that is, relevant to the "claim or defense of any party", and in addition, for good cause, to obtain discovery of any matter relevant to the "subject matter of the action". In some state systems, relevance to the "subject matter of the action" and "not privileged" is all that is required.

75.　See Fed. R. Civ. Proc. 26(b)(1).

76.　See, e.g., Fed. R. Civ. Proc. 26(b)(3).

as to any material fact and that the moving party is entitled to a judgment as a matter of law."[77] In determining whether a party has satisfied its burden of producing evidence that would entitle it to proceed to trial, the court considers the discovery already conducted as well as affidavits of other potential witnesses. With evidence in this form, of course, the court does not assess the strength of the evidence or the credibility of the statements but only whether the evidence presents a "genuine issue of material fact" that should be resolved at a full trial. Either of the parties, or both, may move for summary judgment.

g. Trial

Following the pretrial process, if a case has not been otherwise resolved by summary judgment or settlement, it will be set for trial. The fact finder will be a judge or a jury. In the federal courts, the Seventh Amendment of the Constitution assures a right to trial by jury for any controversy over twenty dollars, where the suit was one that could be brought "at common law." This reference to "common law" relies on the historical distinction between "law" and "equity" to determine whether a party has a constitutional right to a jury trial in the United States today. Because in England a jury was available only in the common law courts and not in equity (the court of Chancery), a jury trial right will attach only if the asserted claim or counterclaim is one that has an historical common law analogue. Most federal cases involving claims that seek damages do give rise to a right to a jury trial. Many state constitutions contain similar provisions, but the jury trial right in the state court is tied to an interpretation of the state and not the federal Constitution. In order to effectuate the "right" to a jury trial, a party must affirmatively make a demand for a trial by jury, or the "right" is waived. In practice, however, most cases are resolved by pretrial motions or are settled, and only about two percent of all federal civil cases are decided by a jury.

At one time, a federal civil jury required twelve members and a unanimous verdict. The Supreme Court of the United States later held that the Seventh Amendment permits less than twelve jurors in a federal civil case. However, unanimity is still required for a federal jury. The size and unanimity requirements in state courts are different, and non-unanimous jury verdicts are permitted in many states. When a jury has been demanded, a panel of prospective jurors will be selected. *Voir dire* of prospective jurors is conducted in order to determine whether a juror has any prior knowledge of the case or involvement with the parties or any particular bias that might affect the outcome of the case, and if so, the juror can be discharged "for cause." A party may also move to strike a juror without cause—via a peremptory challenge—but such challenges are limited. In federal courts, the judge usually conducts the *voir dire*; in many states, the task is for the attorneys for the parties.[78]

---

77. See, e.g., Fed. R. Civ. Proc. 56(c).

78. See generally Stephan Landsman, The Civil Jury in America, 62 Law and Contemp. Probs. 285, 292–293 (1999).

The trial in courts in the United States is conducted by the attorneys for the parties. The trial is continuous with the presentation of both oral and documentary evidence by both sides. The plaintiff proceeds first; plaintiff's lawyer calls witnesses to testify in open court by direct examination.[79] Defendant's lawyer then conducts cross-examination of each witness. These examinations are often followed by redirect and re-cross. The responsibility for introducing evidence either through witnesses or documents is with the lawyers. The judge generally intercedes only when asked to rule on an evidentiary objection, although on occasion, particularly when no jury is involved, may take a more active role and pose a question to the witness.

Largely because of the institution of the jury, there are elaborate rules of evidence governing the admissibility of evidence at trial. However, if the opposing counsel does not raise a timely objection to the admissibility of particular evidence, the evidence will be admitted, any objection having been waived. A striking aspect of American trial practice is the approach to expert testimony.[80] In courts in the United States, experts usually appear as a witness on behalf of one of the parties; the expert will have been chosen, prepared and compensated by the party. The result is often a "battle of experts," with conflicting testimony to be resolved by the trier of fact, often the jury. The rules of evidence in many jurisdictions allow a judge to appoint a neutral expert, but most judges do not exercise the privilege.

Before the case goes to the jury, counsel will make closing arguments. The judge will instruct the jury on the legal rules it is to apply. A jury will usually render a general verdict, merely stating whether the verdict is for the plaintiff or the defendant, and if for the plaintiff, the amount of damages. With a general verdict, the jury does not give reasons for its decision—a feature that other countries have been critical of, leading some civil law systems to refuse to enforce a U.S. judgment based on a jury verdict. In the discretion of the court, a jury can be asked to render a special verdict that will require the jury to respond to particular questions, either in lieu of or in addition to a general verdict.

h. Taking the Case From the Jury and Post-Verdict Motions

Certain procedures unique to American civil procedure are a direct function of the use of juries in the American system and the concomitant attempt to ensure that a jury performs its role of determining the facts and applying the law, as instructed by the judge, to those facts. After the plaintiff has presented its case, and any time before the case is given to

---

79. Thus, the trial in a U.S. court may look substantially different than a trial in England where under the CPR witness statements are substituted for oral evidence-in-chief. See Richard L. Marcus, Putting American Procedural Exceptionalism into a Globalized Context, 53 Am. J. Comp. L. 709, 716–717 (2005).

80. See Oscar G. Chase, American "Exceptionalism" and Comparative Procedure, 50 Am. J. Comp. L. 277 (2002); Langbein, supra note 2, at 835–836 (1985).

the jury, the defendant may request a judgment as a matter of law.[81] The underlying purpose of this motion is to ensure that the jury performs its function and to prevent the jury from deciding a case in favor of a party when there is a lack of evidence to support a jury verdict for that party. For example, if there is no evidence from which a jury could find in the plaintiff's favor on a critical issue that is part of the plaintiff's case, there is no role for the jury and the court will not permit the jury to decide the case. Usually the court will want to hear both sides' evidence, even if it might be inclined to grant the motion. Accordingly, the presentation of the defendant's case will continue, and after presentation of that evidence, the defendant may again make the motion for a judgment as a matter of law in defendant's favor, or may make the motion for the first time if it was not made earlier. Also, the plaintiff may make a motion for judgment as a matter of law if plaintiff believes there is no basis on which a jury could find for the defendant, although usually issues of credibility are for the jury to determine.

In most circumstances, the judge will permit the case to go to the jury rather than grant a motion for judgment as a matter of law. A judge usually prefers this alternative to taking the case from the jury because there is always the possibility that the jury will decide in favor of the movant's position, thereby eliminating any need to decide that question. Also, the judge actually has a second opportunity to determine whether there was a reasonable basis for the jury to decide the case in the way it did since the losing party may make a post-verdict motion for a judgment as a matter of law notwithstanding the jury verdict.[82] Indeed, one of the reasons a judge prefers to allow a case to proceed to verdict is that if an appellate court reverses the trial judge's determination that the case was not one properly for the jury, the jury verdict can be reinstated and a new trial will not be required.

An alternative post-trial motion that may be made by the verdict loser is a motion for a new trial, which may assert various grounds including an error that justifies a new trial or that the verdict was against the clear weight of the evidence. If the post-trial motions are denied, the judge will enter a judgment based upon the jury verdict.

Of course, not all cases are tried by a jury, and when the judge hears a case without a jury, the judge will make findings of fact and conclusions of law prior to entry of judgment.

i. Appeals

Appeals in state and federal courts in the United States are based on the written record of the trial court proceeding. Unlike in many civil law countries, an appeals court does not hear additional testimony or consider additional documents. The record on appeal contains the pleadings and a verbatim transcript of the trial. The parties present their conten-

---

81. In the federal courts, see Fed. R. Civ. Proc. 50(a).

82. In the federal courts, see Fed. R. Civ. Proc. 50 (b).

tions by written briefs, often supplemented by oral argument. Appellate courts are typically multi-member tribunals, with appeals heard before panels of the court.

In some judicial systems in the United States, including the federal system, appeals are only available after a "final decision" by a lower court. In some states, however, interlocutory appeals are permitted, and a party may appeal a procedural ruling, such as the denial of a motion, during the proceedings and before any final judgment is issued.

One of the consequences of "appeal on the record" is that appellate courts in the United States do not exercise plenary review of the findings of fact made by the judge or jury. However, they do review questions of law "de novo," giving no weight to the trial court's conclusions of law. There are some specific matters said to be within the trial court's discretion, such as a motion to grant or deny a new trial, and on those issues, the trial court's ruling will only be overturned for an "abuse of discretion." As for questions of fact, in a case tried by a jury the factual determinations of the jury cannot be reviewed. In a case tried by a judge, the judge's findings of facts will not be overturned unless they are "clearly erroneous."

An appellate court has power to affirm, reverse, vacate, or modify the judgment of the trial court. If it reverses, the court may enter judgment accordingly, or it may remand the case to the trial court for further proceedings.

Decisions are often accompanied by written opinions signed by one of the judge of the panel hearing the appeal. In some systems, provision is made for summary dispositions of appeals without opinion.

3. Conclusion

Procedure in the United States shares a number of traditions with other common law systems, including England—the historical source much of American procedure, including the use of juries to decide questions of fact (although England no longer uses juries in most civil cases). Perhaps most distinct, at least in respect of a comparison with civil law systems of justice, is the embrace of a more adversarial system of justice where the responsibility for both developing and presenting a case rests with the lawyers and where the lawyer's primary obligation is to frame a client's case in as favorable a light as possible. The premise of the American adversary system is that each party will discover and present evidence that will favor its own case and disclose weaknesses in the other side's case; through this bilateral presentation of facts and legal argument, truth will emerge to the impartial decisionmaker.[83] Also, in the United States, as in most common law countries, there is a division of function between pretrial and trial, and formal evidence is

---

83. See Silberman, Stein and Wolff, supra note 53, at 3; Chase, supra note 80, at 276–77.

introduced in what is usually one concentrated trial, even though the proceedings may take place over a number of days or weeks. However, there are a number of features of the American system of justice that are unique even when compared to other common law systems. These include the ability to finance litigation through the contingent fee system, the availability of broad party-initiated pretrial discovery that extends beyond the immediate parties to the lawsuit, the allocation of principal fact-finding to a jury of lay persons, and the relatively passive role of the judge at trial. Such tools, when combined with a philosophy that litigation is the means to develop the common law and serves to articulate social norms and regulate the behavior of both private entities and the government, give civil litigation in the United States a more prominent and substantial role in the social and governmental order than in most other countries of the world.[84]

D. JAPAN*

1. Introduction and Historical Background of Japanese Civil Procedure

As is well known, Japan is a highly industrialized modern country today. Its industrialization and modernization (or westernization) has taken place, however, during the mere past one and one-half centuries. The unique history of modern Japan has left various traces of indigenous and foreign influences on its civil procedure which are of interest from a comparative point of view. In summary, we can find in it a hybrid character of civil law and common law procedure operating in the unique dispute resolution culture of Japan. Most recently, Japan has experienced significant civil procedure reform by a new Code of Civil Procedure of 1996 and further amendments to it in 2003. Commentators see not just a reform of the rules of civil procedure but also a change in the actual practice without which any "reform" would be meaningless.[85]

84. See generally Robert A. Kagan, Adversarial Legalism: The American Way of Law (2001).

* Adapted from Yasuhei Taniguchi, Japan's Recent Civil Procedure Reform: Its Seeming Success and Left Problems, in Trocker and Varano, supra note 20, 91–113.

85. For additional references, see Yasuhei Taniguchi, The 1996 Code of Civil Procedure of Japan—A Procedure for the Coming Century?, 45 Am. J. Comp. L. 767 (1997); Yasuhei Taniguchi, Development of Civil Procedure in Japan: An Experiment to Fuse Civil Law and Common Law, in Festschrift for Prof. Németh 759 (Daisy Kiss and István Varga, eds., 2003); Yasuhei Taniguchi, Between *Verhandlungsmaxime* and Adversary System: In Search for Place of Japanese Civil Procedure, in Festschrift für Karl Heinz Schwab 487 (Peter Gottwald

and Hanns Prütting, eds., 1990); Yasuhei Taniguchi, Civil Procedure: Development of Adversary System in Civil Procedure in Japan, in Japanese Law in Turning Point (Daniel Foote and Veronica Taylor, eds., forthcoming, 2007); Carl F. Goodman, The Somewhat Less Reluctant Litigant: Japan's Changing View Towards Civil Litigation, 32 Law and Pol'y Int'l Bus. 769 (2001).

For a discussion of the new Code of Civil Procedure, see also Takeshi Kojima, Japanese Civil Procedure in Comparative Law Perspective, 46 U. Kan. L. Rev. 687 (1998); Shozo Ota, Reform of Civil Procedure in Japan, 49 Am. J. Comp. L. 561 (2001); Masako Kamiya, Narrowing the Avenues to Japan's Supreme Court: The Policy Implications of Japan's Code of Civil Procedure Reforms, 4 Australian J. Asian L. 53 (2002) (dealing with the adoption by the new Code of Civil Procedure of 1996 of a certiorari-like discretionary appeal to the Supreme

Japan was closed to the outside world until 1853 when American Commodore Perry forced the then Shogunate government of Japan to open the country for commerce. This impact finally led in 1868 to the demise of the Shogun's feudal regime and creation of a new government of the Emperor. The new regime decided to modernize, among many other things, the legal system after the Western models. Students were sent to and advisors were invited from advanced Western countries. Various systems were competing to win adoption for some two decades, first English, then French and finally German. The first comprehensive Code of Civil Procedure was adopted in 1890. This Code was largely a verbatim translation of the German Code of Civil Procedure (*ZPO* of 1877). The most significant departure was the absence of a provision requiring representation of the parties by a qualified lawyer before the district court (first instance court of general jurisdiction) and above. This is explained by the small number of practicing lawyers at the time, a legacy of the previous regime which banned the legal profession as immoral and whose imprint is still noticeable today in the form of a considerable amount of *pro se* litigation.

Apart from some minor changes, the procedural system remained distinctively German as a whole through the first half of the twentieth century. Since adoption of German law occurred in all other fields of law as well, German legal doctrines, legal concepts, and legal terminologies (in Japanese translations) played a predominant role in the Japanese legal scholarship and legal education. The situation had to change in 1945 with the Japanese defeat in the Pacific War. The allied (in fact American) occupation of Japan until 1952 resulted in a considerable Americanization of the Japanese legal system. First of all, the Constitution was rewritten. The new Constitution of 1946 (enforced from 1947) abolished a typical civil law institution—the administrative court—and created an American type Supreme Court of only 15 Justices equipped with a constitutional review power and rule-making power for procedures. The Supreme Court, along with lower courts thereunder, was separated from the Ministry of Justice to become organizationally independent vis-à-vis the legislative and the executive branches. The civil law features of the lower court judiciary were not altered, however, and judges are normally appointed without any law practice experience and gradually promoted within the judiciary. Moreover, they can be posted for a varying term (3 to 10 years) in an administrative position not only within the judiciary (General Secretariat of the Supreme Court) but also in the Ministry of Justice and elsewhere within the executive branch.

2. *Post–War Reform*

Post–War reform of civil procedure in Japan was not extensive when compared with the total reform of the criminal procedure occurring at the same time. Only two provisions of the Code of Civil Procedure were

Court). See also Carl F. Goodman, Justice and Civil Procedure in Japan (2004); and Curtis J. Milhaupt, J. Mark Ramseyer, and Mark D. West, The Japanese Legal System (2006).

changed: Firstly, the provision authorizing the judge to examine evidence *ex officio* was repealed. Secondly, the provision mandating that the presiding judge first examine a witness was amended to require the party who called the witness to ask questions first to be followed by a cross-examination by the adversary party. The judge's intervention was made only supplementary. It goes without saying that the American ideology of adversarial procedure motivated the reform. The original provision—which allowed the judge to ask questions and make suggestions to the parties in an attempt to clarify the matters in dispute and so to guide them to a proper direction—was left intact perhaps because the language of the provision was not mandatory although in practice the judge's clarification was considered a duty and a failure to exercise it properly was held to be a reversible error. However, in the light of adversarialism, as expressed in the two amendments, the Supreme Court held that a failure to exercise clarification was no longer a reversible error. Such case law and these two amendments in the Code seemed to complete a transformation from a judge-dominated procedure into a party-driven adversary procedure.

The reality was not so simple. Lawyers were not ready to practice the adversary system. Moreover, as indicated above, Japanese litigants did not have to retain a lawyer to litigate. The number of lawyers did not increase to catch up with population increase. As of the 1940's and 1950's when the new adversarial ideology was introduced, there were still many litigants without lawyers. The ideal of the adversary system was quite foreign to them. A passive judge who did not exercise clarification often meant a lost case for the party without a lawyer if the other party had one. If both sides were not represented, the judge would be in limbo unless he actively intervened in the process in order to guide the lay parties through clarifications and suggestions. Having realized this reality, the Supreme Court changed its view in the mid–1950's and held that a failure to exercise the clarification power was a reversible error. Ever since, the same position has been kept and even strengthened. Today, the clarification as a judge's duty is a firmly established part of the Japanese procedure. In the light of this change, the aforementioned repeal of the explicit provision for judge's *ex officio* evidence taking must lose most of its significance because the judge may induce a party by way of clarification to produce particular evidence instead of initiating an examination of his own.

The above account may give an impression that Japanese civil procedure has returned to the pre-War state. It is not exactly so. One aspect of adversary procedure introduced during the post-War period is the principal and cross-examination of witnesses by the parties themselves. Although this new method did not at first function well, members of the bar certainly enjoyed the new privilege. As a corollary to the post-War adversary system, lawyers were now encouraged, rather than prohibited as in the pre-War period and in many other civil law countries today, to meet prospective witnesses to better prepare for questioning in court. Despite some criticism from a point of view of efficiency, the new system has generally settled in practice. In the meantime, lawyers have trained themselves in skills of examination, if not so well as in common law countries. Thus, Japanese procedure has gained a truly hybrid character as far as a lawyer appears for both parties.

Here again, however, we must keep in mind an unchanged aspect as *basso continuo* in the tunes of Japanese civil procedure: the recurring problem of lay litigants without a lawyer. This is one of the reasons that the recent new Code of Civil Procedure of 1996 changed the system a bit by allowing the judge to change the order of witness examination with agreement of the parties, so that the judge can now initiate the questioning. The new provision on the face applies to all kinds of litigation, even to one with lawyers for both sides, but lawyers would not normally agree to a change of order. The provision will serve better *pro se* litigation. The issue of *pro se* litigation in fact adds one more element to the civil law— common law hybrid, *i.e.*, a Japanese indigenous element. A considerable amount of litigation is still conducted without any lawyer or with a lawyer for only one side, usually the plaintiff in the district courts, the first instance court of general jurisdiction. Nationwide, about one-fifth of cases have been consistently handled without any lawyer, although the rate is lower in large cities where lawyers are more available. The implication of this, along with other indigenous elements in the setting of Japanese civil procedure, will be discussed later.

It bears noting that a change in attitude among Japanese lawyers greatly contributed to the success of recent civil procedure reform. As described in Chapter 2, The Structure of the Legal Profession, the quality and prestige of the Japanese bar has increased greatly in recent decades.

3.   *Civil Procedure in the Post-War Period*

The newly imported adversarial aspects of Japanese procedure mark a significant departure from civil law practice, where the judge takes responsibility for eliciting information from witnesses although witnesses must be proposed by the parties. Civil law procedures generally adopt the principle of party control or party presentation. But party control stops at presentation of allegation and evidence. In case of testimonial evidence, the party's control would not be complete unless the party is given authority to elicit desired information to support his case from the witness he presents to the court. An essential element of adversarial procedure can be found in this aspect.

Let us examine next how these hybrid characteristics of Japanese procedure are expressed in the mode of hearing in court. The original German type of procedure did not distinguish chronologically the pleading stage and evidence taking stage. These two stages were deliberately made amenable to being mingled and to come one after another as proceedings unfold. Given no constriction of time resulting from the jury system, it was certainly a good policy in order to avoid surprise by evidence and undesirable outcomes resulting from strict preclusion of late submission of new allegations or evidence, thus enabling the judge to reach a substantively just final judgment. But, at the same time, it was accompanied by a danger of inviting delay because there was no real deadline for any procedural action for a party to take. In an attempt to assure that the preparation could be carried out efficiently and completely, a 1926 amendment made the preparatory proceedings semi-obligatory and imposed a preclusion on late factual allegations and proposals of evidence. The post-War reform pursued the same direction by encouraging the parties to prepare well by meeting prospective witnesses beforehand. But with inactive lawyers and ignorant lay litigants, the enforcement of preclusion was felt by judges as inviting only injustice. It is also pointed out that the parties, being afraid of preclusion, tended to submit an excessive amount of hypothetical allegations and evidence, which unnecessarily delayed the whole proceedings. The preparatory proceedings were not used and virtually forgotten.

The typical unfolding of civil litigation which gradually developed during the 100 years of practice is commonly referred to as the "May-rain" or "dentist" method. Hearings take place only intermittently just as the rain in May tends to fall only occasionally in Japan and the dentist treats perhaps everywhere a patient with an interval between visits. What typically happened in Japan was a long dragged out series of short hearings to complete a preliminary stage of identifying the issues to be followed by a series of short witness examination sessions. First, several sessions with an interval of several months were spent exchanging briefs and documentary evidence with clarification requested by the judge or the adversary party. When witness testimony was taken, it was again piecemeal. One witness was examined in a hearing session of 30 minutes and the next hearing would often be a couple of months later to examine a next witness or even to continue to examine the same witness (often cross-examination). As a result of the testimony, a party might wish to amend the pleadings, which was liberally allowed. Thus, the case unfolded only gradually toward a conclusion of the hearing by repeating testimony-taking and pleadings one after another.

Comparing this with American style litigation, an eminent American observer of the Japanese civil procedure, the late Professor Dan F. Henderson, once appropriately remarked that the first half of litigation process in Japan serves only the purpose of *de facto* discovery.[86] If it is so, it is not easy for the judge to narrowly identify the issues of a case in an early stage of proceedings because the parties themselves do not yet know how to formulate the case. In American procedure, an extensive discovery serves that purpose. A cause of the failure of the 1926 reform and the post-War reform is found in that a preparatory procedure was imposed on the parties without giving them a tool to gather information and evidence. Unless the parties are sufficiently informed of the facts

86. Dan F. Henderson, Civil Procedure, Code of, in 1 Kodansha Encyclopedia of Japan 318, 320 (right column 8) (1983).

and evidence to prove them, no real issues can be definitely identified so that the ensuing witness examination may finally resolve the dispute.

The 1996 Code again tried to tackle this problem. It not only reshaped the preparatory proceedings but also expanded the parties' ability to collect information and evidence. Although an adoption of American type discovery was rejected, the Code adopted a new device called "inter-party inquiry" which allows a party to ask for relevant information from the adversary and, more importantly, it expanded the scope of the document production order. The experience for some 5 years under the new Code has shown that the "inter-party inquiry" is not effective because of lack of sanction for non-compliance but the expanded document production order has been working relatively satisfactorily. Since the court is now ready to issue an order, the parties, if requested by the other party, have become generally willing to produce the demanded document voluntarily even without any court order.

A further amendment in the same direction took place in 2003 which, as explained below, enables the parties to collect information and evidence from the prospective adversary or from a third party even before instituting an action. The effectiveness of this new institution is still to be seen. But even without this new device in place, the preparatory proceedings under the new Code seem to have gained certain solid footing in actual practice. It must be remembered, however, that the reform in this respect was not really an innovation by the new legislation. It was rather a codification of a preceding practice. From the mid 1980's, some willing judges with cooperation by willing lawyers started a preparatory procedure commonly called "the argument-settlement session." This was the beginning of the recent civil procedure reform movement which is still continuing today as the next section explains.

4. A New Trend of Judge–Lawyer Cooperation—Successful Preparation and Concentration of Witness Examination

It was a common practice under the old Code that the judge held a special *in camera* session for settlement of dispute often using the technique of caucusing. In such a session, the judge helps the parties (not only lawyers but also often the parties in person) broadly discuss the situation in dispute and seek a settlement. In doing so, the judge as well as the parties often found real issues emerging which encouraged the parties to settle. Therefore, "the argument-settlement session" utilized the same opportunity and technique to find out the real issues and weed out unnecessary issues with agreement of the parties. If a settlement was reached, it was a welcome by-product.

A somewhat similar procedure had been practiced earlier in Germany under the name of "Stuttgart Model." Because of the German origin of the Japanese procedure and a continuing affinity with German procedural scholarship, the Stuttgart Model and its later codification in 1976 were much studied and discussed in Japan. The Supreme Court even sent some young judges to Germany to observe the practice firsthand. Although the "argument-settlement session" was not a direct importation of the Stuttgart Model, it was certainly inspired by the latter. But what led the experiment of "the argument-settlement session" to certain success was a positive cooperation by willing lawyers with the judges who wanted to experiment in this new procedural idea. The judge's initiative could not have gone through without a positive cooperation by the lawyers involved. The main cause of previous failures of various preparatory proceedings was general lack of cooperation by the lawyers.

This type of constructive cooperation between the judge and the lawyer was highly unusual in Japanese legal history. As explained in Chapter 2, The Structure of the Legal Profession, the organized bar and individual lawyers gained an unprecedented self-confidence by the 1980's. The judiciary and individual judges now looked at members of the bar as on a par. The ideological antagonism and mutual mistrust which long characterized the relationship between the bar and the judiciary started to fade, if not entirely. A change in the domestic political climate since the end of the cold war in the international world also helped. Thus, there were noticeable signs that a mutual respect and understanding between the bar and the judiciary have come to existence. This is the background against which the "argument-settlement" experiment became possible. The organized bar no longer flatly rejected a proposal from the judiciary. They themselves formed study groups and made constructive proposals for better management of litigation and the judiciary was willing to listen to them because it also knew that nothing could be achieved in this field without willing cooperation by the lawyers.

The draft of the new Code of Civil Procedure of 1996 was considered by the Consultative Committee of the Ministry of Justice which for the first time included representatives of the organized bar. Their proposals were discussed and some of them were adopted. The afore-mentioned "inter-party inquiry" was one of them. The practice of "argument-settlement session" was codified in a little modified form. Under the new Code enforced from January 1998, the new preparatory procedure has proven largely successful thanks to cooperative lawyers and understanding judges, helped by the new possibility of gathering information and documentary evidence as explained earlier. Particularly noteworthy is the fact that a rather harsh rule of preclusion of late submissions under the old Code has been replaced in the new Code by a mild request by the other party for "explanation" of reason for the delay.

Good preparation is essential for making the evidence taking stage that follows efficient and conclusive. Evidence taking mainly means testimony taking in court. If this stage is conducted in a "May-rain" fashion, the value of good preparation will be largely lost. Moreover, a protracted evidence taking process will inevitably be accompanied by the judge's memory loss which is likely to undermine the correctness of the final judgment. Also, the judge in charge of the case may change before the evidence is concluded—in Japanese practice judges are transferred from one court to another every three years or so. In theory, when this happens, the same witness can be re-examined under the new judge upon demand by a party. But such is never practiced for the sake of time. Thus, the new judge must rely on the record of testimony which is normally not a verbatim transcription but a mere summary rendered by the court clerk.

Therefore, the next problem is how to expedite the testimony taking. The new Code requires the so-called "concentrated witness examination." This means that, as in the common law trial, several witnesses are consecutively examined (and cross-examined) in one continuous hearing session, not in a piecemeal way in the May-rain style.

The importance of witness evidence in Japanese procedure should be underlined here. Traditionally, the Japanese, even those in the business, do not use writing as often and as extensively as practiced in the Western world. A contract even if rendered into a writing tends to be short and summary. A typical business contract traditionally has a last clause saying, "If a dispute arises, both parties will talk sincerely to solve it amicably." There is a feeling that to demand a detailed written agreement at the time of contracting is not a correct thing to do because it may be taken by the other party as a manifestation of distrust and an anticipation of a breach. The substantive law normally does not require a writing for a contract to be enforceable. Procedural law also does not limit evidence to a writing. Therefore, once litigation arises, testimonial evidence often plays a crucial role rather than documentary evidence, which tends to be scarce. This background leads in turn to a crucial role of witness examination in litigation.

The common law type of concentrated witness examination is possible only where the parties (lawyers) are well prepared. Successful concentration requires the cooperation and willingness of the lawyers involved. Concentration will also impose a formidable task upon the busy courts in the scheduling of hearings. Under the May-rain type hearings, literally hundreds of cases have been dealt with simultaneously by a single judge in a piecemeal fashion. If one case takes a whole day, many other cases must be delayed. It is systematically impossible for such a judge to schedule a concentrated testimony taking for one case without affecting the progress of all other cases.

Despite those practical difficulties, concentrated testimony taking is increasingly conducted in varying degrees today. Even examining only two witnesses in one session is great progress from the old practice where only one witness was normally examined in one session sometimes leaving the cross-examination for the next session two to five months later. Concentration of any degree will necessarily lead to a speeding up of the process and avoidance of possible change of the judge. There is a report that in the Tokyo District Court, the largest first instance court of general jurisdiction in Japan, concentration is already practiced by almost all judges if its definition is more than one witness being examined in one session of hearing. There are also many cases where all adopted witnesses are examined in one day, a real common law type of concentration.

It is important, however, to notice that if the lawyers are not willing to conduct witness examination in a concentrated manner, there is no way to enforced it. However, it is said that the lawyers have in fact become more and more cooperative in the concentrated witness examination proposed by the judge as a fruit of well processed preparatory proceedings. Combined with efficient preparatory proceedings, a successful concentration of witness examination would greatly expedite the civil process. As a matter of fact, statistics show that the period from the filing of an action to the termination of the first instance proceedings has been markedly shortened during the last ten years. The following table shows the average time (months) spend between the filing of the complaint and the close of the case in all 50 district courts in Japan:

> Table I: Average time (months) between the filing of a complaint and the closing of a case in all 50 district courts in Japan, including cases of default and termination by settlement or withdrawal

Year	1991	1992	1993	1994	1995	1996	1997	1998	1999	2000	2001	2002
Months	12.2	10.9	10.1	9.8	10.1	10.2	10.0	9.3	9.2	8.8	8.5	8.3

Table I includes cases of default and termination by settlement or withdrawal. The next table shows a more realistic picture in the same years of the average time for contested cases with witness examination:

> Table II: Average time (months) between the filing of a complaint and the closing of a case in all 50 district courts in Japan in contested cases with witness examination

Year	1991	1992	1993	1994	1995	1996	1997	1998	1999	2000	2001	2002
Months	22.7	21.8	21.1	20.9	21.1	21.3	20.8	20.8	20.5	19.7	19.2	18.7

Medical malpractice litigation and intellectual property litigation normally require a longer period of time and they are most likely contested. The following table shows the statistics for medical malpractice cases ("MM," line 1) and intellectual property cases ("IP," line 2), both concluded most likely either by a final judgment or by a settlement:

Year	1991	1992	1993	1994	1995	1996	1997	1998	1999	2000	2001	2002
MM cases	41.6	39.8	42.6	42.0	39.1	37.5	36.7	35.3	34.6	35.5	32.7	30.4
IP cases	31.1	29.6	31.9	23.7	23.7	22.7	25.0	25.7	23.1	21.6	18.3	16.8

Although the reduction of the time period can be said to be remarkable in both categories of litigation, these two types of cases still require a much longer time than ordinary cases in part because of the complicated nature of the dispute and expertise required. The court usually retains an expert witness, but this adds considerable time to the proceeding. It is not uncommon to see a battle of experts in Japanese courts, another sign of adversariness of the Japanese civil procedure.

5. *Further Amendments in 2003*

One of the issues dealt with by the most recent amendment to the Code of Civil Procedure, in force from April 2004, relates to the problem of expertise in court. The new institution called the "expert commissioner" was established by this amendment. The commissioners will be appointed in various fields of expertise and their participation in the proceedings in the capacity of a neutral advisor is anticipated. For example, a chemical expert would participate in the preparatory proceedings in a litigation arising from a pharmaceutical patent to help the judge and the lawyers understand the dispute better and find out the real issue more efficiently. The same rule of disqualification and challenge as those for judges apply to the expert commissioner. Various safeguards are introduced (such as consent of the parties and disclosure of information) to protect the interests of the parties from undue influence of an expert commissioner. It is expected that this new institution will considerably decrease the necessity of appointing a formal expert witness who requires a good deal of time and expense. Commissioners will be paid only a modest fee by the court for the service. However, this will not make a real expert witness unnecessary in proper cases. The amended Code has also streamlined the procedure for expert witness examination.

It would be appropriate at this juncture to explain some other significant points of the 2003 amendment of the Code. There are two more important features which are both directly related to the theme of this chapter:

1. Introduction of the obligatory "Planning of Proceedings": Where the court considers a case to be complicated as, for example, involving industrial pollution damages, medical malpractice, a large construction project, etc., it must establish a chronological agenda for the future procedural steps on the basis of consultation with the parties. The plan must fix the time frames for the preparatory proceedings and for witness examination and provisionally set the anticipated time of conclusion of the hearing and rendition of the final judgment. It is said that the idea was taken from the commercial practice of fixing a delivery date at the time of contract. When the court is retained, it should make a commitment for the delivery date of its final product, *i.e.*, the final judgment, by fixing a time table for necessary steps to be taken before reaching it. Here again a successful plan can be made and complied with only where the court can avail itself of good cooperation by the lawyers concerned. Based on a positive experience under the new Code, the expectation is that such cooperation can be obtained in a good number of important litigation, if not in all.

2. Adoption of pre-filing evidence discovery measures: The 1996 new Code expanded the scope of document production order and introduced a system of inter-party inquiry as described earlier. But these devices are only available after filing of an action. It is sometimes necessary to have sufficient information in order to formulate a com-

plaint. Therefore, the Code now enables the prospective plaintiff to issue a questionnaire to the prospective defendant after having given a notice of the general nature of the intended action. The amendment further provides for assistance by the court for (a) collecting evidence held by a public office or a third person (such as police record of a traffic accident or weather report of a certain date), (b) securing an expert opinion on a specific matter (such as authenticity of a handwriting) or (3) verification by the sheriff of the state of a specific thing (such as present condition of land border in a border dispute). This is in addition to the pre-existing devices for preservation or perpetuation of evidence which are available before institution of an action but the requirement is more stringent because the court must recognize a danger of disappearance of the evidence sought. The fate of this new discovery measure is still to be seen, as there is no sanction for non-compliance.

Better preparation, concentrated witness examination, better scheduling, etc., all require much work and responsibility not only of the participating lawyers but also of the judge in charge. Frequent contact between the court and the lawyers becomes necessary. For that purpose, a competent administrative support system is needed so that the judges can concentrate on their proper tasks. In this respect, the new role of the court clerk should be particularly mentioned here. See the discussion of this development in Chapter 2, The Structure of the Legal Profession. The court clerks are no longer a subordinate officer but an independent role player side by side with the judges. The court clerks posted in litigation management constantly contact the parties (lawyers) for various purposes, for just a scheduling, or for a more substantive matter like clarification of allegations.

6. *Prospects and Conclusion—The Need for Solid Infrastructure*

From a broad comparative point of view, the trend of reform of civil procedure in Japan, both in law and practice, seems to show a direction toward a bifurcation of pre-trial and trial stages typical of common law procedure. It must be remembered, however, that it is not because of an absolute necessity as in the common law system, which was originally based, and still based largely in the United States, on the tradition of the jury trial. Where no such systemic necessity exists, a combination of good preparation and a concentrated witness examination could be brought about only by hard work and cooperation among the judge and the parties. The recent reforms seem to have attained at least a certain degree of success. A judge of the Tokyo District Court who served before and after the reform remarked in an article in 2002, "The present civil procedure in my court may look to an uninformed eye like a procedure in a foreign country. It is so fundamentally different from the situation ten years ago." Moreover, there is currently an optimistic mood and desirable enthusiasm of cooperation among the actors concerned—the judges, the lawyers, and the clerks. But the mood and enthusiasm have a limit unless supported systematically by a necessary infrastructure.

As suggested earlier, it is physically very difficult given the present state of court congestion to conduct a concentrated witness examination because it would affect the hearing schedule of hundreds of other cases. In order to solve this problem, the case load of each judge must be reduced to a manageable size so that the judge can freely schedule concentrated witness hearings for appropriate cases. The main cause for the congestion is a small number of judges in Japan, another infrastructural difference from the German system. There are only about 2,200 judges of full qualification and about 800 summary court judges who can only serve in the lowest level court of limited jurisdiction below the district court. The number of civil cases is smaller than in most Western countries but large enough for the small number of judges and lawyers. It must be recalled, moreover, that most of these cases brought to the court are difficult cases legally and factually because for the Japanese, litigation is the last resort to be used only after all kinds of effort to solve a dispute have failed. Accordingly, the settlement rate of actual cases is only about 30 per cent. Therefore, the judge's burden to hear the cases and to write final judgments is very heavy. They usually work at night and over the weekend to write judgments.

There are numerous infrastructural problems which have been reconsidered on the basis of the 2001 report of the Justice System Reform Council[87] to the then-Prime Minister, Mr. Koizumi. It recommended making the civil justice system more "user friendly" and proposed a radical increase of judges and lawyers as the top priority matter. The organized bar has long been demanding the adoption of the common law type judiciary of lawyer-judges rather than the existing civil law type judiciary of career judges. Currently, the recruitment of judges from the bar is very limited, less than ten a year, mainly because of reluctance on the part of individual lawyers. The report of the Council took a positive posture toward a system change in this respect. If this sort of reform is adopted to staff a substantial part of the judiciary by former practitioners, the landscape of Japanese civil procedure will change drastically. But such a change does not seem to be likely in the near future.[88]

Some smaller but significant infrastructural reforms had already taken place, even before the 2001 report, in the direction of making the court "user friendly." For example, the filing fee which must be paid by the plaintiff and is pro-rated to the amount in controversy was considerably reduced in view of a criticism that it was an onerous obstacle to litigation. It was further reduced in 2003. The so-called round-table court room was introduced even prior to the 1996 Code. This type of

87. An English version of the report is available at the Prime Minister's website: http://www.kantei.go.jp/foreign/judiciary/2001/0612report.html.

88. A small number of young judges are already sent to law firms for two years besides to administrative agencies or private enterprises. As a compromised solution, it has been proposed that every LTRI student aspiring to be a judge should be required to practice for 5 years.

court room has no high platform for the judge. Everybody participating in the proceedings sits at the same large round table, creating an informal atmosphere that facilitates exchanges of documents. Many such court rooms have since been created in district and summary courts.

It will be only after all these large and small infrastructural changes are completed that real civil procedure reform will also be completed. It will take years and hopefully the present mood and enthusiasm will continue to persist to support a lasting effort.

The recent justice system reform movement has paid little attention to the problems of *pro se* litigation. The prevailing view seems to be that *pro se* litigation is a vestige of the past and will fade away when enough lawyers and sufficient legal aid are provided. When *pro se* litigation is necessary because of a shortage of practitioners in an area, an increase of lawyers will be the solution. If a lawyer is not retained because of high cost, an expanded legal aid and the system of loser-pays-winner's-lawyer will be a solution. If a smooth and expedited procedure demands cooperation of the parties, nobody can expect of a lay litigant the same kind of cooperation as of a professional lawyer. An indigenous element of Japanese civil procedure is the existence of a sizable amount of *pro se* litigation—the question is whether this element will or should simply fade away.

This indigenous element has affected Japanese civil procedure as a whole in various ways although it has not yet attracted serious academic attention. *Pro se* litigation set the standard for Japanese civil procedure in May-rain type proceedings in the sense that lawyers were as dependent on the judge's paternalistic guidance in the conduct of litigation as a lay litigant. However, once lawyers have transformed themselves into an independent professional on par with judges, a real difference between the two types of litigation must emerge and may pose a serious practical problem to the court.

In the process of recent civil procedure reform, the problems of *pro se* litigation seem to have been avoided unconsciously or deliberately. There is a widely held simplistic assumption that it is an unnecessary burden on the judge, who therefore normally recommends the lay party to retain a lawyer as soon as possible and many litigants do so. Thus, the main stream of thought is that the *pro se* litigation is an anomaly at least in the district court and above, which should be eradicated by increasing the number of lawyers and expanding the legal aid program. There is also a strong argument that Japan should finally adopt the system of compulsory representation by a lawyer when a sufficient number of lawyers have been secured. This is certainly a possible argument. If this line of development is eventually taken, one important indigenous element of the Japanese civil procedure will disappear.

It is interesting, however, to see that a contrary argument has recently emerged inspired by American studies of law and psychology. These studies show that if a litigant has personally participated in the dispute resolution process he or she has a greater feeling of satisfaction whether or not the outcome is favorable.[89] As a matter of common sense, we can endorse such observation. The nature of the *pro se* litigation and an empirical comparison between the two types of litigation should be studied more seriously with an empirical method and the result must be analyzed from a broader perspective than a simple point of view of efficiency. If we reach a conclusion that the *pro se* litigation is a socially useful device for dispute resolution, a more difficult problem would be how to implement such a legitimate need. Must a new type of procedural scheme be created? What kind of infrastructure is needed to support the system? Should the need instead be satisfied by a sort of ADR mechanism? It is interesting to see how this rather fundamental problem of the Japanese civil procedure will be finally resolved in the years to come.

Some pessimism about the new Code seemed appropriate when it was adopted in 1996. In particular, there was concern that the kind of enthusiasm which supported the experience of the "argument-settlement session" might not be long lasting. Fortunately, pessimism seems to have proved wrong. After six years of enforcement of the new Code, the enthusiasm is still well alive thanks to the larger justice system reform movement which followed the adoption of the new Code of Civil Procedure. A mere enthusiasm cannot support lasting changes unless a suitable infrastructure is provided to sustain the change on a permanent basis. On the other hand, there may be too much optimism about the cooperative relationship between the judiciary and the organized bar. A mutual distrust still does exist. It must exist in any legal system as long as the judge and the lawyer must play a different and often conflicting role. It is a relative matter. In the case of Japan, the present civil court practice under the new Code was made possible largely by a changed attitude of the judiciary and the bar with respect to each other.

III. OTHER SYSTEMS: AN APOLOGIA

By no means do the jurisdictions selected for treatment in this book provide an exhaustive account of the variety of dispute resolution systems found in the world. While the reader will find references to the rules of nations other than England, Italy, Japan, and the U.S. in the chapters that follow, large gaps remain. Notable by their absence are some of the world's largest nations—China, India, and the Russian Federation. Nor will the reader find anything specifically about Africa or the Islamic world. For these omissions we apologize and offer the following explanation. In large part these gaps reflect the limits of the authors' collective expertise—we have followed the time-honored writers' dictum to "write about what you know." Moreover, we contend that insofar as their formal systems of dispute resolution are concerned, many of the nations omitted have been so influenced by the systems

---

89. *See, e.g.,* E. Allan Lind and Tom R. Tyler, The Social Psychology of Procedural Justice (1988); Tom R. Tyler, Citizen Dis-content with Legal Procedures: A Social Science Perspective on Civil Procedure Reform, 45 Am. J. Comp. L. 871 (1997).

discussed in the text that one can infer much about the basics of their approach. This is the case, for example, with India and its neighbor Pakistan. Each of them was subject to British rule and each has—with different modifications—retained the basic structure of English civil procedure as it was at the time of their independence in 1947. The same is true of many of those nations in Africa that were also English colonies, and of Israel, whose processes continue to reflect the British Mandate period (1922–1948). Then there are the many nations that are part of the "civil law world" to which we alluded earlier. These include not only South America but also countries as diverse as Senegal, Korea, Turkey, and Egypt.

The situation in the People's Republic of China and the Russian Federation is more complex. Each is developing a post-socialist legal system in the light of its own distinct traditions. With respect to China, it is said:

> While certainly there are Chinese traditions, and socialist doctrinal requirements in the legal system, the fact of its system being more inquisitorial than adversarial, its "trials" not being recognizable as a single event, its judges playing a larger role in collecting the evidence and examining witnesses, the different role of lawyers (with little cross-examination and little pre-trial discovery) and no juries, merely describes the traditional civil law approach as much as the Chinese approach. However, to be sure, the actual legal and judicial system in China has its distinct "Chinese characteristics" that distinguish it from pure civil law. And, as in all countries, law and how the law is applied in practice must be separately examined and understood.[90]

As to Russia, one contemporary observer acknowledges that "historically, Russia adhered to the continental model" but argues that "[t]he Russian style of civil procedure is not simply a continental or Anglo–Saxon system possessing classical civil and common law features, but a unique system possessing exceptional features that do not exist in either of these traditional approaches."[91] He notes that under the Code of Civil Procedure adopted in 2002 Russian civil litigation shares with the civil law model a leading role for the judge at trial, the absence of a civil jury, the lack of class actions, and the use of court-appointed experts. Like the common law process, however, the judge is not responsible for gathering the evidence and the trial process includes a preliminary session which is "manned mainly by the opposing parties." The role of the judge is unique to Russian process, he argues, because of the manner in which "the court and the disputing parties share an active role in the litigation process."

Readers interested in pursuing any system in depth have a growing number of sources available to them. In addition to the many works

---

90. Ronald C. Brown, Understanding Chinese Courts: Law with Chinese Characteristics xxi (1997).

91. Dmitry Maleshin, New Russian Civil Procedure in the Context of Cross–Cultural Interaction, presented at the 2006 Kyoto Congress of the International Association of Procedural Law, at 1.

devoted to a single nation, descriptions of litigation systems in many of the world's nations can be found in the Encyclopedia of International Commercial Litigation, Anthony Colman, General Editor (1991; Supp. 2005) and the International Encyclopedia of Laws: Civil Procedure, Pict Taelman, General Editor (2001; supp. 2005). A scholarly and sensitive treatment of modern legal systems in the context of traditional dispute resolution is found in Werner Menski, Comparative Law in a Global Context: The Legal Systems of Asia and Africa (2d ed. 2006). An extensive bibliography compiled by the staff of the NYU School of Law Library is available at www.law.nyu.edu/library/foreign_intl/civilproc.

Chapter 2

THE STRUCTURE OF THE LEGAL PROFESSION

I. INTRODUCTION

The legal profession is one of the foundations of every legal system and is essential to its proper functioning. However, there are significant differences in the structure, the attitudes, and the roles of the legal profession which do not necessarily depend on whether a legal system belongs to either the common law or the civil law. The differences begin with legal education, which is graduate and very much professionally oriented in the U.S., while it is undergraduate and general in the civil law world.

> [L]egal education is concerned not with the techniques of problem-solving but with the inculcation of fundamental concepts and principles. * * * Law school is not considered a professional training school but a cultural institution * * * the learning process is passive * * * the student is not trained to handle a concrete case. Above all * * * legal education gives him a strong orientation toward doctrine, as opposed to precedent, and toward the orthodox dogmatic approach of the academic establishment.[1]

In part at least, the above remarks apply to English legal education too. In order to illustrate the differences, excerpts from a celebrated article by Mirjan Damaška will be found in section II. This article is particularly interesting because of the European origins and formation of the author coupled with his long teaching experience in American law schools. Although the essay dates back almost forty years, and many reforms have occurred since then everywhere in the world, the basic differences between the two approaches to legal education still hold valid.

The second difference which we wish to highlight is that "Americans usually think of the legal profession, of a single entity," while the civil

---

1. Mauro Cappelletti, John Henry Merryman and Joseph M. Perillo, The Italian Legal System: An Introduction 89–91 (1967) (hereinafter Cappelletti, Merryman, and Perillo).

lawyers refer to a variety of legal professions open to law graduates, whose initial choice tends to be final. In this respect too England is somehow different from the U.S., since it has distinguished practicing lawyers between barristers and solicitors for centuries. Here and there, the materials will refer also to the changes which are occurring in several European legal systems, including England, following the development of European integration. On the one hand, the fundamental freedoms provided for by the European treaties—freedom of establishment (art. 43), freedom to provide services (art. 49)—have been made applicable to attorneys as well as to any other private professional. On the other hand, the idea of a competitive market is being extended also to legal services. In practice, this means that many traditional restrictions on the exercise of the legal profession—such as, for instance, prohibition of contingency fee agreements, prohibition of advertising, prohibition of, or limitations on, partnerships—are being gradually attenuated, if not abolished. In the long run, the more entrepreneurial and competitive model characterizing the U.S. legal profession may spread also to Europe.

The third great difference concerns the judiciary. There are several indicators of a different status and role for the common law judge: their selection and appointment is not bureaucratic as in the civil law, there is no judicial career as such, their status and prestige in society is immense, and even if a growing role of legislation is widely acknowledged among the sources of law, the common lawyers tend to think of legislation as still serving a kind of supplementary function. John Merryman offers one of the best characterizations of the judge in the two major western traditions (although the comparativist must transcend what Merryman himself called the "folklore" of the traditions):

> [In] the common law world * * * [h]e is a culture hero, even something of a father figure. * * * Many of the great names of the common law are those of judges. * * * We do not like to use such dramatic phrases as 'judicial supremacy', but when pushed to it we admit that this is a fair description of the common law system, particularly in the United States. * * * But in the civil law world, a judge is something entirely different. He is a civil servant, a functionary. * * * The net image is of the judge as an operator of a machine designed and built by legislators. His function is a mechanical one. The great names of the civil law are not those of judges (who knows the name of a civil law judge?) but those of legislators (Justinian, Napoleon) and scholars (Gaius, Irnerius, * * * Pothier, Savigny * * *). The civil law judge is not a culture hero or a father figure. * * * His image is that of a civil servant who performs important but essentially uncreative functions.[2]

2. John Henry Merryman, The Civil Law Tradition 34–37 (2nd ed. 1985).

II. THE EDUCATION OF CIVIL LAWYERS

Mirjan Damaška, A Continental Lawyer in an American Law School: Trials and Tribulations of Adjustment, 116 U. Pa. L. Rev. 1363 (1968).

A. EUROPEAN LEGAL EDUCATION

As in this country, so in European countries there is a great deal of controversy over the aims of legal education and the role universities should play in it. Traditional ideas on curricula as well as methods of instruction are increasingly questioned; new ideas are discussed and, in some countries, experimented with. Yet notwithstanding these winds of change and the considerable differences that exist among various European countries, fluctuation and diversity fade away when viewed from this side of the Atlantic. A distinctive Continental *mos iura docendi* still seems to exist. As I see it, one can distil the essential ingredients of Continental law school experience. This essence involves exposure to what I will call the grammar of law, a panoramic view of the most important fields of law, and some initiation into the patterns of legal reasoning. These three essential ingredients must be treated separately although they are imparted simultaneously.

1. *The Grammar of Law*

While it would be false to imply that grammar is completely absent from American law, the fact remains that there exists no real counterpart to the Continental grammar of law. The difference is perhaps in the degree of refinement and importance of grammar in the two systems.

In order to gain an understanding of Continental legal grammar, Americans should imagine lawyers of an analytical turn of mind à la Hohfeld at work a long time, studying the law as it emerged from legal practice. Americans should further imagine that both the analysts' dissection of law and their generalizations were generally accepted by the legal profession. Let me pursue this hypothesis with specific examples and suggest what the consequences might be for American law.

Many rather amorphous American legal concepts would be subjected to rigorous analysis. An illustration is the concept of jurisdiction with its bewildering number of meanings. Words and phrases like "property," "standing to sue," "security," and "mens rea" also come to mind. In the process of analysis the twilight zone of the concepts would be somewhat reduced, sub-concepts isolated and separately labeled. A richer and more precise legal terminology would appear. Movement would also proceed in the opposite direction, that is toward the creation of more general, sometimes almost cathedral-like concepts. For example, inquiry into what contracts, conveyances and wills have in common would probably result in something similar to the Continental concept of legal transaction (*Rechtsgeschäft, negozio giuridico*). These newly created, broad concepts would become accepted as elements of standard legal terminology. Study would then proceed to the relationships between such legal concepts. Questions would be raised about the relationship of "jurisdictional" to "procedural" issues, of "mistake" to "mens rea."

Inquiry into relationships between concepts would be linked to an investigation into the nature or essence of concepts. For example, what is the nature of "arbitration" or of "pleadings" and "stipulations" in criminal procedure? Pursuit of what is common to the decisional law of seemingly unrelated areas would be conducive to the creation of broader rules (*e.g.*, on misrepresentation in conveyances, contracts, and so forth) and even to the development of principles (*e.g.*, principles of procedure). Almost imperceptibly an urge to establish a rigid network of classification would develop; for example, the question whether we should separate real and personal property would arise. Thus, step by step, the conceptual digestion of the law would result in a network of precise interrelated concepts, broad principles and classificatory ideas. This network is the grammar of law.

* * *

Even anti-conceptualists would, I believe, concur in the traditional justifications advanced by Continentals in defense of their legal grammar.

Let me quickly sketch these often overlapping justifications. In the first place, it is claimed that a well developed legal grammar results in economy of thought. The concepts in such a grammar can be used independently of specific legal rules, just as elements in an algebraic system, and with all the advantages of algebra over arithmetic. Pursuing mathematical analogies, one can say that the urge to generalize results in factoring out common features, thus leading to simplification. A great many heretofore unrelated legal rules can be seen as offshoots of a single more general rule or principle.

A related advantage attributed to legal grammar is clarity of vision, sometimes expressed by the old Latin tag *praxis sine theoria caecus in via*. Broad interrelated concepts facilitate awareness of the ramifications of hypothetical legal situations, notably contemplated changes in the law. Thus law can more easily be tested by logic. It is further believed that profound analysis of the law sometimes fosters a sense of the proper order of analysis. This in turn goes a long way towards shielding the average legal mind from confusion. Finally, it is believed that legal grammar represents an essential prerequisite for the satisfactory drafting of comprehensive legislation and the successful ordering of judge-made law.

The importance attached to legal grammar explains why initiation into it represents one of the minimal requirements of legal education in Continental law schools. Even a casual glance at any student manual will immediately reveal the extent to which "grammatical" considerations dictate the organization and presentation of the body of law.

2. *The Panoramic View*

In addition to an initiation into the grammar of law, the Continental student is also offered what would, to an American lawyer, appear to be a panoramic presentation of the most important fields of law. This comprehensive view of the whole is considered to be of utmost importance. It is feared that if the young lawyer fails to perceive the great contours of private and public law in school, he will seldom acquire an overview later in practice. Entangled in the jungle of practical problems, he will be deprived of the guidance that comes from an awareness of the totality of law in his particular field.

The way in which the panoramic view is offered would be rather startling to in American lawyer. Even aside from discussion of the highly abstract legal issues closely connected with the Continental legal grammar, discourse proceeds most of the time on a level that seems much too abstract to the American legal mind. Statutory or code provisions are systematically presented on a level which seems to provide only vague guidelines for the solution of actual cases. Occasional references to actual cases will almost invariably be made in generalized form. The legal problems in a case will be treated in the abstract, as illustrations of how the court evolved legal rules, adapted to the solution of the case, from the more general ones found in the code or statute. When on a rare occasion the discussion does descend to the level of particular facts, it will be abruptly cut off by the remark that a *questio facti* is involved which does not merit further analysis. The American lawyer would thus discover that, more often than not, where his interest really begins the law teacher's seems to end. A related and similar source of distress to an American would be the paucity of references to the meaning of legal rules in practical operation. He would be shocked to find that as much time is devoted to analysis of legal problems of only academic interest as to problems commonly confronting the courts. Almost never would he find discussion of the influence of procedural considerations on substantive issues. He would be positively annoyed by the method of instruction that still prevails in Continental law schools, with formal and not infrequently somewhat soporific lectures. Faced with professorial assertion on the basis of what to him seemed vague and inconclusive authorities, he would be tempted to think that the teacher was getting his law out of his head. I believe he would soon decide that he could make equally good (or bad) use of his time by reading lectures in the form of *scripta*, or by studying the professor's manual or treatise.

3. *Patterns of Legal Reasoning*

By American standards, Continental law schools give very little training in "how to think like a lawyer." Stimulation of students to participate in problem solving (on the Continental level of discourse), while not unknown, is comparatively insignificant. This is not to say that patterns of thinking are not implanted in students, if only through exposure to the style of thinking of the faculty. Let me present a very cursory sketch of this style, for it is important for my purposes. Very characteristic is an urge to relate particular problems to a whole array of rules, principles and "grammatical" ideas. Logical consistency within the array assumes a very great importance. Seldom does one find the feeling that discussion of rules apart from judicial application is somewhat vacuous. There is a significant lack of the argumentative approach towards the law which permeates the atmosphere of law schools in this country. The moving spirit of analysis is not the desire to find the best argument for a proposition, but rather the quest for the "right" answer to the problem at hand. Conspicuous by its absence is the intertwining of legal and nonlegal arguments so common here.

Comparatively speaking there is also very little preparation in Continental law schools for the practical problems awaiting the student (handling of sources, legal writing, and the like). But even though vocationally oriented education represents an inferior intellectual tradition to the Continental lawyer, I do not think that a typical Continental law professor is insensitive to the needs of practical training. He would agree that a full-fledged lawyer needs practical as well as theoretical preparation. *Theoria sine praxis rota sine axis.* However, he will probably argue that theoretical and practical preparation cannot both be offered in school, and that a choice of priorities must be made. Since in the Continental scheme of things theoretical preparation and a grasp of the whole must precede exposure to the complexities of practice, precedence is given to rendering instruction in the grammar of law and in the grand contours of most important fields of law. It is upon graduation and during the internship period preceding the bar and bench examinations that the student receives a rigorous practical training in how to find the law and write about it.

The three components may now be drawn together. If a Continental student has acquired some mastery of legal grammar, if he has learned the substantive rules as presented in the panoramic view, and if he has gained some grasp of the style of thinking described, he is a successful product of Continental legal education on the university level.

B. The Expectations of a Continental Lawyer

When the Continental law school graduate enters practice, the neatness, simplicity, and purity of the vision of the law imparted to him in school will be somewhat marred. Yet, even after extended legal practice most of the attitudes shaped in school, somewhat modified, will still influence his perception of law. Of course, if he is fresh from law school—as are many foreigners in American law schools—the impact of his legal education will be undiluted in its strength. Some features of the young lawyer's outlook should concern us here.

He will tend to associate at least modern domestic law with a more or less closed and orderly system. He will assume that precise terminology, conceptual specificity, and other elements of the Continental legal grammar are indispensable tools for mature legal analysis. Sensitivity toward logical consistency over relatively wide areas will appear to him to be an attribute of a good lawyer. It will seem natural to be able to gain a panoramic view of legal fields. He will believe that legal discourse of real importance proceeds on the level of rules he is familiar with, and that emphasis on factual questions and too much concern about justice in a given case betray a non-technical, layman's approach—what Max Weber called khadi justice. For him the primary purpose of legal discussion—at least in the academic milieu—will be the quest for right answers rather than partisan arguments.

* * *

C. The Clash Between Expectation and Reality

If there is a measure of truth in the preceding description of expectations, the problems faced by a Continental lawyer attempting to adjust to a typical American law school are not too difficult to fathom. I cannot hope to discuss them all, so I shall limit myself to the most pressing.

* * *

After exposure to the finely shaded rigidities of the Continental legal grammar, the student will discover that it has virtually no analogue in American law, and that very little importance is attached to the conceptual digestion of the law. He will find that definitions, so important to his mind, are viewed with a scepticism reminiscent of classical Roman lawyers.

* * *

Claiming no great discoveries, I can see at least four sources of difficulty. The first is produced by disparities in the level of discourse. As has been repeatedly intimated, the Continental tends to move on the level of abstract rules which to his American counterpart often seem to be only rather vague standards. In contrast, American legal discussion usually proceeds on the more concrete level of what a Continental would consider to be less significant *questiones facti*. Second, the strength of legal arguments differs substantially. Logical consistency over areas too wide for American taste is of very great importance to a Continental mind, which in turn remains closed to many specific arguments much higher on the American scale. In the third place, the Continental conceptual scheme imposes relatively rigid methods of analysis, while the non-grammatical American legal mind remains very flexible. Finally, the very goals of legal discussion frequently will not coincide. The Continental will seek the right solution; his counterpart will display a liberal agnosticism about "right" answers, coupled with a procedural outlook. He will be primarily concerned about good arguments for a case.

III. THE LEGAL PROFESSION vs. THE LEGAL PROFESSIONS

John Henry Merryman, The Civil Law Tradition 101–108 (2nd ed. 1985).

EUROPEAN LEGAL EDUCATION

[T]he division of labor among professional lawyers in the civil law world displays characteristics unfamiliar to the common law world, and particularly to those in the United States. Americans usually think of *the* legal profession, of a single entity. To Americans a lawyer, no matter what kind of legal work he happens to be doing at the moment, is still a lawyer. Although many young graduates start out as private attorneys, government lawyers, or members of the legal staffs of corporations, and stay in those positions for life, it is common for them to change from one branch of the profession to another. During his lifetime a lawyer may do a variety of legal jobs. He may spend a year or so as law clerk to a state or federal judge after graduation from law school. He may spend some time in the office of a district attorney or a city attorney or in the legal office of a state or federal agency; or he may join a corporate law department. He may then move to private practice. If he has a successful career, he may ultimately secure an appointment as a state or federal judge. Americans think it normal for him to move easily from one position to another, and they do not think it necessary for him to have special training for any of these different kinds of work.

Things are different in civil law jurisdictions. There, a choice among a variety of distinct professional careers faces the young law graduate. He can embark on a career as a judge, a public prosecutor, a government lawyer, an advocate, or a notary. He must make this decision early and then live with it. Although it is theoretically possible to move from one of these professions to another, such moves are comparatively rare. The initial choice, once made, tends to be final in the majority of cases. The point of entry into any of these careers is almost always at the bottom, and advancement is frequently as much a function of seniority within the given career as it is of merit. Accumulated experience in another legal career does not give one a head start or any formal advantage in the process of advancement. Consequently the average young lawyer soon finds himself locked into a career from which escape is likely to be too costly to contemplate.

One predictable result is a tendency for the lines that divide one career from another to sharpen. Those involved in one branch of the legal profession come to think of themselves as different from the others. They develop their own expertise, their own career image, their own professional association. Rivalries, jurisdictional problems, and failures of communication between different kinds of lawyers are more likely to occur than they are in the United States, with its single, unified legal profession. * * * Bureaucratization, especially evident in the various governmental legal careers, is measurably greater than in the common law world, where easy lateral mobility among the different branches of the legal profession leads to a quite different mode of entry into and advancement within them.

The tendency of the initial choice of legal career to be final and the resulting sharp separation of each branch of the legal profession from the others combine to produce a number of effects considered undesirable by many civil lawyers. Frequently the career decision is made without an adequate basis for choice, before the young lawyer has been sufficiently exposed to the range of possible legal careers to decide wisely which is the best for him. And the isolation of those in one career from the others, the tendency to identify with only one set of professional interests and functions, encourages a limiting narrowness of attitude and a Balkanization of the legal professions. These are among the reasons why, in certain nations, law graduates are required to undergo a period of practical training, in which they must participate for designated periods in the work of the judiciary, of government lawyers, and of private practice before they can be admitted to any legal career.

* * *

The judiciary provides an obvious and interesting example of the phenomena we are describing. On graduation from law school (or following the period of practical training, where required) the student who wishes to become a judge immediately applies for admission to the judiciary; if selected (often on the basis of a competitive examination), he enters at the bottom of the profession. In a few nations he will attend a special school for judges, but in most he will soon find himself assigned to the lowest in the hierarchy of courts in a remote part of the country. As the result of some combination of seniority and demonstrated merit, he will gradually rise in the judicial hierarchy to more desirable and prestigious judicial positions, and eventually retire. Normally he will compete for desirable positions only against other members of the judiciary. Although appointment to positions on the highest court—a supreme court of cassation or its equivalent—may in theory be open to distinguished practicing lawyers or professors, such appointments are rare. The highest courts, like the lower courts, are likely to be manned exclusively by those who have risen within the judicial career service. The typical judge will never have practiced law or have served in any other branch of the legal profession, except possibly during required practical training following graduation from the university. He will tend to restrict his professional and social contacts to other judges. He will see the law solely from the judge's point of view. He will be a specialist.

The public prosecutor is also a civil servant, and, typically, he has two principal functions. The first is to act as prosecutor in criminal actions, preparing and presenting the state's cases against the accused before a court. In this sense the public prosecutor is like a district attorney in a typical American state. His second principal function, however, is quite different; he is called on to represent the public interest in judicial proceedings between private individuals. Thus he may have the power to intervene, even at the trial level, in a variety of actions of the sort ordinarily considered to be private law matters, involving only the interests of the parties. He may also be required by law to intervene in other matters at the trial level, typically actions involving personal status and family relationships. Finally, in some nations, he may be required to appear and to present his own independent view of the proper interpretation and application of the law in actions before the highest ordinary courts. The theory is that a primary function of such courts is the correct interpretation and application of the law, that parties to cases cannot always be expected to present all the arguments, and that the judges need the assistance of a public prosecutor to assure that an impartial view, in the interest of the law, is presented.

The young university law graduate who wishes to become a public prosecutor ordinarily takes the state examination for this career shortly after he leaves the university or completes his practical training; if successful, he enters at the bottom of the service and begins a lifetime career in it. Recently there has been a tendency in civil law jurisdictions toward "judicialization" of the public prosecutor service, the idea being that since prosecutors perform quasi-judicial functions, they ought to have something of the independence and security of tenure that is given judges. This trend has reached an advanced stage in several nations, most prominently Italy, where the office of public prosecutor has been made a part of the judiciary. However, the career of judge and that of public prosecutor continue even in these nations to be separate careers within the judiciary; although the trend ultimately may be toward a merger of the two functions, this has not yet taken place. In particular, the relationship between the public prosecutor and the ministry of justice, which exercises authority over his work, continues to be quite different from the relationship of the judge to that ministry. Judicialization of the office of public prosecutor has, however, tended to encourage mobility between the judicial and prosecutorial professions.

In some civil law jurisdictions there is no general career of government lawyer * * *. In other countries, there is an office of government attorneys that provides legal services for all state agencies. Even in the former case, appointment and advancement are bureaucratized and regularized. And in either case the difficulty of lateral movement to another branch of the profession tends to fix the government lawyer in his career.

* * *

The advocate is the closest thing one finds in the civil law to the attorney-at-law in the United States. Divisions of this profession into subspecialties (e.g. the French *avocat* and *avoué*; the Italian *avvocato* and *procuratore*) still survive in a few nations, but are rapidly losing their significance. The advocate meets with and advises clients and represents them in court. He may also become involved in helping them plan their business and property affairs. He will be a product of a university law school and, typically, of a period of apprenticeship in the office of an experienced lawyer. He will normally practice in a law office in which he is the only senior lawyer, with one or two junior attorneys associated with him. Although law firms resembling those in the United States are beginning to appear more often in major cities in the civil law world, the general rule still is that of the individual law office; indeed, in some countries partnerships for the practice of law are still forbidden. Frequently there are similar restrictions on the development of corporate law departments or similar "house counsel" arrangements. This kind of restriction is the product of a traditional ideal of the lawyer as a totally independent person who is free to accept or reject clients and who makes his own decisions about how the client's affairs should be handled. However, there is a growing trend toward evasion of such restrictions, so it is not uncommon to find groups of lawyers practicing together in what look like partnerships or corporate law departments in a jurisdiction in which such arrangements appear to be forbidden by statute or by regulation of the bar association. Generally, all practicing advocates must be members of a bar association, which frequently is officially recognized and has the authority to establish rules governing the practice of the profession, including fee schedules. As in the United States and elsewhere, members of the practicing bar are likely to become involved in politics and to move into high public office. Although the matter varies from nation to nation, in many civil law countries the percentage of high public officials who began their careers as practicing lawyers is as high or higher than is the case in the United States.

If the civil law advocate closely resembles our practicing lawyer, any similarity between the civil law notary and the notary public in common law countries is only superficial. The historical origins of the civil law notary and the common law notary public are the same, but the two occupations have developed along very different lines. Our notary public is a person of very slight importance. The civil law notary is a person of considerable importance. The notary in the typical civil law country serves three principal functions. First, he drafts important legal instruments, such as wills, corporate charters, conveyances of land, and contracts. Although advocates sometimes get involved in drafting instruments, the notary continues to do most of this work in civil law nations. * * * Second, the notary authenticates instruments. An authenticated instrument (called everywhere in the civil law world a "public act") has special evidentiary effects: it conclusively establishes that the instrument itself is genuine and that what it recites accurately represents what the parties said and what the notary saw and heard. Evidence that contradicts statements in a public act is not admissible in an ordinary judicial proceeding. One who wishes to attack the authenticity of a public act must institute a special action for the purpose, and such an action is rarely brought. Third, the notary acts as a kind of public record office. He is required to retain the original of every instrument he prepares and furnish authenticated copies on request. An authenticated copy usually has the same evidentiary value as the original.

Notaries are usually given quasi-monopolies. A typical civil law nation will be divided into notarial districts, and in each district a limited number of notaries will have exclusive competence. Unlike advocates, who are free to refuse to serve a client, the notary must serve all comers. This, added to his functions as record office and his monopoly position, tends to make him a public as well as private functionary. Access to the profession of notary is difficult because the number of notarial offices is quite limited. Candidates for notarial positions must ordinarily be graduates of university law schools and must serve an apprenticeship in a notary's office. Typically, aspirants for such positions will take a national examination and, if successful, will be appointed to a vacancy when it occurs, although in some nations the successful aspirant still must purchase the "office" from the owner. Ordinarily there will be a national notaries organization that will serve the same sort of functions for notaries as the national bar association serves for advocates and other organizations for judges, prosecutors, and government lawyers.

We come finally to the academic lawyer * * *. He is the inheritor of the tradition of the Roman jurisconsult and of the medieval scholar, whose opinions, at some periods in the history of the civil law tradition, have had formal authority to bind judges. Formal authority aside, the academic lawyer is generally viewed as the person who does the fundamental thinking for the entire legal profession. His ideas, as expressed in books and articles, and his opinions on specific legal questions raised in litigation or lawmaking, particularly in the areas covered by the basic codes, are of substantially greater importance than the work of academic lawyers in the common law world.

It is not easy to become a professor in a civil law university. The road to appointment to a vacant chair is long, arduous, and full of hazards. The young aspirant to an academic career attaches himself to a professor as an assistant, sometimes with pay and sometimes without. Eventually, after meeting certain more or less formal requirements and publishing a book, he will take a state examination for admission to the category of "private-docent." If he receives this title, he is considered to be qualified for an academic post. When a chair becomes vacant, he will compete for it against other private-docents and, if the post is a desirable one, against professors who hold less prestigious chairs. Throughout this process his progress may depend as much on the influence of the professor to whom he has attached himself as on his demonstrated ability as a scholar. This system gives the professor great power over those who have attached themselves to him and makes them heavily dependent on him for their careers. The result is an academic world composed of professors surrounded by retinues of assistants. These assistants are expected to think and work along the same lines as the professor, and thus "schools of thought" are established and grow. Doctrinal, as well as personal, loyalty is expected by the professor, whose power over the assistant's career enables him to demand it.

The uncertainty of success in pursuit of a professorship is so great that few can afford to gamble exclusively on it. In addition, in many civil law nations professors are not expected to spend all, or even a major portion, of their time at the law school. In Latin America, in particular, their rates of compensation reflect this assumption; they are by any standard extremely low. The formal obligations of the professor are to lecture to his classes a few hours a week and to give examinations (with the help of his assistants) two or three times a year. He is not paid enough for this to live well, and he consequently divides most of his time between another legal career—usually in practice, in the judiciary, or in public office—and his own and his assistants' doctrinal writing. While professors are full-time teacher-scholars in some parts of the civil law world, such as Germany, these are exceptions to the general rule. The trend is in the direction of full time, but it is still only a trend.

Thus an aspirant to an academic position customarily embarks on an additional legal career, both as a hedge against possible failure in the academic world and as an additional source of income, even if he is successful in the competition for a chair. The professor is not full-time and is not expected to be. In the usual case he is also a practicing lawyer, and the prestige of his title as professor may be of most importance to him because of the business it will bring to his law office. An advocate with the title of professor will attract important clients and will be called upon to prepare opinions on legal questions by other lawyers (and also by judges) and be paid for them.

The tendency of the law professor also to be a practicing lawyer produces what appears to common lawyers to be a curious sort of professional schizophrenia. As a lawyer, he will be pragmatic, concrete, and result-oriented. He will follow the problem where it leads him, regardless of boundaries between fields of the law. He will be fact-conscious. He will seek and cite judicial decisions. He will be a tough, partisan advocate. As a professor, he will write and teach in the prevailing doctrinal style, working in the central tradition of legal science. Both his writing and his teaching will prominently display the academic characteristics typical of legal scholarship in the civil law world, and he may even exaggerate such characteristics to overcompensate because he is also a practicing lawyer. He becomes aggressively academic, as a kind of reaction against his practical work as advocate. His life is divided into two separate halves, and he adopts a different professional personality for each.

IV. THE STRUCTURE OF THE LEGAL PROFESSION IN THE CIVIL LAW: GERMANY, FRANCE, ITALY, AND JAPAN

GERMANY

Judges in the civil law are career judges, whose independence is usually guaranteed by the constitution of their respective countries. The following materials concerning Germany, and the other legal systems we are addressing, confirm this general statement.

FUNDAMENTAL LAW (GRUNDGESETZ) OF THE FEDERAL REPUBLIC OF GERMANY OF 1949*

Article 97 [Independence of the judges]

1. The judges are independent and subject only to the law.

2. Judges appointed permanently on a full time basis to an established post can, against their will, be dismissed, or permanently or temporarily suspended from office or transferred to another post or retired before expiration of their term of office only under authority of a judicial decision and only on grounds and in the form provided by law. Legislation may set age limits for the retirement of judges appointed for life. In the event of changes in the structure of the courts or their areas of jurisdiction, judges may be transferred to another court or removed from their office, provided they retain their full salary.

Article 98

(amended 18 March 1971)

1. The legal status of the Federal judges shall be regulated by a Special Federal law.

2. * * * If a Federal judge, in his official capacity or unofficially, infringes upon the principle of the Basic Law or the constitutional order of a Land, the Federal Constitutional Court may decide by a two-thirds majority, upon the request of the Bundestag, that the judge be transferred to another office or placed on the retired list. In a case of an intentional infringement, his dismissal may be ordered.

3. The legal status of the judges in the Laender shall be regulated by special Land laws. * * * The Federation may enact outline provisions, insofar as paragraph (4) of Article 74a does not provide otherwise.

4. The Laender may provide that the Land Minister of Justice together with a committee for the selection of judges shall decide on the appointment of judges in the Laender.

5. The Laender may, with respect to Land judges, enact provisions corresponding with paragraph 2. Existing Land constitutional law remains unaffected. The decision in a case of impeachment of a judge rests with the Federal Constitutional Court.

Peter L. Murray and Rolf Stürner, German Civil Justice 68–72, 85–125 (2004).

ORGANIZATION AND STRUCTURE OF THE GERMAN JUDICIAL SYSTEM

G.   German Judges

The core element of the German system of justice is the German professional judge (*Berufsrichter*). The system requires and expects a

---

* Translation available at http://www.psr. keele.ac.uk/docs/german.htm (Site last visited June 11, 2007).

high standard of energy, competence and integrity on the part of its judges. By the same token, German judges receive thorough training, enjoy strong civil service protection and full judicial independence, and can anticipate careers of esteemed public service in their roles as the main functionaries of Germany's justice system.

German judges hold salaried positions in the judicial branches of the various German states or the federal government. Following a probationary period at the beginning of their careers, they have lifetime tenure. The terms and conditions of their service and their performance are regulated by the German Judges Law (*Deutsches Richtergesetz* or *DRiG*). Ordinarily judges start in the lower branches of the justice system. They may apply for promotion to serve in the Appeals Courts and even the Federal Supreme Courts based on merit and seniority as determined by various appointment committees.

1. Education and Training

The German program for the education and training of judges and lawyers alike is based on the principle of the "complete jurist" (*Volljurist*). That is, every lawyer is given the same basic training required for a person to be appointed as a judge. Although the educational facilities (universities) are administered and funded by the German States, the basic educational requirements to serve as a judge are specified by Federal law. The German Judges Law (*Deutsches Richtergesetz* or *DRiG*) requires that all future judges attend a German university for at least 3 ½ years, after which they must pass a First State Examination (*erstes Staatsexamen*). Following passage of the First State Examination, the judicial candidates are required to fulfil the requirements of a two-year internship (*Referendariat*) with various organs of justice including the judiciary, the state attorney's office, an administrative agency, a private law office, and another justice-related enterprise of the candidate's choice (*Wahlstation*). During the internship each candidate is paid a small monthly stipend by the state. Following this internship there is a Second State Examination (*zweites Staatsexamen*), which covers not only academic subjects but also the practical lessons from the internship. Successful passage of the Second State Examination is the final formal qualification for service in the German judiciary.

A law professor on any German law faculty is automatically qualified for appointment as a full-time or part-time judge regardless of completion of the internship or Second State Examination. Some German law teachers, especially those specializing in procedural law, serve as part time judges on State Appeals Courts located near their universities.

2. Appointment

Most German professional judges (*Berufsrichter*) serve courts maintained by the various German states, and practically all judges, except for some of the members of the Constitutional Court, start their judicial service on a state court. Among the various German states there is some variation in the method of selecting and appointing judges. In some states, such as Hessen, Hamburg, Bremen and Berlin, appointment of new judges involves participation by judicial selection commissions combining elements of the state executive, legislative and judicial branches. In the others the state governmental administration (*Regierung*) or state ministry of justice is responsible for selection and appointment of judges. Under either procedure, candidates apply for judicial vacancies and are evaluated on their merits. High scores on state examinations and other indicia of intellectual ability, industriousness and judicial temperament such as published writings and strong recommendations from senior judges usually carry the most weight in such appointments. Political activity is usually not important in evaluating applicants for entry-level judgeships in the ordinary courts. Most entry-level judges are appointed at the completion of their legal educations soon after completing the second state examination. Occasionally a state's attorney with some years experience will enter the judiciary, much less frequently a jurist from private practice or the academy.

A young judicial candidate is initially appointed a probationary judge (*Richter auf Probe*) for a period not exceeding five years, during which she may be discharged for a simple failure of satisfactory performance. Following successful service as a probationary judge for at least three years, the judge is appointed judge with life tenure (*Richter auf Lebenszeit*). A judge is appointed to a particular court in a particular locality subject only to temporary assignment to service in a corresponding court at another location.

Aside from professors who serve as part time judges, the great majority of German professional judges start and end their legal careers as judges. Normally there is little crossover into the judiciary from other branches of the legal profession, with the exception that sometimes senior public attorneys will become judges after several years of service. Judges very rarely leave the bench to enter private practice. Occasionally a judge may be called to serve as a senior public attorney or state attorney.

The German Constitution provides that a Federal Judicial Selection Committee (*Bundesrichterwahlausschuss*) composed of ministers from the respective states and an equal number of deputies of the German Parliament is responsible for electing judges to the Federal Supreme Courts.

Judges of the Constitutional Court are often not professional judges before their selection, although judges from the Federal Supreme Courts are frequently appointed. The majority of appointees are individual jurists of high public or academic distinction, as befits a court which has the responsibility of safeguarding the constitutional structure of the entire country. Constitutional Court judges are chosen by vote of the respective houses of the German Parliament. Political considerations play a major role in the selection and election of these judges.

3. Compensation, Evaluation and Promotion

German professional judges have a unique status as salaried members of the judicial branches of the states and federation and are entitled to various privileges and protections designed to safeguard their independence. Compensation is generally at a level of a senior academic civil servant or government official and is based largely on the particular judicial position and seniority in service.

German judicial service is hierarchical so far as responsibility, compensation and prestige are concerned. There are a number of levels and positions within the judiciary through which a judge can pass during an active judicial career. In general, compensation, responsibility and prestige are seen to increase with the level of court, starting at the bottom with the Local Courts and leading to the Federal Supreme Courts at the top. Courts such as the State District Courts which sit in tribunals have designated presiding judges (*vorsitzende Richter*) who play larger roles in oral proceedings and enjoy slightly greater prestige and pay than the other sitting judges. Multi-judge Local and District Courts have chief judges (*Präsidenten*) and sometimes deputy chief judges (*Vizepräsidenten*). It is not uncommon that the compensation and prestige of such a position in a jurisdictionally "lower" court might exceed the compensation of an ordinary judge on a "higher" court.

Judges are evaluated for promotion to positions of leadership within a given court and for appointment to higher courts based on experience (seniority) and performance in office. There are also minimum requirements of age or judicial experience for some judgeships. When a vacancy occurs, it is advertised and qualified persons invited to apply. There is no geographic limitation on judges within the system. A Local Court judge from Bavaria can apply for a vacant District Court judgeship in Baden–Württemberg or Berlin. Although there is no formal barrier to movement between the various court systems, ordinary and specialized, movement of judges between court systems is not very common, at least after the several years of judicial activity.

4. Independence

Judicial independence is a fundamental principle of the German Constitution and the framework of its legal system. There are many features and institutions designed to enhance and safeguard the independence and impartiality of Germany's judiciary.

As noted above, German professional judges hold lifetime tenure. They can only be removed by statutorily prescribed judicial proceedings.

German judges, although hierarchically organized, are not subject to orders from superior judges. They are not bound by prior decisions of higher courts other than decisions of the Federal Supreme Courts on remand of the same cases and decisions of the Constitutional Court in similar cases. Matters such as their duties, responsibilities and compensation are all defined as much as possible by statute. The idea is that a judge should be free to do her work without substantive control or interference by higher authority.

* * *

THE GERMAN BAR AND ACCESS TO CIVIL JUSTICE

A. History and Background of Lawyers in Germany

* * *

In Germany, as elsewhere in Europe the legal profession divided itself early on between lawyers who represented clients (*Rechtsanwälte*), and lawyers who served as notaries (*Notare*) drafting contracts, conveyances and wills. Unlike advocate lawyers, notaries generally functioned as systemic neutrals, drafting documents for "the situation" when more than one party was involved. They were and are * * * public officials. In most of the German states the number of notaries is strictly regulated and a notarial practice is a highly coveted and lucrative position.

* * *

B. Current Status, Role and Function of the German Legal Profession

As of this writing it can be said that the German legal profession is at a high point of public esteem and economic success. Lawyers in practice generally enjoy satisfactory incomes and working conditions. More important, they are perceived as being important and effective elements of the system of justice and maintenance of a democratic society. The first section of the German Attorneys Law declares that "the German attorney is an independent organ of the administration of justice." The independence and freedom of the legal profession is seen as a material element in the effort to set boundaries on the power of the state as contemplated by the German constitution. German law also declares and protects the right of members of the legal profession to provide legal advice and represent others in legal matters of all kinds as well as every person's "right to be advised by an attorney of choice in all legal matters and to be represented before all courts, arbitration tribunals or administrative agencies."

As is the case in many countries, the relatively free entry and consequent explosive growth of the profession have led to a perception of overcrowding. And the growth of the international mega-firms may result in some loss of independence for those lawyers from German firms which have merged with or been taken over by the international giants.

It should be noted that only a fraction of those persons who receive a German legal education enter the practice of advocacy. In 1990 only about 35% of German jurists were in private law practice. Of the others, some 14% were serving as judges or public attorneys, 25% held positions in government service, and 26% worked in various capacities in private employment, some as in-house counsel and some in non-legal management positions. As the number of jurists continues to grow, it can be anticipated that a shrinking fraction of the total will find employment in the traditional role of advocates representing clients in court.

C.   EDUCATION AND TRAINING OF GERMAN LAWYERS

Although access to the German legal profession has been liberalized over the last several decades, its educational prerequisites and internship requirements continue to be some of the most rigorous in the world. Basically, in order to practice as an advocate lawyer (*Rechtsanwalt*), one must complete the same program of education and training required for service as a judge or public attorney. This includes, first, a university education of at least 3 ½ years, second, a comprehensive state examination, third, a two-year series of evaluated internships and fourth, a second comprehensive state examination.

* * *

5.   *The Second State Examination*

* * *

Successful passage of this second state examination * * * is the final qualification for a young jurist to serve as a judge or to be admitted to the bar as an advocate attorney (Rechtsanwalt).

D.   ADMISSION TO PRACTICE

1.   *Admission as an Attorney*

Although the basic qualifications for admission to the bar are set forth in federal law, admission to the bar of the various courts is administered by the states.

* * *

Application must be filed with the ministry of justice in the state in which admission is sought. The state ministry of justice in turn refers the application to the bar association (*Rechtsanwaltskammer*) in the judicial district in which the applicant intends to practice. The bar association is required to investigate the application to determine whether any of the statutory grounds for denial of admission exist and file an official report with the ministry of justice within two months of receiving the request. If the bar association reports that there is no statutory ground for denial of admission, the state ministry of justice issues a certificate of admission (*Urkunde*).

* * *

If the bar association's report identifies a statutory ground for denial, the state ministry of justice suspends further action on the application and furnishes a certified copy of the report to the applicant. Within one month of receipt of the adverse report the applicant may file an "application for judicial decision" (*Antrag auf gerichtliche Entscheidung*) in the attorneys court (*Anwaltsgerichtshof*) for the state appeals court district in which she intends to practice. If the attorneys court determines that grounds for denial exist, the application is denied. If the attorneys court finds do ground for denial, the application is deemed granted and the ministry of justice must issue the certificate. If no appeal is filed the application is deemed withdrawn.

2. Admission to Practice in Court

Every German advocate attorney must be admitted to practice by at least one court of ordinary jurisdiction, either a local court, a state district court, or a state court of appeals. Upon admission to practice, each lawyer automatically becomes a member of the bar association of the state appeals court district in which his office is located.

Traditionally a lawyer was permitted to appear in civil matters only before courts to which she had been admitted.

* * *

Recent developments in the European Union have spurred liberalization of bar admission requirements within Germany. Effective January 1, 2000 the traditional "localized admission" (*lokalisierte Postulationsfähigkeit*) was abolished so that now a lawyer admitted to practice before a single German district court can appear in district courts and local courts nationwide. On December 13, 2000 the German Federal Constitutional Court ruled that the traditional ban on simultaneous practice before state district or local courts on the one hand and state appeals courts on the other violated Article 12 of the German Constitution guaranteeing citizens the right to work and practice professions untrammelled by unreasonable government strictures. The result of these developments is that a German lawyer admitted to the bar of any of the ordinary state local, district or appeals courts has the right to appear before all of them.

* * *

4. Foreign Attorneys

Traditionally admission to the German bar and to practice before the German courts was limited to lawyers who had received their full education and training in Germany. However in recent years this tradition has yielded to developments within the EU so that now lawyers from other EU nations have broad access to practice in Germany.

A 1998 European Union Directive requires member states to permit lawyers educated and qualified in other member states to practice under their home state designations in all EU member states. Pursuant to that directive, Germany enacted the Law for the Implementation of the EU Directive on the Law of the Legal Profession (*Gesetz zur Umsetzung von Richtlinien der Europäischen Gemeinschaft auf dem Gebiet des Berufsrechts der Rechtsanwälte*). Now, a lawyer licensed under the laws of another member state can practice in Germany as a "European lawyer" (*europäischer Rechtsanwalt*), but only under the official designation of his home state. Thus, a French lawyer may appear in Germany not as a *"Rechtsanwalt"* but as an *"Avocat"*. However, after three years' continuous practice in Germany, a European lawyer is entitled to automatic admission to the German bar and to practice as a German lawyer under the usual designation of *"Rechtsanwalt"*.

Locally qualified lawyers from other member states may also obtain immediate admission to the German bar by taking a modified entry examination (*Eignungsprüfung*) offered by one of the various German states. The examination is designed to measure "the applicant's professional knowledge and his competence to practice in the profession of an advocate lawyer in Germany". The applicant is examined on civil law and the law regulating the legal profession plus one subject of choice (*Wahlfach*) from each of two choice groups. Successful examinees may obtain immediate admission to practice in Germany on the same basis as German-educated lawyers.

European lawyers who have not established offices in Germany may appear in German courts in behalf of their own clients so long as they are associated with lawyers regularly admitted to practice before German courts.

Lawyers from jurisdictions which are not members of the EU and the European Free Trade Association but are members of the World Trade Organization may practice in Germany as foreign attorneys under the appropriate designation for their home jurisdictions. Their practices, however must be limited to matters involving the law of their home jurisdictions, and international law (*Völkerrecht*). They may participate as "foreign attorney" members of the local bar associations (*Anwaltskammer*) but may not appear before German courts.

5. *The Bar of the Federal Supreme Court*

The Federal Supreme Court has its own exclusive bar of specially admitted appellate advocates. Any person with a civil case before the Federal Supreme Court must be represented by a member of the bar of that court.

* * *

An attorney admitted to practice before the Federal Supreme Court cannot be admitted to practice before any other court. The result of this regime is that the bar of the Federal Court of Justice consists of a small number of elite appellate advocates. As a matter of policy, the value of high quality professional advocacy at the highest appellate level provided by such a restrictive structure must be weighed against the value of new and diverse advocate perspectives which one might expect to find in a more open system.

E. Regulation of the German Bar

Regulation of the German bar is mainly a matter of statutory law. * * * Only the German Federal Bar Association has the authority to enact a Code of Ethics, which implements a framework of state legislation.

* * *

1. The Federal Attorneys Law and the Code of Ethics

The Federal Attorneys Law (*Bundesrechtsanwaltsordnung* or *BRAO*) is the basic code of conduct for German lawyers.

* * *

In 2001, the Federal Bar Association adopted a new Code of Ethics (*Berufsordnung für Rechtsanwälte* or *BORA*) * * *. A code of guidelines of the Association of European Attorneys supplements national law but is not, strictly speaking, legally binding. This code may influence the interpretation of national law and further the harmonization of the different rules of ethics in Europe and worldwide.

* * *

The basic duty of the lawyer is set forth in Section 43 of the Attorneys Code:

> "The attorney must practice his profession conscientiously. He must show himself, within and without the profession, as worthy of the esteem and the confidence which the position of the attorney commands".

This basic provision has been construed, for instance, to prohibit attorneys from extravagant advertising to attract clients, to require an attorney to exercise collegial courtesy in dealing with opposing counsel, to forbid conflicts of interest, and to require attorney confidentiality, even though some of these areas are regulated by other civil and criminal statutes. * * *

2. Bar Associations

A major portion of the Attorneys Code is devoted to the establishment of bar associations (*Anwaltskammer*) and to spelling out the procedures for attorney discipline and disbarment. * * *

H. LAWYERS FEES AND COMPENSATION

In litigated matters German lawyers' fees and compensation are in principle determined by a comprehensive statute prescribing a fixed attorneys fee based on the amount in controversy for every stage of a litigated case * * *.

The compensation scheme of the Attorneys Fee Law is built around the concept of a "fee" * * * for a unit of professional service. A number of statutory sections associate described litigation activities with a specified number of fee units. For instance, the preparation and filing of an ordinary civil case is associated with one fee unit * * *.

The Attorneys Fee Law specifies in tabular form the amount per fee unit at each level of value of the subject matter * * *.

The * * * Law permits clients and their lawyers to enter into agreements providing for payment of compensation to the lawyer at rates and amounts different from those provided in the statutory schedule * * *.

A lawyer and client may not agree on increased compensation based on a favorable outcome * * * compensation computed as a percentage of the recovery is not permitted.[3] Nor may a lawyer agree to accept no compensation or compensation at a rate lower than that prescribed by statute in the event of an unfavourable outcome. These restrictions are designed to prevent extreme price competition * * *.

Fees for litigation have traditionally followed the statutory formula. This is because only the statutory fees may be taxed by the court to the unsuccessful party. Traditionally German lawyers have been reluctant to demand * * * fees which could not be recovered from the other side.

I. LEGAL AID AND ACCESS TO JUSTICE IN MODERN GERMANY

Germany is a world leader in affording its citizens * * * reasonable access to its civil justice system.

1. Out of Court Legal Assistance

The Legal Advice Assistance Act ... was enacted in January 1980 * * * to provide non-litigation legal assistance to indigent persons in certain designated areas * * * As of the present time most states have adopted programs under which indigent persons seeking legal advice assistance apply to the local court authorization. Authorization is granted based on a means test and some screening on the significance of the legal issue on which help is sought * * *.

2. Legal Aid in Civil Litigation

Legal aid in litigation is regulated by federal law * * *

Legal aid is available in all legal proceedings * * * In practice the great bulk of legal aid is rendered in various family court proceedings and to a lesser extent in consumer, landlord tenant, and personal injury cases.

* * * An indigent person who wishes to initiate litigation or defend a case brought against him can either apply to the court directly * * * or * * * go to a lawyer for help in the application process. All lawyers are

---

3. Editors' Note: A recent decision of the Constitutional Court holds unconstitutional the absolute prohibition of contingency fee agreements in all cases, in that it can violate both the client's right of access to justice in civil cases and the attorney's right to practice freely. Consequently, the court required the German Parliament to modify the law against contingency fees agreement within a year. See Bundesverfassungsgericht, 1BvR2576/04 vom 12.12.2006, http://www.bverfg.de/entscheidungen/rs20061212. See also Anthony J. Sebok, How an Important German Constitutional Court Decision May Change the Nature of Law Practice in

eligible and expected to participate in representation of legal aid clients, there is no panel or list * * *.

* * * the Federal Attorneys Law prescribes a different and lower fee schedule for services in legal aid cases * * *.

Legal aid funds are made available only to pay the recipient's own attorney. There are no funds to satisfy the obligations of an indigent person who loses a case and is taxed with the opponent's attorney's fees. The winning opponent is left to collect such funds as best it may.

J. LEGAL COST INSURANCE

It is possible for Germans to protect themselves against the financial impact of having to hire counsel or pay an opponent's lawyers' fees by the purchase of legal cost insurance offered by private insurance companies * * *

A large percentage of ordinary German citizens hold some kind of legal cost insurance policy. Between 1975 and 1990 the gross amount of annual premiums paid by the by Germans for legal cost insurance trebled to a total of over 1.5 billion Euros * * *.

In recent years commercial finance firms have entered the market of underwriting the assertion of plaintiffs' personal injury and other claims in litigation. The finance firm contracts to pay all costs required to be advanced by the claimant, as well as the opponent's costs and fees if the claimant loses. In return the plaintiff assigns to the finance company a portion of the claim on which the suit is to be brought * * * generally between 30 and 50 percent * * *.

Some have criticized this new form of litigation as a circumvention of the prohibition against contingent compensation, and on the ground that it changes the balance between the parties, since there are no such contracts available to potential defendants. On the other hand it has also been argued that the three-cornered finance company-client-lawyer relationship is not subject to some of the theoretical and practical disadvantages of the direct contingency fee arrangement and that it does provide access to justice for some litigants who would not otherwise be able to get into court.

FRANCE

Constitution of the Republic of France (1958).*

Article 64 [Independence]

(1) The President of the Republic shall be the guarantor of the independence of the Judiciary.

Germany, http://writ.lp.findlaw.com/sebok/ 20070313.html.

* Translation available at http://www. oefre.unibe.ch/law/icl/ (Site last visited June 9, 2007).

(2) He shall be assisted by the Superior Council of the Judiciary (Conseil Superieur de la Magistrature).

(3) An organic statute (loi organique) shall determine the status of members of the Judiciary.

(4) Judges may not be removed from office.

Article 65 [Conseil Superieur]

(1) The Superior Council of the Judiciary (Conseil Superieur) shall be presided over by the President of the Republic. The Minister of Justice shall be its vice-president ex officio. He may deputize for the President of the Republic.

(2) The Superior Council of the Judiciary shall consist of two sections, one with jurisdiction for judges, the other for public prosecutors.

(3) The section with jurisdiction on judges shall comprise, in addition to the President of the Republic and the Minister of Justice, five judges and one public prosecutor, one conseiller d'Etat appointed by the Conseil d'Etat, and three prominent citizens who are not members either of Parliament or of the judiciary, appointed respectively by the President of the Republic, the President of the National Assembly and the President of the Senate.

(4) The section with jurisdiction on public prosecutors shall comprise, in addition to the President of the Republic and the Minister of Justice, five public prosecutors and one judge, and the conseiller d'Etat and the three prominent citizens referred to in the preceding paragraph.

(5) The section of the Superior Council of the Judiciary with jurisdiction on judges shall make nominations for the appointment of judges in the Court of cassation, the first presidents of the courts of appeal and the presidents of the tribunaux de grande instance. Other judges shall be appointed with its assent.

(6) [It] shall act as the disciplinary council for judges. When acting in that capacity, it shall be presided over by the President of the Court of cassation.

(7) The section of the Superior Council of the Judiciary with jurisdiction on public prosecutors shall give its opinion on the appointment of public prosecutors, with the exception of appointments to be made by the Council of Ministers.

(8) It shall give its opinion on disciplinary sanctions with regard to public prosecutors. When acting in that capacity, it shall be presided over by the General Prosecutor of the Court of cassation.

(9) An organic statute shall determine the manner in which this article is to be implemented.

Catherine Elliott and Catherine Vernon, The French Legal System 192–201 (2000).

THE LEGAL PROFESSION

PART I: JUDGES AND THE *MINISTERE PUBLIC*

Introduction

This chapter looks at both the judiciary in the civil and criminal court system and judges in the administrative system. In the civil and criminal system, each court has at its disposal, in addition to the ordinary judges who decide cases, a number of civil servants known as *magistrats du parquet* and collectively as the *ministère public* * * * They receive the same training as judges and are considered to form part of the same profession. People can switch from practising as a member of the *ministère public* to sitting as a judge on the bench deciding cases.

Ordinary judges in the civil and criminal courts

The judicial hierarchy

In France, judges are regarded as civil servants providing a service to the public. Appointments to judicial office are made by the President of the Republic, on a proposal of the Minister of Justice (ordonnance of 22 December 1958). This recommendation is really by an independent body known as the *Conseil superieur de la magistrature* (CSM). The composition of this body is regulated by article 65 of the Constitution * * *.

The most senior appointments, namely to the posts of judge of the *Cour de cassation*, First President of the courts of appeal and Presidents of the *Tribunaux de Grande Instance*, are chosen by the CSM. The CSM forwards their nomination to the Minister of Justice and the President of the Republic who will normally appoint that person. Other senior appointments, such as judges to the courts of appeal, are made on the advice of the CSM, which again is customarily followed by the Minister of Justice and the President. More junior appointments are recommended by a separate commission which proposes names to the CSM, to be formally appointed by the Minister of Justice and the President of the Republic. The most junior judges are trainee judges on posting during their studies at the *Ecole Nationale de la Magistrature*.

Termination of appointment and disciplinary action

Article 64 of the 1958 Constitution provides that judges are *inamovibles* (irremovable). This does not mean that their appointment may never be terminated, but that a judge can only be removed on the very limited grounds allowed for by the law. This is mostly contained in the *ordonnance* of 22 December 1958 mentioned above. Any decision to dismiss a judge is taken by the CSM, sitting as a court and presided over by the President of the *Cour de cassation* * * *. The same body may also consider cases where the judgment may include less serious consequences, such as a reprimand or demotion to a less important post. There is no right of appeal from its decisions.

* * *

Independence of the judiciary

It is a fundamental principle of the Constitution that judicial power should be exercised by a judiciary independent of the bodies exercising legislative and executive power, namely Parliament and the government. The 1958 Constitution specifically states in article 64 that this independence is guaranteed by the President of the Republic. However, to achieve independence it is essential that appointments are made by an independent body. To achieve this goal the composition of the CSM was reformed in 1993 to include a larger number of judges, but there is still a significant political membership and further reforms may be introduced in the future. To increase the independence of judges further, they may never be obliged to accept a new post, even one involving promotion.

In addition, to ensure that judges are seen to be independent, the *ordonnance* of 22 December 1958 bars them from practising another profession or carrying on business. Only a limited number of occupations are permitted, such as teaching (with permission) or carrying out artistic activities. They are also forbidden to express political opinions in public. There are, however, many judges whose political opinions are well known, and this does indeed lead the public (rightly or wrongly) to consider that their decisions are influenced by their political views. They can, in particular, legitimately express their views as members of unions protecting judges' interests, though they do not have the right to strike.

The ministère public

* * * [T]he public prosecutor's office is part of a wider body of civil servants that also has a role to play in civil cases. It is known as the *ministère public* or the *magistrature du parquet*. In criminal cases, public prosecutors are parties to the cases. In civil matters, members of the *ministère public* are not usually parties to the litigation, but in important cases they make representations to the court on behalf of the public. Their aim is to thereby ensure that in reaching its decisions the court has the benefit of independent expertise, though it is not bound to follow their advice.

Hierarchy of the ministère public

Appointments to the *ministère public* are made, as for members of the judiciary, by the President of the Republic, on a proposal by the Minister of justice. The CSM, which for this purpose is composed of the President of the Republic, the Minister of Justice, five members of the *ministère public*, one judge of the civil and criminal justice system, and three independent members, also plays a part. However, its recommendations are not considered as authoritative as those for appointments to the bench. It would be more accurate to describe its role as merely consultative. The most important members of the *ministere public* are appointed by the government, and the CSM is not even consulted (article 65–7 of the 1958 Constitution).

* * *

The services of members of the *ministère public* are available to all courts in the civil and criminal system. Members posted to the Tribunal de Grande Instance (TGI) are known as *procureurs de la République*. Those operating in the courts of appeal and the Cour de cassation have the title of *procureur général* or *avocat général*, according to rank. None are allocated to the specialised courts but members may be lent, when required, by the local TGI.

Termination of appointment and disciplinary action

Members of the *ministère public*, unlike the ordinary judiciary, do not benefit from security of tenure. However, before being removed from office they are entitled to a hearing, and the CSM, headed by the public prosecutor of the *Cour de cassation*, is required to give its advice on the matter (article 65–8 of the 1958 Constitution). The final decision is pronounced by the Minister of Justice who will listen to, but need not follow, the CSM's advice.

Independence of the ministère public

The independence of the public prosecutor's office in criminal cases is the subject of much discussion. * * * This is not such an issue in civil cases where the role of the *ministere public* is, in effect, advisory only.

Judges in the administrative courts

There is no *ministère public* as such in the administrative courts. The judges are civil servants who are employed by the Home Office rather than the Ministry of Justice. They have a reputation for acting independently, despite the fact that they are not directly protected by the 1958 Constitution. In a landmark decision of 22 July 1980 the *Conseil constitutionnel* declared that the independence of administrative judges was a fundamental principle of the Republic. They also have the benefit of a number of different laws regulating their profession, which differ according to the court and position of the judge.

PART II: AVOCATS

The *avocats* are the oldest legal profession in France, with origins dating back to Roman times. They are officers of the court, but are independent and have the privilege of self-regulation by their local Barreau, which fulfils a similar function to the English and Welsh Bar, and will for convenience be translated in this text as the 'Bar'. The closest English and Welsh equivalent to *avocats* are barristers. The best have, in common with their English and Welsh counterparts, a public image of performing feats of brilliant oratory in court. French *avocats* did indeed, for the years preceding the latest reforms in 1971 and 1990, concentrate largely on pleading at court hearings. They had ceased, since the 15th century, to deal with the drafting of pleadings and other written parts of legal procedure and in practice did not give much legal advice which was unconnected with litigation. Others had taken on this discarded work. Those responsible for drafting pleadings and the written part of procedures had developed into the independent profession of *avoués* and those specialising in giving legal advice were subsumed separately into the profession of *conseils juridique* (which will be referred to as 'legal advisers'). The Act of 31 December 1971, in effect, merged the professions of *avoués* and that of *avocats* (with the exception of *avoués* at the Court of Appeal which form a separate profession we will look at later). The Act of 31 December 1990 merged the profession of legal adviser with that of *avocat*.

The current role of *avocats* and the organisation of their profession is set out below.

Role of the avocat

The *avocat* has four main roles: acting as an advocate at pre-trial and trial court hearings (known as assistance), drafting written submissions on behalf of the client (known as representation), giving legal advice and drafting documents.

Advocacy

Acting as an advocate before the courts is the traditional role of the *avocat*. A great deal of work is done by the judge during the pre-trial phase, including interviewing witnesses, the suspect and, if necessary, experts. The *avocats* are present at these proceedings where they involve their client and make oral representations on their behalf where necessary. They have a monopoly on the right to make oral pleading in the ordinary courts in criminal cases except where the parties are allowed to plead for themselves. *Avocats* have rights of audience throughout the country, though they are not allowed to act before the two highest courts in the land, the *Cour de cassation* and the *Conseil d'Etat*. A specialist body of senior *avocats* carries that function known as *avocats aux conseils*.

Drafting court documents

The *avocat* drafts pleadings and other written papers required during the pre-hearing stage of proceedings.

* * *

Legal advice

Avocats have no monopoly on giving legal advice, and other legal professionals, such as *notaires* and people with no professional qualification other than a law degree, also give advice in a number of circumstances.

* * *

Non-litigious drafting

Avocats also now draft documents other than pleadings and documents required in the course of litigation. Again, they have no monopoly of such functions * * *.

* * *

Organisation of the profession

Avocats belong to the Bar attached to their local TGI. Each Bar is administered by its own council, elected by its *avocats* (decree of 27 November 1991). Members sit for a period of three years and a third of the members stand for election every year. The President of the Bar Council, known as the *bâtonnier*, is elected by senior *avocats* for a term of two years (Act of 31 December 1971).

The Bar Council exercises a number of functions of which the most important are the calling of new *avocats* to the Bar, and ensuring efficient self-regulation of the Bar by enforcing its rules and disciplinary code. *Avocats* may appeal to the court of appeal against decisions made by the Bar Council.

Since 31 December 1990, individual *avocats* and their local Bars, are also represented by a National Bar Council. This is composed of a number of *avocats* elected according to complex rules which are designed to ensure both individual representation and representation of the interests of the various regional Bars.

PART III: OFFICIERS MINISTERIELS

Important legal functions are carried out by *notaires, avoués, avocats aux conseils*, and *huissiers* who are all officers of the court (*officiers ministériels*). This title refers to legal professionals who are appointed by the Minister of Justice after they have acquired a practice. A practice is usually acquired either by purchasing it from an existing practitioner, or by receiving it under a legacy or a gift. Occasionally the Ministry of Justice will open new practices for which qualified entrants may compete. These will usually be in the suburbs of large towns or other areas where existing practitioners do not meet the legal needs of the local population. Most commonly the new professional acquires the practice of a person who is retiring and proposes the new applicant to the Ministry of Justice. The Minister will then usually grant a certificate of practice to the person proposed by the retiring professional and accept the contract made between the parties for the sale of the existing practice. Conditions may, however, be imposed if, for instance, it is considered that the agreed provisions ask the new practitioner for too high a payment.

Once candidates have acquired both a practice and the required certificate, they become *officiers ministériels* in their chosen profession. The various professions are governed by societies, which perform similar functions to those of the Bar Council in relation to *avocats*. These include responsibility for the training of new applicants and the self-regulation of the profession by enforcing a disciplinary code. The societies are centralised and hierarchical, unlike the various Bar Councils which are locally based. Furthermore, while the societies may themselves enforce minor sanctions such as a reprimand, more serious sanctions, such as requiring a practitioner to resign, must be imposed by the judgment of a court, after an application to the Minister of Justice.

Notaires

* * *

Notaires have three functions:

Drawing up authenticated and enforceable instruments

* * * By tradition many documents, such as sale contracts, are drawn up by *notaires*. In general, there is no legal requirement for such formalities but it is traditional, for instance, for documents involving the transfer of property rights to be executed in this way. The advantage is that there is a presumption that the document is authentic. It is only possible to challenge this, in the case of suspected fraud, by following a complex procedure, and very few cases are brought. In addition, unlike ordinary legal documents, they can be enforced without the need for a separate judgment confirming that the contract is enforceable. Certain documents are by law required to be drawn up by *notaires*, such as marriage contracts and mortgages. * * * The original documents are kept at the *notaire's* office, and parties may only obtain certified copies. These can be endorsed by the *notaire* to allow them to be enforced by the court as if they were originals.

* * *

Giving legal advice

Notaires give legal advice in connection with the types of transaction mentioned above and other matters such as business and commerce.

Acting as officers of the court

Notaires are occasionally required by the court to draft documentation in connection with a divorce settlement or the liquidation of a company.

* * *

Like other *officiers ministériels*, *notaires* belong to their own society. They are also required to take out insurance cover for liability for negligence claims.

Avoués

The law relating to *avoués* is contained in an Act of 2 November 1945 (as amended). This profession used to have a monopoly over the drafting of all court pleadings. In 1971, this role in relation to litigation before courts of first instance was passed to the *avocats*, while the separate profession of *avoués* was kept for the court of appeal. No doubt the profession was initially retained at this level as a first step to full abolition, but the *avoués* at the court of appeal, now a very small profession, have proved useful enough to be retained. The main reason is no doubt the purely practical one that it is convenient for the courts of appeal to be able to rely on a body of lawyers who are well known to them, available at all times and within close proximity of the court. They have accordingly kept their monopoly of this work. The one exception is that parties in cases which do not require such documentation (for example, employment cases) may choose to do the work themselves. The *avoués* have an implied mandate to act as their client's agent in the preparation of all pleadings and it is not necessary for them to be expressly given this status.

Avocats aux conseils

Avocats at the *Conseil d'Etat* and at the *Cour de cassation* have the right both to act as an advocate and draft court pleadings for the two highest courts. They are thereby exercising the equivalent role to the *avocats* before the courts of first instance and the *avoué* and *avocat* jointly before the court of appeal. In doing so they enjoy a monopoly, except that in a limited number of cases parties are allowed to represent themselves.

This profession is governed by an Act of 10 September 1817, as amended by a decree of 28 October 1991, which gives them a unique status. They are, however, *officiers ministériels*, and are required both to purchase a practice and be appointed by the Minister of Justice. The profession is very small with only approximately 80 members at anyone time. Most are experienced *avocats*, and in addition they will have passed a special examination and completed a two-year practical course organised by the *avocats* at the *Conseil d'Etat* and at the *Cour de cassation*. Like the *avocats* and the *avoués*, they have an implied mandate to act as agents for the parties in respect of the particular case and it is not necessary for the parties to appoint them specifically to this status.

ITALY

Constitution of the Italian Republic (1948).*
Article 101

Justice is administered in the name of the people.

Judges are subject only to the law.

Article 102

The judicial function is exercised exclusively by ordinary judges appointed and governed by the rules of judicial organization.

* Translation by Vincenzo Varano, adapted from Mauro Cappelletti, John Henry Merryman, and Joseph M. Perillo, The Italian Legal System 305 (1967).

Extraordinary or special judges shall not be established. It shall be lawful only to establish specialized sections of the ordinary courts for specific subjects, and in these qualified citizens not drawn from the judiciary may participate.

The law will determine the cases and manner in which the people shall participate in the administration of justice.

Article 103

The Council of State and other organs of administrative justice have jurisdiction to protect legitimate interests and, in specific matters indicated by law, subjective rights against the public administration.

* * *

Article 104

The judiciary is an autonomous order independent of any other.

The Superior Council of the Judiciary is chaired by the President of the Republic.

The President and the General Public Prosecutor of the Court of Cassation are members ex officio of the Superior Council.

The other members are elected as to two-thirds by all ordinary judges belonging to the different categories, and as to one-third by Parliament in joint session, from among university professors of law and lawyers with at least fifteen years of practice.

The Council elects a Vice–President from among the members designated by Parliament.

Elected members serve for a term of four years and may not be immediately re-elected.

They are not allowed, while in office, to be registered as members of the legal profession, nor members of Parliament or of a Regional Council.

Article 105

The Superior Council of the Judiciary has the exclusive responsibility to appoint, assign, transfer, promote, and discipline members of the judiciary, in accordance with the rules on judicial organization.

Article 106

Appointment to the judiciary is based on competitive examinations.

The law on judicial organization may allow the appointment or election of honorary judges, to perform all the functions assigned to single judges.

Upon recommendation of the Superior Council of the Judiciary, university professors of law as well as lawyers with at least fifteen years of practice, and registered for practice in highest courts, may be appointed to the Court of Cassation for exceptional merits.

Article 107

Judges may not be removed from office.

They may not be dismissed, suspended, or moved to other offices or functions except with their own consent or following a decision of the Superior Council of the Judiciary, taken for the reasons and with the guarantees of defense provided for by the law on judicial organization.

The minister of justice may initiate disciplinary action.

Judges shall distinguish themselves only by the diversity of their functions.

The public prosecutor's office enjoys the guarantees defined by the law on judicial organization.

Article 108

The rules on the judicial organization and any judicial authority at every level will be established by law.

The law will ensure the independence of judges of special courts, of the office of Public Prosecutor attached to them, and of all those who do not belong to the judiciary, but who participate in the administration of justice.

* * *

Article 110

Except for matters within the competence of the Superior Council of the Judiciary, the organization and direction of all services connected with the administration of justice are vested in the Minister of Justice.

Note on the Italian Legal Professions

1. *Avvocati* (attorneys). At the time of writing there are more than 150,000 practicing lawyers in Italy, registered with some 160 local bars. They are still basically regulated by the antiquated Law of November 27, 1933, n. 1578, which since then has not undergone major changes.

Traditionally, the profession was divided between *procuratori*—i.e., the parties' agents and procedural technicians—and *avvocati*, who prepared and prosecuted the parties' substantive claims and defences. However, the distinction had evolved to such a formality that it was abolished by the law of February 24, 1997, no. 27, merging the two professions into that of *avvocato*. In order to appear before the highest courts—i.e., the Constitutional Court, the Court of Cassation, the Council of State, and the Court of Accounts—*avvocati* must complete eight years of practice, or take an ad hoc examination after one year of practice, most people opting for the former solution.

Admission to the profession is open to law graduates who have completed the required period of apprenticeship in the law office of a qualified attorney, and passed a rather selective bar exam, both written and oral, of a theoretical and a practical nature.

Avvocati must be members of the Bar Association of the tribunal district where their practice is based. The Bar Association "is a semi-autonomous quasi-governmental agency that is responsible for maintaining the rolls of attorneys and for disciplining violators of professional ethics."[4] Their officers are elected by the members of the association.

Traditionally, the legal profession conforms to "the legislative ideal of individual practice. The independent practitioner is idealized because attorneys are deemed to be independent participants in the administration of the law."[5] As a consequence, rigid rules have prohibited for a long time partnerships, any form of advertising, contingency fee agreements, and provided for professional tariffs setting down minimum and maximum fees. It is only very recently that these rules have begun to be relaxed in the name of "liberalization" and "competition" ideals, certainly prompted by the European integration which is affecting the legal profession, as well as any other economic activity, in Italy and elsewhere.

The modernization of the legal profession is still in progress. After the law of February 2, 2001, no. 96, which has introduced a special form of professional association, and some timid openings of the code of ethics to advertising, a very recent statute (the Law of August 4, 2006, n. 248, which is meant in general to favor the economic development and the increase of competition) has unexpectedly and deeply affected the traditional structure of the legal profession among others. Art. 2 of that law, whose declared purpose is to implement such fundamental principles of community law as freedom of competition and freedom of movement of persons and services, and to allow consumers an effective choice and comparison of the services available on the market, attempts at extending the idea of a competitive market to legal services. Consequently, it repeals flatly any provision prohibiting the deviation from minimum fees, the stipulation of contingency fee agreements, the prohibition of advertising the professional specializations, the characteristics of the services offered, and their costs, and many restrictions to professional partnerships. The new law has raised, not unexpectedly, quite some strong reactions (including strikes) on the side of the legal profession, and many other categories—from taxi licensees to pharmacists—whose privileges have also been touched upon. However, at the moment of writing (October 2006) its implementation seems to be certain, because the law meets with a widespread consensus which goes across party lines.

2. <u>Notaries.</u>

Mauro Cappelletti, John Henry Merryman, and Joseph M. Perillo, The Italian Legal System: An Introduction 99–102 (1967).

The Italian *notario* drafts and authenticates important legal instruments, including wills, corporate charters, conveyances, and contracts. Any instrument that on its face purports to have been drafted * * * under the supervision of a notary is known as a "public act" and is conclusive evidence of three things: (1) that it was in fact so drafted and

4. Cappelletti, Merryman, and Perillo, supra note 1, at 93.

5. Id. at 94.

executed; (2) that the recitals and agreements expressed in the instrument are accurate reports of the parties' statements and agreements; and (3) that any fact that the instruments recites to have occurred in the presence of the notary did occur, and any act the instruments recites to have been performed by the notary was in fact performed. The conclusive nature of a public act can be upset only in a *querela di falso*, a special proceeding with criminal overtones.

Successful completion of a difficult national examination is a requirement for admission to the notariat. * * * [T]he candidate must have completed law school and have served a two-year apprenticeship in the office of a notary. When a vacancy occurs in one of the approximately 4,000 notarial positions, preference is given to notaries already in service. Vacancies that are not applied for by incumbent notary are filled by the successful examination candidates * * *.

The keeping, filing, and indexing of notarial records are minutely governed by law. Ordinarily, any notary must retain the original of any instrument he prepares or that is filed with him * * * Upon demand he is required to prepare and deliver a copy of any instrument—except a will—that is in his official custody. A notarial copy * * * has the same evidentiary value as an original.

Although a notary is a public official he receives no salary. * * * The fees charged are rigidly fixed by law and fixed high * * *.

The profession offers its members generous financial rewards and performs a highly useful function. The implicit trust that is granted notaries is rarely abused. Lawyers consider the profession a dull, plodding one, but many envy it for its secure earning power and the universal respect it is accorded.

3.   The Italian Judiciary in Transition. In Italy, as in any other civil law country, the judiciary is made up of several thousand career judges—8,744 presently serving, according to the latest figures published by the Superior Council of the Judiciary. This number includes the public prosecutors (precisely 2,254), who are part of the judicial organization according to the Italian Constitution (art. 107 para. 4). Access to the judiciary depends on the passing of a difficult highly competitive national examination (art. 106, para. 1)—a rule designed to assure that the selection is based only on the ascertainment of technical skills and is immune from political considerations. Successful candidates, after a period of up to two years of apprenticeship as *uditori giudiziari*, become full judges and advance in their career as judges and/or prosecutors.

The Constitution assures both the judiciary as a whole (art. 104, para. 1) and individual judges very strong guarantees of independence. They are subject only to the law (art. 101, para. 2), they are differentiated only by the diversity of their functions (art. 107, para. 4), their career has been made to depend substantially on seniority, following a number of statutes enacted between 1966 and 1979, and they cannot be removed without their consent either from office or from the functions they exercise (art. 107, para. 2). The bulwark of judicial independence, well beyond the proclamations contained in a written text, is the *Consiglio Superiore della Magistratura*, established by art. 104 of the Constitution, which is the governing body of the judiciary. It is the CSM which appoint, promote, discipline and, in general, supervise ordinary judges.

In the chapter on the machinery of justice which Professor Varano wrote in 2001 for the Introduction to Italian Law edited by J.S. Lena and U. Mattei (2002)—which the reader can be referred to for further information on judges and their independence—he anticipated that the center-right coalition led by Mr. Silvio Berlusconi, which had gained the general elections of May 2001 and a large majority in Parliament, had marked the "problem of justice" as a priority on its agenda, mainly as a reaction against the season of "clean hands", i.e. the criminal investigations of the early 1990s which revealed how politics was dominated by corruption, and practically removed from the scene an entire political ruling class and the main political parties (foremost, the Christian Democrats and the Socialists) which had governed Italy for over forty years.

The final outcome of the Legislature, characterised by the ongoing bitter contrast between the executive and the judiciary, is the Law of July 25, 2005, n. 150, which reforms deeply the law on the judiciary in force since 1941, and delegates authority to the Government to implement it through secondary legislation. The law has been criticised by the opposition, by a substantial number of scholars, and by influential associations of judges as undermining the independence of the judiciary and individual judges. The law does not succeed in separating sharply the careers of judge and prosecutor and putting the latter under a closer control of the Minister of Justice, which was the real political objective of the government, but certainly limits severely the possibility of moving from judicial to prosecutorial duties, and vice-versa, throughout a judge's career, which until now has been quite common.

The career of judges is no longer substantially based on seniority, but on a complicated system of internal evaluations and competitions which ends up in submitting the judge to a continuous scrutiny and distract her from the dispatch of judicial work; the law provides that the various judicial offices, and in particular the prosecutorial offices, are more hierarchically structured than it is the case today—to the point, for instance, that it is only the head of the office who bears the responsibility of instituting the prosecution and who is allowed to have contacts with the media. The foregoing are only some of the points of a very complex law which have been more sharply criticised. At the time of writing (October 2006), the new center-left Government which came out from the general elections of April 2006 has not repealed the law, as some observers would have expected, but has limited itself to delay the coming into effect of the implementing decrees concerned with the above mentioned crucial areas until July 2007 so as to modify them.

JAPAN

The Constitution of Japan (1946).*
Article 6

* * *

(2) The Emperor appoints the Chief Judge of the Supreme Court as designated by the Cabinet.

* Translation available in Constitutions of the Countries of the World: A Series of Updated Texts, Constitutional Chronologies and Annotated Bibliographies (A. P. Blaustein and G. H. Flanz, eds., 1971).

Article 76

* * *

(3) All judges shall be independent in the exercise of their conscience and shall be bound only by this Constitution and the laws.

Article 78

(1) Judges shall not be removed except by public impeachment unless judicially declared mentally or physically incompetent to perform official duties.

(2) No disciplinary action against judges is to be administered by any executive organ or agency.

Article 79

(1) The Supreme Court shall consist of a Chief Judge and such number of judges as determined by law. All such judges excepting the Chief Judge shall be appointed by the Cabinet.

(2) The appointment of the judges of the Supreme Court shall be reviewed by the people at the first general election of members of the House of Representatives following their appointment, and shall be reviewed again at the first general election of members of the House of Representatives after a lapse of ten (10) years, and in the same manner thereafter.

(3) In cases mentioned in the foregoing paragraph, when the majority of the voters favors the dismissal of a judge, he shall be dismissed.

* * *

(5) All such judges receive, at regular stated intervals, adequate compensation which shall not be decreased during their terms of office.

Article 80

(1) The judges of the lower courts shall be appointed by the Cabinet from a list of persons nominated by the Supreme Court.

(2) All such judges shall hold office for a term of ten (10) years with privilege of reappointment, provided that they shall be retired upon the attainment of the age as fixed by law.

(3) The judges of the lower courts shall receive, at regular stated intervals, adequate compensation which shall not be decreased during their terms of office.

Yukiko Hasebe, Civil Justice Reform: Access, Cost, and Expedition. The Japanese Perspective, in Adrian A. S. Zuckerman, Civil Justice in Crisis 235–262 (1999).

2.3.   The legal profession.

A would-be lawyer has to pass the National Bar Examination. It is one of the most difficult national examinations. A person who has succeeded in the National Bar Examination then has to complete two years of training at the Legal Training and Research Institute, a state-funded institution. At the end of the two years, he or she has to pass the final qualifying examination. Then, he or she is appointed as an assistant judge or a public prosecutor, or starts practising as an attorney. An assistant judge is restricted to hearing cases as one member of a three-judge panel. He or she is normally promoted to judge after ten years. At this point, he or she is qualified to hear cases as a single-judge court. Thereafter, some judges are promoted to the high court bench, and a small number of them become Supreme Court justices.

Thus, the judiciary of the district court, family court, and the high court is largely composed of so-called 'career judges'. Supreme Court justices are recruited from judges, prosecutors, attorneys, and others, including law professors and ambassadors. Summary court judges are often retired judges.

An attorney (*bengoshi*) has to enroll in one of Japan's local Bar Associations. Together, the Bar Associations constitute the Japan Federation of Bar Associations, which represents the interests of attorneys all over the country.

Yasuhei Taniguchi, Japan's Recent Civil Procedure Reform: Its Seeming Success and Left Problems in The Reforms of Civil Procedure in Comparative Perspective 91, 96–99, 108, 110 (Nicolò Trocker and Vincenzo Varano, eds., 2005).[6]

III. The Situation of the Japanese Bar

For hundreds of years, the Japanese feudal regime banned practice of law as immoral while the judiciary dealt only with the parties in person. Legal profession was officially legitimatized in the 1870s but until the end of the Second World War it did not enjoy neither a prestige nor a power vis-à-vis the judges in particular. The number of practicing lawyers was kept small and lawyers were under a strict governmental supervision. The post-War reform included liberalization of lawyers and a reform of professional training. Now the integrated bar became a fully autonomous body free from any governmental supervision and future lawyers came to be trained together with future judges and prosecutors (procurators) for two years in the Legal Training and Research Institute (LTRI) attached to the Supreme Court. But the pre-War social status of practitioners was not to be improved immediately. Number of lawyers

---

6. See also Yasuhei Taniguchi, The Changing Image of Japanese Practicing Lawyers (*Bengoshi*): Reflections and a Personal Memoir, in Emerging Concepts of Rights in Japanese Law 223 (Harry N. Scheiber and Laurent Mayali, eds., 2007).

has been kept small even till today due to a small *numeros clausus* of the LTRI. It was kept at 500 a year for a long time until about 10 years ago. It has become 1,000 only a couple of years ago.

For a long time since the creation of modern bar as a legitimate profession in the early 1870's, the relationship between the judges and the lawyers was not a good one. These two groups were separated and did not regard each other as partners. The judges, being professionally authoritarian and socially prestigious, formed an elitist group. The lawyers, still suffering a low social status even after being liberated from a governmental supervision after the Second World War, generally could not attract elitist sector of the society and accordingly chose to position themselves as an anti-government and anti-officialdom power. Thus, any proposal by the judiciary or by individual judges, however constructive and reasonable it might be, tended to be received as a sign of oppression and to meet a strong resistance from the organized bar and individual members thereof. The political climate in the post-War period also enhanced this tendency. There was a clear polarization of political forces with a conservative party in power on the one side and Marxist oriented opposition parties (Communist Party and Socialist Party) on the other. The organized bar always sided with the latter.

The situation began to change in the 1980's for various possible reasons. Two most important factors must be mentioned, namely, first, the effect of the post-War united training of prospective judges and lawyers and secondly a qualitative change of the bar. In the pre-War period, according to the general civil law tradition, the judges and lawyers, though studying together in the university had to take a separate entry examination and separate training although the examination was unified since 1934 in the High Civil Service Examination for Judicial Officials. One of the post-War legal reforms was the creation of LTRI mentioned before for a common two years training for prospective judges, prosecutors and lawyers. It was only in the 1980's that those judges and lawyers who went through the new system took the leading positions within the judiciary and the bar.

The mere fact that the future lawyers and the future judges are trained together would not have change the landscape. What has changed the situation was the quality of people who decided to go to practice rather than to the judiciary or to the prosecuting office. From the 1970s more and more graduates of LTRI who would have elected to become judges and prosecutors began to choose to become a practitioner. Not only the number of these people increased but also their quality improved. Many of those whom the judiciary and the prosecuting office wanted to recruit and did try to recruit to their respective organizations declined the invitation and chose the career as practitioner. It used to be the norm that promising young candidates volunteered to be a judge or prosecutor and those who had taken years to pass the extremely competitive National Legal Examination went to the practice. In the 1980's this pattern was reversed. The number of students of LTRI was gradually increased so that a sufficient number of qualified candidates could be secured for the judiciary and prosecuting office. In my view, the change was caused primarily for two reasons.

First, the lawyers' public image started to change in the 1960's when a group of leftist lawyers won public support in pursuing large anti-air or water pollution suits. It was a political rather than legal movement for attacking the governmental policy of the controlling conservative party to push forward the country's economic developments in disregard of environmental and ecological consideration. Famous Minamata Disease case (mercury poisoning in the Minamata Bay area causing many deaths) in the 1960's was representative. This and other similar litigation led to the legislation of the Pollution Control Basic Law in 1967. This was a kind of the bar's activity that was impossible before the War without risking a severe sanction because of strict governmental control over the lawyers. It was instrumental not only for changing the public image of lawyers, but also for helping change the self-image of the lawyers themselves. What used to be a monopoly of the "progressive" leftist lawyers became a part of ordinary practice of any lawyer. The bar gained a new attractiveness as an independent profession serving social justice. This, as a matter of fact, represents another aspect of Americanization brought into Japan through the post-War reform. Though in a lesser degree, litigation in Japan sometimes has played certain political function thanks to the activism of the bar, as typically seen in the United States and elsewhere.

One of the other causes for the popularity of lawyers was, of course, financial. As the Japanese economy expanded and internationalized, a demand for competent lawyers arose and a high starting salary was promised by emerging international law firms. Although the judges and prosecutors are much better paid than ordinary civil servants of equivalent background and age in the executive branch, the income of successful practitioners well exceed that of those in the public sector. In addition, an improved social image of lawyers carried with it an air of freedom and challenge which could not be enjoyed in the bureaucratic career system of the judiciary or the prosecuting office. Thus, there are many reasons why ambitious and capable young men and women came to be attracted to the practice of law. Successful large law firms also aggressively recruited eligible young trainees in the LTRI from early days of their training. All this added a centripetal force toward the practice.

Despite all of these recent trends, the number of lawyers in Japan is still kept very small (currently only about 21,000 lawyers serving 120 million people) compared to that in other industrialized nations. Government has declared that the number will be increased to 100,000, the per capita level in France, in a couple of decades, and as the first step toward this goal the American styled "law schools" have been created. Almost 60 of these new 2–3 years graduate professional schools with more than 5,000 fresh students started operation from April, 2004. The real achievement of this development is to be seen in 10 years. At present, it is still true that the historical vestige of Japanese practicing bar has at least so far contributed the way the Japanese civil procedure is conducted to date. At the same time, it is also true that the post-War legal training reform and the recent popularity of legal practice have had a decisive impact on the success of the recent procedural reform as discussed shortly.

* * *

VII.   *New Role of Court Clerks*

Better preparation, concentrated witness examination, better scheduling, etc., all require much work and responsibility not only of the participating lawyers but also of the judge in charge. Frequent contact between the court and the lawyers becomes necessary. For that purpose, a competent administrative support system is needed, so that the judges can concentrate in their proper works. In this respect, the new role of the court clerk should be particularly mentioned here. Under the Code of Civil Procedure, the court clerks are given the independent authority and responsibility for keeping record of proceedings. In reality, they have been long considered as a second class court officer subordinate to the judges. In addition, under the previous political environment, the court clerks were unionized under a strong leftist orientation and often opposed to the court and the judiciary as an oppressive employer. At about the same time as the bar's attitude toward the judiciary was changing, the attitude of clerks also began to change. The judges who wanted to have more efficient preparatory proceedings and concentrated witness examination gave the clerks a greater responsibility for organizing and managing matters in cooperation with the judge.

Many willing clerks positively responded to this offer of a challenging new role and they proved in fact capable enough to conduct such works. To become a court clerk one must pass a demanding state examination comparable to the National Legal Examination and thereafter go through a rigorous training program for one (for law graduate) or two (for non-law graduate) years in the Court Clerk's Training Institute attached to the Supreme Court. Under this system which was also instituted during the post-War period, the level of the court clerks has been remarkably elevated. The 1996 Code thus transferred some of the judge's responsibilities to the court clerk. It is now the court clerk's responsibility to issue the summary payment order (German *Mahnverfahren*) and to assess the court costs after the conclusion of litigation. Court clerks are now characterized as the "court manager". A busy movie actor or actress cannot perform well in the screen without a competent manager behind him or her. The judge similarly can play his or her proper role better with a good arrangement by the court clerks. The court clerk is no longer a subordinate officer but an independent player side by side with the judge. The court clerks posted in the litigation management constantly contact the parties (lawyers) for various purposes, for just scheduling or for a more substantive matter like clarification of allegations.

Note on Developments in Japan

1. <u>New law schools and National Legal (or Bar) Examination:</u>

The characteristically small size of the Japanese legal profession is about to change thanks to the recent reform of the justice system. The reforms include (1) creation of more than 70 graduate level law schools, graduation from which is now a prerequisite for taking the National Legal Examination (NLE); and (2) a radical relaxation of the pass rate of the NLE, which for decades remained as low as 2 to 3 percent. Another innovation is that any applicant for the NLE can take the examination only three times in the individual's life time.

In 2006, the new law schools produced their first graduates. Starting from that year, there are two types of NLE: a new type of examination which can be taken only by graduates from one of the new law schools subject to an increasing admissions quota; and the old type of examination which will continue for 5 years, subject to a decreasing admissions quota. It is projected that the total number of successful applicants will reach 3,000 in 2010. The number of practitioners, presently about 23,000, is thus expected to reach 50,000 in 2018 and 135,000 in 2056.

Recent NLE statistics of applicants and their success rate are as follows:

Year	Applicants	Passers	Success Rate	
2005	45,885	1,464	3.2%	(old exam only)
2006	35,782	549	1.5%	(old exam)
	2,137[a]	1,009	47.0%	(new exam)
	Total	1,558		
2007[b]	28,016	300		(old exam)
	5,280	1,800~2,200	34-47%	(new exam)
	Total	2,100~2,500		

a   The new law schools which started in April 2004 have two types of students: those who hold an undergraduate law degree and those who hold other undergraduate or graduate degrees. The former can graduate in 2 years while the latter are required to study for 3 years before taking the legal examination. Applicants for the new exam in 2006 were only those who could graduate in 2 years. Applicants in 2007 include fresh graduates who have studied for 3 years and those who failed the 2006 exam.
b   The number of "passers" and the success rate for 2007 are estimated projections.

2. <u>Statistics of choices by graduates from LTRI (judges, prosecutors or practitioners):</u>

Uniform training of future practitioners and judges/prosecutors was started in 1947 as one of the post-War reforms. The training period was two years, with time allocated as follows: (1) the first 4 months for class room education; (2) 16 months in the field (8 months in the court, 4 months in the prosecuting office, and 4 months in a law office); and (3) the last 4 months again for class room education, to be concluded by a final examination. The period of training was shortened to 1.5 years in 1999 in order to accommodate an increased number of trainees; it was decreased again to one year beginning 2007 for graduates of the new law schools. Law schools are expected to provide elementary practical trainings formerly provided at the LTRI. The "1.5 year" program will continue, side by side with the new requirements, until the old examination is terminated in 2011.

The first graduating class of 1949 had only 134 trainees, of which 72 became judges; 44, prosecutors; and 18, practitioners. The following table shows changes in professional choices in every tenth year and in the most recent two years (number of women in parentheses):

Year	Total	Judges	Prosecutors	Bar	Others[c]
1959	282	69	51	157	5
1969	516	84	53	374	5
1979	465	64	49	350	2
1989	470	58	51	360	1
1999	729	97	72	549	11
2005	1,158 (274)	124 (34)	96 (30)	911 (204)	27
2006	1,386 (364)	115 (35)	87 (26)	1,144 (262)	40

[c] "Others" include academics, civil servants, those unknown at the time of survey, etc. The increasing size of the "others" category in recent years seems to reflect a greater difficulty in finding an employment in law firms.

V. THE STRUCTURE OF THE LEGAL PROFESSION IN THE COMMON LAW: ENGLAND AND THE UNITED STATES

ENGLAND

The machinery of justice in England has been undergoing radical changes in the last fifteen years or so. The two branches of the legal profession—barristers and solicitors—were characterized by rules and practices of medieval origin which aimed at protecting the interests of the guilds rather than serving the public interest.[7] At some point, it was inevitable that the profession would have to face the challenges of the market. As to judicial organization, the Human Rights Act 1998 contributes decisively to making certain features of the English judiciary untenable, such as the fusion of executive, legislative, and judicial powers in the Lord Chancellor's office and the ambiguous position of the Appellate Committee of the House of Lords.

As far as the legal profession is concerned, the two branches have lost some of their most peculiar features, and have consequently come closer to each other though they have not been unified. Following the Courts and Legal Services Act 1990, and the Access to Justice Act 1999, barristers no longer enjoy their monopoly over the right of audience before the superior courts, which in turn means that they have lost also their monopoly on appointments to the bench. At the same time, they are no longer prevented from direct contacts with clients.[8]

As to solicitors, also their monopoly on conveyancing has been swept away after centuries by the winds of liberalization of the legal profession: see § 34–37 of the CLSA.

---

7. See Michael Zander, Lawyers and the Public Interest: A Study in Restrictive Practices (1968).

8. The relevant provisions are § 17 and §§ 31–33 (as amended by § 36 of the Access to Justice Act 1999) of the Courts and Legal Services Act 1990.

The twilight of the welfare state has brought about a gradual demise of the Legal Aid and Advice schemes, for which England had been celebrated since 1948. In its place, § 58 of the Courts and Legal Services Act 1990, as amended by § 27 of the Access to Justice Act 1999, have introduced conditional fee agreements ("CFA"). Consider whether a conditional fee agreement is compatible with the principle of equality of arms in that it exposes a defendant to a higher cost of risk whenever a claimant chooses to be represented on a CFA basis.

Zuckerman on Civil Procedure: Principles of Practice 1054–1056 (2nd ed. 2006).

A CFA usually takes the following form. The lawyer agrees not to charge the client any fee in the event of the client being unsuccessful. At the same time, the lawyer agrees with the client a normal hourly fee plus a success fee, in the event of the client being successful in the litigation. The lawyer recovers the hourly fee and the success fee from the unsuccessful party. A CFA would still leave the client liable for the other party's costs, if the client is unsuccessful. The client may also be liable for the expenses that his own lawyers have incurred on his behalf to the extent that they are not recoverable from the other side. To protect himself from such risks the client normally takes out *an after the event* insurance policy (ATE), under which the insurer undertakes to pay the insured litigation liabilities. ATE premiums are recoverable from the losing party, alongside the lawyer's hourly fee and success fee. * * * The availability of CFA representation has improved access to justice [in those areas of litigation in which they are easily available]. However, the fairness of the scheme is far from obvious.

Note on Developments in England

Certain results of the liberalization process are already clearly visible, among them the fact that legal services are now being delivered by a number of other professionals such as legal executives, licensed conveyancers, and patent agents. However, more changes seem to be on their way. A White Paper was published by the Secretary of State for Constitutional Affairs and Lord Chancellor in October 2005, "The Future of Legal Services: Putting Consumers First" and a Draft Legal Services Bill (Cm. 6839) was presented to Parliament in May 2006.

With regard to the judicial organization, the major changes concern the abolition of the Appellate Committee of the House of Lords, and the establishment of a new Supreme Court in its place, the reform of the historic office of the Lord Chancellor, and the new approach to judicial selection.[9] As to the Lord Chancellor's office, it is clear that the Human

---

9. See Chapter III, Organization of the Courts, for a discussion of the Supreme Court of the United Kingdom.

Rights Act 1998, with its emphasis on "independent and impartial tribunal", put definitely under strain the fusion of executive, legislative and judicial powers vested in the Lord Chancellor. The Constitutional Reform Act 2005 has reformed the Lord Chancellor's office as well as the procedure for judicial selection. In fact, the Lord Chancellor is no longer the Speaker of the House of Lords, and does not have any judicial responsibility, which now accrues rather to the Lord Chief Justice who "holds the office of President of the Courts of England and Wales and is Head of the Judiciary of England and Wales" (s. 7). However, as the Secretary of State for Constitutional Affairs, the Lord Chancellor still plays a major role in the selection of judges. Following Part 4 of the 2005 Act, in fact, a newly constituted Judicial Appointments Commission selects the candidates for each vacancy which may occur in any court, from among barristers and solicitors qualified to practice before the superior courts, and indicates them to the Lord Chancellor. The latter will either appoint the candidate or recommend her appointment to the Crown as the case may be, or reject the proposal and ask the Commission to reconsider it. Part 3 of the Constitutional Reform Act provides for a special procedure for the appointment of judges of the Supreme Court, where the Prime Minister too has a role in making the recommendation to the Crown.

As to judicial independence, the Constitutional Reform Act 2005 confirms a long standing tradition, according to which judges of the High Court and above may be removed only by the Queen on an address from both Houses of Parliament. In turn, judicial office holders below the High Court, including Justices of the Peace, continue to be removable by the Lord Chancellor for inability and misbehavior. Another significant innovation of the Act is the provision for disciplinary procedures, applicable when the Lord Chancellor is considering whether to exercise his statutory powers to remove a judicial office-holder, with the concurrence of the Lord Chief Justice, and when the Lord Chief Justice is considering to impose any lesser disciplinary sanction on such office-holder, with the concurrence of the Lord Chancellor.

Given the importance of Justices of the Peace and special tribunals in the English administration of justice, it is not surprising that the Constitutional Reform Act 2005 has affected also their recruitment procedure. In particular, Justices of the Peace and the members of some of the most important tribunals are selected by the Judicial Appointment Commission, and then appointed by the Lord Chancellor (s. 85 and Schedule 14).

THE UNITED STATES

Constitution of the United States.

Article III

Section 1. The judicial power of the United States, shall be vested in one Supreme Court, and in such inferior courts as the Congress may from time to time ordain and establish. The judges, both of the supreme and inferior courts, shall hold their offices during good behaviour, and shall, at stated times, receive for their services, a compensation, which shall not be diminished during their continuance in office.

* * *

1. *Judges*

Henry J. Abraham, The Judicial Process: An Introductory Analysis of the Courts of the United States, England, and France 20–45 (7th ed. 1998).

SELECTION

What principles should govern the selection of the men and women who dispense justice? To raise this question brings us face to face with moral as well as political questions of the greatest importance. However awe-inspiring their functions may be, our judges are still human beings. As such, they make the ultimate decisions in the judicial process. In essence, there are just two basic methods of selection: *appointment* and *election*—no matter who does the actual appointing or electing—although, as we shall see, a compromise between the two modes has been devised and is practiced on certain levels of the judiciary in a good many jurisdictions. A collateral question is whether judges should be members of a career service, as in France and Germany; chosen from a special group of lawyers, as in England (for its above-magistrate-level jurists); or selected through appointments from the legal profession generally, as in the United States. Practices of selection differ in large measure in accordance with the traditions and needs of the country concerned. A crucial consideration here is the very position of the judiciary in the framework of government that provides the rationale for the particular mode adopted and practiced. Under the Roman law tradition of the Continent, the judiciary is a part of the overall administrative hierarchy and, as such, represents a position and profession other than that of the ordinary lawyer. Under the common law system, on the other hand, the judges are drawn exclusively from the ranks of the legal profession, except for certain jurists on the state or local level in the United States. Nevertheless, the guiding principles for the selection and tenure of the judiciary in the three nations that concern us most here—England, France, and the United States—display a commonly held ideal: Judges are expected to be impartial and hence must be given assurance of independence, security, and dignity of tenure. When these requirements are present, the fact that different techniques govern selection in those lands is hardly of great significance.

* * *

THE TWO CHIEF METHODS

The fifty American states (and their local subdivisions) employ at least six diverse types of recruitment systems for their approximately 40,000 (1996) judges: partisan election, nonpartisan election, merit selection at one or more levels of the judicial system, gubernatorial appointment, legislative election, and selection by sitting judges. But the *appointive* method is used exclusively at the federal level of the U.S. government * * *.

Appointment. In the United States, all of the approximately 1,500 (1996) federal judges are appointed by the President, subject to confirmation by simple majority vote of the Senate. Depending on the Chief Executive involved, the President's responsibility (a heavy one) has often been largely delegated to the Attorney General and the Deputy Attorney General. * * * Yet whatever mode is employed, three other crucial factors enter here.

The *first* factor is the obvious need for consultation with the U.S. senator(s) and/or other seats of political power in the home state of the candidate for judicial office, provided these political figures are of the same party as the appointing authority. Thus, care must be taken that the appointee is not "personally obnoxious" to a home-state senator, on pain of having the latter involve the age-old, almost invariably honored custom of "senatorial courtesy" * * *.

[I]t is simply not possible for the President to select a candidate for the bench and see that candidate confirmed without at least the grudging approval of his or her home-state senators. * * *

The *second* factor that has played an increasing significant role in the appointive process of the federal judiciary in the United States, especially since the latter months of the Truman Administration, is the American Bar Association's fifteen-member Committee on Federal Judiciary, established in 1946. * * *

[T]he committee has become a powerful and respected vehicle in the vital initial stages of the nominating process. It does not generate names for judicial vacancies, but it evaluates the qualifications of "persons considered for appointment to the Supreme Court of the United States, Circuit Courts of Appeals, District Courts and the Court of International Trade." After an investigation, customarily lasting from six to eight weeks, it reports to the Justice Department on the qualifications of the prospective nominee. * * *

There is a *third* factor: the increasing evidence of the unquestionably significant influence that sitting and retired members of the Court itself, especially the Chief Justice, have on nominations by consulting with and being consulted by the President and the Attorney General in the selection process of a new Supreme Court Justice. * * *

Election. * * * Election of judges is still widespread in a majority of the states in America, where as recently as 1970 fully 82 percent of the nation's state and local judges ran on various election ballots. Only six states did not have *any* type of elections for judges at any level in 1995. Thus, judges may be elected by the electorate on partisan ballots (e.g., Arkansas and Alabama) or by the legislature (e.g., South Carolina and Virginia). Or, they may run on nonpartisan tickets (e.g., Washington and Michigan), but loyal service in partisan politics normally tends to be a prerequisite for nomination—in line with Jacksonian tradition. Also, although the term of office for most elected judges is on the average six to ten years, for some it extends to fifteen years (e.g., in Maryland). In a few states, the concept of supporting the sitting judge has been adopted when he or she is up for reelection, but this theoretically laudatory practice has been ignored almost as much as it has been observed. Moreover, the mitigating factors that are inherent in the deviations from the straight, partisan, short-term ballot election are found in but a few states, and even in these they are usually confined to the upper echelon of the judiciary.

Other practices worthy of note in this general consideration of selection are those of at least some judges by gubernatorial appointment subject to legislative consent (e.g., Maryland and Maine) and appointment of some, either temporary or permanent, by courts (e.g., Alaska and South Dakota). Massachusetts's commission-selected, gubernatorially appointed judges, except justices of the peace, serve for life, "conditioned upon good behavior"; those of New Jersey, strictly gubernatorially selected, serve for seven years and then, if reappointed, for life terms "during good behavior."

A COMPROMISE?

An intriguing attempt at a compromise between the elective and appointive methods of choosing state judges in America has been advanced and popularized in several different versions by a number of states at some or all appellate and/or trial court levels. * * * This compromise is designed to minimize political influence and provide a degree of security of tenure while retaining an element of popular control. * * *

* * * The Missouri Plan is mandatory for the judges of the Missouri Supreme Court, the state's other appellate courts, the circuit and probate courts in St. Louis and in Jackson County, and the St. Louis Court of Corrections. It is optional, subject to popular referenda, in the thirty-eight other circuits of the state * * *. Under the Missouri version, nonpartisan nominating boards known as the Missouri Appellate Commissions, operating on different court levels, select three candidates. for every vacant judgeship * * *.

The Governor of Missouri is obliged to choose one of the three individuals selected by the Appellate Commission and appoint him or her until the next general election, but not for less than one year ... After this probationary period, the appointee must be approved by the electorate for a full twelve-year term in the appellate courts or for a lesser term in the trial courts, running unopposed on a separate, nonpartisan judicial ballot at the time of the general election. * * *

Generally deemed to be the most innovative and most attractive system of judicial selection extant in the various states, the Missouri Plan combines the democratic notion of accountability to the electorate with an intelligent method of selecting qualified candidates for judicial office. * * *

TENURE OF OFFICE

Essential to the independence of the judiciary is the security of tenure, particularly in the case of appointed judges—our main concern here. Without a lengthy term of office (preferably life), adequate remuneration, and stringent constitutional and/or statutory safeguards against removal, the concept of judicial independence becomes a mockery * * *.

At the *federal* level in the United States of America, all judges of the constitutional courts—those appointed under the provisions of Article III of the constitution (the judicial article)—hold their position during good behavior, which in effect means for life or until they choose to retire. The other federal judges—those of the *legislative* courts, created under the provisions of Article I of the Constitution (the legislative article)— occupy their positions for whatever period Congress may have prescribed at the time of its establishment of the court or in subsequent legislation. In some instances this has meant good behavior tenure for them, too— or, frequently, terms of office ranging between four and fifteen years. The constitutional judges have the additional safeguard, stated in Article III, that their ... compensation ... shall not be diminished during their continuance in office. Hence, although their salaries may be increased during their incumbency, they may not be lowered, short of constitutional amendment of the section concerned. Were a judge of a constitutional court to be removed from office other than in the manner expressly permitted by the Constitution, his salary would indeed be rather drastically "diminished." * * *

Removal. The removal of federal judges who wish to remain on the bench can be effected only by the process of impeachment and conviction. However, not only has it evidently been legal for some time for the Judicial Council of a U.S. Circuit to discipline one of its federal judges by stripping him or her of duties and authority while permitting the retention of both title and salary, in 1980 Congress enacted legislation, the Judicial Councils Reform and Judicial Conduct and Disability Act, creating authority in the judicial councils of the (now thirteen) judicial circuits to discipline, but not to remove, for misconduct all federal judges except those of the Supreme Court. In accordance with constitutional requirements, impeachment for "Treason, Bribery, or other high Crimes and Misdemeanors" may be voted by a simple majority of the members of the House of Representatives, there being a quorum on the floor. Trial is then held in the Senate, which may convict by a vote of two-thirds of the members of the Senate present and voting, if a quorum is present.

2. *Attorneys*

David S. Clark, Legal Education and the Legal Profession, in Introduction to the Law of the United States 13, 16, 28–33 (David S. Clark and Tugrul Ansay, eds., 2nd ed. 2002).

B.   THE LEGAL PROFESSION

No elite profession of the bench and bar arose in the early American republic to parallel the profession in England. Requirements for admission to the bar were loose and became looser toward the middle of the 19th century. In 1840 only 11 of 30 states prescribed a definite period of apprenticeship to become a lawyer; some states required that a person pass an examination (which might involve a few formal perfunctory questions). While formal restrictions were weak, the informal constraints of an open market for legal services—where social and geographic mobility was high—remained an efficient control. Lazy, incompetent, or ineffective lawyers simply had too few clients to survive.

Judges, similarly, varied in training and ability. A majority of judges in the early republic were laymen, especially on the lower courts. These men often came from prominent families or had made their fortune and were active in politics. Once Jacksonian Democracy succeeded in broadening suffrage and the popular control of public office, almost all states abandoned an appointive selection method for judges (often through the legislature or in combination with the governor) and adopted the method of popular election for a term, typically four to eight years. Federal judges, by the U.S. Constitution's mandate, are nominated by the president for life tenure, subject to confirmation by a majority of the Senate. * * * Virtually all federal judges were lawyers and the trend in states was to elect lawyers to the bench (except for the position of justice of the peace, which remained with laymen until late in the 20th century). Most high court judges by the end of the 19th century were successful or ambitious lawyers, who reflected the values of America as an industrializing society run by businessmen and politicians. They were conservative but not aristocratic, an attribute promoted by the elective system. At the lower levels of the judiciary were many examples of venality and incompetence, fostered by the dependence of courts on local politics. The toughest assignments, however, were for federal territorial judges in the West, who accepted the four year patronage job in an often hostile, lawless environment.

In 1850 there were about 24,000 lawyers and law-trained judges in the United States. After the Civil War the great economic transformation from an agricultural to an industrial society increased the demand for lawyers, which together with judges reached 64,000 by 1880 and topped 114,000 in 1900. Judges had more cases to process and the work became more diverse. Lawyers prospered because they were able to adapt in a profession with little governmental or self-regulation. The profession offered upward social and economic mobility to ambitious immigrant and middle class sons. Law was not so stuffy that practitioners could not move in and out of business and politics. Bar associations did try to limit entry by raising standards, but their dream of an elite guild, an English-style bar, could not be imposed on such a porous profession.

The appearance of law firms with more than three partners was the most significant structural development of the post-Civil War period. In 1900 about 70 firms had five or more lawyers, with the majority on or near Wall Street in New York City. The largest firm had ten attorneys. These lawyers avoided lawsuits and left that work for traditional practitioners. Firms grew up to service powerful corporations; they specialized in corporate securities and finance. Other developments included the emergence of salaried lawyers, who worked as in-house counsel to corporations, especially insurance companies and railroads, and government lawyers, who worked for various agencies in the federal government and for city or state governments. For instance, the U.S. Attorney General employed 13 lawyers and the New York City Law Department had 28 attorneys.

* * *

A. A UNIFIED PROFESSION

Admission to a state bar carries with it a license to practice law anywhere within the state and to engage in all types of practice: in a law firm, as an employee of a corporation, or with the government as a prosecutor, judge, or state attorney. There is no distinct judicial or prosecutorial career; there is no division of private practice between barristers and solicitors.

Law graduates in the United States tend to view the legal profession as a single entity, a unified bar. The principal national organization is the ABA, open to any lawyer in good standing in her state. Today the ABA is, on the one hand, a federation of state and local bar associations and other important legal organizations such as the American Law Institute and, on the other hand, a social, educational, and political organization with about half the country's lawyers as members. The ABA's House of Delegates sets ABA policy and elects officers for one year terms. Many educational and social functions are carried out through a large number of sections and committees, such as the International Law and Practice Section, which has over 13,600 members and publishes its own journal, *The International Lawyer*. Since ABA members come from all sectors of the legal profession, its policies and programs have a homogenizing effect. It promulgates a model ethics code that influences state rules, but the ABA itself has no disciplinary power over lawyers.

* * * Most law graduates initially took a job in the private sector, where they typically earned more than the 1998 overall median salary of $45,000. Business paid $50,000 and attorneys who worked in firms with more than 25 lawyers began at over $50,000. It is also apparent that larger law firms have a more expensive clientele and gain efficiency from size, so that those with more than 250 lawyers could pay beginning attorneys—one out of eight of the total—$87,000. Geography also matters. For example, nine percent of the total law jobs were in New York City; employers there paid a median salary of $93,000 in private practice and $66,000 for business. Lawyers in Houston, by comparison, earned $67,000 and $51,200 respectively.

Another factor that acts to unify the profession is the high mobility among the various types of lawyers, which is promoted by two structural circumstances. First, the existence of big law firms, which pay large starting salaries to young graduates, allow the firms to choose which associates they will retain and promote to partner after a six year or so probationary period. Since only about one associate out of three becomes a partner, there is a large pool of experienced attorneys who leave firms, many of whom then work for federal, state, or local governments or for corporations as in-house counsel. Others stay in private practice, either with specialty firms, new firms composed of former associates, or in solo or small firm practice. A second variable that stimulates mobility is the political nature of the appointment or election process for certain attractive government lawyer jobs, including federal judges, state high court judges, and chief prosecutors (U.S. attorney, state attorney general, or local district attorney).

Attorneys after ten or so years experience with an interest in politics will often consider switching careers to enter government or judicial service. There is also a cultural element that emphasizes freedom of movement.

* * *

B. The Number and Type of Lawyers

Table 6 Total Lawyers, 1910 to 2000

Year	Number	Women (Percent)	Per 100,000 Population
1910	114,704		124
1930	160,605		161
1950	214,000	3	141
1960	285,933	3	159
1970	349,000	3	171
1980	513,623	8	226
1990	746,000	19	299
1995	815,258	24	310
2000	877,000	28	319

Table 6 sets out the growth of the American legal profession in this century. The greatest expansion began in the late 1960s and paralleled the student enrollment in law schools. Between 1970 and 1990 the profession more than doubled in size. In 1990 there were 299 lawyers per 100,000 population, a 75 percent increase since 1970 in the relative availability of law-trained persons. During the 1990s the decade's growth rate in the relative number of lawyers declined to a much slower seven percent to reach a ratio of 319 per 100,000 population in 2000, but the absolute number of active lawyers still increased by 131,000 although not yet passing the one million mark. It took a generation for the entry of women in law schools to have a significant impact on the profession. Between 1970 and 2000 the percentage of women lawyers rose from three to 28 percent of the total.

[S]triking is * * * how little the basic distribution pattern of law work appears to have changed since World War II. While the number of lawyers almost quintupled, the relative shrinkage in private practice was about equally met by the expansion of employment by corporations and non-profit organizations. The ratio of lawyers working in the judiciary, for the other branches of government, or in education stayed about the same.

* * *

Within the private practice sector, however, there was a dramatic decline in the relative position of sole practitioners from 1951 to 1970 (from 55 to 37 percent of the legal profession) and a shift toward the use of law firms to provide legal services. This shift occurred with the large expansion of employed lawyers within firms (associates) from four to 19 percent of all lawyers in 1991, although that percentage declined in the mid–1990s as the average lawyer was older in the later period. The ageing bar was reflected in more lawyers becoming partners by the end of the century. The organization, consequently, whether a firm or a corporation, has gradually replaced the entrepreneur within the legal profession.

The law firm excels in functional specialization for the delivery of private legal services, which accommodates the increased complexity of modern society. The United States, the world's leader in the absolute and relative size of its legal profession and in the number of private practitioners, also leads in taking the law firm to its logical extreme. In 1995 there were 702 firms with 51 or more lawyers and the largest firms had over a thousand attorneys. Firms with more than 50 attorneys employed 105,000 lawyers, although the growth rates in these larger firms stalled in the 1990s. As recently as 1960 American law firms were clearly identified with a particular city. Nowadays large law firms operate on a-national and increasingly an international basis with branch and affiliate firms. In 1995 77 percent of the firms with over 100 attorneys had multi state or global branches. In the mid–1990s the largest 100 firms generated fees in the United States over $15 billion, about ten percent of which came from foreign clients.

American law firms come in all sizes; attorneys in private practice are a very heterogeneous group. In urban centers one likely will find large firms (representing major corporations, banks, and governments), specialty firms (handling matters such as patent applications, labor relations, or white-collar criminal defense), small firms (with a general practice based on probate, real estate, and small business matters), and solo practitioners either waiting for the personal injury client or divorce case to walk into the office or more aggressively seeking business at the criminal court. In rural areas private practice is basically one of small firms and solo practitioners carrying on a general practice of whatever the community demands. * * *

Finally, public interest lawyers litigate to promote certain causes, such as protection of the environment (Sierra Club Legal Defense Fund) or promotion of individual liberties (American Civil Liberties Union).

To fully appreciate the distinctive American distribution of lawyers, it is instructive to compare it to that of Germany. In the United States the legal profession as a whole is more highly privatized than in Germany. Only 13 percent of the profession in the U.S. serves as judges or works as government lawyers compared to 42 percent in Germany. The ratio of judges to attorneys in the two countries also shows the much greater role in Germany that judges play to make the procedural system function properly: one judge for 3.4 attorneys in Germany compared to 27.3 attorneys in the United States.

Several factors account for the existence of a large private practice sector in the United States, which is also the situation in other common law countries. One, the emphasis in sources of law on judge-made rules leads to a proliferation of legal materials that makes resolution of legal issues complex and time consuming. * * * In civil law nations, by contrast, codes and scholarly treatises are more efficient organizing tools for quick solution of most legal problems. Two, the common law system of procedure puts a heavy burden on attorneys to discover the facts in a case and even to brief the complicated legal issues for the judge. * * * Civil law countries, alternatively, staff the judiciary and prosecutor offices more fully so that the ratio of judges to attorneys is much higher. In this sense, common law countries have a more privatized judicial procedure. Three, many common law nations are federal in political structure, further complicating legal analysis and stimulating demand for more attorneys.

Chapter 3

ORGANIZATION OF THE COURTS

I. INTRODUCTION

In every legal system, in every legal tradition, courts are the institutions set up by the state to solve disputes according to certain procedures. This does not mean, however, that the institutions which go under the name of "courts" are structured in the same way, and perform the same role everywhere. As a matter of fact, there are some crucial differences between courts in the civil law and the common law legal systems referred to in this book.

We have already seen in Chapter 2 that the judicial personnel staffing the courts is radically different; judges have a different professional background, are selected through different procedures, and enjoy different tenure and prestige. We have also seen that whereas common law systems typically have only one hierarchy of courts in each jurisdiction—though there may be more than one type of first instance court at the base of the hierarchy, such as family courts and surrogate's courts, and courts of general civil jurisdiction—when we turn to the civil law, we have to underline that there is not only one hierarchy of courts—which we refer to as "ordinary" courts, dealing with civil and criminal cases, but several of them. Invariably, due to a more rigid adherence to the principle of separation of powers, there is an autonomous set of administrative courts, and there are countries such as Germany which, in the name of specialization, add separate fiscal, labor and social jurisdictions.

We must also mention that the U.S. courts, which, as Alexis De Tocqueville puts it in "Democracy in America" (see below) are "vested with immense political power", in that they have the right "to found their decisions on the Constitution rather than on the laws." In the civil law systems, constitutional adjudication, in turn, has too much of a political flavour to be left to "ordinary" courts and "ordinary" career judges. As a rule, it has been entrusted to special ad hoc body, usually called the Constitutional court, or Constitutional council as in France. Another major difference concerns supreme courts, their structure and role. In the civil law, they lack the compact, manageable, unitary structure, and the discretion of their common law counterparts. This bears also on their authority, and the precedential value of their decisions, which may be persuasive, even strongly so, but are not binding.

The preceding remarks explain the geography of this Chapter. In sections II and III we shall provide the reader with some more in depth information on the court structure in some representative countries of the civil law—Germany, France, Italy and Japan—and the common law traditions—England and the USA. Section IV will be dedicated to the various models of constitutional review—judicial vs. political, centralized v. decentralized. Section V will describe the role of supra-national courts in Europe, and some comparative remarks on the role of stare decisis will conclude the Chapter (Section VI).

II. CIVIL LAW SYSTEMS: GERMANY, FRANCE, ITALY, AND JAPAN

GERMANY

In some legal systems, including Germany, the basic structure of the court system is sketched out in the Constitution. As to Germany, a federal state, it is worthy of noting that only the highest courts are federal courts; the first instance and appellate courts are state courts.

Fundamental Law (*Grundgesetz*) of the Federal Republic of Germany (1949).*

Article 92 [Court Organization]

Judicial power is vested in the judges; it is exercised by the Federal Constitutional Court, by the federal courts provided for in this Constitution, and by the courts of the States [Länder]

* * *

Article 95 [Highest Courts, Joint Panel]

(1) For the purposes of ordinary, administrative, fiscal, labor, and social jurisdiction, the Federation establishes as highest courts of justice the Federal Court of Justice, the Federal Administrative Court, the Federal Finance Court, the Federal Labor Court, and the Federal Social Court.

(2) The judges of each of these courts are selected jointly by the competent Minister and a committee for the selection of judges consisting of the competent State [Land] ministers and an equal number of members elected by the House of Representatives [Bundestag].

* * *

* Translation available at http://www.psr.keele.ac.uk/docs/german.htm (Site last visited June 11, 2007).

Article 101 [Ban on extraordinary Courts]

(1) Extraordinary courts are inadmissible. No one may be removed from the jurisdiction of his lawful judge.

(2) Courts for special fields of law may be established only by Legislation.

Peter L. Murray and Rolf Stürner, German Civil Justice 37–68 (2004).

A. In General

German civil and criminal justice are dispensed through a nation-wide system of mixed general-jurisdiction and specialized courts. Although the role and jurisdictions of the various German courts differ, they all share certain common institutional features. Each German court is presided over by a professional judge. All professional German judges have a complete legal education and training. All professional judges hold salaried positions in the judiciary of the various German states or in the federal judiciary. Most German judges are full-time. All professional judges are appointed for what becomes lifetime tenure and are insulated from activities which would compromise their judicial independence. All German courts function according to the same basic procedural principles in civil cases. While the following description relates chiefly to the courts of general jurisdiction *(ordentliche Gerichte)* in which most civil business is done, the workings and procedures of the specialized courts are in large part very similar.

An observer of the German justice system is immediately struck by the large number of judges employed in the dispensation of civil and criminal justice in Germany. In the entire world Germany is number one both in the absolute number of professional judges employed as well as the number of judges per capita. As of 1998 the official tally of German professional judges of all kinds was 20,969, or one judge per four thousand German citizens.

This large number of public jurists speaks both to the high importance placed by German policy and culture on formal civil and criminal justice in the courts as well as the large role of the German judge in the processing and determination of civil and criminal litigation. While in other legal cultures the lawyer is considered the key figure in the administration of justice and the protection of legal rights, in Germany the judge takes on a central part of this function. This results in a balance of private resources, represented by the parties and their lawyers, and public resources, represented by the judge and the court staff, that in Germany consists of a somewhat larger proportion of public and a somewhat smaller proportion of private resources than in some other systems.

B. General and Specialized Court Jurisdictions

The legal workload of Germany's justice system is divided between a court system of general jurisdiction and several court systems of specialized jurisdiction. The court system of general jurisdiction *(ordentliche Gerichte)* exercises jurisdiction over all disputes cognizable by law, civil or criminal, which are not confided to the competence of one of the specialized Courts. The principal specialized court systems which exercise jurisdiction of a more or less "civil" nature are the Labor Courts *(Arbeitsgerichte)*, the Administrative Courts *(Verwaltungsgerichte)*, the Social Welfare Courts *(Sozialgerichte)* and the Tax Courts *(Finanzgerichte)*.

An important component of the civil justice system in Germany is the Federal Constitutional Court *(Bundesverfassungsgericht)*, which has the power to determine the constitutional validity of all German legislative enactments, court judgments, and administrative actions.

* * *

C. The Major Specialized Courts

Germany's four major specialized court systems exercise jurisdictions based on the natures of the issues being litigated.

* * *

Each one of these basic specialized court systems operates a complete top-to-bottom judicial establishment with courts of first instance and appeals courts. Each system is crowned by a Federal Supreme Court of last resort. Proceedings in each of the specialized court systems is governed by a specialized procedure code for that court system supplemented by the German Civil Procedure Code *(Zivilprozessordnung* or *ZPO)* which governs to the extent that the specialized code does not otherwise provide.

Although the docket of all of the specialized courts taken together comprises only a fraction of all civil proceedings filed each year in Germany, the number of cases handled is not insignificant. For instance, in 1998 a total of 584,686 complaints were lodged in the various Labor Courts, and 201,543 were filed in Administrative Courts, compared with some 2.5 million in the courts of general jurisdiction.

* * *

1. The Labor Courts

The labor court system, like all of the German court systems, operates as a decentralized system of Labor Courts *(Arbeitsgerichte)* of first instance, Labor Appeals Courts *(Landesarbeitsgerichte)* in the various German states *(Länder)*, and a Federal Supreme Labor Court *(Bundesarbeitsgericht)* exercising an appellate jurisdiction over all of the state labor courts.

The Labor Courts are vested with exclusive jurisdiction over all disputes relating to the employment relationship ... Their jurisdiction also includes disputes between trade unions and employer associations and issues between worker representatives *(Betriebsrat)* and the employer's management.

The first-instance Labor Courts are each staffed with a single professional judge and two lay judges, the latter being selected from lists provided by employers' and labor organizations respectively.

The Labor Appeals Courts *(Landesarbeitsgerichte)* hear appeals on questions of fact and law *(Berufungen)* from decisions of the Labor Courts. Their composition is the same as that of the Labor Courts, one professional judge and two lay judges, again equally from management and labor. Most of the German states have a single Labor Appeals Court which sits in several panels.

Appeals on questions of law or procedure only *(Revision)* from decisions of the Labor Appeals Courts go to the Federal Labor Supreme Court, which sits in Senates composed of three professional judges and two lay judges, the latter representing management and labor interests respectively. A "Grand Senate" *(Grosser Senat)* of sixteen judges of the Federal Labor Supreme Court can be convened to resolve splits among Senates and clarify important legal principles.

* * *

The large number of cases filed each year suggests that German employees and their employers and unions look to the Labor Court as the first line of resolution for the many disputes and frictions that are likely to arise in the employment relationship. The large proportion of such cases that are settled, and the small proportion of Labor Court judgments that are appealed to the Labor Appeals Court (5%) can be seen as testimony to the effectiveness of the court in resolving these disputes and the confidence of the parties in the quality of the decisions rendered.

2.   The Administrative Courts

The Administrative Court system deals with issues of public law other than those sectors confided to specialized courts such as the Social Welfare Courts or the Tax Courts. Challenges to the actions of governmental officers or agencies, as well as all appeals from the decisions of administrative bodies go to the Administrative Courts *(Verwaltungsgerichte)*, which are empowered to consider constitutional issues arising from public action or decisions so long as the constitutional validity of a post war legislative enactment is not in question.

* * *

Much of the law with which the Administrative Courts are concerned is state public law, which can and does vary among the various German states *(Länder)*. The role of the Federal Supreme Administrative

Court thus includes the correct application and interpretation of both federal and state law in harmony with the Constitution and other basic principles underlying the legal systems of all the German states.

3. *The Social Welfare Courts*

Questions of entitlement to social welfare and insurance programs are decided by a system of Social Welfare Courts *(Sozialgerichte)*. This system also consists of three layers, the Social Welfare Courts *(Sozialgerichte)* of the first instance, Social Welfare Appeals Courts *(Landessozialgerichte)* and a Federal Social Welfare Supreme Court *(Bundessozialgericht)*. Procedure in the Social Welfare Courts is governed by the Social Welfare Courts Law *(Sozialgerichtsgesetz* or *SGG)* supplemented by the Civil Procedure Code *(ZPO)*.

The sixty-nine Social Welfare Courts of the first instance sit in tribunals each consisting of one professional and two lay judges. (. . .) Lay members of the tribunals are selected from various organizations depending on the subject matters of the tribunals' workloads. The background and experience of the lay judges often corresponds at least to some degree to the issues being determined by the tribunal. Cases presenting only relatively simple factual and legal issues without fundamental significance may be referred to and decided by single professional judges.

Second instance appeals on law and facts *(Berufungen)* from decisions of the Social Welfare Court are heard by regional Social Welfare Appeals Courts *(Landessozialgerichte),* which sit in panels of three professional judges and two lay judges. Review appeals on questions of law and procedure from decisions of the Appeals Courts are heard by the Federal Social Welfare Supreme Court, which also sits in panels of three professional and two lay judges.

4. *The Tax Courts*

The Tax Courts *(Finanzgerichte)* hear appeals from administrative decisions of the authorities responsible for administration of all forms of taxation (including customs and import duties). First instance proceedings are lodged in the Tax Courts, which sit in panels *(Kammern)* composed of three professional and two lay judges. The Tax Court Law *(Finanzgerichtsordnung* or *FGO)*, supplemented by the Civil Procedure Code *(ZPO)*, governs procedure in the Tax Courts. Review appeals on questions of law or procedure from decisions of the Tax Courts are heard by five-judge panels of the Federal Supreme Tax Court *(Bundesfinanzhof)*.

D. COURTS OF GENERAL JURISDICTION

Germany's courts of general jurisdiction *(ordentliche Gerichte)* represent the bulk of its judicial establishment and are represented at some level in almost every locality in the country. All criminal prosecutions and all civil actions not within the jurisdiction of one of the specialized

court systems are brought in one or the other of the courts of general
jurisdiction.

* * *

Each year Germany's courts of general jurisdiction hear and determine a truly impressive volume of civil litigation. For instance in 1998,
some 2,080,928 civil actions were brought in various Local Courts
throughout Germany. In the same year a total of 505,187 cases (including 100,591 appeals from Local Court judgments) were filed in the State
District Courts. In 1998 the State Appeals Courts received 69,600
appeals from State District Court judgments and another 26,056 appeals
from Local Court judgments in family cases. In the same time period
6,096 cases were appealed to the Federal Supreme Court. These statistics
give a picture of a very busy court system in civil matters.

1.   The Local Courts

The Local Courts *(Amtsgerichte)* are by far the most numerous of
German judicial establishments. As of the end of 1998, there were 693
Local Courts established in all parts of Germany. Even the smallest town
is likely to have a Local Court either within that town or in the
neighboring locality. The ubiquitousness of these courts bespeaks their
role in the German legal culture. These are truly the courts of the
people.

a.   Local Court Jurisdiction

The civil jurisdiction of the Local Courts tends to focus chiefly on
legal matters of consequence to the common citizen, family law cases,
non-contentious probate and inheritance matters, and smaller civil cases.
Currently the Local Courts exercise an exclusive civil jurisdiction over
most civil cases in which the amount in controversy does not exceed
5,000 Euro. Also within the exclusive civil jurisdiction of the Local
Courts are a variety of matters regardless of the amount in controversy.

* * *

b.   *Composition and Procedure of Local Courts*

Civil matters within the jurisdiction of the Local Courts are heard
by single judges. Procedure in the Local Courts is governed by the Civil
Procedure Code, which, however, contains several special provisions
applicable only to Local Court proceedings.

* * *

The simplifications and shortcuts in Local Court procedure reflect
not only the limited jurisdiction of Local Courts in most civil matters,
but also the fact that parties in many Local Court proceedings are not
represented by counsel. Although the presence of lawyers in Local Court
has increased over the years, * * * [t]he system is designed to make it
possible in many cases for a litigant to get a fair shake at justice in the
Local Court without having to hire a lawyer.

2. The State District Courts

The backbone of the German civil justice system is the State District Court *(Landgericht)* of general jurisdiction, of which there are now some 116 in the principal cities and towns throughout Germany. These courts serve as the courts of first instance for the great bulk of serious civil matters and also hear and decide appeals of law and facts *(Berufungen)* from most decisions of the Local Courts. It was for these courts that the Civil Procedure Code was written.

* * *

b. Composition of the State District Courts

The State District Courts generally sit in panels *(Kammern)* of three judges for the more important and difficult cases. For ordinary civil cases, this means three professional judges.

* * *

A presiding judge *(vorsitzender Richter)* of each panel presides at the hearings and largely conducts the proceedings so far as the court is concerned. For most cases the presiding judge will designate one of the other members of the panel as reporting judge *(Berichterstatter)*. The reporting judge is expected to become particularly familiar with the case record *(Akte)* and often will be delegated to write the judgment.

The statute prescribing the composition of the District Court includes an important proviso. The State District Court is to consist of three judges, "insofar as a single judge is not to decide in place of the panel according to the provisions of procedural law."

* * *

By virtue of the 2002 reforms it is now the rule that a member of the panel hears and decides the case as an "original single judge" unless one of the statutory exceptions applies. If a case assigned by statute to a single judge discloses legal or factual difficulties or has fundamental legal significance or if both parties so request, the single judge may refer the case to the full panel. A case not automatically tried by a single judge must still be assigned to an "obligatory single judge" if the case discloses no difficulties or fundamental significance.

* * *

c. Commercial Panels of the State District Courts

German civil justice retains specialized commercial panels *(Handelskammern)* within the State District Courts for the determination of disputes in commercial and business matters *(Handelssachen)*. * * * [T]he provisions setting forth the competence of the commercial panels are not jurisdictional. A judgment rendered by an ordinary panel of the District Court in a matter cognizable by a commercial panel would not be void. Assignment of a case to a commercial panel is a matter of division of judicial business, not judicial power to decide.

* * *

Each commercial panel is staffed by a presiding judge *(Vorsitzender)*, who is a professional State District Court judge, and two honorary judges *(ehrenamtliche Richter)*. The honorary judges are not legally trained, but are required to fulfil demanding professional qualifications within their spheres of commerce and industry.

* * *

Procedure before the commercial panels is governed by the Civil Procedure Code including some special provisions applicable only to matters before commercial panels.

* * *

Although the commercial panels hear only a small percentage of all civil cases filed in the State District Court, often these cases are of great significance to the business community and hence the economy. While the efficacy of participation of honorary judges from the business and commercial community may be subject to debate, in the German legal culture they lend a degree of authenticity and credibility to civil justice that justifies their retention and continued use.

3.   *The State Appeals Courts*

Each of the German states *(Länder)* has at least one State Appeals Court *(Oberlandesgericht)* which exercises an almost exclusively appellate jurisdiction in civil and criminal cases * * *.

The State Appeals Courts are busy. In 1998 some 85,600 civil appeals were filed in German State Appeals Courts.

a.   *State Appeals Court Jurisdiction*

The bulk of the State Appeals Courts' jurisdiction in civil matters consists of second instance appeals on facts and law *(Berufungen)* and various forms of miscellaneous appeals *(Beschwerden)* from judgments *(Urteile)* and other decisions and orders *(Beschlüsse, Entscheidungen)* of the State District Courts. The State Appeals Courts also hear second instance and miscellaneous appeals from judgments and orders of the Local Courts in paternity cases and matters cognizable by the Family Court. These latter bypass the District Courts and go directly to the State Appeals Courts.

Appeals to the State Appeals Courts are as of right, so long as the amount in controversy is more than 600 Euro. In other cases the court which issued the judgment must give permission to appeal.

* * *

b. *Composition and Procedure of the State Appeals Courts*

The State Appeals Courts usually sit in appellate panels or senates *(Senate)* each composed of three professional Appeals Court judges. Each panel is under the chairmanship of a presiding judge, who conducts the oral proceedings. As in the State District Courts, the panels tend to beat least somewhat specialized, even within the overall realm of civil justice.

* * *

Procedure in civil appeals in the State Appeals Courts is governed by the Civil Procedure Code.

* * *

The recent 2001/2002 reforms enlarge the role of the single judge at the appellate level. If a decision subject to appeal was rendered by a single judge, and if the case does not present special difficulties and has no fundamental significance, the appellate court may refer the complete second instance appeal to be heard and decided by a single member of the panel.

4. *The Federal Supreme Court*

The highest court in the German civil justice system is the Federal Supreme Court *(Bundesgerichtshof* or *BGH)*, which sits in Karlsruhe. The Federal Supreme Court is the court of last resort for all criminal and civil matters. Its judges are organized into civil and criminal senates *(Senate)*. The senates are composed of 6–8 judges apiece, but sit in panels each of 5 judges, a Presiding Judge and four others. As of this writing the Federal Supreme Court consisted of 122 judges divided into 5 criminal senates *(Strafsenat)*, 12 civil senates *(Zivilsenate)* and 4 senates dealing with specialized matters. There is a considerable degree of specialization among the various senates.

* * *

In cases posing issues where the decisions of the respective senates seem to diverge, a Grand Civil Senate *(Grosser Senat für Zivilsachen)* composed of judges representing the regular civil senates can be convened to resolve the difference and maintain the unity of the law *(Rechtseinheit)*.

The jurisdiction of the Federal Supreme Court is entirely appellate * * *

Before the 2001 civil justice reforms, there were two significant thresholds which an appeal had to cross in order to reach the Federal Supreme Court. First of all, the case had to involve an amount in controversy of at least 60,000 DM. Smaller cases could only be appealed to the Federal Supreme Court with the consent of the State Appeals Court. Second, even if the case involved more than 60,000 DM, the Federal Supreme Court could reject the appeal if the senate was satisfied that "the legal issue is of no fundamental significance."

As the caseload of appeals to the Federal Supreme Court burgeoned in recent years, more and more frequent use was made of this provision for discretionary rejection of appeals.

* * *

In 2001 following spirited discussion among bench, bar and public, reforms of the Civil Procedure Code designed to relieve the workload on Germany's appellate courts passed the houses of Parliament. These reforms became effective January 1, 2002. Under the new reforms the Federal Supreme Court will now only hear appeals in cases where permission to appeal has been granted by state appellate courts or the Federal Supreme Court itself.

For some time now the Federal Supreme Court has been a very busy court. In 1998 a total of 6067 civil appeals were lodged, of which 163 were by consent of State Appeals Courts and 4056 involved an amount in controversy in excess of the 60,000 DM jurisdictional minimum. Of the latter, the court rendered judgment in 607, and rejected the rest as insubstantial under the previous version of ZPO § 554b. This state of chronic overwork of the nation's highest civil and criminal appeals court has led to periodic calls for enlargement of the court or reform of its procedures, or both.

FRANCE

No provision of the 1958 French Constitution is concerned with the organisation of the courts. The short "Title VIII—The Judiciary" guarantees the independence of the judiciary, and establishes the Conseil Superieur, the governing body of the judiciary whose task is to make that independence effective. The rules governing the various courts are to be found in ordinary statutes. The following materials offer an accurate though brief picture of the organisation of French civil courts.

John Bell, French Legal Cultures 25–32 (2001).

B.   Court Institutions

French court institutions are structured according to four basic principles, the first two of which are structural, while the last two are more operational in character. First, in terms of subject-matter, courts are *specialist* to varying degrees. Certain specialisms are fundamental to the structure of the French court system (and to its substantive law), others result more from convenience than legal principle. Three distinctions are of fundamental importance: between public law and private law, between civil law and criminal law, and between these ordinary courts and the Conseil constitutionnel. There is no court that has even residual jurisdiction over all branches of law. The civil and criminal courts and the administrative courts have both courts of general jurisdiction (juridictions de droit commun) and also specialist courts, described as exceptional courts (juridictions d'exception) or as courts of limited jurisdiction (juridictions d'attribution). Second, in terms of territorial jurisdiction, French courts are *local or regional*. Only at the highest point in the hierarchy is there a national court in any branch of law. * * * Third, in terms of levels of court, the French adhere to the principle of the *right to an appeal* (double degré de juridiction), which entitles the litigant to a hearing at first instance and then on appeal. This right of appeal on law and fact means that there is no leave required for an appeal. There are restrictions on access to the Conseil d'Etat and the Cour de cassation, the national courts at the pinnacle of the public and private law systems, but their functions are primarily to review the legal basis of decisions reached by lower courts, rather than to act as a third level of appeal on the merits. * * * Finally, in terms of *composition*, French courts are traditionally collegial and professional, viz they are composed of a bench of professional judges. As will be seen, there are in fact numerous instances where there is a single judge and where non-professional judges are used.

(1) Civil and criminal courts

* * *

(a) First instance civil courts

There are two general first instance civil courts, the tribunal d'instance and the tribunal de grande instance. Cases are assigned to one or other of these courts depending on their seriousness.

Until 1958, the tribunal d'instance was known as the court of the juge de paix (justice of the peace). It has long been a single-judge court hearing small civil cases. Since 1958, the judges have formed part of the corps of the ordinary judiciary. The 473 courts are located in the main towns of departements, arrondissements and important cantons.

* * *

In 1998 the tribunaux d'instance handed down 452,646 judgments on the merits and 69,034 decisions en référé.

More important civil cases are heard by the 181 tribunaux de grande instance, located in each départment. Some are very large—Paris has over 300 judges, and where this occurs the courts may, in practice, have specialist sections. The tribunal de grande instance deals with family matters (marriage, divorce, affiliation and nationality), as well as cases beyond the jurisdictional limits for the tribunaux d'instance.

The tribunal de grande instance is, by tradition, a collegial court, but there have been sufficient derogations in recent years that, in practice, much of its important civil work is carried on by single judges.

* * *

(c) Specialist first instance courts

There are a number of specialist courts which are spread across the French regions, * * * which are significant within the French legal system viewed as a whole.

A system of commercial courts has existed since 1563, and has survived with little change. The Code de commerce of 1807 entrusted the decision on litigation on commercial matters to these tribunaux commerciaux. Commercial matters are those which arise between commercial people (commerçants), or on commercial matters (eg commercial leases or companies), or about commercial things (eg patents). There are 227 commercial courts of varying sizes in France outside Aisace, and are staffed only by non-professional or 'consular' judges elected indirectly by the members of the local chamber of commerce. In 1998, these courts decided 168,038 cases on their merits and 40,083 decisions by way of référé and also oversaw 68,056 insolvency cases.

Labour courts (Conseils des prud'hommes) also pre-date the Revolution. Napoleon generalised the system to deal with employment issues. There are now 270 Conseils across France, and they are staffed essentially by lay people. The court is paritaire, that is to say it has equal numbers of employers and employees, at least four from each side. In the event of a tie, a professional judge from the tribunal de grande instance will act as the juge départiteur. In 1998, these courts decided 165,947 cases on their merits and 48,680 decisions by way of référé.

A similar *paritaire* court exists in relation to rural leases (3,680 cases on their merits and 270 decisions by way of référé in 1998), although it is always presided over by a juge d'instance. Representation of employers and employees also exists on the tribunaux des affaires de sécurité sociale (129,312 cases in 1998).[1]

(d) The cour d'appel

Appeals on both civil and criminal cases lie to the cour d'appel.
* * *

There are 33 cours located often where the pre-revolutionary Parlements sat, maintaining a significant element of continuity in the French legal tradition. Apart from urgent matters, the cour d'appel is collegial with a minimum of three members, though, civil cases are often heard before a single rapporteur. A typical cour d'appel will have a number of specialist chambers, dealing with civil, social, criminal and juvenile matters. Appeal lies on law and fact. Because there is a file on the case containing all the elements of the evidence reduced to writing produced by the lower civil and criminal courts, it is easy to conduct such an appeal on fact as well as law. Although it is usually sufficient to review the file as presented by the lower Court, the court may order such additional investigations as might seem necessary. In 1998, the cours d'appel heard 209,839 civil appeals and 28,361 criminal cases.

(e) The Cour de cassation

A litigant may make a pourvoi en cassation against a decision of the cour d'appel to the Cour de cassation, created in 1790, which is the only

---

1. Editor's Note: In 2002, a new first instance court was introduced, the so-called *juridiction de proximité*. It is meant to be a court for the solution of minor disputes, closer to the citizens.

national court in France on civil or criminal matters. As its name implies, it is not strictly an appeal court, but merely a body that quashes the rulings of appeal courts for error of law. The normal cassation procedure is that the Cour de cassation merely decides the disputed question of law and then refers it to a different cour d'appel for decision on the merits in the light of its ruling. In 1998, the Cour de cassation decided 19,815 civil matters (resulting in cassation in 19.15% of cases) and 7335 criminal matters (resulting in cassation in only 5.5% of cases).

The Cour de cassation is made up of six chambers, five civil chambers and the sixth dealing with criminal law. It has nearly 200 members * * * The Cour sits normally in panels of five judges . . . . More important cases may be heard by a larger panel of judges within a chamber. To resolve divergences of interpretation and case law, a chambre mixte composed of the Premier President of the Cour together with the president and three senior members of each chambre concerned (anything between 13 and 25 people in total). The Cour sits in plenary session (Assemblée plénière) where a case is appealed from a cour d'appel to which it has been remitted after cassation or where the premier president considers a matter to be of major importance. In such cases, the premier president sits with four members from each of the six chambers (the president, oldest conseiller and two others), a total of 25 judges.

Since 1991, the Cour de cassation gives a ruling (technically an opinion) on a point of law on a preliminary reference from a lower court. This saisine pour avis applies where a case raises a novel legal issue of serious difficulty relevant to a number of cases. An opinion is issued within three months. The Cour sits in a particularly solemn formation to deliver such opinions, being presided over by the First president and attended by the president and oldest conseiller and two other members of each chamber concerned.

In recent times, two measures have been taken to reduce the time taken to decide cases submitted to the Cour de cassation. In the first place, summary decision procedures have been introduced to deal with appeals which lack merit. Since 1981 and where the solution was obvious, the premier president or the president of chamber has discretion to refer a case to a formation restreinte composed of three judges provided neither party objects. Second, in 1979 the Cour de cassation was given power to decide cases without referring them back to another court (cassation sans renvoi). The Cour may enter a definitive judgment where the facts as found by the lower court enable it to apply the correct legal rule or where quashing the decision of the lower court does not require further inquiry into the facts of the case. Only in a very limited way does this procedure turn the Cour de cassation into a trier of fact. The procedure is used frequently in criminal matters, but is rarely used in civil cases.[2]

2. Editor's Note: The *Code de l'organisation judiciaire*, as amended by the Law of June 25, 2001, n. 2001–539, provides now that the formation *restreinte* of the *chambre*

(2) Administrative courts

(a) Public law and private law

Administrative law is the branch of law that is concerned with the powers and organisation of governmental bodies, notably the State. Its central characteristic is the presence of administration as one of the parties to the dispute. The notion of the 'administration' here covers not only national government, but also local authorities, public agencies and public services, ranging from universities to utilities or the regulatory agencies such as the Conseil supérieur de l'audiovisuel. Public law has special rules governing not only the use of powers, but also the rules of contract, the liability of public authorities and employment. By contrast, a private law dispute is one between two individuals or companies.

The precise allocation of disputes to either public law or to private law does pose some difficulties and there is a special court, the Tribunal des Conflits, which exists to resolve them. It is made up of equal numbers of judges from the highest public and private law courts, and the Minister of Justice (Garde des Sceaux) has the casting vote. In 1998, it decided 47 cases.

The consequence of the distinction between public and private law is two-fold: first, the rules of law applicable to a contract or a wrong or to the use of powers are not the same for public bodies as for private bodies; second, any litigation is tried by different courts according to different procedures by different groups of judges, whose background is distinct from that of private law judges. This radical separation between public and private law courts, in its present form, is a feature of the French republican tradition. It was set out in a loi of 16–24 August 1790 and by Napoleon's creation of the Conseil d'Etat in 1799, and was restated by decisions of the Tribunal des Conflits at the beginning of the Third Republic. More recently, it has been declared a fundamental principle recognised by the laws of the Republic by the Conseil constitutionnel.

* * *

(b) The Conseil d'Etat

The oldest of the public law courts is the Conseil d'Etat, set up by Napoleon in 1799, which had many similarities to the King's Privy Council. It was originally a court of first and last instance, but since the creation of the tribunaux administratifs in 1953 and the cours administratives d'appel in 1987, it has increasingly become a supervisory court, with a role as an appeal court in a small number of areas. Its jurisdiction

which the case has been referred to, may reject summarily inadmissable recourses, or recourses "non fondés sur un moyen sérieux de cassation," i.e., not grounded on serious cassational reasons according to art. 131–136 of the COJ (see, e.g., Loïc Cadiet and Emmanuel Jeuland, Manuel de droit judiciaire privé 634–635 (5th ed. 2006)). In other words, it is apparent that France, as well as Germany and other civil law countries, is trying to recuperate the normative function of their supreme courts by allowing them to use case selection discretionary devices.

is typically to review the decisions of the lower administrative courts and to quash them where the law has been wrongly applied. Since 1989, it also gives advisory opinions on the law during litigation when requested to do so on a reference from those courts. It retains some matters as a court of first and last instance.

Its judges are drawn from a distinct corps of the administration around 300 members who have distinguished administrative and judicial careers ... The Conseil is not only a judicial body, it is a major advisor to the government. Accordingly, it is organised into six sections, only one of which is concerned with litigation (the Section du contentieux). This Section du contentieux is then further divided into sous-sections which both prepare cases for decision (the work of instruction) and decide most of the routine cases either their own (a sous-section jugeant seule) or jointly with another sous-section (sous-sections réunies). Important cases of principle or where there are conflicts of case law between different sous-sections will be decided by the whole Section du contentieux. Very important cases are reserved to the Assemblee du contentieux, presided over by the Vice–President and involving the presidents of all the Sections of the Conseil. In 1998, the Conseil d'Etat decided some 10,540 cases.

* * *

(c) The tribunaux administratifs and the Cours administratives d'appel

The tribunaux administratifs and the Cours administratives d'appel are staffed a separate corps of judges from the Conseil d'Etat. These are drawn from the administration and, to an increasing extent, from private practice. * * * They are very much more like the civil courts in their activities.

At the bottom of the pyramid of courts are the tribunaux administratifs. They originate in Napoleon's conseils de préfecture which advised the Prefect. There are now 36 spread across France. Each court is made up of a minimum of a president and three or four judges, though some, such as Paris are very large. They have jurisdiction on most matters arising in their area: contracts, liability, illegal municipal elections or decisions. They now have jurisdiction to enforce their own decisions by way of ordonnance to the administration. In 1998, the tnbunaux administratifs decided 110,966 cases.

Above these are the cours administratives d'appel, created in 1987. These seven cours are located in Bordeaux, Douai, Lyon, Marseilles, Nancy, Nantes, and Paris, and deal with appeals on points of law and fact from the tribunaux administratifs. They are staffed by the same corps of judges, but are presided over by members of the Conseil d'Etat. In 1998, they decided 11,651 cases.

ITALY

The Constitution of 1948 devotes the entire Chapter IV of Part II to "The Judiciary," its organization, and its independence. Some provisions are particularly relevant to the topics discussed in this Chapter and are set out below. See also Articles 101–110, in Chapter 2.*

The Constitution of the Republic of Italy (1948).

Art. 111
(as amended, 1999)

* * *

Recourse shall always be allowed to the Court of Cassation, on the ground of violation of law, against judgments as well as against rulings affecting personal liberty, whether pronounced by courts of ordinary or of special jurisdiction ...

Recourse in Cassation against decisions of the Council of State ... will be admitted only on grounds of jurisdiction.

Notes

1. The above constitutional provisions confirm that Italy, like most civil law countries, is characterized by a plurality of court hierarchies. The most important, though not the only ones, are the ordinary courts on one side dealing with civil and criminal matters, and the administrative courts on the other side dealing generally with public law disputes.

2. The system of civil courts is presently based on the following pattern:

a) The *justices of the peace* are at the bottom of the hierarchy. Law n. 374 of November 21, 1991 provides for the appointment of 4700 justices, distributed over 828 offices for a term of four years renewable only once. The Justices are honorary rather than career judges, they are law graduates, at least thirty years old, and receive compensation based upon the amount of work done. Their civil jurisdiction extends to small claims (up to 14,000 euros in certain subjects), but they also have an interesting subject-matter jurisdiction over neighborhood related controversies (including cases of nuisance), not to mention a broad extra-judicial conciliatory function. They sit as single-judge courts; their decisions may be appealed to the *tribunali*, unless they are based on equity, in which case they can only be attacked before the Supreme Court.

b) The *tribunali* are the (civil and criminal) courts of first instance of general jurisdiction. Presently, there are 164 of them and 218 branch sections. This guarantees that the *tribunali* extend throughout Italy, and that they are very close to the citizens. Following recent reform processes, which are being shared by several civil law countries, they sit as a single judge-court, subject to a limited number of exceptions, concerning cases considered to be more complex.

---

* Translation by Vincenzo Varano, adapted from Mauro Cappelletti, John Henry Merryman, and Joseph M. Perillo, The Italian Legal System 281–313 (1967).

c) There are twenty-six intermediate appellate courts in Italy, each of whom has jurisdiction over a district which generally corresponds to a region of the country. The courts of appeal are divided in several divisions—one of which has jurisdiction over labor appellate proceedings—, and sit in three-judge panels.

The right of appeal has no constitutional basis in Italy, though it is so deeply rooted in tradition as to be considered, as in other civil law countries, a part of the fundamental guarantee of fair hearing in both civil and criminal cases. As a rule, appeal involves a full review of the whole case and is not limited to questions of law.

d) The *Corte di Cassazione*, which sits in Rome, is the highest court in civil and criminal matters, and reviews only errors of law. It is divided into several civil and criminal divisions, each sitting with five judges. In certain cases, especially when there is a conflict between different divisions of the court, or in civil cases when the case involves a question of particular importance, the decision is rendered by a plenary session (*sezioni unite*), sitting as a nine-judge panel.

The *Corte di Cassazione* is based on the French model: this means that it either affirms the judgment from below, which then becomes final, or quashes it, and remand it for a fresh decision to a different court, on the same level as the court that rendered the judgment that has been quashed.

Unlike appeal, review by the Supreme court has a constitutional basis in art. 111, para. 7, *supra*—a peculiar feature of the Italian legal system. The expansive interpretation of that provision by the Court itself, as well as the width of the grounds for review provided for in the codes of procedure, have contributed to flood the Court with several thousand applications every year, making it very difficult for the court to effectively pursue the function of assuring "the exact observance and the uniform interpretation of the law, the unity of national law", required by art. 65 of the law of January 30, 1941, on the judiciary. However, the introduction of filters would not only require a substantial departure from the Italian legal tradition, but perhaps a constitutional amendment as well.

3.   The administrative courts are the *Tribunali amministrativi regionali*, with original jurisdiction, and the *Consiglio di Stato,* which has appellate jurisdiction. The former sit in each Region's capital, and adjudicate in three-judge panels; the latter has three advisory divisions—pursuant to art. 100 of the Constitution, the *Consiglio di Stato* is an advisory as well as a judicial body—, and three judicial divisions, each of whom decides with five judges.

The appointment, career and status independence of administrative court judges differs rather significantly from the ordinary judges, and is regulated by different statutes. The distribution of judicial control of administrative action between the ordinary courts, which have jurisdiction over violations of "subjective rights" by the administration, and the administrative courts, which have jurisdiction over violation of "legitimate interests" by the administration, is extremely complicated. So much so, that the frequent and very difficult borderline problems have led the legislator to vest jurisdiction exclusively in the administrative courts in an increasing number of cases.[3]

4. Statistics indicate that the Italian administration of justice, no matter whether civil or criminal, suffers from a very serious delay. It can be safely said that an average of roughly ten years is needed for the final determination of a civil dispute through the first instance ordinary proceeding, appeal, and Supreme Court. The situation is no better as far as delay before administrative courts is concerned.[4]

JAPAN

Japan is usually considered as sharing many features with the civil law tradition given "its decision to import its modern judicial system from European countries (mainly Germany and France) after it modernized its socio-political system in 1867–68 (Meiji Restoration).[5] Shozo Ota summarizes the Japanese civil justice system as follows:

> Appeals in ordinary civil cases (whose stake values are more than 900,000 yen, about US $9,000) move from district courts to high courts, and high courts to the Supreme Court. In minor cases (whose stake values are not more than 900,000 yen) appeals are taken from summary courts to district courts, and from district courts to high courts.

> One of the characteristics of Japan's judicial system is its small size. The court system is composed of one Supreme Court, 8 high courts (with 6 branch offices), 50 district courts and 50 family courts (both with about 200 branch offices), and 438 summary courts. In 2000, the district courts disposed of 187,070 cases, while the summary courts disposed of 314,533 cases."[6]

The defeat in World War II, and the consequent American occupation until 1952, brought about "a considerable Americanization of the Japanese legal system". The new Constitution of [November 3] 1946 [effective since May 3, 1947] "abolished a typical civil law institution of the administrative court and created an American type Supreme Court of only 15 Justices equipped with constitutional review power and rule making power for procedures. The Supreme Court along with lower courts thereunder was separated from the Ministry of Justice to become organizationally independent vis-à-vis the legislative and the executive branches. But the civil law feature of the lower court judgeship was not altered."[7]

3. See, e.g., Domenico Sorace, Administrative Law, in Introduction to Italian Law 125–158 (Jeffrey S. Lena and Ugo Mattei, eds., 2002).

4. For further information, see Vincenzo Varano, Machinery of Justice, in Lena and Mattei, id. at 99–124.

5. Shozo Ota, Reform of Civil Procedure in Japan, 49 Am. J. Comp. L. 561 n.1 (2001).

6. Id. at 561–562.

7. Yasuhei Taniguchi, Japan's Recent Civil Procedure Reform: Its Seeming Success and Left Problems, in The Reforms of Civil Procedure in Comparative Perspective 91, 93 (Nicolò Trocker and Vincenzo Varano, eds., 2005).

Some provisions of the Japanese Constitution concerning the organization of the courts are reported below—the American influence speaks for itself.

Constitution of Japan.*

Article 76 [Judicial Power]

(1) The whole judicial power is vested in a Supreme Court and in such inferior courts as are established by law.

(2) No extraordinary tribunal shall be established, nor shall any organ or agency of the executive be given final judicial power.

* * *

Article 77 [Judicial Procedure]

(1) The Supreme Court is vested with the rule-making power under which it determines the rules of procedure and of practice and of matters relating to attorneys, the internal discipline of the courts and the administration of judicial affairs.

* * *

(3) The Supreme Court may delegate the power to make rules for inferior courts to such courts.

* * *

Article 79 [Supreme Court]

(1) The Supreme Court shall consist of a Chief Judge and such number of judges as may be determined by law; all such judges excepting the Chief Judge shall be appointed by the Cabinet.

* * *

Article 81 [Jurisdiction of Supreme Court]

The Supreme Court is the court of last resort with power to determine the constitutionality of any law, order, regulation, or official act.

* * *

Note

Under the new Code of Civil Procedure, effective since January 1, 1998, the jurisdiction of the Supreme Court has become largely discretionary.

Under the old Code, a losing party could appeal as of right to the Supreme Court whenever he/she challenged the High Court judgment on the ground of errors either in constitutional interpretation or in application of the law (OC 394). It was not very difficult for a good lawyer to find or to

* Translation at http://www.oefre.unibe.ch/law/icl/ja00000_.html.

construct an error of legal interpretation in a High Court judgment. In other words, the Section 394 of the old Code was not an effective gate keeper.

The new Code limited the grounds of appeal as of right to the Supreme Court. A losing party can appeal only when he/she challenges the High Court judgment on constitutional grounds (NC 312). In addition, the new Code introduced the "discretionary appeal" to the Supreme Court (NC 318), which is similar to the writ of certiorari in U.S. law. The Supreme Court accepts appeals on legal interpretation grounds only when deemed necessary and appropriate (e.g., when the High Court judgment is in contradiction with a Supreme Court precedent).[8]

III. COURTS IN THE COMMON LAW: ENGLAND AND THE UNITED STATES

ENGLAND

Henry J. Abraham, The Judicial Process 270–282 (7th ed. 1998).

It is incorrect to think of the courts of Great Britain or of the United Kingdom as a unified judicial system. For actually three different systems exist in the United Kingdom of Great Britain and Northern Ireland: one for England and Wales, one for Scotland, and one for Northern Ireland * * * The following description is of the judicial system of England and Wales * * *

In the United States, the same tribunals ordinarily have both civil and criminal jurisdiction * * * But in England of today, justice is meted out in two separated judicial hierarchies, one for civil cases and one for criminal cases, although the sitting judges are often the same individuals * * * The separation between civil and criminal court jurisdiction is based on the Supreme Court Act of 1981, the progeny of a series of Judicature Acts that commenced in 1873. The modernizing process between 1873 and 1925 brought order into what had been a truly bewildering array of distinct tribunals. However, unlike France, neither England nor Wales (nor the United States) has a * * * system of administrative courts.

* * *

THE CIVIL COURTS' HIERARCHY

* * *

The County Court. The lower of the two courts of first instance in civil matters is the county court * * * The districts they [the county

---

8. See Ota, supra note 5, at 571–572.

courts] serve are arranged so that a county court is within easy reach everywhere; they are subject to geographic alteration by the Lord Chancellor. There are over 246 county courts (1996), which are administered by the six administrative circuits into which the country is divided. The judges, called "circuit judges" since the Courts Act of 1971, are appointed by the Crown on the advice of the Lord Chancellor.

The circuit judges * * * are likely to live in or near their districts. In courts in London and in busy provincial centres they are likely to sit every day, and less frequently each month in centres where the business is less heavy. In addition to the circuit judge, each county court will have one or more district judges, who are judges appointed by the Lord Chancellor mainly from senior practicing solicitors, although senior barristers are now qualified for appointment. The district judge is not only in charge of the court's office staff but also acts as a junior judge of the court, where he or she will have an exceptionally wide jurisdiction in less significant civil and family work, including the responsibility for conducting informal arbitrations in civil proceedings where not more than £3,000 is claimed, in which no costs are recoverable by the winning side, unlike the usual English practice.

The jurisdiction of the county court underwent a radical alteration following the recommendations of the Civil Justice Review Body, a multidisciplinary team that reported to the Lord Chancellor on the future arrangements for civil justice in England in 1988. These recommendations led to the enactment of Part I of the Courts and Legal Services Act 1990, which gave the Lord Chancellor power to make orders allocating business in civil courts between the high court and the county courts, following consultation with senior judges, and the effect of the first orders made under these powers has been to move a substantial quantity of heavy civil litigation down to the county court. The effect of centralized computerization of bulk claims has, however, reduced the volume of business being handled by individual courts. A large proportion of county court business consists of debt-collecting summonses, which lead to the award of a default judgment against the debtor, which can then be enforced by bailiffs. As a result of computerization a centralized Summons Production Centre issued 1.14 million default summonses on behalf of 128 plaintiffs in 1994–95, an the County Court Bulk Centre processed 318,172 judgments and 217,609 warrants on behalf of 34 plaintiffs in the same period. In contrast, individual courts issued less then 150,000 default summonses. The jurisdiction of the county court in any action founded on contract or tort is now unlimited, and different procedural mechanisms are now used to ensure that the High Court is concerned with the weightier of these cases. In relation to other matters, the High Court and County Courts Jurisdiction Order 1991, made pursuant to the Courts and Legal Services Act 1990, sets out the demarcation lines. In some cases, £30,000 is taken as the relevant value that marks the upper limit of the county court's jurisdiction. The county court is the exclusive forum for almost all litigation between landlords and tenants relating to residential tenancies.

* * *

The High Court of Justice. Immediately above the county court in the hierarchy of the civil courts stands the High Court of Justice. (. . .) It combines original, appellate, and supervisory jurisdiction. In 1873 the former jurisdiction of five different courts was combined to form a single High Court, which was then divided into three separate divisions. It is now (1997) staffed by 98 judges (95 puisne judges and three Heads of Division).

* * *

The three divisions of the "High Court," as it is commonly called, comprise the 63–member Queen's Bench Division, including its president, the Lord Chief Justice of England, who ranks immediately after the Lord Chancellor in the judicial hierarchy; the 18–member Chancery Division, including its president, the Vice Chancellor; and the president and 16 judges of the Family Division (the successor, in 1971 to the former Probate, Divorce, and Admiralty Division).

Of the three, the Queen's Bench Division is by far the largest, partly because its judges have heavy responsibilities in the field of criminal justice and in the steadily increasing work of the Criminal Division of the Court of Appeal. In recent years, the work of both the Commercial Court, which is a composite part of this division, and the judges on the Crown Office List, who are concerned with public law matters and exercise both a supervisory and an appellate jurisdiction, has mushroomed to the extent that seven additional judges were appointed to the division in 1994 * * *. The * * * practice of having a Queen's Bench Division Court of three (or, very rarely, five) judges exercising the supervisory and appellate jurisdiction of the court has now been abandoned, and except for appeals by way of case stated in criminal cases from magistrates' courts of the Crown Court, which are usually heard by a two-judge Divisional Court, most of this work is now handled by a single judge of the court. A three-judge court is convened to hear certain appeals from professional disciplinary tribunals and public law cases of major public importance.

The Chancery Division has exclusive jurisdiction in some cases and concurrent jurisdiction with the Queen's Bench Division in others. * * * Its exclusive jurisdiction includes mortgage actions, revenue proceedings, bankruptcy business, company liquidations, execution of trusts, patent matters, and so on.

* * *

The Family Division has jurisdiction in the areas implied by its name: decrees as to divorce and nullity, judicial separation, and presumption of death and dissolution of marriage; resolution of disputes involving domestic violence or the occupation of the matrimonial home, matrimonial property or maintenance, or over children (adoption or guardianship, residence and contact orders). Although there is no integrated Family Court, the three levels of court (the High Court, county court, and magistrates' courts) operate in conjunction with each other, with cases being transferred, where appropriate, to the appropriate level. It is now the county court that carries the greatest workload in cases arising out of the final breakdown of a marriage, with disputes of particular complexity being referred upwards to the High Court on an ad hoc basis.

* * *

The High Court used to have overall jurisdiction in all cases that were eligible for hearing in the county court as well as those that lay outside that court's jurisdiction, The position is no longer so simple. Certain categories of cases must now be commenced in the County Court: for example, many types of landlord and tenant disputes and claims for personal injury where the value of the action is less than £50,000. In addition, the costs recoverable by a successful plaintiff are restricted in other cases whose financial value does not warrant proceedings in the High Court, and he or she can recover no costs at all on a High Court writ for less than £600.

* * *

The Court of Appeal. Appeals from any of the divisions of the High Court of Justice go to the Court of Appeal, which consists of the Master of the Rolls (England's third-highest judicial officer), who is the presiding judge in the Civil Division of the Court of Appeal, plus thirty-five Lords Justices of Appeal, the regular sitting members—usually in groups of three—who must have had a ten-year High Court qualification or been High Court judges. The Court of Appeal's appellate jurisdiction is primarily concerned with appeal on points of law from the county court or the High Court or a few appellate tribunals. There may also be appeals on fact from the High Court or the county court, but these rarely succeed. In 1994, there were 2,445 applications for leave to appeal to the Court of Appeal. Nine hundred eighty-seven final appeals and 696 interlocutory appeals were set down; these represented cases where leave to appeal had been granted, and a minority of cases where leave to appeal was still granted as a right. As a general rule, in contrast to practices prevalent in the United States' judicial system, there is no unqualified right of appeal in England. It would be entirely accurate to note that * * * the trend is to limit rather than extend judicial review.

* * *

The House of Lords. From the Court of Appeal, if the matter of law involved is deemed to be of sufficient importance, there remains the final path of appeal to the House of Lords (an expensive one—in 1993, £1,000 for printing costs alone was an average expenditure; the cost of reaching the Lords commonly ran to £20,000), provided that the appeal has been certified by the Court of Appeal or granted by the House of Lords itself, a historic right dating back to the practices of the Norman institution of the *magnum concilium,* the Great Council. The Lords do not, of course, sit in a mass body for that purpose (there were 1,193 members in August of 1996, though the average daily attendance was but 290); instead, the legal section of the House of Lords comprises a small, highly skilled, distinguished group of judicial experts, the twelve *Law Lords,* known as the *Lords of Appeal in Ordinary*, plus the Lord Chancellor, the presiding officer of the House of Lords. These twelve (or thirteen) officials, who thus constitute the final court of appeal, are augmented by any other peer who has held, or now holds, high judicial office under the Crown, and is under the age of seventy-five.

This small group of appellate experts, who usually sit in *bancs* of five, was created originally by the Appellate Jurisdiction Act of 1876 to supplement the judicial strength of the House of Lords. It remains the sole kingdomwide judicial body, and as such always has some members from Scotland (usually two) and, on occasion, one from Northern Ireland. These few dignitaries, who are almost always appointed from the ranks of Lords Justices of Appeal or judges of the Court of Session, are all professional, paid judges with life peerages.

* * *

The Judicial Committee of the Privy Council. The Judicial Committee of the Privy Council is the final court of appeal from courts of the United Kingdom dependencies (* * *, Gibraltar, Bermuda) and courts of independent Commonwealth countries that have retained the right of appeal (Antigua and Barbuda, The Bahamas, Barbados, Belize, Brunei, Dominica, The Gambia, Kiribati, Mauritius, New Zealand, St. Christopher and Nevis, St. Lucica, St. Vincent and the Grenadines, Trinidad and Tobago, and Tuvalu). The committee also hears appeals from courts of the Channel Islands and the Isle of Man, the disciplinary and health committees of the medical and allied professions, and some ecclesiastical appeals under the Pastoral Measure 1983.

* * *

Notes

1. The administration of justice in England has been undergoing radical transformations in the last few years, which extend well beyond the organization of the courts to cover the legal professions, including the judicial selection process as well as procedure. As to the organization of the courts, which is the object of this chapter, the reforms that followed the Woolf Report are prompting important changes. For instance, though the distinction between county courts and High Court has been maintained, the adoption of the principle of proportionality and the consequent allocation of cases to different tracks depending on their value and complexity, tends to blur that distinction: "The High Court will tend not to deal with matters less than £ 50,000. Subject to this, the county courts and the High Court

now share the burden of the multi-track case load."[9] This is a vast range of cases from simple contractual disputes to complex commercial cases possibly worthy several million pounds. In the end, sooner or later there may be in England only one court of first instance of general jurisdiction.

The Access to Justice Act 1999 Part IV, and the consequent amendments to the CPR 52 further restricted the possibility to attack a judgment. Now, permission to appeal is required in almost all cases and, unless there are exceptional circumstances, only one level of appeal is permitted. Furthermore, following this reform, all appeals have been limited to a review, and the routes of appeal have been altered so that appeal lies to the next level of judge in the court hierarchy.

The picture would not be complete without a reference to the reforms introduced by some important statutes of constitutional significance.

Following the enactment of the so-called devolution statutes—the Scotland Act 1998, the Government of Wales Act 1998, and the Northern Ireland Act 1998—the Judicial Committee of the Privy Council, in addition to its traditional jurisdiction, has been empowered to consider questions as to whether the Scottish Parliament, the National Assembly for Wales and the Northern Ireland Assembly are acting within their legal powers.

The Constitutional Reform Act 2005, in turn, is a revolutionary statute with momentous implications such as the reform of the Lord Chancellor's office and the method of appointment of judges. It seeks also to make a distinct constitutional separation between the legislature and the judiciary. Part 3 of the Act abolishes, in fact, the Appellate Committee of the House of Lords, and creates a Supreme Court of the United Kingdom giving it the appellate jurisdiction of the House of Lords and the devolution jurisdiction of the Judicial Committee of the Privy Council. The Court will comprise 12 judges—the 'Justices of the Supreme Court'—who are to be appointed, according to a process set out in the Act, by Her Majesty, who will also appoint one of them as the President of the Court and one as the Vice President. The Lords of Appeal currently sitting on the House will become the first members of the new Supreme Court. "The Supreme Court will not be able to strike down legislation as unconstitutional or contrary to the ECHR, and its jurisdiction will be broadly the same as that currently exercised by the House of Lords. It will, however, inherit jurisdiction over devolution matters from the Privy Council. Although the * * * Act was passed in 2005, the provisions establishing the Supreme Court will not be brought into force until it can be properly housed. The government's preferred venue for the new court is Middlesex Guildhall, but the planned refurbishments * * * are unlikely to be complete before the end of 2008."[10]

2. The picture of the administration of civil justice would not be complete without a quick reference to the magistrates' courts and the special tribunals.

The former are usually staffed by lay justices, appointed by the Lord Chancellor following the advice of Local Advisory Committees. They need

---

9. Neil Andrews, English Civil Procedure: Fundamentals of the New Civil Justice System 40 (2003).

10. Walker & Walker's English Legal System 244–245 (Richard Ward and Amanda Wragg, eds., 9th ed. 2005).

not be qualified as members of the legal profession and they serve without pay. There are roughly 30,000 of them. Although the bulk of the jurisdiction of magistrates' courts is criminal, they also have a significant civil jurisdiction. It includes the recovery of certain debts such as income tax, national insurance contributions, charges for utilities, and above all family law matters.

Many disputes are resolved by special tribunals, subject to the supervisory jurisdiction of the High Court, and in some cases to the appellate jurisdiction of the High Court or Court of Appeal. Most special tribunals have been created during the 20th century in order to provide a cheap, quick and informal forum for the resolution of disputes originating in the Welfare state legislation. The disputes which must be brought before special tribunals involve not only the citizen and the administration, but in many cases also private citizens (such as employment cases) and in some case even fundamental rights (such as immigration or unlawful discrimination cases). The composition of tribunals is extremely varied, and includes both legally qualified members and lay members with relevant expertise. The problem with the people serving on the tribunals is their independence, in that they are generally selected and appointed by Ministers, and frequently they have to decide cases concerning those Ministers. The problem has been definitely solved by the Constitutional Reform Act 2005, according to which most tribunal members, as well as judges, will be selected by the new Judicial Appointment Commission.

THE UNITED STATES

Constitution of the United States.
ARTICLE I
* * *

Section 8. [1] The Congress shall have power * * *

[8]   To constitute tribunals inferior to the Supreme Court

* * *

ARTICLE III

Section 1. The judicial power of the United States, shall be vested in one Supreme Court, and in such inferior courts as the Congress may from time to time ordain and establish * * *

Section 2. [1] The judicial power shall extend to all cases, in law and equity, arising under this Constitution, the laws of the United States, and treaties made, or which shall be made, under their authority; to all cases affecting ambassadors, other public ministers and consuls; to all cases of admiralty and maritime jurisdiction; to controversies to which the United States will be a party; to controversies between two or more States; between a State and citizens of another State; between citizens of different States; between citizens of the same State claiming lands under the grants of different States and between a State, or the citizens thereof, and foreign States, citizens or subjects.

[2]   In all cases affecting ambassadors, other public ministers and consuls, and those in which a State will be a party, the Supreme Court shall have original jurisdiction. In all other cases before mentioned, the Supreme Court shall have appellate jurisdiction, both as to law and fact, with such exceptions, and under such regulations as the Congress shall make.

* * *

Alexis De Tocqueville, Democracy in America, Vol. 1, 102–104 (1956 ed.).

Judicial Power in the United States, and Its Influence on Political Society.

THE ANGLO–AMERICANS have retained the characteristics of judicial power which are common to other nations—They have, however, made it a powerful political organ—How—In what the judicial system of the Anglo–Americans differs from that of all other nations—Why the American judges have the right of declaring laws to be unconstitutional—How they use this right—Precautions taken by the legislator to prevent its abuse.

I HAVE thought it right to devote a separate chapter to the judicial authorities of the United States, lest their great political importance should be lessened in the reader's eyes by merely incidental mention of them. Confederations have existed in other countries besides America; I have seen republics elsewhere than upon the shores of the New World alone: the representative system of government has been adopted in several states of Europe; but I am not aware that anv nation of the globe has hitherto organized a judicial power in the same manner as the Americans. The judicial organization of the United States is the institution which a stranger has the greatest difficulty in understanding. He hears the authority of a judge invoked in the political occurrences of every day, and he naturally concludes that in the United States the judges are important political functionaries; nevertheless, when he examines the nature of the tribunals, they offer at the first glance nothing that is contrary to the usual habits and privileges of those bodies; and the magistrates seem to him to interfere in public affairs only by chance, but by a chance that recurs every day.

* * *

The Americans have retained these three distinguishing characteristics of the judicial power: an American judge can pronounce a decision only when litigation has arisen, he is conversant only with special cases, and he cannot act until the cause has been duly brought before the court. His position is therefore exactly the same as that of the magistrates of other nations, and yet he is invested with immense political power. How does this come about? If the sphere of his authority and his means of action are the same as those of other judges, whence does he derive a power which they do not possess? The cause of this difference lies in the simple fact that the Americans have acknowledged the right of judges to found their decisions on the *Constitution* rather than on the *laws*. In other words, they have permitted them not to apply such laws as may appear to them to be unconstitutional.

* * *

Geoffrey C. Hazard, Jr. and Michele Taruffo, American Civil Procedure: An Introduction 51–70 (1993).

The most distinctive characteristic of the courts in the United States is their involvement in determining issues that in other countries are determined outside the courts. Fundamental issues in which the American courts have been instrumental include racial desegregation, abortion, rights of the accused in criminal cases, freedom of speech, and the relationship between religion and the government. In all other modern democracies these issues have been treated almost exclusively as "political" matters. That is, they have been determined by parliamentary legislation, or by the decision of a cabinet composed of parliamentary leaders, or by decisions of the permanent government bureaucracy with which the parliamentary leadership decided not to interfere. The same is true of many issues having lower public visibility but great significance in the world of business and commercial transactions.

The role of the courts in resolving "political" issues has been a central phenomenon of American government since the adoption of the Constitution. The supporters of the Constitution anticipated that the federal court system would restrain the excesses of "faction," by which the Federalists meant popular sentiment. In recent years the role of the courts has been intensely debated in connection with appointments to the U.S. Supreme Court, for example, those of Robert Bork (who was rejected) and of Clarence Thomas (who was confirmed).

The idea that the courts, a nonelective agency of government, can decide fundamental political issues contradicts all conventional theories of democracy. Yet the courts of the United States, the world's longest-established constitutional democracy, perform that very function. The paradox of nondemocratic authority being central in a constitutional democracy has defied political theorists since Tocqueville focused attention on it over 150 years ago. A coherent explanation, if there is one, must be complex. Some insight can be gained by reflecting on the fact that the vehicle for this exercise of judicial authority is ordinary litigation and not some special constitutional process.

Ordinary litigation is available to anyone, at least anyone who can find a lawyer willing to take the case. * * * This right of political access expresses principles of equality and opportunity that are fundamental in American consciousness.

Ordinary litigation calls upon protection of the law, not an exercise of discretion or grace by a government official. * * * A lawsuit, particularly as conducted through the adversary system, as an expression of legal equality, a principle fundamental in American consciousness.

Ordinary litigation summons a citizen, even one having wealth or power, to account for his or her conduct in specific terms and humbling circumstances. The defendant must answer the charges, produce documents from otherwise confidential files, and respond to cross-examination. Judgment is passed by judges who are more or less politically independent and juries comprised of people from, everyday walks of life. This too expresses basic political principles.

Ordinary litigation is conducted in tribunals that deal with the whole range of civil life. On any given day the courts may determine rights between neighbors concerning the use of a driveway; employees and employers over the rights of labor and management; police and criminal suspects over the rules governing arrest; divorcing spouses; consumers and sellers; manufacturers and distributors; rival political candidates; motorists; debtors and creditors; government and taxpayers; and government and the governed. In any given judgment, the courts will have mediated between almost every set of social, economic, and political interests, all in the name of legal justice. The courts represent an institutional version of Plato's ideal philosopher-king, or perhaps the biblical ideal personified in Solomon as king-judge. These images are the products of a strong sense that politics have a moral foundation.

* * *

THE UNIQUE POSITION OF THE SUPREME COURT

The U.S. Supreme Court has a position of authority unlike that of any other judicial tribunal in the world.

The Supreme Court is, first of all, the highest authority in the federal court system. As we have seen, the federal court system has exclusive competence over criminal proceedings for enforcing federal criminal law.

* * *

The federal court system also has exclusive competence of proceedings for judicial review of federal administrative agencies.

* * *

The Supreme Court is the ultimate appellate authority in interpreting the legal standards by which federal administrative agencies are empowered to act.

The federal court system has primary, and in many instances exclusive, competence of civil actions to enforce private rights created by federal statute. Federal rights for civil redress have been created for victims of many legal wrongs * * * The federal courts also have competence in cases concerning use of federal lands, which constitute a substantial portion of the territory of the United States, and matters of admiralty and maritime jurisdiction. The Supreme Court is the ultimate appellate authority in all such litigation.

The Supreme Court has competence as an appellate court to review decisions of state courts that involve questions of federal law * * *. This competence extends not only to civil actions in state courts but to state court criminal cases in which federal legal issues have arisen, such as violations of federal due process requirements.

In exercising its authority in this broad array of legal matters, the Supreme Court speaks as the final interpreter of the Constitution. As such it has appellate authority over federal administrative officials, authority to declare acts of Congress unconstitutional, and authority to direct the President of the United States to comply with the law—as in *United States v. Nixon,* which involved the question of whether the President must comply with a court order to produce documents. The Court has similar appellate authority concerning the validity under federal law of state legislation and acts of state and municipal officials.

These enormous legal powers are not explicitly stated in the Constitution. They were asserted in primal form in the seminal decision of *Marbury v. Madison* in 1803 and have been repeatedly reasserted and expanded in the nearly two centuries since. From time to time the Supreme Court's authority has been challenged.

* * *

The product of these controversies, however, has been a strengthened public commitment to the legitimacy of the Supreme Court's authority and a corresponding acceptance of the authority in the lower federal and state courts.

Peter Hay, Law of the United States: An Overview 46–53 (2002).

A. Introduction

I. *The Civil Suit and Civil Procedure*

This chapter serves to provide an overview of the American court system and of the basics of the law of civil procedure. Again, the principal focus will be on federal law.

"Civil Procedure" as that term is used here, encompasses a wider field and applies to more types of disputes than is the case in many other legal systems, for instance, in those with affinity to the Germanic system. With few exceptions, there are no separate court systems for different types of cases, and there are—basically—but two types of judicial proceedings, in terms of applicable procedural rules—the civil action and the criminal prosecution. Procedure apart, public law matters, labor law disputes, family law and probate cases, contract and tort cases (claims on "obligations" in civil law terminology) and criminal law proceedings all fall within the jurisdiction of the same court: the American judge is a generalist.

In many cases, the judicial proceeding may be preceded by administrative action and proceedings: nevertheless, it is still the court that reviews the administrative action. The rules of the law of civil procedure therefore ultimately govern all legal proceedings except criminal actions

* * *

B. Court Organization and Subject Matter Jurisdiction

I. The Federal Courts

1. Structure

The federal courts are a separate and independent system of courts: "separate" in the sense that—except for the U.S. Supreme Court in federal matters—they do not function as appellate or superior courts for the state courts. The court of first instance (trial court) is the District Court. There is at least one in every state. Larger states are subdivided into regions, each with its own federal **District Court** * * *. As a rule, each District Court will have several judges, but individual cases are ordinarily heard by a single judge. "Bankruptcy cases" are first heard by a "bankruptcy judge" or "referee in bankruptcy." These are inferior tribunals but—because of a party's Constitutional right to a determination by an "Article III judge"—are subject to the supervision of, and review by, the District Court to which they are attached.

The Courts of Appeal review District Court decisions. There are twelve regional Courts of Appeal. These regions, called "circuits" and identified by number (for instance, "Court of Appeals for the Second Circuit") encompass several states * * *. A thirteenth Court of Appeals ("for the Federal Circuit") has limited subject matter jurisdiction. It hears appeals from decisions of the Court of Claims (which has jurisdiction over claims against the federal government), of the Court of Customs and Patent Appeals. A Court of Appeals hears and decides cases with three-judge panels; in special cases, the entire membership of the Court will hear (or rehear) a case: the Court sits "en banc."

Review by a Court of Appeals is more limited than the review by an intermediate appellate court in some other legal systems. American appellate courts—both federal and state—only review the lower court's determinations of questions of law; they do not review the lower court's or jury's determinations with respect to issues of fact.

The U.S. Supreme Court is the highest court in the federal judicial system. It consists of nine judges, appointed for life by the President with the consent of the Senate. The Court does not sit in panels or chambers; it always sits en banc.

2. Subject Matter Jurisdiction

There are only few areas for which federal courts have exclusive jurisdiction, such as in maritime matters and in bankruptcy proceedings. They have concurrent jurisdiction—with state courts—in "federal question cases" and cases based on "diversity of citizenship."

A "**federal question** case" is simply one in which the claim arises from federal law. The exercise of a federal court's "**diversity jurisdiction**" requires that the parties have different ("diverse") citizenship (of different U.S. states or foreign nations), that the amount in controversy exceeds $75,000, and that the controversy does not fall within the exclusive jurisdiction of state courts.

Rules concerning "supplemental jurisdiction" enlarge the subject matter jurisdiction of federal courts. They permit the addition of a claim based on state law to claims invoking the federal court's federal question jurisdiction * * *.

In federal question cases, federal courts apply federal law (statutory or case law). If the case raises questions of state law, however, federal courts may not apply or create federal law *(Erie-doctrine)*. In diversity cases, a federal court therefore ordinarily applies the law of the state in which it "sits," including that state's rules of private international law ("conflicts law"). This means that the federal courts must apply the state's statutory law and the interpretations given to it, as well as other decisional law pronounced by the state's highest court. An underlying policy goal . . . is to ensure decisional uniformity as between federal and state courts addressing like cases in the exercise in their concurrent jurisdiction within the same state.

Art. III of the U.S. Constitution limits the exercise of jurisdiction by federal courts to claims presenting a "**case or controversy.**" The case must involve an actual—not hypothetical—dispute. Further, the claim presented in a federal question case must be "ripe" for decision and the plaintiff must be personally (individually) affected. To have "standing," a plaintiff must satisfy these requirements; there is no federal jurisdiction for abstract claims.

The **political question-doctrine** serves as another limitation upon the exercise of federal jurisdiction. The Constitutional tradition of separation of powers requires that courts do not involve themselves with political questions. Defining "political questions," however, is not easy, an the definition has changed with time and with changing circumstances.

* * *

Startling to many, * * * the U.S. Supreme Court * * * did not consider the doctrine to be a bar to its review of the election procedures of the state of Florida in the presidential elections of November 2000.

Federal procedural law preempts state law in proceedings in federal courts, even when the claim is based on state law (diversity jurisdiction), insofar as it conflicts with state law and claims applicability. In the absence of a federal rule, or when uniform treatment of an issue is not needed, state procedural law may apply.

II. State Courts

1. Structure

Usually, state law also provides for three levels of courts (trial court, intermediate appellate court, and highest court). Many States, however, also provide for special inferior courts below the level of the general trial court, for instance, traffic courts, small claims courts for controversies below a specified amount (such as $2,500), and family courts. Their establishment is designed to ease the case load of the regular courts; formal rules of procedure do not apply to proceedings before them. Because they are special inferior courts, their decisions are subject to review by the regular trial court, which decides the case *de novo*.

The names of state courts vary some from state to state. As in the federal system, the trial court will ordinarily be called "District Court" (but also: Circuit Court, for instance, in Illinois, Michigan, and other states), the intermediate court is the "Court of Appeals" or "Appellate Court" [for a designated area], and the highest court is the Supreme Court.

2. Subject Matter Jurisdiction

State courts have subject matter jurisdiction over all claims except in the limited instances in which federal courts have been allocated exclusive jurisdiction * * *. This means that claims arising under federal law—including under Federal Constitutional law—may be brought in state courts as well as in federal courts (assuming, in both cases, the court's jurisdiction over the parties). When adjudicating claims based on federal law, however, state courts must follow federal judicial precedents.

State courts possess exclusive jurisdiction in matters of family law and succession. In addition, a state court at the situs of immovable property has exclusive jurisdiction over title-related claims.

III. Summary

If the claim arises under federal law, federal courts have competence ("federal question jurisdiction") and state courts are also competent ("general subject matter jurisdiction"), except in the few areas of exclusive federal competence. Federal courts have concurrent jurisdiction with state courts in state law cases, provided that (a) the subject matter does not fall within the exclusive jurisdiction of state courts and that (b) the prerequisites for "diversity jurisdiction" have been satisfied.

Note

As the constitutional provisions reported at the beginning of this section indicate, in the United States, "there are two major types of federal courts from the point of view of their creation and functions: the *constitutional* courts and the *legislative* courts." Constitutional courts are established under Article III of the United States Constitution; legislative courts are established under Article I. It follows that "the safeguards of tenure, salary, and independence that accrue to judges of the constitutional courts * * * are not necessarily present for the judges of the legislative courts." In addition, "legislative courts are endowed with functions that are nonjudicial—that is, legislative and administrative—as well as judicial." * * *.[11]

IV. CONSTITUTIONAL COURTS

John E. Ferejohn, Constitutional Review in the Global Context, 6 N.Y.U. J. Legis. & Pub. Pol'y. 49 (2003).

* * * The United States is virtually unique in having judicial review, if judicial review means a system in which ordinary judges can review and strike down legislation. Other countries that have adopted constitutional review have taken great pains to exclude ordinary judges from having any part in it. This was true at the time of the origination of the new model of constitutional review in Austria after World War I, and it was true in Germany and Italy after World War II. It was true in Spain and Portugal after the collapse of their authoritarian governments. And it was true after the collapse of Soviet hegemony over Eastern Europe. In every case we see that American style judicial review was rejected in favor of something different. We need to pay attention to that basic fact.

Why is it that the form of constitutional review spreading like wildfire is not the American form, but is another form altogether? Why is it that the American style has not been very popular? I think we can get answers to these questions by asking about the circumstances that have given rise to constitutional adjudication over the past half century.

There have been three distinct waves of constitutional adjudication in post-war Europe. The first took place right after World War II in Germany and Italy. The second wave was after the collapse of the Spanish and Portuguese authoritarian governments, and of the Greek dictatorship about quarter century ago. And, the third wave followed the collapse of the Soviet Union about ten years ago. In every case, the nations adopted the same model, pretty much. The choice was always what I shall call the Kelsenian model: specialized constitutional courts, populated by law professors, and never were ordinary judges permitted to participate. No country ever adopted the American practice of judicial review, and in most cases the rejection was explicit and decisive. Why?

Part of the answer, of course, is that in every case I mentioned, a formerly authoritarian system adopted a new constitution and provided for constitutional review in order to enforce constitutional provisions. That was the case in Germany and Italy, obviously, and also in Spain,

11. Henry J. Abraham, The Judicial Process 158–159 (7th ed. 1998).

Portugal, Greece, and the nations previously part of the Soviet empire. These were all cases of failed authoritarian systems with no recent history of democracy or liberty. By contrast, in the old (stable and successful) democracies—Britain, New Zealand, the Netherlands, Sweden—there was no move to create new constitutions, or indeed, any real constitutions at all. And, of course, without a written constitution, there is little need for constitutional courts. The home of contemporary constitutional adjudication, the wildfire, is post-authoritarian systems.

One thing that post-authoritarian systems have in common is that the judges that are still on the bench are implicated, to some extent, in the practices of the previous regime. The citizenry in such circumstances have every sociological reason to be suspicious of how those officials would go about their business. In other words, there exists a characteristic circumstance of distrust. In fact, there's actually a secondary circumstance of distrust arising naturally in post-authoritarian settings, and that is distrust of the lawmakers as well of the judges. In such circumstances, there is a natural desire to place both the positive lawmakers and the law enforcers under constitutional control. The question is how best to do that.

Broadly speaking, the answer for nations that have adopted constitutional review is one that was developed after World War I. Hans Kelsen, an Austrian legal theorist, deserves credit for inventing the model of constitutional adjudication that has become popular over the past few decades. Kelsen, an eminent young legal scholar, happened to be a staff member to a committee charged with framing a new constitution, and was asked to draft the section of it dealing with constitutional review. And that draft constitution created a new institution—a constitutional court of professors—that would have the power to control ordinary legislation.

Kelsen recognized the need for an institution with power to control or regulate legislation. * * * He recognized, too, that constitutional control essentially involves legislative activity. He recognized, in other words, that constitutional adjudication involves legislating as well as judging. The processes by which constitutional adjudicators make or declare general rules are different from those employed in ordinary legislatures, and the considerations and arguments taken into account are different, but constitutional adjudicators are still legislating.

GERMANY

Fundamental Law (*Grundgesetz*) of the Federal Republic of Germany (1949).*

CHAPTER **IX**

Judiciary

Article 92 [Court Organization]

* Translation available at http://www.psr.keele.ac.uk/docs/german.htm (Site last visited June 11, 2007).

Judicial power is vested in the judges; it is exercised by the Federal Constitutional Court, by the federal courts provided for in this Constitution, and by the courts of the States [Länder].

Article 93 [Federal Constitutional Court]

(1) The Federal Constitutional Court decides:

1. on the interpretation of this Constitution in the event of disputes concerning the extent of the rights and duties of a highest federal body or of other parties concerned who have been vested with rights of their own by this Constitution or by rules of procedure of a highest federal body;

2. in case of differences of opinion or doubts on the formal and material compatibility of federal law or State [Land] law with this Constitution, or on the compatibility of State [Land] law with other federal law, at the request of the Government, of a State [Land] government, or of one third of the House of Representatives [Bundestag] members;

2a. In case of differences of opinion on the compatibility of federal law with Article 72 II, at the request of the Senate [Bundesrat], of a State [Land] government, or of a State [Land] parliament;

3. in case of differences of opinion on the rights and duties of the Federation and the States [Länder], particularly in the execution of federal law by the States [Länder] and in the exercise of federal supervision;

4. on other disputes involving public law, between the Federation and the States [Länder], between different States [Länder] or within a State [Land], unless recourse to another court exists;

4a. on complaints of unconstitutionality, being filed by any person claiming that one of his basic rights or one of his rights under Article 20 IV or under Article 33, 38, 101, 103 or 104 has been violated by public authority;

4b. on complaints of unconstitutionality filed by communes or associations of communes on the ground that their right to selfgovernment under Article 28 has been violated by a statute other than a State [Land] statute open to complaint to the respective State [Land] constitutional court;

5. in the other cases provided for in this Constitution.

(2) The Federal Constitutional Court also acts in such other cases as are assigned to it by federal legislation.

Article 94 [Composition of Constitutional Court]

(1) The Federal Constitutional Court consists of federal judges and other members. Half of the members of the Federal Constitutional Court are elected by the House of Representatives [Bundestag] and half by the Senate [Bundesrat]. They may not be members of the House of Repre-

sentatives [Bundestag]. the Senate [Bundesrat], the Government, nor of any of the corresponding bodies of a State [Land].

(2) The constitution and procedure of the Federal Constitutional Court are regulated by a federal statute which specifies in what cases its decisions have the force of law. Such statute may require that all other legal remedies must have been exhausted before a complaint of unconstitutionality can be entered, and may make provision for a special procedure as to admissibility.

ITALY

Constitution of the Republic of Italy (1948).*

Art. 134

(as amended, 1989)

The Constitutional Court shall have jurisdiction over:

Controversies concerning the constitutionality of statutes, and acts having the force of statutes enacted by the State and the Regions;

Conflicts of jurisdiction between the State powers, or between the State and the Regions, or between Regions;

Charges raised against the President of the Republic in accordance with the Constitution.

Art. 135

(as amended, 1967)

The Constitutional Court shall be composed of fifteen judges, one third of them being appointed by the President of the Republic, one third by Parliament in joint session, and one third by the highest ordinary and administrative courts.

The judges of the Constitutional Court will be selected from among judges or retired judges of the highest ordinary and administrative courts, university professors of law, and from among practicing lawyers of at least twenty years' standing.

The judges of the Constitutional Court shall be appointed for nine years, their term beginning the day they are sworn in, and shall not be eligible for reappointment.

At the end of the term, the judge will cease from the office and its functions.

The Court shall elect its President from among its members and according to the provisions established by law. The President shall remain in office for three years, and may be reelected, provided the term of appointment is not exceeded.

* Translation by Vincenzo Varano adapted from Mauro Cappelletti, John H. Merryman, and John M. Perillo, The Italian Legal System 281–313 (1967).

The office of judge of the Court shall be incompatible with membership of Parliament or of a Regional Council, or with the practice of law, and with any other position or office laid down by law.

In proceedings involving charges against the President of the Republic, sixteen lay members will supplement the Court. They will be drawn by lot from a list of citizens, who are qualified to be elected as senators and are designated by Parliament every nine years, according to the same procedures followed for the appointment of judges of the Court.

Art. 136

When the Court declares that a provision of a statute, or an act having the force of a statute, is unconstitutional, the provision shall cease to have any effect from the day following the publication of the decision.

The decision of the Court shall be published and communicated to both Chambers of Parliament and to the interested regional Council, in order for them to take the measures they deem necessary, in the form required by the Constitution.

Art. 137

A constitutional statute will lay down the conditions, forms and terms under which constitutional questions may be raised, and the guarantees of independence of the judges of the Court.

An ordinary statute will lay down the rules necessary for the establishment and functioning of the Court.

No appeal will lie against the decisions of the Constitutional Court.

Mauro Cappelletti, The Judicial Process in Comparative Perspective 132–149 (1989).

II. CENTRALIZED VERSUS DECENTRALIZED JUDICIAL REVIEW

Though the events of the twentieth century brought the West as a whole to see the value of judicial review of legislation, the historical and philosophical differences between the Western states have prevented their adopting identical systems to exercise such control. Deep-seated suspicions of the judicial office, commitments to legal positivism, and other more practical considerations have meant that judicial review in various countries is conducted by different organs of review, which employ different methods, and whose decisions may have different effects.

From a comparative standpoint, one of the most instructive features of any system of judicial review is the state's choice of either a centralized or a decentralized system. The decentralized (or American) system gives all the judicial organs within it the power to determine the constitutionality of legislation. In contrast, the centralized (or Austrian) system confines this power to a single judicial organ.

A. Decentralized Judicial Review

The decentralized model had its origin in the United States, where judicial review remains a most characteristic and unique institution. It is found primarily in several of Britain's former colonies, including Canada, Australia, and India. The American system has also been introduced in Japan under the current Constitution of 1947.

In Europe, as well, the American system has had and still has its analogues. A certain parallel can be found in Swiss law, where * * * the * * * judges have a general power to disregard laws of the cantons in conflict with the Federal Constitution.

Norwegian law, since the end of last century, and Danish law, from the beginning of this century, have also asserted the power of the courts to review the conformity of legislation with the constitution and to disregard, in a concrete case, a law held unconstitutional. * * * A similar power has also been asserted in Sweden * * *.

The rationale behind giving the entire judiciary the duty of constitutional control is, on face of it, both logical and simple, as is apparent from Chief Justice Marshall's opinion in Marbury v. Madison and earlier from the writings of Alexander Hamilton. It is the function of the judiciary * * * to interpret the laws in order to apply them in concrete cases. When two such laws are in conflict, it is the judge who must determine which law prevails and then apply it. When the conflict is between enactments of different normative force, the obvious criterion to be applied is that the higher law prevails. A constitutional norm, if the constitution is rigid, prevails over an ordinary legislative norm in conflict with it ... Hence, one must conclude that any judge, having to decide a case where an applicable legislative norm conflicts with the constitution, must disregard the former and apply the latter.

B. Centralized Judicial Review

* * *

Three principal reasons account for adoption of a centralized system of judicial review in a growing number of civil law countries. These are: first, the Continental conception of the separation of powers; second, the absence of a principle comparable to *stare decisis* in civil law jurisprudence; and third, the unsuitability of the civil law judiciary.

1. The Theory of Separation of Powers

* * * The civil law countries tend to adhere more rigidly to the doctrines of the separation of powers and the supremacy of statutory law. * * * Even today, although the advisability of some sort of control over the constitutionality of legislation is admitted, the essentially political aspects of this function are recognized. The centralized systems therefore refuse to grant this power to the judiciary generally. The ordinary judge must accept and apply the law as he finds it. Several scholars have noted a genuine presumption of legislative validity in these countries. The only attenuation of these notions lies in the power of

ordinary judges to suspend litigation pending reference to the Constitutional Court of a constitutional issue which has been raised below. * * *

2.   *The Absence of Stare Decisis*

* * *

Since the principle of *stare decisis* is foreign to civil law judges, a system that allowed each judge to decide for himself the constitutionality of statutes could result in a law being disregarded as unconstitutional by some judges, while being held constitutional and therefore applied to others. Furthermore, the same court that had one day disregarded a given law might uphold it the next day, having changed its mind about the law's constitutionality. * * *

* * *

* * * [I]n establishing a system of judicial review, the countries to whom the notion of *stare decisis* was foreign had to work with legal instruments very different from those of the United States ... In the former countries it was thought essential to find an adequate substitute for the US Supreme Court. The need was felt for a judicial body capable of giving decisions of general binding effect in cases dealing with the constitutionality of legislation. It was hoped that such special bodies could avoid the conflicts and chaotic uncertainties mentioned above.

3.   *The Unsuitability of the Ordinary Courts.*

* * *

At this point one might enquire why those countries which decided to have a centralized system of judicial review wanted to create special constitutional courts, and did not grant jurisdiction over constitutional matters to the already existing highest court of appeal * * *.

* * * [D]espite their theoretical suitability, the traditional highest courts of most civil law countries were found to lack the structure, procedures, and mentality required for effective constitutional adjudication. First, the European high courts lack the compact, manageable structure of the US Supreme Court. Typical is Germany where there are no less than five high courts * * *. Even within a given high court there are several different divisions, each of which sits and decides cases independently of the other divisions. It is difficult to imagine how, amidst such a welter of judges and jurisdictions, a consistent and carefully considered constitutional jurisprudence could ever be developed.

Procedurally, these courts of last instance are also handicapped by their frequent lack of any discretionary power to refuse jurisdiction, of a device similar to the *certiorari* of the US Supreme Court. To illustrate: the Italian Court of Cassation must hear every case brought before it ... Thus, if the Court of Cassation were to have jurisdiction over constitutional cases as well * * * [t]hese cases would receive neither the time nor the consideration that they require. The situation is very similar for the superior courts of other civil law countries * * *.

Lastly, the bulk of Europe's judiciary seems psychologically incapable of value-oriented, quasi-political functions involved in judicial review. Continental judges are usually 'career judges' who enter the judiciary at a very early age and are promoted to the higher courts largely on the basis of seniority. Their professional training develops skills in technical application of statutes rather than in making policy judgments. The exercise of judicial review, however, is quite different from the usual judicial function of applying the law. * * * [T]he task of fulfilling a constitution often demands a higher sense of discretion than the task of interpreting ordinary statutes. * * *

These, then, seem to be the most important reasons why, when adopting judicial review, several civil law countries chose not to use existing judicial organs and the members of the professional judiciary. Rather, they preferred to introduce entirely new and special judicial bodies, despite the serious problems of co-ordination arising from this choice. These special courts, as all other judicial organs, have full independence and autonomy. However, their members—or at least the majority of them—are not career judges, but * * * are selected from diverse backgrounds and appointed by the highest legislative or executive organs of the state.

Constitution of the Republic of France (1958).*

Title V–Relations between Parliament and Government

Article 34 [Legislative Powers]

(1) All legislation shall be passed by Parliament.

(2) Legislation shall establish the rules concerning:

— civil rights and the fundamental guarantees granted to the citizens for the exercise of their public liberties; the national defence obligations imposed on citizens in respect of their persons or property;

— nationality, status, and capacity of persons, property rights arising out of a matrimonial relationship, inheritance, and gifts;

— determination of felonies and misdemeanors, together with the penalties applicable to them; criminal procedure; amnesty; the creation of new jurisdictions and the status of judges;

— the assessment bases, rates, and methods of collecting taxes of all types; the issuance of currency.

* Translation from http://www.verfass ungsvergleich.de (site last visited June 9, 2007).

(3) Legislation shall likewise determine the regulations concerning:

— the electoral systems of the parliamentary Assemblies and local Assemblies;

— the creation of categories of public establishments;

— the fundamental guarantees granted to civil and military personnel employed by the State;

— company nationalizations and transfers of company ownership from the public to the private sector.

(4) Legislation shall determine the fundamental principles of:

— the general organization of national defence;

— free local government and the powers and resources of local authorities;

— education;

— the rules governing property rights, chattels real, civil and commercial obligations;

— labor and trade-union law and social security.

(5) Finance acts shall determine the financial resources and obligations of the State, subject to the conditions and reservations laid down in an organic act.

(6) Program acts shall specify the objectives of State economic and social policy.

(7) The provisions of this article may be developed in detail and amplified by an organic act.

* * *

Article 37 [Regulations]

(1) Matters other than those that fall within the sphere of legislation shall be determined by regulation.

(2) Legislation concerning these matters may be amended by orders issued after consultation with the Conseil d'Etat. Any such legislative texts introduced after this Constitution has entered into force shall be amended by order only if the Constitutional Council has pronounced that the matters they deal with fall within the field subject to regulation as defined in the preceding paragraph.

* * *

TITLE VII—THE CONSTITUTIONAL COUNCIL

Article 56 [Membership]

(1) The Constitutional Council shall consist of nine members, whose term of office shall last nine years and shall not be renewable. One third of the membership of the Constitutional Council shall be renewed every three years. Three of its members shall be appointed by the President of

the Republic, three by the President of the National Assembly, three by the President of the Senate.

(2) In addition to the nine members provided for above, former Presidents of the Republic shall be *ex officio* life members of the Constitutional Council.

(3) The President shall be appointed by the President of the Republic. He shall have the casting vote in the event of a tie.

Article 57 [Incompatibility]

The office of member of the Constitutional Council shall be incompatible with that of minister or member of Parliament. Other incompatibilities shall be determined by an organic act.

Article 58 [Control of Presidential Elections]

(1) The Constitutional Council shall ensure the regularity of the election of the President of the Republic.

(2) It shall examine complaints and proclaim the results of the vote.

Article 59 [Control of Assembly Elections]

The Constitutional Council shall rule, in the case of a dispute, on the regularity of elections of deputies and senators.

Article 60 [Control of Referendums]

The Constitutional Council shall ensure the regularity of referendums and proclaim the results thereof.

Article 61 [Control of Parliamentary Acts]

(1) Organic acts, before their promulgation, and standing orders of the parliamentary Assemblies, before their implementation, must be submitted to the Constitutional Council which shall rule on their constitutionality.

(2) To the same end, acts of Parliament may, before their promulgation, be submitted to the Constitutional Council by the President of the Republic, the Prime Minister, the President of the National Assembly, the President of the Senate, sixty deputies or sixty senators.

(3) In the cases provided for by the two preceding paragraphs, the Constitutional Council must rule within one month. However, at the Government's request, this period shall be reduced to eight days if a matter is urgent.

(4) In these same cases, referral to the Constitutional Council shall suspend the time limit for promulgation.

Article 62 [Voidability by Control]

(1) A provision declared unconstitutional may not be promulgated or implemented.

(2) The decisions of the Constitutional Council shall not be subject to appeal to any jurisdiction. They shall be binding on the governmental authorities and on all administrative and jurisdictional authorities.

Article 63 [Rules of Procedure]

An organic act shall determine the organizational and operational rules of the Constitutional Council, the procedure to be followed before it, and in particular the periods of time allowed for referring disputes to it.

Mauro Cappelletti, The Judicial Process in Comparative Perspective 153–161 (1989).

I. THE CASE OF FRANCE

In *ancien régime* France the *Parlements*, i.e. the high courts, affirmed their power to control the conformity of legislation to the unwritten *lois fondamentales* of the kingdom. The judges of these courts * * *, however, were so deeply imbued with anti-egalitarian values and so firmly rooted in the feudal structures of pre-revolutionary France that their review power was exercised in an extremely abusive and unpopular manner * * *

* * * post-Revolutionary France has consistently shown a rigid anti-judicial-review approach. This attitude had found its conceptualization in Montesquieu's description of the judges as 'inanimate beings' whose only task should be to apply blindly, automatically, and uncreatively the supreme will of the popular legislature * * * This concept—the French version of 'separation of powers * * * has since represented a basic tenet of political and constitutional philosophy in France, and through French influence, in the rest of continental Europe well into this century * * *

Three episodes * * * are enlightening because they demonstrate the tremendous appeal of judicial review in our time. Indeed, struggling against a powerful tradition, against deeply felt biases, and against structures, processes, and principles which are all adverse to *gouvernement des juges* (as judicial review is still disparagingly labelled by the French), France, too, is adopting a system of judicial review, albeit in a piecemeal and often contradictory manner.

A. Conseil d'Etat

The first episode is represented by a landmark 1959 decision of the *Conseil d'Etat* * * * De Gaulle's Constitution had just been adopted. One of its basic features * * * is to limit the law-making power of Parliament * * * Article 34 of the Constitution of the Fifth Republic limits this jurisdiction by establishing a list of subject-matters belonging to it. All other matters belong to the *pouvoir réglementaire*, i.e. to the autonomous law-making power of the executive (article 37) * * *. By any substantive standards, decrees are not administrative but legislative acts. Therefore, the deeply rooted French repulsion against judicial review of legislation and *gouvernement des juges* should apply to them. This was, in fact, the prevailing theory before the 1959 decision in *Syndicat Général des Ingénieurs-Conseils*, in which the *Conseil d'Etat* established that executive legislation *is* subject to judicial review * * * [and] ascribed itself the power to check the conformity of executive legislation to an undefined, or at most vaguely defined, 'higher law'—the *principes généraux* contained in, or derived from, the *Déclaration des droits de l'homme* of 1789, the Preambles (i.e. the Bills of Rights) of the 1946 and the 1958 Constitutions, and the 'Republican tradition' * * *

B.   Conseil Constitutionnel

* * * The Conseil was seen not as a constitutional court whose task it should be to enforce the preeminence of the constitution vis-à-vis ordinary (parliamentary) legislation, but rather as a mere watch-dog of the newly established law-making prerogatives of the executive branch against potential invasions by Parliament * * *. In a remarkable decision dealing with freedom of association, in 1971 the Conseil Constitutionnel for the first time ceased to be a mere watch-dog of the prerogatives of the executive; rather, it claimed for itself the power and the duty to check the conformity of non-promulgated *lois* not only to articles 34 and 37, but also to the Constitution generally, including those 'general principles' which have constitutional stature and which can be derived from the Magnae Chartae of French constitutional history and the 'Republican tradition'.

C.   Cour de cassation

* * *

* * * In 1975, the supreme ordinary court of France, the Cour de cassation, sat in a most solemn and large composition, the Chambre Mixte, to decide in the case of *Administration des Douanes v. Société Cafés Jacques Vabre* a novel crucial question: whether a regularly promulgated French *loi*, subsequent to, but conflicting with, the law of the European Economic Community, should be refused application by the French judges.

Article 55 of the French Constitution establishes that 'the treaties or [international] accords regularly ratified or approved have, from their publication, an authority superior to that of the laws, upon reservation, for each accord or treaty, of its application by the other party' * * * The Court * * * decided * * * that the judges … are indeed bound not to give application to French legislation if it is in conflict with international treaty law in general, and with community law in particular * * * however, the Cour took care to proclaim that this is not a form of judicial review of the constitutionality of legislation; it is *mere interpretation—* the judges' typical function. It is * * * the natural role of the judge to apply a law having a 'higher authority', rather than a conflicting lower

law, and Community law—or, more generally, international treaty law—
is higher law, *without* being constitutional law.

* * *

The implications of the 1975 decision * * * are extremely far-
reaching. * * * [T]he broad concept of international treaty law must
include the European Convention on Human Rights * * * Thus, a
consistent interpretation of the *Cafés Jacques Vabre* decision leads to a
conclusion which is no less important for being paradoxical. Based on the
traditional prohibition of judicial review of the constitutionality of (parliamentary) legislation, French *lois*, once promulgated, are not subject to
court control; * * * [s]ince *Cafés Jacques Vabre*, however, this basic
prohibition can no longer bind the judges of France wherever French
legislation is in conflict not with the *French* texts and traditions, but
with a *transnational* bill of rights, the European Convention on Human
Rights * * * Judicial review of parliamentary legislation, banished from
the main door of the *national* Constitution, has in fact entered through
the large window of a *transnational* bill of rights. * * *

V. SUPRA–NATIONAL COURTS

A. Introductory Note

There are several "supra-national" courts in the world today. Most
of them deal with disputes between the sovereign states, i.e., the parties
before those courts are the states and not individual litigants interested
in the matter. The International Court of Justice in The Hague and the
WTO Panel and Appellate Body in Geneva belong to that category. On
the other hand, when several sovereign states unite by treaty and create
law to which each member state will be subject, a supra-national court
becomes desirable to enforce the higher norms. The European Court of
Justice and the European Court of Human Rights are examples. A
description of the court structure in Europe would therefore not be
complete without at least a brief look at the courts at those courts. The
former, which was established under the Treaty of Rome of 1957, may be
considered the judicial arm of the European Union (which now includes
27 member States). The latter was established in 1959 in order to
enforce the European Convention of Human Rights and Fundamental
Freedoms, signed in Rome in 1950, and subsequently ratified by 46
States, all of which are members of the Council of Europe.

B. The European Court of Justice

Laws of the European Union are enacted by the European Parliament and the Council of the European Union upon proposals by the
European Commission, which is the executive branch. These laws must
be observed by the member states as their own law. Therefore, these
European laws must be applied by the national courts of each member
state in civil, administrative or criminal cases. When any uncertain issue
of European law arises in the course of litigation in a national court, it

can be referred by the local court to the European Court of Justice (ECJ). This is called a reference for a preliminary ruling, and is regulated by art. 234 of the Treaty on the European Union. A decision of the European Court of Justice then binds not only the particular national court but also other national courts within the EU before which the same problem is raised. There are a considerable number of such references each year not only from the national highest courts but also from national lower courts.

The ECJ sits in Luxemburg and now consists of 27 Judges, one from each member state, and 8 Advocates General. Advocates General are a peculiarly European institution. They attend the arguments, read the briefs and provide the Court with an independent opinion about the issue, which the Court is free to adopt or ignore. The Court may sit as a full court of 13 judges or in Chambers of 3 or 5 judges depending on the nature of cases.

The procedure for handling references for preliminary rulings from a national court is as follows: The national court submits questions to the ECJ about the interpretation or validity of a provision of Community law, generally in the form of a judicial decision in accordance with national procedural rules. When that request has been translated into all of the 23 Community languages by the Court's translation service, the Registry (the secretariat of the Court) notifies the parties to the national proceedings and all the Member States. A notice is published in the Official Journal of the European Union stating, *inter alia*, the names of the parties to the proceedings and the content of the questions. The parties, the Member States and the institutions of the European Union have two months within which to submit written observations to the Court of Justice. As in many Civil Law national systems, a Judge–Rapporteur is appointed by the President and an Advocate General in charge is assigned to the case by the First Advocate General for monitoring the progress of the case. The Judge–Rapporteur summarises the facts alleged and the arguments of the parties. That report is made public. Then, the case is argued at a public hearing, before the bench and the Advocate General. The judges and the Advocate General may put to the parties any questions. Some weeks later, the Advocate General delivers his opinion before the Court of Justice again in open court, analysing the legal aspects of the case and suggesting the response which he or she considers should be given to the problem raised. The judges deliberate on the basis of a draft judgment drawn up by the Judge–Rapporteur. Decisions of the Court of Justice are taken by majority and no record is made public of any dissenting opinions.

The ECJ has a lower court called The Court of First Instance. Its jurisdiction, however, does not extend to entertaining references from national court of the member states. Its jurisdiction is limited to actions brought by natural or legal persons against acts of Community institutions, or actions brought by the member states against the Commission of the European Union. Its decisions can be appealed to the European Court of Justice.

For more information about the European Court of Justice, see the Court web site: http://curia.europa.eu. See also Michael Dougan, National Remedies Before the Court of Justice (2004).

C. The European Court of Human Rights

Peter L. Murray & Rolf Stürner, German Civil Justice, 65–68 (2004).

The European Court of Human Rights * * * exercises a kind of supranational quasi-appellate jurisdiction over matters involving human rights guaranteed by the European Convention on Human Rights * * *. Signatories to this convention are not only the Member States of the European Union, but nearly all European countries including Russia and Turkey. A party asserting violation of a basic human right guaranteed by the Convention * * * must first exhaust all available administrative or judicial appeals in the signatory state, including in the case of Germany, resort to the Federal Constitutional Court. Human rights litigants remaining unsatisfied can apply to the European Court of Human Rights in Strasbourg. A decision by the European Court of Human Rights is binding on German parties, the German government and the German courts. The European Court of Human Rights may render a declaratory judgment which will then be implemented by national judicial relief or it may grant monetary compensation.

Note

Clearly, the remarks by Murray and Stürner on the European Court of Human Rights (CHR), though made from the German perspective, are substantially applicable to the other Member States of the European Union or to the other signatories of the European Convention on Human Rights respectively.

The following description of the organization of the ECHR is found on the Court website, www.echr.coe.int/ECHR, which may be consulted for further detail.

Organization of the European Court of Human Rights

1. The Court, as presently constituted, was brought into being by Protocol No. 11 on 1 November 1998. This amendment made the Convention process wholly judicial, as the Commission's function of screening applications was entrusted to the Court itself, whose jurisdiction became mandatory.

2. The provisions governing the structure and procedure of the Court are to be found in Section II of the Convention (Articles 19–51). The Court is composed of a number of judges equal to that of the Contracting States (currently forty-six). Judges are elected by the Parliamentary Assembly of the Council of Europe, which votes on a shortlist of three candidates put forward by Governments. The term of office is six years, and judges may be

re-elected. Their terms of office expire when they reach the age of seventy, although they continue to deal with cases already under their consideration.

Judges sit on the Court in their individual capacity and do not represent any State. They cannot engage in any activity which is incompatible with their independence or impartiality or with the demands of full-time office.

3.   The Plenary Court has a number of functions that are stipulated in the Convention. It elects the office holders of the Court, i.e. the President, the two Vice–Presidents (who also preside over a Section) and the three other Section Presidents. In each case, the term of office is three years. The Plenary Court also elects the Registrar and Deputy Registrar. The Rules of Court are adopted and amended by the Plenary Court. It also determines the composition of the Sections.

4.   Under the Rules of Court, every judge is assigned to one of the five Sections, whose composition is geographically and gender balanced and takes account of the different legal systems of the Contracting States. The composition of the Sections is varied every three years.

5.   The great majority of the judgments of the Court are given by Chambers. These comprise seven judges and are constituted within each Section. The Section President and the judge elected in respect of the State concerned sit in each case. Where the latter is not a member of the Section, he or she sits as an ex officio member of the Chamber. If the respondent State in a case is that of the Section President, the Vice–President of the Section will preside. In every case that is decided by a Chamber, the remaining members of the Section who are not full members of that Chamber sit as substitute members.

6.   Committees of three judges are set up within each Section for twelve-month periods. Their function is to dispose of applications that are clearly inadmissible.

7.   The Grand Chamber of the Court is composed of seventeen judges, who include, as ex officio members, the President, Vice–Presidents and Section Presidents. The Grand Chamber deals with cases that raise a serious question of interpretation or application of the Convention, or a serious issue of general importance. A Chamber may relinquish jurisdiction in a case to the Grand Chamber at any stage in the procedure before judgment, as long as both parties consent. Where judgment has been delivered in a case, either party may, within a period of three months, request referral of the case to the Grand Chamber. Where a request is granted, the whole case is reheard.

VI.   STARE DECISIS: A COMPARATIVE PERSPECTIVE

Konrad Zweigert and Hein Kötz, Introduction to Comparative Law 259–265 (3d ed. 1998).

II

According to a view expressed in England in 1934 by GOODHART, the critical difference between Continental and English methods of legal thinking lies in the doctrine of the *binding force of precedent (stare decisis)* * * *. At first sight this view seems plausible even today. The doctrine lays down that every English court is bound by all decisions handed down by courts superior to it in the hierarchy; and, until quite recently, the doctrine laid down that the superior courts, namely the Court of Appeal and the House of Lords, were bound to treat their *own* previous decisions as absolutely binding. A previous decision is 'binding' in the sense that it must be followed whether it forms part of a series of similar decisions or whether it stands quite alone, whether it was handed down the previous year or a century ago, and even if the rule it lays down now seems inappropriate because of altered social circumstances or for some other reason. It had always been recognized in England that courts which were faced with the task of discovering the law should take note of previous decisions and follow them whenever this seemed proper on the facts of the case.

* * *

But it was only in the late nineteenth century that the doctrine took the rigorous form we have sketched above—decisions binding even if the result seems repellent to the judge, superior courts bound by their own decisions; it was a product not of legislation but of judicial decision; the courts forged their own fetters.

Of course English judges have devised various ways and means which enable them to 'distinguish a precedent', that is, to avoid following a previous decision which is unsatisfactory. A previous decision is binding only where the basic reason underlying the decision, the so-called 'ratio decidendi', covers the instant dispute. But in many cases it is extremely doubtful what the 'ratio decidendi' of the previous decision is, and what is merely 'obiter dictum'. Take the case where a mother suffers a nervous shock as a result of witnessing a traffic accident in which her child is killed, and a court grants her claim for damages against the careless driver. The *ratio decidendi* of this decision will certainly cover a subsequent case in which, all the other facts being the same, a *father* witnesses the death of his child, but it is not clear that the *ratio decidendi* of the first decision would require the driver to be held liable in a later case where the child was only injured or merely endangered instead of being killed, or where the plaintiff was not a relative of the child. Before the judge can resolve these questions he must scrutinize the precedent keenly, he must examine the arguments presented by the advocates before him, but above all he must carefully sift any related decisions handed down before or after the precedent in question: this intellectual process follows certain rules of the judicial art but it is open at every step to the influence of conscious or unconscious *value-judgments*.

* * *

The attitude of *American* courts in this matter is more flexible still. Legal publishers in the United States issue hundreds of volumes of judicial decisions every year without making any critical selection of them and the mass of material is so enormous that it is virtually impossible to expect that *all* relevant precedents be taken into account. But more than this, the political, social, and economic development of the United States has been so dramatic and the consequent alterations in the substance of the legal order so swift that the superior courts could never have adopted the view that they were absolutely bound by their *own* previous decisions. It was clear that the *Supreme Court,* dealing with constitutional matters, had to be free to depart from a previous decision ('to overrule a precedent') since otherwise the only way to overcome its obsolete decisions would have been by amending the *text* of the Constitution, an extremely complex and slow procedure requiring the ratification of three-quarters of the component states. But in the *states* as well the highest courts have shown an increasing readiness in the last few decades to ask whether the rules laid down in the case-law, even those which have repeatedly been confirmed in a series of decisions, are still in touch with the needs and interests of the times.

Even in England it seems that the doctrine of binding precedent is not accepted as wholeheartedly as it was some years ago. Indeed, the most objectionable part of the doctrine, the rule that the House of Lords was strictly bound by its own previous decisions, was abandoned in 1966. This did not, as one might have expected, occur by Act of Parliament or in the course of a judicial decision; instead the Lord Chancellor simply made a declaration ('Practice Statement') in open court in the name of all the Law Lords.

* * *

A quick look round the Continent shows that matters are not really very different there. It is true that there is never any legal rule which compels a judge to follow the decisions of a higher Court, but the reality is different. In practice a judgment of the Court of Cassation or of the Bundesgerichtshof in Germany today can count on being followed by lower courts just as much as a judgment of an appeal Court in England or in the United States. This is true not only when the judgment of the superior court follows a line of similar decisions; in practice even an isolated decision of the Bundesgerichtshof in Germany enjoys the greatest respect, and it is very rare and not at all typical for a judge openly to deviate from such a decision. In France the situation is much the same:

* * *

Accordingly it is hardly an exaggeration to say that the doctrine of *stare decisis* in the Common Law and the practice of Continental courts generally lead to the same results: 'The practical differences ... are microscopic' * * * In fact, when a judge can find in one or more decisions of a supreme court a rule which seems to him relevant for the decision in the case before him, he will follow those decisions and the rules they contain as much in Germany as in England or France. Of course in order to be able to *follow* a rule, the judge must first have extracted it from the case-law; and in the *method of extracting such rules* there are still very considerable differences between the Common Law and the Civil Law.

The common law judge's technique of approaching the case-law and extracting its rules and principles is the product of a mature and workmanlike tradition of 'reasoning from case to case'.

* * *

This inductive way of thinking, based on the particular factual problem of the case, and the intensive treatment of precedents associated with it are not to be found in Continental law, at any rate not to anything like the same extent. This is because Continental judges, in Italy and France rather more than in Germany, are still imbued with the old positivistic idea that deciding a case involves nothing more than 'applying' a particular given rule of law to the facts in issue by means of an act of categorization; indeed, they often entertain the further supposition that ideally the rules of law to be 'applied' are *statutory* texts. But in fact everyone knows that in really difficult cases the statutory text, if there is one, is too vague to provide a solution, and that the case can only be solved by engaging with the rules, principles, and maxims developed by judges in previous decisions. Nevertheless the traditional tropes are still trotted out, as can be seen in the style of judgments in France and Italy, and also in those of the supreme courts in Germany.

A striking piece of evidence for this is the grudging manner in which the facts of a case are treated in Continental judgments. We have already mentioned that the French Court of Cassation often does no more than make cryptic allusions to them .... The Courts in Germany are required by § 3I3 par. 2 ZPO to give 'only a brief statement of the essential' facts and claims based on them. Even so, when the judgment is printed in periodicals or law reports there is a characteristic tendency to curtail or even to omit it—a proceeding which the Common lawyer would find unthinkable. Again, the French Court of Cassation does not even quote its *own* previous decisions, much less say why it follows one decision rather than another. Of course the judges of the Court of Cassation do in fact go through the case-law with great care, but they like to give outsiders the impression that the judgment springs from the text of the statute at a wave of the magic wand of subsumption * * *. Above all, judgments of supreme courts on the Continent still sometimes reflect the traditions of the authoritarian state of a hundred years ago: judgments should primarily be impersonal acts of state which parade the majesty of the law in front of citizens in awe of authority; therefore they must not let it emerge that judges reach their decisions through a hesitant and doubtful balancing of the pros and cons of concrete solutions of the problem thrown up by the 'case', rather than by sheer intellect and cold logic.

Another indication of how underdeveloped the art of 'reasoning from case to case' remains is the uncritical use made of the 'headnotes' (Leitsätze) which precede published judgments all over the Continent.

These headnotes present a very brief and abstract version of the essential legal proposition basic to the court decision but they omit the underlying facts or only hint at them and never give the reasoning on which the decision was founded. Common Law countries also have these 'headnotes' but they serve the judge only as a preliminary indication of the probable content of the decision which follows and never as a substitute for its investigation in detail. On the Continent, on the other hand, these headnotes, pried loose from their roots in the facts, are often treated as independent polished formulas and used in legal practice much as if they were statutory rules. In Italy, indeed, this occurrence is facilitated by the fact that most decisions of the Court of Cassation are published only in the form of headnotes *(massime);* it thus becomes practically impossible to go back to the facts of the case and discover the real scope of the headnote. In reality the principles contained in these headnotes should be treated only as working hypotheses which must be subjected to critical scrutiny in the light of later cases and the altering needs of life, for they may have to be extended or limited or refined; courts on the Continent no doubt often do this subconsciously, but they far too rarely let outsiders know, and thus be in a position to check, that they are doing so.

* * *

Mauro Cappelletti, The Doctrine of Stare Decisis and the Civil Law: A Fundamental Difference—Or No Difference at All? in Festschrift für Konrad Zweigert zum 70. Geburtstag 381–393 (Herbert Bernstein, Ulrich Drobnig and Hein Kötz, eds., 1981).

* * *

A powerful "convergence of trends" between the Civil Law and the Common Law is * * * apparent, and I have myself analyzed several of its aspects on various occasions. It seems to me however that in making the arguments which led them to the above * * * general conclusion, Professors *Zweigert* and *Kötz* have excessively de-emphasized one difference between the two major legal families which, in my opinion, remains of substantial importance. Speaking of the * * * doctrine of stare decisis *Zweigert* and *Kötz* not only deny the validity today of Professor *Goodhart's* opinion, expressed in 1934, that such doctrine represents "the fundamental distinction between the English and the Continental legal method" * * * but they go further and deny the difference altogether or at least deny that it has any practical importance * * *

To support this position, Professors *Zweigert* and *Kötz* cite, on the one hand, a number of developments in England and the United States which have surely attenuated the rigidity of the *stare decisis* doctrine, including the famous 1966 Practice Statement which affirmed the House of Lords' power to overrule itself. On the other hand, they assert that, in practice, the precedential impact of a decision made by, say, the French *Cour de Cassation* or the German *Bundesgerichtshof* is now comparable to that of a decision made by a court of last resort in the Common Law countries. * * *

As much as I believe in the convergence of trends mentioned above, I am nevertheless convinced that in the statement just quoted there is some exaggeration which I hope to clarify.

* * *

I will make three orders of comments: the first is based on the organization of the higher courts in Continental Europe and in Common Law countries; the second, on a historically rooted bias of the Continental European traditions against judicial discretion; and the third, on some sociological considerations concerning the judiciaries in the two legal families.

(i) It is well-known that the structure of the higher courts system is profoundly different in Continental Europe from that prevailing in England, the United States, an other Common Law countries. The former system lacks the compact, manageable, unitary structure which is typical of the latter. In France and Italy, for instance, there are at least two separate highest courts, one for ordinary civil and criminal questions and one for administrative problems, whereas in Germany there are as many as five such courts, one each for ordinary civil and criminal, administrative, tax, labor, and social matters. Even within a given higher court, we usually find a number of different divisions (*Senate, Chamber, Sezioni*); and each division sits and decides cases independently, to a large extent, of the other divisions. Furthermore, usually many more judges belong to a division than are necessary to decide a case; hence the individual judges called to take part in decisions by a division may vary from case to case.

It is easy to understand that this diffuse organization of the higher courts system in Civil Law Europe brings about an inevitable consequence—a more diffuse authority of both organs themselves and their decisions. In particular, the authority of such decisions is much more diluted than that of decisions made by a compact court composed of a few judges and placed at the apex of a unitary judicial system, such as, for instance, the American Supreme Court or the House of Lords.

(ii) This factor is further aggravated in Civil Law countries by a procedural rule which is rooted in a centuries-old history of distrust in governmental—and, more specifically, in judicial—discretion. A device similar to the writ of *certiorari*, which would give a higher court the discretionary power to decide only some of the cases brought to it, is clearly inconsistent with that tradition.

* * *

The result is that, in principle, the higher courts of Continental Europe must hear every case brought before them. The decisions thus given every year by the *Cour de Cassation*, the *Bundesgerichtshof*, or the *Corte di cassazione*, run into the thousands. In his recent exemplary study on the supreme courts in a number of countries, Professor *André Tunc* pointedly describes this characteristic as representing the "*summa divisio*", the most fundamental difference, between the type of higher courts which we can find in Common Law countries and that prevailing in Continental Europe.

* * *

What is involved here is not only a problem of time pressures and constraints upon careful examination of the questions to be decided. Also a psychological problem is involved, for the selection of the cases to be decided helps the court to gain a fuller awareness of its own mission.

* * *

(iii) The precedential authority of higher court decisions in the Continental systems is further reduced by the type of personnel which prevails in those courts.

Typically the professional training of career judges, who are promoted to a higher courts largely on the basis of seniority, develops skills in technical rather that in policy-oriented decision-making. The *jurisprudence* of such judges, as of all judges, may well be nevertheless inevitably creative; yet its creativity is hidden and, as it were, attenuated. "Le juge français"—Professor *René David* says—"n'aime pas se mettre en évidence en créant des règles de droit." Indeed, career judges tend toward anonymity. Like their authors, decisions given by such judges rarely emerge in bold relief; they are, more often than not, standard and almost mechanical "applications" of the law.

* * *

To sum up, it seems certain to me that, contrary to the statement quoted above, it is, if not wrong, at least greatly exaggerated to deny that there is any visible difference between the impact—and, of course, what is meant is essentially a *law-making, i.e., a binding* impact—of higher court decisions in the Common Law and in the Civil Law systems.

* * *

[W]hen Professors *Zweigert* and *Kötz* affirm that, "in reality", the impact of higher court decisions is equal in the two families, they appear to be themselves, for once, the victims of that centuries-old prejudice. That impact cannot be measured merely in terms of "rules".

* * *

I am sure that the authors * * * are ready to agree with me that a better manner of measuring that impact would be one which considers institutions and personnel, cultures and attitudes as well as rules, for the authority of the rules themselves is conditioned and qualified by those real-world elements. I therefore suggest that the difference between Common Law and Civil Law is not merely one concerning "die Methode der Ermittlung solcher Regeln", but is also, and primarily, a difference concerning the quality and degree of the *authority*, of the *creativity*, indeed of the *binding* and/or *law-making character* of the "Regeln" themselves.

* * *

4. A practical example will demonstrate that the difference of opinions expressed above is not one of nuance or appearance alone.

* * *

It is well known that in our century, and especially after World War II, a number of Civil Law countries have adopted a system of judicial review of the constitutionality of legislation. This is, of course, an old institution in the United States, where the accepted principle since, at least, 1803 has been that all the courts—higher and lower—have the power, and indeed the duty, not to apply a law which appears to them to be in conflict with the Constitution.

* * *

In Civil Law countries, on the contrary, the opposite "centralized" system prevails. I have called such a system "centralized" because, in principle, the power is entrusted to a special, newly created constitutional court.

* * *

As far as I can see, the reasons for the need felt by Civil Law countries to follow the more difficult road—to build up a third (or indeed, as in Germany, a sixth) branch within the judicial system—are essentially those I discussed in previous Sections of this Article. To make a long story short, I would limit myself to saying that it was clearly felt that the structure and organization of the traditional courts—and ultimately, of the traditional higher courts-, the characteristics of a career judiciary, and the traditional biases against judicial discretion and creativity, all these elements militated against the possibility of entrusting the new and challenging task to the existing courts. Constitutional decision-making demands that kind of careful consideration which it is unrealistic to expect from courts which are submerged under thousands of cases they are obliged to decide; it requires a high degree of creativity and of policy-oriented balancing of interests and values, which bureaucratic, routine-oriented judges can hardly provide. Finally, constitutional decisions need that kind of final, or virtually final, authority—I would dare say *stare decisis*-like authority, or, if one prefers, law-making authority—which for the reasons discussed above is largely missing or much too diluted in the decisions of the traditional courts, even supreme courts, in the Civil Law world.

* * *

I hope the above pages * * * are not misleading. They are not intended to bring comparative analysis several decades back—to the time when comparative law scholarship became ecstatic in discovering the Common Law doctrine of *stare decisis* and tried to use it as a *passepartout* to understand the "fundamental" differences between Civil Law and Common Law. I am myself convinced that there is no sharp cleavage between the two major legal traditions, not even as to the topic discussed in this article. I do after all agree with Professors *Zweigert* and *Kötz*—as well as with Professor *David* and others—at least to the extent that I too recognize that a decision by the *Cour de Cassation*, the *Bundesgerichtshof*, or any other supreme court of Continental European nations, is a relevant precedent, which is rather likely to be followed by lower court.

* * *

Perhaps the real difference of my approach consists in the fact that it is * * * less "juristic". I think that a more complete understanding can be gained by introducing in our analysis all the elements of the problem: institutions and their organizations, biases and traditions, sociological backgrounds and attitudes of those who run the "machinery". From this more complex point of view, I have drawn a conclusion which is probably midway between *Goodhart*'s and *Zweigert*'s. *Stare decisis* is still an important difference, even though, admittedly, a diminishing one.

Chapter 4

INITIATING A LAW SUIT, DEFINING THE ISSUES, GATHERING THE EVIDENCE

I. INTRODUCTION

In this Chapter we consider the introductory stages of a civil action, focusing on procedures in England, Germany, Japan, and the United States, though some reference will also be made to French and Italian law. The procedures examined here serve the general purpose of informing the parties and the court of the nature of the claims and defenses and the factual contentions that underlie them. They range along a continuum that begins with the basic acts of formally commencing the action and notifying the defendant that the law suit has been brought and continues through the various devices by which the contentions and facts are revealed. To put it so baldly should not obscure the reality that the sometimes conflicting litigation strategies of the adversaries lead to conflicts over what must be revealed, and when. As you learn about the varieties of approaches in the systems scrutinized, think about how they serve the general procedural goals of fairness, accuracy, efficiency, and legitimacy.

II. INITIATING PROCEEDINGS

The bringing of legal proceedings normally involves two steps: (1) the formal initiation of the lawsuit, the claim, in an appropriate court, and (2) its service upon the defendant. We may refer to these as the process of commencement, or initiation, and the process of notification. These processes serve distinct functions. A process of commencement marks the formal start of the legal process, the precise time of which is important for a number of purposes. Most importantly, the precise time of initiation is crucial in determining whether the claim has met any relevant limitation period, beyond which the claim becomes time-barred. Furthermore, commencement of proceedings brings into play a variety of process rules, such as the requirement that the claimant should serve or notify the claim to the defendant within a specified period of time.

The process of commencement must satisfy two basic practical requirements. It must not depend upon the co-operation of the defendant, for otherwise the defendant would be able to prevent the claimant from initiating proceedings. Furthermore, the time of commencement must be capable of precise ascertainment, so as to enable determination of whether a claim has been brought within the limitation period. It follows that the commencement process must be capable of being carried out unilaterally, simply and quickly.

By contrast, notification requires communication to another party. Unlike commencement, it is not just a matter of formality. It is a fundamental requirement of justice that proceedings should be brought to the notice of the affected parties. Accordingly, while the act of formal initiation of a claim marks the formal commencement of proceedings, the litigation process becomes fully engaged only when the claim form has been served on the defendant. Service is the means by which court documents are brought to the attention of parties to legal proceedings. Service, especially of the formal document that initiates a claim, is no mere formality. The right to fair trial or due process, whether at common law or under the ECHR, whether under German constitutional law (in particular the right to be heard according to Art. 103 sub. 1 Basic Law (Grundgesetz)) or the 14th Amendment of the USA constitution, demands that every litigant should have timely notice of any proceedings affecting his interests and a reasonable opportunity to respond. Defendants must therefore be notified of a claim made against them. All parties must receive notice of any court hearing due to be held, of any document to be presented at a hearing, of any witness to be called, of any amendment to another party's statement of case, and of any other document that might be used in the proceedings.

It should, however, be noted that the notion of commencement is context-dependent. It can have different meanings in different contexts.[1] For the purpose of determining whether proceedings have commenced within any relevant limitation period, the time of formal initiations is the relevant time. In some other contexts the time of commencement may be the time of notification or service rather than the time of formal initiation. For instance, a court is seized of jurisdiction for the purpose of arts 21, 22 of the Lugano Convention on Jurisdiction and the Enforcement of Judgments in Civil and Commercial Matters 1998 (Civil Jurisdiction and Judgments Act 1982, Sch 3C) when service has taken place, not when the claim form has been issued.[2] A further qualification deserving notice is that in England the parties have considerable process obligations even before the formal initiation, in that they have to follow certain pre-action protocols before commencing proceedings.[3]

---

1. Cf Canada Trust Co v Stolzenberg (No 2) [2002] 1 AC 1, [2000] 4 All ER 481 (HL), per Lord Steyn.

2. Dresser UK Ltd v Falcongate Freight Management Ltd, The "Duke of Yare" [1992] 2 All ER 450, 467–468 (CA), but cf.

Canada Trust Co v Stolzenberg (No 2) [2002] 1 AC 1, [2000] 4 All ER 481 (HL).

3. Civil Practice Rules 1998, Practice Direction (Protocols) (The White Book Service 2006).

ENGLAND

Under the Civil Procedure Rules 1998 (CPR), the main method of commencement is the CPR 7 claim form (also known as Part 7 claim), which is applicable in the majority of claims. The date of issue of the claim form is crucial for the purpose of limitation because a claim is considered to have commenced on the date of issue.

Contents of the claim form: A claim form identifies the claimant and the defendant. It instructs the defendant to satisfy the claimant's claim or, alternatively, to acknowledge service of the claim form on an attached form and state whether he intends to contest the claimant's claim. The defendant is warned that unless he satisfies the claim or returns the acknowledgment stating that he intends to contest the claim, the claimant may obtain a default judgment without further notice to the defendant. The claim form must contain a concise statement of the nature of the claim. The statement must be sufficient to inform the defendant of the underlying grounds for the claim, but avoid excessive detail. Next, the claim form must include a description of the remedy that the claimant seeks, such as the repayment of a debt, damages, injunction and the like. Where the claimant does not claim a specified amount of money, the claim form must include a statement of value, in order to enable the court to allocate the case to the correct court and the correct track. Additional matters that must be set out in the claim form are specified by some practice directions, such as further details that have to be included where the claim form is to be served out of the jurisdiction (PD 7A, 3.5). By far the most important special requirement concerns information about funding arrangements. A successful party represented on the basis of a conditional fee agreement (CFA) may be able to recover from his opponent not only the normal costs, but also the success fee, which the party undertook to pay his lawyers, and the premium of an after the event litigation costs insurance (ATE). These are very important pieces of information because they could well affect the opponent's attitude to litigation. For example, a defendant who learns that the claimant is supported by a conditional fee agreement and litigation costs insurance, would know that the claimant is unlikely to be deterred by funding considerations, that the claimant's lawyers are sufficiently confident of success that they are prepared to forego their fee in the event that their client loses and, moreover, that if the claimant wins, the defendant's costs would be considerably higher.

Civil Procedure Rules 1998, Part 7—How to start proceedings (The White Book Service 2006)—CPR 7.2.

> (1) Proceedings are started when the court issues a claim form at the request of the claimant.

(2) A claim form is issued on the date entered on the form by the court.

The act of issuing a claim form consists of stamping the court's stamp on the claim form submitted to it by the claimant. In *Salford City Council v Garner* [2004] EWCA Civ 364 the Court of Appeal examined the question of when the landlord began proceeding for possession:

> 17. * * * In this case the claim form was issued on 11th November 2002. That is the date on which proceedings were started for the purpose of the Civil Procedure Rules.
>
> 18. Nevertheless, in a note at paragraph 5 of the Practice Direction supplemental to Part 5 of the Civil Procedure Rules— under the heading, "Start of Proceedings"—there appears the following:
>
>> "1. Proceedings are started when the court issues a claim form at the request of the claimant: see rule 7.2. But where a claim form as issued was received in the court office on a date earlier than the date on which it was issued by the court, the claim is 'brought' for the purposes of the Limitation Act 1980 and any other relevant statute on that earlier date.
>>
>> The date on which the claim form was received by the court will be recorded by a date stamp either on the claim form held on the court file or on the letter that accompanied the claim form when it was received by the court."
>
> [In the present case] * * * the court is asked to decide * * * whether proceedings were begun in this case on 7th November 2002 (which is the date on which the documents were handed over at the Salford County Court office) or on 11th November 2002 (which is the date on which the claim form was issued and the proceedings started for the purposes of the Civil Procedure Rules).
>
> Was the document filed when it was delivered to the court building, by being put through the court letter box; or was it necessary that the court should be open for business at the time, so that some action could be taken in relation to the document. In Van Aken [v London Borough of Camden [2002] EWCA Civ 1724] this court came to the conclusion that all that was required, under the relevant provision of the rules, was that the document be delivered to the court offices. It was not necessary that something should be done to or with the document when it was received at the court offices. But in the course of their judgments this court distinguished between that case and the case in which, under the relevant rule, it was necessary for there to be

some action taken in relation to the document which had been delivered. For an example of the latter case, see the judgments in this court in <u>Aadan</u> [v Brent London Borough Council [2002] 32 HLR 848], where the requirement was delivery to a court officer.

25. Adopting that distinction, what is required in order to begin proceedings? The answer to that seems to me clear enough under the Rules. What is required to begin proceedings is that the proceedings should be started. And proceedings are started by the issue of a claim form by the court. That, in this case, took place on 11th November 2002. In my view, that was the date on which the landlord began proceedings for possession for the purposes of section 130 of the Housing Act 1996.

26. I am fortified in that view by consideration of the difficulties which will ensue if the date of receipt by the court office is taken as the date on which proceedings are begun. If that were the position the tenant would not be able to rely on the date endorsed on the claim form issued and served upon him. He would have to inquire of the court office whether the claim form had been received by that office on an earlier date. And he would have to do that not only for the purposes of section 130 of the 1996 Act, but also for the purposes of section 128(5) of the Act. I do not think that Parliament could have included, when enacting those provisions, that the tenant should not be able to see, from the claim formed served upon him, whether the requirements which they impose had been met.

Note on Pre-action Protocols Required in England

Although in theory the start of legal proceedings in England continues to be marked by the issue of the claim form, in practice the process starts much earlier. Under the CPR parties to a dispute are required to comply with pre-action protocols before commencing proceedings. The pre-action protocols require prospective claimants to notify prospective defendants of their claim. Thereafter the parties are expected to engage in a meaningful exchange of information in order to see whether the dispute could be resolved without proceedings and, if proceedings appear necessary, to reach a mutual understanding of the issues and the core evidence. These requirements are not directly enforceable, but the courts have considerable powers to attach adverse consequences to non-compliance with protocols, especially in terms of costs, once proceedings have started. Even where the dispute settles before the issuing of a claim form, failure to comply with protocols may have adverse costs consequences if costs-only proceedings take place. Such proceedings may be commenced where the parties have reached an agreement on all issues, including liability for costs, but have failed to agree the amount of those costs (CPR 44.12A).

THE UNITED STATES

Jack H. Friedenthal, Arthur R. Miller, John E. Sexton, and Helen Hershkoff, Civil Procedure: Cases and Materials 213 (9th ed. 2005).

All states have statutes of limitations that fix specific time limits within which various categories of actions must be brought. They are supplemented by bodies of law that define when various causes of action are said to "accrue," the point when the limitations clock begins to run on an action, and the circumstances in which the running of the clock is suspended or "tolled" because a plaintiff for some reason has been prevented from timely assertion of her rights. See generally *Developments in the Law—Statutes of Limitations,* 63 Harv.L.Rev. 1177 (1950). Although statutes of limitations generally are deemed "procedural," their impact decidedly is "substantive"—a plaintiff loses the opportunity to invoke the assistance of the courts to obtain relief for an otherwise valid claim. Almost the first duty of a lawyer for a potential plaintiff is to determine, by the most conservative estimates, the latest possible day for commencing an action.

When is a suit "commenced" for purposes of a statute of limitations? In some states, an action is not deemed "commenced" until process is served on the defendant. In these states, a defect in service can be fatal to the plaintiff's claim, because the statute of limitations may run before the plaintiff has a chance to correct his error. In federal court, when the underlying cause of action is based on federal law, Rule 3 governs when the action is commenced. Thus, the suit is commenced when a copy of the complaint is filed with the district court. West v. Conrail, 481 U.S. 35, 107 S.Ct. 1538, 95 L.Ed.2d 32 (1987). However, when the underlying cause of action is based on state law, state law will govern when the action is commenced. See Walker v. Armco Steel Corp., 446 U.S. 740, 100 S.Ct. 1978, 64 L.Ed.2d 659 (1980).

As a separate matter, it is noteworthy that Rule 4(m) requires a federal court to dismiss without prejudice an action when the defendant has not been served within 120 days of the filing of the complaint, if the plaintiff fails to show "good cause" for not completing service within that time. * * *

If service is promptly attempted but improperly made, should a federal court dismiss the action without prejudice, or should it merely quash service and order the plaintiff to re-serve? The general view has been that the court has discretion in this matter—discretion that is exercised with an eye toward the circumstances of the case. Courts dismiss when the plaintiff has little likelihood of effecting proper service. In cases in which the plaintiff cannot hope to acquire jurisdiction over the defendant through proper service, keeping the action alive unnecessarily burdens the courts. On the other hand, when the plaintiff can make proper service quickly, courts generally quash the faulty service without prejudice to the plaintiff to serve again. See, e.g., Romandette v.

Weetabix Co., 807 F.2d 309, 311 (2d Cir.1986) ("[A] case in which proper service could be yet obtained.").

Federal Rules of Civil Procedure

Rule 3 Commencement of Action

A civil action is commenced by filing a complaint with the court.

Rule 4 Summons

(a) Form.

The summons shall be signed by the clerk, bear the seal of the court, identify the court and the parties, be directed to the defendant, and state the name and address of the plaintiff's attorney or, if unrepresented, of the plaintiff. It shall also state the time within which the defendant must appear and defend, and notify the defendant that failure to do so will result in a judgment by default against the defendant for the relief demanded in the complaint. The court may allow a summons to be amended.

(b) Issuance.

Upon or after filing the complaint, the plaintiff may present a summons to the clerk for signature and seal. If the summons is in proper form, the clerk shall sign, seal, and issue it to the plaintiff for service on the defendant. . . . .

(c) Service with Complaint; by Whom Made.

(1) A summons shall be served together with a copy of the complaint. The plaintiff is responsible for service of a summons and complaint within the time allowed under subdivision (m) and shall furnish the person effecting service with the necessary copies of the summons and complaint.

GERMANY

The German Code of Civil Procedure (*Zivilprozessordnung*—ZPO) requires the formal initiation of the claim in the appropriate court by filing the statement of claim as well as serving it upon the defendant (§ 253 sub. 1 ZPO).* The claim must fulfil certain requirements in order to be served: § 253 sub. 2 ZPO stipulates that the claim "must" designate (1) the parties and the court and (2) a concise statement of the subject matter, the grounds for the claim as well as a request for a specific remedy. Further, the claim "shall" also include the value of the

---

* Translations of the German rules are, throughout this Chapter, if possible, based on Charles E. Stewart (trans.) German Commercial Code and Code of Civil Procedure in English (2001) and S.L. Goren, (trans.) The Code of Civil Procedure rules of the Federal Republic of Germany of January 30, 1877 and the introductory act for the Code of Civil Procedure rules of January 30, 1877. As of January 1990.

subject matter if the jurisdiction of the court depends thereupon and the subject matter of litigation is not an ascertained sum of money (§ 253 sub. 3 ZPO). Additionally, § 253 sub. 4 ZPO refers to the general provisions concerning the preparation of written pleadings which also apply to the statement of claim. These rules are set out in the §§ 130 *et seq.* ZPO. They require, *inter alia*, that the party or the legal representative provide details of factual circumstances supporting the petition (§ 130 no. 3 ZPO) as well as the designation of the evidence by which the party will prove its factual allegations (§ 130 no. 5 ZPO).

The date of filing of the claim is as important in German civil procedure as it is in England. § 167 ZPO stipulates that the date of delivering the statement of claim to the court office is crucial in determining whether the claim has met a limitation period or a time-limit. In cases where service is necessary to meet these deadlines, service is deemed to take place at the time of filing the document, provided that the document is then soon served on the other party. Although the claim is not legally pending before it is properly served upon the defendant, the claimant may nevertheless meet any relevant deadline unilaterally.

In respect of money claims legal proceedings may start with a form of summary proceedings called *Mahnverfahren* (§ 688 ZPO). The claimant may apply to a special *Amtsgericht* (municipal court, as distinguished from the *Landgericht*—district court) for a summary notice, a kind of summary judgment, in cases of claims for an ascertained sum of money. This purely formal procedure does not involve any examination of the merits of the case. It is usually handled by a judicial clerk (*Rechtspfleger*) and not a judge. Upon simple request by means of special claim form the court issues a document, the summary notice, called *Mahnbescheid*, which demands the defendant to pay within two weeks from the time of service of the summary notice. The defendant may object to the notice. The defendant has to do so in order to avoid enforcement proceedings against him since otherwise the court issues an enforceable copy of the summary notice, the *Vollstreckungsbescheid*. This document resembles a default judgement and is again subject to objection. The defendant may stop the enforcement by providing security. If the defendant objects, the file will then be send to the appropriate court, which must already be designated in the initial application, and be listed for a hearing (§ 696 ZPO).

German Code of Civil Procedure

§ 253 [Statement of claim]

(1) The claim is raised by service of a written pleading (statement of claim).

(2) The statement of claim must contain:

1. the designation of the parties and of the court;

2. the concise statement of the subject matter and grounds of the claim raised, as well as a specific petition for remedy.

(3) The statement of claim shall further specify the value of the subject matter if the jurisdiction of the court depends thereon and the subject matter of litigation is not an ascertained sum of money, and also a statement whether there are grounds against the assignment of the case to a single judge.

* * *

§ 130 [Contents of written pleadings]

The preparatory written pleadings shall contain:

the designation of the parties and their legal representatives by name, profession or trade, place of residence and position as party; the designation of the court and of the subject matter; the number of attachments;

the applications that the party intends to make in the court session;

particulars of factual circumstances supporting the petitions;

the declaration concerning the factual allegations of the opponent;

the designation of the evidence to be relied on by the party to prove or rebut statements of fact, as well as a declaration with respect to the evidence designated by the opponent;

* * *

§ 167 [Retroactive effect of service]

If service is necessary to meet a time limit, or to recommence a time limit or to suspend the expiry of a time limit pursuant of § 204 of the Code of Civil Law, this effect is deemed to occur at the time of filing of the application or the declaration, provided that service is effected soon.

JAPAN

Takeshi Kojima, Japanese Civil Procedure in Comparative Law Perspective, 46 U. Kan. L. Rev. 687, 697 (1998).

A lawsuit still generally begins with filing a document—called the complaint—with a court. The complaint plays the basic role of specifying and particularizing the claim of the plaintiff. The new code gives the complaint a two-fold function: in addition to the specification and particularization of the claim itself, it requires that "the operative fact-basis of the claim" be specified as well as relevant important indirect facts that relate to the cause of action. Evidence should be itemized and written out according to each point to be proved. This represents a new policy. The role of the complaint is to disclose all of the important facts and evidence at an early stage as well as to identify the nature of the claim. If the presiding judge feels that the complaint is inadequate, he or she will order the plaintiff to supplement it. If the plaintiff does not revise the complaint satisfactorily, the judge will order that the complaint be rejected. If the complaint is found proper, the court must serve the complaint on the defendant. At the same time, the presiding judge must designate the dates of a hearing and notify the parties.

The Code of Civil Procedure of Japan.*

(Form of institution of suit)

Article 133. A suit shall be instituted by filing a complaint with the court.

2. A written complaint shall contain the following matters:

(1) The parties and legal representatives;

(2) The gist and ground of a claim.

(Service of complaint)

Article 138. A complaint shall be served on the defendant.

* * *

(Designation of date for oral proceedings)

Article 139. When a suit has been instituted, the presiding judge shall designate the date for oral proceedings and summon the parties to appear.

III. NOTIFICATION OF PROCEEDINGS

While the issue of the claim form marks the formal start of proceedings, the litigation process becomes fully engaged only by the act of service of the claim form. For this reason the time of notification or service of the formal document initiating the proceedings (the claim form in England) is the reference point for calculating the time for all subsequent process steps. For instance, CPR 7.4(1) states that the claimant must serve particulars of claim with the claim form, or within 14 days of the service of the claim form. The defendant then has 14 days from the time of service of the particulars of claim to respond (CPR 15.4(1)(a)).

Since the entire litigation timetable refers back to the service of the claim form, the time of service must be capable of being established with certainty by the litigants and by the court, in order to enable them to carry out their litigation functions in an efficient and orderly manner. The need for certainty and clarity lies at the foundation of any notifica-

---

* Translation in EHS Law Bulletin Series, EHS Vol. II, No. 2300 (2005).

tion system. Different systems meet these requirements in different ways.

ENGLAND

A distinction needs to be drawn between notification or service and filing. In England filing consists of delivering a document to the court office. CPR 2.3(1) states that " 'filing', in relation to a document, means delivering it, by post or otherwise, to the court office". The rules specify which documents must be filed and usually also indicate a time for doing so. Broadly speaking, all documents relating to major steps in the proceedings must be filed. Filing is of great importance because it is essential that the court should possess all the relevant documents that are necessary for the proper discharge of its management responsibilities.

Where personal service is involved, service of the claim form and its notification are one and the same thing because personal service involves delivering the process to the defendant himself. But a system of postal service gives rise to a distinction between service and notification. This is because the fact that a document has been posted (or sent by fax or email or placed in a letter box) does not necessarily guarantee that the document has actually come into the possession of the defendant and seen by him. A party or a court that serves a document would normally know when and how service (ie transmission) was carried out but not necessarily whether the document reached its destination. Modern methods of service must therefore be backed up by presumptions of notification that span this gap and enable the process to progress even where the served party has not responded.

Given that there is variety of means by which court documents may be served, ranging from personal service to service by electronic means, the rules indicate in relation to each of these service modes what it is necessary to do in order to comply with a deadline. Thus, where the rules authorise service of the claim form by first class post, they must also specify whether compliance with the deadline for service requires that the posted claim form should reach the defendant before the deadline, or whether it is enough that it should be posted before the deadline. If the latter is the case, the rules must determine whether it is sufficient that the claim form should be placed in a post box at the last minute before the expiry of the deadline or whether it must be posted with time to spare, so that in the normal course of things it will be delivered to the defendant before the expiry of the deadline.

In designing rules for determining compliance with time limits, the legislature also has regard to social welfare considerations, otherwise parties serving documents would be free to trouble their opponents at times that are normally devoted to rest or worship. Policy decisions must therefore be taken at the rule-making level whether to permit service on days such as Christmas Day and public holidays.

Civil Procedure Rules (The White Book Service, 2006)

CPR 7.5 Service of a claim form

(1) After a claim form has been issued, it must be served on the defendant.

(2) The general rule is that a claim form must be served within 4 months after the date of issue.

(3) The period for service is 6 months where the claim form is to be served out of the jurisdiction.

CPR 7.6 Extension of time for serving a claim form

(1) The claimant may apply for an order extending the period within which the claim form may be served.

(2) The general rule is that an application to extend the time for service must be made—

(a) within the period for serving the claim form specified by rule 7.5; or

(b) where an order has been made under this rule, within the period for service specified by that order.

(3) If the claimant applies for an order to extend the time for service of the claim form after the end of the period specified by rule 7.5 or by an order made under this rule, the court may make such an order only if—

(a) the court has been unable to serve the claim form; or

(b) the claimant has taken all reasonable steps to serve the claim form but has been unable to do so; and

(c) in either case, the claimant has acted promptly in making the application.

* * *

CPR 6.2 Methods of service—general

(1) A document may be served by any of the following methods—

(a) personal service, in accordance with rule 6.4;

(b) first class post; * * *

(c) leaving the document at a place specified in rule 6.5;

(d) through a document exchange in accordance with the relevant practice direction; or

(e) by fax or other means of electronic communication in accordance with the relevant practice direction.

THE UNITED STATES

Not all legal systems provide as wide a range of means of effecting service as is found in England. Under U.S. federal law, for example, service by first class post is only valid if the defendant waives service of a summons. According to Rule 4(d)(2) of the Federal Rules of Civil Procedure the defendant is under the duty to avoid unnecessary costs of serving the summons. To avoid these costs, the plaintiff may therefore notify the defendant of the commencement of the action and request the defendant to waive this form of service. In this special situation only notice and request may be dispatched through first-class mail or other reliable means. Service of the summons which becomes necessary if the defendant does not comply with the plaintiff's request has to be effected by delivering the summons and the complaint on the person individually, by leaving the copies thereof behind at the residence or by delivering the copies to an authorized agent (cf. Rule 4(e)). In this case the defendant has to bear all the costs of service.

Jack H. Friedenthal, Arthur R. Miller, John E. Sexton, and Helen Hershkoff, Civil Procedure: Cases and Materials 196–197 (9th ed. 2005).

Notice of a suit is given by the service of process upon the defendant. Each jurisdiction has a set of rules governing the correct methods of making service. Traditionally, process consists of a copy of the plaintiff's complaint, together with a summons directing the defendant to answer. Service of process is made by personal delivery of the summons and complaint to the defendant. Other methods of service, such as delivery by mail, have assumed greater importance since the advent of long-arm statutes.

The procedure governing service of process in federal actions was changed significantly in 1983, and again in 1993. * * * In 1983, Congress chose a system of service by mail modeled after the one used in California. See Cal.Code Civ.Pro. § 415.30. The summons and complaint could be sent by ordinary first class mail, together with a form for acknowledging receipt of service. If the acknowledgment form was not returned, plaintiff had to effect service through some other means authorized by the Rules. In order to encourage defendants to execute and return the form, the Rule directed the court to order a defendant who did not cooperate to pay the costs incurred by the plaintiff in making personal service, unless the defendant could show good cause for failing to return the acknowledgment form.

This system was not always successful because it relied on the defendant's cooperation in returning the acknowledgment form. Thus, after a decade of use, Rule 4 was revised again in 1993. The most significant change was that the "service by mail" provision was replaced by Rule 4(d), which strongly encourages waiver of formal service. Under this modification, an action commences when the plaintiff sends a form (Form 1A) entitled "Notice of Lawsuit and Request for Waiver of Service of Summons," or similar document, by mail or some other "reliable" means. Domestic defendants have thirty days from the date on which the waiver was sent to return the waiver; otherwise they will be charged with the costs associated with providing formal service. Along with the threat of paying for the costs of service, defendants receive a positive incentive in that they are allowed sixty days after the date on which the waiver was sent to answer the complaint if the waiver is returned in a timely fashion. Note that even under the new rule, if a plaintiff is confronting a statute of limitations deadline in a state in which the statute continues to run until a defendant is served, formal service sometimes may still be the wisest course of action, because the defendant may refuse to waive service.

Rule 4, in several subdivisions, sets forth specific means of making personal service on, among others, individuals, corporations, partnerships, and other associations subject to suit under a common name. In addition, Rule 4(e)(1) provides an alternative to these methods by broadly authorizing the use in federal courts of the procedures governing the manner of service prescribed by the law of the state in which the District Court is sitting.

Federal Rule 4(f) makes provision for service of process in a foreign country, affording American attorneys with a flexible framework to permit accommodation of the widely divergent procedures for service of process employed by the various nations of the world. This accommodation is necessary in order to avoid violating the sovereignty of other countries by committing acts within their borders that they may consider to be "official" and to maximize the likelihood that the judgment rendered in the action in this country will be recognized and enforced abroad. Service of process in a foreign country and other procedural aspects of civil litigation having multi-national incidents are discussed in Baumgartner, *Is Transnational Litigation Different?*, 25 U. Pa. J. Int'l Econ. L. 1297 (2004).

The 1993 revision of the Federal Rules expressly provides in Rule 4(f) that "any internationally agreed means reasonably calculated to give notice" may be used to effect service on persons outside the United States. The most important internationally agreed means concerning service of process are contained in the Hague Service Convention, which as of 2002 has been adopted by fifty countries. (Convention on the Service Abroad of Judicial and Extrajudicial Documents in Civil or Commercial Matters, The Hague, 1965, 20 U.S.T. 361, T.I.A.S. No. 6638, 658 U.N.T.S. 163, reproduced (with declarations by the contracting states) in 28 U.S.C.A. following Fed.R.Civ.P. 4). See Tamayo, *Catch Me If You Can: Serving United States Process on an Elusive Defendant Abroad*, 17 Harv. J.L. and Tech. 211 (2003). The heart of the Convention is a requirement that each Contracting State establish a Central Authority, which will receive and execute requests for service from judicial authorities in other Contracting States, and will see that a certification that service has been effected is returned to the court of origin. Service may be made either in accordance with the law of the nation in which service is to be made or (unless incompatible with that law) by a particular method requested by the applicant. 1 Ristau, *International Judicial Assistance (Civil and Commercial)* § 4–3–1 (rev. ed. 1990).

There are, however, several circumstances involving foreign defendants not governed by the Hague Convention. Most significantly, the Convention does not govern in those countries that are not Contracting States. Furthermore, the United States Supreme Court held in VOLKS-WAGENWERK AKTIENGESELLSCHAFT v. SCHLUNK, 486 U.S. 694, 108 S.Ct. 2104, 100 L.Ed.2d 722 (1988) that the Convention applies only if service actually is made *abroad,* rather than on the domestic subsidiary of a foreign corporation deemed to be the corporation's involuntary agent for service of process.

Federal Rule of Civil Procedure Rule 4 Summons

* * *

(d) Waiver of Service; Duty to Save Costs of Service; Request to Waive.

> (1) A defendant who waives service of a summons does not thereby waive any objection to the venue or to the jurisdiction of the court over the person of the defendant.

> (2) An individual, corporation, or association that is subject to service under subdivision (e), (f), or (h) and that receives notice of an action in the manner provided in this paragraph has a duty to avoid unnecessary costs of serving the summons. To avoid costs, the plaintiff may notify such a defendant of the commencement of the action and request that the defendant waive service of a summons. . . .

> If a defendant located within the United States fails to comply with a request for waiver made by a plaintiff located within the United States, the court shall impose the costs subsequently incurred in effecting service on the defendant unless good cause for the failure be shown.

* * *

(e) Service Upon Individuals Within a Judicial District of the United States.

Unless otherwise provided by federal law, service upon an individual from whom a waiver has not been obtained and filed, other than an infant or an incompetent person, may be effected in any judicial district of the United States:

> (1) pursuant to the law of the state in which the district court is located, or in which service is effected, for the

service of a summons upon the defendant in an action brought in the courts of general jurisdiction of the State; or

(2) by delivering a copy of the summons and of the complaint to the individual personally or by leaving copies thereof at the individual's dwelling house or usual place of abode with some person of suitable age and discretion then residing therein or by delivering a copy of the summons and of the complaint to an agent authorized by appointment or by law to receive service of process.

GERMANY

Filing the statement of claim is only the first step of starting civil proceedings in a German court. For the lawsuit to become fully engaged service of the claim upon the defendant is necessary (§ 253 sub. 1 ZPO). In addition, § 271 sub. 1 ZPO prescribes that the statement of claim must be served without delay. Service of the statement of claim follows the general rules on service of documents under the ZPO, which are contained in the §§ 166 *et seq.*

Service, understood as the proper use of one of several approved methods of communicating court documents, has the same purpose under German law than it has under English law: to notify the defendant of the process and thereby give him an opportunity to be heard. In the words of the Federal Constitutional Court:

> The purpose of service is to provide evidence of the time of the transmission, the exact point of which has important procedural effects. In relation to the addressee service shall allow him to take notice of the document served and to arrange for his defence or claim accordingly. Insofar the rules on service help to give effect to the right to be heard.[4]

Since also the German rules on service have to comply with the modern social conditions in which they operate, the German legislator reformed the law on service of documents with effect from 1 July 2002 in an attempt to simplify the process. The two basic rules of the reformed law are: (1) documents are to be served on the person concerned, i.e. in the case of the statement of claim on the defendant (§§ 253 sub. 1, 166 sub. 1 ZPO) and (2) service is now generally effected by the court (§ 166 sub. 2 ZPO).

Like in England, postal service (§ 168 ZPO) is the most common way of service nowadays, although many different forms of service are available. The provisions concerning service by the court regulate in detail how service is to be effected and at what time it is deemed to be effected in cases where direct service is not feasible. Generally, seven different forms of service can be distinguished: (a) Handing over the document at the court office (§ 173 ZPO), (b) transmission or similar forms of delivery with notice of receipt (§ 174 ZPO), (c) service by

4. BVerfG [1984] Neue Juristische Wochenschrift 2567, 2568.

certified mail with return receipt (*Einschreiben mit Rückschein*) according to § 175 ZPO, (d) delivery by postman, judicial clerk or bailiff/marshal (§§ 177–178 ZPO), (e) leaving the document at the residence or on the business premises (§ 178 ZPO), (f) putting the document in the mail box (§ 180 ZPO) and (g) deposit for pickup (§ 181 ZPO).

Additionally, § 179 sent. 1 ZPO provides a simple solution for the case where the addressee refuses unwarrantedly acceptance of the document: The document shall be served by being left behind at the addressee's residence or on his business premises. These methods must be employed according to a specified hierarchy. Alternative service (*Ersatzzustellung*) according to § 178, for example, requires that the deliverer does not encounter the addressee at his residence or on his business premises, so that direct service is not feasible. Similarly, the document may only be left in the mail box, if alternative service according to § 178 is not feasible.

Under German law no presumptions that span the gap between transmission and actual reception of documents are necessary since the exact date of reception by the defendant can easily be determined. This is either the time of handing over the document or leaving the document behind at the residence, office or letter box.

German Code of Civil Procedure

§ 166   [Service]

Service is the notification of a document to a person in the form specified in this Section.

Documents, the service of which is regulated by law, shall be served ex officio, unless a different rule applies.

§ 167   [Retroactive effect of service]

If service is necessary to meet a time limit, or to recommence a time limit or to suspend the expiry of a time limit pursuant of § 204 of the Code of Civil Law, this effect is deemed to occur at the time of filing of the application or the declaration, provided that service is effected soon.

§ 168   [Tasks of the court office]

The court office effects service pursuant to §§ 173 to 175. It can order a postal authority in the sense of § 33 sub. 1 of the Postal Law (*Postgesetz*) or a judicial clerk to effect service. * * *

The presiding judge or another member of the trial court designated by him may order a bailiff/marshal or another public authority to effect service, if service according to subparagraph 1 appears to fail.

§ 170   [Service on agent]

For a person lacking capacity to litigate service shall be effected on his statutory agent. Service on the person lacking capacity to litigate is ineffective.

If the addressee is not an individual person, service on the director suffices.

If there are several statutory agents or directors service on one of them suffices.

§ 171 [Service on appointed representative]

Service on the appointed representative has the same effect as service on the represented party. The appointed representative has to provide a certificate of authorization.

* * *

§ 173 [Service by delivery at the court office]

A document may be served on the addressee or his appointed representative by delivery at the court office. In proof of service it shall be noted on the document as well as in the court files that delivery took place for the purpose of service and the time when this occurred. * * *

§ 175 [Service by certified mail with return receipt]

A document may be served by certified mail with return receipt. The return receipt sufficiently proves service.

§ 177 [Place of service]

Service may be effected in any place where the person on whom service is to be made is found.

§ 178 [Alternative service at residence, office, and community dwelling]

If a person, on whom service shall be effected, is not found at his residence, on the business premises or in the community dwelling where he lives, the document may be served at the residence upon an adult family member, an adult servant of the family or a permanent adult cohabitant; on the business premises upon one of the employees; in community dwellings upon the director or one of his representatives.

* * *

§ 179 [Service when acceptance is refused]

If the acceptance of service is refused without legal basis, the document to be served shall be left behind at the residence or on the business premises. If the addressee has no residence or if there are no business premises, the document to be served shall be send back. The document is deemed to be served at the time of refusal of acceptance.

§ 180 [Alternative service by deposit in letter box]

If service pursuant to § 178 sub. 1 no. 1 or 2 is not executable the document may be deposited in a letter box or similar device belonging to the residence or business premises, which the addressee provided for postal receipt and which is suitable for safe storage in the usual manner. Service is deemed to be effected when the document is deposited. The person serving shall note the date of service on the envelope of the document served.

JAPAN

Hideyuki Kobayashi and Yoshimasa Furuta, Products Liability Act and Transnational Litigation in Japan, 34 Tex. Int'l L. J. 93, 101–103 (1999).

In Japan, service of process is considered to be an exercise of the sovereign power of the national government. As a result, it is always carried out by a court clerk or other government official. The court official must have process served ex officio, either by a bailiff or through special mail service under the direction of the court clerk. Service made in violation of statutory provisions is null and void. Several types of service of process, described below, are provided for in the CCP.

1. Service by Delivery

Service by delivery is the basic method of service of process in Japan. This requires the tendering of a copy of the document by hand to the addressee. Service by delivery must be made at the domicile, place of residence, place of business, or office of the person who is to receive service. If there is doubt as to whether a person has a domicile, residence, place of business, or office in Japan, then service may be made at any place where he or she may be found. The same applies to a person who does not refuse to accept the service. In practice, service by delivery is usually carried out by a mail delivery person, under the court clerk's direction, by means of special mail service.

2. Substituted Service

Substituted service is generally a permissible alternative to service by delivery if the person to be served is not found by the bailiff or mail delivery person at the places specified above. Substituted service is effected by delivery to a personal representative, employee, or occupant of the same premises as the person who is to receive service, provided that the person has sufficient intelligence to understand that service is being made.

3. Service by Leaving the Document

If the person to whom the document is tendered refuses to accept service without justifiable reason, the bailiff or mail delivery person may lawfully serve the document by leaving it where service would otherwise have been made.

4. Service by Registered Mail

If service by the foregoing methods fails, the court clerk may send a copy of the document by registered mail. This type of service is deemed to have full effect at the time of delivery.

5. Service Abroad

Service in a foreign country is effected by entrusting it to the relevant authorities in that country.

6. Service by Public Notice

Service by public notice may be relied upon only if (1) the party's domicile, residence, or other place for service is unknown, (2) service by registered mail has failed, or (3) service cannot be effected in a foreign jurisdiction. Public notice may be used by the permission of a court order upon motion. The court may order service by public notice ex officio if the court finds it necessary to avoid delay. Subsequent service on the same party is made by public notice ex officio.

Service by public notice is carried out by posting a notice on the courthouse bulletin board. Initial service by public notice takes effect when two weeks has elapsed (six weeks if the addressee is abroad) from the date of the posting of the notice, while subsequent service takes effect on the day following the posting date.

7. Personal Service

Personal service by private attorneys or process servers is not allowed in Japan. Litigants or their attorneys from common law countries sometimes contemplate personal service in Japan for litigation pending in their countries. Under Japanese law, however, such personal service will constitute an infringement of Japanese sovereignty, and Japanese courts would find the service invalid.

8. Service of Process for Foreign Proceedings

Because service of process is considered to be an exercise of sovereign power, only the Japanese government or its duly appointed officials can serve process within the territory of Japan. Unless otherwise specifically provided for in international conventions, treaties, or bilateral intergovernmental agreements to which Japan is a signatory, the Japanese government or its duly appointed officials will not serve process for foreign proceedings.

The Code of Civil Procedure of Japan.*

(Service executing organ)

Article 99. Except as otherwise provided, the service shall be effected by mail or by a bailiff.

* Translation in EHS Law Bulletin Series, EHS Vol. II, No. 2300 (2004).

2. In the case of service by mail, a person who is engaged in postal service shall be an official effecting service.

(Service by court clerk)

Article 100. A court clerk may effect service by himself to a person who has appeared for the case in the court to which the court clerk belongs.

(Principle of service by delivery)

Article 101. Except as otherwise provided, service shall be effected by delivering a document to a person who is to receive the service.

(Place of service)

Article 103. The service shall be made at the domicile, place of resident, place of business, or office (hereinafter referred to as "domicile, etc." in this Section) of a person to whom service is to be made. Provided that, the service to the legal representative may be made at his business place or office.

2. If the place provided for in the preceding paragraph is unknown or there is any trouble for making service at such place, the service may be made at another persons' domicile, etc. where a person who is to receive service is in work on the basis of legal acts such as employment and entrustment (hereinafter referred to as the "place of work"). The same shall apply when a person who is to receive service (excluding one provided in paragraph 1 of the following Article) states that he will receive service at the place of work.

IV. IDENTIFYING THE ISSUES

ENGLAND

In Anglo–American law service of initiating process on the defendant will warn him that a claim has commenced against him and will give him a general idea of its nature, but the precise issues in dispute are still to be identified. Until the parties have identified the matters in dispute, they do not know what they have to prove or disprove and the court does not have a controversy requiring resolution. The process of identifying the issues in dispute is carried out by an exchange of documents between the parties. This exchange in known in common law countries as exchange of pleadings and in contemporary English law as exchange of statements of case. Pleadings or statements of case are documents exchanged by the parties, in which they indicate their positions on the subject matter of the claim.

Once the parties have stated their positions and defined the issues, the Court cannot go behind the parties' pleaded cases to take account of matters which are known to it to be the case, nor is the Court permitted to take account of matters that the parties may attempt to put in evidence but which is outside the scope of their pleaded cases.

In England the term "statement of case" includes the claim form, particulars of claim where these are not included in a claim form, defence, or reply to defence, and any further information given in relation to them voluntarily or by court order under rule 18.1 (CPR 2.3(1)). Although the claim form is considered a statement of case, the first statement of case to advance the claimant's case in a fully informative way is the *particulars of claim*. For this reason the defendant does not need to respond until the particulars of claim have been served on him. The particulars of claim may be included in the claim form. As we have already noted, the parties are also required to comply with pre-action protocols before commencing proceedings. Since the protocols require prospective claimants to notify prospective defendants of their claim and the parties are then expected to engage in a meaningful exchange of inform, they should have a general idea of the nature of the claims and defenses before the action is formally commenced.

Once the particulars of claim have been served, a defendant who wishes to resist the claim must respond by serving his own statement of case: the *defence*. In most cases, the exchange of particulars of claim and defence should suffice to identify and define the issues. Occasionally however, the claimant may deem it necessary to serve a reply to the defence in order to make admissions, put forward an assertion in response to something contained in the defence or in order to cut down the issues. After the reply, if any, no party may serve any statement of case without the court's permission (CPR 15.9).

In England all statements of case must be verified by a *statement of truth*. The aim is to ensure that assertions are not made by litigants in which they have no honest belief, and to discourage parties from pleading speculative cases in the hope that some evidence will come to light during discovery (disclosure) or at trial.[5]

Civil Procedure Rules (The White Book Service, 2006).

CPR 22.1 Documents to be verified by a statement of truth

(1) The following documents must be verified by a statement of truth—a statement of case; * * *.

CPR 22.2 Failure to verify a statement of case

(1) If a party fails to verify his statement of case by a statement of truth—

(a) the statement of case shall remain effective unless struck out; but

---

5. Clarke v. Marlborough Fine Art (London) Ltd (Amendments) [2002] 1 WLR 1731.

(b) the party may not rely on the statement of case as evidence of any of the matters set out in it.

(2) The court may strike out a statement of case which is not verified by a statement of truth.

(3) Any party may apply for an order under paragraph (2).

CPR 7.4 Particulars of claim

(1) Particulars of claim must—

(a) be contained in or served with the claim form; or

(b) subject to paragraph (2) be served on the defendant by the claimant within 14 days after service of the claim form.

(2) Particulars of claim must be served on the defendant no later than the latest time for serving a claim form.

CPR 16.4 Contents of the particulars of claim

(1) Particulars of claim must include—

(a) a concise statement of the facts on which the claimant relies;

Note

In the particulars of claim the claimant must state the facts that are necessary to establish a complete cause of action. The test is whether the facts relied upon would, if proved, entitle the claimant to the remedy he seeks, or possibly to a different remedy. A claim for damages for breach of contract, for example, must allege a contract, a breach thereof and a resulting loss. Similarly, a claimant who seeks damages for negligence must state facts that give rise to a duty of care, establish a breach of that duty, and identify the injury suffered as a result.

Civil Procedure Rules (The White Book Service, 2006).

CPR 9.2 Defence, admission or acknowledgment of service

When particulars of claim are served on a defendant, the defendant may—

(a) file or serve an admission in accordance with Part 14;

(b) file a defence in accordance with Part 15, (or do both, if he admits only part of the claim); or

(c) file an acknowledgment of service in accordance with Part 10.

CPR 16.5 Content of defence

(1) In his defence, the defendant must state—

(a) which of the allegations in the particulars of claim he denies;

(b) which allegations he is unable to admit or deny, but which he requires the claimant to prove; and

(c) which allegations he admits.

(2) Where the defendant denies an allegation—

(a) he must state his reasons for doing so; and

(b) if he intends to put forward a different version of events from that given by the claimant, he must state his own version.

(3) A defendant who—

(a) fails to deal with an allegation; but

(b) has set out in his defence the nature of his case in relation to the issue to which that allegation is relevant, shall be taken to require that allegation to be proved.

(4) Where the claim includes a money claim, a defendant shall be taken to require that any allegation relating to the amount of money claimed be proved unless he expressly admits the allegation.

(5) Subject to paragraphs (3) and (4), a defendant who fails to deal with an allegation shall be taken to admit that allegation.

Note

The defendant's response has to address the points made in the particulars of claim. Accordingly, the defendant must state which allegations in the particulars of claims he denies, which he admits and which he is unable to admit or deny but which he requires the claimant to prove (CPR 16.5(1)). A defendant who fails to admit allegations that are plainly true may be penalised in costs. Indeed, a claimant may demand specific admission by serving a notice to admit under CPR 32.18. Where the defendant denies the claimant's allegations, he must state the reasons for his denial; and if he intends to advance a different version of events from those stated by the claimant, he must set out his own version. The function of the defence is to provide a comprehensive response to the particulars of claim so that when the two documents are read together one can learn precisely which matters are in dispute.

THE UNITED STATES

In the United States, the parties' are notified of their respective claims and defenses in the "pleadings," i.e., the complaint served by the plaintiff and the answer served by the defendant in response. The answer may also include a counterclaim; if it does, the plaintiff will serve a reply. The service of additional pleadings is required to add other parties. The general guiding concept of "notice pleadings" means that the parties need not plead facts in detail. In American litigation the parties are expected to learn those details through pretrial discovery. Moreover, the judge has discretionary authority to schedule a pretrial conference with the attorneys soon after the exchange of pleadings for the purpose of exploring and narrowing the issues, scheduling discovery, motions, and the trial, and facilitating settlement. See F.R.Civ. Proc. 7, 8, 16.

Jack H. Friedenthal, Arthur R. Miller, John E. Sexton, and Helen Hershkoff, Civil Procedure: Cases and Materials 510–511, 517–520 (9th ed. 2005).

The Burden of Pleading and the Burden of Production

The burden of pleading an issue usually is assigned to the party who has the burden of producing evidence on that issue at trial, although "the burden of pleading need not coincide with the burden of producing evidence." Hamabe, *Functions of Rule 12(b)(6) in the Federal Rules of Civil Procedure: A Categorization Approach,* 15 Campbell L. Rev. 119, 172 (1993). Typically, plaintiff must put forth evidence on certain matters basic to the claim for relief or he cannot prevail. In a slander action, for example, plaintiff must introduce evidence that the remarks were made, that they were published, and that he was injured thereby. If plaintiff rests his case without producing evidence on any one of these issues, the court will dismiss the action and enter judgment for defendant. Therefore plaintiff must plead those matters he must prove. The rationale for the rule is simple. If plaintiff cannot legitimately allege the existence of each of the basic elements of his claim, it may be assumed that he could not introduce evidence on them at trial.

On the other hand, plaintiff normally does not have to plead matters on which defendant must introduce proof. If plaintiff were required to plead the nonexistence of every defense, not only would the pleading be long, complex, and fraught with danger for a plaintiff who omitted a remote possibility, but also the pleadings would not reveal, in any direct way, precisely upon which defenses defendant actually intended to rely. By placing the burden of pleading defenses on defendant, the court and parties know exactly on which of the many possible defenses he intends to introduce evidence, thus making preparation for trial and the actual work at trial more manageable. Once defendant has established a defense at trial, plaintiff will then have a second burden of production, this time to introduce evidence as to facts that will avoid defendant's defense. For example, if defendant proves that allegedly slanderous statements were made to plaintiff's prospective employer under conditions that rendered the statements privileged, plaintiff then must carry the burden of producing evidence showing that the statements were made maliciously and solely with intent to injure plaintiff, thereby vitiating the defense. Obviously, plaintiff is not required to plead, in the original complaint, matters to avoid defenses, since he cannot tell which defenses will be raised until the answer is filed. In some jurisdictions plaintiff is required to set forth matters that avoid the defendant's defenses in a second pleading, which serves as a reply to the answer; in other jurisdictions the decision whether to require a reply is left to the trial court's discretion.

Matters of avoidance are limited and well recognized so that a reply is most often unnecessary.

Swierkiewicz v. Sorema N. A., 534 U.S. 506 (2002).

Certiorari to the United States Court of Appeals for the Second Circuit. JUSTICE THOMAS delivered the opinion of the Court.

This case presents the question whether a complaint in an employment discrimination lawsuit must contain specific facts establishing a prima facie case of discrimination * * *. We hold that an employment discrimination complaint need not include such facts and instead must contain only "a short and plain statement of the claim showing that the pleader is entitled to relief." Fed. Rule Civ. Proc. 8(a)(2).

I

Petitioner Akos Swierkiewicz is a native of Hungary, who at the time of his complaint was 53 years old. In April 1989, petitioner began working for respondent Sorema N. A., a reinsurance company headquartered in New York and principally owned and controlled by a French parent corporation. Petitioner was initially employed in the position of senior vice president and chief underwriting officer (CUO). Nearly six years later, Francois M. Chavel, respondent's Chief Executive Officer, demoted petitioner to a marketing and services position and transferred the bulk of his underwriting responsibilities to Nicholas Papadopoulo, a 32–year-old who, like Mr. Chavel, is a French national. About a year later, Mr. Chavel stated that he wanted to "energize" the underwriting department and appointed Mr. Papadopoulo as CUO. Petitioner claims that Mr. Papadopoulo had only one year of underwriting experience at the time he was promoted, and therefore was less experienced and less qualified to be CUO than he, since at that point he had 26 years of experience in the insurance industry.

Following his demotion, petitioner contends that he "was isolated by Mr. Chavel TTT excluded from business decisions and meetings and denied the opportunity to reach his true potential at SOREMA." * * * Petitioner unsuccessfully attempted to meet with Mr. Chavel to discuss his discontent. Finally, in April 1997, petitioner sent a memo to Mr. Chavel outlining his grievances and requesting a severance package. Two weeks later, respondent's general counsel presented petitioner with two options: He could either resign without a severance package or be dismissed. Mr. Chavel fired petitioner after he refused to resign.

Petitioner filed a lawsuit alleging that he had been terminated on account of his national origin in violation of Title VII of the Civil Rights Act of 1964, 78 Stat. 253, as amended, 42 U.S.C. § 2000e et seq. (1994 ed. and Supp. V), and on account of his age in violation of the Age

Discrimination in Employment Act of 1967 (ADEA), 81 Stat. 602, as amended, 29 U.S.C. § 621 et seq. (1994 ed. and Supp. V). * * * The United States District Court for the Southern District of New York dismissed petitioner's complaint because it found that he "ha[d] not adequately alleged a prima facie case, in that he ha[d] not adequately alleged circumstances that support an inference of discrimination." * * * The United States Court of Appeals for the Second Circuit affirmed the dismissal * * *. We granted certiorari, * * * and now reverse.

II

Applying Circuit precedent, the Court of Appeals required petitioner to plead a prima facie case of discrimination in order to survive respondent's motion to dismiss. * * * In the Court of Appeals' view, petitioner was thus required to allege in his complaint: (1) membership in a protected group; (2) qualification for the job in question; (3) an adverse employment action; and (4) circumstances that support an inference of discrimination. * * *

The prima facie case * * *, however, is an evidentiary standard, not a pleading requirement. * * * [T]his Court has reiterated that the prima facie case relates to the employee's burden of presenting evidence that raises an inference of discrimination. * * *

This Court has never indicated that the requirements for establishing a prima facie case * * * also apply to the pleading standard that plaintiffs must satisfy in order to survive a motion to dismiss. * * *

In addition, under a notice pleading system, it is not appropriate to require a plaintiff to plead facts establishing a prima facie case because * * * [this] framework does not apply in every employment discrimination case. For instance, if a plaintiff is able to produce direct evidence of discrimination, he may prevail without proving all the elements of a prima facie case. * * *

Under the Second Circuit's heightened pleading standard, a plaintiff without direct evidence of discrimination at the time of his complaint must plead a prima facie case of discrimination, even though discovery might uncover such direct evidence. It thus seems incongruous to require a plaintiff, in order to survive a motion to dismiss, to plead more facts than he may ultimately need to prove to succeed on the merits if direct evidence of discrimination is discovered.

* * * Given that the prima facie case operates as a flexible evidentiary standard, it should not be transposed into a rigid pleading standard for discrimination cases.

Furthermore, imposing the Court of Appeals' heightened pleading standard in employment discrimination cases conflicts with Federal Rule of Civil Procedure 8(a)(2), which provides that a complaint must include only "a short and plain statement of the claim showing that the pleader is entitled to relief." * * * This simplified notice pleading standard relies on liberal discovery rules and summary judgment motions to define disputed facts and issues and to dispose of unmeritorious claims. * * *

Rule 8(a)'s simplified pleading standard applies to all civil actions, with limited exceptions. Rule 9(b), for example, provides for greater particularity in all averments of fraud or mistake. * * * This Court, however, has declined to extend such exceptions to other contexts. In Leatherman [v. Tarrant County Narcotics Intelligence and Coordination Unit, 507 U.S. 163, 113 S.Ct. 1160, 122 L.Ed.2d 517 (1993), a civil rights action involving municipal liability under 42 U.S.C. § 1983] we stated: "[T]he Federal Rules do address in Rule 9(b) the question of the need for greater particularity in pleading certain actions, but do not include among the enumerated actions any reference to complaints alleging municipal liability under § 1983. Expressio unius est exclusion alterius." 507 U.S., at 168, 113 S.Ct. 1160. Just as Rule 9(b) makes no mention of municipal liability under Rev. Stat. § 1979, 42 U.S.C. § 1983 (1994 ed., Supp. V), neither does it refer to employment discrimination. Thus, complaints in these cases, as in most others, must satisfy only the simple requirements of Rule 8(a).

Other provisions of the Federal Rules of Civil Procedure are inextricably linked to Rule 8(a)'s simplified notice pleading standard. * * * If a pleading fails to specify the allegations in a manner that provides sufficient notice, a defendant can move for a more definite statement under Rule 12(e) before responding. Moreover, claims lacking merit may be dealt with through summary judgment under Rule 56. The liberal notice pleading of Rule 8(a) is the starting point of a simplified pleading system, which was adopted to focus litigation on the merits of a claim. * * *

Applying the relevant standard, petitioner's complaint easily satisfies the requirements of Rule 8(a) because it gives respondent fair notice of the basis for petitioner's claims. Petitioner alleged that he had been terminated on account of his national origin in violation of Title VII and on account of his age in violation of the ADEA. * * * His complaint detailed the events leading to his termination, provided relevant dates, and included the ages and nationalities of at least some of the relevant persons involved with his termination. * * * These allegations give respondent fair notice of what petitioner's claims are and the grounds upon which they rest. * * * In addition, they state claims upon which relief could be granted under Title VII and the ADEA.

Respondent argues that allowing lawsuits based on conclusory allegations of discrimination to go forward will burden the courts and encourage disgruntled employees to bring unsubstantiated suits. * * * Whatever the practical merits of this argument, the Federal Rules do not contain a heightened pleading standard for employment discrimination suits. A requirement of greater specificity for particular claims is a result that "must be obtained by the process of amending the Federal Rules, and not by judicial interpretation." Leatherman, [507 U.S.], at 168, 113 S.Ct. 1160. Furthermore, Rule 8(a) establishes a pleading standard without regard to whether a claim will succeed on the merits. "Indeed it may appear on the face of the pleadings that a recovery is very remote and unlikely but that is not the test." Scheuer [v. Rhodes], 416 U.S. [232], at 236, 94 S.Ct. 1683[, 1686, 40 L. Ed.2 90, 96 (1974)].

For the foregoing reasons, we hold that an employment discrimination plaintiff need not plead a prima facie case of discrimination and that petitioner's complaint is sufficient to survive respondent's motion to dismiss. Accordingly, the judgment of the Court of Appeals is reversed, and the case is remanded for further proceedings consistent with this opinion.

It is so ordered.

Federal Rules of Civil Procedure
Rule 8 General Rules of Pleading

(a) Claims for Relief.

A pleading which sets forth a claim for relief, whether an original claim, counterclaim, cross-claim, or third-party claim, shall contain (1) a short and plain statement of the grounds upon which the court's jurisdiction depends, unless the court already has jurisdiction and the claim needs no new grounds of jurisdiction to support it, (2) a short and plain statement of the claim showing that the pleader is entitled to relief, and (3) a demand for judgment for the relief the pleader seeks. Relief in the alternative or of several different types may be demanded.

(b) Defenses; Form of Denials.

A party shall state in short and plain terms the party's defenses to each claim asserted and shall admit or deny the averments upon which the adverse party relies. If a party is without knowledge or information sufficient to form a belief as to the truth of an averment, the party shall so state and this has the effect of a denial. Denials shall fairly meet the substance of the averments denied. When a pleader intends in good faith to deny only a part or a qualification of an averment, the pleader shall specify so much of it as is true and material and shall deny only the remainder. Unless the pleader intends in good faith to controvert all the averments of the preceding pleading, the pleader may make denials as specific denials of designated averments or paragraphs, or may generally deny all the averments except such designated averments or paragraphs as the pleader expressly admits; but, when the pleader does so intend to controvert all its averments, including averments of the grounds upon which the court's jurisdiction depends, the pleader may do so by general denial subject to the obligations set forth in Rule 11.

(c) Affirmative Defenses.

In pleading to a preceding pleading, a party shall set forth affirmatively accord and satisfaction, arbitration and award, assumption of risk, contributory negligence, discharge in bankruptcy, duress, estoppel, failure of consideration, fraud, illegality, injury by fellow servant, laches, license, payment, release, res judicata, statute of frauds, statute of limitations, waiver, and any other matter constituting an avoidance or affirmative defense. When a party has mistakenly designated a defense as a counterclaim or a counterclaim as a defense, the court on terms, if justice so requires, shall treat the pleading as if there had been a proper designation.

(d) Effect of Failure To Deny.

Averments in a pleading to which a responsive pleading is required, other than those as to the amount of damage, are admitted when not denied in the responsive pleading. Averments in a pleading to which no responsive pleading is required or permitted shall be taken as denied or avoided.

(e) Pleading to be Concise and Direct; Consistency

(1) Each averment of a pleading shall be simple, concise, and direct. No technical forms of pleading or motions are required.

(2) A party may set forth two or more statements of a claim or defense alternately or hypothetically, either in one count or defense or in separate counts or defenses. When two or more statements are made in the alternative and one of them if made independently would be sufficient, the pleading is not made insufficient by the insufficiency of one or more of the alternative statements. A party may also state as many separate claims or defenses as the party has regardless of consistency and whether based on legal, equitable, or maritime grounds. All statements shall be made subject to the obligations set forth in Rule 11.

(f) Construction of Pleadings

All pleadings shall be so construed as to do substantial justice.

Rule 11 Signing of Pleadings, Motions, and Other Papers; Representations to Court; Sanctions

(a) Signature.

Every pleading, written motion, and other paper shall be signed by at least one attorney of record in the attorney's individual name, or, if the party is not represented by an attorney, shall be signed by the party. * * * Except when otherwise specifically provided by rule or statute, pleadings need not be verified or accompanied by affidavit. * * *

(b) Representations to Court.

By presenting to the court (whether by signing, filing, submitting, or later advocating) a pleading, written motion, or other paper, an attorney or unrepresented party is certifying that to the best of the person's knowledge, information, and belief, formed after an inquiry reasonable under the circumstances,—

(1) it is not being presented for any improper purpose, such as to harass or to cause unnecessary delay or needless increase in the cost of litigation;

(2) the claims, defenses, and other legal contentions therein are warranted by existing law or by a nonfrivolous argument for the extension, modification, or reversal of existing law or the establishment of new law;

(3) the allegations and other factual contentions have evidentiary support or, if specifically so identified, are likely to have evidentiary support after a reasonable opportunity for further investigation or discovery; and

(4) the denials of factual contentions are warranted on the evidence or, if specifically so identified, are reasonably based on a lack of information or belief.

(c) Sanctions.

If, after notice and a reasonable opportunity to respond, the court determines that subdivision (b) has been violated, the court may, subject to the conditions stated below, impose an appropriate sanction upon the attorneys, law firms, or parties that have violated subdivision (b) or are responsible for the violation.

* * *

Rule 12 Defenses and Objections—When and How Presented—By Pleading or Motion—Motion for Judgment on the Pleadings

(a) When Presented.

(1) Unless a different time is prescribed in a statute of the United States, a defendant shall serve an answer

* * *

(b) How Presented.

Every defense, in law or fact, to a claim for relief in any pleading, whether a claim, counterclaim, cross-claim, or third-party claim, shall be asserted in the responsive pleading thereto if one is required, except that the following defenses may at the option of the pleader be made by motion: (1) lack of jurisdiction over the subject matter, (2) lack of jurisdiction over the person, (3) improper venue, (4) insufficiency of process, (5) insufficiency of service of process, (6) failure to state a claim upon which relief can be granted, (7) failure to join a party under Rule 19.
* * *

(c) Motion for Judgment on the Pleadings.

After the pleadings are closed but within such time as not to delay the trial, any party may move for judgment on the pleadings. If, on a motion for judgment on the pleadings, matters outside the pleadings are presented to and not excluded by the court, the motion shall be treated as one for summary judgment and disposed of as provided in Rule 56, and all parties shall be given reasonable opportunity to present all material made pertinent to such a motion by Rule 56.

(d) Preliminary Hearings.

The defenses specifically enumerated (1)-(7) in subdivision (b) of this rule, whether made in a pleading or by motion, and the motion for judgment mentioned in subdivision (c) of this rule shall be heard and determined before trial on application of any party, unless the court orders that the hearing and determination thereof be deferred until the trial.

* * *

GERMANY

As in common law countries, German procedure seeks to define the scope of the dispute and the controversies upon which the court will be called to decide at the trial. But the method employed to this end is different. The first steps towards this end are already taken by the initial exchange of written pleadings, i.e. the statement of claim (§ 253 ZPO) and the statement of defence (§ 277 ZPO). Both the statement of claim and the statement of defence require the parties to state the exact facts of their respective version of the case and to adduce evidence for each disputed fact, e.g. nominate witnesses, refer to documents and other pieces of evidence that support their case (cf. § 130 ZPO).

Although the written pleadings are meant to establish in advance the relevant facts and the means of evidence, in more complicated cases this written introductory stage often only sets the broad frame of the lawsuit. Therefore, this introductory stage is usually followed by the preparatory procedural stage in which aspects like the applicable law, the factual basis of the case and the available means of evidence are further clarified. This phase of the process informs both the parties and the court about the different aspects of the legal controversy and anticipates or replaces in part the taking of evidence in the main hearing. Thus the exchange of information does not only help the parties to prepare themselves for oral arguments but is also allows the court to manage the case properly. It is the court that is in charge of administering the case in an effective and efficient manner. § 273 ZPO sets these requirements out clearly: it is the court's duty to prepare the final main hearing by taking the required procedural steps in due time.

In order to identify the relevant factual and legal issues before the main hearing, the judge can proceed in two distinct ways. The first possibility is to schedule an "early first session" (*früher erster Termin*) according to § 275 ZPO. The second way is to order the defendant to submit a written pleading as an answer to the statement of claim in a preliminary written proceedings according to § 276 ZPO (*schriftliches Vorverfahren*). In practice, the preparation of the final main hearing sometimes consists of a series of preparatory hearings during which the court may order the production of documents to the opponent and the court, ask for written expertises by court appointed experts for the information of the parties and the court or written statements of witnesses as a preparation of oral testimony.

Furthermore, in order to thoroughly prepare the main hearing and to generally promote proceedings, the court has to ensure that the parties make comprehensive and sufficient submissions. As part of the court's general duty to prepare the main hearing and clarify the issues, the court has an obligation to give hints and feedback to the party's assertions. According to § 139 ZPO the judge is obliged to discuss the case with the parties and, in particular to notify the parties of defects in their pleadings. At all stages of the proceedings, the court must give the parties the opportunity to mend any defects by correcting or supplementing their pleadings. Thus the court may ask for better particulars of the case, to admit facts, to offer better or more evidence or to improve legal arguments. In the course of this process the court must order the parties to bring forward all the evidence required in good time before any hearing. The German procedure seeks to ensure that the court helps inexperienced parties to avoid making obvious procedural mistakes.

The line between good case management and biased assistance towards one side or the other is admittedly hard to define. Since both parties have to be treated as equals, the judge may under no circumstances help one party more generously than the other. The assistance is strictly limited to procedural issues that are concerned with the conduct of the litigation proceedings. The judge is not empowered to help a party in arguing its case, e.g. advising a party to invoke the defence of an expired limitation period or rise the question whether a certain document or piece of evidence that has not been mentioned before in the pleadings exists. Therefore, the discretionary power has to be executed very carefully.

It follows that while both English law and German provide a process for identifying the issues prior to adjudication, the methods chosen are very different and the court's involvement in the process varies greatly.

German Code of Civil Procedure

§ **138**   [Duty to submit facts; Duty of truthfulness]

(1) The parties' statements with respect to factual circumstances shall be complete and truthful.

(2) Each party shall reply to allegations by the opponent.

(3) Facts which are not expressly denied shall be deemed as admitted, unless the intention to deny them is manifest in other statements of the party.

(4) A declaration of lack of knowledge concerning facts is only permissible with respect to facts as constitute neither the acts of such party nor the object of her perception.

§ **139**   [Substantial control of proceedings]

(1) The court shall, to the extent necessary, discuss with the parties the factual and legal aspects of the dispute and ask questions. It shall ensure that the parties make timely and complete statements with respect to all relevant facts, in particular supplement any inadequate statement of facts, designate the evidence and make the pertinent applications.

(2) The court may only base its decision, provided that it does not only concern an ancillary claim, on an aspect of case, which a party apparently ignored or deemed irrelevant if it has drawn attention to this aspect and offered the party the chance to make a statements in this respect. The same applies with respect to an aspect that the court assesses differently than the parties.

(3) The court shall draw attention to any misgivings that obtain with respect to matters to be considered ex offico.

(4) * * *

(5) * * *

§ **272**   [Determination of procedure]

(1) The action shall usually be dealt with in a comprehensively prepared session for the oral hearing (main hearing).

(2) The presiding judge shall either schedule a time for a preliminary first session for an oral hearing (§ 275) or order a preliminary written proceeding (§ 276).

(3) The conciliatory hearing and the oral hearing shall be held as soon as possible.

§ **273**   [Preparation of session]

(1) The court shall give directives for the required preparatory measure in a timely manner.

(2) For the purpose of preparing each session, the presiding judge or a member of the trial court designated by him may:

1. require the parties to supplement or clarify their preparatory pleadings, and in particular set a time limit for statements with regard to certain aspects of the case that need clarification;

2.   request public authorities or a public official to provide documents and to furnish official data;

3.   order the appearance in person of the parties;

4.   summon witnesses on whom the parties rely, and experts to appear at the oral hearing;

§ 275   [Early first session]

(1) In order to prepare the early first session for oral hearing the presiding judge or a member of the trial court designated by him may set a time limit for the defendant to file a written defence. Otherwise the defendant shall be requested to inform the court without delay, in a written pleading prepared by his lawyer to be appointed, of any means of defence which will be presented.

(2) If the proceedings will not be completed at the early first session for the oral hearing, the court shall issue all orders necessary for the preparation of the main session.

(3) The shall set a time limit for the filing of a written defence if the defendant has not yet or not adequately responded to the statement of claim and no time limit has been set pursuant to subparagraph 1 sentence 1.

(4) The court may, during the session or after the defence is filed, set a time limit for the claimant to reply in writing to the defence. * * *

§ 276   [Preliminary proceedings in writing]

(1) If the court does not order an early first session for an oral hearing, it shall request the defendant, when he is served with the statement of claim, to notify the court in writing within a fixed period of two weeks from the time of service of the statement of claim in the event he intends to defend against the claim; the claimant is to be informed of the request. At the same time, a time limit of no less than two more weeks shall be set for a written statement of defence. * * *

(3) The presiding judge may set a time limit for the claimant to reply in writing to the statement of defence.

§ 277   [Statement of defence; replication]

(1) In the statement of defence the defendant shall bring forth his means of defence to such extent as, in the circumstances of the case, is in accordance with a diligent and expeditious conduct of litigation. * * *

(3) The time limit for filing the defence pursuant to § 275 sub. 1 first sentence, sub. 3 is at least two weeks.

§ **279** [Oral hearing]

(1) If a party does not appear at the conciliatory session or if the conciliatory session proves unsuccessful, the oral hearing (early first session or main hearing) shall follow immediately. Otherwise the date for the oral hearing is to be set immediately.

(2) At the main session the taking of evidence shall immediately follow the exchange of arguments.

(3) Following the taking of evidence, the court shall again discuss with the parties the factual and legal circumstances of the case, and also, insofar as already possible, the result of the taking of evidence.

§ **282** [Timeliness of presentation]

(1) Each party shall present at the oral hearing its means of attack and of defence, in particular allegations, denials, pleas, objections, evidence and objections to evidence, in such a timely manner as is, in the state of the proceeding, in accordance with a diligent and expeditious conduct of litigation.

(2) Applications as well as means of attacks and of defence, to which the opponent is presumably unable to make submissions without prior inquiries, shall be communicated in writing in such a timely manner to enable the opponent to gather the necessary information.

(3) Protests with respect to the admissibility of the claim shall be presented by the defendant at the same time and prior to his appearance in the main issue. * * *

JAPAN

Takeshi Kojima, Japanese Civil Procedure in Comparative Law Perspective, 46 U. Kan. L. Rev. 687, 704–706 (1998).

3. Issue–Identifying Procedure

It was the practice under the former code that after the allegations were submitted as to the abstract operative facts, plenary hearings were held about once a month or once in two months. This practice made it difficult to keep the case in focus. To overcome this problem, the new code provides three choices: "preparatory plenary hearings," "proceedings preparatory to the plenary hearing," or "preparation by documents only." The court may choose which of these procedures to use after hearing the opinions of the parties. Of these three procedures, the "proceeding preparatory to the plenary hearings" is the most important and is regarded as an especially useful device to prepare for the concentrated hearing. A requirement common to all three issue identifying-procedures is that at the end of the procedure the court should make it clear what facts are to be proved in the later proof-taking. The effects of these procedures are not strict. There is an adversary party's right to ask questions (kitsumon-keu) and the party's duty to make explication (setsumei-gimu), but the right to raise issues and evidence later is not precluded.

a.   Preparatory Plenary Hearings

Under this procedure, the court may begin the plenary hearing by identifying and organizing the issues and evidence, if the court finds that is necessary. This preparation in open court may be used in cases in which parties are numerous or where a good deal of public concern or interest has been demonstrated.

b.   Proceeding Preparatory to the Plenary Hearings

This procedure is conducted by the court to which the complaint is assigned if the court determines that a separate preparatory hearing is necessary to identify and organize the issues and the evidence. This is the most commonly used among the three issue-identifying procedures. The court must consider the opinions of the parties before ordering this preparatory proceeding.

This proceeding must be conducted on a date when both parties are able to attend. The proceedings must be open to such people whom the court may admit as proper, unless either of the parties has requested closure and the court finds that closure is warranted. In short, preparatory plenary hearings are usually partially open to the public. Proceedings preparatory of plenary hearings can be conducted by a telephone conference if a party resides far away from the court or there is some other proper reason. However, at least one of the parties must be present in court.

The range of activities on the day of this proceeding is considerably expanded as compared to the former code. The court may rule on the production of evidence and on other matters that could be decided out of court. The court examines evidence in the form of documents and quasi-documents. As documents are the basic element of factual determination, examination of documents and quasi-documents provides a firm ground for identifying the real issues.

c.   Preparation by Documents Only

The court may hold the case preparation by documents only without either party present, if both live far away from the court or there is some other proper reason to use this procedure. In such a case, a due date must be fixed for submission of documents. A telephone conference may also be held if the parties or the court believes it is necessary.

Japanese Code of Civil Procedure.*

Article 161. (Preliminary document)

    1.   Oral argument shall be prepared for in writing.

* Translation by Masatoshi Kasai and Andrew Thorson, and included as end material in Takaaki Hattori and Dan Fenno Henderson, Civil Procedure in Japan (Yasuhei Taniguchi, Pauline C. Reich, and Hiroto Miyake, eds., Rev. 2nd ed. 2004).

2. Preliminary documents shall include the following matters:

    i.   offensive and defensive measures;

    ii. statements against the claims and offensive or defensive measures of the adversary party.

3. During an oral argument at which the adversary party is not present in court, facts shall not be asserted except for those facts written in preliminary documents (provided that they have been served on the adversary party or the adversary party submits a document stating that they were received by the adversary party).

Arrangement Proceedings of Point at Issue and Evidence *(Sôten oyobi Shôko no Seiri Tetsuzuki)*

Article 164. (Commencement of preliminary oral argument)

The court may, upon determining it necessary to arrange points at issue and evidence, conduct preliminary oral argument under the provisions of this subsection.

Article 165. (Confirmation of facts which should be proven, etc.)

1. The court shall confirm with the parties the facts which should be proven by the following examination of evidence at the end of the preliminary oral argument.

2. The presiding judge may, upon determining it proper, cause the parties to submit a document which summarizes the conclusions of the arrangement of points at issue and evidence in the preliminary oral argument at the conclusion thereof.

Article 167. (Advancement of offensive or defensive measures after conclusion of preliminary oral argument)

A party who advanced offensive or defensive measures after the conclusion of preliminary oral argument shall, if the adversary party requests, explain to the adversary party the reason why such measures could not *have* been advanced before the conclusion of preliminary oral argument.

Preparations for Argument Proceedings—*(Benron Junbi Tetsuzuki)*

Article 168. (Commencement of preparations for argument proceedings)

The court may, upon determining it necessary for conducting the arrangement of points at issue and evidence, after hearing opinions of the parties, refer the case to preparations for argument proceedings.

Article 173. (Statement of conclusion of preparations for argument proceedings)

The parties shall state the results of preparations for argument proceedings in oral argument.

Preparatory Proceedings by Document—*(Shomen ni yoru Junhi Tetsuzuki)*

Article 175. (Commencement of preparatory proceedings by document)

In cases where a party resides in a remote place or in any other cases deemed proper, the court may, after hearing opinions of the parties, refer the case to preparatory proceedings by document (this shall mean proceedings to arrange points at issue and evidence by submittal of preliminary documents, etc., without the appearance of parties. Hereinafter it shall mean the same).

Article 176. (Measures, etc., of preparatory proceedings by document)

1.   Preparatory proceedings by document shall be conducted by the presiding judge. However, in a high court they may be conducted by a commissioned judge.

2.   The presiding judge or a commissioned judge in a high court (in the following paragraph referred to as "the presiding judge, etc.") shall designate the period prescribed in Article 162.

3.   The presiding judge, etc., may, upon determining it necessary, hold a conference with both parties, regarding matters relating to the arrangement of points at issue and evidence or any other matters which are necessary for the preparations for oral argument, by means which enable the court and both parties to communicate simultaneously by transmission and reception of voice * * *.

ITALY

In Italy, the court tends to be closely involved in the identification of the issues.

Michele Taruffo, Civil Procedure and the Path of a Civil Case, in Introduction to Italian Law 166–168 (Jeffrey S. Lena and Ugo Mattei, eds., 2002).

IV.   Pleadings

The plaintiff commences civil proceedings by filing a complaint and having it served upon the defendant in the manner specified by law. The complaint must identify the *judge*, the *parties*, and the *claim* that is submitted to the court. The hearing at which the parties should appear before the judge must also be indicated. The *statement of claim* is aimed at defining the nature of the claim that the plaintiff has filed in the clearest and most complete way. Correspondingly, a detailed and possibly complete *statement of the facts* at issue is required, together with the legal arguments supporting the claim. The complaint must include the offer of evidence, oral and written, and the request for relief addressed to the judge (in effect, what judgment the judge is being requested to deliver). An especially important provision concerns the requirement of an analytical and complete statement of the legally relevant facts. It is usually said that the rationale for such a requirement is the need to have the claim clearly and completely identified by the plaintiff from the outset of the case in order to avoid uncertainties, prevent wasting time, and allow a quick assessment by the judge of the logical relevancy of evidence. Speaking in American terms, the Italian system is one based upon *fact pleading*, rather than bare notice pleading, although the intent and effect of the fact-based pleading is clearly to inform the defendant that there has been a claim filed against him or her. Therefore, it is assumed that by reading the complaint, the defendant will receive complete and detailed information not only about the subject matter of the claim, but also about the specific facts at issue, the legal arguments proposed, and the evidence offered by the plaintiff.

Within a period of time fixed by the law (twenty days before the hearing, indicated by the plaintiff for the first appearance of the parties in court), the defendant may file the answer. The answer is a written pleading that is roughly symmetrical to the plaintiff's complaint, since it contains all of the defendant's defenses. Different defense strategies are available. Defendants may limit themselves to a denial of the plaintiff's statements of fact and/or of law, but can also propose affirmative defenses by stating new facts that may block or eliminate the legal effects of the material facts stated by the plaintiff. In such cases, these facts should be completely and analytically stated (another feature of the fact-pleading system), since defendants are also required to establish their own versions of the case, in adequate terms, in the first pleading. Defendants will also develop legal arguments and offer any relevant evidence which may support their versions of the facts of the case. If the defendant has a right that can be asserted against the plaintiff, then a counterclaim shall be filed in the same pleading. The counterclaim shall also include a complete statement of the relevant facts, and an offer of evidence supporting such facts.

Theoretically the initial pleadings of the parties, taken together, should provide the judge and the parties with a complete statement of the case, including opposing versions of the factual and legal issues. In some simple cases, this may in fact occur. But things are often much more complicated.

On the one hand, it may be that the plaintiff has affirmative counter-defenses that may be opposed to the defendant's defenses or counterclaims. The law, therefore, allows the plaintiff to file such defenses later, at one of the hearings during the preparatory phase. On the other hand, the law allows a sort of fragmentation of the defendant's defenses, insofar as they may be filed at a later part of this phase (i.e. the defendant may appear and file a counterclaim but postpone the defenses to a later moment). Moreover, the law allows both parties, to make amendments to their first pleadings at the second hearing before the judge. At the same hearing, both parties are allowed to adjust or change their claims and defenses, and even to file new claims under certain conditions determined by the law. Finally, both parties are allowed to allege new circumstantial facts and to offer new evidence at a later hearing (it may be the third or the fourth one, and may take place several months or even more than one year after the filing of the complaint). All of this happens very frequently. It is clear, therefore, that the first pleadings are just the beginning of a complex and long phase of the proceedings, which is devoted just to achieving a reliable and reasonably complete definition of the legal and factual issues representing the actual "content" of the case as it is viewed by both parties. In fact, only at the end of this phase will the court and the parties be fully aware of the real nature of the case.

If one considers that the preparation of the case may require several months (or even a couple of years, in the worst case), and that many months or even some years may be necessary for the presentation of evidence ... , it is clear that first instance proceedings going from the complaint to the judgment may frequently be a very long, burdensome, and complex enterprise. It is also clear that this situation does not foster an effective administration of justice and an adequate protection of the parties' rights and interests. In order to reduce to some extent the awful consequences of such a system recent reforms—in 1973 for labor disputes, and in 1990 in general—introduced various kinds of provisional remedies. One primary example of these reforms is the court's obtaining power to issue orders in the course of ordinary proceedings in a sort of anticipation of certain possible contents of the final judgment. The aim of these orders is to allow the parties to receive some protection of their rights or interests, although with provisional and inconclusive effects, without waiting until the final decision is delivered. These orders may be issued, on a party's motion, under the following circumstances: (i) when a party has written proof of a right concerning the payment of a precise sum of money or the delivery of determined movable goods; (ii) when the adverse party does not deny the other party's right to receive a specific sum of money; (iii) in limited cases, when a party proves a right to receive a partial payment; and (iv) after the presentation of evidence, again, when a party has the right to receive a sum of money or the delivery of certain goods. In most cases, these orders are immediately enforceable, so that the interested party rapidly achieves some concrete effects. At any rate, the function of these orders is to anticipate some parts of the final judgment, which will actually layout the final statement of the parties' rights.

FRANCE

Loïc Cadiet, Civil Justice Reform: Access, Cost, and Delay. The French Perspective, in Civil Justice in Crisis 298–301 (Adrian A.S. Zuckerman, ed., 1999).

3.2. Commencement of ordinary proceedings

In principle, initiating the trial is up to the parties. However, the court only becomes *seized* of the case once a judge is in charge of the dispute. There needs to be a distinct act which can be recorded on the books (role) of the court.

3.2.1. *Requests which do not seize the Court—writs and "common requests"*

The issue of a writ is an act of the public officer of the court (*huissier*). By a writ, the plaintiff summons his opponent before the court. The common request is an act of both the parties by which they indicate to the judge their respective claims, the points on which they disagree and their legal arguments. Designed like a courteous substitute for a writ, the common request is an innovation of the new Civil Procedural Code. It is very rarely used, as it demands at least minimal co-operation between the parties. This is often impossible in contentious matters.

3.2.2. *Requests which do seize the Judge: request, declaration and voluntary appearance*

The initial request and the moment when the court is *seized* merge into one and the same operation when the initial request itself necessitates the intervention of the court. This happens in the case of the voluntary appearance of the parties before the judge. Thus the *Tribunal d'instance* and the Commercial Court are seized when the parties sign the record testifying their voluntary appearance.

3.2.3. *Effects of the court being seized.*

Although *seizing* the court has different specific consequences for each jurisdiction, it also entails some general procedural consequences. Firstly, the case is entered on the list of cases with which the court is seized. Each case on the list takes its turn on a specific assigned date. Secondly, the court clerk opens a procedure file for each case so listed. This file is the official record of the case. It will be referred to in case of an application, or an appeal. It is especially important in oral proceedings.

3.3. *Preliminary investigation of the case (L'instruction de l'affaire)*

The preliminary investigation of the case is an important step in the French civil process. It is within this period that the necessary procedural steps are completed to put the dispute into shape for hearing and decision (*mise en état*).

The form of the preliminary investigation differs between different courts. The Code contains the specific rules for each jurisdiction. Sometimes a specific investigation is undertaken before trial by a designated judge, as happens in the *Tribunal de Grande Instance* and the Court of Appeal. These two courts have a mainly written procedure. Sometimes the case is investigated at the trial itself, as in the Commercial Court, the *Tribunal d'instance*, and the Labour Court. These courts have a largely oral procedure. The key is the level of complexity of the case at the time when the Court is *seized*. Accordingly, even before the *Tribunal de Grande Instance* there are "fast tracks", cases on which are sent directly for hearing on the merits (*l'audience*). Conversely, especially in complex commercial cases, the case may go through a full separate preliminary investigation, under the authority of the *juge-rapporteur*.

Whatever the jurisdiction *seized*, the preliminary investigation phase always has the same object: putting the case into shape for decision. Most often, while the preliminary investigation is underway, parties will tend to narrow down the object and the grounds of their claim in their respective statements. More importantly, during the investigation, they will exchange, and present the judge with, the factual basis of their claim.

The rules of evidence are the same in all courts. On the whole, evidence may be adduced in two ways: by "written materials", or by "investigation measures". In this context, "written materials" means evidence which existed before the judicial intervention, whereas "investigation measures" means those created for the purposes of the court case, using the procedures of the court. In theory, there is a hierarchy between these different means of gathering evidence. An investigation measure ought to be ordered only if the party making an allegation does not have sufficient materials to prove it without the investigation measure. In practice, this is not the case. Investigation measures are quite easily ordered, especially the appointment by the court of an expert. This is not quite in the spirit of the new Code and it does, of course, increase delay and costs. This is especially true for the *Tribunal de Grande Instance* and the Commercial Court. Other jurisdictions do not face quite the same difficulty, especially the Labour Court, where the amount of litigation is high, and therefore few investigation measures are ordered.

3.4   Hearing and argument

Hearings are characterised mainly by publicity and orality. Orality of hearings is a trait common to all civil courts in France, even the *Tribunal de Grande Instance* where the preliminary investigation takes a mainly written form. Even the *Cour de Cassation* has recognised the parties' right to an oral hearing. This is all very well, but both practice and theory tend to minimise the importance of orality. In practice, oral hearings have tended to lose their importance before the civil courts. Most often they take the form of no more than brief oral observations, either made spontaneously, or in answer to questions from the judge. The President of the Court has a discretionary power to end the oral hearing when he thinks fit. Sometimes, the hearing is dispensed with altogether, in favour of the *dossier de plaidoirie*. The development of preliminary investigation of cases, the congestion of the courts, and the weight of judges' preliminary hearings, tend to explain this development, for which advocates must also bear responsibility. The new Civil Procedural Code emphasises this trend, with its decrease in orality.

Publicity of hearings does not call for much discussion. Part of the right to a fair trial, under article 6 § 1 of the European Convention on Human Rights, the principle of publicity can not be dispensed with, except in cases prescribed by statute. Statutory provision has been made in the case of non-contentious matters, and in certain matters relating to capacity (divorce, for example).

3.5   Chronology

In principle, it is always possible to fix a date for the hearing in advance. This date is normally known as soon as the initial request is made in oral proceedings. In written proceedings, a date is set on completion of the *mise en état*. The hearing must then take place on the date fixed. Hearings generally take any time from a few minutes to several hours.[43] If the parties agree, or if there is a legitimate reason, of greater significance than a mere personal circumstance, it is possible to ask the judge to postpone the case to a later date (*remise/renvoi*). The decision to postpone is regarded as a matter of judicial administration, and is in the discretion of the judge. Once oral argument begins the hearing may not be interrupted.

The hearing is conducted before the president. In addition, the clerk keeps the record of the hearing (the *plumitif*).[44] Speaking order during the hearing is determined by law. The plaintiff puts his or her case first, then the defendant, and then the public prosecutor (if he is involved). The president and judges may decide to hear the parties again, if they require further argument on the facts or on the law.

The hearing is closed by the president, as soon as he or she considers the court is sufficiently well informed.

V.   LEARNING THE FACTS—DISCOVERY

ENGLAND

Access to court would not enable citizens to obtain adequate protection for their rights, unless the courts were able and willing to assist them to secure the evidence they need in order to establish those rights. Accordingly, all modern systems employ some compulsory measures to secure relevant evidence. Most systems empower the court to summon witnesses and compel them to testify, most systems impose sanctions for perjury, and many systems authorise the court to order delivery up of documents or real evidence. In common law systems the right of access to evidence is taken much further.

---

43. [Editor's Note: footnote in original]: Here the difficulty of using the word "trial" in the context of the French civil process becomes apparent. There is clearly nothing very much like an English-type trial about the hearing in the French civil context.

44. [Editor's Note: footnote in original]: Keeping this record, which is signed by the President and the Court Clerk after each hearing, allows those concerned to check whether all the legal requirements have been complied with.

Common law systems provide more comprehensive facilities of access to evidence than their continental counterparts.[6] It is in the public interest, Lord Lloyd said, 'that all relevant material should be available to courts when deciding cases. Courts should not have to reach decisions in ignorance of documents or other material which, if disclosed, might well affect the outcome'.[7] 'It would be artificial and undesirable', Lord Woolf CJ has more recently observed, 'for the actual evidence, which is relevant and admissible, not to be placed before the judge who has the task of trying the case'.[8] There is therefore a general presumption in common law systems that all relevant evidence is admissible and should be accessible. The commitment of these systems to assisting litigants to discover and obtain relevant evidence is demonstrated by the variety of devices they place at the service of litigants for the purpose of gaining access to evidence.

In *Flight v Robinson*[9] Lord Langdale MR said:

However disagreeable it may be to make the disclosure, however contrary to [a party's] personal interests, however fatal to the claim upon which he may have insisted, he is required and compelled, under the most solemn sanction, to set forth all he knows, believes, or thinks in relation to the matters in question * * *. [By this means] the greatest security * * * is afforded, for the discovery of all relevant truth, and by means of such discovery, this Court * * * has, at all times, proved to be of transcendent utility in the administration of justice.

One of the more distinctive features of common law systems of litigation has been the discovery process, whereby litigants are able to see each other's documents in advance of the trial. Access to relevant documentary material that is in the hands of other parties to the dispute promotes equality of arms and contributes to the ascertainment of truth. Mutual pretrial disclosure helps reduce information and resource inequality. It increases the prospects of settlement by enabling litigants to make an early and well-informed assessment of their respective chances of success in the litigation.

It should be stressed that in modern English procedure disclosure is but one component of what has come to be known as the 'cards on the table approach'. This approach seeks to ensure that parties to a dispute are able to find out as much as possible about each other's case as early as possible, so that no party is taken by surprise and so that the court is appraised well before the trial of the nature and extent of the evidence.

---

6. PF Schlosser 'Trial and Court Procedures in Continental Europe' in C Platto (ed) Trial and Court Procedures Worldwide (1991) Lord Chancellor's Advisory Board on Family Law [London]; W Habscheid and S Berti 'European Summary' in C Platto (ed) Pre-Trial and Pre–Hearing Procedures Worldwide (1990).

7. R v Derby Magistrates' Court, ex p B [1996] 1 AC 487 at 510, [1995] 4 All ER 526 at 543–544 (HL).

8. Jones v University of Warwick [2003] EWCA Civ 151, [2003] 3 All ER 760, [2003] 1 WLR 954.

9. Flight v Robinson (1844) 8 Beav 22, 50 ER 9, respectively at pp 33–34 and at pp 13–14.

While the advantages of discovery have been plain for a long time, what had been insufficiently appreciated or articulated before the Woolf Reports on *Access to Justice* was that there could be too much disclosure as well as too little disclosure. Discovery could be very laborious and very costly without producing worthwhile results. It is clear that the further we move away from documents with a direct connection to the issues, the less likely it is that the documents will make a substantial contribution to the resolution of the issues. Far from clarifying the facts, an excess of documents may tend to complicate and confuse the issues and undermine the court's ability to get to the truth. It is therefore not only in the interests of economy that the disclosure process needs to be controlled but also in the interest of truth finding.

The disclosure arrangements under the CPR seek to avoid the waste and the excesses of the previous system without losing the principal advantages that mutual disclosure of documents are meant to produce. The CPR impose a constraint of proportionality, which seeks to ensure that the benefits of disclosure are not outweighed by the effort and the cost that have to be invested in the process. Under the CPR, disclosure in the majority of cases is limited to *standard disclosure*, which effectively includes only documents of direct relevance to the issues. However, the court has the power to direct more extensive disclosure in those few cases that are likely to benefit from a deeper and wider search for documents.

The disclosure regime under the CPR is broadly as follows. An informal disclosure process would normally take place even before commencement of proceedings. The pre-action protocols call for meaningful pre-action exchanges between prospective parties, including exchanges of relevant documents. The formal disclosure process is largely governed by CPR 31, which applies to fast track and multi-track proceedings (limited disclosure is provided for the small claims track by CPR 27.2). In the fast track and multi-track there is also substantial scope for obtaining pre-action compulsory disclosure from prospective parties and even from non-parties. Where there is a real prospect of litigation, potential parties may seek an order compelling potential adversaries to disclose directly relevant documents so as to enable them to assess the advisability of litigation. Once proceedings have commenced, disclosure may be obtained from non-parties in certain circumstances. Similarly, the victim of a wrong may obtain from a non-party disclosure of the identity of the wrongdoer or other information that is crucial to his ability to bring proceedings in order to vindicate his rights.

There are two main exceptions to the right of inspection, as distinguished from the obligation of disclosure of the existence of documents. The first exception concerns situations where the disclosing party has a right or duty to withhold a document from inspection. A right to withhold a document from inspection exists where a party is entitled to legal professional privilege or to the privilege against self-incrimination. A duty to withhold a document may exist where disclosure would be harmful to the public interest. Second, the court may exempt a party from the obligation of disclosure on an ad hoc basis, for instance, where inspection would be disproportionate to the needs of the case (CPR 31.3(2)). However, there is no exception to the right to inspect a document that has been mentioned in a statement of case, in a witness statement, in a witness summary, or in an affidavit (CPR 31.14).

Where a party refuses to disclose a document or facilitate its inspection, the court may exercise its general powers to enforce compliance, including dismissal of the party's statement of case.

Civil Procedure Rules (The White Book Service, 2006).

CPR 31.2 Meaning of disclosure

A party discloses a document by stating that the document exists or has existed.

CPR 31.3 Right of inspection of a disclosed document

(1) A party to whom a document has been disclosed has a right to inspect that document except where—* * *

(b) the party disclosing the document has a right or a duty to withhold inspection of it; . . .

(2) Where a party considers that it would be disproportionate to the issues in the case to permit inspection of documents within a category or class of document disclosed under rule 31.6(b)—

(a) he is not required to permit inspection of documents within that category or class; but

(b) he must state in his disclosure statement that inspection of those documents will not be permitted on the grounds that to do so would be disproportionate.

CPR 31.5 Disclosure limited to standard disclosure

(1). An order to give disclosure is an order to give standard disclosure unless the court directs otherwise.

CPR 31. 6 Standard disclosure—what documents are to be disclosed

Standard disclosure requires a party to disclose only—

(a) the documents on which he relies; and

(b) the documents which—

(i) adversely affect his own case;

(ii) adversely affect another party's case; or

(iii) support another party's case; * * *

CPR 31.7 Duty of search

(1) When giving standard disclosure, a party is required to make a reasonable search for documents falling within rule 31.6(b) or (c).

(2) The factors relevant in deciding the reasonableness of a search include the following—

(a) the number of documents involved;

(b) the nature and complexity of the proceedings;

(c) the ease and expense of retrieval of any particular document; and

(d) the significance of any document which is likely to be located during the search.

(3) Where a party has not searched for a category or class of document on the grounds that to do so would be unreasonable, he must state this in his disclosure statement and identify the category or class of document.

CPR 32. 8 Duty of disclosure limited to documents which are or have been in a party's control

(1) A party's duty to disclose documents is limited to documents which are or have been in his control.

(2) For this purpose a party has or has had a document in his control if—

(a) it is or was in his physical possession;

(b) he has or has had a right to possession of it; or

(c) he has or has had a right to inspect or take copies of it.

CPR 31.10 Procedure for standard disclosure

(1) The procedure for standard disclosure is as follows.

(2) Each party must make and serve on every other party, a list of documents in the relevant practice form.

(3) The list must identify the documents in a convenient order and manner and as concisely as possible.

(4) The list must indicate—(a) those documents in respect of which the party claims a right or duty to withhold inspection; and (b) (i) those documents which are no longer in the party's control; and (ii) what has happened to those documents.

(5) The list must include a disclosure statement.

(6) A disclosure statement is a statement made by the party disclosing the documents—(a) setting out the extent of the search that has been made to locate documents which he is required to disclose; (b) certifying that he understands the duty to disclose documents; and (c) certifying that to the best of his knowledge he has carried out that duty.

CPR 31.14 Documents referred to in statements of case etc.

(1) A party may inspect a document mentioned in—(a) a statement of case; (b) a witness statement; (c) a witness summary; or (d) an affidavit.

CPR 31.16 Disclosure before proceedings start

(1) This rule applies where an application is made to the court under any Act for disclosure before proceedings have started.

(2) The application must be supported by evidence.

(3) The court may make an order under this rule only where—

(a) the respondent is likely to be a party to subsequent proceedings;

(b) the applicant is also likely to be a party to those proceedings;

(c) if proceedings had started, the respondent's duty by way of standard disclosure, set out in rule 31.6, would extend to the documents or classes of documents of which the applicant seeks disclosure; and

(d) disclosure before proceedings have started is desirable in order to—(i) dispose fairly of the anticipated proceedings; (ii) assist the dispute to be resolved without proceedings; or (iii) save costs.

CPR 31.17 Orders for disclosure against a person not a party

(1) This rule applies where an application is made to the court under any Act for disclosure by a person who is not a party to the proceedings.

(2) The application must be supported by evidence.

(3) The court may make an order under this rule only where—

(a) the documents of which disclosure is sought are likely to support the case of the applicant or adversely affect the case of one of the other parties to the proceedings; and

(b) disclosure is necessary in order to dispose fairly of the claim or to save costs.

Note on Respect for Confidentiality and Privacy

A tension may arise between, on the one hand, the interests of the administration of justice in seeing that disputes are resolved in accordance with all the relevant evidence, and on the other hand the interests of the parties or non-parties in protecting their confidences and their private affairs. Where the court is asked to limit documentary or testimonial disclosure in order to protect some other interest, the starting point is that no one has a right to withhold documents or information on the grounds that to do so would violate an obligation of confidence or would amount to an invasion of privacy.[10] However, the court may consider such interests in the exercise of its discretion.

An illustration of the exercise of this discretion is provided by *Science Research Council v Nassé*.[11] The House of Lords dealt with two cases in which claimants complained of discrimination in employment and sought disclosure of confidential reports relating to other candidates for appointment. It was held that such confidential documents were not protected by public interest immunity. However, an order of disclosure was discretionary. In exercising that discretion the court should not order discovery unless it was necessary either for disposing fairly of the proceedings or for saving costs. When exercising that discretion, in relation to confidential documents, the court should in the interests of justice have regard to (a) the fact that the documents were confidential and that to order disclosure would involve a breach of confidence and (b) the extent to which the interest of third parties would be affected by disclosure. The court was not bound to order discovery of all documents which were relevant if, for example, the information could be obtained from other sources. If however discovery was necessary for fairly disposing of the proceedings discovery must be ordered notwithstanding the documents' confidentiality. In deciding whether discovery was necessary for that reason the tribunal should first inspect the documents and consider whether justice could be done by special measures, such as covering up confidential but irrelevant parts of the documents, substituting anonymous references for specific names, or, in rare cases, a hearing in camera. In the instant case the House of Lords concluded that discovery should not have been ordered in either of the two cases without the respective tribunals first inspecting the documents and applying the above test.

Note on Search Orders

In 1976 the seminal case of Anton Piller KG v Manufacturing Processes [1976] Ch 55 brought into existence the civil search order, which prior to the CPR was known as an *Anton Piller* order. The jurisdiction to make such orders has since been put on a statutory basis by the Civil Procedure Act 1997, § 7:

> 7.   Power of courts to make orders for preserving evidence, etc.
>
>   (1) The court may make an order under this section for the purpose of securing, in the case of any existing or proposed proceedings in the court—the preservation of evidence which is or may be relevant, or the preservation of property which is or may be the subject-matter of the proceedings or as to which any question arises or may arise in the proceedings.
>
>   (2) A person who is, or appears to the court likely to be, a party to proceedings in the court may make an application for such an order.

10. Alfred Crompton Amusement Machines Ltd v Comrs of Customs and Excise (No 2) [1974] AC 405, [1973] 2 All ER 1169.

11. Science Research Council v Nassé; BL Cars Ltd (formerly Leyland Cars) v Vyas [1980] AC 1028, [1979] 3 All ER 673.

(3) Such an order may direct any person to permit any person described in the order, or secure that any person so described is permitted—to enter premises in England and Wales, and while on the premises, to take in accordance with the terms of the order any of the following steps.

(4) Those steps are—to carry out a search for or inspection of anything described in the order, and to make or obtain a copy, photograph, sample or other record of anything so described.

(5) The order may also direct the person concerned—to provide any person described in the order, or secure that any person so described is provided, with any information or article described in the order, and to allow any person described in the order, or secure that any person so described is allowed, to retain for safe keeping anything described in the order.

A search order is normally made without notice and before service of originating process on the respondent. It directs the respondent (who is usually a defendant) to permit authorised persons described in the order to enter the respondent's premises in order to search, inspect, copy or take away items described in the order. The order may direct the respondent to provide the authorised persons with information or article described in the order and to allow such person to remove for safe keeping anything described in the order. A search order, it must be stressed, does not authorise forcible entry or the doing of anything without the consent or co-operation of the person to whom the order is directed. A refusal to allow entry and to comply with the requirements of the order may amount to contempt of court.[12]

The guidelines, which are set out in Practice Direction to CPR 25, Interim Remedies, seek to ensure that oppressive practices are avoided. They seek to safeguard the interests of the defendant and to ensure that a search process is carried out with appropriate regard for the defendant's interests and with the utmost propriety.

A search order must contain an undertaking by the applicant to serve the application notice, the evidence in its support and any order made on the respondent as soon as practicable and an undertaking to pay any damages which the court considers that the applicant should pay to the respondent (PD 25A, 5). If made without notice, the order must contain a return date for a further hearing in the presence of all the parties.

THE UNITED STATES

Jack H. Friedenthal, Arthur R. Miller, John E. Sexton, and Helen Hershkoff, Civil Procedure: Cases and Materials 735–736 (9th ed. 2005).

Modern discovery serves a number of purposes that are important to individual litigants and to the civil justice system as a whole. From the private perspective, the first, and least controversial, is the preservation

---

12. Practice Direction (Judgments and Orders) para. 9.1.

of relevant information that might not be available at trial. Basically, this objective relates to the testimony of witnesses who are aged or ill or who will be out of the jurisdiction at the time the trial commences. The earliest discovery procedures in the federal courts were designed primarily for this purpose. See *Developments in the Law—Discovery,* 74 Harv. L.Rev. 940, 949 (1961). The second purpose is to ascertain and isolate those issues that actually are in controversy between the parties. There is little dispute that it is appropriate for one party to ask whether another party contests the existence or nonexistence of a fact that the pleadings formally have put in issue. A third purpose of discovery is to find out what testimony and other evidence is available on each of the disputed factual issues. Prior to discovery, a party could ascertain these matters only through private investigation; if, for example, a witness refused to discuss a matter with a party, there was no way to learn the substance of that witness's testimony in advance of trial. As a result, cases often turned on the parties' relative access to the facts and their ability to keep certain matters secret until the trial. Views about discovery reflect a division between those who favor broad discovery to obviate all traces of surprise and those who allege the need for privacy of investigation and development of evidence.

In addition to facilitating the fair and efficient conduct of individual litigation, discovery also promotes important public interests. Judge Higginbotham, of the United States Court of Appeals for the Fifth Circuit, explains:

> Over the years access to the powerful federal engine of discovery has become central to a wide array of social policies. Congress has elected to use the private suit, private attorneys-general as an enforcing mechanism for the anti-trust laws, the securities laws, environmental laws, civil rights and more. In the main, the plaintiff in these suits must discover his evidence from the defendant. Calibration of discovery is calibration of the level of enforcement of the social policy set by Congress.

Higginbotham, *Foreword,* 49 Ala. L. Rev. 1, 4–5 (1997). Professor Carrington adds:

> Private litigants do in America much of what is done in other industrial states by public officers working within an administrative bureaucracy. Every day, hundreds of American lawyers caution their clients that an unlawful course of conduct will be accompanied by serious risk of exposure at the hands of some hundreds of thousands of lawyers, each armed with a subpoena power by which misdeeds can be uncovered. Unless corresponding new powers are conferred on public officers, constricting discovery would diminish the disin-

centives for lawless behavior across a wide spectrum of forbidden conduct.

Carrington, *Renovating Discovery,* 49 Ala. L. Rev. 51, 54 (1997).

* * *

Relevance under the Federal Rules is limited by the concept of proportionality, introduced by amendment in 1983 and currently set out in Rule 26(b). The reporter to the Advisory Committee that first adopted the principle of proportionality called it a "180–degree shift" in discovery philosophy. * * * The goal of proportionality is "to promote judicial limitation of the amount of discovery on a case-by-case basis to avoid abuse or overuse of discovery * * *." 9 Wright, Miller and Marcus, Federal Practice and Procedure: Civil 2d § 2008.1 (1994). In response to reports that lawyers and judges were not abiding by the principle of proportionality, the discovery rules were again amended in 2000 to underscore this limitation.

Federal Rules of Civil Procedure

Rule 26 General Provisions Governing Discovery; Duty of Disclosure

(a) Required Disclosures; Methods to Discover Additional Matter.

(1) Initial Disclosures.

Except in categories of proceedings specified in Rule 26(a)(1)(E), or to the extent otherwise stipulated or directed by order, a party must, without awaiting a discovery request, provide to other parties:

(A) the name and, if known, the address and telephone number of each individual likely to have discoverable information that the disclosing party may use to support its claims or defenses, unless solely for impeachment, identifying the subjects of the information;

(B) a copy of, or a description by category and location of, all documents, data compilations, and tangible things that are in the possession, custody, or control of the party and that the disclosing party may use to support its claims or defenses, unless solely for impeachment;

(C) a computation of any category of damages claimed by the disclosing party, making available for inspection and copying as under Rule 34 the documents or other evidentiary material, not privileged or protected from disclosure, on which such computation is based, including materials bearing on the nature and extent of injuries suffered; and

(D) for inspection and copying as under Rule 34 any insurance agreement under which any person carrying on an insurance business may be liable to satisfy part or all of a judgment which may be entered in the action or to indemnify or reimburse for payments made to satisfy the judgment.

* * *

(2) Disclosure of Expert Testimony.

(A) In addition to the disclosures required by paragraph (1), a party shall disclose to other parties the identity of any person who may be used at trial to present evidence under Rules 702, 703, or 705 of the Federal Rules of Evidence.

(B) Except as otherwise stipulated or directed by the court, this disclosure shall, with respect to a witness who is retained or specially employed to provide expert testimony in the case or whose duties as an employee of the party regularly involve giving expert testimony, be accompanied by a written report prepared and signed by the witness. The report shall contain a complete statement of all opinions to be expressed and the basis and reasons therefor; the data or other information considered by the witness in forming the opinions; any exhibits to be used as a summary of or support for the opinions; the qualifications of the witness, including a list of all publications authored by the witness within the preceding ten years; the compensation to be paid for the study and testimony; and a listing of any other cases in which the witness has testified as an expert at trial or by deposition within the preceding four years.

(C) These disclosures shall be made at the times and in the sequence directed by the court. In the absence of other directions from the court or stipulation by the parties, the disclosures shall be made at least 90 days before the trial date or the date the case is to be ready for trial or, if the evidence is intended solely to contradict or rebut evidence on the same subject matter identified by another party under paragraph (2)(B), within 30 days after the disclosure made by the other party. The parties shall supplement these disclosures when required under subdivision (e)(1).

(3) Pretrial Disclosures.

In addition to the disclosures required by Rule 26(a)(1) and (2), a party must provide to other parties and promptly file with the court the following information regarding the evidence that it may present at trial other than solely for impeachment:

(A) the name and, if not previously provided, the address and telephone number of each witness, separately identifying those whom the party expects to present and those whom the party may call if the need arises;

(B) the designation of those witnesses whose testimony is expected to be presented by means of a deposition and, if not taken stenographically, a transcript of the pertinent portions of the deposition testimony; and

(C) an appropriate identification of each document or other exhibit, including summaries of other evidence, separately identifying those which the party expects to offer and those which the party may offer if the need arises.

Unless otherwise directed by the court, these disclosures must be made at least 30 days before trial. Within 14 days thereafter, unless a different time is specified by the court, a party may serve and promptly file a list disclosing (i) any objections to the use under Rule 32(a) of a deposition designated by another party under Rule 26(a)(3)(B), and (ii) any objection, together with the grounds therefor, that may be made to the admissibility of materials identified under Rule 26(a)(3)(C). Objections not so disclosed, other than objections under Rules 402 and 403 of the Federal Rules of Evidence, are waived unless excused by the court for good cause.

(4) Form of Disclosures; Filing.

Unless the court orders otherwise, all disclosures under Rules 26(a)(1) through (3) must be made in writing, signed, and served.

(5) Methods to Discover Additional Matter.

Parties may obtain discovery by one or more of the following methods: depositions upon oral examination or written questions; written interrogatories; production of documents or things or permission to enter upon land or other property under Rule 34 or 45(a)(1)(C), for inspection and other purposes; physical and mental examinations; and requests for admission.

(b) Discovery Scope and Limits.

Unless otherwise limited by order of the court in accordance with these rules, the scope of discovery is as follows:

(1) In General.

Parties may obtain discovery regarding any matter, not privileged, that is relevant to the claim or defense of any party, including the existence, description, nature, custody, condition, and location of any books, documents, or other tangible things and the identity and location of persons having knowledge of any discoverable matter. For good cause, the court may order discovery of any matter relevant to the subject matter involved in the action. Relevant information need not be admissible at the trial if the discovery appears reasonably calculated to lead to the discovery of admissible evidence. All discovery is subject to the limitations imposed by Rule 26(b)(2)(i), (ii), and (iii).

(2) Limitations.

By order, the court may alter the limits in these rules on the number of depositions and interrogatories or the length of depositions under Rule 30. By order or local rule, the court may also limit the number of requests under Rule 36. The frequency or extent of use of the discovery methods otherwise permitted under these rules and by any local rule shall be limited by the court if it determines that: (i) the discovery sought is unreasonably cumulative or duplicative, or is obtainable from some other source that is more convenient, less burdensome, or less expensive; (ii) the party seeking discovery has had ample opportunity by discovery in the action to obtain the information sought; or (iii) the burden or expense of the proposed discovery outweighs its likely benefit, taking into account the needs of the case, the amount in controversy, the parties' resources, the importance of the issues at stake in the litigation, and the importance of the proposed discovery in resolving the issues. The court may act upon its own initiative after reasonable notice or pursuant to a motion under Rule 26(c).

(3) Trial Preparation: Materials.

Subject to the provisions of subdivision (b)(4) of this rule, a party may obtain discovery of documents and tangible things otherwise discoverable under subdivision (b)(1) of this rule and prepared in anticipation of litigation or for trial by or for another party or by or for that other party's representative (including the other party's attorney, consultant, surety, indemnitor, insurer, or agent) only upon a showing that the party seeking discovery has substantial need of the materials in the preparation of the party's case and that the party is unable without undue hardship to obtain the substantial equivalent of the materials by other means. In ordering discovery of such materials when the required showing has been made, the court shall protect against disclosure of the mental impressions, conclusions, opinions, or legal theories of an attorney or other representative of a party concerning the litigation.

A party may obtain without the required showing a statement concerning the action or its subject matter previously made by that party. Upon request, a person not a party may obtain without the required showing a statement concerning the action or its subject matter previously made by that person. If the request is refused, the person may move for a court order. The provisions of Rule 37(a)(4) apply to the award of expenses incurred in relation to the motion. For purposes of this paragraph, a statement previously made is (A) a written statement signed or otherwise adopted or approved by the person making it, or (B) a stenographic, mechanical, electrical, or other recording, or a transcription thereof, which is a substantially verbatim recital of an oral statement by the person making it and contemporaneously recorded.

(4) Trial Preparation: Experts.

(A) A party may depose any person who has been identified as an expert whose opinions may be presented at trial. If a report from the expert is required under subdivision (a)(2)(B), the deposition shall not be conducted until after the report is provided.

(B) A party may, through interrogatories or by deposition, discover facts known or opinions held by an expert who has been retained or specially employed by another party in anticipation of litigation or preparation for trial and who is not expected to be called as a witness at trial, only as provided in Rule 35(b) or upon a showing of exceptional circumstances under which it is impracticable for the party seeking discovery to obtain facts or opinions on the same subject by other means.

(C) Unless manifest injustice would result, (i) the court shall require that the party seeking discovery pay the expert a reasonable fee for time spent in responding to discovery under this subdivision; and (ii) with respect to discovery obtained under subdivision (b)(4)(B) of this rule the court shall require the party seeking discovery to pay the other party a fair portion of the fees and expenses reasonably incurred by the latter party in obtaining facts and opinions from the expert.

(5) Claims of Privilege or Protection of Trial Preparation Materials.

When a party withholds information otherwise discoverable under these rules by claiming that it is privileged or subject to protection as trial preparation material, the party shall make the claim expressly and shall describe the nature of the documents, communications, or things not produced or disclosed in a manner that, without revealing information itself privileged or protected, will enable other parties to assess the applicability of the privilege or protection.

(c) Protective Orders.

Upon motion by a party or by the person from whom discovery is sought, accompanied by a certification that the movant has in good faith conferred or attempted to confer with other affected parties in an effort to resolve the dispute without court action, and for good cause shown, the court in which the action is pending or alternatively, on matters relating to a deposition, the court in the district where the deposition is to be taken may make any order which justice requires to protect a party or person from annoyance, embarrassment, oppression, or undue burden or expense, including one or more of the following:

(1) that the disclosure or discovery not be had;

(2) that the disclosure or discovery may be had only on specified terms and conditions, including a designation of the time or place;

(3) that the discovery may be had only by a method of discovery other than that selected by the party seeking discovery;

(4) that certain matters not be inquired into, or that the scope of the disclosure or discovery be limited to certain matters;

(5) that discovery be conducted with no one present except persons designated by the court;

(6) that a deposition, after being sealed, be opened only by order of the court;

(7) that a trade secret or other confidential research, development, or commercial information not be revealed or be revealed only in a designated way; and

(8) that the parties simultaneously file specified documents or information enclosed in sealed envelopes to be opened as directed by the court.

If the motion for a protective order is denied in whole or in part, the court may, on such terms and conditions as are just, order that any party or other person provide or permit discovery. The provisions of Rule 37(a)(4) apply to the award of expenses incurred in relation to the motion.

* * *

(g) Signing of Disclosures, Discovery Requests, Responses, and Objections.

(1) Every disclosure made pursuant to subdivision (a)(1) or subdivision (a)(3) shall be signed by at least one attorney of record in the attorney's individual name, whose address shall be stated. An unrepresented party shall sign the disclosure and state the party's address. The signature of

the attorney or party constitutes a certification that to the best of the signer's knowledge, information, and belief, formed after a reasonable inquiry, the disclosure is complete and correct as of the time it is made.

GERMANY

Common law discovery does not exist in German civil procedure. There is neither a specific phase during the proceedings in which the parties have to collect their evidentiary material nor a general duty of comprehensive disclosure of all relevant facts and evidence. According to the procedural conception of the German Code of Civil Procedure, the taking of evidence takes place during the main hearing. The relevant facts therefore have to be gathered during the preparatory stage of the proceedings between the initial pleadings and the final main hearing. Which evidence has to be disclosed and taken depends on the issues of the case that cannot be clarified during the exchange of the pleadings and particulars of the case. Since every factual assertion in a written pleading has to be accompanied with a designation of the evidence that proves the assertion (§ 130 ZPO), the interplay between party submissions and court case management lead to the establishment of the relevant facts and evidence that then form the basis of the final judgment.

In regard of the allegations of fact the burden of proof originates from the substantive civil law. The rule is that each party must offer the evidence and eventually prove all the asserted facts which are necessary to justify its claim or defence unless the other party does not dispute a fact or set of facts. This basic principle that each party has to make its own case goes along with the so-called golden rule of German disclosure duties, which follow the *nemo tenetur* principle: 'A party is not obliged to give the weapons into the other party's hands.'[13]

This does not mean, however, that disclosure of (unfavourable) evidence is unknown in German courts. Disclosure of evidence does exist, although it differs from the English model both in its structure and in its scope. German disclosure can be described as a 'patchwork' system,[14] as it is not as neatly regulated in the German Code of Civil Procedure as it is in the CPR but consists of a mixture of different specific claims for disclosing evidence, which can be found either in procedural law or in substantive law.

From a procedural point of view, the basic provision for gathering the relevant facts is § 138 ZPO. It stipulates that the parties are obliged to make comprehensive and truthful allegations of fact. A litigant may neither lie nor withhold deliberately any relevant information, including harmful evidence. Where a party's submissions are unclear or ambiguous

---

13. BGH [2000] Neue Juristische Wochenschrift 1108, 1109.

14. Peter Schlosser, Die lange deutsche Reise in die prozessuale Moderne, Juristenzeitung 599, 604 (1991).

as regards the factual circumstances of the case, the court will order it to provide the necessary clarifications during the proceedings.

Since the parties do not have a general procedural right to obtain the relevant information, they have to rely on their personal knowledge and on the material in their possession. Furthermore, parties may only make submissions in relation to facts, which are directly relevant for the determination of the legal right in dispute. If the other side contests an allegation, the judge will then take evidence in order to verify the point in dispute.[15] However, evidence is taken not only if the court deems it necessary but also on a party's application.

The substantive law recognises a right to obtain information in certain circumstances. Thus, German law contains both substantive and procedural disclosure rights. Substantive disclosure rights are scattered throughout innumerable statutes of the civil law. Where no statutory right exists, the courts may grant disclosure on a good faith or 'equity' basis.[16] The substantive disclosure rights have to be enforced in separate court proceedings. However, since these rights exist independently of any litigation, information can often be obtained without any proceedings. Thus German law provides a system of free-standing rights to information. In legal proceedings the court may order production of documents in relation to which such a right exists (§ 422 ZPO). It may oblige the opposing party to produce a document if the party wishing to rely on this documentary evidence is entitled to demand the production of the document under the substantial civil law.

By contrast to substantive disclosure rights, specific procedural disclosure rights are scarce. One of them is granted in § 423 ZPO, which stipulates that a party has to disclosure those documents on which it relies in its submissions. The 2001 reform of the ZPO introduced a new procedural right to documentary disclosure. § 142 ZPO now provides that the court may order the other party or a non-party to disclose a specific document if one of the parties refers to it in its submissions. This provision therefore allows a party to refer to a specific document, which is in the other's party possession, and requests its disclosure. The court has discretion whether to grant the order or not. When exercising this discretion, the court has to balance the interest of the requesting party to prove a relevant fact of its case against the other party's interest of confidentiality. However, procedural orders for documentary disclosure are not directly enforceable. All the judge can do if a party refuses to comply with the order is to take this behaviour into account in its final decision, i.e. to draw adverse inferences from non-compliance. Finally, a party may also initiate separate evidentiary proceedings, which are available if there is a risk of loss of evidence or if the determination of certain facts may help to avoid litigation.

---

15. Leo Rosenberg Karl–Heinz Schwab and Peter Gottwald, Zivilprozessrecht 738 (16th ed. 2004).

16. See, e.g., BGH [1994] Neue Juristische Wochenschrift 1958.

Where a party lacks knowledge as to potentially relevant facts, it may make allegations without precise knowledge as to their truthfulness. Only completely arbitrary submissions 'out of the blue' are forbidden.[17] Therefore, parties who wish to obtain a particular piece of evidence often make an application to the court on mere speculation. In these cases, the party sometimes does not meet its obligation to make substantial factual allegations, so that the court might disregard such allegations as being insufficiently founded.

Like their Common Law counterparts, however, the German system has always been aware that a party cannot present detailed facts or offer specified means of evidence, if it lacks sufficient knowledge of these facts of evidence. This problem is encountered where the relevant facts are within the opponent's peculiar sphere of knowledge or that of a non-party. Since 'fishing' for evidence that is not directly relevant is contrary to general principles of German civil procedure, parties are sometimes in dire straits regarding their access to crucial information. In such a case, German courts may nevertheless order the production of documents on the basis of more general factual allegations or a more general description of a class of documents in the possession of the opponent or a third party.

Thus, the courts grant access to evidence where the disparity of information between the parties threatens to impede justice and reliable knowledge of the facts depends on a mosaic of circumstantial facts.[18] In 1989 for example, the Federal Supreme Court (*Bundesgerichtshof*) allowed a medical student who had been infected by a virus to inspect the research records of the university hospital where she had been working. The court granted access to all documents within a period of six years in order to enable the student to search for information concerning research activities involving this virus. The court lowered the standard for her 'substantial' allegation that the research might have caused her illness. Although the court formally upheld the doctrine that unspecified probing for evidence is prohibited, it ordered disclosure because the files were reasonably calculated to lead to the discovery of admissible evidence.[19] One might justifiably call this probing for evidence as a "fishing expedition", as long as it is understood that "fishing" is not *per se* objectionable but may be dictated by the needs of justice. The *Bundesgerichtshof* rendered a similar decision the following years, in which the court granted discovery and evidence adopting a liberal interpretation of the requirement of specificity with regard to the factual and evidentiary allegations.[20]

German Civil Procedure Code

§ 138   [Duty to submit facts; Duty of truthfulness]

17. BGH [1996] Neue Juristische Wochenschrift 1826, 1827.

18. See, e.g., BGH [1987] Neue Juristische Wochenschrift 1201.

19. BGH [1989] Neue Juristische Wochenschrift 2947–48.

20. BGH [1995] Neue Juristische Wochenschrift 2111; BGH [1992] Neue Juristische Wochenschrift 1967.

(1) The parties' statements with respect to factual circumstances shall be complete and truthful.

(2) Each party shall reply to allegations by the opponent.

(3) Facts which are not expressly denied shall be deemed as admitted, unless the intention to deny them is manifest in other statements of the party.

(4) A declaration of lack of knowledge concerning facts is only permissible with respect to facts as constitute neither the acts of such party nor the object of her perception.

§ 142   [Order to produce documents]

(1) The court may order a party or a third party to produce documents and other records in her possession to which a party referred. * * *

(2) Third parties are not obliged to produce documents to the extent to which this production cannot be reasonably expected or they can invoke a right not to testify according to the §§ 383 to 385. * * *

§ 143   [Order to produce files]

The court may order the parties to produce those files in their possession that consists of papers concerning the proceedings and decision of the subject matter.

§ 144   ZPO [evidence by inspection; experts]

(1) The court may order to take evidence by inspection or by an expert. For this purpose it may order a party or a third party to produce an object in her possession and it may set a time-limit to do so. It may also order tolerating the measure according to sentence 1, as long as it does not concern a residence.

(2) Third parties are not obliged to produce documents to the extent to which this production cannot be reasonably expected or they can invoke a right not to testify according to the §§ 383 to 385. * * *

(3) The procedure is regulated by the provisions on evidence by inspection at request or expert evidence.

§ 422   [Duty to produce documents under the Civil Code]

The opposing party is obliged to produce the document if the party offering the evidence is entitled to demand the relinquishment or the production of the document under the provisions of the (substantive) civil law.

§ 423   [Duty to produce documents in case of reference]

The opposing party is also obliged to produce the documents in his possession to which he referred in the course of offering evidence, even if that occurred in a preparatory pleading.

Note on Privileges in Germany

Privileges under German law mirror the entangled discovery rules, as the ZPO lacks a comprehensive set of privilege rules. Only witness privileges are sufficiently regulated in §§ 383–390. A witness may, for example, invoke the privilege against self-incrimination according to § 384 no. 2 ZPO. Other provisions protect special confidential relationships, e.g. communications with lawyers, doctors or priests. The duty of truth and faithfulness under § 138 ZPO is also limited by privileges, including the privilege against self-incrimination. Confidential business information is protected as well. In this respect, the definition of 'confidential' is subject to the court's discretion and is determined on a case-by-case basis.

Parties have no protection of privilege against substantive disclosure rights for the following reason. Substantive disclosure rights are normally based on a pre-existing legal relationship, which imposes a special responsibility on the parties. They lead to an increased duty of care, the violation of which triggers disclosure duties. These disclosure duties therefore come only into existence after the specific interests of the parties have been assessed and balanced against each other. Thus they may not be circumvented by privileges.

German Civil Procedure Code

§ 383   [Refusal to testify for personal reasons]

(1) The following are entitled to refuse to testify:

the person engaged to be married to a party;

the spouse of a party, also when the marriage no longer subsists;

2a. the registered partner of a party, also when the registered partnership no longer subsists;

those who are or were related in the direct line to a party or related by marriage, collaterally related to the third degree or collaterally related by marriage to the second degree;

clergymen with respect to matters entrusted to them in the exercise of their pastoral duties;

persons who collaborate in the preparation, production or distribution of periodicals or broadcasts in their professional capacity, or did so in the past, with respect to the person of the editor, contributor or source of contribution with regard to contributions and documents, as well as with respect to information related to them with regard to their activities, to the extent that it deals with contributions, documents and information for the editorial part;

persons to whom matters are entrusted by virtue of their office, profession or trade, which are to be kept secret due to their nature or by law, with respect to the facts to which the duty of secrecy pertains.

(2) The persons designated in nos. 1 to 3 above shall be informed of their right to refuse to testify before they are examined.

(3) The examination of persons designated in nos. 4 to 6 above shall, also when testifying is not refused, not be directed to facts with regard to which it is apparent that evidence cannot be given without the violation of the duty of secrecy.

§ 384   [Refusal to testify for objective reasons]

Testimony may be refused

with respect to questions, the answer of which would cause for the witness or a person related to him in the manner specified in § 383 nos. 1 to 3 a direct financial loss;

with respect to questions, the answer to which would disgrace the witness or a witness related to him or her in the manner specified in § 383 nos. 1 to 3 or would involve the jeopardy of his or her prosecution for a crime or infraction;

with respect to questions that the witness could not answer without disclosing an act or trade secret.

JAPAN

Takeshi Kojima, Japanese Civil Procedure in Comparative Law Perspective, 46 U. Kan. L. Rev. 687, 701–704 (1998).

b.   Preparation for Plenary Hearings

    i.   Preliminary Documents

Each party has a duty to investigate carefully the factual relations on the basis of witness testimony and other evidence. Each party must prepare for the plenary hearing by organizing documents and evidence. They must submit these documents in advance of the hearing in adequate time for the other party to make its preparation.

The defendant must specify his or her defenses corresponding to the items on the complaint submitted by the plaintiff, and describe the important relevant facts and evidence for each point to be proved. Even if these supporting points cannot be set out due to unavoidable reasons, the defendant must turn in the documents that supplement the preliminary documents as soon as they are available. If one party denies the facts asserted by the other party in the preliminary documents, the party is required to set out the reasons for the denial (sekkyoku hinin or riutsuki hinin).

ii. Inquiry in Writing Between the Parties

Each party may, during the course of the litigation, submit a written inquiry to the other party, asking for answers to questions that are necessary to prepare the inquiring party's case. A duty of cooperation is imposed on the parties in litigation. This system is borrowed from the interrogatory practice, one of the tools for discovery in American civil procedure. Its aim is to enable one party to collect information that is in the possession of the other party and is needed for preparation of the case, and thus to rectify uneven availability of information between the parties. This procedure is supposed to work without the court's participation, and is administered by exchanging inquiries and replies between the parties.

The party to whom the inquiry is addressed has the duty to reply according to the principles of good faith and trust. If the requested party fails to reply or returns an incorrect reply, however, there is no direct penalty. Thus, the success of this system depends largely on the parties' sincere cooperation.

iii. Document Production Order (Subpoena Duces Tecum)

Among the various types of evidence, written documents generally are the most unevenly distributed. So, the scope of the evidence the court may require to be produced, which is in the possession of a party or a third party, can be the decisive element in the outcome of the litigation.

There is no comprehensive provision for discovery in the new code. However, a document production order may be said to be a functional equivalent of one of the forms of American discovery. The new code seeks to expand the scope of the document production order. The old code had imposed the duty to produce written documents under a few specified conditions. The new code has imposed a general obligation to submit the documents under a broader set of conditions. Under the new code, the document production order can be used to gain access to all types of documents unless they fall into the following categories: documents that might violate the privilege against self-incrimination; privileged communications of lawyers or doctors; technical or trade secrets; or documents made exclusively for the use of the holder (documents for self-use).

There were a substantial number of decisions under the old code that gave broad meaning to the concept of self-use documents, or those concerning the relations between the holder and the party. In view of this tendency toward broad construction of the permissible categories under the old code, it may be that the excluded categories under the new code will be narrowly construed. For instance, the meaning of documents for self-use that are exempted from the general disclosure obligation is not clear. This category has usually been understood to mean documents that are created for the exclusive use of the creator and other concerned persons. Such documents were understood to be free from disclosure to outsiders. Examples would include an individual's diary or documents circulated within a business firm (ringisho). How much that meaning may be changed will become more clear with the accumulation of court decisions in the future.

Since the new code has not introduced general provisions for discovery, despite the expansion of the scope of the document production order, there are some procedural difficulties in asking the court to order the submission of documents. It is necessary, for instance, to particularize the requested documents. On this point, the new code provides special treatments for such problems. First, the requirement of specifying the documents requested in a motion for the production order has been relaxed. When it is extremely difficult to identify the documents' title or contents, it is sufficient to state the factors that enable the holder of it to differentiate that one from others. In such a case, the requesting person may ask the court to order the holder to clarify the documents' titles or contents, but there is no direct penalty if the holder does not follow this order. Second, if there is a dispute as to whether general documents may be exempted from the duty to submit and the court is required to make a ruling on this point, it may order the holder to submit the document to the court. The judge can then inspect the contents of the document in chambers to determine whether it should be exempted or not. In this provision, the new code has adopted the in-camera inspection procedure from American law. Third, the court may order submission of the document without such sections or parts as are unnecessary to be examined or produced in court. This provision removes the doubt that lingered in the former code.

The original draft of Article 222(1) and (2) would have limited the ability to subpoena administrative documents. It would have required a reference to be made to the supervising administrative agency for approval of the production of the documents. However, the agency could not turn down the request unless it found that the approval may hamper the public interest or cause an extreme burden in the performance of the administration. This provision was not adopted by the Diet because, in its view, this provision could be used by the administrative agencies to hold back information. Within approximately two years after the promulgation of the new code, a provision will be added to the code on this point in light of the Freedom of Information Act that will soon be enacted.

iv. Preservation of Evidence

If the court thinks that without a prior examination of evidence it would be difficult to examine it later, the court may order the examination before the time for examination in the ordinary course of procedure. This is a device to preserve evidence even before the lawsuit starts. It was proposed that the use of this procedure could be so expanded as to work as discovery in the United States does, but the new code did not contain a specific provision for this purpose. It may be possible that by interpretation the function of these provisions can be extended somewhat for the purpose of discovery. In any event, it is regrettable that the new code did not adopt the expanded scope of examination in advance, such as independent examination procedure by a neutral expert in Germany.

Note on Privileges in Japan

The exchange of information is also subject to various evidentiary privileges. Consider these additional provisions under the Japanese procedural code and how they affect the discovery process.

The Code of Civil Procedure of Japan.*

(Inquiry by party)

Article 163. A party may, during the pendency of the litigation, make inquiry in writing to the other party to answer in writing within a reasonable period fixed, with regard to the matters necessary for preparing for assertion or proof. Provided that, this shall not apply if such inquiry fans under any of the following items:

(1) Inquiry which is not concrete nor individual;

(2) Inquiry to insult or embarrass the other party;

(3) Inquiry to overlap with the inquiry already made;

(4) Inquiry to request opinions;

(5) Inquiry to require unreasonable expenses and time in order that the other party may answer;

(6) Inquiry as to the matters similar to such matters as may reject testimony in accordance with the provision of Article 196 or Article 197.

(Examination of government official)

Article 191. When examining a government official or a person who was a government official as a witness regarding official secrets, the court shall obtain approval of the competent supervising government office (in the case of a member of the House of Representatives or House of Councilors or a person who was a member thereof, approval of the House concerned; in the case of the Prime Minister

* Translation in EHS Law Bulletin Series, EHS Vol. II (2005).

or other Minister of the state, or a person who held such post, approval of the Cabinet).

2. The approval mentioned in the preceding paragraph may not be refused except when it may injure public interests or cause serious impediments to the performance of official duties.

(Right to refuse to testify)

Article 196. A witness may refuse to testify if his testimony relates to such matters as a witness or a person having any of the following relationship with a witness may be prosecuted or convicted. The same shall apply if the testimony relates to the matters to bring disgrace on such person.

(1) A person who is or was a spouse, relative of blood within the fourth degree of relationship or relative by affinity within the third degree of relationship, of a witness;

(2) A person who is a guardian of a witness or under the guardianship of a witness.

(Right to refuse to testify)

Article 197. In the following cases, a witness may refuse to testify:

(1) The case mentioned in Article 191 paragraph 1;

(2) Where a witness who is or was a doctor, dentist, pharmacist, druggist, mid-wife, lawyer (including a Gaikokuho–Jimu–Bengoshi), patent attorney, defense counsel, notary public, or person being engaged in religion, prayer, or worship as an occupation is questioned with regard to the fact which he has obtained knowledge in the exercise of his professional duties and he should keep secret;

(3) Where a witness is questioned with regard to the matters on technological or professional secret.

2. The provision of the preceding paragraph shall not apply where a witness has been exempted from the duty to keep secret.

Note

As forecast in the preceding article by Kojima, a series of provisions for ordering production of government documents passed the Diet in 2001. The adopted new version gives the court the power to examine in camera an allegedly secret document to determine whether it is privileged. Relevant provisions follow:

(Obligation to produce document)

Article 220. A holder of a document may not refuse the production thereof in the following cases:

(1) When the party himself is in possession of the document to which he has referred in the litigation;

(2) When the person going to prove is entitled to demand from the holder of the document the delivery or the perusal thereof;

(3) When the document has been drawn up for the benefit of the person going to prove or for the legal relations between the person and the holder thereof.

(4) In addition to the cases mentioned in the preceding three paragraphs, when the document does not come under any of the following;

   a. A document stating therein the matters provided for in Article 196 as to a holder of the document or a person having relationship mentioned in each item of Article 196 with a holder of the document;

   b. The documents concerning secrets in respect of government officials' duties, which have an apprehension that the public peace would be disturbed or that serious inconvenience would be caused to the performance of official business by their production;

   c. A document stating therein the fact provided for in Article 197 paragraph 1 item (2) or the matter provided for m item (3) of the said paragraph which is not exempted from the duty to keep secret;

   d. The document to be offered only for the use of a holder of a document (excluding those used by government officials organizationally in the case of documents possessed by the State or local public entities);

   e. The documents concerning lawsuits pertaining to criminal cases or the records of cases concerning juvenile protection, or the documents seized under those cases.

(Application for order for production of document)

Article 221. An application for an order for production of a document shall clarify the following matters;

(1) Indication of the document;

(2) Gist of the document;

(3) The holder of the document;

(4) The fact to be proved;

(5) The ground for obligation for production of the document.

   2. An application for an order for production of a document on the ground for the obligation for production of a document arising from the case mentioned in item (4) of the preceding Article, may not be made unless the offering of documentary evidence is required to be made by the application for an order for production of a document.

(Procedure for specifying document))

Article 222. If, in the case where an order for the production of a document has been applied for, it is extremely difficult to clarify the matter mentioned in item (1) or (2) of paragraph 1 of the preceding Article, at the time of the application it shall be sufficient to clarify, as a substitute for such matter, the matter which enables the holder of a document to distinguish the document under the application. In this case a notice shall be made to the court requesting the holder of a document to clarify the matter mentioned in item (1) or (2) of the said paragraph as to the said document.

5. If a notice under the provision of the preceding paragraph has been made, the court may request the holder of a document to clarify the matters mentioned in the latter part of the said paragraph except when it is clear that an application for an order for production of a document is groundless.

(Order for production of documents)

Article 223. The court shall, if it deems the application for an order for production of documents well-founded, order the holder of a document to produce it by ruling. In this case, if the document contains part deemed to be unnecessary to be examined or part not to be deemed to be under obligation for production, the court may order the production of the document except such part.

2. The court intending to order a third person to produce a document shall examine the third person.

3. The Court shall, in case that a motion of the order to produce documents has been made because that the documents concerning secrets in respect of government officials' duties fall under the case mentioned in Article 220 item (4) is the ground for obligation to produce documents, except the case it is apparent that the motion is not sustainable, regarding if the said documents fall under the documents mentioned in b. of the said item, hear the opinion of the competent supervising Government Office (with respect to the documents concerning secrets in respect of members' duties of the House of Representatives or the House of Councilors, respective Houses, and with respect to the documents concerning secrets in respect of duties of the Prime Minister and other Ministers of State, the Cabinet; hereinafter the same in this Article). In this case, the said competent supervising Government Office shall, if it states the opinion to the effect that the said documents fall under the documents mentioned b. of the said item, show the ground.

4. In the case of the preceding paragraph, if the competent supervising Government Office stated the opinion to the effect that the said documents fell under the documents mentioned in Article 220 item (4) b. because there are fears mentioned in the following from the production of the said documents, the Court may, limited to the case the opinion is not sufficient to be considered to have reasonable ground, order the person who possesses the documents for their production.

(1) The fear that the national security is impaired, the fear that the relationship of trust with other countries or international organization is broken, or the fear to be disadvantaged on the negotiations with other countries or international organizations,

(2) The fear that inconvenience is caused on prevention, suppression or investigation of crimes, sustainment of action, execution of punishment and stabilization of other public safety and order.

5. In the case of the former part of paragraph 3, the competent supervising Government Office shall, if it states opinion concerning the documents described pertaining to the matters regarding technological or occupational secrets of a third person other than the person who possesses the concerned documents, except if it states opinion to the effect that they fall under the documents mentioned in Article 220 item (4) b., beforehand, hear the opinion of the said third person.

6. The court may, if it deems it necessary to decide whether the document under an application for an order for production of a document comes under any of the documents mentioned in a. through d. of item (4) of Article 220, have the holder of the document to present the said document. In this case, no one may request the disclosure of the presented document.

7. An immediate Kokoku-appeal may be filed against the ruling on an application for an order for production of documents.

(Effect of party's non-compliance, etc. with order for production of document)

Article 224. If a party does not comply with an order for the production of a document, the court may admit the truth of the assertion of the other party relating to a statement of the document.

2. When a party has destroyed a document which he is bound to produce or otherwise has made it impossible for use with the object of hindering its use from the other party it shall be the same as the preceding paragraph.

3. In the cases provided for in the preceding two paragraphs, if it is extremely difficult for the other party to make a concrete assertion relating to a statement of the document and to testify to the facts to be proven by the said document on other evidence, the court may admit the truth of the assertion of the other party relating to such facts.

Note on Pre-action Discovery

In 2003, the Japanese Code of Civil Procedure was further amended to add a new chapter containing eight articles providing certain devices for pre-action discovery from an opposing party and from third parties. The relevant provisions are:

The Code of Civil Procedure of Japan.*

(Inquiries prior to the institution of action)

Article 132–2. In the cases where a person to institute an action gave the previous notice for instituting an action to a person to be a defendant in writing (hereinafter the said notice shall be referred to as the "previous notice" in this Chapter) may, to the person who received such previous notice, only within the limit of four months counting from the day of giving such previous notice, prior to institute an action, regarding the matters clearly necessary for preparing the contention or proof in the case of instituting an action, with fixing appropriate period, inquire in writing to let him/her answer in writing. Provided that, this shall not apply if such inquiry falls under any of the following respective items.

(1) Inquiries falling under any of the respective items of Article 163;

(2) Inquiries regarding the secret matters concerning private life of the other party or the third parties, which arouse fears to hinder social life of such other party or the third parties if they answer them;

(3) Inquiries regarding the matters concerning trade secrets of the other party or the third parties.

2. With respect to the inquiries regarding the secret matters concerning private lives of the third parties provided in item (2) of the preceding paragraph or regarding trade secrets of the third parties provided in item (3) of the said paragraph, those provisions shall not apply in the cases where such third parties gave consent to the other party's answering to them.

3. In the writing of previous notice shall describe the purport of request and essential points of controversy pertaining to the action to be instituted.

4. The inquiries under paragraph 1 shall not be made on the basis of the previous notice which is the repetition of a previous notice already made.

* Translation in EHS Law Bulletin Series, EHS Vol. II (2005).

Article 132–3. A person who received the previous notice (hereinafter referred to as the "person receiving previous notice" in this Chapter) may, if, to the person giving previous notice, he/she replied to such previous notice by a writing describing the purport of pleadings in answer for the purport of request and essential points of controversy under paragraph 3 of the preceding Article which are written in such previous notice, to the person giving previous notice, only within the limit of four months counting from the day of receiving such previous notice, prior to institute an action, regarding the matters clearly necessary for preparing the contention or proof in the case of being instituted an action, with fixing appropriate period, inquire in writing to let him/her answer in writing. In this case, the provisions of the proviso of paragraph 1 of the said Article and paragraph 2 of the said Article shall apply mutatis mutandis.

2.   The inquiries under the preceding paragraph shall not be made on the basis of replies for the previous notice which is the repetition of a previous notice already made.

(Adopting measures regarding collection of evidence prior to the institution of action)

Article 132–4. A Court may, upon motion of the person giving previous notice or the person receiving previous notice who replied under paragraph 1 of the preceding Article, regarding those to be evidence clearly necessary for proving in the case where an action pertaining to the said previous notice is himself/herself, with hearing the opinion of the other party for such previous notice or such reply (hereinafter referred to as simply "the other party" in this Chapter), adopt the measures mentioned in the following pertaining to such collection prior to the institution of the action. Provided that, this shall not apply if it deems not adequate because of the conditions, such as the time necessary for such collection or the burden of the person to be entrusted is inadequate.

(1) To entrust the holder of the documents (including the articles provided in Article 231; hereinafter the same in this Chapter) to forward such documents;

(2) To entrust a government or other public office, governments or other public offices of foreign countries, or other organizations, such as a school, a chamber of commerce and industry or an exchange (referred to as the "government or public office, etc." in item (2) of paragraph 1 of the next Article) to conduct necessary investigation;

(3) To entrust the person having technical knowledge and experience to state the opinion based on such technical knowledge and experience;

(4) To order execution officers to investigate the shape of articles, relation of possession and other actual conditions.

2.   * * *

Note on Discovery Reforms

Nicolò Trocker and Vincenzo Varano, Concluding Remarks, in The Reforms of Civil Procedure in Comparative Perspective 255–258 (Nicolò Trocker and Vincenzo Varano, eds., 2005).

7.   The diffusion of forms of discovery

The European codes of the 19th century strictly adhered to the principle *nemo tenetur edere contra se*, i.e., the principle that no party has to help her opponent in her inquiry into the facts, and did not provide for instruments capable of eliciting from the parties all of the preconstituted items of evidence which might be necessary for the decision of the case. More recently, however, the idea gained ground, gradually and not without difficulty, that if procedure aims at getting as close as possible to the truth concerning the litigated issues, it must rely on techniques through which each party can have access to items of evidence not in her possession.

In France, art. 10 of the Code Civil, as amended in 1972, introduces a general duty of procedural discovery, by providing that "each party must bring her contribution to the administration of justice in view of the ascertainment of truth", and that the party who avoids this duty once she has been legally asked to perform it, without any justification, can be forced to fulfill it through the imposition of an *astreinte*, without prejudice of damages. Art. 11 of the *"dispositions liminaires"* of the new code of civil procedure reaffirms the obligation of the parties to contribute to the proof taking stage, and specifies that it shall be sanctioned, as far as the disclosure of documents is concerned, through the power of the judge to order the payment of an *astreinte*.

The French lead has been followed by the German *Zivilprozessnovelle* of 2002, which has introduced the power of the judge to order parties or third parties to disclose documents in their possession, on the simple basis that they may be useful to the ascertainment of the facts of the case. Commentators do not hesitate to define the new wording of § 142 of the ZPO as one of the most meaningful innovations of the recent reform. Professor Walter writes in his Report that "these newly established obligations to producing documents can—with regard to the German tradition of procedural law—be called close to revolutionary", and underlines their analogies to the pretrial discovery of documents of the (Anglo) American procedural tradition, warning however that the so called fishing expeditions continue to be forbidden in German law.

Also the Dutch Code, following the Procedural Law Reform Act of 2002, has introduced a technique designed to assure the acquisition of documents which the parties cannot produce without the collaboration of the opponents or third parties in their possession (art. 22). If a party does not comply, the judge can draw the conclusions she considers appropriate. The Dutch Reporters add that the reform has also introduced a "decidedly revolutionary . . . general article in which it is stipulated that parties and their representatives are obliged to 'fully and truthfully' supply facts that are relevant for the judge's decision. Here too the sanction: if the stipulation is not met, the judge can draw conclusions he considers appropriate".

The Spanish solution, adopted by the new *Ley de Enjuiciamento Civil*, provides that each party, without resorting to the judge, can ask from the opponent, pending the case, the disclosure of documents in her possession. It is interesting and somewhat original, though it may raise doubts about its effectiveness, since the disclosure procedure is not supported by any sanction for the case of non compliance.

All the instruments we have just talked about, introduced by recent European procedural reforms, have a common character, that of being part of the proof taking stage. In other words, they are aimed at obtaining information useful to the ascertainment of specific facts which have come to be discussed in the proceeding through the preliminary stage. As we have already indicated, they cannot be used before the "thema probandum" has been specified. However, the need to obtain the necessary information cannot be considered only in view of reaching the final decision of the case. In many cases, it would be extremely useful to have those information also when the problem is to decide whether, and eventually against whom, to bring a suit, or whether, and within which limits, to settle the case.

Interestingly enough, comparative research shows important trends in this direction. This is the case of France, where courts have interpreted art. 145 of the NCPC so as to facilitate the securing of documents from an opponent or third parties before, and independently from litigation on the merits, even beyond the requirement of there being a reason to conserve or establish facts upon which a solution of the dispute may depend. In this way, a party will be able to understand whether to initiate a suit and against whom, and whether it may be to look for an extrajudicial settlement of the dispute. These seem to be strikingly similar goals as those pursued by the American pretrial discovery when it is used in view of clarifying the controversy.

Professor Taniguchi, in turn, informs us in his Report that Japan, after having adopted in 1996 "a new device called 'interparty inquiry', which allows a party to ask for relevant information from the adversary, and expanded the scope of the document production order", has introduced an amendment in 2003 "which enables the parties to collect information and evidence from the prospective adversary or from a third party even before instituting an action". Professor Taniguchi further explains that the reason for this amendment is that "it is sometimes necessary to have sufficient information in order to formulate a complaint", in order, in other words, to better define the scope of the controversy and to better prepare it.

The pre-action protocols introduced in England by the new Rules (CPR 26.4 e 31.16) are also of the utmost interest: as we have already mentioned (*supra*, § 2), they are exchanges of information between the prospective parties taking place before the beginning of the proceeding, so as to see whether on their basis a conciliation might be possible. In Italy too, the recent proposal of the Vaccarella Committee goes in an analogous direction, in that it gives the attorneys the possibility of gathering evidentiary information in view of prospective litigation, by asking public agencies to disclose documents, by hearing witnesses and asking written statements from them, by securing statements of facts from public officials. This is a truly preliminary discovery, the value of which is stronger than the mere acquisition of information. In fact, all the material which has been gathered through it can be used freely in the course of the proceeding and can be freely evaluated by the judge, who is also free to decide whether to order the renewal of the preliminary evidentiary activities. Also, the proposal has been made to use the procedure of preservation of evidence (*istruzione preventiva*) very much in the same way as the French courts have interpreted art. 145 NCPC. Obviously, the danger of this kind of proposals and trends, is that the principle of immediacy may be substantially attenuated, i.e. the principle according to which there must be identity between the judge who takes the evidence and the judge who decides. In other countries, commentators have underlined the danger that techniques of this kind may end up in "fishing expeditions".

In any case, when we deal with such techniques as discovery, allegedly typical of the common law procedural models, we cannot conclude the comparison by saying that the civil law countries do not have any discovery. Within any system of law or justice one must be careful about comparing individual elements of the system without sufficient consideration of the system as a whole. In fact, and by way of example, in our legal systems there are several important provisions of substantive law which create a "right of information", in the context of specific legal relationships. Such substantive legal rights can be enforced judicially, and are functional to gain factual information from private parties or from the administration in order eventually to start a proceeding. In general, we should also remember that our pleadings are *fact pleadings*, the statement of claim must include the precise indication of the subject matter, the legal foundation of the claim, as well as a specific prayer for relief. This means that most of the work has to be done by the lawyers who have to verify before they file the claim whether there are sufficient facts substantiating the claim. This means also that, if and when the lawyers decide to bring the suit and do file the claim, they do not need as much as their common law, and especially American, counterparts to fish for facts and information.

Chapter 5

RESOLVING THE CASE IN THE FIRST INSTANCE COURT: THE TRIAL AND ANALOGOUS PROCESSES

I. INTRODUCTION

In this Chapter we look at the stage of the case called (at least in the common law system) the "trial." Principal differences between the litigation process in the civil law world and the common law countries concerns what is called the "trial" in the common law courts. The differences are so profound that the word "trial" is not ordinarily used to describe the process by which a civil law judge hears and resolves the case. The phrase that is commonly used to include both models is the "first instance" procedure.

Important differentiating features of the common law trial are (1) the use of the jury as fact-finder (in some but not all common law jurisdictions); (2) the continuous presentation of the evidence to the fact-finder over whatever period of time is necessary; (3) the separation of the evidence into the "plaintiff's case" and the "defendant's case" (4) attorney control of the order of presentation; (5) attorney questioning of the witnesses; (5) party-selected experts; and (6) a verbatim "record" of the proceedings at a common law trial versus a judge-made summary called the "dossier." Describing the different "flavor" of the two kinds of process, Professor John Langbein puts it this way: "Countless novels, movies, plays, and broadcast serials attest to the dramatic potential of the Anglo–American trial. * * * German civil proceedings have the tone not of the theatre but of a routine business meeting—serious rather than tense."[1]

II. THE STRUCTURE OF THE "FIRST INSTANCE" PROCEEDING

The differences in the structure of the "trial" and the civil law "first instance proceeding" are ably summarized by the ALI–UNIDROIT Principles of Civil Litigation:

---

1. John H. Langbein, The German Advantage in Civil Procedure, 52 U. Chi. L. Rev. 823, 831 (1985).

Civil-law litigation in many systems proceeds through a series of short hearing sessions—sometimes less than an hour each—for reception of evidence, which is then consigned to the case file until an eventual final stage of analysis and decision. In contrast, common-law litigation has a preliminary or pretrial stage (sometimes more than one) and then a trial at which all the evidence is received consecutively.[2]

According to Professor Rolf Stürner, a "third model" is now in use in Germany, Spain and England:

> It could be described as the "main hearing model." After a written introductory stage (pleading stage) comes a period of preparatory clarification regarding the applicable law, the factual basis of the case, and the available means of evidence. This preparatory procedural stage serves not only to inform the parties and to enable them to prepare for the main hearing, it is also designed to inform the court or the judge and to anticipate or replace in part the taking of evidence in the later main hearing (production of documents to the opponent and the court, written expertises for the information of the court and the parties, written statements of witnesses as a preparation or anticipation of oral testimony, etc.) Only those relevant issues that remain unclarified during this preparatory stage will be tried in the final concentrated main hearing, where evidence not already received will be presented and taken and where the parties will make their concluding arguments.[3]

As you will have seen from the previous chapter, the civil law practice of hearing evidence during a series of sessions with the judge reduces the need for American-style pretrial discovery. But this contrast between the concentrated "trial" of the common law world and the series of "short hearings" of the civil law affects the process in other ways as well. The following excerpts from John Langbein's often-cited article describe the differences and their impact in more detail. Professor Langbein argues that the civil law structure of the first instance process offers many advantages.

John H. Langbein, The German Advantage in Civil Procedure, 52 U. Chi. L. Rev. 823, 826–832 (1985).

I. OVERVIEW OF GERMAN CIVIL PROCEDURE

There are two fundamental differences between German and Anglo–American civil procedure, and these differences lead in turn to many

---

2. ALI/UNIDROIT Principles of Transnational Civil Procedure 6 (2006).

3. Rolf Stürner, The Principles of Transnational Procedure, An Introduction to Their Basic Conceptions, in Rabels Zeitschrift 224–225 (2005).

others. First, the court rather than the parties' lawyers takes the main responsibility for gathering and sifting evidence, although the lawyers exercise a watchful eye over the court's work. Second, there is no distinction between pretrial and trial, between discovering evidence and presenting it. Trial is not a single continuous event. Rather, the court gathers and evaluates evidence over a series of hearings, as many as the circumstances require.

* * *

Judicial Preparation. The judge to whom the case is entrusted examines these pleadings and appended documents. He routinely sends for relevant public records. These materials form the beginnings of the official dossier, the court file. All subsequent submissions of counsel, and all subsequent evidence-gathering, will be entered in the dossier, which is open to counsel's inspection continuously.

When the judge develops a first sense of the dispute from these materials, he will schedule a hearing and notify the lawyers. He will often invite and sometimes summon the parties as well as their lawyers to this or subsequent hearings. If the pleadings have identified witnesses whose testimony seems central, the judge may summon them to the initial hearing as well.

Hearing. The circumstances of the case dictate the course of the hearing. Sometimes the court will be able to resolve the case by discussing it with the lawyers and parties and suggesting avenues of compromise. If the case remains contentious and witness testimony needs to be taken, the court will have learned enough about the case to determine a sequence for examining witnesses.

Examining and Recording. The judge serves as the examiner-in-chief. At the conclusion of his interrogation of each witness, counsel for either party may pose additional questions, but counsel are not prominent as examiners. Witness testimony is seldom recorded verbatim; rather, the judge pauses from time to time to dictate a summary of the testimony into the dossier. The lawyers sometimes suggest improvements in the wording of these summaries, in order to preserve or to emphasize nuances important to one side or the other.

Further Contributions of Counsel. After the court takes witness testimony or receives some other infusion of evidence, counsel have the opportunity to comment orally or in writing. Counsel use these submissions in order to suggest further proofs or to advance legal theories. Thus, nonadversarial proof-taking alternates with adversarial dialogue across as many hearings as are necessary. The process merges the investigatory function of our pretrial discovery and the evidence-presenting function of our trial.

II. JUDICIAL CONTROL OF SEQUENCE

From the standpoint of comparative civil procedure, the most important consequence of having judges direct fact-gathering in this episodic fashion is that German procedure functions without the sequence rules to which we are accustomed in the Anglo–American procedural world. The implications for procedural economy are large. The very concepts of "plaintiff's case" and "defendant's case" are unknown. In our system those concepts function as traffic rules for the partisan presentation of evidence to a passive and ignorant trier. By contrast, in German procedure the court ranges over the entire case, constantly looking for the jugular—for the issue of law or fact that might dispose of the case. Free of constraints that arise from party presentation of evidence, the court investigates the dispute in the fashion most likely to narrow the inquiry. A major job of counsel is to guide the search by directing the court's attention to particularly cogent lines of inquiry.

Suppose that the court has before it a contract case that involves complicated factual or legal issues about whether the contract was formed, and if so, what its precise terms were. But suppose further that the court quickly recognizes (or is led by submission of counsel to recognize) that some factual investigation might establish an affirmative defense—illegality, let us say that would vitiate the contract. Because the court functions without sequence rules, it can postpone any consideration of issues that we would think of as the plaintiff's case—here the questions concerning the formation and the terms of the contract. Instead, the court can concentrate the entire initial inquiry on what we would regard as a defense. If, in my example, the court were to unearth enough evidence to allow it to conclude that the contract was illegal, no investigation would ever be done on the issues of formation and terms. A defensive issue that could only surface in Anglo–American procedure following full pretrial and trial ventilation of the whole of the plaintiff's case can be brought to the fore in German procedure.

* * *

The episodic character of German civil procedure—Benjamin Kaplan called it the "conference method" of adjudication—has other virtues: It lessens tension and theatrics, and it encourages settlement. Countless novels, movies, plays, and broadcast serials attest to the dramatic potential of the Anglo–American trial. The contest between opposing counsel; the potential for surprise witnesses who cannot be rebutted in time; the tricks of adversary examination and cross-examination; the concentration of proof-taking and verdict into a single, continuous proceeding; the unpredictability of juries and the mysterious opacity of their conclusory verdicts—these attributes of the Anglo–American trial make for good theatre. German civil proceedings have the tone not of the theatre, but of a routine business meeting—serious rather than tense. When the court inquires and directs, it sets no stage for advocates to perform. The forensic skills of counsel can wrest no material advantage, and the appearance of a surprise witness would simply lead to the scheduling of a further hearing. In a system that cannot distinguish between dress rehearsal and opening night, there is scant occasion for stage fright. In this business-like system of civil procedure the tradition is strong that the court promotes compromise. The judge who gathers the facts soon knows the case as well as the litigants do, and he concentrates each subsequent increment of fact-gathering on the most important issues still unresolved. As the case progresses the judge discusses it with the litigants, sometimes indicating provisional views of the likely outcome. He is, therefore, strongly positioned to encourage a litigant to abandon a case that is turning out to be weak or hopeless, or to recommend settlement.

Note

The "episodic" hearing process described by Professor Langbein is a feature of civil law procedure generally, although, as described by Professor Stürner, above, the "main hearing model" now favored in Germany and some other countries combines elements of the concentrated common law trial and the classic episodic civil law process. The "main hearing" reform was motivated by the reality that the episodic process can too-often drag on unduly. Professor Taniguchi has noted that the problem of delay due to the episodic or, as he calls it the "May-rain" or "dentist" method of litigation. See the section on Japan in Chapter 1. As noted there, "Hearings take place only intermittently just as the rain in May tends to fall only intermittently in Japan and the dentist treats perhaps everywhere a patient intermittently. What typically happened in Japan was a long dragged-out series of short hearings to complete a preliminary stage of identifying the issues to be followed by a series of short witness examination sessions." Japanese reformers have attempted to remedy the situation by concentrating the evidence-taking sessions so that more than one witness at a time is heard and fewer hearings are needed.

Japan is hardly alone in having encountered delays stemming in large part from the episodic hearing approach of the civil law system. The situation in Italy seems even worse. According to Professor Michele Taruffo: "The most important, not to say tragic, problem of Italian civil justice is that justice is often awfully delayed, which means that it is frequently denied."[4] He notes that while the average length for a "first instance proceeding" in 1996 in Europe was 17 months, in Italy it was 36 months.[5] A major cause of Italian litigation delay has been attributed to the process under which "the development of the proceeding requires an excessive number of formal and bureaucratic passages and hearings, with long intervals * * * "[6]

As described in the following article, English procedure was reformed in 1999 to grant extensive managerial powers to the judge in the interest of improving the efficiency of the litigation process.

---

4. Michele Taruffo, Recent and Current Reforms of Civil Procedure in Italy, in The Reforms of Civil Procedure in Comparative Perspective 217 (Nicolò Trocker and Vincenzo Varano, eds. 2005).

5. Id. at 222.

6. Id. at 224. Blame is also laid at the feet of the bar: "The average Italian lawyer is strongly oriented to provoke delays and unnecessary fragmentation of the proceeding simply because these tactics raise the amount of the fees she may charge." Id. at 223–224.

Neil Andrews, A New Civil Procedure Code for England: Party–Control "Going, Going, Gone," 19 Civil Justice Quarterly 19 (2000).

Introduction and background

The 1999 Rules

This article explains the background to the momentous changes of April 1999, when Lord Woolf's new procedural code took effect. [Lord Woolf was the principal author of a Report that provided much of the impetus for the 1999 changes—Eds.] The Civil Procedure Rules (hereafter "CPR") proclaim themselves to be a new procedural code.

* * *

Lawyers around the world are interested to discover not just the details of the English reforms to civil procedure but to what extent these new rules alter the traditional pattern of English litigation. Certainly the new code has reshaped the relationship between the parties, their lawyers and the courts. The next few years are likely to reveal the full extent of this shift of procedural control from the parties to the courts. * * *

Certainly, the new rules represent the greatest shake-up in civil procedure since the 1870s, when the common law and equity jurisdictions were fused in a combined High Court, or since the withering of civil juries during the last 100 or so years. It is surprising, therefore, that the merits of "case-management", the jewel in the new procedural crown, were not tested in a pilot-scheme (outside the Commercial Court, where case-management has been practised for some time).

Reasons for change

The three major problems of the old system of civil procedure identified by Lord Woolf corresponded with those already described in the Civil Justice Review in 1988: the high cost of litigation, delay and complexity. The layman might cynically regard these as the unholy trinity of consequences which flow once a lawyer gets hold of a dispute.

Lord Woolf added to these the problem of the present adversarial "culture": "the adversarial process [namely the absence of judicial control] is likely to * * * degenerate into an environment in which the litigation process is too often seen as a battle field where no rules apply." As a Chancery judge has reported: "In cases before me I have had 'blue chip' firms carrying on at their clients' expense feuds with each other in the form of vitriolic correspondence and total non-co-operation during the trial, where I have had to act as a mediator between them. If the price of impressing clients is indulging in these tactics, it is a price which no [practitioner] can afford to pay consistently with his duty to the Court, and the sanctions for breach of this duty must be real enough to deter recurrence."

Lord Woolf also referred to the wasteful present system which leads to "every aspect of the case [being] fully investigated [by the parties]. This encourages excessive work and cost on issues which are often recognised from an early stage to be peripheral."

The old law: party-control or the adversarial principle

Where the dominant principle is a pure and unmodified adversarial concept of civil proceedings, it is the parties who dictate at all stages the form, content and pace of litigation.

Although somewhat diluted in the preceding 10 years or so, English procedure as recently as 1998 exhibited a highly concentrated form of the adversarial principle.

* * *

Civil litigation was regarded as essentially a private dispute conducted before an official. Again in [Sir Jack] Jacob's words:

> Under the adversary system, the basic assumptions are that civil disputes are a matter of private concern for the parties involved, and may even be regarded as their private property, although their determination by the courts may have wider, more far-reaching, even public repercussions, and that the parties are themselves the best judges of how to pursue and serve their own interests in the conduct and control of their respective cases, free from the directions of or intervention by the court.

* * *

The traditional system rested on a number of additional presuppositions: that the parties were both legally represented; that their lawyers were roughly of the same calibre; that each of the party's lawyers was predominantly concerned to advance his client's interest, so that the overall attainment of justice was a by-product of the collision of adversaries; and finally, it rested on the view, which became perhaps too complacent, that the court itself seldom needed to intervene to safeguard the public interest or even to carry out independent research to check the parties' legal submissions.

Now that the public interest has been defined as including the achievement of speed, efficiency and proportionality in civil litigation, it has become possible to say "the judges are the masters now".

The New Framework

The New Starting Point and the Break with the Past

Lord Woolf's major decision is that judicial management of civil litigation will be the key-stone of his overall strategy:

> There should be a fundamental transfer in the responsibility for the management of civil litigation from litigants and their legal advisers to the courts.

The only aspects of the old adversarial system which will be untouched by this new wave of reform are the following:

(1) a party's decision to initiate proceedings;

(2) the selection of a remedy (this aspect was not fully discussed by Lord Woolf);

(3) a party's decision unilaterally to withdraw either a claim or a defence; (of course, the parties can also bilaterally settle the case);

(4) a decision to seek enforcement of a judgment or other order;

(5) a party's decision to seek an appeal (with or without a court's permission to appeal); but the closure of the Court of Appeal to appellants lacking judicial permission to appeal is a significant check against this aspect of private initiative.

Case-management

After April 1999 the parties do not enjoy as much autonomy as they have hitherto possessed. The court's impressive and daunting array of managerial powers is listed at the forefront of the 1999 code. The court, especially through its case-management powers, will be expected to curb the parties' tendency to take inappropriate steps or to prosecute the case in an oppressive, disproportionate, inefficient or unfair fashion.

[T]here will be a radical break with the past. The courts will take much greater charge of the conduct of the litigation than has hitherto been characteristic in English civil proceedings, except perhaps within the Commercial Court which has been in the vanguard during the last decade. Judicial control will involve case-management and the exercise of various powers of initiative. The courts will be able to issue directions at a case-management conference, or a pre-trial review, or both. The expectations concerning such conferences are described in detail. The court will endeavour to fix the trial date or trial period as soon as possible after allocation of the case to this track.

The range of the court's new powers

Generally, the court will have various powers to ensure procedural efficiency. Thus CPR, r. 3.1 states that the court can (among other things):

shorten or extend periods for procedural compliance; or

adjourn or re-arrange hearings; or

stay a proceeding; or

decide the order in which issues are to be tried; or

hold a preliminary hearing; or

"take any other step or make any other order for the purpose of managing the case and furthering the overriding objective."

The amplitude of this final phrase demonstrates that control of civil procedure has truly moved away from the parties to the courts: the procedural centre of gravity has now shifted, perhaps irreversibly.

The court's powers of initiative

The court has powers to make orders of its own initiative without waiting for a party to apply. This power exists "except where a rule or some other enactment provides otherwise."

Striking out

The new rules preserve pre-existing grounds for striking out. * * * Under the 1999 rules, the court has power to strike out, in whole or in part, a statement of case (a phrase which includes both the claimant's and defendant's statement of the issues) on three newly specified grounds:

(a) "the statement of case discloses no reasonable grounds for bringing or defending the claim"; or

(b) "the statement of case is an abuse of the court's process or is otherwise likely to obstruct the just disposal of the proceedings"; or

(c) "failure to comply with a rule, practice direction or court order."

It appears that this power of striking out can be exercised whether or not a party makes an application to the court.

Impact of the 1999 rules in specific contexts

The modification of the adversarial principle will be extensive, as the following list of contexts reveals.

(a) Judicial influence upon issues to be tried

The court will become involved in the formulation of the issues to be tried. It will have a hand in the formulation of the "statement of case" (old style "pleadings"). The court can order clarification or supplementation of matters in dispute. Conversely, pleadings must be "concise". The Court of Appeal has emphasised, especially in the context of defamation actions, that pleadings should be proportionate and take into account the fact that much supplementation occurs through the exchange of witness statements so that the danger of surprise is slight.

The court also has the power of its own initiative to add or substitute new parties. Furthermore, the ... court, during the process of case management, must ensure "that the issues between the parties are identified and that the necessary evidence is prepared and disclosed."

(b) Ordinary witnesses

The court * * * can restrict the number of witnesses (both lay and expert) used by each party.

If a party intends to call a particular witness, the latter's proposed evidence-in-chief must be prepared in written form, signed and then served on the other parties. The witness statement will normally stand as evidence-in-chief. The statement must be supported by a statement of truth by the witness or his legal representative (the same applies to an expert's report). It is an act of contempt of court to make a dishonest and false statement and then to purport to verify this by a statement of truth.

* * *

Trial

Since April 1999 the court is required to take charge of the conduct of trial. There is little chance that a trial judge acting under the 1999 rules will suffer the fate of a 1950s High Court judge: gentlemanly dismissal by the Lord Chancellor for having asked too many questions at trial.

Thus the court since April 1999 can "control the evidence by giving directions as to (a) the issues on which it requires evidence; (b) the nature of the evidence which it requires to decide those issues and (c) the way in which evidence is to be placed before the court." It can also exclude admissible evidence and can limit cross-examination.

These combined powers remove any possibility of the parties setting the evidential agenda at trial in the teeth of judicial opposition. Once more, the court has the final word. Misapplied, these wide powers might threaten a serious loss of impartiality and the risk of pre-judgment by the court. It must be hoped that they will be used with sensitivity, since the highest duty of the court is not the pursuit of efficiency and speed but the obligation to deal with actions at all stages "justly".

Impact of the 1999 changes on lawyers

New rules emphasise that a litigation lawyer's foremost duty is to respect the abstract interests of justice, rather than blindly to be propelled by the adversarial vectors of contractual, tortious, fiduciary and professional duties to their client.

An important precursor to the new rules is this judicial statement:

* * * the balance between the advocate's duty to the client and the advocate's duty to the court must reflect evolutionary change within the civil justice system. If evolutionary shifts are necessary to match civil justice reforms they should * * * be towards strengthening the duty to the court.

The new rules also proclaim:

The parties are required to help the court to further the overriding objective.

That objective requires, among other things, the quest for justice, equality, efficiency, proportionality and due speediness in the conduct of litigation.

Section 42 of the Access to Justice Act 1999 imposes on all advocates (barristers or solicitors) "a duty to the court to act with independence in the interests of justice", as well as a duty to comply with prescribed professional rules, and "[both sets of duties] shall override any obligation which the person may have * * * if it is inconsistent with them."

Reception by the profession

How will Lord Woolf's new interventionist style of litigation be received by litigants and lawyers? Will they not resent being pushed around by judges, some of whom might be at least perceived to be over-zealous, fussy, ill-motivated and even tyrannical? No doubt, Lord Woolf expects judges under his new system will display exemplary professionalism, efficiency and fairness:

> * * * judges have to be trusted to exercise the wide discretions which they have fairly and justly in all the circumstances, while recognising their responsibility to litigants in general not to allow the same defaults to occur in the future as have occurred in the past. When judges seek to do that, it is important that this court should not interfere unless judges can be shown to have exercised their powers in some way which contravenes the relevant principles.

It was certainly reassuring to the hundreds of practitioners at a conference in 1998 to hear May L.J. state that judges under the 1999 rules should not seek to "bash the parties and their lawyers". Much will depend on the quality of judges, their system of training, and measures to ensure accountability.

Consider this comment by an American scholar:

> Managerial judges frequently work beyond the public view, off the record, with no obligation to provide written, reasoned opinions, and out of reach of appellate review.

And the present Lord Chief Justice has said:

> * * * [B]oth the trial judge and Court of Appeal must be constantly alert to the paramount requirements of justice: justice to the plaintiff and justice to the defendant. To expedite the just despatch of cases is one thing; merely to expedite the despatch of cases is another. The right of both parties to a fair trial of the issues between them cannot be compromised.

* * *

Conclusion

"Times change and procedure develops."

The 1999 changes, although radical and still largely unalloyed by judicial interpretation, must not be mistaken for a canonical set of eternally applicable rules and principles. The subject will always involve compromises between competing values and principles, which represent each generation's attempt to meet the perennial challenges of civil procedure.

THE UNITED STATES

Federal Rule of Civil Procedure 16—Pretrial Conferences; Scheduling; Management

(c) Subjects for consideration at Pretrial Conferences. At any conference under this rule consideration may be given, and the court may take appropriate action, with respect to

(1) the formulation and simplification of the issues * * *

* * *

(4) the avoidance of unnecessary proof and of cumulative evidence * * *

* * *

(14) an order directing a party or parties to present evidence early in the trial with respect to a manageable issue that could, on the evidence, be the basis for a judgment as a matter of law under Rule 50(a);

(15) an order establishing a reasonable limit on the time allowed for presenting evidence, and

(16) such other matters as may facilitate the just, speedy, and inexpensive disposition of the action.

ENGLAND

Civil Procedure Rules, Rule 1.4 (The White Book Service 2006).

(1) The court must further the overriding objective [i.e., to deal with cases justly—Eds.] by actively managing cases.

(2) Active case management include—

(a) encouraging the parties to co-operate with each other in the conduct of the proceedings

* * *

(b) deciding promptly which issues need full investigation and trial and accordingly disposing summarily of the others;

(c) deciding the order in which issues are to be resolved

* * *

(g) fixing timetables or otherwise controlling the progress of the case;

(h) considering whether the likely benefits of taking a particular step justify the costs of taking it ;

* * *

(l) giving directions to ensure that the trial of a case proceeds quickly and efficiently.

GERMANY

Code of Civil Procedure*

§ **272** (1) The action shall be treated generally in a comprehensively prepared session for oral argument (main hearing).

(2) The presiding judge shall either schedule a time for a preliminary first session for oral argument or order a preliminary written proceeding.

(3) The oral argument shall be held as soon as possible.

§ **273** (1) The court shall effect necessary preparatory measures in a timely manner. At every stage of the proceedings, the parties shall be influenced to make timely and complete declarations.

(2) for the purpose of preparing each session, the presiding judge or a member of the court designated by him or her may:

> (i) require the parties to supplement or clarify their preparatory pleadings, and to deliver documents and other objects suitable for deposit with the court, and without limiting the generality thereof, to set a time period for the clarification of certain points requiring clarification ...

§ **275** * * * (2) In the event that the proceeding shall not be concluded at the initial preliminary session for oral argument, the court shall issue all orders necessary for the preparation of the principal session. * * *

§ **278** (1) The state of facts and the status of the dispute shall be established by the court at the principal hearing session. The parties present shall be heard in person to such end.

(2) The taking of evidence shall immediately follow in a defended trial. Following the taking of evidence, the state of facts and of the dispute shall again be discussed with the parties.

(3) A legal point which a party shall have obviously overlooked or held unimportant may be relied upon by the court for its decision * * *.

JAPAN

Code of Civil Procedure**

Article 2 *Responsibility of court and parties*

Courts shall make efforts to secure that civil actions be conducted with justice and speed, and parties shall conduct civil actions in accordance with good faith and trust.

---

* Translation in German Commercial Code and Code of Civil Procedure in English (Charles E. Stewart, trans., 2001).

** Translation in Code of Civil Procedure and Rules of Civil Procedure of Japan (Ma-satoshi Kasai and Andrew H. Thorson, trans., 1999).

Article 148 (1) The presiding judge shall control the oral argument. (2) The presiding judge may allow statements or prohibit persons who do not comply with orders from making statements.

Article 149 (1) The presiding judge may question the parties or require them to present evidence on matters of fact and law, on a date set for oral argument or on an occasion other than such date, in order to clarify the relationships involved in the litigation.

Article 151 (1) The court may take the following dispositions in order to clarify the relationships involved in the litigation:

1. order the appearance of a principal party or the legal representative of the principal party on a date set for oral argument;

2. have a person, who manages or assists in business for a party and who is deemed proper by the court, make statements on a date set for oral argument;

3. order the production of such items as documents concerning the litigation, documents referred to in the litigation and other articles which are in the possession of a party;

4. inspect or order an expert opinion.

III. THE ROLE OF THE JUDGE AND ATTORNEY AT THE HEARING

As the preceding excerpts about the structure of the first instance proceeding suggest, the behavior of the judge varies considerably across different legal systems. Markedly, in the civil law system, "the court rather than the parties' lawyers takes the main responsibility for gathering and sifting evidence, although the lawyers exercise a watchful eye over the court's work."[7] In this section we focus on the differing roles of the lawyers and the judge in organizing the proceeding and questioning the witnesses. As you read these materials, bear in mind that in most systems, whether common or civil law, the judge has power to order departure from normal practices. Indeed, many commentators contend that the most pronounced trend in procedure all over the world has been the growth of judicial discretionary authority.

Oscar G. Chase, Law, Culture, and Ritual: Disputing Systems in Cross–Cultural Context 62–65 (2005).

A significant difference between American litigation and that used in the civil law countries concerns the role of the judge: the American remaining largely passive during the trial except when called upon by

---

7.   Langbein, supra note 1, at 826.

not the judge who decides what evidence is needed, and it is the attorneys who present the evidence through the examination of witnesses and presentation of documents. A fictional American lawyer once caught the predominant view admirably when he offered the opinion that an American judge "is sworn to sit down, shut up, and listen."

* * *

John Langbein accordingly claims that the " 'grand discriminant' " between the American and Continental legal cultures is "adversarial versus judicial responsibility for gathering and presenting the facts." Germany, which is in this regard typical of many civil law countries, can accordingly serve as a basis for examining the point in more detail. The German judge has a statutory "duty" to clarify issues, which involves the court deeply in the development of the case. "Always examining the case as it progresses with understanding of the probably applicable norms, the court puts questions intended to mark out areas of agreement and disagreement, to elucidate allegations and proof offers and the meaning of matters elicited in proof-taking* * *. The court leads the parties by suggestion to strengthen their respective positions, to improve upon, change, and amplify their allegations and proof offers and to take other steps. It may recommend that the parties take specific measures in the litigation." The court, acting on recommendations from the parties, decides whether to hear a particular witness and the order in which the witnesses will be heard and documents presented.

"One of the most notable differences" between the process at the common law trial and the oral hearing in the civil law process "is the method of interrogating witnesses." In the civil law countries it is the judge who alone or predominantly questions the witnesses. * * *.

Like other Continentals the German judge has a control over the actual interrogation of the witnesses that is particularly telling:

In the ordinary case there is relatively little questioning by the lawyers or parties. What there is of it is generally conducted direct rather than through the court. For the lawyer to examine at length after the court seemingly has exhausted the witness is to imply that the court has not done a satisfactory job—a risky stratagem.

Thus, what is arguably the most important role of American trial lawyer—examination and cross-examination of witnesses—is almost entirely ceded to the Continental judge.

To be sure, recent changes in American litigation rules have tended to enhance the role of the court in relation to the parties: the whole concept of "managerial judging" centers on the power and responsibility of the judge to move the case along, to promote settlement if possible, and at the very least to get to the trial promptly. One could argue that in this respect there has been a convergence between the systems, a point made forcefully by Adrian Zuckerman. But the critical difference, "the grand discriminant," remains constant. It is still the American lawyer— not the court—that is responsible for gathering and presenting the proof.

It is still the American lawyer—not the court—who is responsible for choosing the witnesses and for questioning and cross-examining them. Notwithstanding the ritualized elevation of the American judge— through honors of place, dress and forms of address, it is the parties, through their lawyers, who dominate the trial itself. Note, too, how the differential in the American and Continental judicial powers parallels the differential in their powers to find the facts—the weaker American must often cede power to the lay jury.

The case for common law/civil law convergence is much stronger when we use England as the exemplar of the common law and look at the new English Civil Procedure Rules. Neil Andrews, describing "extensive * * * modification of the adversarial principle," notes that the new rules not only include greater pre-trial managerial powers but also grant the British judge more power to control the trial, to prescribe the evidence required and the means of its presentation. Judicial questioning of witnesses will apparently become much more frequent. This is not the case in the United States.

When we look at the power of the judge to find and determine the law applicable to the case, we find that the American judge has the power that is at the heart of the common law system—the power to make law by developing and applying new legal norms. The common law tradition allows the judge to help shape the law through legal decisions that become part of the corpus of *stare decisis*. The civil law counterpart, considered to be merely *"la bouche de la loi,"* is theoretically limited to applying the law as set forth by the legislator. She cannot "make" law. Is the greater role of the Continental judge at trial trivialized because in the law-making the American judge is the more powerful? In my view, this difference does not contradict my central point that in the courtroom, as between the judge and the litigants, the former is more powerful on the Continent. The point is also buttressed by the Continental judge's authority to take note of and apply law that has not been argued by the parties, whereas the U.S. counterpart is in general limited to deciding the case on the basis of law actually relied upon by the parties.

* * *

* * * Michele Taruffo argues that the allocation of authority between the parties on one hand, or the court, on the other, reflects such cultural factors as "the trust in individual self help rather than in the State as a provider of legal protection; the trust in lawyers rather than judges, or vice-versa; different conceptions of the relationships among private individuals and between individuals and the public authority; different conceptions of whether and how rights should be protected and enforced and so forth."

Notes

1.   Amendments to the German Code of Civil Procedure (the ZPO) in 2002 augmented the judge's role in the litigation. As amended, ZPO § 139 requires the judge to "alert the parties as soon as possible" to his own view of the merits of the case, *see* Gerhard Walter, The German Civil Procedure Reform Act 2002: Much Ado About Nothing? in Nicolò Trocker and Vincenzo Varano, eds., The Reforms of Civil Procedure in Comparative Perspective 67, 75 (2005).

2.   In Italy, on the other hand, reform has accorded more control to the lawyers at the expense of traditional judicial control over case preparation, as explained in the following excerpt.

Michele Taruffo, Recent and Current Reforms of Civil Procedure in Italy, in The Reforms of Civil Procedure in Comparative Perspective 224–227 (Nicolò Trocker and Vincenzo Varano, eds., 2005).

Faced with the problems of civil justice, the current government entrusted selected groups of experts (judges, lawyers and academics) with the task of preparing procedural reforms mainly aimed at reducing the delays of civil proceedings.

The main feature of what is proposed as a new model for the ordinary civil proceedings, in corporate cases as well as—possibly—in any other case, is a radical reform of the preparatory phase of such proceedings: a reform that is conceived and advertised in the name of the so-called "privatization" of civil justice. In the terms of the two texts just mentioned, "privatizing" means that the preparatory stage of the proceeding should be—so to say—taken away from the hands of the judge and entrusted exclusively to those of the parties' lawyers. No more "managerial judges", therefore, but only "managerial lawyers", if one assumes that it is not an oxymoron.

Going further into the details: the proceeding should consist of essentially two phases. The first phase begins with the notice of the statement of claim: the notice is served by the plaintiff directly to the defendant, without submitting the case to the judge. This phase ends up when one of the parties files a request to the judge for the fixation of a hearing before the court; then the judge makes a decree that concludes the preparation of the case and fixes the date of a hearing that will be devoted to the discussion of the case. The second phase consists of this hearing, in which the case is discussed, the evidence is presented, the case is conclusively argued by the lawyers, and eventually the final judgment is delivered by the judge (see art. 16, text *a*). * * *

The most important part of the reforms that we are considering is the "new" procedural model that is adopted for the preparation of the case. The core of this model is that this phase of the proceeding will consist *only and exclusively* of the exchange of a number of written pleadings and briefs between the parties' lawyers, without having any contact with the judge. The rules regulate the first two pleadings for each party (arts. 2, 4, 6 and 7, text *a),* but it is also provided that the exchange of briefs can continue much further, without any limit concerning the number of writings or the time allowed (a time limit is provided only by art. 7 of text *a*, but no limit is provided by text *b*). All this may be put to an end only when a party will feel satisfied and will ask the judge to fix the hearing for the presentation of evidence (art. 8, text *a*).

Therefore, the guiding idea is that the case should be prepared *only* by the parties' lawyers, without any intervention, control or management by the judge, by means of an exchange of a possibly unlimited amount of writings, and that such an exchange of briefs will keep going on until one of the lawyers will be tired of it. The assumptions underlying such a guiding idea are clearly the following:

(a) the judge should have no role at all in the preparation of the case;

(b) the best preparation of the case is made by the lawyers alone;

(c) the best way of preparing the case is to allow the exchange of a virtually unlimited number of briefs;

(d) the length of this phase of the proceeding and the size of the paperwork should be freely determined by the parties' choice;

(e) only a party may decide that the moment has come to submit the case to the judge.

Note

The procedural reforms described by Professor Taruffo came into force for some commercial cases in January, 2004. It is noteworthy that even prior to these changes Italian judges were far from "managerial" in their handling of cases. "While it is true that some rules of the Italian Code of Civil Procedure vest the judge with several powers concerning the direction and the management of cases, one must consider that in practice these powers are used very lightly, since the prevailing attitude of judges is not to interfere with the management of the case, leaving that task to the parties." Michele Taruffo, Civil Procedure and the Path of a Civil Case, in Introduction to Italian Law 165 (Jeffrey S. Lena and Ugo Mattei, eds., 2002).

As we see from the following excerpt, French procedure gives the presiding judge a good deal of discretion with regard to the presentation of evidence.

Frédérique Ferrand, The Respective Role of the Judge and the Parties in the Preparation of the Case in France, in The Reforms of Civil Procedure in Comparative Perspective 28–29 (Nicolò Trocker and Vincenzo Varano, eds., 2005).

The judge of the preparation can also order an inquiry (*enquête*) at the request of one party or *ex officio*. The order states the facts to be proved. The judge of the preparation (or another judge if no preparatory stage takes place) is charged to hear the witnesses who give evidence under oath. The evidence of witnesses is given in an adversary manner before the judge in charge of the inquiry. The powers of the judge are large; he can interrogate the witnesses, confront him to another witness or to the parties. The examination is led by the judge. The parties' lawyers can only propose questions to the judge who decides whether they are relevant. There is no cross-examination. The court clerk draws up a record of all the stages of the inquiry and of the evidence from the judge's dictation.

But most of the time, witnesses are not directly heard by the judge of the preparation or by the court during the final hearing. French practice often uses *affidavits,* written testimony. In order to ensure the probative value of affidavits, French law requires that the author's civil status appears with his relationship, if any, with the parties (family links, subordination, co-operation or community of interests). It must be entirely hand-written by the author, dated and signed, with the proof of his identity (most often a photocopy of the identity card). A false affidavit exposes one to penal sanctions. Written testimony is more flexible and gains time, but does not guarantee the truth and spontaneity of the witness. The judge is free (pouvoir souverain) to accept or to refuse to hear as a witness persons who have written an affidavit.

The judge can also decide to do himself personal verification (Art. 179 NCPC, *vérifications personnelles du juge*) and to go to the scene, but this happens rarely because in practice, judges do not have enough time for that. The judge can also require that the parties should appear personally in order to hear them and to ask them some questions (*comparution personnelle des parties*). But this seems to happen rarely because the results are often not convincing. In case of a personal appearance of a party, the judge may request this party to make a declaration under oath (*serment supplétoire*) but this also happens rarely.

He can also ask a specialist his opinion on a point of fact which requires specialised knowledge (findings, consultation or expertise: constatations, consultation or expertise). Expert advice can only concern a point of fact raising a technical problem. Expert proceedings are regulated in detail by the New Code of Civil procedure. * * *

Note

French law (like some other civil law systems) allows a person with a civil claim to institute a criminal proceeding, called the *action civile* which is then prosecuted by that person along with the ordinary prosecutorial officials. In the following excerpt, an eminent French attorney claims that overuse of the process requires substantial limiting reforms.

Daniel Soulez Lariviere, Overview of the Problems of French Civil Procedure, 45 Am. J. Comp. L. 737, 745–746 (1997).

[S]pecific provisions of French law concerning victims entitle them to bring suit before the criminal courts, and the number of victims who are now choosing to do so is quite overwhelming, causing problems of public policy and flying in the face of common sense. Because a party claiming damages in criminal proceedings is automatically represented by the State, it has at its disposal the entire State police machinery with which to wage its own private war, which may or may not be justified, in conditions which are much more gratifying than in the civil courts. As long as, in certain cases, civil hearings remain considerably undervalued, and the judges are not given sufficient authority, greater numbers of victims of all kinds will abandon the civil courts in favor of the criminal courts. All of a sudden what was simply a particularity of the French system—the strong position of the victim—will become a major flaw in emotional cases, with the state prosecutor having to bow to the dictates of parties claiming damages, which may well be associations using the services of professional teams of lawyers, technical experts and media consultants. The state prosecutors are constantly aware of the pressure of public opinion, as expressed through such associations.

Similarly, even in the business world, the strategy of seeking remedy in the criminal courts is becoming a means of harming, blackmailing and destabilizing a rival company for claimants who have very little hard evidence, but who take advantage of the State apparatus to wage their own private war, acquiring the services of the police free-of-charge. In order to re-establish the equilibrium, the law would have to try and de-penalize an antiquatedly over-criminalized legal system, which inflates the importance of the criminal courts, although this would require great courage.

IV. EVIDENCE AND PRESENTATION OF PROOF

Mirjan R. Damaška, Evidence Law Adrift 12–17 (1997).

Virtually all observers agree that the intense preliminary screening of evidence constitutes a salient trait of the Anglo–American fact-finding style. This trait is primarily the product of institutional arrangements regarding the policing of the receipt of evidence. But the screening is also anchored in normative considerations: it is the law that supplies the criteria for separating admissible from inadmissible information. We should hence not be surprised to find that exclusionary rules are widely considered a hallmark of Anglo–American evidence. From a comparative standpoint, however, this is another gross exaggeration: only a small subset of exclusionary rules is truly idiomatic to the common law. To identify this subset, a quick reconnaissance of the Continental legal landscape is in order.

Extrinsic exclusionary rules. Rules rejecting probative information for the sake of values unrelated to the pursuit of truth are clearly not limited to the world of Anglo–American justice. A piquant example is testimonial privileges: not only are they widespread on the Continent, but they often assume broader forms-much more encompassing than in the law of any common law country. Thus, in addition to refusing to answer self-incriminating questions, in many European jurisdictions witnesses can refuse to answer questions potentially capable of incriminating members of their family. Some countries go even further and dispense witnesses from the duty to answer any question likely to dishonor them or expose them to direct financial loss. Other countries grant parties in civil litigation a general dispensation from the duty to testify. Indeed, so expansive are some of these testimonial privileges that one wonders how the lawgivers' promises can be kept without seriously harming the interests of justice.

* * *

Intrinsic exclusionary rules. Rules typical of common law can be found only among those that reject probative information, on the belief that its elimination will enhance the accuracy of fact-finding. Consider threshold demands on the probative force of evidence. It is daily routine in Anglo–American courtrooms to oppose admission of evidence on the ground that its significance is too slight or that its connection with material facts of the case is too remote. There is no real analogue to this routine in Continental trials.

Although it is not precisely true that Continental systems are ready to admit all logically relevant information, when all demands on the minimal probative potential of evidence are duly accounted for, they still appear remarkably unexacting by comparison with those of the Anglo–American law.

More peculiar and also more important are common law rules rejecting probative material on the theory that it might be overestimated or on the theory that its probative value is overshadowed by its "prejudicial" capacity—its capacity to unfairly predispose the trier of fact toward a particular out-come. The hearsay rule is by far the best known example of exclusion on the first of these two grounds. Although countries outside of the common law's compass are not unaware of hearsay dangers, their reaction to them seldom assumes the form of exclusionary rules. Where it does, as is sporadically the case in criminal procedure, the embrace of the exclusionary option is rooted as much in due process values as it is in the desire to protect the adjudicator from unreliable information. With minor qualifications, then, derivative information is readily available to Continental fact finders, especially in written form and in the form of hearsay remarks by firsthand witnesses. Expressed in short-hand, typical strictures against hearsay—more important in criminal than in civil cases—convey no more than the following message to the adjudicator: "Use original sources of information whenever they are reasonably available. When you feel you must rely on a derivative source, explain in a written opinion the reasons that impelled you to give credence to information that is usually of inferior value."

One also scans the legal map of Europe in vain for analogues to common law provisions that prohibit character evidence, evidence of collateral misdeeds, or similar information about a person's past life. The few rules that can be located on this subject are intended not to enhance the accuracy of fact-finding but to impose side-constraints on the pursuit of truth for the sake of extrinsic policy reasons. Again, this does not suggest that Continental law fails to realize the risks of relying on inferences from propensity evidence. It is generally acknowledged as improper to assume that just because an accused has a criminal record or has committed a collateral bad act he is more likely to have committed the crime with which he is now charged-or, in civil matters, that just because a person was negligent in the past, he is likely to have been similarly culpable in the occurrence *sub judice*. But Continental evidentiary theory focuses only on whether information from a person's past has probative value: if it is probative, it can and should be used in adjudication. Absent from mainstream Continental thought is the concern that propensity information, although probative, could be accorded more weight than it deserves or that it could generate unfair bias against a litigant. The worry that dirty linen from a person's past could obscure whatever relevance propensity inferences might possess is hence a distinctive concern of Anglo–American evidence law.

What final lesson is suggested by this breathtaking tour of Continental legal landscapes? It turns out that exclusionary rules per se are indeed not uniquely characteristic of common law evidence. We enter genuine common law territory only as we examine the rejection of probative information on the ground that it may be misused. Only this motive for the exercise of the exclusionary option is the common law's true *nonpareil*.

Michele Taruffo, Civil Procedure and the Path of a Civil Case, in Introduction to Italian Law 168–170 (Jeffrey S. Lena and Ugo Mattei, eds., 2002).

The general principle concerning the admission of evidence is that evidence is admitted by the judge when it is *relevant* and *legally admissible*. Relevancy depends on the logical connection of the single item of evidence with the facts of the case. * * *

The legal admissibility of evidence is determined by various rules limiting or excluding some types of evidence under special circumstances recognized by law. The most important exclusionary rules deal with cases in which the only evidence admitted consists of *written documents*. In this realm, the Italian legal system follows the traditional French model, according to which several types of contracts can be proved only by means of written evidence. With oral (and particularly testimonial) evidence excluded * * * In other cases, the exclusion is based on the assumption of the relatively lower reliability of testimonial evidence. There are additional specific rules of exclusion. For instance, non-parties who might possibly intervene in the case are not allowed to testify. Moreover, parties cannot be heard as witnesses, although they can make probative statements in the form of either confessions or oaths. On the other hand, there is nothing similar to the American hearsay rule, since secondhand testimony is ordinarily admitted (although the court may order the examination of the "firsthand" witness when possible, and the probative weight of hearsay evidence should be cautiously assessed).

Another important group of rules excluding evidence is aimed at the protection of several types of secrets. These rules are the Italian equivalent of Anglo–American rules concerning privileges * * *

On the basis of the standards of relevancy and admissibility, the court makes a selection from the evidence offered by the parties and determines what evidence will actually be presented. The order admitting or excluding the various items of evidence is issued by the court at the end of the phase devoted to the preparation of the case. * * *

Oral evidence includes three main items. Testimony may be given by any non-party who knows anything relevant to the facts in issue. From the Anglo–American perspective, it is no doubt remarkable that the parties and third parties *cannot* testify as witnesses; even potential third parties are not competent to testify. The parties can be—or according to the law *should* be, but sometimes this does not actually occur—examined by the judges in an informal way and without swearing to tell the truth (the so-called *interrogatorio libero*), but this is not testimony in the proper sense. This kind of examination is aimed only at clarifying the subject matter of the case, and possibly inducing the parties to settle their dispute.

A *civil confession* may be made by a party who admits that a fact contrary to his or her interest is true. * * * The admission of the truth of such a fact is a *legal proof*, which means that such a statement is binding both upon the court and the parties. * * *

Another legal proof is the *civil oath*. The civil oath may take three different forms: first, it may be initiated by a party challenging the other party to swear the truth of a favorable material fact * * * under threat of religious and moral sanctions and criminal sanctions in the case of perjury; secondly, it may be initiated by the court when there is some evidence of a fact but the court thinks it should be supported by a sworn statement * * * and thirdly, it may be initiated by the court simply in order to determine the value of something * * * In any case, if the oath is taken, its outcome is strictly binding for both the judge and the parties.

Note

In addition to the differences between the rules of evidence in Continental countries and those applicable in American courts, the courts apply different rules to expert testimony. This is described in the next passages.

John H. Langbein, The German Advantage in Civil Procedure, 52 U. Chi. L. Rev. 823, 835–841 (1985).

The European jurist who visits the United States and becomes acquainted with our civil procedure typically expresses amazement at our witness practice. His amazement turns to something bordering on disbelief when he discovers that we extend the sphere of partisan control to the selection and preparation of experts. In the Continental tradition experts are selected and commissioned by the court, although with great attention to safeguarding party interests. In the German system, experts are not even called witnesses. They are thought of as judges' aides.

Perverse incentives. At the American trial bar, those of us who serve as expert witnesses are known as "saxophones." This is a revealing term, as slang often is. The idea is that the lawyer plays the tune, manipulating the expert as though the expert were a musical instrument on which the lawyer sounds the desired notes. I sometimes serve as an expert in trust and pension cases, and I have experienced the subtle pressures to join the team—to shade one's views, to conceal doubt, to overstate nuance, to downplay weak aspects of the case that one has been hired to bolster. Nobody likes to disappoint a patron; and beyond this psychological pressure is the financial inducement. Money changes hands upon the rendering of expertise, but the expert can run his meter only so long as his patron litigator likes the tune. Opposing counsel undertakes a similar exercise, hiring and schooling another expert to parrot the contrary position. The result is our familiar battle of opposing experts. The more measured and impartial an expert is, the less likely he is to be used by either side.

At trial, the battle of experts tends to baffle the trier, especially in jury courts. If the experts do not cancel each other out, the advantage is likely to be with the expert whose forensic skills are the more enticing. The system invites abusive cross-examination. Since each expert is party-selected and party-paid, he is vulnerable to attack on credibility regardless of the merits of his testimony. A defense lawyer recently bragged about his technique of cross-examining plaintiffs' experts in tort cases. Notice that nothing in his strategy varies with the truthfulness of the expert testimony he tries to discredit.

A mode of attack ripe with potential is to pursue a line of questions which, by their form and the jury's studied observation of the witness in response, will tend to cast the expert as a "professional witness." By proceeding in this way, the cross-examiner will reap the benefit of a community attitude, certain to be present among several of the jurors, that bias can be purchased, almost like a commodity.

Thus, the systematic incentive in our procedure to distort expertise leads to a systematic distrust and devaluation of expertise. Short of forbidding the use of experts altogether, we probably could not have designed a procedure better suited to minimize the influence of expertise.

The Continental tradition. European legal systems are, by contrast, expert-prone. Expertise is frequently sought. The literature emphasizes the value attached to having expert assistance available to the courts in an age in which litigation involves facts of ever-greater technical difficulty. The essential insight of Continental civil procedure is that credible expertise must be neutral expertise. Thus, the responsibility for selecting and informing experts is placed upon the courts, although with important protections for party interests.

Selecting the expert. German courts obtain expert help in lawsuits the way Americans obtain expert help in business or personal affairs. If you need an architect, a dermatologist, or a plumber, you do not commission a pair of them to take preordained and opposing positions on your problem, although you do sometimes take a second opinion. Rather, you take care to find an expert who is qualified to advise you in an objective manner; you probe his advice as best you can; and if you find his advice persuasive, you follow it.

When in the course of winnowing the issues in a lawsuit a German court determines that expertise might help resolve the case, the court selects and instructs the expert. The court may decide to seek expertise on its own motion, or at the request of one of the parties. The code of civil procedure allows the court to request nominations from the parties—indeed, the code requires the court to use any expert upon whom the parties—but neither practice is typical. In general, the court takes the initiative in nominating and selecting the expert.

The only respect in which the code of civil procedure purports to narrow the court's discretion to choose the expert is a provision whose significance is less than obvious: "If experts are officially designated for certain fields of expertise, other persons should be chosen only when special circumstances require." One looks outside the code of civil procedure, to the federal statutes regulating various professions and trades, for the particulars on official designation. For the professions, the statutes typically authorize the official licensing bodies to assemble lists of professionals deemed especially suited to serve as experts. In other fields, the state governments designate quasi-public bodies to compile such lists. For example, under section 36 of the federal code on trade regulation, the state governments empower the regional chambers of commerce and industry (Industrie- and Handelskammern) to identify experts in a wide variety or commercial and technical fields. That statute directs the empowered chamber to choose as experts persons who have exceptional knowledge of the particular specialty and to have these persons sworn to render professional and impartial expertise. The chamber circulates its lists of experts, organized by specialty and subspecialty, to the courts. German judges receive sheaves of these lists as the various issuing bodies update and recirculate them.

Current practice. In 1984 I spent a little time interviewing judges in Frankfurt about their practice in selecting experts. My sample of a handful of judges is not large enough to impress statisticians, but I think the picture that emerges from serious discussion with people who operate the system is worth reporting. Among the judges with whom I spoke, I found unanimity on the proposition that the most important factor predisposing a judge to select an expert is favorable experience with that expert in an earlier case. Experts thus build reputations with the bench. Someone who renders a careful, succinct, and well-substantiated report and who responds effectively to the subsequent questions of the court and the parties will be remembered when another case arises in his specialty. Again we notice that German civil procedure tracks the patterns of decision-making in ordinary business and personal affairs: If you get a plumber to fix your toilet and he does it well, you incline to hire him again.

When judges lack personal experience with appropriate experts, I am told, they turn to the authoritative lists described above. If expertise is needed in a field for which official lists are unavailing, the court is thrown upon its own devices. The German judge then gets on the phone, working from party suggestions and from the court's own research, much in the fashion of an American litigator hunting for expertise. In these cases there is a tendency to turn, first, to the bodies that prepare expert lists in cognate areas; or, if none, to the universities and technical institutes.

If enough potential experts are identified to allow for choice, the court will ordinarily consult party preferences. In such circumstances a litigant may ask the court to exclude an expert whose views proved contrary to his interests in previous litigation or whom he otherwise disdains. The court will try to oblige the parties' tastes when another qualified expert can be substituted. Nevertheless, a litigant can formally challenge an expert's appointment only on the narrow grounds for which a litigant could seek to recuse a judge.

Preparing the expert. The court that selects the expert instructs him, in the sense of propounding the facts that he is to assume or to investigate, and in framing the questions that the court wishes the expert to address. In formulating the expert's task, as in other important steps in the conduct of the case, the court welcomes adversary suggestions. If the expert should take a view of premises (for example, in an accident case or a building-construction dispute), counsel for both sides will accompany him.

Safeguards. The expert is ordinarily instructed to prepare a written opinion. When the court receives the report, it is circulated to the litigants. The litigants commonly file written comments, to which the expert is asked to reply. The court on its own motion may also request the expert to amplify his views. If the expert's report remains in contention, the court will schedule a hearing at which counsel for a dissatisfied litigant can confront and interrogate the expert.

The code of civil procedure reserves to the court the power to order a further report by another expert if the court should deem the first report unsatisfactory. A litigant dissatisfied with the expert may encourage the court to invoke its power to name a second expert .... When, therefore, a litigant can persuade the court that an expert's report has been sloppy or partial, that it rests upon a view of the field that is not generally shared, or that the question referred to the expert is exceptionally difficult, the court will commission further expertise.

A litigant may also engage his own expert, much as is done in the Anglo–American procedural world, in order to rebut the court-appointed expert. The court will discount the views of a party-selected expert on account of his want of neutrality, but cases occur in which he nevertheless proves to be effective. Ordinarily, I am told, the court will not in such circumstances base its judgment directly upon the views of the party-selected expert; rather, the court will treat the rebuttal as ground for engaging a further court-appointed expert (called an *Oberexperte*, literally an "upper" or "superior" expert), whose opinion will take account of the rebuttal.

To conclude: In the use of expertise German civil procedure strikes an adroit balance between nonadversarial and adversarial values. Expertise is kept impartial, but litigants are protected against error or caprice through a variety of opportunities for consultation, confrontation, and rebuttal.

The American counterpart. It may seem curious that we make so little use of court appointed experts in our civil practice, since "[t]he inherent power of a trial judge to appoint an expert of his own choosing is virtually unquestioned" and has been extended and codified in the Federal Rules of Evidence and the Uniform Rules of Evidence (Model Expert Testimony Act). The literature displays both widespread agreement that our courts virtually never exercise this authority, and a certain bafflement about why.

While "simple inertia" doubtless accounts for much (our judges "are accustomed to presiding over acts initiated by the parties"), a comparative example points to a further explanation. The difficulty originates with the locktight segmentation of our procedure into pretrial and trial compartments, and with the tradition of partisan domination of the pretrial. Until lately, it was exceptional for the judge to have detailed acquaintance with the facts of the case until the parties presented their evidence at trial. By then the adversaries would have engaged their own experts, and time would no longer allow a court-appointed expert to be located and prepared. Effective use of court-appointed experts as exemplified in German practice presupposes early and extensive judicial involvement in shaping the whole of the proofs.

Richard W. Hulbert, Comment on French Civil Procedure, 45 Am. J. Comp. L. 747, 749 (1997).

When controverted issues of fact, particularly facts of a technical nature, do arise to be dealt with, the French practice will almost invariably leave the resolution of them to an expert appointed by the court. The appointee will conduct an investigation outside the courtroom, under no formal rules of evidence or relevance, at sessions to which the parties are convoked with full freedom to present their views and those of their experts or other representatives, orally or in writing. The result of the *expertise* is a report that in principle the judge need not accept, but in the absence of other evidence, it is difficult to see how it could be rejected, provided that the judge is satisfied that the *expert* has done what he was commissioned to do and that no material procedural irregularities have been committed in the course of the *expertise.*

Note

In England the Civil Procedure Rules of 1998 (CPR) effected substantial changes in the use of expert witnesses in that country's courts:

> Expert evidence was a cause of much unnecessary cost and delay under the pre-CPR system due to the culture of confrontation that permeated the use of experts in litigation. * * * To remedy the shortcomings of the old system the CPR adopt three radical measures. First, the use of experts is placed under the complete control of the court. No party may rely on expert evidence without the court's permission (CPR 35.4(1)). Parties are no longer free to call as many experts as they wish. Second, an expert's primary duty is to help the court to arrive at a correct decision on matters within his expertise, rather than advance one or other of the parties' causes (CPR 35.3(1)). Lastly, the rules seek to promote party co-operation in the employment of experts, even before the start of proceedings, and to encourage the use of joint experts wherever possible.[8]

V. DECISION MAKERS

Oscar G. Chase, Law, Culture, and Ritual: Disputing Systems in Cross–Cultural Context 55 (2005).

The civil jury. "The jury is one of America's venerated institutions." It has achieved and maintained an importance in American trials that is unparalleled elsewhere in the world. While the jury retains a lively role in criminal cases in most English-speaking nations (but not in the rest of the world), it is striking that in no other nation does the jury play the role in civil litigation that it has in the United States. The right to a jury trial in civil cases in the U.S. is historic and iconic: it was added to the Federal Constitution by the Seventh Amendment as one of the Bill of Rights ratified in 1791. In 1938, when the Federal Rules of Civil Procedure were promulgated, its drafters thought it desirable to include a provision reminding readers that "The right of trial by jury as declared by the Seventh Amendment to the Constitution or as given by a statute of the United States shall be preserved to the parties inviolate." The Seventh Amendment and the Federal Rules apply only in federal litigation, but the right to a jury in civil cases is found in state constitutions as well.

* * *

---

8. Zuckerman on Civil Procedure: Principles of Practice 713 (2nd ed. 2006).

Contrariwise, juries have never been used in civil cases in any of the countries that follow Continental procedure. The power of the jury in the American tradition has been called "[t]ruly astonishing in the Continental view * * *." And England, where it originated, has abandoned the civil jury in all but a very few kinds of cases. Other common law jurisdictions have followed suit.

Alan B. Morrison, Courts, in Fundamentals of American Law 57, 75–79 (Alan B. Morrison, ed., 1996).

TRIAL

A very small percentage of the cases filed are actually tried in United States courts—state or federal. Some cases are simply withdrawn without any attempt at proceeding; others are dismissed either on the motion of the defendant to dismiss or for summary judgment; a very large portion are settled with the plaintiff obtaining some, but less than all, of the relief sought in the complaint; and the remainder, generally about 10 percent, go to trial. Some cases are settled for relatively modest sums, where the plaintiff has little chance of prevailing, but the defendant is willing to pay something simply to avoid further costs and attorney's fees. Most of the settlements, how ever, are based on the assessments of the parties that there are risks on both sides, and that a settlement is in the interest of everyone, rather than risking an all or nothing verdict at trial.

One aspect of American trials has made all litigants conscious of the risks of litigation: the role of the jury. In the federal system, both parties have a right to a trial by a jury, composed of between six and twelve persons, on all claims involving money damages (Rule 38). The Seventh Amendment to the United States Constitution guarantees the right for claims in excess of $20 'in suits at common law' where there was a right to trial by jury, which includes personal injury and breach of contract claims. In the more than 200 years since the Seventh Amendment became law, many new types of actions have been created, and the courts have held that, even if the cause of action is new, if it is of the type for which there would have been a jury trial in 1789, then the claim is one for which there is a right to a jury trial today, even if the claim was first created in 1989. Although the Seventh Amendment applies only to trials in federal courts, most state constitutions contain similar rights to trial by jury.

Juries are picked from the lists of eligible voters in the geographic area covered by the court, and the members serve for relatively brief periods of time, as an obligation of their citizenship. They are compensated, but only minimally, and they are often asked to decide extremely difficult and important disputes. The larger panels of potential jury members are selected by lot, from which individual jurors are excused if there is some reason to believe they would not be impartial-such as being a friend or a relative of a party or of a lawyer in the case. In addition, there is an opportunity for each side to exclude up to three other jurors without specific cause, in winnowing the larger group down to the actual jury, plus one or two alternates. Generally, lawyers use this right, known as a 'preemptory challenge', to remove potential jurors whom they believe would be more favorable to the other side. The Supreme Court has recently limited preemptory challenges to assure that jurors are not excluded based on considerations such as race or sex.

At the trial, which is open for any person to attend (subject to space limitations), the parties present their documentary evidence and witnesses in court, rather than through affidavits, with the plaintiff going first, followed by the defendant, and then any rebuttal by the plaintiff. The party calling the witness asks questions first and then the other side is allowed to question ('cross-examine') the witness. Judges are permitted to ask questions of any witness, but they generally refrain from doing so, especially in jury trials. At the conclusion of the evidence, each side's lawyer is entitled to summarize its case in an effort to persuade the jury to accept its version of the facts. Then the court gives the jury instructions, which are a translation of the law into terms that the jury can understand and apply, and the jury then leaves the courtroom, to discuss the case and vote in secret. In federal courts, the verdict must be unanimous, but in many states the verdict may be by majority of jurors. In most cases the jury will issue a general verdict—'we find that the defendant was not negligent', or 'we find the defendant liable and award plaintiff S100,000'-and in some cases the jury will be asked to answer specific questions, and the judge will then apply the law, a process known as a 'special verdict' (Rule 49). One reason for using special verdicts, especially in complex cases, is to be certain that the jury follows the law, instead of deciding the case on its notions of justice, or because it does not understand the judge's instructions on the legal rules that apply.

The task of the jury is to decide all factual issues. Among the most significant are issues of credibility—whom to believe when there is sharply contrasting testimony. Another vital role of the jury is setting damages, which is particularly significant where the plaintiff has sustained a physical injury, and she seeks compensation for pain and suffering, a determination which is obviously not subject to a precise numerical calculation. It is particularly because of the wide discretion given jurors on setting the amounts of damages that many cases are settled, rather than risking either a very high or a very low verdict.

While the jury controls the determinations of fact, the judge remains in control of the law. The judge's role is evident in several ways. First, at the conclusion of the plaintiff's case, the judge is often asked to rule that the plaintiff has failed to put on sufficient evidence to establish her claim as a matter of law, even if all disputed factual issues on which evidence has been presented are resolved in her favor (Rule 50(a). That motion, formerly known as a 'motion for a directed verdict', now referred to as a 'motion for judgment as a matter of law', is similar to a motion for summary judgment; it resolves the legal issue in favor of the defendant based upon the evidence presented at trial, whereas the motion for summary judgment is decided based on the evidence presented before trial. In either case, if there are genuine disputed issues of material fact, the court may not grant the motion.

Secondly, in a number of cases, the court will be in doubt as to whether to grant such a motion, but often will deny it and allow the defendant to put on its case and then have the jury reach its decision, If the jury decides in favor of the defendant, then the motion becomes moot. But if the jury rules in favor of the plaintiff, the court has the right to review the situation again, this time also considering the defendant's case, in determining whether there was sufficient evidence to permit the jury to find for the plaintiff (Rule 50(b)). If the judge concludes that there was insufficient evidence on the plaintiff's side, then it may enter a judgment in favor of the defendant, despite the contrary result reached by the jury. The court's power to overturn a jury verdict can also be exercised in favor of a losing plaintiff, but that occurs much less often because generally juries show more sympathy to injured plaintiffs than to defendants. Thus, although the jury is said to be the ultimate arbiter of factual disputes, the court retains the power to assure that the jury does not abuse this power by making unjustifiable factual findings that have the effect of negating the law.

The court has another alternative, to grant a new trial where it believes that, while the evidence may have been legally sufficient, it would be unfair to allow the judgment to stand because the great weight of the evidence pointed to a different result. Such a ruling is often made in cases where the damages are believed by the court to be excessive, or in a few cases inadequate, in which case there would be a retrial only on the issue of damages, but not on liability. The court can also make its ruling on a new trial conditional, by saying to the parties, for example, 'if you are willing to accept $100,000, instead of the $200,000 that was awarded, I will not order a new trial; otherwise there will be a new trial on damages'. It is then up to the parties (which generally means the winning side) to decide whether to accept that offer (known as a remittitur) since the court cannot force them to do so; it can simply order a new trial if they do not.

Although many trials are before juries, there are some cases in which there is no right to trial by jury (such as claims against the United States for personal injuries) or in which the parties may choose to have the case resolved by the judge. While it would be an unusual case in which a person injured in an accident would elect to have the case tried by a judge rather than a jury, there are cases in which both parties prefer a judge for a number of reasons. Among these are the complexity of the case; the fact that the judge may be highly regarded by everyone and/or be very familiar with the case by having ruled on motions along the way; the fact that the case can be presented more quickly before a judge than before a jury; or that for a variety of logistical reasons, the case must be tried in segments, and the judge is better able to handle the stopping and starting than would a jury. But if one party has properly demanded a jury trial, both sides must consent before the case can be tried by a judge alone (Rule 38(d)).

If a case is tried by a judge, the trial proceedings are generally similar to those before *a jury,* except that the judge will often admit evidence that might be kept from the jury on grounds of relevance or possible prejudice. At the end of the case, or often several weeks thereafter, the judge will issue a ruling in which she is required to make findings of fact and conclusions of law, which are more detailed than a decision by a jury. In many cases, the judge will ask the parties to submit proposed findings, sometimes before trial and some-times after trial, to assist the court and to sharpen the issues.

Peter L. Murray and Rolf Stürner, German Civil Justice 307–312 (2004).

1.   FREE EVALUATION OF PROOF

If decision of the case requires resolution of a factual issue, the court is required to evaluate the evidence relating to that issue and make a factual de-termination based on that evidence. In performing this function the court is not constrained by rules or rankings of proof, but can evaluate most forms of evidence according to its sound judgment and common sense.

ZPO § 286 prescribes:

"The court is to decide upon consideration of the entire content of the arguments and the results of reception of evidence according to its free conviction whether a factual assertion is to be regarded as true or untrue. The reasons which led to the court's convictions are to be stated in the judgment."

The principle of "free evaluation of proof" *(freie Beweiswürdigung)* is only qualified with respect to certain forms of documentary evidence, which on some issues can be given either prima facie, or conclusive weight.

At the same time, the court is not free to credit or discredit factual proof arbitrarily or whimsically. A German judge is expected to be able to articulate reasons for crediting or discrediting evidence and to explain the conclusions drawn from the evidence. So, for instance, if the court believes the testimony of one fact witness in preference to that of another, the court must be in a position to give reasons for its choice in the judgment. If the court draws a conclusion from proven facts, the court must be able to justify the conclusion by reference to either logic or experience.

2.   ROLES OF PARTIES AND COUNSEL

In analyzing the evidence, the court ordinarily will be bound by the parties' admissions and stipulations of fact *(Gestiindnisvertrcige.)* If the parties have agreed that the facts are to be determined based on a particular evidentiary record (e.g. solely from identified documents), their stipulation will be honored, except to the extent that the court can call for proof on its own motion (e.g. naming an expert witness).

The court must also make sure that the parties have opportunity to comment on the evidence received and the conclusions to be drawn before the court reaches its own findings and conclusions of fact. Following the reception of evidence the court must discuss anew with the parties the factual and legal issues in the case and, to the extent then possible, the results of the reception of evidence: The parties and their counsel are invited to address by oral argument the credibility of the evidence received as well as the conclusions to be drawn from it. If the proof is complex or circumstances other-wise suggest it, the parties are to be allowed reasonable opportunity to prepare their arguments and responses or to submit arguments in writing. Sometimes the result of reception of evidence may lead a party to designate additional evidence that should be received in order that the court get a complete factual picture. Proof which has not been exposed to party comment and argument may not be used as the basis for a judicial finding or determination. This insistence on party input after evidence has been received is another expression of the constitutionally based right to be heard *(rechtliches Gehör)* in German civil justice.

Usually this discussion with the parties and counsel occurs at the same hearing at which the evidence is presented. If the evidence was received by a single member of the panel or another judge, the parties are to be given the opportunity to argue the conclusions to be drawn from the evidence before the actual court which is to decide the case.

The process of addressing the evaluation of evidence affords opportunity for the interplay between judge and parties which is an essential feature of German civil justice. Good practice, if not specific rule language, mandates that the court share with the parties or their counsel its tentative conclusions and impressions from the reception of evidence, thus giving the parties opportunity to focus their arguments, to consider the offering of additional evidence, or to attempt to resolve the case.

The requirement that factual findings and conclusions be articulated and logically or experientially supported, as well as the opportunity for comprehensive review of such findings and conclusions on appeal, mean that considerable attention is paid to the logical and systematic evaluation of evidence by lawyers and judges. There is considerable literature on the process by which the judge evaluates evidence and draws factual conclusions. Although German lawyers may appear to play a secondary role in connection with the reception of evidence by the court, their arguments on how the evidence should be analyzed and what conclusions should be drawn can have a crucial effect on what the court does with that evidence. The attorney must listen carefully to a witness's testimony, and then be in the position to argue effectively why the court should, or should not credit the testimony, and conclusions should or should not be drawn from it, These arguments are based on considerations of consistency of the testimony with undisputed facts, other testimony, the laws of nature or human experience, the existence of bias or interest which might color the testimony, likely innocent and nefarious causes for a witness's testimony to diverge from the attorney's version of the case, and similar common-sense matters.

3. Standard of Proof in Civil Cases

In order to determine a fact in dispute, the court must be "convinced" *(überzeust)* that the fact exists, without setting an unrealistic standard of certainty. Such a level of conviction may be difficult to describe. Termed sufficient have been "a degree of certainty useable for practical life; or "such a high degree of probability as would quiet, without eliminating, the doubts of a person of reasonable and clear perception of the circumstances of life."

How high this probability must be is the subject of some dispute. Some scholars suggest that "more likely than not" should suffice. Others contend that a standard of probability akin to that of the common law would open the floodgates of liability. In practice theoretical formulations of degrees of conviction may be of little importance. The court will in the final analysis base its determinations on such evidence as is reasonable to expect, considering the circumstances of the case, the nature of the issue and the kind and amount of evidence available. One must remember that the German judge does not merely evaluate the presentation of others, but actively participates in the process of the reception and evaluation of the evidence, and in a sense, develops his own degree of conviction.

The requirement that the court have a subjective conviction of the truth of facts found and conclusions drawn does not prevent the court from relying on methods of proof which provide only a statistical likelihood of accuracy. For instance, blood tests or DNA-analyses, which associate persons to a high degree of statistical probability, can be used as the basis for a determination of parenthood.

The court can also reach a fact conclusion based on *prima fade* evidence *(Anscheinsbeweis)* in the absence of a contrary explanation. In many kinds of cases direct evidence of a fact in issue may be difficult for the proponent of that fact to procure. When in ordinary experience the facts proved are linked with a particular standard of care or causation, such standard of care or causation may be inferred in the absence of another explanation for the facts proved. So, for instance, if a motorist hits a pedestrian on the sidewalk, in the absence of other evidence the motorist's negligence can be inferred because in ordinary experience motor vehicles are not driven on the sidewalk unless the driver is careless. In the absence of an alternative explanation, prima facie evidence can give rise to a sufficiently convincing inference of the existence of the experientially-linked fact as to justify a fact finding.

Proof of damages raises particular problems in a regime which requires reasoned justification for all findings and conclusions. It is often difficult to determine the amount of damages with enough logical particularity as to with-stand rigorous rational analysis. For instance, how can the court determine with logical particularity the monetary amount of damages that should be awarded for pain and suffering sustained by an injured plaintiff? How can the court be "convinced" that any particular figure of damage is "true"? The same is often true of the causal link between the actions giving rise to legal liability and the damages assertedly flowing from those actions.

ZPO § 287 attempts to mitigate the standard of conviction required for proof of damages or causation of damage. Issues of the degree or the causation of damage are to be determined by the court's "free conviction in consideration of all the circumstances." This standard is generally believed to be somewhat less demanding than the standard of conviction required for other kinds of facts. The court is authorized to determine in its discretion the extent of specific evidence or expert testimony to be required or allowed on issues of causation and extent of damage. The court is required in its judgment to outline the "factual bases for the assessment" *(tatsächlichen Grundlagen der Schätzung)*, but is not required to provide a logical justification of the details.

The boundary between those facts subject to the "full conviction" standard of § 286 and the relaxed standard of § 287 is subject to dispute. The Federal Supreme Court has indicated that a claimant must fully convince the court that it was actually "affected" *(betroffen)* by the act or omission of the defendant.

Once the affectedness *(Betroffensein)* has been shown to the complete conviction of the court, the milder standard of § 287 applies to the determination of the extent of the affectedness and the numerical assessment of money damages.

There are also judicial decisions which have allowed a relaxed standard of proof under circumstances when to require proof to a standard of "full conviction" *(voile Uberzettgung)* would result in making a class of claim impossible of enforcement as a practical matter. For instance, a party claiming casualty insurance proceeds based on theft of an auto which unexplainedly disappeared at night is not expected to prove to the full conviction of the court that it was stolen. Proof of circumstances consistent with theft will usually be accepted as sufficient.

Note

What features of the civil and common law proceedings will best promote the goals of efficiency, accuracy, and justice? Is one of these systems better overall on any or all of those goals?

Chapter 6

SHORT–CUTS TO JUDGMENT AND PROVISIONAL REMEDIES

I. INTRODUCTION

This Chapter surveys procedural devices that allow for the summary, accelerated, or expedited consideration of particular kinds of claims. Although short-cut procedures can be found in almost all modern legal systems, they differ from nation to nation in terms of their technical design, the circumstances of their use, and the court's willingness to deploy them. Short-cut remedies typically fall into two categories: first, those that produce a final judgment on an expedited or summary basis; and second, those that offer provisional relief during the pendency of a lawsuit. Although conceptually distinct, summary and provisional remedies often work together in the same lawsuit, implicating important issues of fairness, cost, and proportionality.

This Chapter opens with a brief overview of the history and justification for summary and provisional remedies, drawing on insights from both civil law and common law systems. The Chapter then turns to summary procedures, selecting for comparison those that allow for the disposition of a claim without resort to oral testimony. The Chapter then examines summary procedures designed for the resolution of "small claims"—disputes involving a relatively modest sum of money. The Chapter closes with a section on provisional remedies, looking at the purposes they are expected to serve, selected national examples, and the special role of the "*Mareva*" injunction.[1] The growth of transnational markets, resulting in large numbers of cross-border disputes, has heightened the importance of provisional remedies as a way to ensure security and predictability in a global economy. The materials in this section relate in important ways to the later Chapter on the enforcement of judgments, and should also be examined in tandem with the Chapter on transnational litigation. As with any comparative analysis, be sure to

---

1. The term "*Mareva* injunction" takes its name from a pair of cases decided by the English Court of Appeals: Nippon Yusen Kaisha v. Karageorgis [1975] 3 All ER 282, [1975] 1WLR 1093; Mareva Compania Naviera SA v. International Bulk Carriers SA [1975] 2 Lloyd's Rep 509.

consider the political and social context of the procedures under review, relating their scope and application to other features of the legal system of which they are a part.

II. SUMMARY AND PROVISIONAL REMEDIES: HISTORY AND CONTEMPORARY CONTEXT

"There is a widespread perception," Adrian A.S. Zuckerman writes, "that the administration of civil justice is failing to meet the needs of the community."[2] His concern with "the problems of high costs and excessive delays" is shared by other commentators in both civil and common law systems. Some legal systems have responded to this perceived problem by establishing, adapting, or expanding the use of summary or accelerated procedures that are intended to streamline or expedite the dispute-resolution process. The current interest in short-cut remedies should not obscure the long pedigree that such procedures hold, tracing back to Roman Law as well as to the emergence of equity jurisdiction. Consider this historical account:

> The term "summary" as applied to civil procedure had its origin in the *summatim cognoscere* of the Roman Law. In the late Middle Ages it was applied by the Italian jurists to that simplified and abbreviated form of procedure prescribed by the decretal *Saepe contingit* (1306) of Pope Clement V, which came to form the substratum of most of the modern Continental systems, as well as in considerable measure of the Anglo–American chancery and admiralty procedures. Briegleb, in his classic study, assails the correctness of this application on the ground that the Roman *summatim cognoscere* was not a merely simplified and abbreviated version of the ordinary procedure, but a form characterized by a provisional and incomplete hearing and eventuating in a more or less provisional order,—a form, that is to say, to which our proceeding on application for temporary injunction would offer a fairly close analogy. According to his view, the curtailed ordinary form is not a "summary procedure" in any true sense, but one which is much more accurately denoted by the name "planary," bestowed upon it by some of the fourteenth century jurist, or "expedited" (*schleunig*) employed by Briegleb himself. Nevertheless, the term "summary" became firmly established in Continental usage, as applicable to both sorts of variant procedure: namely, to that which differed from the ordinary form only in its elements of simplicity and abridgement, as well as to that which was guided by the principle of the Roman *summatim cognoscere*. In our own [common law] system the term is familiar enough, but has never had the same extensive field of application or found as its subject the same organized structure as on the Continent. Blackstone's only reference to summary procedure is in the

2. Adrian A. S. Zuckerman, Preface, in Civil Justice in Crisis: Comparative Per- spectives of Civil Procedure *v* (Adrian A.S. Zuckerman, ed., 1999).

matter of criminal jurisdiction, whose proceedings he distinguishes as regular and summary.[3]

A comparative analysis of short-cut procedures can be enhanced by introducing an economic perspective into the discussion. As the preceding Chapters make plain, all procedural rules implicate concerns of efficiency, accuracy, and fairness. Summary and provisional remedies, which emphasize expedition, illuminate the possible trade-offs with particular clarity. Geoffrey P. Miller explains these trade-offs as follows:

> The law-and-economic analysis of litigation sees a trade-off between two costs: the costs of the procedure in question, and the costs of error. The existence of such a trade-off is quite clear-cut. As the procedures involved in resolving a dispute become more and more summary, the probability that the finder of fact or law will make an error will usually increase. * * * From the standpoint of welfare economics, the efficient result (holding certain other factors equal) would be a system that minimized the *sum* of the two costs–the costs of erroneous results (inaccuracy), on the one hand, and the costs of the applicable procedures, on the other. * * * [W]e cannot be confident that reducing the costs of litigation (for example, by streamlining procedures or eliminating unnecessary requirements) will inevitably reduce delay in the courts. While it is true that streamlining the procedures will reduce delay in individual cases, other things equal, this effect may be swamped by the increased quantity of litigation filed. Paradoxically, streamlining procedures may actually have the effect of increasing, not decreasing, delay in the courts, depending on the shape of the demand curve for litigation. If demand for litigation is highly elastic over the relevant range, even slight reductions in costs of litigation will result in large increases in case filings.[4]

III. SHORT-CUTS TO JUDGMENT: SUMMARY REMEDIES IN ENGLAND, GERMANY, ITALY, JAPAN, AND THE UNITED STATES

Almost all civil and common law procedural systems include summary, abbreviated, or expedited devices that allow the decision maker to resolve a dispute in a shorter period than that required by a full or "ordinary" plenary proceeding. Short-cut devices of this sort cover a broad range of mechanisms but share overlapping concerns: to avoid delay, to reduce cost, and to achieve some measure of proportionality between the nature of the dispute and the resources expended for its resolution. Beyond these overall goals, summary remedies reveal a great deal of variation from country to country, making it difficult to set out an all-encompassing taxonomy for comparative analysis.

3. Robert Wyness Millar, Three American Ventures in Summary Civil Procedure, 38 Yale L. J. 193, 193–194 (1928–1929).

4. Geoffrey P. Miller, The Legal–Economic Analysis of Comparative Civil Procedure, 45 Am. J. Comp. L. 905, 906–910 (1997).

A few examples can illustrate the range of short-cuts to judgments. Civil law procedural codes provide for special proceedings in a number of specific substantive contexts such as debt collection and landlord-tenant cases. For example, the Italian code authorizes the *procedimento di ingiunzioni* in cases in which the creditor has documentary proof of a right to payment or to the delivery of movable goods. As a safeguard, the debtor is permitted to challenge the judgment in a subsequent action; the procedure also cannot be used if the debtor resides outside Italy.[5] The *ingiunzione* procedure has widespread importance in Italy: "Every year in Italy courts issue more *ingiunzione* decrees than judgments after ordinary proceedings * * *."[6] Common law procedural codes likewise provide for special proceedings to meet particular substantive needs; in the United States, all state judicial systems authorize summary proceedings for eviction in landlord-tenant disputes.[7] In England, the judge's case management powers go hand-in-hand with the underlying efficiency aims of special proceedings and reflect the underlying principles of proportionality and individual justice.

This section focuses on summary procedures that rely exclusively on documentary evidence. As you review the examples that follow, consider the specific ways in which each procedure streamlines the decision making process: whether the procedure applies only to specialized claims (e.g., the German *Urkunden- und Wechselprozess*, for checks, negotiable instruments, and other similar documents); whether the procedure applies only to uncontested claims (e.g., the German *Mahnverfahren*, or "civil warning system"); whether the procedure allows for the entry of partial judgment (e.g., the United States summary judgment motion); whether the procedure permits the presentation of defenses (e.g., the English summary judgment motion); and other specific details that affect the role that the procedure plays in the overall system of justice. In particular, consider how the judge's case management powers affect the overall operation of summary proceedings and how other factors—the availability of discovery, the concentration of the trial, the use of lay decision makers—might create litigant preferences, whether favorable or not, for short-cut devices. Finally, although particular short-cut remedies may share the same terminology, do not automatically assume that their scope and operation are identical.

ENGLAND

Civil Procedure Rules, Part 24—Summary Judgment (The White Book Service 2006).

5. See Enzo L. Vial, Italian Civil Procedure, in Foreign Courts: Civil Litigation in Foreign Legal Cultures 266 (Volkmar Gessner, ed., 1996).

6. Sergio Chiarloni, Civil Justice and Its Paradoxes: An Italian Perspective, in Zuckerman, supra note 2, at 272.

7. See Mary B. Spector, Tenants' Rights, Procedural Wrongs: The Summary Eviction and the Need for Reform, 46 Wayne L. Rev. 135 (2000). The author criticizes state summary eviction procedures that emphasize "speed rather than fairness." Id. at 137.

Grounds for summary judgment

24.2 The court may give summary judgment against a claimant or defendant on the whole of a claim or on a particular issue if—

(a) it considers that—

(i) that claimant has no real prospect of succeeding on the claim or issue; or

(ii) that defendant has no real prospect of successfully defending the claim or issue; and

(b) there is no other compelling reason why the case or issue should be disposed of at trial.

Neil Andrews, English Civil Procedure: Fundamentals of the New Civil Justice System 505–507 (2003).

A. Nature

[The summary judgment] procedure [set out in the Civil Procedure Rules, Part 24] allows claimants or defendants to gain final judgment if they can show that their opponent's claim or defence lacks a 'real prospect' of success. It is a swift and streamlined procedure, enabling the applicant to avoid the delay, expense, and inconvenience of taking the case to trial.

B. Background

Summary judgment in favour of claimants was introduced in 1855 in favour of creditors to deal with the problem of dishonoured bills of exchange. This recognized the need to provide speedy justice against defendants who dishonour cheques, or fail to make payment under other types of bills of exchange or letters of credit. Indeed the old ' * * * Order 14 procedure' was described as one of the great procedural successes of the previous 150 years.

* * * [Civil Practice Rule] Part 24 makes three main changes to the system of summary judgment. These are:

(1) * * * CPR Part 24 makes summary procedure available to both claimants and defendants; and so defendants can use this procedure to attempt to dismiss a bad or threadbare claim;

(2) the kernel of the new test in CPR Part 24 is whether the relevant party's claim or defence has a 'real chance of success' at trial; this test allows the court to reject bad claims or defences slightly more readily than under the old * * * Order 14;

(3) the court can now initiate a summary judgment hearing under CPR Part 24, without waiting for a party to make such an application.

C. Connection with "the Overriding Objective"

* * * Summary judgment is an early exemplar of proportionality * * * for if the defendant's defence lacks merit what point can there be

in allowing him to delay the claimant's judgment? Similarly, if the claimant has no real prospect of success, what point can be there be in allowing him to spin out a bad claim?

* * * But summary judgment embodies other aspects of the 'Overriding Objective' because this accelerated and relatively stream-lined procedure can:

—save expense;

—speedily dispose of claims and defences;

—help to allot to an action 'an appropriate share of the court's resources, while taking into account the need to allot resources to other cases';

—finally, it can promote settlement of an action * * *; even cursory examination by the court of a case's merits during summary judgment will provide the litigants with strong clues as to the likely result at trial * * *.

GERMANY

German Code of Civil Procedure.*

§ 592

A claim, the object of which is the payment of a certain sum of money or the delivery of a certain quantity of other fungible pieces of property or bills of exchange, may be asserted in a trial by record in the event that all the facts necessary for the support of the claim can be proved by documents. A claim arising out of a mortgage, a land charge, annuity charge or a mortgage on a ship shall be equal to a claim, the object of which is the repayment of a sum of money.

§ 689

(1) The summary proceedings shall be conducted by the Lower Courts. Machine processing shall be permitted. In such case, submissions should be dealt with no later than on the business day following the day of filing.

(2) The Lower Court before which the movant has his or her general venue shall have exclusive jurisdiction. In the event that the movant has no general domestic venue, the Lower Court Schöneberg in Berlin shall have exclusive jurisdiction. The first and second sentence shall be applicable also to the extent that other provisions specify another exclusive jurisdiction.

(3) The governments of the respective states shall be empowered to assign, by means of regulations, summary proceedings cases arising in the district of one or several State Superior

* Translation in The German Commercial Code and Code of Civil Procedure in En-glish 337, 366 (Charles Stewart, trans. 2001).

Courts to one municipal court, in the event that that would bring about a more expeditious and practical settlement. The governments of the states may also delegate such power to the state judicial authorities by means of a statutory order. Several states may agree among themselves to confer jurisdiction on a Lower Court beyond their boundaries.

Peter L. Murray and Rolf Stürner, German Civil Justice 425–428 (2004).

DOCUMENTARY AND CHECK PROCEEDINGS

The German civil justice system has long recognized a special accelerated procedure for claims based solely on checks, other negotiable instruments, and similar documents. If a claim is for a sum certain and the cause of action can be proved solely through documentary evidence the plaintiff has the option to follow the special written document and check procedure (*Urkunden- und Wechselprozess*). The idea is to provide a relatively fast and inexpensive means to collect sums due where all of the material relevant to the cause of action is in writing.

If the documentary and check process is elected, the plaintiff must so indicate in the complaint and attach all checks, notes or other documents on which the claim is based. Counterclaims are not permitted. The only admissible proof is documentary proof (*Urkundenbeweis*) which the court can consider without the need for witness testimony to establish relevance or authenticity. * * *

The defendant may raise objections (*Einrede*) to the cause of action asserted by the plaintiff, and may substantiate the objections with documentary proof of its own. If the court finds the complaint legally sufficient and supported by the documentary evidence, and finds any objections of the defendant legally insufficient, or insufficiently supported, the court will enter judgment for the plaintiff in the amount substantiated by the documentary evidence. If the documentary evidence supports the position of the defendant, the complaint will be dismissed. If the defendant raises a legally sufficient objection or defense (*Einrede*) which will require proof beyond the documentation submitted by the parties, the court enters a provisional judgment (*Vorbehaltsurteil*) against the defendant "reserving his rights", and the case remains pending for ancillary proceedings (*Nachverfahren*) to determine the sufficiency of the objection or defense. The plaintiff may obtain execution on the provisional judgment, but if the ancillary proceedings result in vacation of the judgment, the plaintiff will be liable for damages sustained by the defendant by reason of execution of the vacated judgment.

* * *

CIVIL WARNING PROCEEDINGS

If a creditor believes that its claim is not likely to be contested by the debtor, and wishes to avoid the cost and expense of commencing an ordinary lawsuit, it may elect to use the "civil warning procedure" (*Mahnverfahren*) to collect the claim. In a large number of cases the receipt of the official warning notice from the court will produce voluntary payment. If the claim is actually not disputed, the warning procedure can result in an enforceable court order and execution. If the defendant gives notice that the claim is disputed (*Widerspruch*), it will proceed as an ordinary lawsuit.

ITALY

Michele Taruffo, Civil Procedure and the Path of a Civil Case, in Introduction to Italian Law 159, 161–162 (Jeffrey S. Lena and Ugo Mattei, eds., 2002).

* * * [I]n the Italian procedural system a variety of proceedings exist. Aside from the "ordinary" proceedings, considered a kind of general model, there are several "special" proceedings that are used when the case deals with particular matters. The most important examples of special proceedings concern labor disputes and landlord-tenant cases. In such matters, the law takes into consideration the peculiar need for a speedy resolution of disputes. Accordingly, streamlined procedural rules apply, with the aim of a quicker and more effective disposition of cases. Therefore, an important preliminary decision is whether the particular case falls into one of the legally recognized categories covered by these special regulations, and hence whether the procedure employed to dispose of the case will be abbreviated and relatively tolerable compared with the more lengthy "ordinary" cases.

Other special procedures are used in areas such as divorce or bankruptcy because of the special nature of the subject matters involved. On the other hand, there are no special proceedings for commercial cases, which are tried and decided by ordinary civil courts according to the common procedural rules (with limited special provisions concerning some types of evidence).

An important type of "special" proceeding is a peculiar form of summary judgment that is frequently used for the collection of debts called the *procedimento di ingiunzione*. This procedure is available to the creditor with written proof of his or her right to a monetary payment or to the delivery of movable goods. In such cases, the creditor may obtain from the court a decree *inaudita altera parte* (*i.e.* without hearing from the debtor) with an order of payment issued to the debtor. This may occur even within a few hours, and the order may be made immediately enforceable. If the debtor thinks that it has been wrongly issued, the order may be attacked in subsequent proceedings. These special proceedings are very useful because of their summary nature, and their rapidity and effectiveness. However, they may be used only for the protection of the creditor in legal relationships that are based on written documents and have a determined content.

Alexander Layton and Hugh Mercer, eds., European Civil Practice, Vol. 2, 334 (2nd ed. 2004).

A summary payment order (*decreto ingiuntivo*) may be granted in a special, abbreviated form of proceedings, in which the merits of the claim are summarily established, initially *ex parte*, entitling the claimant to an order for payment or delivery. The summary order will become ineffective if not served within 60 days in Italy, but the procedure may not now be used against defendants outside Italy. In order to have a right to defend himself, the defendant must then take the initiative. If he enters an objection, the proceedings are converted into ordinary proceedings on the merits, obliging the claimant to prove his case fully.

A summary payment order is obtained by presenting a claim in form of *ricorso* to the *giudice di pace* or *tribunale* judge. To obtain an order, the claimant must provide written proof of a liquidated and due debt for a sum of money, or a determined quantity of fungible goods (*fungiblie*).

Dismissal of the claim for payment order does not prevent reformulation of the claim. Where on the other hand it is successful, the court makes an order for the other party to pay or deliver within a period of 40 days from the date of service. There is specific notice that defence may be entered within that period, but that in the absence of opposition there may be execution of the court order. Further, in certain types of case, on application, the judge may issue a provisional enforcement order, which requires the debtor specifically to perform the obligation without delay, even if the proceedings are subsequently defended. These are particular cases founded on a bill of exchange, cheque, stock certificate or deed executed before a notary, banker's draft, or in a case where delay will cause grave prejudice.

JAPAN

The Code of Civil Procedure of Japan.*

Book V—Special Provisions Concerning Litigation of Bills and Cheques

(Requirements for litigation of bills)

Article 350. With respect to suits for the purpose of claiming monetary payment of bills and indemnification of damages incurred by legal interest rate incidental thereto, a trial and a decision under litigation of bills may be demanded.

    2. A statement demanding a trial and a decision under litigation of bills shall be contained in a petition.

* Translation in EHS Law Bulletin Series, EHS Vol. II, No. 2300 (2004).

(Prohibition of cross action)

Article 351. A cross-action may not be filed in a litigation of bills.

(Limitation of examination of evidence)

Article 352. Examination of evidence may be made in the litigation of bills only with respect to documentary evidences.

2. The order for producing documents or the entrustment for sending documents shall not be made. The same shall also apply to the order for producing or the entrustment for forwarding such objects bearing handwriting or seal impressions as may be used for comparison.

Book VII: Summary Procedure

(Requirements for pressing for payment)

Article 382. With respect to claims for payment of money and other substitutes thereof or a certain quantity of negotiable securities, the court clerk may issue a pressing for payment upon motion of a creditor. Provided that, this provision shall apply only in cases where such pressing may be served without resorting to the service by publication in Japan.

Takaaki Hattori and Dan Fenno Henderson, Civil Procedure in Japan 9.04 (Yasuhei Taniguchi, Pauline C. Reich, and Hiroto Miyake, eds., Rev. 2nd ed. 2004).

ACTIONS ON BILLS OR CHECKS

Because of the need for speed and effectiveness in resolving actions on promissory notes, bills of exchange and checks, the [Code of Civil Procedure of Japan] provides for special proceedings in such cases.

Although these cases are by nature ordinary actions, the CCP subjects them to some special rules for expeditious disposition of this type of case. The major features are summarized briefly below:

(1) These actions may be brought in the district or summary court (depending on the disputed amount) in the place where payment is to be made as shown on the face of the instrument or in the courts having territorial competence under ordinary rules;

(2) When the provisions for these special proceedings are invoked in the complaint, the judge must designate a date for a session as soon as possible, and hold a hearing in the form of formal oral proceed-

ings (*kôtô benron*). In practice, a date is usually set within two weeks after filing;

(3) No counterclaim is allowed in these actions;

(4) Only documentary evidence, including the note, bill or check, is admissible as evidence, provided, however that witnesses including parties may be examined for the sole purpose of authenticating the documents or proving presentation for payment. Examination of evidence by a requisitioned judge or investigation by other court agencies is not allowed;

(5) A judgment in favor of the plaintiff must always carry the declaration of provision execution (*karishikkô sengen*), which enables the plaintiff to initiate compulsory execution for collection even when the defendant has brought an objection to the judgment and the cases continues as explained in (6) below;

(6) As a rule, the losing party may not appeal to a superior court, although he or she may object (*igi*) to the judgment in the same court. If there is an objection, the same court, unless it dismisses the objection as defective, hears the case in an ordinary proceeding and either sustains its former judgment, or, after reversing its former judgment, renders a new one based on the entire proceeding. When the losing defendant brings an objection, he or she can apply for a stay of execution by proving *prima facie* a good cause for reversal, which may be granted with security.

THE UNITED STATES

Federal Rule of Civil Procedure 56 Summary Judgment.

(a) For Claimant. A party seeking to recover upon a claim, counterclaim, or cross-claim or to obtain a declaratory judgment may, at any time after the expiration of 20 days from the commencement of the action or after service of a motion for summary judgment by the adverse party, move with or without supporting affidavits for a summary judgment in the party's favor upon all or any part thereof.

(b) For Defending Party. A party against whom a claim, counterclaim, or cross-claim is asserted or a declaratory judgment is sought may, at any time, move with or without supporting affidavits for a summary judgment in the party's favor as to all or any part thereof.

(c) Motion and Proceedings Thereon. The motion shall be served at least 10 days before the time fixed for the hearing. * * * A summary judgment, interlocutory in character, may be rendered on the issue of liability alone although there is a genuine issue as to the amount of damages.

(d) Case Not Fully Adjudicated on Motion. If on motion under this rule judgment is not rendered upon the whole case or for all the relief asked and a trial is necessary, the court at the hearing of the motion, by examining the pleadings and the evidence before it and by interrogating counsel, shall if practicable ascertain what material facts exist without substantial controversy and what material facts are actually and in good faith controverted. * * *

(e) Form of Affidavits; Further Testimony; Defense Required. Supporting and opposing affidavits shall be made on personal knowledge, shall set forth such facts as would be admissible in evidence, and shall show affirmatively that the affiant is competent to testify to the matters stated therein. * * *

(f) When Affidavits Are Unavailable. Should it appear from the affidavits of a party opposing the motion that the party cannot for reasons stated present by affidavit facts essential to justify the party's opposition, the court may refuse the application for judgment or may order a continuance to permit affidavits to be obtained or depositions to be taken or discovery to be had or may make such other order as is just.

(g) Affidavits Made in Bad Faith. Should it appear to the satisfaction of the court at any time that any of the affidavits presented pursuant to this rule are presented in bad faith or solely for the purpose of delay, the court shall forthwith order the party employing them to pay to the other party the amount of the reasonable expenses which the filing of the affidavits caused the other party to incur, including reasonable attorney's fees, and any offending party or attorney may be adjudged guilty of contempt.

Arthur R. Miller, The Pretrial Rush to Judgment: Are the "Litigation Explosion," "Liability Crisis," and Efficiency Clichés Eroding Our Day in Court and Jury Trial Commitments?, 78 N.Y.U. L. Rev. 982, 1017–1019, 1042, 1071 (2003).

A primitive form of summary judgment appeared in the United States as early as 1732 in Virginia, but the motion was not widely used until the early 1900s. In the federal courts it was available under the Conformity Act of 1872 if it existed in the forum state's procedure. Consistent with the English rule limiting the motion to actions for fixed monetary amounts, summary judgment was available only at law. Most of the early versions of the motion in this country either embraced the same actions as did the English rule or were modestly more extensive. For example, many states permitted the motion in purely American types of action, such as suits against public officers or against private citizens acting in a quasi-fiduciary relationship with the plaintiff. * * *

* * *

By 1938, summary judgment was available in virtually all actions at law in most parts of the country. The procedure's utility was magnified by the federal courts' adoption of simplified pleading when Rule 8(a) replaced what essentially had been fact pleading in code states under the Conformity Act. Although the federal pleading regime has the virtue of simplicity and abjures technicalities, it has permitted cases initiated with ambiguous, extremely broad, and, occasionally, frivolous complaints to survive into the discovery phase. To deal with pleadings of this character and the dramatic expansion of claim and party joinder, the contemporaneously adopted Rule 56 was designed to provide a mechanism by which unsupportable claims can be terminated before trial.

* * *

[In 1986, the United States Supreme Court handed down a trilogy of cases involving summary judgment that makes the granting of a Rule 56 motion against the plaintiff more likely.] * * * As a result, a defendant is likely to resort to the motion more readily if she fears a jury will be sympathetic to the plaintiff or the claims asserted. Moreover, if judges are more receptive to granting summary judgment, defendants naturally will be encouraged to invoke the procedure. Indeed, the "new" motion has been perceived as a "ruthlessly efficient interception device," especially since "some plaintiffs with prospects for success at trial cannot readily or economically assemble a prima facie case before trial."

* * *

Overly enthusiastic use of summary judgment means that trialworthy cases will be terminated pretrial on motion papers, possibly compromising the litigants' constitutional rights to a day in court and jury trial. * * * All of this is reinforced by the "litigation explosion" and "liability crisis" rhetoric and a culture of management that gives the judge a sense of familiarity with the dispute that emboldens pretrial disposition.

IV. SHORT-CUTS, CONTINUED: TREATMENT OF SMALL CLAIMS IN ENGLAND, ITALY, JAPAN, AND THE UNITED STATES

This section examines the procedural treatment of small claims—disputes that put at issue relatively modest financial sums. As John Baldwin observes, commenting on the use of small claims procedures in England and Wales, it is generally recognized "that the costs of pursuing many kinds of civil action in the courts are wholly disproportionate to the amounts of money at stake, and it is now widely accepted that it is intolerable for the costs of civil litigation to exceed the sums of money that are in dispute."[8] The monetary value ascribed to the small claim varies from country to country, as does the significance of the dispute and the mechanisms used to achieve resolution. Devices include the establishment of courts with specific jurisdiction (i.e. competence) to hear small claims, regardless of the substantive issues involved; the use of streamlined or simplified procedures; the reliance on lay representation; and an emphasis on non-adversarial methods such as mediation and arbitration. In the materials that follow, consider whether a nation's decision to use special procedures for small claims or to channel such claims to specialty courts is related to the civil law or common law background of the procedural system overall.

ENGLAND

Civil Procedure Rules, Part 26–Case Management—Preliminary Stage (The White Book Service 2006).

Scope of Each Track

26.6—(1) The small claims track is the normal track for—

(a) any claim for personal injuries where—

(i) the financial value of the claim is not more than £ 5,000; and

(ii) the financial value of any claim for damages for personal injuries is not more than £ 1,000;

(b) any claim which includes a claim by a tenant of residential premises against his landlord where—

(i) the tenant is seeking an order requiring the landlord to carry out repairs or other work to the premises (whether or not the tenant is also seeking some other remedy);

(ii) the cost of the repairs or other work to the premises is estimated to be not more than £ 1,000; and

(iii) the financial value of any other claim for damages is not more than £ 1,000.

Zuckerman on Civil Procedure: Principles of Practice 482–489 (2nd ed. 2006).

Efficient case management consists in economical and effective allocation of procedural resources. The idea behind the overriding objective is that the investment of resources in any given dispute should be no more than is required for a fair and expeditious resolution of the dispute. The process adopted for the resolution of disputes, in other words, should be proportionate to the needs of the dispute in hand. However, if every claim required its own judicially crafted bespoke procedure, the

---

8. John Baldwin, Small Claims in the County Courts in England and Wales: The Bargain Basement of Civil Justice? 153 (1997).

task of adjusting process to dispute could end up consuming excessive procedural resources, with the result that insufficient resources would be left for the adjudication of the merits of disputes. To avoid such waste the CPR provide template procedures which will be suitable for the majority of cases, while maintaining sufficient flexibility within these procedures to cater for diversity of importance and complexity of disputes.

There are three procedural tracks to which defended claims are allocated. Subject to important qualifications that will be mentioned in due course, these tracks are as follows. The small claims track is intended for claims of up to £5,000. It offers a quick and informal process, shorn of technicalities, which can be undertaken without the need for legal representation. Claims with a value between £5,000 and £15,000, which are expected to be tried in a one-day hearing, are allocated to the fast track. Fast track litigation is conducted under tight timetables and normally follows standard directions designed to bring a case to trial within 30 weeks. The multi-track caters for cases of higher value, complexity or importance and allows for greater flexibility, depth of investigation and judicial involvement in the pre-trial stage. However, even here the aim is to use standard directions as much as possible so that litigation may be conducted with as the least possible hands-on judicial involvement. Claims with no financial value are allocated to the most suitable procedural track.

* * *

The small claims track is designed to offer an expeditious and uncomplicated procedure for disposing of modest claims. Disclosure is more limited than in the other tracks. Expert evidence may not be called without court permission. Costs for legal representation are not normally recoverable * * *. Other than interim injunctions, no other interim remedy is available on this track.

ITALY

European Commission, European Judicial Network in Civil and Commercial Matters (2006).[9]

Justice of the Peace

* * * The *giudice di pace* is an honorary position, not a career judge and is nominated by the *Consiglio Superiore della Magistratura* on the basis of fixed requirements (including a law degree); the office is held for a period of four years, which may be renewed once.

The *giudice di pace* adjudicates individually. There are approximately 4,700 *giudici di pace* in Italy, distributed in 848 offices throughout the national territory (as of January, 2003). They are remunerated in the form of a fee for work carried out.

---

9. The materials provided are available on the European Commission website, http://ec.europa.eu/civiljustice/org_justice/ org_justice_ita_en.htm#2 (Site last visited February 6, 2007).

Jurisdiction

The *giudice di pace* has jurisdiction in cases relating to chattels of a value of up to €2 582.28 or actions for compensation for damage caused by vehicles or boats up to a value of €15 493.71. For some disputes definitively regulated by law, he has jurisdiction regardless of value. These include disputes relating to the use of facilities in houses which are jointly owned. Territorial jurisdiction follows the common rules in the *Codice di Procedura Civile* (Code on Civil Procedure).

The parties before the *giudice di pace* may conduct their own defence if the value of the proceedings does not exceed € 516.46; in other cases the assistance of a defence lawyer is required, although the *giudice di pace* may authorise the parties to conduct their own defence in view of the nature and scale of a particular case.*

* * *

Proceedings are simplified and almost entirely oral. They tend to favour conciliation, which should constitute the natural conclusion of this type of economically small-scale dispute.

The *giudice di pace* gives judgment in compliance with the relevant laws; in cases with a value of less than € 1 032.91 he follows the principles of general equity. He also decides in accordance with general equity in cases provided for by the law and, if their rights are alienable, where the parties request that he do so.

Contesting decisions

Judgments may be appealed before the Court, unless they are given in accordance with equity or cannot be appealed (e.g. in the case of administrative sanctions), in which cases the only recourse is an appeal to the *Corte di cassazione*.

JAPAN

The Code of Civil Procedure of Japan.**

Book VI—Special Provisions Concerning Litigation of Small Claims

(Requirements, etc. for litigation of small claims) * * *

Article 368. In summary courts, with respect to suits claiming payment amounting to six hundred thousand yen (¥600,000) or less, a trial and a decision under litigation of small claims may be demanded. Provided that, such demand may not be made in excess of the number of times, as prescribed by the Rules of the Supreme Court, in the same year in the same summary court.

* * *

---

* Editor's Note: emphasis in original.   ** Translation in EHS Law Bulletin Series, EHS Vol. II, No. 2300 (2004).

(Prohibition of cross-action)

Article 369. A cross-action may not be filed in litigation of small claims.

(Principle of one day trial)

Article 370. In litigation of small claims, except when there are special circumstances, the trial shall be completed on the date for oral proceedings to be made for the first time.

2. The parties concerned shall produce all means of attack or defense before the date or on the date mentioned in the preceding paragraph. Provided that these provisions shall not apply when oral proceedings have been continued.

Carl F. Goodman, Justice and Civil Procedure in Japan 483–487 (2004).

The Summary Court is established at a level below the District Court. In civil cases, in addition to handling conciliation cases * * *, it is similar to a small claims court in that it handles cases involving claims that do not exceed 1,400,000yen. In addition to the typical procedure applicable to most cases, the Summary Court has a special "one-day" procedure for the handling of cases involving less than 300,000yen.*

* * *

As is the case with small claims courts in the United States, procedures in the Summary Courts are simplified. The Complaint in Summary Court does not need to be in writing but can be stated orally. In addition the statement of the case need not be as detailed as in District Court. Although the principle of Oral Argument applies to Summary Court cases, Preparatory Documents such as in the District Court need not precede the Oral Argument although briefs may be utilized. Where a writing is utilized and is served on the opposition party, failure of the opposing party to appear may constitute a default, unless the party not appearing has filed a writing contesting the claims or defenses. A defendant in a Summary Court matter may file a counterclaim that exceeds the jurisdictional limits of the Summary Court. In such situation the case is transferred to the District Court.

* * *

The new "one-day" trial procedure is an innovation of the 1996 Code. The procedure applies to cases where the amount in dispute is 300,000yen or less. The plaintiff may at the time of initiating the case request that small claims—"one-day"—procedures be utilized. To avoid small claims matters brought by debt collectors clogging up the one-day trial procedure, a party may only apply for one-day trial ten times in any one year before any particular Summary Court. The defendant has the

---

* Editor's note: The amount has been raised to ¥ 600,000.

option of demanding that normal Summary Court procedures be followed but must do so prior to making any presentation at Oral Argument. The defendant can exercise this option in writing prior to appearing for the Oral Hearing or orally at the hearing. If the defendant exercises the option to have the matter heard by ordinary procedure, the clerk must immediately advise the plaintiff unless the option is exercised orally and the plaintiff is present and thus obtains notice through hearing the objection to the one-day procedure. * * * If the judge determines that the matter not be heard by the one-day procedure, the clerk must notify the parties to this effect. A default may not be taken on a one-day trial case if the defendant has been served by publication—in such a case the matter must be handled as a normal Summary Court proceeding.

Except for special circumstances (determined by the court) the court is to complete the case within one-day and render its decision immediately after hearing the case on the single day. Testimony is taken immediately. The court may use audio telecommunications equipment to take the testimony of witnesses not present in the courthouse. Because of the immediacy of witness testimony there is no need to file written statements concerning testimony. The court may require a party to personally appear even if the party appears by a representative (bengoshi or Legal Scrivener).

In a one-day trial the court may frame an order so as to provide some protection to a losing defendant. This represents a reason why a defendant may not object to the one-day trial procedure. Thus, the court has authority (and the plaintiff cannot appeal from the court's exercise of its authority) to spread the payment of the judgment out over a three-year period and to waive the payment of pre-suit delinquency charges as long as the payment schedule is maintained.

A losing party has no right of appeal to a higher court. The losing party may, within two weeks of the decision, file an *objection* to the determination. If objection is filed, the matter is returned to the Summary Court for proceeding as if the matter had been an ordinary case. The court retains discretionary authority to order a payment schedule in lieu of immediate payment and may still waive pre-filing delinquency payments. Neither party may appeal the final determination of the Summary Court.

THE UNITED STATES

Bruce Zucker and Monica Her, The People's Court Examined: A Legal and Empirical Analysis of the Small Claims Court System, 37 U.S.F. L. Rev. 315, 317–318 (2003).

Following the lead of the establishment of the initial small claims court in Kansas in 1912, every state in the United States has created some form of a small claims court system. Although the financial claims limits, methods of procedure, and overall structure vary from state to state, the concept is essentially the same: relatively minor disputes involving dollar amounts that are insufficient to warrant processing the case through the normal court procedure justify expedited and simplistic handling.

United States small claims courts are often considered courts of equity. That is, they are not necessarily bound by the letter of the law. These courts have flexibility to use more holistic approaches to problem solving and dispute resolution than what is typical. "In most judges are going to do what makes sense to them, even if this means setting aside legal formalities." Moreover, traditional rules of evidence and court processes do not apply. "The rules of small claims courts emphasize conciliation and pragmatism over winning, and many rules of evidence and civil procedure have been simplified to allow maximum access to the courts by individuals unable to afford an attorney."

* * *

Throughout the United States, the [dollar] limit varies: Virginia has the lowest dollar limit ($1,000) and the highest limits are in Georgia and Tennessee, with limits of $15,000. Some commentators have suggested that small claims court limits should be raised to $20,000 on a nation-wide basis.

V. PROVISIONAL REMEDIES: COMPARATIVE OVERVIEW

This section surveys provisional remedies and the role that they are designed to serve in the legal systems of which they are a part. Provisional remedies include such devices as temporary restraining orders, preliminary injunctions, and attachment. As Xandra E. Kramer observes, "Provisional and protective measures can be found in every developed legal system. The rules concerning these measure, and especially the requirements for obtaining such a measure, as well as the contents and their scope, are however quite different."[10] The rise of cross-border disputes has heightened the significance of national variation in the availability of provisional relief. Provisional remedies thus play an important part in transnational litigation and should be reconsidered in connection with Chapter 11.

A. JUSTIFICATIONS AND CURRENT PROBLEMS

A leading commentator explains, "Interim orders serve many and varied purposes, but they all have one common denominator in that they are not designed to provide a final resolution to the matter in dispute. Rather they are intended to achieve some procedural end or to regulate

10. Xandra E. Kramer, Harmonisation of Provisional and Protective Measures in Europe, in Procedural Laws in Europe: To-wards Harmonisation 305 (Marcel Storme, ed., 2003).

the parties' conduct pending litigation."[11] On the one hand, provisional remedies ensure that a worthy claimant does not suffer an erosion of rights simply because of the time it takes to bring a litigation to final judgment. On the other hand, such remedies may impose a major burden on a defendant, depriving him or her of the use of property during the pendency of a suit without a plenary consideration of rights and interests. Both civil law and common law procedural systems take into account a number of factors in determining whether provisional relief ought to be provided. The English courts refer to these factors as "the balance of convenience" or the "balance of justice";[12] the Italian courts examine whether "there would be a danger to the applicant's rights if the remedial processes of the court were delayed (*periculum in mora*)" and also whether "the applicant probably has a right to a favorable final judgment (*fumus boni juris*)."[13] Pressures to harmonize provisional remedies across nations reflect the increased importance of a global marketplace, the desire to encourage cross-border transactions, and the different bases on which to assert personal jurisdiction over a defendant. The materials in this section explore the justifications for provisional remedies and some current problems with their use.

Stephen Goldstein, Recent Developments and Problems in the Granting of Preliminary Relief: A Comparative Analysis, 40 Revue Hellenique de Droit International 13 (1987–1988).

All legal systems have long recognised the need to provide the plaintiff with provisional relief of various types so as to insure that, during the pendency of the legal proceedings, the defendant does not take actions that would prevent the plaintiff from proving his cause or would frustrate the possibility of enforcing the plaintiff's judgment if one is obtained.

* * * [P]rovisional relief is, by definition, relief provided before the plaintiff has proven the defendant's liability. In other words, the coercive power of the courts is sought to be brought to bear, whether in the form of sequestration of the defendant's property or by an order directed against him personally to restrain from acting as he otherwise would— e.g., a temporary injunction. This, indeed, is a drastic step—a restraint of the defendant's property or liberty prior to a definitive adjudication of his liability.

Given this clash of competing interests it is no wonder that different legal systems have, at different times, reached varying results as to the types of provisional remedies which they recognise and the conditions under which such remedies will be granted.

---

11. Zuckerman on Civil Procedure: Principles of Practice 296 (2nd ed. 2006).

12. For a discussion of this standard, see id. at 305–337.

13. Mauro Cappelletti, John Henry Merryman, and Joseph M. Perillo, The Italian Legal System: An Introduction 125 (1967).

By the nature of litigation there must be some lapse of time between the initiation of an action and its completion. Thus, in all jurisdictions and in all historical periods the problem of provisional remedies necessarily arises. However, the problem becomes exacerbated when there are extensive delays in the judicial process which cause the length of time between the initiation of an action and its completion to be measured not in terms of months, but in years—indeed, four, five years or more in many jurisdictions.

Moreover, the situation becomes even more worse when during this lengthy period of time the value of the plaintiff's claim may be reduced by inflation or when the plaintiff is a relatively poor individual who needs to have his claim satisfied in order to continue to provide sustenance for himself and his family.

George A. Bermann, Provisional Relief in Transnational Litigation, 35 Colum. J. Transnat'l L. 553, 558–559 (1997).

The aims of provisional relief are essentially the same whether the need arises in transnational or in purely domestic litigation. Perhaps its principal purpose is to ensure that assets within the jurisdiction of the court will remain available for satisfaction of an eventual money judgment. It is easy enough to place this need in a transnational context by imagining, in a case brought by party A against party B in country X, that the assets of party B located in country Y will be needed to satisfy an eventual judgment, and that those assets are at risk of disappearance.

In a sense, the pre-judgment attachment of assets as security merely illustrates a broader purpose of provisional relief, namely to help preserve the *status quo* pending litigation. But preserving the *status quo* clearly may mean other things as well, such as protecting the subject matter of the dispute or preventing further harm while the litigation is underway. Here, too, transnational applications of provisional relief are easily imagined, as when the subject matter of the dispute before the courts of country X is physically present in country Y and there is reason to fear for its survival.

Put in still broader terms, provisional relief may be thought of simply as a means of enhancing in some fashion the effectiveness of pending litigation. Provisional relief typically is sought from the same court as the one in which the litigation whose efficacy is in question is pending, but that will not necessarily be the case; it may well be sought to enhance the effectiveness of litigation pending elsewhere. Provisional relief becomes truly transnational when the two courts in question belong to two independent States. * * *

B. PROVISIONAL REMEDIES IN THE EUROPEAN UNION AND OTHER NATIONAL EXAMPLES

Provisional remedies play a critical role in disputes involving cross-border activity by preventing a defendant from disposing of assets in a rush to evade an eventual order of liability.

The availability of interim relief is complicated by variations in jurisdictional regimes among different national systems; one question that divides commentators is whether it is ever appropriate to issue interim relief on "the mere presence of assets within a country ... in respect of those assets."[14] As is well known, discussion at The Hague in connection with the negotiation of an international treaty to address jurisdiction and the enforcement of judgments has stalled, in part, over disagreement about provisional remedies and the obligation to recognize and enforce such interim relief.[15] Within the European Community, the Brussels Regulation, which replaced the earlier Brussels Convention on Jurisdiction and the Recognition and Enforcement of Judgments,[16] deals specifically with provisional relief affecting member states and provides for the recognition of interim orders under specified conditions.[17] Although a trend toward harmonization is clearly visible among European nations in their approach to interim relief, other countries, and in particular the United States, remain exceptional in their refusal to enter provisional remedies that have extra-territorial effect.

This section offers background information about the availability of interim relief in disputes involving the courts of member states of the European Union. By way of counter-point, this section closes by focusing on Japan and the United States.

EUROPEAN UNION

European Union, Council Regulation on Jurisdiction and the Recognition and Enforcement of Judgments (2002).

Section 10—Provisional, including protective, measures

> Article 31: Application may be made to the courts of a Member State for such provisional, including protective, measures as may be available under the law of that State, even if, under this Regulation, the courts of another Member State have jurisdiction as to the substance of the matter.

---

14. Comm. on Int'l Civil and Com. Litig., Int'l L. Ass'n, Principles on Provisional and Protective Litigation 18, quoted in Russell J. Weintraub, How Substantial Is Our Need for a Judgments–Recognition Convention and What Should We Bargain Away to Get It?, 24 Brook. J. Int'l L. 167, 208–209 (1998).

15. For a discussion of these debates, see Linda J. Silberman and Andreas F. Lowenfeld, The Hague Judgments Convention—and Perhaps Beyond, in Law and Justice in a Multistate World: Essays in Honor of Arthur T. von Mehren 132–133 (James

A.R. Nafziger and Symeon C. Symeonides eds., 2002).

16. This volume takes up the topic of the Brussels Regulation and its treatment of jurisdiction in Chapter 11.

17. See generally Panagiota Kelai, Comment—Provisional Relief in Transnational Litigation in the Internet Era: What is in the U.S. Best Interest?, 24 J. Marshall J. Computer and Info. L. 263, 289 (2006); Peter Gottwald, Principles and Current Problems of Uniform Procedural Law in Europe under the Brussels Convention, 1997 St. Louis–Warsaw Transatlantic L.J. 139 (1997).

Manuel Juan Dominguez, Using Prejudgment Attachments in the European Community and the U.S., 5 J. Transnat'l L. and Pol'y 41, 42–45 (1995).

* * * The Brussels Convention eliminates many of the problems associated with enforcing judgments in foreign jurisdictions. Brussels Convention members recognize judgments from other states without any special procedures. As a result, judgments are more exportable between the [European Community] member states, and economic activity is promoted.

The Brussels Convention also addresses the use of interim relief, e.g. attachment. This is an important aspect of the Brussels Convention, because a judgment, even if recognized by another jurisdiction, would be of no use if the defendant can remove assets before the final judgment can be executed. Interim relief prevents defendants from removing assets from the jurisdiction. Article 24 of the Brussels Convention states that interim relief "may be available under the law of that State, even if * * * the courts of another Contracting State have jurisdiction as to the substance of the matter."[18] Article 24 allows a plaintiff or creditor to attach the assets of a defendant or debtor in one contracting state, even if the state does not have jurisdiction in the main proceeding. For example, a plaintiff may petition a French court to attach property located in France, even though the main proceeding is being held in a German court.

A. REQUIREMENTS UNDER ARTICLE 24 OF THE BRUSSELS CONVENTION

Article 24 has four requirements for creditors seeking prejudgment attachments. First, the measures required must be provisional and may be protective. Second, the measures must be available as a remedy in the state in which they are being sought. Third, the measures must fall within the scope of the Brussels Convention. Lastly, the courts in one of the contracting states must have subject matter jurisdiction over the main proceeding from which the provisional relief is derived.

In order to understand the scope of the first condition "provisional" relief must be defined. Provisional relief is temporary in nature and is directly related to the outcome of the proceedings in the main action. In other words, "[i]f the relief granted under Article 24 would fully satisfy the plaintiff's cause of action, then [the relief] is not provisional."

As well as provisional, the relief must be available as a remedy in the state where the assets are located. A common problem occurs when a plaintiff wants to petition a European court for a remedy, and the main proceeding is being held in a different country. For example, the English court in *Republic of Haiti v. Duvalier* [[1989] 2 W.L.R. 261 (Eng. C.A. 1988)] addressed whether the remedy sought must exist in the nation

---

18. Editors' Note: Article 24 has since been renumbered and currently is Section 10, Article 31.

adjudicating the main proceeding. *Duvalier* held that English courts do not require the existence of similar remedies.

Article 24 also requires that all interim measures fall within the scope of the Brussels Convention. Article 1 states that "[t]his convention shall apply in civil and commercial matters whatever the nature of the court or tribunal" but does not apply in "revenue, customs or administrative matters." The specific exclusions found in Article 1 imply that public law matters do not fall within the scope of the convention. Therefore, if a contracting state is adjudicating a public matter, a plaintiff cannot obtain provisional relief associated with the matter in another contracting state.

An issue arises as to whether provisional proceedings ancillary to the excluded main proceedings are *per se* excluded from the Convention, or whether their exclusion hinges on how closely related they are to subject matter that is excluded from the Convention. The European Court seems to have resolved this issue by holding that for provisional proceedings to be omitted, they must be closely connected to the subject matter of the public adjudication. For example, a plaintiff who is applying for a provisional remedy arising from the probate of a will in a foreign proceeding, is not *per se* excluded. To determine whether the jurisdiction exists under Article 24, the court must determine whether the provisional remedy correlates with an issue closely connected to probate or with some other private dispute associated with the case. For example, if the probate dispute is related to the ownership of property, and the parties prove that a contract dispute arose before the probate proceeding, the conflict could then be construed as an actual private disagreement which falls under the scope of the convention.

The last element of Article 24 requires that one of the signatory states have jurisdiction over the main substantive proceeding. Usually a state's national rules determine whether that state has jurisdiction over the main proceeding, but jurisdiction can also be determined by the Convention. Additionally, the Convention does not require that the main proceeding in the foreign signatory state be underway.

An exception exists to the last requirement of Article 24 regarding jurisdiction. If proceedings of substance are in a non-signatory state, like the United States, then Article 24 does not apply. Article 24 does not apply in cases where the defendant is not summoned. In addition, if proceedings are held *ex parte* because the defendant was not served prior to the proceeding, then the interim relief is not enforceable.

B. PURPOSE OF THE BRUSSELS CONVENTION

The purpose of the Brussels Convention is to promote a universal system of judgment recognition. This purpose is frustrated if defendants are permitted to move their assets before a judgment can be executed. Therefore, the ability to freeze or attach a defendant's assets is critical for the success of the Brussels Convention.

ENGLAND

Civil Procedure Rules, Part 25—(The White Book Service, 2006).

Orders for interim remedies

25.1—(1) The court may grant the following interim remedies—

(a) an interim injunction;

(b) an interim declaration;

(c) an order—

(i) for the detention, custody or preservation of relevant property;

(ii) for the inspection of relevant property;

(iii) for the taking of a sample of relevant property;

(iv) for the carrying out of an experiment on or with relevant property;

(v) for the sale of relevant property which is of a perishable nature or which for any other good reason it is desirable to sell quickly; and

(vi) for the payment of income from relevant property until a claim is decided;

(d) an order authorizing a person to enter any land or building in the possession of a party to the proceedings for the purposes of carrying out an order under subparagraph (c);

(e) an order * * * to deliver up goods;

(f) an order (referred to as a "freezing injunction")—

(i) restraining a party from removing from the jurisdiction assets located there; or

(ii) restraining a party from dealing with any assets whether located within the jurisdiction or not;

(g) an order directing a party to provide information about the locating of relevant property or assets or to provide information about relevant property or assets which are or may be the subject of an application for a freezing injunction.

(h) an order (referred to as a "search order") * * * (order requiring a party to admit another party to premises for the purpose of preserving evidence, etc.);

(i) an order * * * (* * * for disclosure of documents or inspection of property before a claim has been made);

(j) an order * * * (* * * in certain proceedings for disclosure of documents or inspection of property against a non-party);

(k) an order * * * (* * * for interim payment) * * *;

(l) an order for a specified fund to be paid into court or otherwise secured, where there is a dispute over a party's right to the fund;

(m) an order permitting a party seeking to recover personal property to pay money into court pending the outcome of the proceedings and directing that, if he does so, the property shall be given up to him;

(n) an order directly a party to prepare and file accounts relating to the dispute;

(o) an order directing any account to be taken or inquiry to be made by the court; and

(p) an order * * * on the enforcement of intellectual property rights * * *.

Zuckerman on Civil Procedure: Principles of Practice 296–297 (2nd ed. 2006).

The range of interim orders that the court may make is very extensive. Broadly speaking, an interim order is an order made by the court directing a party, and sometimes a non-party, to do or refrain from doing an action in connection with the litigation. * * * Some interim orders are no more than case management orders, e.g., orders designed to assist a party to obtain evidence or carry out inspection of property. Others, such as interim injunctions, aim to provide protection for rights pending litigation, such as an interim injunction to restrain a defendant from pulling down a building that is subject to litigation. Interim orders are mostly used pending litigation, but they may also be used after final judgment, such as a freezing injunction in aid of the enforcement of a judgment.

* * * [B]roadly speaking, [the Civil Practice Rules authorize] * * * two different types of interim orders, which have little in common apart from the fact that they are connected with legal proceedings but are not meant to finally determine the issues in these proceedings. The first type consists of orders designed to protect substantive rights (usually the rights in issue in the case) during the proceedings or to deal with them in some way; "protective orders". The second type consists of measures designed to facilitate access to information or to regulate the litigation process in some way; "process orders". Clearly, there is a profound difference between an order restraining a defendant from pulling down a disputed building and an order directing disclosure of documents or directing a person to allow the inspection of property.

FRANCE

Loïc Cadiet, Civil Justice Reform: Access, Cost, and Delay. The French Perspective, in Civil Justice in Crisis: Comparative Perspectives of Civil Procedure 291, 301–304 (Adrian A. S. Zuckerman, ed., 1999).

For many years, French justice, like all other systems, has faced the dramatic consequences of the exploding volume of litigation. The long delays and high costs which this explosion causes are, to a certain extent, the counterpart of democratized access to law and justice. Although several reforms have been initiated, one should not forget that the current difficulties originate largely from the fact that the resources of the justice system have not risen proportionately to the sharp increase in the volume of litigation with which courts have been faced. The solution to the crisis is essentially financial.

* * *

3.6.   Special types of 'ordinary' proceedings

Not all contentious proceedings lead to a final adversarial judgment, extinguishing the claim between the parties. Ordinary proceedings are not the only form of procedure in use before the courts. The Code also contains provisions governing specific types of proceedings which lack one or other of the elements of the contentious and adversarial proceedings. The two main forms are: *référé* proceedings; and *ex parte* proceedings.

3.6.1   Référé *proceedings*

3.6.1.1.   Increase and diversification

While the 1806 Code only envisaged a *référé* before the president of the *tribunal civil* (the ancestor of the *tribunal de grande instance*), who could order urgent measures where there was no serious defence to be made on the merits of the case, the new Code now recognizes other purposes for the *référé* and opens the way to *référé* proceedings before any court (apart from the *Cour de Cassation*, of course).

Traditionally the *référé* was a means of rapidly obtaining a provisional measure pending a decision on the merits of the claim. Conservatory measures, such as a provisional prohibition (on the sale of a book alleged to infringe copyright, or to contain defamatory material, for example), or a provisional suspension (prohibiting the opening of a new shop alleged to be in breach of restraint of trade agreements, for example), do not affect the final decision of the judge. This classical *référé* is maintained by the new Code as the general type. However, new and specific types of *référés* slowly appeared. These do not necessarily share the features of the ordinary *référé*, especially the requirements of emergency and absence of serious objection on the merits. Thus a 'new' *référé* proceeding may be taken with the aim of obtaining: (*a*) a preliminary investigation, outside the context of a full court case (*référé in futurum*); (*b*) the provisional payment of a sum of money as damages, even up to the whole of the sum claimed; (*c*) conservatory measures (like the English injunction) to prevent impending damage or to force a troublesome interference to cease immediately. The *référé* judge also has the power to order somebody to fulfil his obligations, as by performing a contract, or delivering or replacing goods (the *référé-injonction*).

3.6.1.2. *Référé* procedure

The court is normally seized of a *référé* by way of a writ for a specific hearing at a certain time and date, usually on a day set aside for such cases. If the situation is urgent or, for some reason, the nature of the dispute requires it, the judge may make an order that the writ be served for a specific hour of a day, even a bank holiday or a Sunday (the 'hour to hour' *référé*). Access to such urgent procedures is granted (or refused) on the *ex parte* application of the party concerned.

In most such cases, the judge will sit alone to decide the *référé* claim presented to him. However, the law gives the judge two other options. He may adjourn the case for consideration as a *référé* by a collegiate bench of the court at a specific future date. He may also decide that the case is not suitable for determination under the *référé* procedure, but is urgent, in which case he has the power to authorize the plaintiff to serve his writ for hearing on a specific day. These two techniques are different, even though they tend to merge in practice. In the latter case, the procedure leads to a judgment on the merits. In the former case, the resulting order is still a *référé* order, which is provisional by nature, rather than final and conclusive. The judge who will consider the merits of the case does have not [sic] any obligation to follow the order. Yet, the *référé* order does have legal effects. Binding, albeit provisionally, it can be immediately enforced, even if an appeal is lodged at the court of appeal. However, conditions such as provision of security or a guarantee can be attached to its enforcement.

Référé orders tend, in fact if not in law, to have the effect of a final, definitive decision on the merits of the case in hand. In practice, the *référé* procedure has become the normal summary procedure for resolving uncomplicated civil claims.

3.6.2. Ex parte *applications*

3.6.2.1. *Ex parte* procedure

Ex parte applications are governed by Articles 493 to 498 of the new Civil Procedural Code. The resulting decisions are classified as neither 'adversarial' nor final. The *ex parte* procedure may be used when the court can be persuaded that there are good reasons why the plaintiff should not call his opponent to court in opposition to the application before the order is made. It is sometimes necessary to maintain a degree of discretion for a provisional measure to be effective.

3.6.2.2. Special regime for interlocutory injunctions

The Code also creates certain specific interlocutory injunctions, which are obtained using the *ex parte* application procedure. The injunction to pay a sum of money (*injonction de payer*) is available from the *tribunal d'instance* and the commercial court, for a civil or commercial debt. The mandatory injunction (the order to do something) is available from the *tribunal d'instance* in cases where the complaint is made of a failure to perform obligations (*injonction de faire*). The *injonction de faire* has not really been used at all. The procedure might as well be abolished. However, the *injonction de payer* is far more popular. * * * Although the injunction is initially granted *ex parte*, an opportunity is allowed to the debtor for him to explain the reasons for his failure or refusal to pay. At this stage, the case is effectively sent back to the court on the merits, like any other claim for payment (in apparent contradiction of the essentially summary and *ex parte* nature of the initial procedure). The key to understanding the popularity of the procedure is to realize that the option of opposing the injunction is often not exercised, and therefore it does not affect the efficiency of the whole scheme. If the defendant does not oppose the injunction within the legal period, the injunction produces all the effects of a properly 'adversarial' judgment on the merits, without any possibility of appeal to the court of appeal.

GERMANY

German Code of Civil Procedure.*

§ 916

(1) Detention shall be effected to secure execution against movable or immovable property, on account of a money claim or another claim that can be turned into a money claim.

(2) The admissibility of a seizure shall not be excluded by the fact that the claim is deferred or conditional, unless the conditional claim shall have no present asset value because of the remoteness of the possibility of occurrence of the condition.

§ 929

(1) Orders of seizure require a writ of execution only in the event that the execution is to be carried out on behalf of a creditor other than the one designated in the order or against a person other than the debtor designated in the order.

(2) The execution of an order of seizure shall not be permissible in the event that a month shall have expired since the date on which the older was notified or served on the party at whose request it was issued.

(3) The execution is permissible before the service of the order of seizure on the debtor. It is, however, ineffective in the event that the service is not carried out within a week after its execution and before the expiration of the period fixed therefor in the preceding paragraph.

§ 930

---

* Translation in The German Commercial Code and Code of Civil Procedure in English 445, 447–48 (Charles E. Stewart, trans. 2001).

(1) The execution of a seizure of chattel shall be effected by means of an attachment. The attachment shall be carried out in accordance with the same principles as any other attachment and gives rise to a lien with the effects laid down in § 804. The court issuing the order of seizure shall be competent for the attachment of a claim in its capacity as court of execution.

(2) Attached money and the part of proceeds due to a creditor in a division procedure shall be deposited.

(3) The court of execution may order on motion that a chattel, in the event that it is exposed to a considerable loss [in] value or in the event that its safekeeping would result in disproportionate expenses, be sold by auction and the proceeds be deposited.

Manuel Juan Dominguez, Using Prejudgment Attachments in the European Community and the U.S., 5 J. Transnat'l and Pol'y 41, 47–49 (1995).

In Germany, the procedures for obtaining provisional protection in the civil courts can be found in the Code of Civil Procedure. A plaintiff seeking provisional relief may choose seizure or a provisional injunction as a remedy. Each remedy is used not to satisfy the creditor, but to preserve the creditor's rights. A provisional injunction is used to preserve personal rights or to tentatively resolve a disputed legal relationship, while seizures are used to ensure that property is preserved for execution. This Section will concentrate on an analysis of seizures.

1. REQUIREMENTS FOR SEIZURE IN GERMANY

When a plaintiff applies for an order of seizure, the order may be applied either against assets, both movable and immovable, or against the person of the debtor. An order against the person of the defendant may result in the defendant's detention or other restriction of his freedom. This order is usually not granted due to its detrimental effect on an individual's liberty. The order against the person of the debtor will be granted only if an order against the assets of the defendant would not be sufficient to protect the plaintiff.

For a German court to enter an order of seizure, Article 917 of the Code of Civil Procedure requires that the plaintiff prove that "the execution of a judgment would be frustrated or made substantially more difficult" without the order. Implicit in this statement is a requirement that the deterioration of a defendant's financial position be imminent. Proof of deterioration would include a showing that the defendant is squandering any remaining assets, or that there are signs that the defendant intends to do so. The application for the order of seizure must include the amount of the claim and an amount that a defendant may deposit to have the order removed.

Another possible ground for a seizure order is a deliberate breach of a contract by the defendant which is detrimental to the plaintiff. An example of such a detrimental breach would be a showing that the defendant committed a criminal offense by damaging the plaintiff's property.

When a seizure order is granted, the order generally applies to all the assets belonging to the defendant. Selection of assets does not take place until the order is executed. The seizure order may be issued *ex parte* and may even be executed before the defendant is served, but the defendant must be served within one week. Seizure and provisional orders "must be enforced within one month of pronouncement of the decision or service thereof on the applicant."

A defendant may try to revoke the order by claiming the plaintiff has not instituted the seizure proceedings in the main action. The court, at its discretion, may then impose a time limit on the plaintiff to begin such proceedings. The plaintiff's failure to do so will cause the order to be revoked. A defendant may also revoke the order on appeal or by claiming changed circumstances.

Plaintiffs must also be aware of the liabilities which can arise from an unjustified seizure. When plaintiffs lose in a main proceeding, their orders are deemed unjustified, and they must pay damages to the defendant. Plaintiffs are also liable for damages if they do not serve the defendant or begin the main proceedings within the time specified by the court.

2. The Availability of Seizure to a Plaintiff from Non-E.C. States

Since Germany is one of the original signatories to the Brussels Convention, a plaintiff who has instituted or plans to institute a proceeding in a signatory state may utilize German attachment procedures to freeze the assets of the defendant. To freeze the assets of the defendant, a plaintiff must apply for an order of seizure. However, a plaintiff who begins proceedings in countries outside of the E.C. may have a problem obtaining an order of seizure from a German court.

a. *Basic Requirements under the Civil Code and Case Law*

One commentator addressing this issue has stated:

> The German Law of Civil Procedure well establishes, however, that a creditor who has been directed to introduce his pecuniary claim underlying the attachment within a certain time-limit may raise that action in a foreign court; provided that the judgment of such foreign court would be entitled to recognition and enforcement in Germany.

Again, as in the case of France, the ultimate issue is whether Germany will recognize and enforce the judgment of a non-signatory state. * * *

ITALY

Alexander Layton and Hugh Mercer, eds., European Civil Practice, Vol. 2, 332–333 (2nd ed. 1989).

One of the most important types of provisional measure is attachment (*sequestro*). It is used to preserve property by ordering that it be kept under custody with a prohibition on its disposal. When attachment is directed at ensuring that an asset is preserved to ensure the satisfaction of a future money judgment, it is called *sequestro conservativo*. When it relates to the preservation of real or personal property (the ownership or possession of which is in dispute), or the preservation of books, ledgers, records, samples or anything else of an evidential value, it is called *sequestro giudiziario*.

* * *

A second specific form or provisional measure is *denuncia di nuova opera*, which lies against any person who has undertaken building work in the course of the preceding year, provided that the work is still unfinished. If the complainant can show either that he has suffered damage or that there is a risk of damage from the new work, the court will make an order restraining the work or compelling the defendant to provide security to compensate for any damage. A third type of measure, *denuncia di danno temuto*, which is related, enables the court to make a restraining order when damage is threatened from the condition of an adjoining property.

In addition to these specific powers, the court has power under Art. 700 of the CPC [Civil Procedure Code of Italy] to hear applications for *provvedimenti di urgenza*, (urgent measures) wherever none of the specific provisional remedies mentioned above is not available. This is a procedure by which a party may be enjoined to do or refrain from doing some act so as to prevent irreparable damage being done to the claimant's interests pending the outcome of the main trial. The remedy is also available prior to commencement of proceedings, on condition that these are commenced within 30 days of the injunction.

Vincenzo Varano, Civil Procedure Reform in Italy, 45 Am. J. Comp. L. 657, 657–661 (1997).

Throughout the years, it has become almost commonplace among Italian as well as foreign commentators, that the Italian system of civil procedure introduced by the code (CPC) of 1940, effective since 1942, amended in 1950, is at best inefficient. In fact, although delay seems to characterize, to a greater or lesser extent, most contemporary legal systems, the level of delay reached in Italy has become intolerable, so as to amount to a real denial of justice, and to give rise to many complaints to the European Court of Human Rights for violation of art. 6, para. 1 of the European Convention for the Protection of Human Rights and Fundamental Freedoms.

* * *

A source of relief from such a serious situation which deteriorated steadily year after year, as the statistics show, has come from the increasing resort to summary adjudication on the one hand; and from the enactment of a number of partial reforms on the other, which aimed at accelerating the unfolding of civil proceedings in certain areas.

The Italian legal system, as any other, makes available to potential litigants a variety of summary proceedings and provisional remedies. The basis of the former is the need to avoid to the parties and the administration of justice the cost of the ordinary full proceeding, which would not be justified by a real dispute between the parties. The basis of the latter is the need to avoid that the plaintiff may suffer a serious or even an irreparable damage before he can have a final enforceable judgment, thereby assuring the effectiveness of the right of action guaranteed by art. 24, para. 1 of the Constitution.

Resort to summary adjudication has increased dramatically in recent decades, and has also been encouraged by the legislator who has introduced a variety of anticipatory remedies (see, e.g., art. 24 of the law of December 24, 1969, no. 1990 which provides for interim payments in civil liability cases arising from the circulation of motor vehicles; or art. 18, para. 4 of the law of May 20, 1970, no. 300, which provides for an interim reinstatement of dismissed workers), and provisional remedies capable of becoming final no matter whether the action on the merits is not initiated or is discontinued (see, e.g., art. 28 of the law of May 20, 1970, no. 300, on anti-union activities; or arts. 1 to 5 of the law of December 9, 1977, no. 903 on equal treatment of male and female workers). In this context, a particular importance has been acquired by the catchall provision of art. 700 CPC which allows the court to grant "urgent relief" when there is a danger of immediate and irreparable injury and no specific remedy is available. Important as this phenomenon has been, it is nonetheless worrying for a number of reasons, the most important of which are the impairment of due process guarantees and the fact that judges and lawyers have come to consider "normal" (better to say, the only effective form of judicial protection) what should rather be considered extraordinary.

* * *

* * * [A]rt. 74, para. 2 of the law no. 353 of 1990 (introducing a number of new articles in the body of the CPC–art. 669–bis through 669–quaterdecies) is concerned with the rationalization of the provisional relief procedure * * *. [I]t is important that the reform has addressed a number of problems which had become particularly acute with the uncontrolled explosion of this form of adjudication.

* * * [T]he procedure for obtaining the various orders has been substantially unified, contrary to the pre-reform undesirable proliferation of different procedural models. * * * Other sections provide, in turn, for the bond which the judge may ask the applicant to post, the duration of provisional orders, the power of the judge to modify or revoke it, the hearing which must be held within 15 days from the order granting the remedy ex parte, the introduction of an immediate control of the order before a different judge within strict time limits. In general, the reform tends to a more balanced respect of the *audi alteram partem* principle.

JAPAN

Civil Provisional Relief Act (Law No. 91, 1989) (*Minji Hozen Hô*).*

Article 1. (Tenor)

The provisions of this Act shall govern the provisional attachment of property, provisional disposition of subject-matter in dispute, and provisional disposition to establish a provisional state of affairs relating to a right in the principal case of civil action (hereinafter referred to jointly as "civil provisional relief"), except as otherwise provided by other laws and ordinances, in order to secure the future execution of a right in the principal case of a civil action.

Article 2. (Execution Authorities and Court of Provisional Relief)

(1) The court may, upon the motion of a party, order civil provisional relief (hereinafter referred to as "order of provisional relief").

(2) Civil provisional relief may, upon the motion of a party, be executed by either a court of an execution officer (hereinafter referred to as "execution of provisional relief").

(3) In cases where an execution of provisional relief is to be enforced by a court, the court of execution shall be the court which is authorized under this Act to execute it; in cases where executorial disposition of provisional relief is to be enforced by an execution officer, the court of execution shall be the district court to which the execution officer is attached.

Article 3. (Discretionary Oral Argument)

A judgment with respect to proceedings of civil provisional relief may be rendered without hearing oral argument.

Article 4. (Provision of Security)

(1) The provision of security pursuant to the provisions of this Act shall be effected by means of depositing money or valuable instruments which the court ordering the provision of security deems appropriate, with the depository located within the jurisdiction of the district court having jurisdiction over the situs of the ordering court or the court of execution or by other means prescribed by the Rules of the Supreme Court. Provided that, if the parties have

* Translation in Doing Business in Japan,
App. 6D (Zentaro Kitagawa, ed., 2005).

entered into a special contract which provides otherwise, such contract shall govern.

* * *

Article 6. (Exclusive Jurisdiction)

The jurisdiction of the court provided for under this Act shall be exclusive.

Article 7. (Mutatis Mutandis Application of the Code of Civil Procedure)

Except as otherwise provided, the provisions of the Code of Civil Procedure shall apply *mutatis mutandis* to proceedings for civil provisional relief.

Article 8. (Rules of the Supreme Court)

Except as otherwise provided by this Act, the particulars necessary for proceedings of civil provisional relief shall be prescribed by the Rules of the Supreme Court.

* * *

Article 9. (Clarification)

The court, when it determines that it is necessary to clarify a party's allegation concerning the facts at issue, may permit the person whom the court deems appropriate and who is managing the party's affairs or assisting in the management of the party's affairs, to make a statement about the facts in issue on a date set for oral argument or a questioning.

Article 10. (Questioning by a Commissioned Judge)

The court may have a commissioned judge hear the case at a questioning.

* * *

Article 12. (Jurisdictional Court)

(1) The proceedings of a case with respect to an order of civil provisional relief shall be under the jurisdiction of the court which has jurisdiction over the principal case, or the district court that has jurisdiction over the district where the property to be provisionally attached or the subject-matter in dispute is located.

(2) The court which has jurisdiction over the principal case shall be the court of first instance. Provided that however, in cases where the principal case is pending in an appellate court, it shall be the appellate court.

(3) In cases where the property to be provisionally attached or the subject-matter in dispute is an obligation-right (as defined in Article 143 of the Civil Execution Act; this definition shall, hereinafter, apply throughout this Article)

the obligation-right shall be deemed to exist at the place of the general forum of the obligor of the obligation-right (hereinafter referred to as "the third-party obligor"). * * *

Article 13. (Motions and Preliminary Showing)

(1) A motion for provisional relief shall be implemented by stating the relief demanded, the right or the relationship involving the rights to be protected and the necessity for such provisional relief.

(2) The party shall make a preliminary showing of the existence of the right or the relationship involving the rights to be protected by provisional relief, and of the necessity for such provisional relief.

(3) Neither a deposit of security money nor an oath as to the truth of the party's allegations may be substituted for the preliminary showing provided for in the preceding paragraph.

Article 14. (Security for Orders of Provisional Relief)

(1) An order or provisional relief may be issued either with the requirement that the party seeking it provide a security or the condition that the execution of such relief is subject to the provision within a reasonable time period, or without the requirement that the party provide a security.

* * *

Article 19. (Immediate Kōkoku–Appeal of Court's Denial)

(1) In cases where a motion for an order of provisional relief is denied, the obligee may file an immediate *kōkoku*–appeal within the peremptory term of two weeks from the receipt of notice of denial.

* * *

Article 20. (Necessity of Orders of Provisional Attachment)

(1) An order of provisional attachment may be issued when there is a fear that future compulsory execution with respect to a monetary obligation-right would be impossible or that there would be considerable difficulty in enforcing such right.

* * *

Article 23. (Necessity of Orders of Provisional Disposition)

(1) An order of provisional disposition of subject-matter in dispute may be issued when there is a fear that realization of the obligee's right would be impossible or there would be considerable difficulty in enforcing such right due to a change in circumstances.

(2) An order of provisional disposition may be issued to establish provisionally the state of affairs of the oblige when it is necessary to avert significant damage or imminent risk to the oblige with respect to the right at issue.

* * *

Takaaki Hattori and Dan Fenno Henderson, Civil Procedure in Japan 6–7—6–12 (Yasuhei Taniguchi, Pauline C. Reich, and Hiroto Miyake, eds., Rev. 2nd ed. 2004).

§ 6.04   Provisional Remedies: Introduction

Provisional remedies are procedural devices designed to ensure the enforceability and effectiveness of a future judgment for the plaintiff or prospective plaintiff. They are regulated by the Civil Provisional Remedies Law of 1989 (*Minji hozen-hô*) (hereinafter CPRL) and the Civil Provisional Remedies Rules of 1990 (*Minji hozen kisoku*) (hereinafter CPRR) both in effect as of January 1, 1991. The CPRL and the accompanying rules have brought several improvements to the prior system by making relief swifter and more effective while better safeguarding the respondent's procedural rights.

There are two basic types of provisional remedies, provisional attachment (*kari-sashiosae*), and provisional disposition (*kari-shobun*). Provisional disposition is further divided into two types: provisional disposition with respect to the subject matter in dispute (*keisôbutsu ni kansuru kari-shobun*) and provisional disposition temporarily fixing the state of affairs with respect to the legal relationship in dispute (*kari no chii wo sadameru kari-shobun*). Plaintiffs frequently apply for these remedies prior to or during an action.

In addition to these remedies, similar remedies are available for use in special proceedings such as various insolvency proceedings and conciliation under the special statutes dealing with various types of issues and subject matter. The purpose of these special provisional remedies is also to ensure that an effective remedy may be granted by a final disposition (such as declaration of bankruptcy, successfully completed conciliation, etc.) They will be considered separately under the various headings for special proceedings (see infra § 10.06 and Ch. 11), but generally speaking the principles adopted by the CPRL will apply.

§ 6.05   Provisional Attachment

[1]   Requirements

Provisional attachment is a procedure whereby a debtor's property may be temporarily attached, thereby preventing the debtor from disposing of his or her property. The attachment secures execution of a future judgment on a monetary claim (or a claim which can be converted into a monetary claim). All types of debtors' property are subject to attachment: movable and immovable, tangible and intangible, even a debtor's claims against third parties; thus, "attachment" includes garnishment. Attachment may be authorized even when the creditor's (applicant's) claim is not yet due or is conditional.

An application (*shinsei*) for provisional attachment must be based upon a reasonable apprehension that a favorable judgment for the applicant would lose its practical effect unless provisional attachment is ordered. This apprehension will be deemed reasonable if based upon objective facts, such as the behavior of the debtor, but not if based only upon subjective anxieties of the applicant. Furthermore, provisional attachment will not be granted if the creditor has sufficient other security (mortgages, pledges, or preferential rights) or if he or she is in a position to immediately pursue the execution of his or her claim through other means, such as a notarial deed having the force of a judgment.

[2]   Competent Court

The only courts competent to order provisional attachment are (1) the district court which has the jurisdiction over the place where the property to be attached is located, and (2) the court which has the jurisdiction over the main action.

In case of provisional attachment on a debtor's claim against a third party, the claim shall be deemed to be located at the domicile of the third party debtor. In case of property, other than real property, ships, movables and claims, whose transfer needs to be registered, the property shall be deemed to be located where it is registered.

In case of urgency, the presiding judge of the court where the action is pending may decide on the application.

[3]   Procedure

An application for provisional attachment must be in writing and state the requested order, the claim to be secured by provisional attachment and the need for attachment. The requested order shall specify the property to be attached except in case of an attachment on movables.

The claim to be secured and the need for attachment must be proved prima facie (*somei*) through the use of evidence which can be examined immediately. The oral proceeding in open court, which is mandatory for a more formal judgment proceeding (*hanketsu tetsuzuki*), is discretionary in provisional remedy cases and the court may decide the case based on the application and evidence presented by the applicant to support his or her case, with or without interrogation (*shinjin*) of the applicant or both parties. In practice, an ex parte proceeding based on examination of documents is used in most provisional attachment cases. In appropriate cases, however, the court in additional will hear orally only the applicant without giving any notice to the respondent.

When it orders attachment, a court must determine the amount of money the opponent must deposit to stay the attachment or to have an already effected attachment removed.

[4]   Security

A court usually issues a provisional attachment order either after the applicant has furnished such security as ordered by the court or on the condition that its execution may be allowed only after the applicant has furnished such security as ordered by the court. That is to say, in the latter case, an order is issued without the furnishing of any security, but an actual attachment is possible only after the security has been furnished.

The furnishings of security shall be made by depositing money or such bonds or stock as are approved by the court at the National Deposit Office (*Kyôtakusho*) attached to the Local Bureau of the Ministry of Justice (*Chihô Homukyoku*) or by other means prescribed by the Supreme Court Rules.

THE UNITED STATES

Federal Rules of Civil Procedure.

Rule 64 Seizure of Person or Property.

> At the commencement of and during the course of an action, all remedies providing for seizure of person or property for the purpose of securing satisfaction of the judgment ultimately to be entered in the action are available under the circumstances and in the manner provided by the law of the state in which the district court is held, existing at the time the remedy is sought, subject to the following qualifications: (1) any existing statute of the United States governs to the extent to which it is applicable; (2) the action in which any of the foregoing remedies is used shall be commenced and prosecuted or, if removed from a state court, shall be prosecuted after removal, pursuant to these rules. The remedies thus available include arrest, attachment, garnishment, replevin, sequestration, and other corresponding or equivalent remedies, however designated and regardless of whether by state procedure the remedy is ancillary to an action or must be obtained by an independent action.

Rule 65 Injunctions.

> (a) Preliminary Injunction
>
> > (1) Notice. No preliminary injunction shall be issued without notice to the adverse party.
> >
> > (2) Consolidation of Hearing With Trial on Merits. Before or after the commencement of the hearing of an application for a preliminary injunction, the court may order the trial of the action on the merits to be advanced and consolidated with the hearing of the application. Even when this consolidation is not ordered, any evidence received upon an application for a preliminary injunction which would be admissible upon the trial on the merits becomes part of the record on the trial and need not be repeated upon the trial. This

subdivision (a)(2) shall be so construed and applied as to save to the parties any rights they may have to trial by jury.

(b) Temporary Restraining Order; Notice; Hearing; Duration. A temporary restraining order may be granted without written or oral notice to the adverse party or that party's attorney only if (1) it clearly appears from specific facts shown by affidavit or by the verified complaint that immediate and irreparable injury, loss, or damage will result to the applicant before the adverse party or that party's attorney can be heard in opposition, and (2) the applicant's attorney certifies to the court in writing the efforts, if any, which have been made to give the notice and the reasons supporting the claim that notice should not be required.
* * *

(c) Security. No restraining order or preliminary injunction shall issue except upon the giving of security by the applicant, in such sum as the court deems proper, for the payment of such costs and damages as may be incurred or suffered by any party who is found to have been wrongfully enjoined or restrained. No such security shall be required of the United States or of an officer or agency thereof.

The provisions of Rule 65.1 apply to a surety upon a bond or undertaking under this rule.

* * *

Charles Alan Wright, Arthur R. Miller, and Mary Kay Kane, 11A Federal Practice and Procedure 2d § 2931 (2005).

Rule 64, which has not been amended since it was adopted, authorizes the use of provisional remedies at the commencement of and during the course of an action. These remedies provide for seizure of a person or property for the purpose of securing satisfaction of the judgment ultimately to be entered in the action. What these remedies are, and the circumstances under which they are available, is determined by the law of the state in which the district court is held, subject to any applicable statute of the United States and to constitutional limitations. Although the statute from which Rule 64 was derived was limited to "common-law causes," the rule applies generally to "an action" and it has been held that this "must be interpreted to mean any and all actions, common-law and statutory * * *."

New York Civil Practice Law and Rules § 6001 (McKinney's 2005).

Kinds of provisional remedies; when remedy available to defendants.

The provisional remedies are attachment, injunction, receivership and notice of pendency. On a motion for a provisional remedy, the plaintiff shall state whether any other provisional remedy has been secured or sought in the same action against the same defendant, and the court may require the plaintiff to elect between those remedies to which he would otherwise be entitled; for this purpose, seizure of a chattel in an action to recover a chattel is a provisional remedy. A cause of action contained in a counterclaim or a cross-claim, and a judgment demanded thereon, shall entitle the defendant to the same provisional remedies to which he would be entitled if he were the plaintiff, the party against whom the judgment is demanded were the defendant and the cause of action were contained in a complaint.

David D. Siegel, New York Practice 492–493 (4th ed. 2005).

CPLR 6001 lists the four official provisional remedies, each of which is then given its own article for the law applicable to it. The four are attachment (Article 62), injunction (Article 63), receivership (Article 64), and notice of pendency (Article 65). The notice of pendency is more commonly known as "lis pendens". To these four may be added a few others which, while not actually "provisional", are provisional-like and are traditionally treated as part of the family. They are the order to seize a chattel in a replevin action, procedure for which is in Article 71 of the CPLR, and the order of sequestration in a matrimonial action, supplied by §§ 233 and 243 of the Domestic Relations Law.

The four provisional remedies are "provisional" in the sense that they afford the plaintiff some kind of security or protection while the action is pending, but they operate only as interim devices which, at least theoretically, do not effect any permanent divestiture against the defendant. They may come close, however, and in any event they do inflict deprivations, even if only "provisional". This engendered a series of constitutional determinations that reduced the freedom with which the remedies used to be granted. The constitutional limitations are discussed as an independent topic in the next section and are the subject of brief reminders as they become relevant.

Broadly viewed, and subject to elaboration and detail as each of the remedies is separately treated in ensuing sections, the provisional remedies operate this way:

Attachment seizes the defendant's property and prevents the defendant from using it during the pendency of a money action unless the defendant discharges the attachment with a bond, whereupon the bond substitutes for the attached property and the plaintiff gets just as much security that way.

Injunction operates to require the defendant to maintain a specified status quo during the pendency of the action, usually with an instruction not to do a given act (a negative rather than positive direction).

A receiver takes possession of designated property of the defendant and protects it during the pendency of the action, preventing the defendant from selling it, squandering it, or abusing it.

The lis pendens, which is merely a paper the plaintiff files in a county clerk's office, puts the world on notice that the plaintiff has a claim to a described parcel of real property and that anyone who buys it or lends money on the strength of it or otherwise relies on the defendant's unfettered ownership of it does so subject to whatever the pending action decides to be the plaintiff's right.

The order to seize a chattel, a provisional-like remedy, is available only in a replevin action. It is not officially "provisional" because it can result in the plaintiff's actually getting the chattel before the action goes to judgment. We mention it here * * * only to show why the seizure order does not officially qualify as "provisional".

The same may be said of sequestration, a device used to seize property of a spouse or parent in a matrimonial action, thus enabling support and other money obligations to be paid out of the sequestered assets. Since the property seized may actually be expended—sold and reduced to money and the money used to support the family during the action—the sequestration device, too, falls beyond the merely "provisional" frame.

Each of the remedies is available only in certain categories of actions or under designated conditions. For each of the four provisional remedies, the opening section of its CPLR article states those categories and conditions.

All the remedies require a court order except the lis pendens, which the plaintiff merely files. The reader should note whether the motion for the order must be on notice, or may be ex parte. Some are available ex parte. For those the constitution is on close watch.

VI. PROVISIONAL REMEDIES, CONTINUED: A COMPARATIVE LOOK AT THE *"MAREVA"* INJUNCTION

This Chapter closes with a comparative examination of a specific provisional remedy: the eponymous *"Mareva"* injunction, a judicially crafted procedure which bars a defendant from transferring assets outside the jurisdiction of the rendering court during the pendency of a lawsuit. The purpose of the *Mareva* order is to ensure that at the end of the day assets are available through which to enforce a hard fought judgment. The fact that the order seriously curtails the defendant's use of assets that are not formally implicated in the lawsuit raises serious questions of fairness. Moreover, the extraterritorial effects of the order implicate concerns of sovereignty and other national policies. Courts vary significantly in their approach to this question; however, the conceptual fault line does not appear to be that between common law and civil law systems. As you review the materials that follow, consider the extent to which different approaches to the *Mareva* injunction can be explained by, or at least rationalized by, discrete aspects of different national legal systems. This section looks first at the history of the *Mareva* litigation in order to provide some factual context for the materials that follow.

Mark S. W. Hoyle and assisted by Mark Walsh, Freezing and Search Orders 1–2 (4th ed. 2006).

1.1   In May 1975, Japanese shipowners issued a writ against Greek charterers, claiming various sums of hire owing for three ships that had been chartered by the defendants. The plaintiffs feared that the charterers would take steps to remove their funds from the jurisdiction of the English courts, and so effectively negate any judgment eventually entered against them. Accordingly, four days after issue of the writ, the shipowners applied *ex parte* to the High Court for an interim injunction restraining the defendants from removing outside those of their assets within the jurisdiction. The purpose behind this application was of course to ensure that some funds would remain available, against which execution could be made of the judgment the plaintiffs were almost certain to obtain. The circumstances of the case were such that the money was clearly owing, and there was little question of an arguable defence, so that summary judgment was likely. From a practical point of view, therefore, the plaintiffs wanted to preserve the *status quo* until the mechanics of enforcement could recover some, if not all, of the judgment debt.

1.2   Unfortunately, it had not previously been the practice of the English courts to grant an injunction in circumstances where the order was sought to restrain a defendant from disposing of his own property on the grounds of a likelihood that the plaintiff would recover judgment against him. Consequently, following on this established practice, [the presiding judge] * * * refused the shipowner's application.

1.3   No previous plaintiff had appealed against such a refusal, whether because the sums claimed did not warrant challenging what many practitioners considered too rigid a rule to be changed without statutory intervention, or for other valid reasons, but in this case there was an immediate appeal, which came before the Court of Appeal for judgment on 22 May 1975. No cases were cited in argument, and the hearing was again *ex parte*. After a sufficient, but brief, review of the facts, the appeal was allowed, and an injunction was granted restraining the defendant charterers from disposing of their assets in England outside the jurisdiction * * *.

Uppermost as a consideration was the fear that if some restraint were not imposed the funds would be sent overseas and be difficult to recover, if not irrecoverable. * * *

* * *

Thus began the practice which is now undoubtedly one of the most useful to a party faced with an opponent who is likely to so arrange his affairs as to frustrate a court judgment or arbitral award against him. * * *

ENGLAND

Civil Procedure Rules, Part 25—Interim Remedies (The White Book Service, 2006).

Orders for interim remedies

25.1—(1) The court may grant the following interim remedies—

* * *

(f) an order (referred to as a "freezing injunction")—

(i) restraining a party from removing from the jurisdiction assets located there; or

(ii) restraining a party from dealing with any assets whether located within the jurisdiction or not;

(g) an order directing a party to provide information about the location of relevant property or asserts or to provide information about relevant property or assets which are or may be the subject of an application for a freezing injunction.

Zuckerman on Civil Procedure: Principles of Practice 359–361 (2nd ed. 2006).

Although there are no formal means of discovering in advance of judgment the defendants' creditworthiness, a claimant would not normally bring proceedings unless he is confident that the defendant has sufficient resources for satisfying a judgment. Once he has commenced proceedings, the claimant runs a risk that by the time he comes to enforce a favourable judgment, the defendant will be left with no means of satisfying it and his investment in litigation would have been wasted, especially if he is unable to even recover his costs. We may refer to this risk as the risk of unenforceability of judgment. In some jurisdictions, a claimant may obtain security for judgment to protect him from this risk. Although English law does not as a matter of principle recognise a procedure for security for judgment, in 1975 the Court of Appeal developed the "Mareva injunction" for dealing with a particular type of risk of unenforceability. The objective of a freezing assets order is to prohibit the party against whom it is granted from dissipating his assets to defeat a judgment that the party obtaining the order may in due course obtain against him.

Although it is the case that English law does not provide a general power to order security for judgment, such security may nevertheless be obtained in certain limited circumstances. [Civil Practice Rule] 3.1(5) states that the "court may order a party to pay a sum of money into court if that party has, without good reason, failed to comply with a rule, practice direction or a relevant pre-action protocol". * * *

The first two cases in which the Mareva jurisdiction was first recognised involved claims for damages against foreign defendants who were likely to remove their assets from the jurisdiction of the English court in order to defeat judgment as soon as they learnt of the proceedings against them. It was held that the court had the power to order a defendant to refrain from dealing with his assets pending litigation in order to prevent the defendant from evading the court's jurisdiction by dissipating or hiding his assets. Freezing injunctions, it was explained, were the law's response to "the 'ploy' of a defendant to make himself 'judgment proof' by taking steps to ensure that there are no available or traceable assets on the day of judgment; not as a result of using the assets in the ordinary course of business or for living expenses, but to avoid execution by spiriting his assets away in the interim."

* * * [A] freezing injunction restrains the defendant from dealing with assets to which the claimant makes no claim of right whatsoever. Such a serious interference with the defendant's property requires cogent justification, especially in view of the fact that the law does not normally allow claimants to obtain security for judgment. * * * It may be said that dissipation of assets to avoid judgment subverts the administration of justice just as much as the destruction of evidence in order to prevent the court from establishing the truth. This rationale stresses the effect of evasion on the court's authority. A somewhat different rationale invokes the right of access to justice. It may be said that by putting himself beyond the reach of the court, the defendant is effectively undermining the claimant's right to seek effective court adjudication and enforcement of his rights. Accordingly, the jurisdiction to grant freezing injunctions may be seen as a means of preventing unscrupulous defendants from defeating the court's jurisdiction to enforce rights and denying the claimant an effective access to court. * * *

FRANCE

Mark S. W. Hoyle and assisted by Mark Walsh, Freezing and Search Orders 194–196 (4th ed. 2006).

11.26 The French practice of *saisie conservatoire* has frequently been compared to the *Mareva* injunction. * * *.

I Freezing the Assets of one party to Litigation (or Arbitration) pending the final judgment (or Award) at the request of another party

(1) The applicable statute, code and/or procedural provisions giving the court jurisdiction.in the country where the order is granted.

The freezing of assets in France is governed by the law of 9 July 1991 and the decree of 31 July 1992. The freezing order can cover any property, tangible or intangible, belonging to the debtor or to any third party who is a debtor of the debtor. The power to freeze the debtor's assets is normally vested in a special jurisdiction named *"juge de l'execution"*. The proper venue will typically be determined by the debtor's domicile or headquarter. The judge can be seized at anytime but if the freezing order is granted prior to the action on the merits of the case, a claim must then be filed in a constraining time limit (one month from the date the seizure is made. It must be noted that the creditor is granted a three-month time period to implement the order from the date it was granted by the judge).

The fact that arbitration proceedings are pending or about to start does not preclude the creditor from obtaining freezing orders.

It should be noted that French courts are not allowed to grant a "worldwide" freezing order that allows freezing of all the assets of the person against whom it is granted which are located overseas as well as in the country where the order is granted.

However, French courts can be petitioned to give effect to such a "worldwide" freezing order when granted overseas.

(2) The tests to be applied (must there be a risk shown of dissipation of money/assets, and a risk of destruction of documents/subject-matter?)

The tests to be applied is defined by Article 67 of the law of 9 July 1991 which provides that all persons whose receivables seem to be undisputed, may request from the judge the authorization to carry out freezing measures over the debtor's assets, without prior notice, if they justify circumstances that are likely to threaten the recovery of the receivables.

The judge will pay special attention to the likelihood of a debtor's insolvency or any maneuvers to conceal assets. In practice, French judges are rather liberal in granting the freezing of assets located within the French territory.

(3) Whether an applicant for such remedies has to provide a financial bond or guarantee in case the respondent suffers loss from the orders.

French law no longer authorizes judges to impose a financial bond or guarantee on the creditor when requesting a freezing order. Typically, the judge will make his decision on the basis of the evidence provided by the creditor and will only determine whether the test described above is satisfied.

(4) Can order be made in the absence of the respondent, and how does he have them discharged?

Orders are typically granted in the absence of the respondent. The plaintiff generally files a request for a freezing order with the judge without the debtor being informed of the proceedings. It is only once the freezing orders are implemented that the debtor will be aware of the measure.

The debtor is then entitled to challenge the freezing order before the judge who granted it by proving that the conditions set out in Article 67 of the law have not been fulfilled and/or that the formal requirements have not been followed by the creditor in implementing the order.

(5) Do the courts recognize similar orders made overseas in proceedings pending there (for example, does the French court recognize and enforce an Order of the English Court freezing assets (A) in England, and/or (B) worldwide?)

French courts may recognize Freezing Orders granted abroad.

When such an order is rendered by courts located within the European Union, French courts will decide whether to enforce it in view of the liberal criteria set forth by the Council Regulation No. 44/2001 of 22 December 2000 on jurisdiction and the recognition and enforcement of judgments in civil and commercial matters.

It should be noted, however, that the application of the liberal above-mentioned regulation will only be permitted when the debtor could have been in position to request an adversary hearing in the state where the order was made before recognition and enforcement were sought in the state where the assets are located.

It is worth mentioning that the French Supreme Court (*Cour de Cassation*) recently ruled that a *"Mareva injunction"* * * * granted by the London High Court of Justice should be recognized by French courts.*

GERMANY

Jens Grunert, Interlocutory Remedies in England and Germany: A Comparative Perspective, 15 Civil Justice Quarterly 18, 20–21, 26–27 (1996).

The two main procedural devices for the interlocutory process in Germany are *Arrest*, paras. 916–934 ZPO and *einstweilige Verfügung,* paras. 935 *et seq.* ZPO.

The German equivalent of the *Mareva* injunction is the ordinary *Arrest*. The Code of Civil Procedure provides for protection of the judgment creditor or plaintiff against an empty judgment by allowing the attachment of assets (movable or immovable property) belonging to the potential judgment debtor, under paras. 916 *et seq.* ZPO. The *Arrest* will give the creditor a temporary guarantee either through the partial or total attachment of the debtor's assets. The purpose of the attachment order (*Arrestbefehl*) is the temporary protection of monetary claims or claims which may become money claims. The terms of the injunction are at the court's discretion, provided that an injunction must never finally dispose of, but only secure, a claim. It follows that the creditor cannot obtain satisfaction through the *Arrest* but can only block the assets of the defendant.

The main difference between *Arrest* and *Mareva* injunction is that the German instrument operates as a general order *in rem*, while the *Mareva* injunction constitutes merely a relief *in personam*, prohibiting the defendant from removing assets out of the jurisdiction or dealing with them within the jurisdiction pending trial of the action. Thus the *Mareva* injunction does not have the scope of comparable remedies as the *Arrest*, that is to enable the plaintiff to obtain the attachment of the defendant's assets before the judgment. Therefore the *Mareva* injunction has, unlike the *Arrest* under German law, no direct legal effect with regard to the assets in question. An additional act of execution, as in the German proceedings, is unnecessary for the enforcement of the provisional measure. In Germany the creditor is not yet protected with the issuance of the *Arrest*. The order for *Arrest* is only the title which has to be executed.

The *einstweilige Verfügung* or temporary injunction is the procedural instrument which comes closest to the interlocutory injunction under English law. It offers protection to the plaintiff by granting an interim or temporary order to preserve claims other than money claims, that is, claims arising from individual performance and non-performance. The temporary injunction may be granted to prevent the threatened change of existing conditions which may render impossible or more difficult the realisation of a right of one of the parties, or, if the preliminary adjudication of a legal dispute is necessary.

The *einstweilige Verfügung* is the appropriate remedy, for example, when an individual is building a house and crosses the boundary be-

* Editors' note: footnotes omitted.

tween his own and his neighbour's property. Furthermore, the *einstweilige Verfügung* can be obtained in cases where the plaintiff wants to prevent infringements of intellectual property rights or to secure claims for specific performance. The court has a wide sphere of judicial discretion in respect to the order that it may make and is only restricted in that the order must be made suitable to afford an effective remedy in the circumstances of the case.

* * *

In contrast to ordinary proceedings in Germany, as a specific feature of the interlocutory process, it is entirely at the discretion of the court and optional to deal with the application with or without an oral hearing. The applicant may state his "wish" that the court should refrain from an *inter partes* hearing but he cannot force the court to do so. If the protective measure is granted *ex parte* the defendant can raise an objection according to paras. 924, 925 ZPO. The judge is then given an opportunity to review his order in the light of the arguments brought forward by the other side.

1.   *The* ex parte *Arrest (attachment of assets)*

Para. 921 I ZPO provides that the decision to make an order for *Arrest* may be given without an oral hearing. The court might be of the opinion that an oral hearing is not necessary at the interlocutory stage and the application may therefore be determined without the opponent being present and heard.

When the order for *Arrest* is made without an oral hearing the opponent has usually no opportunity at all to bring forward his legal position. In such cases he receives notice of the interlocutory proceedings having been commenced when he is served with the order. There is no right of appeal against the decision of the court to deal with the application without an oral hearing. In practice an oral hearing at which both parties are heard is ordered by the court only in cases of a complicated nature or where the facts are not clear, that is, where the court feels doubtful about the matter, in order to avoid injustice to the parties. In those cases an oral *inter partes* hearing takes place unless there is a danger of the debtor taking steps to frustrate enforcement. The decision is usually taken without an oral hearing, however, as the element of surprise often determines the success of the *Arrest*. para. 921 I ZPO sets no further condition for an ex parte process. The aim of the provision is the speedy disposal of applications for an *Arrest*.

2.   *The* ex parte *einstweilige Verfügung (temporary injunction)*

In contrast to the provisions for *Arrest,* the German legislature has enacted an additional requirement for the *einstweilige Verfügung*. The court granting a "temporary injunction" may only refrain from oral and therefore *inter partes* proceedings in cases of particular urgency for the creditor (paras. 937 II, 942 IV ZPO). In practice, however, the courts interpret the term "cases of urgency" fairly liberally and grant readily the *einstweilige Verfügung* without an oral *inter partes* hearing. Therefore the threshold of urgency can be overcome easily. Despite the rule-exception-relation in accordance with the ZPO, in practice a multitude of "temporary injunctions" are issued *ex parte*.

* * *

JAPAN

Yutaka Yazawa, The Importance of Effective Legal Systems—Provisional Remedies in Litigation, in Commercial Law in a Global Context: Some Perspectives in Anglo–Japanese Law 231, 236 (Barry A. K. Rider, Yutaka Tajima, and Fiona Macmillan, eds., 1998).

'Provisional attachment' has a similar effect to the English Mareva injunction. It allows the plaintiff to obtain an order from the court that prevents the defendant from disposing or otherwise dealing with his property, whether moveable or immovable. Its purpose is to preserve the assets in order to prevent a monetary claim becoming difficult or impossible to execute. 'Provisional disposition' is very roughly similar to all other kinds of injunction order that can be obtained in the English court.

THE UNITED STATES

David Capper, The Need for *Mareva* Injunctions Reconsidered, 73 Fordham L. Rev. 2161, 2161–2165 (2005).

American courts have been deprived of a most useful tool created by the common law courts in England—the *Mareva* injunction—because of a 5–4 decision of the United States Supreme Court in *Grupo Mexicano de Desarrollo, S.A. v. Alliance Bond Fund, Inc.* [527 U.S. 308 (1999)]. In this case the Supreme Court reversed the decision of the U.S. Court of Appeals for the Second Circuit, and erroneously condemned, in dicta, all *Mareva* injunctions in a case where such relief would probably not have been granted in England or the other common law jurisdictions that use it. It is the essence of this essay that the usefulness of the *Mareva* injunction must be reconsidered and approved. The beauty of the *Mareva* injunction—before a decision on the merits—is that claimants can protect their potential judgments at an early time in a dispute when the location of assets against which judgment may be enforced is not a game of hide and seek. Of course, the law of fraudulent conveyances, by state statute or as included in the federal Bankruptcy Act, permits the recapture of assets, the disposal of which rendered a debtor insolvent. But this is often a fruitless and expensive chore, seldom producing sufficient assets to satisfy the judgment; hence the utility of the *Mareva* injunction to freeze assets before they can be concealed. * * *

* * *

A *Mareva* injunction is an interlocutory (normally ex parte) injunction restraining a defendant in civil litigation from disposing of assets so as to render itself judgment proof. It operates in personam against the defendant and does not confer upon the plaintiff any rights in the assets or enhanced priority in the event of the defendant's insolvency. * * *

While the early *Mareva* decisions in England certainly did break new ground, the change was not as revolutionary as a majority of the Supreme Court "made out." The only major common law jurisdiction where the *Mareva* injunction has not flourished is the United States. To persuade a court to grant this relief a litigant normally has to prove the following:

1. A cause of action within the jurisdiction of the court asked to grant relief. This is necessary because the plaintiff's claim for *Mareva* relief is to prevent the disposal of assets that would frustrate the enforcement of judgment in that action. * * * Today in the United Kingdom, this is more of an exception than a rule because the Civil Jurisdiction and Judgments Acts of 1982 and 1991 allow British courts to grant *Mareva* relief in support of proceedings going on in European Union and European Economic Area countries. Indeed the Civil Jurisdiction and Judgments Act of 1982 (Interim Relief) Order 1997, made pursuant to section 25(3) of the 1982 Act, has now authorized the High Court to grant interim protective measures in aid of overseas proceedings generally.

2. A "good arguable case" on the merits of that cause of action. In *Grupo Mexicano* it was stressed that the plaintiffs were almost certain to win their case, but "good arguable case" means something rather less than that. English courts have resisted the temptation to explain the concept in percentage terms because most *Mareva* applications are ex parte and prospects of success cannot be quantified. In essence, "good arguable case" means that on the material before the court the plaintiff appears to have real prospects of success. Doubts about the plaintiff's chances of success at trial can go against it either because the court thinks there is insufficient support for a "good arguable case" or in the exercise of the court's overall discretion.

3. A real risk that any judgment the plaintiff obtains in the proceedings will go unsatisfied. Originally, it was necessary to show that assets were at risk of being transferred out of the jurisdiction, but by the 1980s courts were showing signs of extending the injunction/procedure to disposals of assets within the jurisdiction. Section 37(3) of the Supreme Court Act of 1981 confirmed the matter as far as England was concerned and other jurisdictions have followed suit. Courts in the Republic of Ireland apparently insist on evidence that the defendant *intends* by its disposal of assets to render itself judgment proof. If this is really the position of Irish courts, it is different from other jurisdictions which appear only to insist on a risk of disposal for no good reason, such as meeting obligations to other creditors.

4. That it is just and convenient to grant relief. No authority need be cited here because the proposition is an elementary one. An injunction is an equitable remedy and subject to the discretion of the court. Should it appear that there are significant doubts about the

plaintiff's claim for relief or that excessive hardship would be caused to the defendant then relief can be refused. What normally happens is that the injunction is granted on an ex parte application and any reasons why relief should not be granted are considered if the defendant applies to discharge or vary the injunction.

The above are the most significant matters that a plaintiff must prove. Some other important features of *Mareva* injunctions should also be stated at this stage. Although they are interlocutory orders, *Mareva* injunctions can be granted after judgment and normally are continued after judgment. They are usually granted against assets within the jurisdiction of the court, but in a series of cases in the late 1980s the English Court of Appeal extended relief to extraterritorial assets. As equity acts in personam and not against the defendant's assets, there was no reason why the court could not reach extraterritorial assets. But a major practical consideration, of which courts were already well aware, was highlighted by this development. To make a *Mareva* injunction stick it is necessary to serve it on third parties, particularly banks that are holding the defendant's assets, and enjoin them from allowing the assets to be disposed of. Certain procedural safeguards have to be built into the injunction to protect third parties from other liabilities to which they might otherwise be subject. * * *

Mareva injunctions contain a number of procedural and other safeguards for the protection of the defendant. If granted, the usual order is limited to the maximum amount of the plaintiff's claim. Because most applications are made ex parte there is a duty on the applicant to make full and frank disclosure of all matters of relevance of which the court should be aware. * * * As with all interlocutory injunctions, the applicant usually has to give an undertaking in damages to compensate the defendant should it become clear later that the injunction should not have been granted, for example, when the defendant successfully applies to the court to discharge the injunction. The practice of some courts, such as the Chancery Division in England, is to review *Mareva* injunctions at an *inter partes* hearing a short time after the grant of an ex parte order. As an alternative to discharge of the order, the defendant may seek a variation that allows payments to be made to third parties in the ordinary course of business or reasonable expenditure to be incurred. The order normally specifies a sum for reasonable living expenses but this may have to be adjusted in light of information the defendant puts before the court.

Justice Scalia's opinion in *Grupo Mexicano* argued that there was nothing new about debtors not paying debts or preferring creditors. This is, with respect, a disturbingly complacent view of the reality of modern civil litigation. * * * Whether evading legal liabilities through disposal of assets is new or not, it is a real and serious phenomenon. Failure to deal with it allows the legal process to be treated with contempt. Probably, at least, the extent of the problem is a feature of modern technology which enables assets to be whisked away in an instant—a matter only grudgingly acknowledged by Justice Scalia.

Chapter 7

APPEAL

I. INTRODUCTION

The institution of appeal against a judgment at first instance serves both public and private purposes. The private purpose represents the litigant's interest in protecting his rights by obtaining a correction of judicial error. The public purpose centres on the need to clarify and develop the law, to maintain high standards of adjudication, and more generally to promote public confidence in the administration of justice. However, the distinction between private and public interests is not altogether clear-cut. Individual litigants could be motivated by a desire to obtain clarification of the law rather than just protecting their immediate rights. Equally, the public interest is not confined to the clarification of the law but extends to the avoidance of error even if it affects only individual litigants, because public confidence in the administration of justice depends on the public perception that the courts can put right their own mistakes and avoid injustice. Other considerations too influence the availability of appeal procedures and their nature. Thus the need for finality of litigation and for certainty in the law may argue for both strict time limits and for limitations on the number of appeal. Even the need for clarification and development of the law may suggest limiting appeal opportunities, because an excess of judicial views on points of law could render the law uncertain. The greater the number of appeals to which a judgment can be subjected and the more intrusive appellate interference, the more likely it is that judicial views will differ and the less predictable the outcome of litigation would become.

In this Chapter we consider a variety of different systemic approaches to the appellate process. Note that the related topic of the organization of appellate courts has been treated in Chapter 3, so we will refer to the differences in appellate structure only insofar as they directly affect the process. What, then, are the points at which we see the greatest variations in appellate procedures?

—Can the appellate court receive new evidence?

—Is the judgment of the first instance court enforceable while an appeal is pending?

—Can the appellate court issue a new judgment or is it limited to striking the decision below and remanding for further consideration?

—Is there a right to appeal or does the appellate court have discretionary control over its own docket?

—Is appeal limited to appeals from final judgments?

—Are constitutional issues heard by ordinary appellate courts or are they reserved for a designated Constitutional Court?

Although space does not permit treatment of all of these questions, do keep them in mind as you read the materials that follow.

ALI/UNIDROIT Principles of Transnational Procedure 47 (2006).

Historically, in common-law systems appellate review has been based on the principle of a "closed record," that is, that all claims, defenses, evidence, and legal contentions must have been presented in the first instance court. * * * Historically, in civil-law systems the second-instance court was authorized fully to reconsider the merits of the dispute, but there is variation from this approach in many modern systems. In a diminishing number of civil-law systems a proceeding in the court of second instance can be essentially a new trial and is routinely pursued. * * * In some systems, the parties must preserve their objections in the first-instance tribunal and cannot raise them for the first time on appeal.

II. EUROPEAN APPELLATE SYSTEMS IN GENERAL

J.A. Jolowicz, Introduction: Recourse Against Civil Judgments in the European Union: A Comparative Survey, in Recourse Against Judgments in the European Union 1–11 (J.A. Jolowicz and C.H. van Rhee, eds., 1999)

I.   The nature of the final recourse

[I]n all the countries of the European Union there is more than one level of jurisdiction and in most there are three.

If attention is directed to the character of proceedings at the highest level of jurisdiction (which will here be called the 'Supreme Court'), the countries of the European Union apparently fall into three categories. First, there are those in which all proceedings subsequent to first instance are described and regarded as procedures of appeal. Secondly there are those which distinguish between the second level 'appeal' and the third level '*Revision*'. Finally there are those which distinguish between the second level appeal and the third level '*cassation*'. In their original conceptions, the differences between appeal, *Revision* and *cassation* are substantial differences of kind: a Court of Appeal considers questions of fact as well as of law and replaces the decision of the court below with its own; a court of *Revision* also commonly replaces the decision of the court below with its own, but considers only questions of law; a court of *cassation* considers only questions of law and simply quashes a defective decision; it cannot substitute its own decision and must remit the case for fresh decision elsewhere.

The distinctions between appeal, on the one hand, and, on the other, *Revision* or *cassation* as the case may be, continue to be stressed in the countries in which they are drawn. In particular, *cassation* is seen as something so different from appeal that the two can scarcely be spoken of in the same breath: legislative exclusion of certain cases from 'appeal', for example, does not carry with it exclusion from *cassation* but, rather, has the effect of making recourse to the Court of *cassation* immediately available.

In a few countries *cassation* still survives in something approximating to its original form. In general, however, the procedure recognised as *cassation* in many European countries today has moved so far from the original model of post-Revolutionary France that the differences between *cassation*, on the one hand, and *Revision* or even appeal, on the other, are significantly reduced.

First, many Courts of *cassation* now have the power to replace decisions which contravene substantive law provided only that a new decision can be formulated on the basis of the facts as found in the court below. This, of course, is characteristic of courts of *Revision* or appeal, but it is also true that such courts, like courts of *cassation* even if less frequently, may also have to remit a case for fresh decision elsewhere. This occurs, for example, where the error of the court a quo related to procedure rather than to substance or where it becomes apparent that new findings of primary fact are necessary.

Secondly, the concept of what constitutes a question of law for the purposes both of Courts of *cassation* and of Courts of *Revision* has almost everywhere been expanded, especially through use of such ideas as that the qualification of the facts is itself a question of law, or that the Court may intervene where the motivation of the court below in relation to the facts is inadequate.

In Supreme Courts which are Courts of appeal, and so of fact, there is no incentive to enlarge the concept of a question of law, and in the Scandinavian countries an appellate court can rehear the oral evidence given below; it may, indeed, be bound to do so if the decision at first instance depended on the credibility of such evidence. In the common law countries, on the other hand, where witnesses are not ordinarily reheard, appellate courts may and do restrict the kind of decisions of fact which they are willing to reopen; given the importance at first instance of oral testimony and the judge's assessment of the credibility of witnesses, findings of primary fact are unlikely to be reconsidered. Questions of inference and questions of the qualification of facts will, however, be reconsidered, and these are just the questions now held in many Courts of *cassation* or *Revision* to be questions of law.

Finally, it may be mentioned that even the fundamental idea that only decisions against which no appeal is available are susceptible to *cassation*, has lost some of its force. In at least three countries the possibility exists that a case may reach the Court of *cassation* even before the avenue of appeal has been exhausted and, indeed, dispensing with it. Though the conditions for this are not the same everywhere, it resembles the so-called 'leap-frog' form of appeal which, in England, may enable a decision at first instance to be taken directly to the Supreme Court—the House of Lords—omitting the Court of Appeal.

It is, of course, important not to overstate the point here sought to be made, and many experts in procedural law would probably still deny it altogether. Nevertheless, when the image is drawn on a canvas broad enough to contain all the legal systems of the European Union, the clear impression is left that the differences between appeal, *Revision* and *cassation* are, to put it no higher, much less marked than once they were. This has not, however, prevented the language and the habits of thought of the different systems from surviving largely intact.

A particular, and particularly important, illustration of this phenomenon can be seen in countries whose Supreme Court is a Court of *cassation*. There, any similarity between appeal and *cassation* continues to be denied and, in general, it continues to be insisted that access to the Court of *cassation*, unlike that to a Court of appeal, shall be virtually unconditional, provided that all possibilities of appeal have been exhausted. This is not, of course, to say that the right of access to the Court of *cassation* may not become time-barred nor is it to say that the grounds on which the Court may be seised are unrestricted. It is to say that control of access on a case by case basis is not only non-existent but is virtually unthinkable. The nearest approach to such a form of control seems to have been the device, introduced in 1979 in France, of a '*formation restreinte*' in the Court of *cassation*, consisting of three rather than the usual five judges, which could exclude a case from consideration by the Court if it was inadmissible or 'manifestly unfounded'.

Only two years later, however, the '*formation restreinte*' was made part of the Court itself since it was given the power of judgment in cases for which the solution is straightforward. Such control of access to the Court of *cassation* as had briefly existed, disappeared.

Alongside insistence that access to a Court of *cassation* shall be unrestricted, it also continues to be said that, in contrast with the appeal which is concerned with the justice inter partes of the decision under consideration, the principal, if not the only, concern of *cassation* is with the law. In practice, however, and even if it were still true in substance as well as in form, this does not serve to distinguish Courts of *cassation* from Courts of *Revision* or appeal. Like Courts of *cassation*, Courts of *Revision* are formally restricted to questions of law and, as in Courts of *cassation*, the concept of a question of law has been enlarged. As for Supreme Courts which are Courts of appeal. 'Leave to appeal' is generally required, and legislation in the Scandinavian countries makes it clear that, subject to a few exceptions, such leave will be granted only where a point of general legal interest is involved; despite the absence of relevant legislation in England, the same is true in practice for the House of Lords.

If there is here another point of similarity between appeal, *Revision*, and *cassation* at the Supreme Court level, there is a striking difference between the case loads of the different kinds of Supreme Court. In the French Court of *cassation*, for example, about 20,000 cases are decided each year and in the Italian it is not much less. It is difficult to see that the judges of these courts can have the time to give full consideration to complex questions of law. In Germany, the largest European country, the 200 judges of the Supreme Court (of *Revision*) decide some 3,000 cases a year while in England the House of Lords (a Court of Appeal) decides a mere 50 civil cases or less.

A partial explanation of such disparities lies in the fact that the right of recourse is unrestricted only where the Supreme Court is a court of *cassation*. In Supreme Courts of *Revision* or appeal recourse is usually conditional upon the grant of leave, and this provides a means whereby the caseload can be controlled. Nevertheless, it is believed that persistence of habits of thought is no less, and perhaps more, influential. To take just the two extreme cases by way of example, in England recourse to the Supreme Court is and always has been regarded as exceptional; in France it is and always has been regarded as a matter of right.

II.   The right of appeal

Whatever the nature of the recourse to the Supreme Court, a form of recourse against first instance. decisions, recognised as 'appeal', exists throughout the European Union. Whatever the differences in the nature and scope of the appeal in different countries, the appeal has, everywhere, the characteristics that the appellate court is not restricted to consideration of questions of law alone and that, normally, the decision on appeal replaces the decision at first instance. The nature and scope of the appeal is considered below. First, however, it is necessary to consider the extent to which a right of appeal exists.

In England all appeals are said to be 'statutory', which means that the law does not give the status of a general principle to the rule of double instance. * * *

In other countries, with the exception of Austria and Finland, where the right of (first) appeal is unfettered, the position is in general as for the Irish Supreme Court, that is to say that, from a decision at first instance, an appeal is available unless the law otherwise provides. Special provisions may apply to interlocutory decisions, but so far as final decisions are concerned, the availability of appeal is commonly regulated by reference to the value of the case in question.

Usually the value of a case to qualify for appeal is relatively low * * *

III.   Leave to appeal: final decisions

1.   THE REQUIREMENT OF LEAVE

In countries whose Supreme Court is a Court of *cassation*, the requirement of leave to appeal is for all practical purposes unknown. In countries where the Supreme court is a court of *Revision*, leave to appeal to that Court is, or may be, required, but appeal is as of right for the ordinary appeal (*Berufung*) from first instance judgments. The same is true for Finland and Ireland, but in both Denmark and Sweden leave is required for a first appeal if the amount involved is less than a certain figure—in Denmark, less than US$1,500 and in Sweden less than US$5,000. In England leave is always required for appeal to the House of Lords but, formerly, appeal to the Court of Appeal from final decisions was by right, except for decisions of the County Court with a value less than US$8,000. Implementation of reforms with effect from 1999 has resulted in a requirement of leave for all appeals to the Court of Appeal.

2. THE GRANT OF LEAVE

In some countries including England and, in effect, Austria, it is the general rule that where leave to appeal is required it may be granted by either the court *a quo* or by the court *ad quem*, but, at least in England, it is increasingly the case, especially for appeals to the House of Lords, for the Court *a quo* to refuse leave so as to enlarge the opportunity for the court ad quem to control its own case load. The same control is exercised in Sweden, where it is the court *ad quem* only which has power to give leave. In Germany, and in Austria, where the case is worth less than US$20,000, leave for *Revision* is given by the court *a quo*, but the Supreme Court can refuse to hear a case even if leave has been given. In Denmark and Finland a special panel of judges decides on applications for leave.

3. GROUNDS FOR THE GRANT OF LEAVE

The grounds on which leave to appeal to the Supreme Court may be granted, where such leave is required, have already been briefly mentioned. In Denmark and Sweden, where leave to appeal from a first instance decision is required in cases of relatively low value it is similarly provided that leave should be given only if a decision of the appellate court is necessary to give guidance on the application of the law. In England the (non-statutory) rule is less severe: leave should be granted unless the appeal has no realistic prospect of success and, even if that criterion is not satisfied, leave might still be granted if the case raises a point which should be considered at the appellate level.

IV.   The nature and scope of the appeal

The definition of appeal given above—that an appellate court is not restricted to questions of law and that its decision normally replaces the decision at first instance—says little about the process of appeal as such or the nature and scope of an appellate court's reconsideration of the case. In fact, from this point of view, the systems in operation in the European Union reveal such differences one from another that systematic comparison is difficult; the difficulty is compounded by differences in first instance procedures, especially the difference between procedures which make extensive use of oral evidence given at a 'trial', on the one hand, and those in which oral evidence plays a less important role, on the other. As a general proposition, the common law and the Scandinavian countries fall into the first group and the 'civil law' countries into the second. In what follows, systems with each of these two broadly defined procedures at first instance are separately considered.

1) Systems in which oral evidence at 'trial' is the primary mode of proof

In Ireland, on appeal from the District to the Circuit Court and from the Circuit Court (as a court of first instance) to the High Court if the decision was based on oral evidence, the oral evidence will be reheard on appeal, and there is no restriction on new evidence or argument. This form of appeal comes close to being a 'second first instance'. In the Scandinavian countries the appeal is only slightly less all-embracing. There, the rehearing of oral evidence on appeal is possible and may even be mandatory if the decision turns on its credibility. On the other hand, new allegations of fact and new evidence may be presented only if good cause is shown why they were not presented at first instance.

In England, and also in Ireland on appeal from the High Court as a court of first instance to the Supreme Court, oral evidence is not reheard and the appellate court must ordinarily rely on a transcript of the evidence given at first instance. This means that the appellate court will not reconsider first instance findings of fact which turn on the credibility of witnesses. On the other hand, there is no formal rule against the introduction of new claims or defences: the parties' written pleadings, which between them fix the subject matter of the litigation, may, with the leave of the court, be amended at any time and the appellate court has power to admit 'further evidence.' In reality, however, that power is severely restricted and it is inconceivable that leave to amend the pleadings would be given if the proposed amendment would introduce allegations of fact not considered at the trial. Though formally described as an appeal 'by way of rehearing', the appeal is no more than a 'rehearing' on the basis of a written transcript of evidence and for this reason is necessarily less than complete.

2) Systems in which oral evidence is not the primary mode of proof

Within this group of countries forms of appeal can be found from the extreme of a system in which the appellate court's ability to reconsider questions of fact is severely limited to a system which comes close to being a 'second first instance'. In some countries the powers of the appellate court even extend to the decision of issues which have not been considered at all at first instance. This calls for separate mention, below. The least extensive appeal in this group is, probably, that used in Portugal since the reforms of 1995–1996. The oral evidence at first instance is recorded only on the request of a party, and if no request is made the appellate court will not even have a transcript. If there is no transcript, decisions of fact can only be altered on appeal if no oral evidence was used at first instance, if the original decision was plainly inconsistent with the documents in cause, or if a supervening document capable in itself of overturning the documentary evidence which was before the court below, is produced on appeal. If there is a transcript, the appellate court may modify findings of fact, but only those of which the appellant specifically complains.

Though differently structured, the Austrian system is not, in principle, much more extensive than the Portuguese: evidence will not be retaken on appeal or further evidence admitted and claims and defences cannot be extended. There are, however, circumstances in which oral evidence may be heard as, for example, if it is necessary to reconsider its evaluation or if the court of first instance had declined to hear certain evidence, considering it to be irrelevant. In Spain and Italy the position is ostensibly the same, but the exceptions seem to be more generous, and this is true also for France where the definition of a new demand, as applied by the courts, is such that, in practice, the exclusion is not rigorously applied. In Greece, where new claims and defences are also excluded, new evidence may be admissible provided that its admission involves, no alteration to the original basis of the action.

In Belgium new demands are admissible on appeal provided only that they are the subject of contradictory argument and that they are based on facts invoked in the original claim, but it is the appeal in the Netherlands which probably comes closest to a 'second first instance'. There the parties may, in principle, change the original claim or defence, as the case may be, and new evidence is freely admissible.In Germany, the '*Berufung*' is in principle also a second first instance, but, though evidence can be taken afresh, the appellate court will normally rely on the record of the evidence taken below. Furthermore, by what is regarded as a constitutionally controversial rule, claims and defences can be admitted for the first time on appeal only if they could not have been adduced at first instance. The German appeal thus falls short of being truly a second first instance.

3) 'Evocation'

In Belgium and to a lesser extent in France, Luxembourg and the Netherlands, the appellate court may sometimes decide for itself issues which had not previously been decided or even considered at first instance.

The rule in Belgium, described as the '*effet d ǫvolutif renforc*', is broadly stated and is to the effect that on every appeal from a final or an interlocutory judgment the appellate court is seised of the entire case on its merits. This sweeping provision, though somewhat restricted by the appellant's ability to confine his appeal to certain aspects only of the case and by an explicit requirement in the law that, in certain circumstances, the case be returned to the court of first instance, seems to leave no discretion to the appellate court: if the rule applies that court is automatically seised of the entire case.

That is not the case in the other countries where what is called '*evocation*' may be allowed, for there the appellate court has a discretion whether to retain the case for full decision itself or to return it to the court below. Nevertheless, in all these countries the appellate court, once seised of an appeal, may on occasion dispose finally of the case on its merits even though the decision appealed against did no such thing: to a greater or lesser extent, the appeal has become a *'voie d'achévement'*, the advantages of which, from the point of view of procedural economy are obvious. Equally obvious, however, is the derogation from the principle of double instance involved, and for this reason the development remains controversial.

V.   Enforceability of judgment subject to recourse.

As a general rule, and, it seems, with the sole exception of Austria, the availability of recourse to the Supreme Court, whether a court of *cassation*, *Revision* or appeal, does not automatically deprive the judgment of the court below of immediate enforceability. On the other hand, a stay of execution is, in many countries, a possibility, with or without the provision of security. In Italy, for example, a stay of execution pending decision in the Supreme Court may be ordered if execution of the judgment would create severe and irreparable hardship, or if adequate security is given by the party seeking a stay.

As regards the availability of appeal to the (intermediate) appellate court, the common law principle is that there is no suspensive effect. First instance judgments are immediately enforceable unless a stay of execution is ordered. In the 'civil law' and Scandinavian countries, on the other hand, the traditional principle is to the opposite effect: in accordance with the so-called suspensive effect of the appeal, a judgment at first instance is not enforceable until the time for appealing has expired or, if an appeal is brought, until it has been disposed of. In Austria and Finland, the traditional principle retains most of its force, but elsewhere its severity has been modified by the development of 'provisional execution' ordered by the judge of first instance or the appellate court and even, in some cases, actually prescribed by law. In some countries such as Luxembourg, it appears, provisional execution is rarely ordered but in others, such as Sweden, it is common and, indeed, money and default judgments are immediately enforceable unless the losing party provides security or applies successfully for a stay of execution.

The traditional principle has been subjected to criticism in more than one country and its total reversal has now been recommended in an important official report on the reform of civil procedure published in France in 1997. At the time of writing, however, it is only in Italy that such a reversal has been enacted. In that country it has been the rule since the coming into force of a law of 1990 that all judgments of first instance are immediately enforceable unless the appellate court, on request, agrees to a stay of execution for grave cause.

Nicolò Trocker and Vincenzo Varano, Concluding Remarks, in The Reforms of Civil Procedure in Comparative Perspective 264–265 (Nicolò Trocker and Vincenzo Varano, eds., 2005).

Appeals to courts of last resort

A final word must be dedicated to appeals, and in particular to appeals to courts of last resort. Traditionally, this is another important area of differences between civil and common law.

In fact, the civil law tradition has always considered access to the Supreme Court for violation of the law as a matter of right.

* * *

To begin with, the structure and composition of supreme courts is different from that prevailing in common law countries. In Italy, for instance, the Court of Cassation is subdivided into civil and criminal panels, each sitting with 5 judges. A total of some 140 judges are attached to the Court. A more diffuse authority and a weaker precedential of their decisions are among the consequences of the different structure.

As to the consequences of access as of right, though limited to questions of law, on the workload and backlog of the court, first, roughly 25,000 civil appeals are brought in a typical year before the Court, while the Court disposes of roughly 20,000 of them, and the backlog amounts to over 50,000 civil cases. Secondly, as we have already said, a civil proceeding before the Court has an average duration of 824 days, i.e. almost three years! Clearly, figures of this magnitude do not allow the court to perform effectively the function of a supreme court, which is that of doing justice as between the parties, but also, and perhaps foremost, that of keeping the law straight and update, assuring the exact observance and the uniform interpretation of the law.

Until recently, the situation of other supreme courts within the civil law tradition was quite similar. None of them, for reasons deeply rooted in our history and culture, had any discretionary case selection power. Things are changing in this respect too, though not in Italy.

It is the case of Germany, where § 543 of the ZPO, as reformed in 2001, has replaced the former jurisdiction of the Federal Supreme Court, partly based on the amount at stake, allowing review by the BGH when the case has an importance of principle, or when the need to guarantee the uniformity of case law requires the decision of the highest court. In practice, a system of "leave" operates nowadays in Germany, which vests in the BGH pretty much the same discretion which the supreme courts of the common law traditionally enjoy. This should enable the Court to concentrate its work on the development of the law and the formation of a unified case law.

In France, a *"Loi organique"* of June 2001 allows the *"formations resteintes"* of the Cour de cassation to reject summarily inadmissible recourse, or recourses not grounded on *"moyens sérieux de cassation"*.

In Spain, following the new code enacted in 2000, recourse to the Supreme Court is limited to controversies above a certain value (rather trivial, to be sure: 150 euros), or when the recourse either deals with fundamental rights or has a cassational interest (e.g., when the lower court's decision contrasts with the consolidated case law of the *Tribunal Supremo*).

Last but not least, the Austrian reform of 2002 has introduced also for appeals to the Supreme Court in labor and social security cases the requirement of an "important legal question". In this country, too, the Supreme Court is clearly emphasizing the function of unifying and developing national law, and strengthening the precedential value of its decisions.

Sergio Chiarloni, Civil Justice and Its Paradoxes: An Italian Perspective, in Civil Justice in Crisis 267 (Adrian A.S. Zuckerman, ed., 1999).

4.2   The increase in appeals to the *Corte di Cassazione*

The *Corte di Cassazione* is the Italian Supreme Court. This court oversees the uniform interpretation of the law throughout Italy. While the number of first instance cases has decreased, the number of appeals to the *Corte di Cassazione* has seen an opposite trend. Just over 3,000 appeals were submitted annually during the 1960s. The number has now grown to more than 17,000 per year. This increase in workload has had two consequences: decisions are delayed; and, more importantly, uniformity in interpretation of the law is lost, due to the large number of judges required. Thus, the *Corte di Cassazione* is no longer able to guarantee: the equal treatment of litigants throughout the country; the predictability of its decisions; and the high prestige of its members as supreme judges. Instead, the court has become a sort of judicial supermarket, where lawyers can be sure to find any precedent they need to plead the case of their client.

9.2.3.4 Filtering the access to the *Corte di Cassazione*

* * *

Some have argued that, the traditional uniformity function of the *Corte di Cassazione* ought to be relaxed. They approve of the behaviour of the present judges of this court, who increase the legal disorder by their contradictory decisions. This approval is based on two implicit assumptions: a radical conception of the creative function of jurisprudence; and a belief that the interpretative discretion of the lower court judges, should be matched by the same discretion within the *Corte di Cassazione*.

These assumptions lead to unacceptable conclusions. Pluralism in the interpretation of laws by the Supreme Court is not acceptable. The existing pluralism of the Court is only and accident, due to its large number of judges (approximately 450).

In order for the *Corte di Cassazione* to fulfil the task of ensuring uniform application of the law, there is only one way. There must be a drastic reduction in the number of appeals, and a concomitant reduction in the number of judges. This solution concerns both the *Corte di Cassazione* and the courts of appeal. Detailed statistical data are not available. However, as any court professional in Italy knows, the chances of successfully appealing to the courts of appeal depends more on questions of law (such as improper application or incorrect interpretation of laws) than on questions of fact. Thus, it would be entirely reasonable to restrict the ambit of appeals, as in common law countries, to questions of law only. In this way, appeals to the *Corte di Cassazione* could be confined to new and/or controversial questions.

III. ENGLAND

The term *routes of appeal* or *destination of* appeals are the modern terminology used for identifying the court to which an appeal must be made. The appellate routes are established by the Access to Justice Act 1999 (Destination of Appeals) Order 2000, made under § 56 of the Access to Justice Act 1999.

The general principle is that an appeal lies to the next level of judge in the court hierarchy. Thus, an appeal from a decision by a district judge (the junior or procedural county court judge) in the county court lies to a circuit judge (the senior county court judge), and from a county court decision by a circuit judge to a High Court judge. In the High Court, appeals lie from a master or district judge of the High Court (ie, the procedural judge) to a High Court judge. All these appeals are heard by a single judge. An appeal from a High Court judge lies to the Court of Appeal. Appeals to the Court of Appeal may be heard by one or more Lord Justices. Normally, appeals to the Court of Appeal are heard by a two or three judge court. Finally, an appeal from the Court of Appeal lies to the House of Lords, which sits in panels of five or more Law Lords. However, this scheme is subject to important exceptions, and exceptions to the exceptions, all of which render the charting of the routes of appeal a fairly complex exercise.

Zuckerman on Civil Procedure: Principles of Practice 832–835, 866–867, 882 (2nd ed., 2006.)

23.4 The present appeal arrangements, for which the ground was laid in s.54 of the Access to Justice Act 1999, are designed to resolve the tension by reconciling these competing interests. The overarching principle is proportionality, which is of course embedded in the overriding objective. Proportionality dictates that once the parties have had an adequate opportunity to present their case and a judicial decision has been taken, any further judicial investigation by way of appeal should be reserved for those cases that really require it. The general principle is that appeals and appellate interference must be kept to the bare minimum compatible with the need to avoid injustice. This minimalist approach governs both the availability of a full appeal process and the extent of appellate interference, where an appeal is entertained.

23.5 Accordingly, subject to very few exceptions, appeals require court permission. Permission would normally be given only where the appeal has a real chance of success or there is a public interest in doing so. The aim is to avoid waste of valuable court resources by weeding out hopeless appeals and focusing appellate attention on matters of real significance to the parties and the general public. As already noted, the general principle is that if the lower court has considered the merits and an appeal court has decided that an appeal has no real prospect of success, there is little justification for devoting further appellate attention to the case and the litigation should be at an end.

23.6 The minimalist approach similarly shapes the nature of appellate jurisdiction. An appeal is not meant to provide a second round of the adversarial process, in which the parties present their case once more before a higher court. Instead, an appeal is confined to a scrutiny of the lower court's decision. As a general rule, therefore, appeals are normally confined to a review of the lower court's decision. Lower court decisions are accorded a large measure of respect; as long as the lower court has not committed an obvious mistake of fact, or an error of principle, or followed a seriously defective procedure, the appeal court will not disturb its decision.

23.7 The policy of restricting appeals to a review of the lower court's decision is founded not only on the need to economise the use of resources. It is also founded on the belief that lower courts should bear the main responsibility for the conduct of litigation and its outcome. Appeal courts must defer to lower courts' decisions, unless a decision is clearly wrong, in the sense that it is contrary to established principle or that no reasonable judge could have reached the conclusion in question. Thus the relationship between lower courts and appeal courts is not one of deference but one of interdependence and supervision.

* * *

23.10 The new system is founded on six general principles:

(1) An appeal cannot be mounted without court permission, subject to very few exceptions. Such permission may be given either by the court against whose decision an appeal is sought, or by the appeal court.

(2) There is no appeal against the grant of permission to appeal. There is no appeal from a decision of an appeal court refusing permission to appeal, if the decision is given after a hearing.

(3) The principal criterion for permission to appeal is whether the appeal has a real prospect of success, though permission may also be given if there is some other compelling reason for hearing an appeal.

(4) An appeal would normally be by way of a review of the decision of the lower court.

(5) In all but exceptional cases only one appeal is allowed. A second appeal can only be made with the permission of the Court of Appeal, to which all second appeals lie, and which must be satisfied that the appeal raises an important point of principle or practice, or that there is some other compelling reason for the Court of Appeal to hear a second appeal.

(6) The Court of Appeal is not merely a venue for appeals, but is also intended to provide authoritative guidance in most areas of law and practice. This is particularly so in the area of civil procedure, where it is the Court of Appeal, rather than the House of Lords, that lays down general guidelines and establishes normative standards for the conduct of litigation. Accordingly, permission to appeal to the House of Lords is reserved for a small number of cases which give rise to legal points of great general public importance.

* * *

23.12 The appeal system is consistent with the right to fair trial, notwithstanding its parsimonious provision of appellate consideration of first instance decisions. ECHR [European Convention on Human Rights], Art.6 does not impose an obligation on contracting states to set up courts of *cassation* or appeal. The right of access to justice is satisfied by the provision of an adequate first instance hearing. A right of appeal is merely an additional opportunity to persuade the court of the validity of one's position. However, states that do provide an appeal procedure are required to ensure that litigants should enjoy the fundamental guarantees contained in Art.6 at the hearing of appeals. For example, it is a breach of ECHR Art.6 to refuse to hear an appeal because the accused has not surrendered to custody prior to the appeal.

23.13 The manner in which Art.6 applies to courts of appeal or to courts of *cassation* depends on the nature of the proceedings concerned. In determining compliance with the right to fair trial account must be taken of the entirety of the proceedings conducted in the domestic legal order and the appeal court's role in them. For example, the ECtHR has held that, provided that there has been a public hearing at first instance, the absence of a public hearing before a second or third instance may be justified by the special features of the proceedings at issue. It has been held that applications for permission to appeal and appeals involving only questions of law may be disposed of solely on the basis of written submissions. Lastly, a lower court must give reasons for its decision in order, amongst other things, to enable parties to exercise any right of appeal they may have. The general obligation to provide a reasoned decision applies to appellate decisions too, but it is commensurate with the nature of the appellate jurisdiction. When an appeal court dismisses an appeal it may simply endorse the reasons for the lower court's decision rather than give detailed reasons of its own.

23.14 In any event, the imposition of a requirement of permission to appeal cannot be regarded as a restriction on the availability of an opportunity for a reassessment of first instance decisions because the permission hearing itself offers an opportunity for reassessment. "There is no substantial restriction", Sir Andrew Morritt V.-C. explained, "and certainly no intrinsically unjust restriction on the right of appeal, since there is ... no reason in justice why a person should be entitled to occupy the time of the court, and put opposing parties to expense and trouble, in conducting appeals which have no real prospect of success and where there is no other compelling reason why the appeal should be heard".

* * *

23.108 Clearly, the main consideration concerns the appeal's prospect of success. The nature of the "real prospect of success" test is similar to the test employed in relation to summary judgment and elaborated by Lord Woolf in *Swain v Hillman* [[2001] 1 All E.R. 91, CA]. Attention is drawn to the fact that the wording of CPR 52.3(6) has now been slightly changed. As originally drafted the opening words were "Permission to appeal will only be given where etc". The change has of the verb to "may" was intended to stress that the court has discretion in the matter and that such discretion must be exercised in accordance with the overriding objective, which includes considerations of proportionality. Accordingly, the test turns on the usefulness of the appeal exercise. An appeal hearing is justified if there is a real prospect that it could make a difference to the outcome, otherwise resources and time would be wasted in vain. Where a first appeal is hopeless because of binding authority, the possibility of a second appeal thereafter could be sufficient to fulfil the threshold condition of a real prospect of success.

* * *

23.110 Permission to appeal may also be given where there is "some other compelling reason why the appeal should be heard" (CPR 52.3(6)(b)). This ground is independent of prospects of success. It might seem odd, on the face of it, that an appeal court should be willing to entertain a hopeless appeal. However, an appeal to the Court of Appeal and occasionally even the House of Lords may be justified in order to provide an authoritative ruling on a matter of general public importance, even if the outcome is foregone.

23.111 An example is provided by the application of a paralysed and terminally ill person to be allowed assisted suicide, which went all the way up to the House of Lords and subsequently to the ECtHR. However firmly the High Court or the Court of Appeal may have decided the matter, and however well founded in principle and authority the first and second decision may have been, the public was entitled to expect a pronouncement on the matter from the highest court in the land. In such situations the test of a compelling reason (which in that case meant a compelling reason for further judicial consideration) relieves the court of the necessity of assessing its prospects of success. Cases of this kind are more likely to arise in public law cases, but there may well be other cases in which this facility could be usefully employed. It is arguable that there may be a compelling reason for an appeal where the appellant does not wish to challenge the order of the lower court, but only the grounds on which it was founded. This may happen, for example, where an appellant wishes to disturb one of the lower court's findings in order to ensure that he is not held bound by it in future litigation (see also discussion below concerning appeals on hypothetical issues).

23.154 A distinction is drawn between appeal by way of review and appeal by way of re-hearing. Broadly speaking, the former consists of a scrutiny of the lower court's decision, which will be disturbed by the appeal court only if it was wrong or involved a serious irregularity. A review is not intended to re-try the issues but merely to examine lower court decisions for errors or irregularities. In a re-hearing, by contrast, the appeal court addresses the issues afresh regardless of whether the lower court's decision was defective. Subject to very few exceptions, appeals are now limited to a review of the lower court's decision. Most significantly, under the modern appeal regime, unlike in the past, appeals from a case management decision given by a district judge or a master to a circuit judge or a High Court judge are now by way of review, not by way of re-hearing.

H.L. v. Canada (Attorney General), 2005 SCC 25, Supreme Court of Canada, Justice Fish.

A. The Applicable Standard of Review: Introduction

Fact finding in the litigation context involves a series of cerebral operations, some simple, others complex, some sequential, others simultaneous. The entire process is generally reserved in Canada to courts of first instance. In the absence of a clear statutory mandate to the contrary, appellate courts do not "rehear" or "retry" cases. They review for error.

The standard of review for error has been variously described. In recent years, the phrase "palpable and overriding error" resonates throughout the cases. Its application to all findings of fact—findings as to "what happened"—has been universally recognized; its applicability has not been made to depend on whether the trial judge's disputed determination relates to credibility, to "primary" facts, to "inferred" facts or to global assessments of the evidence.

Nor has the standard been said to vary according to whether we are concerned with what Hohfeld long ago described as "evidential" or "constitutive" facts (see W. N. Hohfeld, *Fundamental Legal Conceptions as Applied in Judicial Reasoning and Other Legal Essays* (1923)), at p. 32. Nor, put differently, has the standard been said to vary according to whether our concern is with direct proof of a fact in issue, or indirect proof of facts from which a fact in issue has been inferred.

"Palpable and overriding error" is at once an elegant and expressive description of the entrenched and generally applicable standard of appellate review of the findings of fact at trial. But it should not be thought to displace alternative formulations of the governing standard. In *Housen*, for example, the majority (at para. 22) and the minority (at para. 103) agreed that inferences of fact at trial may be set aside on appeal if they are "clearly wrong". Both expressions encapsulate the same principle: an appellate court will not interfere with the trial judge's findings of fact unless it can plainly identify the imputed error, and that error is shown to have affected the result.

In my respectful view, the test is met as well where the trial judge's findings of fact can properly be characterized as "unreasonable" or "unsupported by the evidence". In *R. v. W. (R.)*, [1992] 2 S.C.R. 122, McLachlin J. (as she then was) explained why courts of appeal must show particular deference to trial courts on issues of credibility. At the same time, however, she noted (at pp. 131–32) that

"it remains open to an appellate court to overturn a verdict based on findings of credibility where, after considering all the evidence and having due regard to the advantages afforded to the trial judge, it concludes that the verdict is unreasonable."

The statutory framework in criminal matters is, of course, different in certain respects. But as a matter of principle, it seems to me that unreasonable findings of fact—relating to credibility, to primary or inferred "evidential" facts, or to facts in issue—are reviewable on appeal because they are "palpably" or "clearly" wrong. The same is true of findings that are unsupported by the evidence. I need hardly repeat, however, that appellate intervention will only be warranted where the court can explain why or in what respect the impugned finding is unreasonable or unsupported by the evidence. And the reviewing court must of course be persuaded that the impugned factual finding is likely to have affected the result.

* * *

Moreover, procedural changes governing civil appeals in England that took effect in May of 2000 do not appear from subsequent decisions of the Court of Appeal to have altered substantially the previous approach to appellate review * * *.

Civil Procedure Rules 1998. Part 52—Appeals (The White Book Service 2006).

52.3 Permission

    (1) An appellant or respondent requires permission to appeal—

        (a) where the appeal is from a decision of a judge in a county court or the High Court, except where the appeal is against—

            (i) a committal order;

            (ii) a refusal to grant habeas corpus; or

            (iii) a secure accommodation order made under section 25 of the Children Act 1989(1); or * * *

    (2) An application for permission to appeal may be made—

        (a) to the lower court at the hearing at which the decision to be appealed was made; or

(b) to the appeal court in an appeal notice.

* * *

(3) Where the lower court refuses an application for permission to appeal, a further application for permission to appeal may be made to the appeal court.

(4) Where the appeal court, without a hearing, refuses permission to appeal, the person seeking permission may request the decision to be reconsidered at a hearing.

(5) A request under paragraph (4) must be filed within 7 days after service of the notice that permission has been refused.

(6) Permission to appeal will only be given where—

(a) the court considers that the appeal would have a real prospect of success; or

(b) there is some other compelling reason why the appeal should be heard.

52.7 Stay

Unless—

(a) the appeal court or the lower court orders otherwise;

* * *

an appeal shall not operate as a stay of any order or decision of the lower court.

52.10 Appeal court's powers

(1) In relation to an appeal the appeal court has all the powers of the lower court.

(2) The appeal court has power to—

(a) affirm, set aside or vary any order or judgment made or given by the lower court;

(b) refer any claim or issue for determination by the lower court;

(c) order a new trial or hearing;

(d) make orders for the payment of interest;

(e) make a costs order.

52.11 Hearing of appeals

(1) Every appeal will be limited to a review of the decision of the lower court unless—

(a) a practice direction makes different provision for a particular category of appeal; or

(b) the court considers that in the circumstances of an individual appeal it would be in the interests of justice to hold a re-hearing.

(2) Unless it orders otherwise, the appeal court will not receive—

    (a) oral evidence; or

    (b) evidence which was not before the lower court.

(3) The appeal court will allow an appeal where the decision of the lower court was—

    (a) wrong; or

    (b) unjust because of a serious procedural or other irregularity in the proceedings in the lower court.

(4) The appeal court may draw any inference of fact which it considers justified on the evidence.

(5) At the hearing of the appeal a party may not rely on a matter not contained in his appeal notice unless the appeal court gives permission.

52.13 Second appeals to the court

(1) Permission is required from the Court of Appeal for any appeal to that court from a decision of a county court or the High Court which was itself made on appeal.

(2) The Court of Appeal will not give permission unless it considers that—

    (a) the appeal would raise an important point of principle or practice; or

    (b) there is some other compelling reason for the Court of Appeal to hear it.

IV. THE UNITED STATES

Alan B. Morrison, Litigation, in Fundamentals of American Law 61–82 (Alan B. Morrison, ed., 1996).

In the federal court system and in most state courts, the party that loses is entitled to at least one appeal as a matter of right. In addition, in the federal system, a party who loses an appeal may request that the United States Supreme Court hear the case, but review is discretionary in virtually all cases, and the Court hears less than 3 percent of all the cases in which it is asked to rule. The percentage of cases given a second level of review is somewhat larger in most state court systems, but even then it is still relatively rare in civil cases. Cases from state courts can reach the Supreme Court, on a discretionary basis, but only if they present questions of federal statutory or constitutional law.

In general, a person in the federal system has a right to appeal an adverse ruling only at the conclusion of the case. This principle, known as finality, is different from the practice in many state courts where many rulings made during the course of the proceeding, referred to as "interlocutory decisions", may be appealed at the time, as well as at the end of the case. There are a few exceptions to the finality rule in the federal courts, such as the granting or denying of a request for a preliminary injunction which would remain in effect until the trail can be held, as well as certain other matters which as a practical matter would unreviewable at the end of the case if they are not reviewed when they are made.

On the appeal, the issues to be decided are principally questions of law, which are decided "de novo": i.e., the appeals court takes a full and fresh look at the legal issues and will not affirm the decision unless it independently concludes that the trail court made the right rulings. Even when the appeals court finds that the trail judge has made an error, for example, the jury instructions were mistaken in some respect, the judgment may still be upheld if the error is found to be harmless in light of all the circumstances. As it is sometimes put, a party is entitled to a fair trial, not a perfect trial.

Although appellate rulings are generally limited to questions of law, there are two exceptions. First, a party, most often a defendant, will argue that there was insufficient evidence to support the plaintiff's case, and thus as a matter of law the jury should not have been permitted to reach the verdict that it did. Appeals courts will entertain such contentions, not to decide whether the jury was correct in its findings, but only whether, under the law, there was enough relevant evidence to permit the jury to decide the question in favor of the prevailing party. Thus, if a reasonable jury could have reached a conclusion that this jury did, the appeals court will not disturb the verdict simply because it would have reached the opposite result. That power, though rarely exercised, is essential to assuring that juries do not take the law into their own hands by finding facts necessary to produce the outcome they desire.

Secondly, where the facts are found by a judge instead of a jury, an appeals court will overturn a finding if it concludes (as it rarely does) that the trial judge was 'clearly erroneous'. Appeals courts are more willing to reverse a judgment because there was a failure to produce any evidence on a critical point, because the law as given to the jury was incorrectly stated, or because the plaintiff's factual proof did not entitle it to prevail under the existing law. But even these reversals are relatively rare.

There is a third category of issues arising on appeals in which the trial court is almost never overruled. They involve exercises of the court's discretion on matters such as whether additional discovery should be stopped because it has become unduly burdensome, whether further cross-examination should be allowed of a witness, or whether a particular juror should have been excused for cause. In all of those instances the trial judge is exercising her informed discretion about how best to handle the case, and the appeals court, largely in recognition of the need to allow the trial judge flexibility and of her ability to assess first hand all the relevant factors, almost never finds that the trial judge abused her discretion, which is the standard for issues such as these.

Unlike the trial court where there are live witnesses, appeals are decided entirely on the factual record developed in the district court. The losing party writes a document known as a 'brief', which is often as much as 50 pages in length, and the prevailing party then responds, with a brief of similar length, followed by a relatively short reply by the appealing party. The case is assigned to a panel of three judges of the court of appeals who generally, but not in all cases, hear an oral presentation by the lawyers and have the opportunity to ask questions about it. Following oral arguments, which generally last someplace between a half an hour and an hour, the judges discuss the case in private and, some time later, issue a ruling. Until the appeals courts became very busy, there used to be a written opinion explaining the decision in most cases, but that is becoming increasingly less a part of appellate practice. Now, especially when the court affirms the decision below, there is often only a one or two sentence order, sometimes with a brief explanation accompanying it. In perhaps half of the cases, the court issues a lengthy opinion, but that number is decreasing, and in some courts the percentage is far less than that. If a judge disagrees with the result she may write a dissenting opinion, which occurs fairly often. In addition, a judge who may agree with the result may disagree, at least in part, with the rationale in the majority opinion, and may write a 'concurring' opinion that expresses his preferred rationale.

Although statistics are somewhat misleading, or at least inconclusive, the party who prevails in the trial court wins in well over half, and probably dose to two-thirds to three-quarters, of the cases appealed. Thus, a party who loses a case in a trial court must give serious thought to whether the appeal is worth the time, the money for lawyers' fees and preparing the record, and additional effort, even where the ruling appears to be wrong or unjust.

Note

As noted in the preceding excerpt, appeals in the federal judiciary of the United States may ordinarily be taken only from final judgments of the trial court. See also 28 U.S.C.A. §§ 1291 and 1292. Most states follow this practice, but New York is a major exception, "allowing appeals to the state's intermediate appellate court—the Appellate Division—in a great many situations in which no final judgment has been rendered."[1] Describing the availability of interlocutory review under New York law, a leading commentator emphasizes the fact "that there is hardly a question of practice that cannot be appealed; and, if a matter is said to be addressed to the court's discretion or favor, this may mean a more limited scope of review but will rarely affect appealability. Appeals on practice matters are legion, ranging far and wide over questions of venue, parties, consolidation and joint trial, pleading and pre-trial disclosure."[2]

---

1. Jack H. Friedenthal, Arthur R. Miller, John E. Sexton, and Helen Hershkoff, Civil Procedure: Cases and Materials 1064 (9th ed. 2005).

Questions concerning the issues subject to review are an important aspect of the scope of appellate review in the United States. Another important topic involves whether appellate review is mandatory or discretionary. Both of these issues are explored in the following excerpt.

Jack H. Friedenthal, Arthur R. Miller, John E. Sexton, and Helen Hershkoff, Civil Procedure: Cases and Materials 1090, 1107 (9th ed. 2005).

ISSUES SUBJECT TO REVIEW

There are a number of well-defined limits on the scope of appellate review. First, the alleged errors must appear in the trial-court record. Thus it is vital during the course of pretrial preparation as well as during trial itself that an attorney make certain that all rulings and evidence that might form the basis for an appeal be formally recorded. Second, an aggrieved party must have promptly objected to the trial court regarding rulings or events that the judge could have corrected or ameliorated. Normally an error is waived unless a proper objection was taken. Third, even if the issue that the appellant seeks to have reviewed has been presented properly below and has not been waived, it must not constitute "harmless error"—that is, it must have affected substantial rights. Finally, an alleged error must be presented to the appellate court in appellant's brief and the relevant portions of the trial-court record must be brought to the appellate court's attention.

* * *

COURTS ABOVE APPELLATE COURTS—DISCRETIONARY RE-VIEW

For many years, Congress had provided in 28 U.S.C. §§ 1254 and 1257 that the Supreme Court was *required* to review certain decisions of the federal courts of appeals and of state courts in situations involving the validity of state laws under the Constitution, treaties, or laws of the United States. In fact, the requirement was somewhat illusory because the Court took the position that it had jurisdiction only if the case involved a "substantial federal question." Zucht v. King, 260 U.S. 174, 43 S.Ct. 24, 67 L.Ed. 194 (1922). Many such appeals therefore were dismissed because the issue was considered remote or already well-settled.

In 1988, Congress amended Sections 1254 and 1257 to provide that such decisions receive no special treatment, but shall be reviewed, as are most others, only if the Supreme Court, in its discretion, grants a petition for a writ of certiorari.* * *

2. Korn, Civil Jurisdiction of the New York Court of Appeals and Appellate Divi-sions, 16 Buff. L. Rev. 307, 322 (1967), quoted in id.

The most important restriction on Supreme Court review of state-court decisions regarding federal claims is that the judgment necessarily must turn on a federal question and that it not rest upon an independent state ground. Even if the decision is based on alternative grounds, one federal and one state, review will be denied. Zacchini v. Scripps–Howard Broadcasting Co., 433 U.S. 562, 568, 97 S.Ct. 2849, 2853–54, 53 L.Ed.2d 965, 971–72 (1977).

Beginning in the late 1980's, however, the trend began to reverse and the size of the Supreme Court's docket began to decrease:

> From 1971 through 1988, the United States Supreme Court was hearing and deciding an average of 147 cases each Term. * * *

> In the 1989 Term, the number of plenary decisions dropped to 132. That alone would not necessarily have signaled any change. But in 1990 the number dropped still further, to 116. Thereafter, with one trivial exception, the plenary docket continued to shrink. The 1995 Term, which came to and end in 1996, yielded only 77 plenary decisions—half the number that the Court was handing down a decade earlier.

Hellman, *The Shrunken Docket of the Rehnquist Court*, 1996 Sup. Ct. Rev. 403, 403 (1996). "In the October 1999 term, the United States Supreme Court continued its decade-long trend of deciding fewer than 100 fully argued cases. The Court decided on the merits 79 cases in 74 opinions, representing less than four percent of paid petitions and approximately one percent of all petitions." George and Solimine, *Supreme Court Monitoring of the United States Courts of Appeals En Banc*, 9 Sup. Ct. Econ. Rev. 171, 172 (2001).

Title 28, United States Code—Judiciary and Judicial Procedure

28 U.S.C. § 1291 Final decisions of district courts

The courts of appeals * * * shall have jurisdiction of appeals from all final decisions of the district courts of the United States * * *

28 U.S.C. § 1292. Interlocutory decisions

(a) Except as provided in subsections (c) and (d) of this section, the courts of appeals shall have jurisdiction of appeals from:

(1) Interlocutory orders of the district courts of the United States * * * or of the judges thereof, granting, continuing, modifying, refusing or dissolving injunctions, or refusing to dissolve or modify injunctions, except where a direct review may be had in the Supreme Court;

> (2) Interlocutory orders appointing receivers, or refusing orders to wind up receiverships or to take steps to accomplish the purposes thereof, such as directing sales or other disposals of property;

(3) Interlocutory decrees of such district courts or the judges thereof determining the rights and liabilities of the parties to admiralty cases in which appeals from final decrees are allowed.

(b) When a district judge, in making in a civil action an order not otherwise appealable under this section, shall be of the opinion that such order involves a controlling question of law as to which there is substantial ground for difference of opinion and that an immediate appeal from the order may materially advance the ultimate termination of the litigation, he shall so state in writing in such order. * * * *Provided, however,* That application for an appeal hereunder shall not stay proceedings in the district court unless the district judge or the Court of Appeals or a judge thereof shall so order.

28 U.S.C. § 1254. Courts of appeals; certiorari; certified questions

Cases in the courts of appeals may be reviewed by the Supreme Court by the following methods:

(1) By writ of certiorari granted upon the petition of any party to any civil or criminal case, before or after rendition of judgment or decree;

(2) By certification at any time by a court of appeals of any question of law in any civil or criminal case as to which instructions are desired, and upon such certification the Supreme Court may give binding instructions or require the entire record to be sent up for decision of the entire matter in controversy.

28 U.S.C. § 1257. State courts; certiorari

(a) Final judgments or decrees rendered by the highest court of a State in which a decision could be had, may be reviewed by the Supreme Court by writ of certiorari where the validity of a treaty or statute of the United States is drawn in question or where the validity of a statute of any State is drawn in question on the ground of its being repugnant to the Constitution, treaties, or laws of the United States, or where any title, right, privilege, or immunity is specially set up or claimed under the Constitution or the treaties or statutes of, or any commission held or authority exercised under, the United States.

Federal Rules of Civil Procedure

Rule 61 Harmless Error

No error in either the admission or the exclusion of evidence and no error or defect in any ruling or order or in anything done or omitted by the court or by any of the parties is ground for granting a new trial or for setting aside a verdict or for vacating, modifying, or otherwise disturbing a judgment or order, unless refusal to take such action appears to the court inconsistent with substantial justice. The court at every stage of the proceeding must disregard any error or defect in the proceeding which does not affect the substantial rights of the parties.

Rule 62 Stay of Proceedings to Enforce a Judgment

* * *

(c) Injunction Pending Appeal.

When an appeal is taken from an interlocutory or final judgment granting, dissolving, or denying an injunction, the court in its discretion may suspend, modify, restore, or grant an injunction during the pendency of the appeal upon such terms as to bond or otherwise as it considers proper for the security of the rights of the adverse party. If the judgment appealed from is rendered by a district court of three judges specially constituted pursuant to a statute of the United States, no such order shall be made except (1) by such court sitting in open court or (2) by the assent of all the judges of such court evidenced by their signatures to the order.

(d) Stay Upon Appeal.

When an appeal is taken the appellant by giving a supersedeas bond may obtain a stay subject to the exceptions contained in subdivision (a) of this rule. The bond may be given at or after the time of filing the notice of appeal or of procuring the order allowing the appeal, as the case may be. The stay is effective when the supersedeas bond is approved by the court.

* * *

(g) Power of Appellate Court not Limited.

The provisions in this rule do not limit any power of an appellate court or of a judge or justice thereof to stay proceedings during the pendency of an appeal or to suspend, modify, restore, or grant an injunction during the pendency of an appeal or to make any order appropriate to preserve the status quo or the effectiveness of the judgment subsequently to be entered.

V. GERMANY

Peter Gottwald, Civil Procedure in Germany after the Reform Act 2001, 23 Civil Justice Quarterly 338, 345–350 (2004).

II. THE REORGANISATION OF THE FIRST APPEAL
AS A MEANS OF CORRECTING ERRORS

As long ago as the debates surrounding the introduction of the German Imperial Code of Civil Procedure of 1877 opinion was divided as to whether first appeals should take the form of retrial of the case, or merely act as a corrective review of the first instance decision. The more extensive opinion prevailed at that time. According to s.525 CCP (old version) the case had to be completely reheard by the appellate court. The actual practice of the appellate courts has however evolved over the past few decades into a two-stage process. The initial stage of an appeal focused on a review of the first instance decision; that review confined itself to the pleaded grounds of appeal. Only if that review disclosed further grounds for concern as to the probity of the first instance decision would the appellate court move to the second stage, a full rehearing of the matter.

At present the legislator authorises the appellate review of first instance findings, under s.529 sec.1 No.1 CCP, if there is a sound basis for concluding that they are incorrect or incomplete. The novel aspect of this form of review is that the appeal court's doubts must arise from concrete indications of such error in the stated grounds for appeal (s.520 sec.3 sent.2 No.3 CCP). Whilst this new form of appellate review may superficially appear to have effected a paradigm change in the nature of appeal hearings. As is clear from an assessment of the actual practice of the appellate courts prior to its introduction it is, in reality, much less of a change. Given this it is difficult to comprehend the basis for the enraged protests of lawyers, which went as far as nationwide public petitions and a national protest meeting in Berlin, which greeted the abrogation of s.525 CCP. The reforms have however gone further than this merely superficial change, and have introduced novel restrictions on the scope of parties' rights on a first appeal.

1. Restrictions to Submit New Allegations

The right to submit new allegations or fresh evidence has been restricted radically. Under s.531 sec.2 No.3 CCP, facts, already existing while proceedings had been pending at first instance, may be submitted to the appellate court only, if the party did not fail to submit them at first instance negligently. Through this provision the legislator clearly places the burden on parties to ensure that all relevant facts already in existence are submitted to the court of first instance, and that parties are not permitted to keep relevant facts or information in reserve for deployment on appeal. Only in exceptional cases where the party, applying an objective test, cannot be blamed for nonsubmission of factual allegations will such evidence be adducible at an appellate hearing. Such exceptional circumstances might arise, for example, if the failure to adduce such evidence at first instance arose due to a procedural error on the court's part, or if the court of first instance overlooked certain aspects of the evidence, or wrongly regarded some aspects of it as irrelevant and the parties, for that reason only, did not adduce it (cf. s.531 sec.2 Nos 1 and 2 CCP). If the court of first instance and the appellate court arrive at differing interpretations of the law relevant to the case before them the parties must be given the opportunity to make such submissions of those matters of fact as are necessary to the appellate court to enable it to properly apply the law. Under the new law of appeal errors or mistakes made by the court of first instance shall not inhibit the parties' ability to present their case on appeal. Under the old s.528 CCP, fresh arguments could be precluded only where settlement of the issues before the appellate court was not delayed by their due consideration, or where the party did not apologise for the delay. If the court of first instance had fixed a deadline by which arguments had to be submitted to it for the first instance hearing a party who wants to adduce such evidence on appeal had to prove good cause before fresh arguments. If however the court of first instance had not fixed any such deadline fresh arguments could be submitted without the need to show cause unless the party failed to submit them at first instance due to gross negligence. In any case, the crucial point was that the introduction of fresh argument on appeal could be precluded only if it delayed the settlement of appellate proceedings. If the appeal hearing could not however be scheduled for at least 9 or 12 months after the statements of appeal had been submitted, as was regularly the case, the court would generally accept any fresh evidence or argument that could be placed before it during that time. Consequently, the preclusion rules whilst strict in theory were seldom observed in practice. The new rules eschews the prior rule's flaws, and its consequences, as it compels the parties to submit all their arguments to the court of first instance. If however an appellate court decides that nonetheless it will permit a party to adduce fresh argument or evidence, in order to decide the case on what might be said to be the whole of the evidence, no remedy exists for the other party to the action. The, aggrieved, party cannot for instance seek a further appeal of the appellate court's judgment on points of law, and request a fresh judgment made without a consideration of the belated arguments. Most judges fully agreed with this fundamental reform of the first appeal; lawyers have also familiarised themselves with the changed requirements.

2. *The Single Judge sitting in the Court of First Appeal*

The legislator has also provided the means whereby a panel sitting as a court of first appeal can transfer any appeal against decisions of single judges sitting at first instance and all cases classified as "simple" to a single appellate judge for final decision (s.526 sec.1 CCP). It remains to be seen whether the introduction of this procedure was well advised since it may put some judge in a delicate situation, especially if a probationary judge sitting as a single appellate judge overrules the judgment of a presiding judge of the district court.

3. *Order Rejecting an Appeal*

Whilst the reorganisation of appellate proceedings to a means of control in the interest of the parties seems to be proper, I have grave doubts about the new power granted to appellate courts to reject appeals that have neither prospects of success nor raise any question of general importance by a non-appealable order made without oral hearing having taken place (s.522 sec.2 CCP). The power to reject obviously groundless appeals without an oral hearing, by court order, seems to me to be quite proper. But it is doubtful whether the absence of any remedy against such an order, by s.522 sec.3 CCP, accords with the fundamental nature of the Code of Civil Procedure system as a whole, or even with the constitutional requirement of access to justice. This is the case because an appellate court may deprive the parties of any further appeal against its own decision, even if it touches very delicate or fundamental questions merely by rendering its decision to reject an appeal by order and not by judgment. It is obvious that such a power is open for misuse. The legislator took the view that by requiring an appellate court panel to give a unanimous decision to order the rejection, and through requiring written notice to be served in advance of such an order on the parties that the panel was considering such an order, combined with the possibility to remonstrate, that the possibility of misuse would be precluded. Obviously those who place their trust in such considerations have never been committee members, where the committee has been required to settle a delicate issue by unanimous vote: after realising that the issue is delicate the members of the committee will regularly follow the proposal of the chairman to dispose of the problem without much debate. Practical experience, so far, shows that some appellate courts have made no use whatsoever of their new power, whereas others reject up to 60 per cent of all appeals by such order. This highly divergent of practice is ample proof that some degree of standardisation is required to control the exercise of this power.

III. THE NEW SYSTEM OF PERMISSION TO FINAL APPEAL

Under the old law any judgment with a gravamen in excess of 60,000 Deutschmarks was susceptible to a further and final appeal before the Federal Supreme Court. However it only had to accept the final appeal if it raised a question of general legal importance, or if the judgment of the first appellate court was based on an error of law (s.544b CCP). Following the reforms this final appeal is now only available where the first appellate court grants permission to appeal, or where the Federal Supreme Court itself grants such permission. Permission to appeal by the Federal Supreme Court is only available in cases where the first appellate court has refused permission to appeal, the gravamen is worth in excess of €20,000 and it raises an issue of fundamental importance (s.543 sec.1 CCP). This reform is considerably more radical than the reform of the law relating to first appeals. The Committee for the Preparation of a Reform of the Civil Procedure had by 1961 already recommended the restriction of final appeals to cases of fundamental importance. When reforming the law of final appeal in 1975 the legislator at only the very last minute decided not to adopt this system but to open access to final appeals for all financially important cases, whilst granting the Federal Supreme Court some discretionary power to as to whether it would hear a particular appeal. The existence of this discretionary power to accept or reject final appeals was however short-lived. Soon after the introduction of the 1975 law the Federal Constitutional Court overruled this discretion and held that the Federal Supreme Court was obliged to accept final appeals under the Basic Law even where there was no issue of fundamental importance if it was likely that the appeal might succeed due on the basis that the judgment appealed was founded on a relevant error, or violation, of law. In practice, two thirds of all final appeals were not accepted by order without reason but after thorough review of the case by the reporting judge. This system was ideal for parties as they could submit any economically important case to the Federal Supreme Court and receive, at the least, a careful examination of the appellate judgment by the reporting judge even if, ultimately, the final appeal was formally not accepted. In the eyes of the public and of most Supreme Court judges this system was highly unsatisfactory, because two thirds of the work of the Supreme Court judges consisted in the preparation of unpublished reports for the deliberation of the court and was, in the end, merely done for the benefit of the waste-paper basket.

1. *Practical Consequences of the new System of Permission*

The new scheme of access to final appeal has had a number of consequences for the culture of appeal. Final appeals are no longer available to every high value case. On the other hand low value cases can now be submitted to the Federal Supreme Court if the first appellate court takes the view that the cases raises an issue of fundamental importance. As might have been expected this change in the principal of access to final appeal has resulted in less high value cases, and more low value cases, being heard by the Federal Supreme Court. Because lawyer's fees for cases heard on final appeal are based on the amount in dispute, this development has resulted in a substantial drop in the income of lawyers who are exclusively registered to appear before the Federal Supreme Court. This has rendered doubtful the survival of the specialised Federal Supreme Court bar.

2. *Obvious Errors in Law and Procedural Errors*

Even in cases where permission to hold a final appeal is granted for public interest reasons, the appeal remains of interest to the parties concerned: the basis for the appeal maybe an issue of fundamental public importance but the remedy sought affects the parties to the action. Given the primacy of party interest in bringing, and setting the scope of, the final appeal, the Federal Supreme Court can only rule on such issues of wider importance where litigants themselves raise those issues before the court. The court's role as a forum to resolve issues of public importance is therefore limited: it can do so only where litigants raise issues before it. It should be remembered however that the right of access to the Federal Supreme Court is protected by the constitutional guarantee of access to justice.

To reduce Federal Supreme Court's workload the legislator abolished the right to final appeal's, which were solely based on the violation of fundamental procedural rights. Gross violations of fundamental procedural rights are, however, still classified as errors that justify a judgment in any case being overruled. As a result of the reforms however, the grant of permission for a final appeal is only given if such errors also violate basic constitutional rights, for example, the right to be heard, the right to a legally competent judge, or the guarantee of access to justice as part of due process of law. In such a case the divisions of the Federal Supreme Court admit the final appeal, by granting a complaint against the refusal of permission to appeal, because of the fundamental importance of the case, or as a means to guarantee uniform court practice. The criteria for obtaining permission to appeal are not however fulfilled if the fundamental procedural error happened in an individual case, or if there is an obviously bad judgment even in a high value case, where the error seems to concern just a single case without any danger of imitation in court practice. Such estimation, however, is very uncertain. Cases which are currently regarded as being exceptional may become daily practice in the courts of tomorrow without that alteration of practice being foreseeable. Because obvious errors of law seriously undermine the courts' authority and the rule of law, reversing judgments that contain such errors should be regarded as an issue of fundamental importance. Such a stance appears to be practicable as the Federal Supreme Court would have a wide discretion, and cases involving obvious errors of law by a court of second instance (e.g. first appellate courts) are uncommon. In my opinion access to final appeals could have been further restricted by the legislator, for example through the introduction of a system of certiorari as practiced by the US Supreme Court. But if he wanted to consider parties' interests more intensively the review should not fall short to the constitutional guarantees of due process.

3. *Settlement of Final Appeal by Court Order*

On the other hand I can see no reason why the Federal Supreme Court must sit in full division to hear any final appeal and is not authorised to correct obvious errors of law or to reject obviously unfounded final appeals by sitting in a chamber of three judges and by written court order.

German Code of Civil Procedure.*

§ 511

The final judgment in the first instance shall be subject to the appeal on facts.

§ 511a

(1) In litigation with respect to monetary claims, an appeal on facts shall be impermissible in the event that the value of the subject of the complaint does not exceed one thousand five hundred German Marks.

(2) In disputes about claims arising from a landlord-tenant relationship with respect to residential space, or with respect to the terms of such a landlord-tenant relationship, appeal on facts shall also lie in the event that the Lower Court deviates from a decision of a Superior State Court or of the Federal Supreme Court and the decision is based on such deviation.

§ 513

(1) A default judgment may be not be contested by way of appeal by the party against whom it was given.

(2) A default judgment, against which an appeal properly considered is not admissible, shall be subject to appeal to the extent that it is based on the fact that there shall have been no case of default. Section 511 a shall not be applicable.

§ 520   Effective as of January 1, 2000

(1) In the event that the appeal shall have not been dismissed as impermissible, a date shall be fixed for hearing and the parties notified thereof. The fixing of date for hearing may be omitted in the event that a preliminary proceeding in writing appears necessary for the final preparation of the principal session.

(2) The presiding judge or the appellate court may allow a period for the appellee to enter a written opposition to the appeal and a period for the appellant to file a written opinion on the opposition to the appeal. In the case of paragraph 1 sentence 2, the appellee shall be granted a period of not less than a month for filing a written opposition to the appeal. Section 277 (1), 2 and 4 shall be applicable analogously.

(3) Along with the notice pursuant to paragraph 1 sentence 1 or the fixing of a period pursuant to paragraph 2 sentence 2 within which the appeal is to be answered, the appellee shall be instructed that he or she must be represented before the Superior State Court by an attorney admitted to practice before such court. The provisions of § 274 (3) shall be applicable analogously to the period that must lie between the notification of the time of the hearing and hearing.

§ 522

(1) The cross-appeal shall lose it validity in the event that the appeal shall have been withdrawn or dismissed as not admissible.

---

* Translation in German Commercial Code and Code of Civil Procedure in English (Charles E. Stewart, trans., 2001).

(2) In the event that the appellee joined a file appeal within the period allowed for appeal, he or she shall be deemed as having lodged the appeal independently.

§ 522a

(1) The joinder shall be effected by filing the joinder of appeal in writing in the appellate court.

(2) Reasons for the joinder of appeal must be filed before the expiration of the period allowed for the appeal (§ 519 (2)) and, to the extent that it is filed after the expiration thereof, within the joinder of appeal.

(3) The provisions of § 518 (2), 4 of § 519 (3), 5 and of §§ 519a, 519b shall be applicable analogously.

§ 529

(1) Waivable objections relating to the permissibility of the complaint that, contrary to §§ 519 or 520 (2), were not made in a timely manner may only be accepted in the event that the party adequately excuses the delay. The same shall be applicable to waivable new objections relating to the permissibility of the complaint in the event that the party should have presented them in the first instance.

(2) In lawsuits with respect to monetary claims, the appellate court shall not examine the exclusive jurisdiction or the jurisdiction of the Labor Court on its own motion; a plea of defect of the defendant shall be excluded in the event that he or she pleaded to the principal issue in the first instance without the plea of defect and he or she fails to offer a sufficient excuse therefor.

§ 531

The violation of a statutory provision with respect to procedure in the first instance may be pleaded in the appellate instance in the event that the party shall have already lost his or her right to plead a defect in the first instance pursuant to § 295.

§ 542

(1) In the event that the appellant fails to appear at the time fixed for hearing, his or her appeal shall be dismissed on motion in a default judgment.

(2) * * *

§ 543

(1) A statement of facts may be left out in the judgment and, to the extent that the appellate court is in agreement with the grounds of the contested decision, it may also omit the recital of the grounds of the decision.

(2) In the event that an appeal on issues of law (revision) lies, the statement of facts shall include a concise presentation of the state of facts and of the action based on the oral presentation of the parties. A reference made to the contested judgment as well as to written pleadings, records and other documents shall be permissible, to the extent that the judging of pleas advanced by the parties by the highest court of appeal (Revisionsgericht) is not substantially rendered more difficult thereby.

§ 545

(1) An appeal on issues of law (revision) against final judgments of the State Superior Courts (Oberlandesgericht), as appellate instances, lies in accordance with the following provisions.

(2) The revision shall not be allowed against judgments by which a decision is made with respect to the issuance, modification or cancellation of a custody order or an interim disposition. The same shall be applicable to judgments with respect to a premature vesting order in expropriation proceedings or in partition proceedings.

§ 578 [Reopening of Proceedings)

(1) The reopening of a trial concluded by a final judgment can take place by means of an action for annulment or an action for restitution.

(2) In the event that both actions are brought by the same party on different parties, the proceeding and decision with respect to the action for restitution shall be suspended until final judgment on the action for annulment.

§ 579

(1) The action for annulment arises:

1. In the event that the court giving the judgment was not properly constituted:;

2. In the event that a judge, who by virtue of the law was excluded for officiating as a judge, participated in making the decision, to the extent that such impediment is not ineffective as the result of an unsuccessful challenge or appeal;

3. In the event that a judge participated in making the decision although he or she had been rejected on account of presumed partiality and the motion for rejection had been declared well founded;

4. In the event that a party was not represented in the proceedings as required by law, unless he or she expressly or tacitly consented to the conduct of the proceedings.

(2) In the cases designated in nos. 1 and 3, an action shall be excluded in the event that the annulment could have been asserted by appeal.

§ 580

An action for restitution arises:

1. In the event that the opponent, by confirming on oath a statement on which the judgment is based, is guilty of intentionally or recklessly violating his or her oath;

2. In the event that a document on which the judgment is based was falsely drawn up or falsified;

3. In the event that, in case of a testimony or expert opinion on which the judgment is based, the witness or the expert is guilty of a punishable violation of the duty of speaking the truth;

4. In the event that the judgment is secured by the representative of the party or of the opposing party by a criminal offense committed relating to the lawsuit;

5. In the event that a judge who, with respect to the action, is guilty of a punishable violation of his or her official duties vis-á-vis a party participated in making the judgment;

6. In the event that the judgment of a regular court, an earlier special court or of an administrative court, on which the judgment is based, shall have been set aside by another final judgment;

7. In the event that the party discovers:

   a. a prior final judgment given in the same matter; or

   b. another document, the use of which would place him or her in a position to bring about a decision more beneficial for him.

VI. FRANCE

Alexander Layton and Hugh Mercer, European Civil Justice, Vol. 2, 51.092–51.100 (2nd ed. 2004).

France–Civil Procedure Appeals

1. Introduction

Procedural law distinguishes between two categories of appeals (*voies de recours*): ordinary appeals and extraordinary appeals. Ordinary appeals are an appeal in the strict sense (*appel*) and an opposition against a judgment entered in default or against certain other judgments. Extraordinary appeals are third party opposition (*tierce opposition*), a petition for review (*recours en révision*) and an appeal to the *Cour de cassation (pourvoi en cassation)*. In addition, there are various special forms of appeal relating to specific matters, notably a *contredit* against some of the rulings on a question of jurisdiction. . . .

2. Ordinary appeals

Appel. An *appel* is the normal means of recourse from a judgment made by any court of first instance, and is brought before the *cour d'appel* for the region in which the court appealed from is located. An *appel* may not be brought against a judgment for less than €3,800. The time-limit for lodging an *appel* is generally one month in the case of a judgment in a contentious matter and 15 days in the case of a summary order or a judgment in a non-contentious matter. The time-limits for appealing do not apply to a cross-appeal, which may be raised at any time in the appellate proceedings. The appellant is called the *appelant*; the respondent, the *intimé*; and a cross-appellant, the *appelant titre incident*. The appeal is initiated by the appellant's *avoué* filing a *declaration d'appel* with the court. This is then sent by post to the respondent requiring him to appoint an *avoué*. The appellant must file his *conclusions d'appel* within four months from the *declaration d'appel*. The procedure is then the same as that in the *tribunal de grande instance*.

Unless the judgment is provisionally enforceable, enforcement of the judgment is stayed while the time for the lodging of an appeal is running or until the appeal is disposed of. A judgment which is provisionally enforceable may be stayed on summary application to the principal president of the *cour d'appel*.

An *appel* involves a consideration *de novo* of matters of both fact and law. The *cour d'appel* will review the whole case and fresh evidence may be submitted, although no new claims may be advanced. It can vary or set aside the judgment of the court below. The respondent may himself raise an incidental cross-appeal, either against the appellant, or against another respondent, or against a person who was a party to the decision at first instance.

Opposition. An application to set aside a judgment which is not subject to *appel* and which is entered in default (*a jugement par defaut*) is called an opposition and is made to the court which gave the judgment. It has already been described above. In addition, the procedure for setting aside an *injonction de payer* is also called *opposition*.

3. *Extraordinary appeals*

The bringing of an extraordinary appeal does not generally have the effect of staying execution; but a stay of execution may sometimes be obtained in an appropriate case. Application is generally made by the *référé* procedure.

Tierce-opposition. This is an appeal whereby a judgment may be set aside or varied on the application of a person (the third party) who has an interest in the judgment but who was not a party to it. In an appropriate case, it may be brought by the creditors or assignees of a party if the judgment was obtained in fraud of their rights or on other sufficient grounds. As regards the third party, it reopens the matters of fact and law in the judgment challenged in the application. The application is made to the court which gave the judgment and it may generally be made at any time within 30 years from the date of the judgment; but if the third party was served with notice of the judgment, the time-limit for making the application is two months from the date of service of the notice, provided that the notice clearly indicated that time-limit and the means by which the judgment could be challenged.

Recours en révision. This is a procedure whereby a party may apply to set aside a judgment which has become *res judicata*. It is available only on the ground that the judgment was obtained by fraud or on similar grounds. The application for a stay must be made within two months from the date when the applicant had knowledge of the grounds for review on which he relies and he must not have been able to raise those grounds before the judgment became *res judicata*.

Pourvoi en cassation. An appeal to the *Cour de cassation* may only be brought on a point of law and generally only against a decision which is not appealable by *appel or opposition.* The nature of the appeal has been described above. The *pourvoi en cassation* must normally be brought within two months, although this time-limit is subject to many exceptions. It does not generally have the effect of preventing the judgment appealed against from becoming *res judicata,* and thus it does not suspend its enforceability.

VII. JAPAN

Takeshi Kojima, Japanese Civil Procedure in Comparative Law Perspective, 46 U. Kan. L. Rev. 687, 715–717 (1998)

E. *Appeals*

The new code introduces a system of discretionary appeal to the Supreme Court. Discretion is given both with respect to appeals from judgments (*jokoku*-appeal) and appeals from interlocutory orders and rulings (*kokoku*-appeal). The *jokoku*-appeal is effected by the Supreme Court's acceptance of the judgment of an intermediate level court known as a high court. The *kokoku*-appeal depends upon permission being given by the high court for the appeal of interlocutory rulings and orders of the high court. The reform aims to improve the whole system of appeal by introducing flexibility with the possibility of restriction in *jokoku*-appeal and expansion in *kokoku*-appeal.

1. *Jokoku*–Appeal by Acceptance of the Supreme Court

The Japanese court system consists of three tiers of courts. The lower two can determine issues of fact as well as law, but the highest court—the Supreme Court—only considers questions of law. The first appeal is either to a high court or a district court. The court of first appeal continues hearings on facts, and the parties are allowed to produce new evidence.

The second appeal is to either a high court or the Supreme Court. The new code made few revisions as to the second appeal to a high court, but it includes important revisions as to the second appeal especially to the Supreme Court.

The second appeal may lie as a matter of right in cases where there is an alleged contravention of the Constitution or some other absolute reason for appeal. In other cases, discretionary appeal to the Supreme Court is allowed where a violation of law influenced the judgment. This idea of appeal at the court's discretion derives from Anglo–American law, and is influenced to some extent by German law. Upon a motion for appeal, the Supreme Court may accept those cases where the lower court decision is irreconcilable with Supreme Court precedents or some important issues in interpreting law are involved. For instance, appeal to the Supreme Court is accepted when the lower court decision is inconsistent with precedents, when there is no precedent of the Supreme Court on the issue, or when it is necessary to overturn a precedent. The new code introduces the discretionary appeal system because the Supreme Court needs to make meaningful use of the Justices' time for important cases by strictly limiting those appeals taken for the purpose of prolonging the rendering of the final judgment, or where the ostensible reason is the violation in interpreting law but where the real motive is dissatisfaction with the facts found by the lower court.

2. *Kokoku*–Appeal by Permission

The new code introduces appeal by permission and allows an appeal of an order or ruling to the Supreme Court when the high court that rendered the challenged ruling or order has permitted the ruling or order to be appealed. Its purpose is to dispel the situation existing under the old code where undesirable chaos could be caused by irreconcilable rulings or orders among the eight high courts as to important issues. Appeals for the reason of violation of law were not permitted from non-final rulings or orders. The new system of appeal of such rulings by permission will contribute to bringing about coherence in the application and interpretation of law, especially in the fields of Civil Execution Law and Civil Preservation Law.

Note

The period within which an appeal (*koso appeal*) must be filed is quite short in Japan, normally two weeks. Interestingly, the appeal notice is filed with the court which gave the judgment against which the appeal is made. A preliminary review will then take place to examine whether the appeal notice complies with the requirements of the rules, such a precise identification of the order appealed. If following such review the appeal is accepted, the presiding judge of the *koso* appeal will set a date for the first oral hearing.

The appeal is a continuation of the trial process and the appeal court may therefore entertain arguments on both questions of fact and law. The appellant may raise on appeal fresh arguments, though the fact that he has not done so in the lower court may be held against him or her. However, it is not normally necessary for the appeal court to hear the evidence afresh since it will have before it the record of the first instance court.

An appeal normally stays execution, but the court has the power to order execution even pending an appeal. If, at the conclusion of an appeal, the appeal court concludes that the appeal was made merely in order to delay execution, it may order the appellant to pay penalty up to 10 times the value of the appeal filing fee.[3]

Japanese Code of Civil Procedure.[*]

Article 281. (Judgment against which Kôso-Appeal may be made, etc.)

---

3. For a more detailed explanation, see Carl F. Goodman, Justice and Civil Procedure in Japan 432–434, 438–439, 440–441 (2004).

[*] Translation by Masatoshi Kasai and Andrew Thorson, and included as end material

in Takaaki Hattori and Dan Fenno Henderson, Civil Procedure in Japan (Yasuhei Taniguchi, Pauline C. Reich, and Hiroto Miyake, eds., Rev. 2nd ed. 2004).

1.   A Kôso-Appeal may be made against a final judgment rendered by a district court in the first instance or against a final judgment rendered by a summary court. However, this shall not apply to cases where both parties have, following the entry of a final judgment, agreed not to make a Kôso Appeal but reserved the right to make a *jôkoku-appeal.*

Article 294. (Declaration of provisional execution *of* judgment in first instance)

The kôso-appellate court may, upon motion, by ruling, make a declaration of provisional execution only regarding any part of the judgment in the first instance against which no appeal has been made.

Article 311. (Court of last resort)

1.   A *Jôkoku-Appeal may* be made to the Supreme Court against the final judgment of a high court acting in the second instance or the first instance, and to a high court against the final judgment of a district court acting in the second instance.

2.   In cases of the proviso of the provisions of Article 281, paragraph 1, a *Jôkoku-Appeal may* be made directly to the Supreme Court against the judgment of the district court and to the high court against the judgment of the summary court.

Article 312. (Grounds for jôkoku-appeal)

1.   A jôkoku-appeal may be made based upon the grounds that there is an alleged misinterpretation or any other contravention of the Constitution in the judgment.

2.   A jôkoku-appeal may also be made based upon any of the following grounds. However, with regard to the grounds referred to in item iv, this shall not apply to cases where ratification has been made in accordance with the provisions of Article 34, paragraph 2 (including those cases to which it applies mutatis *mutandis* in Article 59).

> i.   the court rendering judgment was not composed according to law
>
> ii.   a judge, who was prohibited by law from doing so, participated in the judgment
>
> iii.   provisions regarding exclusive jurisdiction have been contravened
>
> iv.   there existed some defect in the authorization of the legal representative or advocate, or in the necessary authority granted to such representative for the act of litigation
>
> v.   provisions concerning public oral argument have been contravened
>
> vi.   the judgment was made without giving the reason therefor, or where the reasons given are not consistent

3. A *Jôkoku-Appeal to* a high court may also be made based upon the grounds that a contravention of laws or ordinances clearly influenced the judgment.

Article 318. (Motion for acceptance of jôkoku—appeal)

1. In cases where the court to which a *jôkoku-appeal.* shall be made is the Supreme Court, the Supreme Court may, upon motion, by ruling, and as the court of last resort, accept a case in which the original judgment* includes an adjudication which contradicts the precedent of the Supreme Court (if there is no such precedent, the precedent of the *Taishin' in,*** or of a high court as the court of last resort or the kôso-appellate court), or any other case which is deemed to include an important matter relating to interpretation of laws or ordinances.

[* "Original judgment" means a judgment against which the appeal is made.]

[** "The *Taishin' in,*** means the Grand Court, or the Supreme Court of Japan under the *Meiji*-Constitution (The Constitution of the Empire of Japan) and related laws.]⁴

2. The motion referred to in the preceding paragraph (hereinafter referred to as "motion for acceptance of *jôkoku-appeal)* shall not be made on the grounds provided for in Article 312, paragraphs 1 and 2.

3. In the cases referred to in paragraph 1, the Supreme Court may, upon determining that there are unimportant reasons among the reasons given for a motion for acceptance of *jôkoku-appeal,* exclude the unimportant reasons.

4. In cases where there is a ruling under paragraph 1, it shall be deemed that the jôkoku-appeal has been made. In such cases, with regard to the application of the provisions of Article 320, the reasons given in a motion for acceptance of a *jôkoku-appeal.* except for reasons excluded under the preceding paragraph, shall be deemed the reasons for the *jôkoku-appeal.*

5. The provisions of Articles 313 to 315 inclusive and Article 316, paragraph 1 shall apply mutatis *mutandis* to a motion for acceptance of *jôkoku-appeal).*

Article 328. (Decision against which kôkoku-appeal may be made)

1. A kôkoku-appeal may be made against a ruling or an order dismissing a motion relating to the litigation proceedings without proceeding to oral argument.

2. A kôkoku-appeal may be made against a ruling or an order made in a matter that cannot be adjudicated by such ruling or order.

Article 338. (Grounds for retrial)

1. In cases where any of the following grounds exist, an appeal against a final judgment which has become final and binding may be made by means of a petition for retrial. However, this shall not

---

4. Editors' Note: This refers to the Old Constitution of 1889 of the Empire of Japan.

apply to cases where the party asserted the grounds in a prior kôso-appeal or *jôkoku-appeal. or* has not asserted them although such party had knowledge thereof.

i. the court rendering judgment was not composed according to law

ii. a judge, who was prohibited by law from doing so, participated in the judgment

iii. there existed some defect in the authority of the legal representative or advocate, or in the necessary authorization granted to such representative for the act of litigation

iv. a judge who participated in the judgment committed a crime in connection with the judge's official duties in relation to the case

v. the party was led to make a confession or was prevented from advancing offensive or defensive measures which would affect the judgment, by virtue of a criminally punishable act of another person

vi. a document or any other object used as evidence for the judgment has been forged or fraudulently changed

vii. evidence for the judgment was based on the false statement of a witness, an expert witness, an interpreter, or a sworn party or legal representative

viii. a civil or criminal judgment or any other decision or administrative disposition on which the judgment was based has been changed by a subsequent decision or administrative disposition

xi. the decision omitted major factors which might affect the judgment

x. the judgment against which the appeal has been made contradicts a judgment which previously became final and binding

2. In cases where any of the grounds referred to in items iv to vii inclusive of the preceding paragraph exists, a petition for retrial may be filed only if, with regard to the acts to be punished, the judgment for conviction or decision for a nonpenal fine has become final and binding, or it is impossible to obtain a judgment for conviction or a decision for a nonpenal fine for reasons other than lack of evidence.

3. In cases where a judgment has been entered in the kôso-appeal instance upon the merits of the suit, a petition for retrial against the judgment of the first instance may not be filed.

ITALY

Michele Taruffo, Civil Procedure and the Path of a Civil Case, in Introduction to Italian Law 175–177 (Jeffrey S. Lena and Ugo Mattei, eds., 2002).

VII.   Appeals

Within time limits fixed by law, the losing party may file an appeal against the first instance judgment. Such an appeal will usually be tried and decided by an intermediate appellate court. The appeal is of right. That is, no leave is required and there are no conditions or limits (except in the case of very small claims, *i.e.* for judgments delivered by a justice of the peace for an amount up to one million lire). The claim may deal with any feature of the first instance judgment that may make the decision "unjust": for instance, the appeal may be grounded on errors of fact concerning the evaluation of proofs, on errors of law concerning the choice, interpretation, and application of the governing rule, or on both types of errors. On the other hand, the appellate court may revise any aspect of the appealed judgment. If the appeal is found to be well-founded, the appellate court makes a new decision on the merits of the case, by reconsidering both facts and law. This decision will take the place of the first instance decision. There is no trial *de novo* in the first instance court (except for a few cases in which the first instance judgment is found to be invalid for specific procedural reasons). Although the appellate court may take into consideration any kind of factual and legal error, the admissibility of fresh evidence in the appellate proceedings is limited to the items of evidence that could possibly lead the court to reverse the decision of the lower court. No other new evidence is admitted. Therefore, the appellate court will make a new judgment on the facts, but rely mainly on the same evidence that was presented in the first instance proceedings. This is the outcome of a recent change in Italian civil procedure—the traditional system used to admit fresh evidence before the appellate court, allowing this court to make a completely new decision on the facts of the case. The rule was changed in 1990 with the aim of accelerating appellate proceedings, but also of deterring people from filing appeals in the hope of attaining a new judgment on a different evidentiary basis. For the same reasons, new claims and new defenses are not admitted in appellate proceedings.

The judgment delivered by the intermediate appellate court is final and enforceable. However, a further appeal may be filed in the Italian Supreme Court (*Corte di Cassazione*, the court of last resort) for civil disputes in the Italian system. It is worth stressing that the appeal to the Supreme Court is granted not only by the ordinary rules of the Code of Civil Procedure, but also by art. 111 para. 7 of the Italian Constitution. Along the same lines as the traditional French model that inspired the Italian system, the Supreme Court is only a court "of legitimacy." That is to say, the main role of this court is to check whether the lower court interpreted and correctly and validly applied substantive and procedural legal rules. The basic function of the court is, in fact, to ensure the legality and legitimacy of the legal system as a whole, and also to help to achieve an adequate degree of uniformity in the interpretation and application of the law. Therefore, an appeal to the Supreme Court may be grounded only upon errors of law. Such errors may concern the violation of both procedural and substantive rules. Besides, a very peculiar ground of appeal to the Supreme Court deals with the opinion supporting the decision of the lower court: if the justificatory opinion does not exist, or if it is not sufficient or contradictory, an appeal may be filed to the Supreme Court. In accordance with the role of the Supreme Court, no evidence is admitted (though no new evidence is actually needed) in proceedings before the Court.

When the Supreme Court finds that the appeal is well-grounded, it quashes the judgment and send s the case back to a lower court (usually another intermediate appellate court) for a new judgment. The Supreme Court states the legal rule that the lower court is required to follow when making its new decision on the case. No fresh evidence is admitted in these further proceedings. Therefore, the new judgment is based upon the legal principle stated by the Supreme Court, and possibly upon a new consideration of the facts and evidence that was presented in the earlier phases of the proceedings. However, in accordance with a recent reform, there are some cases in which the Supreme Court may make a decision on the merits of the whole case, including the facts. This may happen when the Court quashes the judgment of the lower court, but finds that a new judgment on the merits may be delivered without any reconsideration of the facts at issue. Then the Supreme Court may "take the facts as they were established" by the lower court and deliver a new final judgment on the merits of the case directly.

Two other devices of attack against a judgment must be considered. First, a non-party who is affected by a judgment delivered between the proper parties, because of a substantive connection among legal situations, may challenge that judgment in order not to be "touched" by its effects (this device is called the *opposizione di terzo*), since a judgment may only be effective between the subjects that were the proper parties in the proceedings.

Also, if a final judgment (even if it is already *res judicata*) conflicts with another judgment *res judicata*, if it is considered the effect of a fraud by either one of the parties or the judge; or if it is found that the judgment is based on a clear mistake or on evidence that is discovered to be false; or if new relevant evidence is found after the end of the proceedings, such a judgment may be challenged by means of a specific device called *revocazione*.

Chapter 8

AGGREGATION OF PARTIES, CLAIMS, AND ACTIONS

I. INTRODUCTION

This Chapter compares and contrasts joinder devices in selected civil and common law systems. The mechanism of joinder allows litigants to aggregate parties, claims, or actions within a single proceeding. In theory, the availability of joinder opens the courthouse door to larger numbers of claimants who might otherwise be barred from seeking relief because of the cost or inconvenience of litigation. Joinder devices are therefore critical tools in affording access to justice. In practice, however, the use of joinder in any particular case may undermine an individual's ability to participate fully in a lawsuit and so interfere with autonomy values. In these situations, joinder—aimed at promoting efficiency, preventing duplication, and effectuating complete relief—comes into conflict with the overriding aim of achieving justice for the individual litigant. Adrian Zuckerman, focusing on recent reforms to the English procedural system, locates this potential tension in a more general context:

> The overriding objective [of the revised Civil Procedure Rules] consists in "enabling the court to deal with cases justly" (CPR 1.1(1)). Doing justice is the goal of any enlightened system of civil litigation. However the notion of doing justice is capable of a variety of interpretations. Under the previous system the notion of justice was interpreted merely as indicating the need to arrive at a judgment that was correct as a matter of fact and of law, i.e., achieving rectitude of decision. It was thought that the court's function was doing justice on the merits and no more. The CPR break with this tradition by establishing that doing justice on the merits is not the sole overarching principle. The overriding objective adds two other vital procedural imperatives to the imperative of doing substantive justice: deciding cases within a reasonable time, and using no more than proportionate resources.[1]

---

[1] Zuckerman on Civil Procedure: Principles of Practice 3 (2nd ed. 2006).

Most of the joinder devices surveyed in this Chapter adhere to an individualistic model of adjudication. Although their details differ across nations, these devices share important similarities in terms of structure and operation. First, joinder devices tend to build on a two-party structure—referred to as bilateral or bipolar—in which an aggrieved party initiates suit by asserting a claim against the alleged wrongdoer. From this basic model, joinder devices permit increasing degrees of complexity. For example, a claimant might be permitted to aggregate its own claims with those of another injured party in one suit against a common adverse party; an alleged wrongdoer might be permitted to assert counterclaims against the putative victim or to join together with other defendants in a single lawsuit; and strangers to a lawsuit might be allowed to join an on-going proceeding to protect rights and interests that are implicated in the lawsuit. Second, joinder devices reflect two modes of operation: voluntary, which leaves the decision whether or not to aggregate up to the parties (usually subject to conditions such as jurisdictional limits); and mandatory, which leaves the decision up to the court as a condition of proceeding to judgment.

In addition to these traditional devices, some procedural systems include aggregation mechanisms that depart from the individualistic approach by permitting a party—whether an individual claimant, an associational entity, or a government official—to represent the interests of others who do not personally appear in the lawsuit. The class action is the best known of the representative devices and for a long time was unique to the United States. However, even in countries that do not use the class action, adjudicative devices, such as the "public action," may be available to resolve collective harms. Some legal systems rely on social welfare legislation to achieve similar goals. The European Union, with its push toward harmonization, has spurred member nations to adopt new forms of representative actions that draw some inspiration from the American model but differ in important ways.

This Chapter opens with materials that explore the functional justifications for aggregation; moves to illustrative examples of voluntary and mandatory aggregation devices within an individualistic framework; turns to the special problem of claims for reimbursement or contribution; discusses class, representative, and collective actions; and concludes by looking at aggregation devices that allow for the consolidation of separate lawsuits, filed in different courts or before different judges, in a single proceeding.

As you read the examples that follow, do not be lulled into a simple comparison of procedures that, at least on the surface, appear to be similar because of comparable language or scope of application. As with every legal rule, consideration must be given to political, cultural, and other factors that give joinder devices "a quite different significance than they appear to have" from one's own legal perspective.[2] In particu-

---

2. Kenneth W. Graham, Jr., The Persistence of Progressive Proceduralism, 61 Tex. L. Rev. 929, 934 (1982–1983).

lar, consider how a procedural system's approach to judicial authority, as reflected in case management powers, potentially affects the design and operation of joinder rules.

II. THE FUNCTION AND GOALS OF AGGREGATION DEVICES

Conceptually, joinder mechanisms adhere to an individualistic model of adjudication. Central to this model is the principle of party autonomy, which many commentators view as critical for protecting personal liberty against the power of the state. Rolf Stürner posits that a

> common concept of procedural liberty and autonomy is the self-evident basis of the Romance, Germanic, and Anglo–American procedural tradition, even though the procedure codes of many countries do not contain special provisions that describe or define this fundamental concept. This homogeneity reflects a piece of common political culture that places the personal rights of the individual citizen in the centre of economic and legal activity and makes the individual a central figure of state order and economy.[3]

To the extent that joinder devices depart from the principle of individual autonomy, commentators justify aggregation in terms of efficiency, fairness, and theories of representation. The excerpts in this section explore the various goals that aggregation devices in different national systems are expected to achieve.

Ernst J. Cohn, Parties, in International Encyclopedia of Comparative Law 38, 42 (1976).

It is often desirable that several parties should join as plaintiffs or defendants in the same proceedings in order to avoid conflicting decisions and the multiplication of law suits. On the other hand, a defendant may be embarrassed by having to face a large number of plaintiffs, and *vice versa*. Further, plurality of parties may result in extending unnecessarily the scope and duration of the proceedings. All systems therefore agree that plurality is permissible in certain cases only, where some form of connection exists between the various parties on either side.

The definition of this connection as well as its legislative treatment differs considerably. Some legal systems permit the court to compel a joinder of parties in suitable cases. Others confine themselves to securing some measure of joint conduct of the proceedings by the several plaintiffs or defendants. A distinction is made between cases where the connection between the various parties is particularly intimate (here referred to as compulsory plurality) and those in which, though existing, it is less intimate (here referred to as permissive plurality). Permissive

---

3. Rolf Stürner, The Principles of Transnational Civil Procedure: An Introduction to Their Basic Conceptions, in 692 Rabels Zeitschrift für ausländisches und internationals Privatrecht 201, 221–222 (2005).

372 AGGREGATION OF PARTIES, CLAIMS, & ACTIONS Ch. 8

plurality means that the court can decide on the merits of the case without a joinder of all concerned. It does not mean that all parties joined have done so voluntarily.

* * *

All systems agree that there are a number of cases in which the connection between the parties is so intimate that the rules dealing with permissive plurality are insufficient to meet the special needs of these cases. There is, however, a wide divergence of views as to both the nature of the cases in question and the manner in which they should be treated.

There are a number of cases in which rules of substantive law require an action to be brought or defended by a number of persons acting jointly. Where this is so, an action brought or defended by only some of the total number required, must in general fail. Plurality in such cases may be said to be necessary. This is an inevitable result of a rule of substantive, not of procedural law. * * *

There remain a number of other cases in which, on grounds of legal logic, or of equity, or of overwhelming convenience, it seems most desirable that on the one hand parties who have not joined the proceedings should be compelled by court order to join them and that on the other hand there should be some measure of joint conduct of the proceedings. A number of legal systems have, however, valued the freedom of each party to conduct his own case so highly that they have not permitted any joinder by compulsion.

Richard D. Freer, Avoiding Duplicative Litigation: Rethinking Plaintiff Autonomy and the Court's Role in Defining the Litigative Unit, 50 U. Pitt. L. Rev. 809, 813–815 (1989).

Packaging eliminates duplicative litigation, and thus generally is more efficient than repetitive litigation from a societal standpoint; scarce judicial resources need to be expended only once to unravel the facts of a dispute. It is certainly more efficient for the party who otherwise would be subject to multiple actions, since he may avoid duplicated expenses on discovery, attorneys' fees, and the like. Others may benefit as well; the litigation expenses saved may be used to compensate deserving plaintiffs or may allow the defendant to avoid bankruptcy.

Addressing all related claims in a single action will often resolve the overall dispute more quickly than entertaining multiple suits. Every claim and defense is placed before one judge, who can oversee and streamline all aspects of the case, including discovery and perhaps settlement. The parties litigate once, put the matter behind them, and get on with their lives, which may augur toward the psychological well-being of some parties, or toward restoring market confidence in a commercial entity involved in litigation.

Inclusive joinder also promotes fairness. The would-be nonparty is protected from practical harm which may flow from litigation in her absence. Likewise, inclusive joinder avoids the possibility of imposing multiple liability or inconsistent obligations on the defendant. The avoidance of inconsistent judgments fosters public faith in the administration of justice.

Of course, packaging is not a panacea. If compelled, it may create litigation of claims which otherwise might not have been asserted and may force joinder of persons who otherwise might not sue or be sued. It can, in some circumstances, hinder settlement, since a single obstreperous party may thwart the agreement of the others. Moreover, packaging can create management problems on two levels. First, it makes pleadings, motions, discovery, and trial more complicated simply by injecting more claims, defenses, and parties. Second, it can create tension, if not open hostility, among counsel jockeying for control of the litigation. Most, if not all, of the problems in the former category can be addressed by a variety of management tools available to the court. The latter problem requires a judge willing and able to supervise and oversee a division of labor or to appoint lead counsel. These problems are thereby addressed by an involved and active judge, fitting the increasingly apt model of the judge as case manager.

III. PERMISSIVE JOINDER OF CLAIMS AND PARTIES

A corollary of litigant autonomy is the right of a plaintiff to associate with other claimants in a single lawsuit. The principle of party equality extends this right to defendants. As Michele Angelo Lupoi explains, focusing on party and joinder rules in Italy, "The parties are the masters of the procedure also in so much as only they can determine the objective scope of the dispute, through the claims, objections and counterclaims they raise against each other in their respective defences."[4] The procedural systems under review allow parties to exercise a right of association through the mechanism of permissive joinder, a device that leaves the decision to aggregate almost entirely in the hands of the litigants themselves. Some commentators see in permissive joinder a principle of voluntarism which they characterize as "highly consistent with an adversarial system, in which plaintiffs seek to structure the litigation to their best advantage. If joinder is not strategically advantageous, then plaintiffs are not compelled to join additional plaintiffs or defendants."[5] It follows, however, that the parties' strategic interest in aggregation may be "far from ideal" and, indeed, run counter to systemic goals of efficiency and proportionality.[6] Permissive joinder devices are not unique

---

4. Michele Angelo Lupoi, Italy, 2 International Encyclopedia of Laws: Civil Procedure §§ 44–46 (2002).

5. Jay Tidmarsh and Roger H. Transgrud, Complex Litigation: Problems in Advanced Civil Procedure 71 (2002).

6. Id. at 72.

to common law systems; they also are used in civil law systems traditionally characterized as "inquisitorial."

This section sets out examples of permissive joinder devices from selected countries. Consider the ways in which differences among the provisions can be ascribed to the procedural system of which they are a part. In thinking about this question, how might jurisdictional and regional divisions within a single court system limit a party's ability to aggregate claims against a defendant in a single judicial proceeding? Do you find any relation between the managerial powers of the presiding judge and the scope of permissive joinder devices? What other factors might explain differences in permissive joinder claims?

ENGLAND

Civil Procedure Rules, Part 19—Parties and Group Litigation (The White Book Service 2006).

Parties—General. 19.1 Any number of claimants or defendants may be joined as parties to a claim.

Civil Procedure Rules, Part 20—Counterclaims and Other Additional Claims (The White Book Service 2006).

Purpose of this part. 20.1 The purpose of this Part is to enable counterclaims and other additional claims to be managed in the most convenient and effective manner.

Scope and interpretation. 20.2 (1) This Part applies to—

(a) a counterclaim by a defendant against the claimant or against the claimant and some other person;

(b) an additional claim by a defendant against any person (whether or not already a party) for contribution or indemnity or some other remedy; and

(c) where an additional claim has been made against a person who is not already a party, any additional claim made by that person against any other person (whether or not already a party).

Zuckerman on Civil Procedure: Principles of Practice 501 and 145 (2nd ed. 2006).

English law has a long standing preference for completeness in adjudication.

* * *

The court has extensive powers under CPR 19 to add or substitute parties. It may exercise its powers on the application of any party, or on the application of the person who wishes to become a party * * *.

* * *

A defendant to a claim may wish to add a claim or a party to the proceedings. He may wish to bring an action against the claimant * * *. The purpose of CPR 20 is to enable counterclaims and other additional claims to be managed in the most convenient and effective manner * * *.

GERMANY

German Code of Civil Procedure.*

§ 59—Several persons may jointly sue as joined parties or be sued in the event that they have a common legal relationship with respect to the object of litigation or in the event that their rights or obligations arise from the same factual and legal ground.

§ 60—Several persons may also jointly sue or be sued as joined parties in the event that rights or obligations of the same nature and of a substantially similar factual and legal basis constitute the object of the litigation.

§ 61—Unless otherwise provided by the Civil Code or this Act, the joined parties have the status of individual parties vis-à-vis the opposing party such that the actions of one of the joined parties shall not affect the others to their benefit or detriment.

§ 62—Each joined party shall be entitled to prosecute the litigation; all joined parties shall be summoned to all hearings.

Peter L. Murray and Rolf Stürner, German Civil Justice 198–199, 200 (2004).

A plaintiff may join as many claims for relief as he has against the named defendant. There is no requirement that the claims be factually or legally related so long as the subject matter jurisdiction and venue of the court are correct for each claim and so long as the form of procedure is the same for all claims.* * *

By the same token, the plaintiff is permitted to assert less than all of its claims, even claims based on the same facts, occurrence or document, against the defendant. For instance, if the defendant had given the plaintiff a promissory note for 100,000 Euros, and the note had come due, the plaintiff would not be required to sue for the entire 100,000 Euros at once, but could sue for any part of the entire sum without prejudicing his right to sue for the balance at a later time. A partial complaint can permit the plaintiff to test the legal and factual sufficiency of a claim without being exposed to costs

* Translation in the German Commercial Code and Code of Civil Procedure in En-   glish 203–204 (Charles E. Stewart, trans. 2001).

based on a large amount in controversy in the event of an adverse decision.

* * *

The classic conception of civil litigation in Germany involves two parties, Plaintiff (*Kläger*) and Defendant (*Beklagter*). Multiple persons or entities may join or be joined in these roles when the claims asserted by or against them are legally or factually related. Such persons are referred to as comprising a "suit group" (*Streitgenossenschaft*). Persons with completely unrelated claims generally cannot assert them in the same suit.

ITALY

Mauro Cappelletti and Joseph M. Perillo, Civil Procedure in Italy 125 (1965).

Joinder of parties * * * is appropriate in a large variety of instances and may encompass joinder of plaintiffs, of defendants, and of third party defendants.

Permissive joinder is allowed for reasons of practical convenience and to avoid multiplicity of suits. Parties may be joined when two or more claims are connected by the *causa petendi*, the *petitum*, or common issues. The claims joined on one of these grounds remain distinct and each may be decided differently. At the request of all the parties, or if the court on its own initiative feels that the joinder will unduly delay or burden the proceeding, the cases may be severed.

JAPAN

The Code of Civil Procedure of Japan.*

(Conditions of joint litigation)

Article 38—If the rights or liabilities which are the subject-matter of a suit are common to two or more persons or are based on the same ground in fact and in law, such two or more persons may sue or be sued as co-litigant. The same shall apply if the rights or liabilities which are the subject-matter of a suit are of the same kind and are based on the same kind of ground in fact and in law.

Takaaki Hattori and Dan Fenno Henderson, Civil Procedure in Japan 5–14 and 7.03 (Yasuhei Taniguchi, Pauline C. Reich, and Hiroto Myake, eds., Rev. 2nd ed. 2004).

To promote practical convenience or to avoid a multiplicity of suits, two or more parties may sue or be sued in one action (*tsûjô kyôdô soshô*). Such a joinder is allowed if the following requirements are met:

---

* Translation in EHS Law Bulletin Series, EHS Vol. II, No. 2300 (2004).

(1) The rights or liabilities in controversy are common to the parties;

(2) The rights or liabilities in controversy are based on the same facts and law; or

(3) The rights or liabilities in controversy are of the same kind and are based on the same kind of legal and factual ground.

In cases of permissive joinder of parties, each co-litigant is treated as independent of the other co-litigants vis-à-vis the adverse party. He/she may present his/her own claim, defense, or evidence, and, generally, prosecute his/her own case separately. Neither procedural acts done by one co-litigant nor acts done by the adverse party against him/her will affect other co-litigants. Nor do judgments for (or against) one of the co-litigants bind other co-litigants. In practice, however, it is not uncommon for co-litigants to jointly present defenses and tender evidence, and to co-operate in other ways.

*   *   *

Joinder of claims is permissible when the following three requirements are met:

(1) the same rules of procedure must govern the adjudication of each of the claims;

(2) joinder is not specially prohibited by law;

(3) the court must be competent to adjudicate at least one of the claims joined.

To be joined, claims need not be related. It is believed that if joined from the beginning, multiple claims are unlikely to cause defendant undue difficulty or unduly to delay the proceedings.

THE UNITED STATES

Federal Rules of Civil Procedure.

Rule 18 Joinder of Claims and Remedies.

> (a) Joinder of Claims. A party asserting a claim to relief as an original claim, counterclaim, cross-claim, or third-party claim, may join, either as independent or as alternate claims, as many claims, legal, equitable, or maritime, as the party has against an opposing party.

> (b) Joinder of Remedies; Fraudulent Conveyances. Whenever a claim is one heretofore cognizable only after another claim has been prosecuted to a conclusion, the two claims may be joined in a single action; but the court shall grant relief in that action only in accordance with the relative substantive rights of the parties. In particular, a plaintiff may state a claim for money and a claim to have set aside a conveyance fraudulent as to that

plaintiff, without first having obtained a judgment establishing the claim for money.

Rule 20 Permissive Joinder of Parties.

(a) Permissive Joinder. All persons may join in one action as plaintiffs if they assert any right to relief jointly, severally, or in the alternative in respect of or arising out of the same transaction, occurrence, or series of transactions or occurrences and if any question of law or fact common to all these persons will arise in the action. All persons (and any vessel, cargo or other property subject to admiralty process in rem) may be joined in one action as defendants if there is asserted against them jointly, severally, or in the alternative, any right to relief in respect of or arising out of the same transaction, occurrence, or series of transactions or occurrences and if any question of law or fact common to all defendants will arise in the action. A plaintiff or defendant need not be interested in obtaining or defending against all the relief demanded. Judgment may be given for one or more of the plaintiffs according to their respective rights to relief, and against one or more defendants according to their respective liabilities.

(b) Separate Trials. The court may make such orders as will prevent a party from being embarrassed, delayed, or put to expense by the inclusion of a party against whom the party asserts no claim and who asserts no claim against the party, and may order separate trials or make other orders to prevent delay or prejudice.

Robert G. Bone, Mapping the Boundaries of the Dispute: Conceptions of Ideal Lawsuit Structure from the Field Code to the Federal Rules, 89 Colum. L. Rev. 1, 104–107 (1989).

The federal rule drafters marked a sharp distinction between permissive and compulsory party joinder. Rule 20 established the basic permissive joinder scheme. Section (a) set out the joinder requirements, and section (b) gave the trial judge broad discretion to order separate trials whenever desirable for reasons of trial convenience. In addition, Rule 21 made clear that dismissal was not an appropriate response to misjoinder.

The most striking feature of the federal permissive party joinder rules is the absence of any reference to the concept of "interest in." The omission reflected the fundamental change in beliefs about law that characterized the reform movement. The rule drafters rejected the right-remedy approach and the idea of a rights network that gave meaning to the code's "interest in" concept. Instead, they followed the pragmatic approach to ideal lawsuit structure, and as a result, they drafted a set of rules that placed few limits on joinder and gave the trial judge wide latitude to create convenient litigating units.

The rule drafters contemplated a two-step inquiry for permissive joinder analysis. First, Rule 20(a) required a certain commonality among all the prospective parties to a single lawsuit. They had to share a common question of law or fact, and they had to be connected with the same "transaction, occurrence, or series of transactions or occurrences." While persons related in this way could litigate together, a lawsuit consisting of all such persons was not necessarily the ideal litigating unit. The test for optimal lawsuit structure was "trial convenience," and the trial judge applied that test in the second part of the joinder analysis. Rules 20(b) and 21 gave the judge broad discretion to carve up plaintiff's lawsuit into smaller litigating units if trial convenience so required. The result of this two-step process was one or a number of lawsuits each ideally suited for adjudication as a unit.

Some commentators criticized Rule 20 for imposing threshold limits on joinder. They pointed to Rule 18, which allowed unlimited joinder of claims, and argued that the same approach ought to apply to party joinder as well, leaving it to the trial judge to divide the whole into convenient litigating units.

* * *

Rule 20(a) was modeled on similar permissive joinder provisions in the English Judicature Act and on rules in states such as New York, Illinois and California inspired by the English example. The drafters may have felt more comfortable with an existing rule that had proven itself in practice even though the rule contained limitations difficult to justify in theory, and they may have felt that a rule with precedential support would more easily pass Supreme Court and congressional scrutiny.

This treatment of Rule 20(a) suggests that the rule drafters invested the commonality requirements with little, if any, normative significance for the scope of the ideal adjudicative unit. "Trial convenience" was the crucial determinant.

* * *

IV. MANDATORY JOINDER OF CLAIMS AND PARTIES

As we have seen, devices authorizing voluntary joinder, whether of claims or parties, generally leave the decision to aggregate in the parties' own hands. By contrast, mandatory joinder provisions impose aggregation as a condition of the court's proceeding to judgment. The justifications for mandatory joinder rules vary, as do their scope and application. Some systems justify mandatory joinder on prophylactic grounds to protect the defendant against double liability or inconsistent obligations. Mandatory joinder also is used to protect a nonparty's interest if no other practical means exist to achieve that goal. Mandatory joinder might also be required by a substantive rule of law. Finally, mandatory joinder provides a way to increase efficiency and to avoid duplicative litigation. Looking at mandatory joinder rules in the federal courts of the United States, one commentator urges greater use of such compulsory aggregation, even at the apparent expense of party autonomy: "A plaintiff is entitled to due process, but has no right to sole possession of center stage; we need to tell the prima donna of the legal world that she must work with some co-stars."[7] In the examples that follow, consider the different problems that the mandatory joinder rules might be intended to solve and how they relate to other aspects of the procedural system of which they are a part, such as jurisdictional limits, specialty courts, or attitudes toward judicial management.

ENGLAND

Civil Procedure Rules, Part 19—Parties and Group Litigation (The White Book Service 2006).

Change of parties—general

19.2—(1) * * *

(2) The court may order a person to be added as a new party if—

(a) it is desirable to add the new party so that the court can resolve all matters in dispute in the proceedings; or

(b) there is an issue involving the new party and an existing party which is connected to the matters in dispute in the proceedings, and it is desirable to add the new party so that the court can resolve that issue.

(3) The court may order any person to cease to be a party if it is not desirable for that person to be a party to the proceedings.

(4) The court may order a new party to be substituted for an existing one if—

(a) the existing party's interest or liability has passed to the new party; and

(b) it is desirable to substitute the new party so that the court can resolve the matters in dispute in the proceedings.

* * *

19.3 Provisions Applicable Where Two or More Persons are Jointly Entitled to a Remedy

(1) Where a claimant claims a remedy to which some other person is jointly entitled with him, all persons jointly entitled to the remedy must be parties unless the court orders otherwise.

(2) If any person does not agree to be a claimant, he must be made a defendant, unless the court orders otherwise.

---

7. Richard D. Freer, Avoiding Duplicative Litigation: Rethinking Plaintiff Autonomy and the Court's Role in Defining the Litigative Unit, 50 U. Pitt. L. Rev. 809, 813 (1989).

(3) This rule does not apply in probate proceedings.

Zuckerman on Civil Procedure: Principles of Practice 502 (2nd ed. 2006).

Since the jurisdiction under CPR 19 is guided by the preference for completeness of adjudication, the court may order a person to be added as a party where this is necessary in order to resolve all the matters in dispute in the proceedings, or where there is an issue between an existing party and the proposed party, which is connected to the proceedings and it is desirable to resolve that issue in the same proceedings * * *.

Since participation in litigation is voluntary, a person can be added as a claimant only with his written consent * * *. If the presence of such a person is necessary but he refuses to consent to becoming a claimant, he must be joined as a defendant. For example, where a claimant claims a remedy to which others are jointly entitled, the others must be joined as claimants or, if they refuse, they must be joined as defendants * * *.

GERMANY

Peter L. Murray and Rolf Stürner, German Civil Justice 202–203 (2004).

Joinder of either plaintiffs or defendants is required "if the disputed legal relationship of all members of the suit group can only be determined on a unitary basis, or if the suit group is a necessary one for another reason." The requirement for a single decision binding multiple claimants or defendants can arise out of procedural law or substantive law. Joinder can be required, for instance, if claimants who can act only jointly seek to assert a joint claim, or if certain kinds of collective liability are asserted against a group of defendants. Required joinder is frequently encountered in claims asserted *in rem* in behalf of or against real estate owned in condominium or, in real estate matters, in behalf of or against a group of heirs of one or more testators.

The Civil Procedure Code is silent as to the consequences of failure to join a necessary party. Logically it would seem that if joinder is in fact legally necessary, inclusion of the necessary parties would be a prerequisite to suit (*Prozessvoraussetzung*), and failure to include all necessary parties would lead to procedural dismissal without prejudice (*Prozessabweisung*). Although the claim may be legally allowable, if the substantive law requires that the right in question be asserted by the entire group, the complaint will be considered unfounded (*unbegründet*). On the other hand, it is clear that once the necessary parties have been joined, a party's later failure to participate in the proceeding will not result in an individual adverse judgment. Contrary to the usual rule, a defaulting necessary party is bound by the actions taken by the active members of the suit group, who are said to "represent" (*vertreten*) the absent party for such purposes.

ITALY

Michele Angelo Lupoi, Italy, International Encyclopaedia of Laws: Civil Procedure Vol. 2, § 44 (2002).

The judge may, at certain conditions, order joinder of a third party on his own motion, but this is not an exception to the principles exposed so far, since it is for the parties and the parties only to extend their defences and claims against the third party (and *vice versa*).

Mauro Cappelletti and Joseph M. Perillo, Civil Procedure in Italy 125–126 (1965).

Joinder of parties is necessary when there is a unity of interest of the parties plaintiff or defendant in the substantive right underlying the claim or defense. A proceeding for the division of a *condominio* provides a typical example of a case in which joinder is necessary; all of the owners must be joined. If all those united in interest have not been made parties to the action, the court must order their joinder within a peremptory period. A judgment issued in the absence of a necessary party is *inutiliter datum*; that is, it has no effect even upon the participating parties.

JAPAN

Code of Civil Procedure of Japan.*

(Joint Litigation of Necessity)(1)

Article 40. When the subject of an action is to be confirmed conjointly only in respect of the entire body of co-litigants, any act of procedure by one of them shall take effect only in favor of the entire body.

2.   If it is provided for in the preceding paragraph, any act of procedure done by the other party against one of the co-litigants shall take effect for the entire body.

3.   In the case providing for in paragraph 1, should there be any cause for interruption or stay of proceedings in regard to one of the co-litigants, such interruption or stay shall take effect for the entire body.

4.   The provision of Article 32 paragraph 1 shall, with respect to Joso-appeal [i.e., Jôkoku or kôso] instituted by one of the co-litigants in the case providing for in paragraph 1, apply mutatis mutandis to the acts of procedure which should be done by a person under curatorship or a person under assistance who is

---

* Translation in EHS Law Bulletin Series, EHS Vol. II, No. 2300 (2004).

another co-litigant or by a guardian or other legal representatives of another co-litigant.

(Joint litigation requested for simultaneous trial)

Article 41. In cases where the relations between the right which is the subject of a suit against one of co-defendants and right which is the subject of a suit against the other of the co-defendant are unable to be legally coexistent, an argument and decision shall be made unseparatedly upon request of a plaintiff.

2. The request mentioned in the preceding paragraph shall be made until conclusion of an oral argument in the appeal instance.

3. In the case mentioned in paragraph 1, the appeal case relating to each co-defendant is under pending separately in the same appellate court, an oral argument and a decision shall be made unitedly.

Takaaki Hattori and Dan Fenno Henderson, Civil Procedure in Japan 5–16—5–17 and 7.03, note 223 (Yasuhei Taniguchi, Pauline C. Reich, and Hiroto Myake, eds., Rev. 2nd ed. 2004).

A party's joinder is compulsory, or, in Japanese terminology, necessary *per se*, if the subject matter of an action cannot be determined in the party's absence (*koyû hitsuyôteki kyôdô soshô*). If necessary parties have not been properly joined, the court must dismiss the action. * * *

When indispensable parties have been joined, procedural acts of any one of the co-litigants benefits all of them, but may not prejudice any of the co-litigants including the one who has so acted. On the other hand, the acts of an adverse party affect all opposing co-litigants. For example, the appearance of one co-defendant will suffice to prevent a default judgment against any co-defendant, including an absentee. An appeal by one co-defendant will be effective for all.

* * *

There are cases in which two or more persons may sue or be sued separately (accordingly, they are not cases of necessary joinder *per se*), but if they sue or are sued jointly, a consistent judgment must be given to all of them. According to the predominant view and judicial precedents, such is the case where a judgment against one of them would also bind the others. This kind of joinder is called semi-necessary joinder (*ruiji hitsuyôteki kyôdô soshô*). For example, any shareholder may bring an action to have a corporate resolution annulled, and joinder of the other shareholders is not necessary. However, a judgment for the plaintiff would bind all of the shareholders. * * *

The procedural rules that apply to necessary joinder *per se* also apply to semi-necessary joinder. In addition, if actions which could have been brought jointly as semi-necessary joinder are brought separately, the courts will usually consolidate these separate actions into one action for the convenience of both the court and the parties.

* * *

Compulsory joinder of claims is unknown to Japanese procedure. However, if a plaintiff files several actions in the same court against the same defendant at the same time, the defendant may apply for joinder of oral proceedings * * * to avoid undue inconvenience, although the court is not necessarily bound to grant the application.

J. Mark Ramseyer and Minoru Nakazato, Japanese Law: An Economic Approach 146–147 (1999).

If a court cannot partition a judgment among several parties, at least in theory they *must* join. For example, two people who jointly bought land from [an individual] drafted the purchase agreement as though they had bought it from his son. To confirm their title, they later sued the son. Mid-stream in the litigation, one of them withdrew. Held the Supreme Court: (1) Compulsory joinder applied; (2) therefore, the suit could not proceed without both; and (3) therefore, once they had joined, neither could independently withdraw. If a party to the compulsory joinder rule does not initially join the suit, the other may not sue without him. When one community sued to establish its right to the common, the court required that it join all its members. Their rights—if they were rights at all—were rights in common. Compulsory joinder applied, and if anyone refused to join, the suit could not proceed.

* * *

* * * The mandatory joinder rules * * * will prevent some victims of collective harms from obtaining even injunctive relief. Take the citizens of the city of Buzen. For environmental reasons, seven of them sued to enjoin a new power plant. Because they demanded relief whose effects extended beyond themselves, they could not proceed. The law provided for no class actions, and unless all citizens joined, no one had standing to sue.

THE UNITED STATES

Federal Rule of Civil Procedure 19 Joinder of Persons Needed for Just Adjudication.

(a) Persons to Be Joined if Feasible. A person who is subject to service of process and whose joinder will not deprive the court of jurisdiction over the subject matter of the action shall be joined as a party in the action if (1) in the person's absence complete relief cannot be accorded among those already parties, or (2) the person claims an interest relating to the subject of the action and is so situated that the disposition of the action in the person's absence may (i) as a practical matter impair or impede the person's ability to protect that interest or (ii) leave any of the persons already parties subject to a substantial risk of incurring double, multiple, or otherwise inconsistent obligations by reason of the claimed interest. If the person has not been so joined, the court shall order that the person be made a party. If the person should join as a plaintiff but refuses to do so, the person may be made a defendant, or, in a proper case, an involuntary plaintiff. If the joined party objects to venue and joinder of that party would render the venue of the action improper, that party shall be dismissed from the action.

(b) Determination by Court Whenever Joinder Not Feasible. If a person as described in subdivision (a)(1)-(2) hereof cannot be made a party, the court shall determine whether in equity and good conscience the action should proceed among the parties before it, or should be dismissed, the absent person being thus regarded as indispensable. The factors to be considered by the court include: first, to what extent a judgment rendered in the person's absence might be prejudicial to the person or those already parties; second, the extent to which, by protective provisions in the judgment, by the shaping of relief, or other measures, the prejudice can be lessened or avoided; third, whether a judgment rendered in the person's absence will be adequate; fourth, whether the plaintiff will have an adequate remedy if the action is dismissed for nonjoinder.

(c) Pleading Reasons for Nonjoinder. A pleading asserting a claim for relief shall state the names, if known to the pleader, of any persons as prescribed in subdivision (a)(1)-(2) hereof who are not joined, and the reasons why they are not joined.

Carl Tobias, Rule 19 and the Public Rights Exception to Party Joinder, 65 N.C. L. Rev. 745, 766–767 (1987).

* * * Rule 19 instructs courts to find initially whether absentees have the type of interest in the litigation to be considered parties needed for just adjudication under rule 19(a). If absentees are needed, judges then must determine whether joinder is feasible pursuant to rule 19(a)'s joinder limitations respecting subject matter jurisdiction, venue, and service of process. If these requirements are satisfied, courts are commanded to order absentee joinder. When absentee joinder is found infeasible, judges must next find under rule 19(b) whether it is more equitable for the plaintiff's action to continue or to be dismissed. This subdivision contemplates that courts will examine first its four stated factors, especially those implicating the plaintiff's forum needs and potential absentee prejudice, then examine additional pertinent considerations, and perhaps value and balance all the relevant factors. Judges should also consider options less Draconian than dismissing the plain-

tiff's case or proceeding without absentees, if alternatives are available. Only after making this detailed inquiry should courts determine whether it is more fair for the plaintiff's litigation to be dismissed or to continue. Dismissal is to be premised on a judgment that absentees are "indispensable," while continuing is to be based on the decision that absentees are not indispensable. But both determinations are conclusory ones meant to attach only at the very end of the process described. The drafters who amended rule 19(b) * * *, and the Supreme Court Justices applying the new version * * *, expressly admonished judges to determine whether absentees are indispensable only *after* treating relevant considerations. For instance, Justice Harlan emphasized that saying a "court 'must' dismiss in the absence of an indispensable party . . . puts the matter the wrong way around: a court does not know whether a particular person is 'indispensable' until it has examined the situation to determine whether it can proceed without him."

V. JOINDER AND THE RIGHT TO RECOVER REIMBURSEMENT: THE EXAMPLE OF IMPLEADER

In some lawsuits, a finding of liability against the defendant may allow that party to seek contribution or indemnification from a third party who was not sued in the original action. To avoid the need for a separate lawsuit, some systems offer special aggregation devices that allow the defendant to join the third party in the original litigation. One commentator explains:

> When *A* sues *B* there is often a third party, *C*, who may ultimately be liable to *B* for all or some part of the damages which *A* might recover. This liability over may be based on such legal relationships as those which arise from a contract of indemnity for loss or liability or a right to contribution from a joint tortfeasor. If it were necessary for *B* to institute a separate action to recover reimbursement from *C*, the issue or *B*'s liability to *A* would often have to be relitigated between *B* and *C*, since *C*, not a party to the original litigation, would generally not be bound by the prior determination. Even if *B* could obtain a wholly consistent result against *C*, the courts would have been burdened by two trials and *B* might have been seriously handicapped by having to satisfy *A*'s judgment long before his recovery over from *C*.[8]

The common law device of impleader, found in the United States and in England, traces to the practice of "vouching to warranty," but differs by allowing "a party who may be liable over to be directly joined as a third party defendant, rather than merely vouched in."[9] Despite its

---

8. Developments in the Law: Multiparty Litigation in the Federal Courts, 71 Harv. L.Rev. 877, 906 (1958).

9. Matt Neiderman, Vouching in Under the U.C.C.: Its History, Modern Use, and Questions About Its Continued Viability, 23 J. L. and Com. 1, 16 (2003).

common law roots, some form of impleader practice exists in many civil law systems. What are the comparative advantages of permitting a defendant to join claims for contribution or reimbursement in the original case, rather than requiring the filing of a separate, later lawsuit? Do you see any disadvantages to the aggregated approach?

ENGLAND

Civil Procedure Rules, Part 20—Counterclaims and Other Additional Claims (The White Book Service 2006).

Defendant's additional claim for contribution or indemnity from another party

20.6—(1) A defendant who has filed an acknowledgment of service or a defence may make an additional claim for contribution or indemnity against a person who is already a party to the proceedings by—

(a) filing a notice containing a statement of the nature and grounds of his additional claim; and

(b) serving the notice on that party.

(2) A defendant may file and serve a notice under this rule—

(a) without the court's permission, if he files and serves it—

(i) with his defence; or

(ii) if his additional claim for contribution or indemnity is against a party added to the claim later, within 28 days after that party files his defence; or

(b) at any other time with the court's permission.

Zuckerman on Civil Procedure: Principles of Practice 148–149 (2nd ed. 2006).

A claim for contribution or indemnity brought by a defendant against another person (whether already a party or not) must be advanced as an additional claim. A claim for contribution is an assertion of a right to recover from another person all or part of the amount that the defendant might be found liable to pay in the proceedings on the grounds that the other person contributed to the loss in respect of which the defendant is sued. This may happen, for instance, where pedestrian claims compensation against the driver who ran him down and the driver asserts that another driver contributed to the accident and should bear some or all of the liability for the loss.

* * *

Claims for indemnity or contribution may on occasion present tricky case management problems. For instance, a defendant, who makes an additional claim for contribution or indemnity against a non-party, may be interested in the resolution of this additional claim before deciding how to resist the main * * * claim that has been made against him.

* * * [The relevant portion of the Civil Procedure Rules] does not expressly mention the need for the court to give directions as to the management of the case, but the court has ample case management powers to direct that the claim for contribution or indemnity should be dealt with first, if this is a sensible way of proceeding.

GERMANY

German Code of Civil Procedure.*

§ 72

(1) A party who believes that he or she could, in the event of an unsuccessful outcome of the proceeding, claim warranty or indemnity against a third party or is asserting the claim of a third party, may, prior to the final decision in the matter, move to join such third party.

(2) The third party shall be entitled to join additional third parties.

Peter L. Murray and Rolf Stürner, German Civil Justice 208 (2004).

German civil procedure does not allow a defendant who has a claim for reimbursement, contribution or indemnity against a third party simply to add the third party to the suit. In such a case the defendant must defend the suit as best it can and then proceed separately against the third party in the event of an unfavorable outcome.

A defendant in such a position can, however, obviate potential objections by the third party based on inadequate defense of the claim by filing and serving the third party with a "notice of pending suit" (*Streitverkündung*) and inviting the third party to participate as an auxiliary intervenor. Once the notice has been given, the third party will be bound by the outcome between the original parties to the same extent as if it had intervened on its own.

ITALY

Mauro Cappelletti and Joseph M. Perillo, Civil Procedure in Italy 125–127 (1965).

Joinder of parties, either permissive or necessary, is appropriate in a large variety of instances and may encompass joinder of plaintiffs, of defendants, and of third party defendants.

* * *

---

* Translation in The German Commercial Code and Code of Civil Procedure in English 206 (Charles E. Stewart, trans. 2001).

Involuntary intervention may be effectuated at the initiative of one of the parties or by order of the curt. Usually it will be the defendant who will take steps to effectuate joinder of a new party. A tenant who has been sued by third parties regarding his right to occupy rented premises may call in his lessor. A merchant sued for breach of warranty may call in his supplier. If the involuntary intervention is ordered by the judge, the order is not directed at the party to be joined, but at the original parties. Should they fail to take the necessary steps to call in the third party, the case is stricken from the docket.

THE UNITED STATES

Federal Rule of Civil Procedure 14 Third Party Practice.

(a) When Defendant May Bring in Third Party. At any time after commencement of the action a defending party, as a third-party plaintiff, may cause a summons and complaint to be served upon a person not a party to the action who is or may be liable to the third-party plaintiff for all or part of the plaintiff's claim against the third-party plaintiff. * * *

(b) When Plaintiff May Bring in Third Party. When a counterclaim is asserted against a plaintiff, the plaintiff may cause a third party to be brought in under circumstances which under this rule would entitle a defendant to do so.

(c) Admiralty and Maritime Claims. When a plaintiff asserts an admiralty or maritime claim * * *, the defendant or person who asserts a right * * *, as a third-party plaintiff, may bring in a third-party defendant who may be wholly or partly liable, either to the plaintiff or to the third-party plaintiff, by way of remedy over, contribution, or otherwise on account of the same transaction, occurrence, or series of transactions or occurrences. * * *

Jack H. Friedenthal, Mary Kay Kane, and Arthur R. Miller, Civil Procedure 380–382 (4th ed. 2005).

Impleader, or third-party practice, is the procedural device enabling the defendant in a lawsuit to bring into the action an additional party who may be liable to the defendant for all or part of any damages the defendant ultimately may owe the original plaintiff. This additional party is known as a third-party defendant, and the original defendant who brings an impleader claim is called the third-party plaintiff. Unlike counterclaim procedure, impleader is entirely optional; the defendant may assert the claim against the third party in a completely separate action.

* * *

Federal Rule 14 governs impleader in the federal courts; similar provisions are found in a number of states. * * * Using this provision, defendant may implead someone whom the plaintiff could not sue directly as, for example, when the statute of limitations would have barred an action against that person by the original plaintiff. This is because a third-party plaintiff's right of indemnity or subrogation does not arise until liability is found in the original claim.

* * *

In federal practice, and in many states, impleader of a third party because she is directly liable to the plaintiff in the original action is forbidden. Accordingly, impleader is not suitable when the defendant believes that someone other than himself is responsible for the breach of legal duty giving rise to plaintiff's claim. A defendant sued for negligence, for example, cannot implead a third party on the theory that that person's negligence was totally responsible for plaintiff's injury. When a third party's conduct furnishes a complete defense against the defendant's liability, the defendant may raise that conduct defensively in the answer but may not use it as a foundation for impleader. If the plaintiff has brought separate actions against two defendants, one of them who claims that the other is solely responsible for plaintiff's harm may be able to effectuate joinder by consolidating the actions.

VI. COLLECTIVE OR REPRESENTATIVE ACTIONS

The contemporary treatment of group harms presents an issue of endless fascination to those interested in the comparative study of civil procedure. Developments in this area have been complex and of relatively recent vintage. Michele Taruffo observes: "In the 1960s, the landscape of group litigation was almost completely bare, with the only significant example being the U.S. class action regulated by Rule 23 of the Federal Rule of Civil Procedure. This situation has changed over the years and is now much more interesting, but also much more complicated."[10] He continues:

> In some countries—even in civil law jurisdictions—the problem of group litigation (or, as it is sometimes defined, the problem of the judicial protection of collective, diffuse, and super-individual interests and rights) has been dealt with in several ways: new statutory regulations, developments in case law, theoretical debates, and projects for reform. Much of the complexity of the present situation is due to the fact that such problems have been—and still are— approached from very different perspectives and with different strategies. The class action lawsuit in the U.S. system has evolved significantly and has been adopted, with significant changes and adaptations, in other countries, including those with civil law systems. However, many other countries, mainly in continental Europe, did not follow the class action model and have adopted different

10. Michele Taruffo, Some Remarks on Group Litigation in Comparative Perspec- tive, 11 Duke J. Comp. and Int'l L. 405, 405 (2001).

approaches to the problem of group litigation. Most of these countries do not conceive of this problem in general terms and take into consideration only particular instances of collective interests, such as those involved in consumer and environmental protection.[11]

As you consider developments in this area, be attentive to the fact that different legal systems may use mechanisms that have the same name but work in different ways and to different effect. Recent commentary explains:

> To begin with, it is impossible to equate U.S. and European legal terminology concerning the term "class action." The term is well understood in the U.S. and has a virtually uniform meaning throughout the country. This is not the case in Europe. In some European countries, the English term "class action" is used but does not necessarily mean that the procedures are the same as those in the United States. In countries that have procedures somewhat similar to U.S. class actions, such as the Netherlands, a statute for those procedures has been enacted but avoids even a local language version of what could be confused with the specific term "class action." For example, the Dutch Civil Code simply refers to "a legal proceeding which extends to similar claims of different persons." More often a local language term is used, which will usually not reflect similarities with U.S. practices.
>
> Even when the terms are expressed in English (as in the U.K. or Ireland) or are translated into English, one is still faced with a variety of terms that do not reveal whether there are any similarities with U.S. class actions. For instance, Ireland uses the terms "MPL" (multiparty litigation), "GLO" (group litigation order), and "group action" (also used in the UK). "Group action" is also the direct translation of the German term (*Gruppenklage*), the Swedish terms (*grupptalan, grupprättegång*) and the Lithuanian term (*ieskinys grupes vardu*). Some European countries prefer the idea of a "public lawsuit" (e.g., Greece, Portugal) or "collective lawsuit" (e. g., Estonia, Poland, Romania, Spain) or "combined lawsuit" (Hungary) but without revealing what is or would be intended by "public" or "collective" or "combined."
>
> Procedures somewhat akin to the U.S.-style class action exist in various European statutes whose names contain some of this specific terminology. However, those procedures may be dispersed and intermingled into consumer protection statutes, various civil code and code of civil procedure rules, and within specific statutes relating to securities regulation, environmental protection, or unfair competition. It is as if, in order to understand class action procedures in California, one had to piece together separate information from the Civil Code, the Unruh Act, the Code of Civil Procedure, the California Rules of Court, the Business and Professions Code, the Labor

---

11. Id. at 405–406.

Code, and the Tom Banes Civil Rights Act, without ever encountering the general and familiar term "class action."

Even finding what looks like a European class action statute or procedure (or draft legislation proposing such a law) does not mean that there will always be functional parallels with Rule 23 of the Federal Rules of Civil Procedure or with U.S. state law class action analogues. For instance, the Swedish *grupprättegång* rules are considerably more detailed than federal Rule 23 and are set out in a special Swedish statute on the subject. The rules in Lithuania, however, are contained in a single sentence in the Code of Civil Procedure.

Despite these lexicological difficulties, one can use the term "class action" to refer to any European procedure in which one or more plaintiffs seek a civil legal remedy in a national court or a procedure in which any such remedy may be sought on their behalf.[12]

A. JUSTIFICATIONS FOR COLLECTIVE OR REPRESENTATIVE ACTIONS

As you weigh the justifications for collective or representative actions, consider the ways in which political and economic developments—within countries and across the global economy—are exerting pressure toward procedural convergence. At the same time, in what ways do you think cultural or other factors might explain the persistence of broad national difference in this area? What are the advantages and disadvantages of the United States preference for adjudication of group harms relative to the greater reliance placed on legislative and political solutions in legal systems elsewhere in the world?

Mauro Cappelletti, Vindicating the Public Interest Through the Courts: A Comparativist's Contribution, 25 Buff. L. Rev. 643, 645–648 (1975–1976).

Our contemporary society—or, to use a more ambitious term, our civilization—is frequently characterized as a "mass production-mass consumption" civilization. That characterization reflects, no doubt, a typical feature of modern economies in all parts of the world—"massification." But this feature extends far beyond the economic sector; it characterizes social relationships, feelings, and conflicts as well. * * *

* * *

Indeed, more and more frequently the complexity of modern societies generates situations in which a single human action can be beneficial or prejudicial to large numbers of people, thus making entirely inadequate the traditional scheme of litigation as merely a two-party affair.

---

12. Louis Degos and Geoffrey V. Morson, Class System: The Reforms of Class Action Laws in Europe Are as Varied as the Nations Themselves, 29–Nov. Los Angeles Lawyer 32–34 (2006).

For example, false information divulged by large corporations may cause injury to all who buy shares in that corporation; an antitrust violation may damage all who are affected by the unfair competition; the infringement by an employer of a collective labor agreement violates the rights of all his employees; the imposition of an unconstitutional tax or the illegal discontinuance of a social benefit may be detrimental to large communities of citizens; the discharge of waste into a lake or river harms all who want to enjoy its clean waters; defective or unhealthy packaging may cause damage to all consumers of these goods. The possibility of such mass injuries represents a characteristic feature of our epoch.

As a rule, however, the individual alone is unable to protect himself efficiently against such injuries. Even if he has a legal cause of action, other factors may preclude judicial relief: his individual right may be too "diffuse" or too "small" to prompt him to seek its protection; excessive costs may obstruct his legal action in court; he may fear the powerful violator; he may even be unaware of his right. It is necessary to abandon the individualistic, essentially laissez-faire, 19th-century concept of litigation, a concept which awards the right to sue, if at all, solely to the subject personally aggrieved in his own narrowly-defined individual rights * * *. The new social, collective, "diffuse" rights and interests can be protected only by new social, collective, "diffuse" remedies and procedures. * * *

Thomas D. Rowe, Jr., Foreword—Debates Over Group Litigation in Comparative Perspective: What Can We Learn From Each Other?, 11 Duke J. Comp. and Int'l L. 157, 157–158 (2001).

Modern societies all face in varying degrees the problem of possible liability for actual injuries, and prevention of threatened ones, to large numbers of people, with the injuries resulting from a single event or product or other common cause. The sources of injury or threat can vary greatly—a tragedy such as a hotel fire or airplane crash; widespread distribution and use of a drug or other product such as asbestos, tobacco, or Fen-phen; claimed violations of civil or human rights; environmental pollution; and business practices such as alleged price-fixing, misleading statements affecting values of publicly held securities, insurance overcharges, and violation of consumer protection laws.

However parallel the problems, the responses of different legal systems have varied widely among nations, with varying emphases on class actions, group litigation by associations or unions, regulatory enforcement, social compensation schemes, and other approaches. In the United States the class action has for the last third of a century been the most prominent but by no means exclusive mode—and has been a focus of much controversy. Only a few other nations have adopted the class action device even to a limited extent; and in many countries, particularly the civil law systems of continental Europe, resistance to the class action is strong, and responses to widespread-injury problems are sometimes limited.

How well legal systems respond, in whatever forms, to such problems is vital for reasons both concrete and philosophical. Effective national and international markets and financial systems require considerable transparency; perceived lack of the enforceable rule of law can hinder investment and growth. Unrighted wrongs can leave victims uncompensated, under-deter harmful conduct, and foster social resentment. Government enforcement, although essential, is sometimes inadequate due to underfunding, "capture" by targets of regulation, or worse. Also, public enforcement is often more effective at stopping or preventing conduct than at assuring compensation for harms inflicted, and individual rather than collective private enforcement is often not worth pursuing when losses to most or all victims are small—even if the harms are widespread, and the gains to violators (as with small overcharges to large numbers of consumers) great. At the same time, there is considerable concern for possible abuses in devices like the American class action, with some criticizing small recoveries to class members along with large fees to class counsel, "lawyer-driven" litigation, and weak suits forcing settlements because of their *in terrorem* value.

Michele Taruffo, Some Remarks on Group Litigation in Comparative Perspective, 11 Duke J. Comp. and Int'l L. 405, 406–409 (2001).

A very general and fundamental distinction can be drawn when considering the purposes that may be pursued by means of group or class litigation. In practice, these purposes can be combined in various degrees and in several ways, but theoretically, they may be kept separate for the sake of simplicity.

A.   COMPENSATION OF INDIVIDUAL HARMS

The first important purpose is to compensate individual harms. In many cases, it may be said that litigation is *damage oriented*, since it is aimed at achieving a judgment granting damages to a class or a group of injured or harmed people and charging the wrongdoer with the obligation to pay compensation. The ultimate goal is to indemnify each member of the group for the harm suffered. Here, we are mainly—although not exclusively—in the domain of torts, and the most important situation is that of mass tort litigation. There is no need to emphasize that this category of damage oriented actions includes a wide range of subject matters—examples include the classic case of a plane crash, the well-known cases of Agent Orange or asbestos exposure, the use of defective products or harmful pharmaceuticals, and tobacco addiction. These kinds of cases may be distinguished from each other in many ways (nature of the injury or loss suffered, type of causation, number of people involved, size of compensatory or punitive damages granted, etc.).

However, they share the fundamental aim of providing relief in terms of monetary compensation for the individual harms, injuries, or losses that have been suffered by (more or less numerous) classes or groups of people because of the same unlawful actions.

B. Achievement of Changes

The second purpose is to achieve changes in the practice of some subjects, in the regulation of legal transactions, or in legally relevant behavior. Since, generally speaking, actions of this kind are brought in order to obtain new regulation of matters or behaviors according to particular values and standards considered preferable for the protection of the subjects involved, they may also be said to be *policy oriented*. This category of actions is extremely broad and internally differentiated. For instance, one may bring such an action to affect changes in commercial practices (contractual clauses, fair competition, advertising, labeling of products, etc.) with the aim of protecting consumers. Alternatively, an action might be brought with the aim of enforcing civil rights and changing the functioning—or even the structure—of private or public institutions (i.e., banks for financial and commercial practice, schools in cases of racial desegregation, and prisons and hospitals in cases of structural or institutional injunctions). The regulatory changes that are pursued by means of this kind of litigation may concern private or public regulations. * * *

It is easy to observe that these (and many other) situations are extremely varied and may occur in a number of different areas within modern legal systems. However, they have a fundamental character in common: litigation is used as a means to protect and enforce collective rights and interests by setting aside illegal practices and behavior and by achieving directly—or provoking indirectly—the adoption of new standards or rules.

B. CLASS ACTIONS: THE UNITED STATES APPROACH

No procedural device provokes greater academic controversy than the United States rule concerning class actions. Arthur R. Miller, who served as the Reporter to the Advisory Committee on Civil Rules of the Judicial Conference of the United States, observes:

> Class action adherents would have us believe it is a panacea for a myriad of social ills, which deters unlawful conduct and compensates those injured by it. Catch phrases such as "therapeutic" or "prophylactic" and "[taking] care of the smaller guy" are frequently trumpeted. Its opponents have rallied around characterizations of the procedure as a form of "legalized blackmail" or a "Frankenstein Monster."[13]

This section presents an overview of the class action rule in the United States, situating the practice in some of the more distinctive

---

13. Arthur R. Miller, Of Frankenstein Monsters and Shining Knights: Myth, Reality, and the "Class Action Problem," 92 Harv. L. Rev. 664, 665 (1979).

features of the American legal culture, such federalism, adversarialism, and entrepreneurial incentives. As a contrast, this section also includes a strong criticism of the class action device from a commentator who speaks from a "European" perspective and emphasizes the traditions of the Italian civil law system.

UNITED STATES

Federal Rule of Civil Procedure 23 Class Actions.

(a) Prerequisites to a Class Action. One or more members of a class may sue or be sued as representative parties on behalf of all only if (1) the class is so numerous that joinder of all members is impracticable, (2) there are questions of law or fact common to the class, (3) the claims or defenses of the representative parties are typical of the claims or defenses of the class, and (4) the representative parties will fairly and adequately protect the interests of the class.

(b) Class Actions Maintainable. An action may be maintained as a class action if the prerequisites of subdivision (a) are satisfied, and in addition:

> (1) the prosecution of separate actions by or against individual members of the class would create a risk of
>
> > (A) inconsistent or varying adjudications with respect to individual members of the class which would establish incompatible standards of conduct for the party opposing the class, or
> >
> > (B) adjudications with respect to individual members of the class which would as a practical matter be dispositive of the interests of the other members not parties to the adjudications or substantially impair or impede their ability to protect their interests; or
>
> (2) the party opposing the class has acted or refused to act on grounds generally applicable to the class, thereby making appropriate final injunctive relief or corresponding declaratory relief with respect to the class as a whole; or
>
> (3) the court finds that the questions of law or fact common to the members of the class predominate over any questions affecting only individual members, and that a class action is superior to other available methods for the fair and efficient adjudication of the controversy. The matters pertinent to the findings include: (A) the interest of members of the class in individually controlling the prosecution or defense of separate actions; (B) the extent and nature of any litigation concerning the controversy already commenced by or against members of the class; (C) the desirability or undesirability of concentrating the litigation of the claims in the particular forum; (D) the difficulties likely to be encountered in the management of a class action.

(c) Determining by Order Whether to Certify a Class Action; Appointing Class Counsel; Notice and Membership in Class; Judgment; Multiple Classes and Subclasses.

(1) (A) When a person sues or is sued as a representative of a class, the court must—at an early practicable time—determine by order whether to certify the action as a class action.

(B) An order certifying a class action must define the class and the class claims, issues, or defenses, and must appoint class counsel under Rule 23(g).

(C) An order under Rule 23(c)(1) may be altered or amended before final judgment.

(2) (A) For any class certified under Rule 23(b)(1) or (2), the court may direct appropriate notice to the class.

(B) For any class certified under Rule 23(b)(3), the court must direct to class members the best notice practicable under the circumstances, including individual notice to all members who can be identified through reasonable effort. The notice must concisely and clearly state in plain, easily understood language:

- the nature of the action,

- the definition of the class certified,

- the class claims, issues, or defenses,

- that a class member may enter an appearance through counsel if the member so desires,

- that the court will exclude from the class any member who requests exclusion, stating when and how members may elect to be excluded, and

- the binding effect of a class judgment on class members under Rule 23(c)(3).

(3) The judgment in an action maintained as a class action under subdivision (b)(1) or (b)(2), whether or not favorable to the class, shall include and describe those whom the court finds to be members of the class. The judgment in an action maintained as a class action under subdivision (b)(3), whether or not favorable to the class, shall include and specify or describe those to whom the notice provided in subdivision (c)(2) was directed, and who have not requested exclusion, and whom the court finds to be members of the class.

(4) When appropriate (A) an action may be brought or maintained as a class action with respect to particular issues, or (B) a class may be divided into subclasses and each subclass treated as a class, and the provisions of this rule shall then be construed and applied accordingly.

(d) Orders in Conduct of Actions. In the conduct of actions to which this rule applies, the court may make appropriate orders: (1) determining the course of proceedings or prescribing measures to prevent undue repetition or complication in the presentation of evidence or argument; (2) requiring, for the protection of the members of the class or otherwise for the fair conduct of the action, that notice be given in such manner as the court may direct to some or all of the members of any step in the action, or of the proposed extent of the judgment, or of the opportunity of members to signify whether they consider the representation fair and adequate, to intervene and present claims or defenses, or otherwise to come into the action; (3) imposing conditions on the representative parties or on intervenors; (4) requiring that the pleadings be amended to eliminate therefrom allegations as to representation of absent persons, and that the action proceed accordingly; (5) dealing with similar procedural matters. The orders may be combined with an order under Rule 16, and may be altered or amended as may be desirable from time to time.

(e) Settlement, Voluntary Dismissal, or Compromise.

(1) (A) The court must approve any settlement, voluntary dismissal, or compromise of the claims, issues, or defenses of a certified class.

(B) The court must direct notice in a reasonable manner to all class members who would be bound by a proposed settlement, voluntary dismissal, or compromise.

(C) The court may approve a settlement, voluntary dismissal, or compromise that would bind class members only after a hearing and on finding that the settlement, voluntary dismissal, or compromise is fair, reasonable, and adequate.

(2) The parties seeking approval of a settlement, voluntary dismissal, or compromise under Rule 23(e)(1) must file a statement identifying any agreement made in connection with the proposed settlement, voluntary dismissal, or compromise.

(3) In an action previously certified as a class action under Rule 23(b)(3), the court may refuse to approve a settlement unless it affords a new opportunity to request exclusion to individual class members who had an earlier opportunity to request exclusion but did not do so.

(4) (A) Any class member may object to a proposed settlement, voluntary dismissal, or compromise that requires court approval under Rule 23(e)(1)(A).

(B) An objection made under Rule 23(e)(4)(A) may be withdrawn only with the court's approval.

(f) Appeals. A court of appeals may in its discretion permit an appeal from an order of a district court granting or denying class action certification under this rule if application is made to it within ten days after entry of the order. An appeal does not stay proceedings in the district court unless the district judge or the court of appeals so orders.

(g) Class Counsel.

(1) Appointing Class Counsel.

(A) Unless a statute provides otherwise, a court that certifies a class must appoint class counsel.

(B) An attorney appointed to serve as class counsel must fairly and adequately represent the interests of the class.

(C) In appointing class counsel, the court

(i) must consider:

- the work counsel has done in identifying or investigating potential claims in the action,

- counsel's experience in handling class actions, other complex litigation, and claims of the type asserted in the action,

- counsel's knowledge of the applicable law, and

- the resources counsel will commit to representing the class;

(ii) may consider any other matter pertinent to counsel's ability to fairly and adequately represent the interests of the class;

(iii) may direct potential class counsel to provide information on any subject pertinent to the appointment and to propose terms for attorney fees and nontaxable costs; and

(iv) may make further orders in connection with the appointment.

(2) Appointment Procedure.

(A) The court may designate interim counsel to act on behalf of the putative class before determining whether to certify the action as a class action.

(B) When there is one applicant for appointment as class counsel, the court may appoint that applicant only if the applicant is adequate under Rule 23(g)(1)(B) and (C). If more than one adequate applicant seeks appointment as class counsel, the court must appoint the applicant best able to represent the interests of the class.

(C) The order appointing class counsel may include provisions about the award of attorney fees or nontaxable costs under Rule 23(h).

(h) Attorney Fees Award. In an action certified as a class action, the court may award reasonable attorney fees and nontaxable costs authorized by law or by agreement of the parties as follows:

* * *

(4) Reference to Special Master of Magistrate Judge. The court may refer issues related to the amount of the award to a special master or to a magistrate judge * * *.

Linda Silberman, The Vicissitudes of the American Class Action—With a Comparative Eye, 7 Tul. J. Int'l and Comp. L. 201, 201–218 (1999).

[T]he American class action has been molded in a system that (1) relies on a strong adversary tradition, (2) is powered by entrepreneurial lawyering, (3) is comfortable with a culture of robust judicial lawmaking, and (4) is complicated by the intricacies of an expansive dual system of courts. * * *

A second theme that emerges from the story of class actions in the United States is that it cuts across different substantive areas of law. Although the treatment of class actions so far has generally been trans-substantive—i.e. a one-size rule that fits all—more recent developments suggest class action reform should be approached in particular substantive contexts and as a part of substantive law reforms. * * *

* * *

I. A Brief Account of Rule 23 Practice Over the Years

Historically, the class action in the United States was limited in its use and confined to those with a tight community of interest. Its critical feature was that it bound all persons who were members of the class despite the fact that they were not parties to it. For that reason the "true" class action extended only to those whose rights could be said to be "joint, common, or secondary." The federal courts also recognized a device—known as the "spurious class action"—that was used primarily to obviate joinder problems but formally bound only those who were named parties to the litigation. However, an additional feature of the spurious class action was to allow absent members to intervene *after* the judgment, thereby taking advantage of a favorable outcome in the litigation.

In 1966, rule 23 of the Federal Rules of Civil Procedure was revised to construct a tri-part classification of different types of class action possibilities, some with different requirements, but all imposing the critical feature of binding absent members. All class actions were required to meet numerosity, commonality, and typicality requirements and the class representative was required to "fairly and adequately" represent the interests of the entire class. With respect to rule 23(b)(1) class actions, the requirements encompassed what had been traditionally the "true" class actions, where rights were "joint" or "common," at least in terms of the relief requested. Interestingly, the most typical class actions—derivative actions by shareholders and actions relating to unincorporated associations—were carved out in special provisions; and the (b)(1) action was defined to embrace situations which could give rise to incompatible standards of conduct or impair as a practical matter the interests of other members of a group. A second type of class action—the (b)(2) action—was directed toward class injunctive and declaratory relief. The third type of action, known as the (b)(3) action, was the most revolutionary in that it gave binding effect to an action brought as a class where the relationship between the parties was greatly attenuated and largely the result of persons who found themselves similarly situated because of conduct by the defendant. As a result, extra protections were imposed for class certification in these situations, including individual notice to absent class members and the ability to opt out of the class. Professor Arthur Miller, writing in 1979, argued persuasively that the rulemakers who brought about the 1966 revision to rule 23 probably did not perceive the dramatic effects that these amendments would create. And although I believe Professor Miller was correct in attributing the flexing of rule 23's muscles in the 1970s to societal changes and the general increase in "public law" litigation, there was a clear sense of the importance of the change to rule 23(b)(3) which effectively bound absent class members (who shared only questions of law or fact in common) unless they exercised their privilege to opt out of the suit.

Whatever the intention of the 1966 class action amendments, the effect of Federal Rule 23(b)(3) was to facilitate the aggregation of relatively small claims that were not otherwise individually economically viable to pursue into a group claim. As a result, the availability of class action litigation dramatically increased. The growth of these types of "damage" class actions can be attributed in part to entrepreneurial lawyering generated by contingent fees available in the class context where lawyers for a plaintiff class in a massive damage can collect fees from a common fund if successful. Alternatively, the specter of huge damage awards against defendants in a class action suit and the expense of litigating these large suits in a system without cost-shifting frequently led defendants to settle even marginal cases, with the settlement often including substantial attorneys' fees for the class lawyers.

In the immediate period following the 1966 class action amendments, class action suits proliferated. There was much enthusiasm for the class action as a device that could be instrumental in providing access to justice for economically disadvantaged groups, and the new rule was being construed in liberal fashion leading to an abundance of class certifications.

* * *

* * * For judges who previously perceived the class action as the cause of their docket problems, they now found in it one of their solutions. Mass tort actions, particularly those involving asbestos claims, threatened to overwhelm the federal court system. A variety of solutions were contemplated, experimented with, and rejected. Finally, "class action" settlements were brokered as a means to resolve some of this mass litigation. The use of the class action in this context was somewhat surprising in light of the caution expressed in the Advisory Committee Note to the 1966 amendments to rule 23 that the "mass accident" case was ordinarily not appropriate for a class action. * * *

* * *

The incentives operating in settlement class actions can often work to the disadvantage of absent class members. Plaintiffs' attorneys begin with substantial leverage because class actions are burdensome and difficult to defend. Defendants have strong incentives to settle class actions to avoid the substantial litigation costs associated with litigation. Plaintiffs' attorneys may procure a limited recovery for class members but a generous attorneys' fee for themselves; and the defendants want to buy whatever "global peace" they can achieve by "binding" the largest group at the least cost. Judges, for their part, see a way of clearing masses of cases from their calendars.

* * *

As the reported case decisions reveal, it is important to have a "check" on a court's ruling on whether or not to certify a class. Recognizing the impact that a certification ruling has, the Advisory Committee on Civil Rules recently promulgated Rule 23(f), which authorizes interlocutory appeals from grants or denials of class action certification at the appellate court's discretion. Interestingly, this same Committee considered broader revisions to rule 23, including a specific subsection on settlement classes. * * *

* * *

II. The Autonomy/Entity Tension and the Requisite Protections Necessary for Class Action Treatment

In a recent article, Professor David Shapiro has highlighted competing conceptualizations of the class action. As Professor Shapiro's article illustrates, the class action can be viewed as an aggregation of individual claims where autonomy must be preserved wherever possible and consent is an important value to sustain class action viability. Alternatively, the class action can be perceived as a vehicle which by its very nature demands the surrender of individual interests in order to pursue collective action for the entity. Professor Shapiro allies himself with the "entity" model of group litigation, and recommends legislative reforms to accomplish new substantive standards necessary to accommodate the reconceptualized view of the class action. I share some of Professor Shapiro's sympathies here, but I do not think a "pure" entity model can work on a trans-substantive basis. For particular types of actions, such as tobacco and asbestos causes, it should be possible to enact legislation that will achieve certain kinds of trade-offs and provide particular "entity" relief at the expense of private individual claims. But I believe these changes must be achieved within a particular contextual and substantive framework. * * *

* * *

In the United States some of the complications of class actions are due to the nature of nationwide classes and the possibilities of parallel litigation in the context of the federal system. * * *

One observation to be made is that substantial responsibility for protecting the rights of absent class members rests with the judge. To some degree, the context of the adversary system limits the information that a judge has at her disposal in evaluating the worth of the claims not only in the instant but in other parallel or even future litigation. While this is a serious problem for an adversary system, I do not think civil law systems would be any more comfortable with the centrality of the judge's role to protect the interests of absent class members. Indeed, they might well find such a role less congenial. As Professor Claudio Consolo wrote in a paper a few years ago, the civil law judge plays a much more "passive" role on matters of this kind, and would feel disabled from exercising choice and responsibilities on these social values and comparative costs and benefits.

* * *

III.   THE SPECIAL PROBLEMS OF FEDERALISM

Some of the class action problems to which I have alluded will resonate with other judicial systems, but many of the difficulties associated with class actions in the United States are directly attributable to the operation of the class action in a federal system. * * *

* * *

The potential for parallel litigation and overlapping class litigation may be unique to the American federal system. The lack of formal mechanisms to consolidate or prioritize conflicting class litigation proceeding simultaneously in state and federal courts is not only inefficient but also creates the danger of "reverse actions." In the class setting, where competing teams of plaintiffs' attorneys often file suits in the wake of newsworthy events such as corporate takeovers, unexpected share declines, or investigation of defective products, each group wants its lawsuit to go forward and generate fees for plaintiffs' attorneys. The consequences are many. * * *

* * *

IV.   CONCLUSION

Some abuses of the class action system may have resulted from the failure to foresee and to guard against its myriad uses. The procedural history of the American class action highlights key issues that should be addressed by those countries embarking upon the class action experiment. Perhaps the American experience may help other systems to put the class suit to its best use and prevent its worst abuses.

Richard B. Cappalli and Claudio Consolo, Class Actions for Continental Europe? A Preliminary Inquiry, 6 Temp. Int'l and Comp. L.J. 217, 261–264 (1992).

Several "obstacles" have been advanced as retarding, if not totally impeding, the adoption of a class action in civil law systems. * * * The first such barrier is a practical one. Practical problems are those which the legislator can eliminate with strokes of the pen. That no class suit presently exists within the Italian Code of Civil Procedure does not preclude the Italian Parliament from inserting one, either generically or as a process attached to a specific set of rights. Inconsistencies with existing rules would have to be reconciled. As examples, the *procura* (power of attorney) required for each represented party would have to be required only of the named party and not absentee class members; attorneys would have to be permitted to advance the class' litigation costs and to collect a fair compensation for their special litigation risks and efforts, even if such meant a payment contingent upon success and assessed against the fund created for the class' benefit. In addition, special management and sanctioning powers might have to be vested in class action judges to enable them to accomplish the multiple management tasks required to shepherd this complex litigation along at a reasonable pace. If it is believed that the typical Italian trial judge in the *tribunali* has insufficient experience and inclination toward such involvement, then special panels can be created in the *tribunali* or even the courts of appeal for processing class actions. Over time these panels could gain experience in managing class suits as has the federal trial bench in the United States.

Describing this cluster of obstacles and the like as "practical problems" is not meant to minimize their weightiness but merely suggests they are essentially political judgments that involve a weighing of competing values. If an Italian or other European legislator sees a predominating value in the social and economic justice achieved by class action, then the values implicit in the "blocking" rules will have to be sacrificed or the rules reshaped to accommodate the greater value.

The second potential barrier to the class action adoption in civil law systems consists of conceptual and philosophic problems. These issues are more deeply rooted because they involve a country's fundamental, perhaps unalterable, modes of thought. One such problem which comes immediately to attention is Article 24 of the Italian Constitution, which guarantees to all people the right to assert legal claims. Because the class device is an "empowering" mechanism, that is, one which facilitates the bringing of claims, it is difficult to conceive that the Italian Constitutional Court would invalidate a class process enacted by the country's parliament in order to encourage the assertion of rights. The existing constitutional jurisprudence eliminates economic requirements which violate Article 24 by inhibiting or blocking court access to those without means. Should the Italian Parliament aim to overcome such obstacles by using the fiscal power of the class, one sees an actualization of Article 24 and not a violation. Indeed, one even finds hints in *la dottrina* that Article 24 may impose a positive duty on the legislature to create access systems and procedures. Extrapolating from that idea, an argument can be made that there is a constitutional right to class proceedings—though the development of this proposition will have to await another day!

The final obstacle to consider is difficult * * * to elucidate: the Italian, or more broadly, "civilian" legal mind. * * * The study of law in continental Europe is quite unlike our pragmatic, "problem solving" focus; it is dominated by dogmatics, i.e., a focus on legal abstractions and the inter-relationship of juridical concepts. In the classroom, the European professor plunges into the comprehensive codes and meticulously extracts every possible meaning, nuance, and cross-reference out of every word and phrase. He likewise endlessly massages concepts when he creates *dottrina* through his scholarship. This approach moves directly with the Continental lawyer into offices and courtrooms and legislatures * * *. In such a mindset, the focus is what exists in the codes and not the problems which exist in the society. This creates a triple bind for the civilian jurist who is asked to appreciate the American class action: first, it cannot be related to any existing legal institution, making it "inconceivable;" second, the class suit violates the dogma of individual litigation control—the "exaggerated individualism" which dominates European civil procedure—making it anti-doctrinal; and third, it is a practical, untidy, problem-solving device, making it distasteful.

C. COLLECTIVE ACTIONS ON BEHALF OF CONSUMERS AND OTHERS: DEVELOPMENTS WITHIN THE EUROPEAN UNION AND ELSEWHERE

The preceding excerpt emphasizes the individualistic model that continues to dominate civil justice systems in many countries outside the United States. However, even within this traditional model, procedures exist allowing for "group actions" that are designed to resolve collective harms in a single lawsuit:

> One type of group action permits consumer associations or other interest groups to initiate lawsuits for the protection of individual, as well as collective, interests. Although the French *action en représentation conjointe* seeks collective protection of the individual interests of a category of plaintiffs, it differs from the class action in that it requires an explicit power of attorney from all members of the "class" and the plaintiff must be an entity, not an individual.[14]

The European Union has issued directives regarding consumer interests that have spurred the adoption of new forms of group actions

---

14. Richard H. Dreyfuss, Class Action Judgment Enforcement in Italy: Procedural "Due Process" Requirements, 10 Tul. J. Int'l and Comp. L. 5, 10 (2002).

in participating countries. This section surveys some of these developments. It also includes illustrative examples of other collective devices that treat similar concerns. How do these new forms of group litigation differ from the United States class action? Notice that in some countries, such as England, the representative mechanism authorizes consumer organizations to initiate claims on behalf of similarly situated individuals, but the government is responsible for designating those organizations that can play this representative role. Do you see similarities between this limitation, presumably aimed at ensuring the integrity and capacity of the representative entity, and the requirement under United States law that the court approve the adequacy of the class representative? What are the relative strengths and weaknesses of these two approaches? The consumer action differs in important ways from the United States class action, but also from a "pure" individual action. For example, under the German consumer model, the *"Verbandsklage"*:

> the association does not sue as an agent or as a representative of the members of the affected group, nor if they are also members of the association: the association vindicates a common, diffused or collective interest that is different from the rights of the individuals. Therefore, the individuals are never adversely affected by the judgment rendered in the association's suit: they just can use it in some cases by way of issue preclusion against the same adversary (unless they actively join in the litigation or explicitly confer an agency power to the association).

> Since the subject matter of the litigation does not include the individual rights, the passive individuals are not parties to the action and are not liable for any cost and fee: they are just supposed to contribute spontaneously to the efforts of the association. Therefore, the system does not overcome completely the problem of free riding, because cost-sharing is not automatic. However, the mechanism of the association can create links between the members of the dispersed group that can reinforce it in the long run (although never eliminating the gap between cohesive and dispersed groups).[15]

EUROPEAN UNION

Directive 98/27/EC of the European Parliament and of the Council of 19 May 1998 on injunctions for the protection of consumers' interests (OJ L 166, 11.6.1998, p. 51).

> Whereas current mechanisms available both at national and at [European] Community level * * * do not always allow infringements harmful to the collective interests of consumers to be terminated in good time; whereas collective interests mean interests which do not include the cumulation of interests of individuals who have been harmed by an infringement; whereas

---

15. Andrea Giussani, The "Verbands-klage" and the Class Action: Two Models for Collective Litigation in Procedural Laws in Europe: Toward Harmonisation 389, 389–391 (Marcel Storme, ed., 2003).

this is without prejudice to individual actions brought by individuals who have been harmed by an infringement;

* * *

Article 1

Scope

1. The purpose of this Directive is to approximate the laws, regulations and administrative provisions of the Member States relating to actions for an injunction referred to in Article 2 aimed at the protection of the collective interests of consumers included in the Directives listed in the Annex, with a view to ensuring the smooth functioning of the internal market.

2. For the purpose of this Directive, an infringement shall mean any act contrary to the Directives listed in the Annex as transposed into the internal legal order of the Member States which harms the collective interests referred to in paragraph 1.

Article 2

Actions for an injunction

1. Member States shall designate the courts or administrative authorities competent to rule on proceedings commenced by qualified entities within the meaning of Article 3 seeking:

> (a) an order with all due expediency, where appropriate by way of summary procedure, requiring the cessation or prohibition of any infringement;

> (b) where appropriate, measures such as the publication of the decision, in full or in part, in such form as deemed adequate and/or the publication of a corrective statement with a view to eliminating the continuing effects of the infringement;

> (c) insofar as the legal system of the Member State concerned so permits, an order against the losing defendant for payments into the public purse or to any beneficiary designated in or under national legislation, in the event of failure to comply with the decision within a time-limit specified by the courts or administrative authorities, of a fixed amount for each day's delay or any other amount provided for in national legislation, with a view to ensuring compliance with the decisions.

2. This Directive shall be without prejudice to the rules of private international law, with respect to the applicable law, thus leading normally to the application of either the law of the Member State where the infringement originated or the law of the Member State where the infringement has its effects.

Article 3

Entities qualified to bring an action

For the purposes of this Directive, a 'qualified entity' means any body or organisation which, being properly constituted according to the law of a Member State, has a legitimate interest in ensuring that the provisions referred to in Article 1 are complied with, in particular:

> (a) one or more independent public bodies, specifically responsible for protecting the interests referred to in Article 1, in Member States in which such bodies exist and/or

> (b) organisations whose purpose is to protect the interests referred to in Article 1, in accordance with the criteria laid down by their national law.

* * *

Article 7

Provisions for wider action

This Directive shall not prevent Member States from adopting or maintaining in force provisions designed to grant qualified entities and any other person concerned more extensive rights to bring action at national level.

Edward F. Sherman, Group Litigation Under Foreign Legal Systems: Variations and Alternatives to American Class Actions, 52 DePaul L. Rev. 401, 418–419 (2002).

In 1998, the European Parliament and Council issued the "European Directive on Injunctions for the Protection of Consumers' Interests," which had to be implemented into national law by the end of 2000. The directive provided that rights of action would be assigned to "qualified entities" that are either organizations (such as consumer associations) or independent public bodies (such as administrative agencies). Such entities would be allowed to file "group litigation" on behalf of a specifically defined group of people adversely affected by a defendant's conduct.

The title of the directive is something of a misnomer, as an injunction, as well as damages, may be sought in some countries in certain situations. The term "consumers' interests" is broadly interpreted, comprehending suits to vindicate rights under consumer protection, competition, and fair contract practices. However, European "group representation" is much more limited than the American class action, requiring advance determination of the right to serve as a representative rather than allowing the American "self-selective" approach.

The European group representation model differs dramatically from the American model in its conception of who should be empowered to sue on behalf of others and what degree of cohesiveness is required to qualify as a group for purposes of representation. Professor Harald Koch has described the philosophy behind the [European Union] approach:

> There is no method of self-appointment of an individual champion (plaintiff) and no concept of an individual private Attorney General, whose initiative is fostered by fee incentives or by an alluring contingency fee arrangement. To be sure, this may be well deserved because of the risk assumed and the attorney's hard work; however, in the European tradition—although this may be slightly over-simplified—we entrust the public interest to public institutions rather than to private law enforcers. By doing so, we must put up with all of the problems of a poorly-motivated, cumbersome, and perhaps understaffed bureaucracy, as well as the question of legitimacy of representation. Under such a system, the interests of individual victims of unlawful behavior tend to be neglected in larger and more autonomous organizations.

Christopher Hodges, Europeanization of Civil Justice: Trends and Issues, 26 Civil Justice Quarterly 96, 119–123 (2007).

Might the European Union introduce a harmonised class action mechanism? The possibility of consumer collective or class actions was first raised in the EU context in a Commission paper of 1984. This noted the common legal tradition of the then Member States, irrespective of whether they came from civil law or common law traditions, that no individual is entitled to institute legal proceedings unless he or she establishes a direct personal interest. The interests of a number of consumers, or of consumers generally, was entrusted to either the public prosecutor's office, or to an authorised public body, or some form of action brought by an individual on behalf of other individuals, or the defence of the collective interests of consumers was sometimes entrusted to associations that satisfied certain criteria. The Commission concluded in 1984 that it was not possible to propose binding harmonisation of national mechanisms on collective actions, since there was too much complexity and diversity amongst the national systems.

However, various Community measures have adopted the mechanism of empowering consumer organisations to take enforcement action under consumer protection provisions. Such provisions are found in the Directives for misleading advertising, unfair contract terms, cross-border injunctions for breach of specified consumer protection Directives, the Regulation on consumer protection co-operation and the recent Directive on unfair business-to-consumer commercial practices * * *.

The European Commission has recently signalled its interest in introducing a class action claim mechanism across Europe. A study of the "analysis and evaluation of alternative means of consumer redress other than individual redress through ordinary judicial proceedings" was commissioned in 2006. The Commission will be strengthened by a 2006 survey which found that 74 per cent of Europeans would be more willing to defend their rights in court if they could join with other consumers who were complaining about the same thing. It is an interesting question whether the Commission would have jurisdiction to propose harmonising legislation on a general rule of law that permitted a class action, as opposed to a specific mechanism to enhance consumer protection. In any event, the Commission would presumably not consider that it has the political support of the Member States to proceed with such a proposal unless a sufficient number of Member States were to have existing general national legislation on class claims, but that state of affairs is now not far off.

ENGLAND

Civil Procedure Rules, Part 19—Parties and Group Litigation (The White Book Service 2006).

Representative parties with same interest

19.6—(1) Where more than one person has the same interest in a claim—

(a) the claim may be begun; or

(b) the court may order that the claim be continued, by or against one or more of the persons who have the same interest as representatives of any other persons who have that interest.

(2) The court may direct that a person may not act as a representative.

(3) Any party may apply to the court for an order under paragraph (2).

(4) Unless the court otherwise directs any judgment or order given in a claim in which a party is acting as a representative under this rule—

(a) is binding on all persons represented in the claim; but

(b) may only be enforced by or against a person who is not a party to the claim with the permission of the court.

(5) This rule does not apply to a claim to which rule 19.7 applies.

Neil Andrews, English Civil Procedure: Fundamentals of the New Civil Justice System 974, 977 (2003).

Group litigation is now the favoured form of multi-party procedure. The essence of such litigation is that a set of claimants or defendants are shepherded into the same procedural pen. They can then travel together the long road to trial without it being necessary to consider a plethora of separate issues, many of which might raise the same or very similar questions of fact or law.

* * *

New rules were added to [England's Civil Practice Rules 1998] Part 19 in 2000 to implement recommendations for reform of the system of group litigation. * * *

The essence of group litigation is that the court takes control of the proceedings, having delineated a cluster of claims which justify a Group Litigation Order * * *. Such an order provides for 'the case management of claims which give rise to related issues of fact or law'. Most group litigation concerns claims by a plethora of claimants. But the rules also state that a Group Litigation Order can include a claim brought against a plurality of defendants.

Edward F. Sherman, Group Litigation Under Foreign Legal Systems: Variations and Alternatives to American Class Actions, 52 DePaul L. Rev. 401, 422–424 (2002).

An English procedure for "representative proceedings" has been available for over two hundred years at common law, although it was used infrequently because of narrow court interpretations. It permitted a person to take legal action on behalf of persons who had "common issues" arising from "the same interest" in a claim against the same defendant. It was given a definitive interpretation in the House of Lords decision *Duke of Bedford v. Ellis* in 1901. In that case, a group of market stallholders were allowed to pursue a class action to assert a statutory right in relation to allocation of certain stalls in Covent Garden. Lord MacNaughten said that the requirement of "the same interest" is satisfied if the representative can show a common interest or common grievance and that the relief sought is beneficial to all. * * *

By 1989, it was accepted that claims for damages were not automatically excluded from the operation of the rule merely because they were made severally by numerous plaintiffs.

Like American class actions, representative proceedings can begin without the court's permission, and the representative does not need to be appointed or elected by the group. Curiously, there seems to be less court supervision than in the United States; the court does not monitor nor normally need to approve settlements. Limitations on damages, however, have been said to be "the reason why the English representative action remains a procedural backwater rather than a flourishing style of multi-party litigation." Damages cannot be awarded without reference to the particular loss suffered by members of the class, and "the arithmetic of individual loss must be totted and tabulated painfully and precisely." The court can award damages in a representative action only where: (i) the class members' loss can be readily ascertained at the time of judgment; or (ii) the class members have waived their rights to individual receipt of damages and instead wish their compensation to be paid to a body enjoying care of their interests.

Given the shortcomings of English representative actions, amendments to the Civil Procedure Rules were made in 2000 to allow courts to issue Group Litigation Orders providing for "the case management of claims which give rise to related issues of fact or law." This is essentially a consolidation device that has elements of the American transfer of federal court cases with common questions to a single court by the judicial panel on multidistrict litigation. A court may delineate a cluster of claims as appropriate for a Group Litigation Order. The court to which the cases are assigned is the "management court," although different judges can be responsible for managing various facets of the litigation. The solicitors are expected to form a Solicitors' Group. Parties who want to join the group litigation must "opt in," in contrast to representative proceedings that "can effectively take place behind the backs of class members without their knowledge, participation or control." A group member is liable, if the group loses, to pay "an equal proportion, together with all the other litigants, of the common costs," as well as "the amount of individual costs incurred by the defendant in meeting that particular litigant's claim."

Representative proceedings and group litigation orders continue to develop in the United Kingdom, but are still a far cry from American class actions. In addition, limitations on contingent fees and the "loser pays" rule considerably curtail the entrepreneurial aspects of American practice. Lord Steyn, a Lord of Appeal in Ordinary, explained at a conference that English senior judges "are opposed to a 'litigious society,' that is, an over-excited tendency for citizens and businessmen to 'blame and claim' by bringing actions in the ordinary courts rather than pursuing grievance procedures through political systems of democratic accountability, pressure groups, ombudsmen, arbitration, conciliation, etc." Nevertheless, growing EU interest in group litigation, the influence of huge British solicitor firms capable of undertaking class actions, and internal pressure in the United Kingdom for more fluid forms of legal practice (as seen in proposals to allow limited contingent fees and to give solicitors greater rights of audience at court) seem to militate in favor of an expansion of UK representative or group procedures.

GERMANY

Christopher Hodges, Europeanization of Civil Justice: Trends and Issues, 26 Civil Justice Quarterly 96, 117–118 (2007).

* * * The prevailing view among German lawyers for many years was that there was no need for a class action mechanism, and that all claims could be resolved individually, but this belief was demolished by litigation brought by 15,000 individual claimants against Deutsche Telecom, who claimed that the company overvalued assets before a share sale

in 2000. The German Procedural Code does not permit these similar claims to be managed in some co-ordinated fashion, and the judges who were in charge of the many individual claims recognised that they needed some new powers, such as to try specimen "lead claims" and in the meanwhile stay the majority of other claims. The position of German investors was adversely compared with the fact that a class claim by investors in Deutsche Telecom in the United States was settled there for over US $120 million.

Accordingly, in 2005, Germany passed the Capital Investors' Model Proceeding Law, which provides for a test case to be brought in relation to a claim for damages or for specific performance by investors or shareholders in takeover offer situations. Following a public announcement of a court's acceptance of the initial petition, if nine further similar cases occur within four months, the first court will decide which questions are common, and the questions will then be decided by the Higher Regional Court, with no opt-out provision in relation to any of the individual cases, which remain stayed pending resolution of the selected common questions. In addition, Germany's Consumer Ministry has asked two law professors to draft a general class action law.

Act on the Initiation of Model Case Proceedings in respect of Investors in the Capital Markets, Kapitalanleger–Musterverfahrensgesetz vom 16. August 2005 (BGBI. I S. 2437) entered into force on Nov. 1, 2005: KapMuG Geltung ab 01.11.2005 bis 31.10.2010.[16]

Part 1

Application for Establishment of a Model Case; Reference Procedures

Section 1

Application for Establishment of a Model Case

(1) By application for the establishment of a model case, in a proceeding at first instance, in which

1. a claim for compensation of damages due to false, misleading or omitted public capital markets information or

2. a claim to fulfillment of contract, which is based on an offer under the Securities Acquisition and Takeover Act,

is asserted, the establishment of the existence or non-existence of conditions justifying or ruling out entitlement or the clarification of legal questions may be sought (establishment objective), provided the decision in the legal dispute is contingent thereupon. Applica-

---

16. The materials provided are available at http://www.bmj.bund.de/files/-/1110/Kap MuG_english.pdf (Site last visited March 15, 2007).

tion for the establishment of a model case may be made by the plaintiff and the defendant. Public capital markets information means information directed at a great number of investors regarding facts, circumstances and statistical as well as other company data which relate to an issuer of securities or an offer of other investments.

* * *

(2) Application for the establishment of a model case shall be made with the court trying the matter and shall include indication of the establishment objective and the public capital markets information. * * * The applicant shall substantiate that the decision on the application for the establishment of a model case may have significance for other similar cases beyond the individual dispute concerned. The respondent shall be granted opportunity to submit a written pleading on the matter.

* * *

Section 2

Public Announcement in the Complaint Registry

(1) The court trying the matter shall announce publicly an admissible application for the establishment of a model case in the electronic Federal Gazette under the title "Complaint Registry pursuant to the Capital Markets Model Case Act" (Complaint Registry). A decision on public announcement shall be given by order of the court trying the matter. There shall be no possibility to appeal such order. * * *

* * *

(2) Access to the Complaint Registry shall be open to everyone free of charge.

* * *

Section 16

Effect of the Model Case Ruling

(1) The model case ruling shall be binding on the courts trying the matter, whose decisions depend on the establishment made on the model case or the legal question to be resolved in the model case proceedings. * * *

(2) Upon final and binding conclusion of the model case proceeding, the interested parties summoned shall only be heard in legal disputes brought against the opposing party which assert that the main party's presentation of the case was inadequate, provided that, on account of the stage the model case proceeding was in at the time they were sum-

moned or on account of statements and actions of the main party, the interested parties summoned were hindered from availing themselves of means of contestation or defense, or such means of contestation or defense of which they were not aware were not availed of by the main party, either intentionally or due to gross negligence.

(3) The model case ruling shall also have effect for and against the interested parties summoned, who did not intervene in the appeal on points of law proceeding.

Michael Stürner, Model Case Proceedings in the Capital Markets—Tentative Steps Towards Group Litigation in Germany, 26 Civil Justice Quarterly 250, 256–266 (2007).

THE REMEDY: BASIC FEATURES OF THE KAPMUG

The KapMuG entered into force on November 1, 2005. * * * Section 1 of the Act provides that it applies on claims for compensation of damages due to false, misleading or omitted public capital markets information or claims to fulfilment of contract which is based on an offer under the Securities Acquisition and Takeover Act (*Wertpapiererwerb-sund-übernahmegesetz*). The scope of application of the KapMuG is obviously rather narrow, since it applies only to claims related to the capital markets. Moreover, the legislator has opted for a test phase of five years, after which the Act will be ineffective. It is the intention of the legislator, however, to enlarge the scope of application of the KapMuG.

* * *

The KapMuG operates in three different phases: model case proceedings start with an opening phase in which the Regional Court (the Lower Court), on the application of no less than 10 parties, orders the initiation of intermediary proceedings and determines the legal or factual issues to be decided there. In the second phase the pending claims will be suspended as the model question is decided by the competent Regional Appellate Court (the Higher Court) which appoints one or several model claimants. Finally, in the third phase again the Lower Court decides every single case on the basis of the results obtained in the preceding phase. It is important to note that the KapMuG operates exclusively as an intermediary process for similar claims which are already pending.

THE OPENING PHASE

The Need for an Application by the Parties

An application for the establishment of a model case may be made by any claimant or defendant. It is the objective of the model case to clarify the existence or non-existence of conditions justifying or ruling out entitlement or to decide legal questions. In the application the objective of the establishment as well as the relevant public capital markets information have to be stated. There is no power of the court to open the model case proceedings *ex officio.* * * * [U]nder the KapMuG the court cannot act on its own initiative. The principle of party prosecution is still very much dominating the multi-party situation. There will be no model case proceedings if the parties do not apply for it even though the court would regard it as an imperative of procedural economy.

Every application is being registered in the electronic complaint registry. Other potential applicants and even other potential claimants are thus informed about the possible model case proceedings. Within four months after the first application for the establishment of a model case, at least nine other applications must be made to the court trying the matter or to any other court in Germany where similar cases are pending. Those applications must relate to the same subject matter. This is a relatively ample definition of which applications are related. Identity of applications is not required. It is sufficient if applications concern different aspects of a claim, but the same subject matter. Applications relating to the same prospectus, but to different capital market information contained in that prospectus, are related applications. The same is true for contradictory applications (e.g. one by claimant that the prospectus was false, one by defendant that the prospectus was correct) or for claims against different defendants (e.g. one claim against the company, another against its directors).

Proceedings in which an application has been made are interrupted *ex lege.* Owing to the goals of expedition and efficiency, no appeal lies against the decision to interrupt proceedings. This is potentially unfair to the defendant because even though a claimant has no case and his or her claim will eventually fail, he or she will participate in the model case proceedings. However, there is some scope for procedural skirmishes, since there lies an appeal against the order of the court not to allow the application for model case proceedings.

The Effect of Successful Applications

If at least 10 related applications have been made within the period of 4 months, all the other proceedings will be suspended as the model case is deferred to the Regional Appellate Court (*Oberlandesgericht*), which is bound by the decision of the Lower Court. Parties cannot appeal this decision even if they are not content with the legal or factual issues to be decided in the model case proceedings.

If the requirements for the establishment of a model case are not met (e.g. if there are not enough applications relating to the same subject matter or due to the inadmissibility of some applications), the Lower Court refuses the existing applications and continues trying the different matters. Such a decision may be appealed according to s.252 of

ZPO like any other decision of the court by which the suspension of proceedings is denied.

Thus, the concept of a "class" is still alien to German law. An investor who wants to be party to the model case proceedings will have to file a statement of case. There is no other way to benefit from the model case decision of the Higher Court. If the Lower Court has ordered to defer the case to the Higher Court to decide the model case, every new claim filed with any court in Germany will be suspended automatically.

* * *

The Second Phase: Model Case Proceedings

In principle, the model case proceedings follow more or less familiar patterns. In an adversarial context, claimants and defendant(s) bring forward arguments and defences as to the model question. To facilitate proceedings, one or several model claimants are chosen who "lead" the case. However, they are not representatives of the other claimants. In case the Higher Court appoints an expert witness, the parties do not have to pay any advance for the costs. * * * In the end the losing party, or parties, as the case may be, has to bear all those costs.

Selecting a Model Claimant

Once the Lower Court has ordered to initiate model case proceedings, intermediary proceedings start before the Higher Court. As a first step, the Higher Court has to appoint a so-called model claimant. According to the Act there is a presumption that the claimant with the highest individual claim will be the model claimant. Alternatively, the Higher Court can appoint a different claimant, for instance when a large number of claimants is represented by one law firm. The discretion of the Higher Court has to be exercised with an eye on the objective of the Act that the model case is run smoothly and that the model claimant will not withdraw his or her claim. Thus, a race to the courtroom which would be the effect of a strict first-come-first-served approach is not encouraged. However, there is a certain probability that the model claimant will be chosen amongst the first 10 claimants: since not all files can be transferred to the Higher Court, the Lower Court will probably lodge only the files of the first 10 applicants. For practical reasons, the Higher Court will normally choose the model claimant from these applicants.

The model claimant is not a representative of the other claimants. This leads to problems in cases where the claim of the model claimant does not contain all the points of dispute of the establishment objective. The model claimant does not have any obligation to make propositions or to raise defences as to all of these points. Thus, all the other parties have to pursue their own interests by filing statements of case. This, in turn, leads to an increase of statements. The only remedy will be to appoint several model claimants to cover all the points of dispute. If the model claimant withdraws his claim, the court will have to appoint a new model claimant.

Once the model claimant has been chosen, there is an electronic publication on the website of the Federal Ministry of Justice. From this moment, all the other pending cases where the decision depends on the establishment to be made or the legal question to be solved are being suspended. It does not matter whether or not an application for the establishment of a model case has been (successfully) made in that particular case. This presupposes that the court has had scrutiny of all the pending cases to determine if they depend on the model question.

The Role of the Other Claimants

The other claimants have the status of interested parties summoned (*Beigeladene*). Their role has been designed according to the model of the intervening third party. Interested parties summoned are meant to support the model claimant.

Interested parties summoned do not automatically get all the statements of case of the model claimant unless they expressly request it. Moreover, there is no way to request statements of case of other interested parties summoned, the reason for this being again procedural economy. Thus their right to be heard is impaired as they may not get all the factual information the court disposes of to decide the model question. Regardless of that all the claimants are bound by the model case decision. According to KapMuG, s.12, a statement of case of an interested party summoned may not contradict the statements of case of the model claimant. * * *

An expansion of the subject matter in the model case is possible within the framework of the establishment objective on application of any party. * * *

Decision in the Model Case Proceedings

Settlement

During the model case proceedings, settlement of the model question remains possible. However, the model claimant does not have the power to settle the model case on behalf of all the other claimants: all of the parties concerned must give their consent. * * *

The Model Case Decision

Where the model case is not being settled, the Higher Court renders a decision on the model question. Section 14(1) of the KapMuG remains silent on the contents of the model case decision. * * *

As the Higher Court is only entrusted with the task to decide the model case, it does not render judgment for each individual claimant. After the decision of the Higher Court, the different proceedings continue separately before the Lower Court. The model case decision provides but one piece for the jigsaw of each case; the other pieces are to be found by the Lower Court according to the normal procedural rules.

The Binding Effect of the Model Case Decision

With regard to the main goal of the model case proceedings, procedural economy, the Lower Court or Lower Courts, as the case may be, are bound by the model case decision of the Higher Court. Even those interested parties summoned who have withdrawn their claim after the model case proceedings start are bound by the model case decision. By withdrawing a claim, a party only escapes liability for the costs of the model case. However, a claimant who has withdrawn his or her claim before the public announcement of the order for a model case is not bound by the model case decision.

* * * Appeal

The model case decision can be appealed; the appeal will be heard by the Federal Court of Justice (*Bundesgerichtshof*). Rather surprisingly, all the parties, including interested parties summoned, have a right to appeal. This reflects the principle of party autonomy; the model claimant is not representing the other claimants. If none of the model claimants appeals the model case decision, the first interested party summoned to commence appellate proceedings will be the model case appellant. Those claimants who did not explicitly join the appeal are still bound by the decision of the appellate court.

An appeal will further delay the model case decision. Even those parties who are content with the decision of the Higher Court cannot obtain judgment—their claims remain suspended during the appellate proceedings. German civil procedure which is anyway notorious for its generous appellate regime gives the parties further possibilities to protract. Given the number of claimants it is almost certain that at least one of them will challenge the model case decision.

THE THIRD PHASE: JUDGMENT IN THE INDIVIDUAL CASES

After the model case question has been decided by the Higher Court and possible appeals have been disposed of, the Lower Court(s) will then decide all the individual cases on the basis of the model case decision. The court(s) will have the opportunity to deal with the specific issues each case presents, namely the individual amount of damages, questions of expiry of the limitation period, proof of the causal link between the inaccuracy of the capital markets information and the acquisition of shares, and so on. All of the normal procedural principles of the ZPO apply. The court can consolidate actions according to s.147 of ZPO, if it thinks fit.

THE PROBLEM OF COSTS

It is well known that the costs system works as an important regulatory mechanism. * * *

[U]nder German law contingency fees are not permitted (although in reality a success bonus seems not to be totally uncommon). The concept of the KapMuG conceives the model case proceedings only as an intermediary step, not as an entirely separate action. Therefore, the model case will not give counsel any extra fee even though his or her workload increases considerably. Consequently, there is only little financial incentive for lawyers to act as counsel to the model claimant. * * *

However, there is an incentive for a lawyer to collect as many clients as possible since under the German costs system fees are increasing in proportion to the amount in dispute. Some law firms are specialising in lucrative claims in the capital markets. For those firms there is a massive incentive to be counsel to the model claimant to ensure a maximum presence in legal and other media. Moreover, there is growing co-operation between those firms and lawsuit funding companies. The lawsuit is funded by the company on a success fee basis which facilitates the decision for an investor to bring an action.

As usual, the losing party has to bear all the costs. In case the model question is decided in favour of defendant, every claimant has to bear a proportionate share of the costs of the model case proceedings. * * *

The Future of Aggregate Litigation in Germany

The KapMuG tries to achieve the impossible: providing for an efficient way to deal with mass litigation and safeguarding individual process rights like the right to be heard and rectitude of decision at the same time. It is a timid step towards a general recognition of the fact that multi-party situations require a new definition of the scope of basic procedural principles. * * *

[A]fter the test phase of the KapMuG the German legislator will surely expand the scope of application of the group litigation. Possible areas include claims related to financial services, competition law and consumer protection. Another potential field apt for multi-party situations is mass torts, as they may occur in cases of product liability, environmental liability or pharmaceutical product liability.

The question remains: where does this development lead to? Behaviour control of actors on the global market will always be necessary. The traditional, European approach is regulation, the more modern one, advocated by the US legal system, is private law enforcement. Instead of introducing more regulatory instruments, investors and their lawyers are entrusted with the enforcement of public laws by private supervision. They act as private attorney-generals. Quite clearly, legislators in Europe are increasingly fond of that latter approach.

ITALY

Richard H. Dreyfuss, Class Action Judgment Enforcement in Italy: Procedural "Due Process" Requirements, 10 Tul. J. Int'l and Comp. L. 5, 10–14 (2002).

A provision in the Italian Code of Criminal Procedure permits entities, such as associations "representative" of interests harmed by the crime in question, to participate in the criminal proceeding and to exercise the same procedural rights and powers which the Code grants to the person *offesa dal reato*, or crime victim. The entities, however, must first obtain the consent of the crime victim. Moreover, where an entity can show that it incurred immediate and direct damages from a crime perpetrated against another, the entity has the right to claim restitution and damages *(azione civile)* within the context of the respective criminal proceeding instead of commencing a separate civil action after the criminal adjudication. In addition, an Italian statute expressly permits associations of manufacturers, consumers, and other interested associations to claim restitution and damages within the context of criminal proceedings concerning the marketing of dangerous foods, even if these entities are unable to show that their damages were an immediate and direct consequence of the crime.

The European Union Directive [98/27/EC] on injunctions for the protection of consumers' interests defines certain "qualified entities" that, as representative organizations, may be empowered to bring actions on behalf of consumers. To comply with European Union principles for the protection of consumers' interests, Italy enacted Law No. 281 of July 30, 1998. Law No. 281 provides that formally recognized consumer associations may bring lawsuits to protect common interests, principally through injunctions. The statute does not contemplate actions for damages.

JAPAN

The Code of Civil Procedure of Japan.*

Parties

Section 1—Capacity for being Parties and Litigation Capacity

(Appointed parties)

Article 30. A large number of parties having a joint interest and not coming under the provision of the preceding Article may appoint from among them one or more persons who is or are to act as a plaintiff or defendant for all the parties.

2.   When, subsequent to the pendency of the action, a person or persons acting as a plaintiff or defendant have been appointed in accordance with the provision of the preceding paragraph, other parties shall withdraw from the action as a matter of course.

3.   Persons who have a joint interest with a plaintiff or defendant during the pendency of the action and are not parties may appoint a plaintiff or defendant, as a person who is to act as a plaintiff or defendant for themselves.

4.   Persons who have appointed a person who is to act as a plaintiff or defendant in accordance with the provision of para-

* Translation in EHS Law Bulletin Series, EHS Vol. II, No. 2300 (2004).

graph 1 or the preceding paragraph (hereinafter referred to as the "appointers"), may cancel such appointment or change the parties who are appointed (hereinafter referred to as the "appointed parties").

5. Anyone of the appointed parties loses his qualifications upon death or other grounds, other appointed parties may do acts of procedure for all the parties.

Yasuhei Taniguchi, The 1996 Code of Civil Procedure of Japan—A Procedure for the Coming Century?, 45 Am. J. Comp. L. 767, 782–783 (1997).

With a rising interest in consumer protection measures, the adoption of a class action has been discussed for decades. As early as 1975, one of the then opposition parties presented a class action bill to the Diet. An academic group published its own draft named "Group Representative Action Law." One of Tokyo's bar associations did the same thing later. But due to strong opposition from the industry circles, none of these proposals became law. In the current civil procedure reform project, class action law suits were again an issue in the beginning, but soon faded away.

The New Code, however, introduced a mild improvement to the pre-existing "election of party" or "representative action" procedure. This is procedure not existing in the German Code, created by the Japanese drafters of the 1926 amendment, inspired by the "representative unit" in the English equity courts. In this version of "representative action," where more than two persons or entities have a common interest, one (or more) of them can be appointed by the other(s) as the representative for an action on behalf of all. The "representative action" has not been used actively, but the institution was much publicized when a consumer group used it in the 70's against oil companies to recover damages resulting from an overpricing of fuel oil at the time of the first oil crisis. One of the requirements under the present law is that all the represented persons must be individually identified before a representative action is filed. The New Code now makes it possible for anyone who wants to join an already started representative action to elect the same plaintiff as his representative. The plaintiff then amends the complaint to include the claim of the joining person (Art.144). There was a proposal until the last stage of drafting to the effect that the court would publish a notice in newspapers about this possibility, but it was dropped from the final version of the New Code, on the grounds that the court should not give an impression to the public that it underwrites the legitimacy of the action. Consequently, the plaintiffs must publicize their suit by themselves in order to recruit other claimants. In any event, the procedure is far different from a real class action.

Carl F. Goodman, Japan's New Civil Procedure Code: Has It Fostered a Rule of Law Dispute Resolution Mechanism?, 29 Brook. J. Int'l L. 511, 589–592 (2004).

Unlike U.S. law, Japanese civil procedure does not provide for class action suits. In Japan, each allegedly injured party must separately claim damages. However, Japanese law does recognize the "representative action." In a representative action suit, numerous parties are named as plaintiffs. From these plaintiffs, a small group is designated to represent the entire plaintiff group in the litigation. In this fashion, one case can try the issues and facts common to all claims made by the entire group of plaintiffs. Unlike the U.S. class action, however, all the plaintiffs must in fact be real plaintiffs who appear in the case, and the plaintiffs do not represent others similarly situated who did not join in the lawsuit.

The writers of the New Code of Civil Procedure were aware of the U.S. style class action and were aware of the existing opinion that Japanese law should permit class actions. The idea of permitting U.S. style class actions was rejected by the New Code, but the "representative action" was modified to permit parties to join the action after the complaint had already been filed. This joinder provision was seen as a step towards greater access to the court process, placing the New Code somewhere between the Old Code and the U.S. class action.

Note

New provisions (Arts. 12–48) were added in 2006 to the Japanese Consumer Contract Law of 2001 (effective, June 2007), adopting a European Union-type consumer organization injunction suit. In order for a consumer protection organization to bring such a suit, the organization must first be certified as an "eligible organization" by the government (i.e., the Prime Minister).

D. LEGISLATIVE APPROACHES TO COLLECTIVE HARMS

Representative joinder devices, such as the class action, depend on the courts to resolve complex social matters. At least some commentators associate these devices, and especially the United States class-action rule, with a culture of "adversarial legalism" that is characterized by "lawyer-dominated litigation in dispute resolution, policy making, and policy implementation."[17] By contrast, some legal systems rely predominately on social welfare legislation to resolve mass harms, using professional bureaucracies, rather than judicially-staffed courts, to administer programmatic details. In the excerpts that follow, commentators assess the advantages and disadvantages of relying on legislative, rather than court-centered, solutions to the problems generated by mass harm. This section closes with materials describing the claims mechanism adopted by the United States in the wake of the attack on the World Trade Center in New York on September 11, 2001. How does this court-centered mechanism compare with the legislative approaches to collective injury used in legal systems elsewhere?

17. David Nelken, Beyond Compare? Criticizing "The American Way of Law," 28 Law and Soc. Inquiry 799, 800 (2003); see generally Robert A. Kagan, Adversarial Legalism: The American Way of Law (2001).

Linda S. Mullenix, Lessons From Abroad: Complexity and Convergence, 46 Vill. L. Rev. 1, 27–31 (2001).

One of the most striking features of the ways in which European civil law and other common law countries resolve aggregate litigation is through legislation. Thus, some countries have resolved mass disaster claims by enacting legislation to provide compensation for injured claimants. India, for example, passed national legislation to resolve claims arising from the industrial accident in which lethal gas was released from a chemical plant operated by Union Carbide India Limited in Bhopal in December 1984. In addition, Japan passed legislation to compensate the child victims whose pregnant mothers had ingested thalidomide in the 1960s. Often these legislative remedial schemes are financed by public funds as well as contributions from the private malfeasors.

* * *

The United States has been slow to embrace legislative solutions to aggregate mass torts or mass disasters. For more than sixty years, Congress has resisted attempts to resolve asbestos litigation through national legislation. Indeed, the rare congressional initiative has been for the opposite purpose, to immunize potential defendants from liability in advance of mass torts. For example, Congress enacted a statute to relieve swine flu manufacturers of liability for any claims arising from use of the vaccine.

* * * [T]he theme of convergence with regard to legislative solutions for mass torts and other aggregate litigation is striking. The United States created the class action rule, but has steadfastly avoided substantive legislative solutions to aggregate litigation. Most civil law countries, in contrast, have steadfastly avoided the class action rule, but have provided for substantive legislative solutions to aggregate claims. At the beginning of the twenty-first century, however, civil law countries are now embracing class action-like statutory schemes, and the American Congress is giving new scrutiny to substantive legislative solutions to mass torts. By the end of the century, all countries may have some version of a class rule, with parallel substantive legislation for resolving specialized aggregate tort claims.

Anita Bernstein, Formed by Thalidomide: Mass Torts as a False Cure for Toxic Exposure, 97 Colum. L. Rev. 2153, 2158–2161 (1997).

Outside the United States, thalidomide exposure generated criminal and civil litigation that frequently resulted in state and private compensation of victims. In September 1965, German prosecutors charged nine industry executives with manslaughter and intent to commit bodily harm. The manufacturer, Chemie Grünenthal, eventually agreed to establish a fund of DM 100 million to compensate the victims, a fund to which the West German government, recognizing its responsibility both as a social welfare state and as a government that had been remiss in writing and enforcing licensing laws, also agreed to contribute. Thalidomide victims in Japan brought class actions against two drug manufacturers and the Ministry of Health and Welfare, which concluded with both the drug manufacturers and the state admitting liability. In Britain, a group of parents brought a lawsuit against Distillers, the British licensee, and won a settlement of about £54,000 per child, topped off with £5 million of government funds to offset the income tax due on the settlement awards. A lawsuit against a Canadian distributor resulted in a settlement of about $200,000 per child and the establishment of a federal compensation fund of about $8.5 million.

Legislatures were also active in addressing the thalidomide disaster. Germany adopted the Pharmaceutical Law of 1976, which aimed at forestalling and repairing a thalidomide-scale tragedy in the future, compensating drug-injured victims, and obliging pharmaceutical manufacturers to carry insurance. In Sweden, under "the gun of alternative legislation by the Ministry of Justice," pharmaceutical manufacturers agreed to "voluntary" group insurance that would compensate drug-injured claimants beyond the levels of Swedish social security. Legislative responses to thalidomide in Japan included the Drug Side–Effect Injury Relief Fund Act, passed by the Diet in 1979, and the Pharmaceutical Affairs Law, administered by the Ministry of Health and Welfare. Under this legislation new drugs must be approved prior to introduction into the market, and must be overseen after introduction into the market, with attention to toxicity and efficacy. Drug regulation in Canada, relatively elaborate before the thalidomide disaster, was increased along the lines of the United States model.

In addition to spurring changes in the domestic law of many countries, the thalidomide experience contributed to a variety of legal changes at the international and supranational level. The European products liability statute of 1985, popularly called "the Directive," imposed comprehensive products liability reform on the European Union, generally in the direction of stricter liability than what had prevailed at the national level. Thalidomide shaped the 1985 Directive in several ways, bringing to the fore a concern with nonprivy bystanders, unforeseeable risks, and personal injury (rather than economic loss, even though the jurisdictional basis of the European Union is commercial). Scholars link both the Directive and its predecessors—including the 1977 Strasbourg Convention on Product Liability and the 1978 Pearson Royal Commission recommendations—with a public sentiment for reform derived from the devastation of thalidomide in Europe.

Perhaps influenced by the observation that Grünenthal had marketed thalidomide worldwide, the European Union promulgated numerous directives pertaining to the regulation of pharmaceuticals and related products such as medical devices. These regulatory efforts receive additional support by frequent communication between the European Union and regulatory agencies in the United States and Japan as well as international agencies, including the World Health Organization and the Council of Europe. The European Agency for the Evaluation of Medicinal Products, often described as the European counterpart to the FDA, now approves new drugs for marketing in the European Union, and monitors drug safety in the common market. Historical links between this international regulatory scheme and thalidomide may be inferred.

Kenneth R. Feinberg, Speech: Negotiating the September 11 Victim Compensation Fund of 2001: Mass Tort Resolution without Litigation, 19 Wash. U. J.L. and Pol'y 21, 21–26 (2005).[18]

Most of you have some idea about the September 11th Victim Compensation Fund, but let me remind everybody about this federal law. Established by Congress within two weeks after 9/11, the law states that anybody who is eligible, who lost a loved one on 9/11, or who was physically injured on 9/11 could voluntarily elect to come into the fund by the deadline, which was December 22, 2003. You do not have to, but if you elect to come into the fund, the law sets out a calculation of dollars that you are entitled to tax-free, averaging about two million dollars per claim. If you would rather litigate against the airlines, the World Trade Center, the security guards, Massport, the Port Authority, Boeing, go ahead. You can do that, but if you do, you must litigate in federal court in New York City, and there is a cap on the aggregate damages that the airlines and the World Trade Center will have to pay. * * * Ninety-seven percent of all eligible families came into the program. There are today only eighty people litigating 9/11 death claims in federal court. About ten families did nothing—paralyzed with grief, clinically depressed. They did not come into the fund, and they did not litigate. * * *

When the law was passed, it created a tremendous delegation of authority to one person—the Special Master—appointed by the Attorney General. And there was no appropriation of money. Whatever it costs, the U.S. Treasury will pay for it out of petty cash. (Seven billion dollars out of petty cash!) The Special Master will review the claims and authorize the checks. The Treasury will cut the check, tax-free. For death claims, we paid anywhere from $500,000 to $7.1 million tax-free. For injury claims, we paid anywhere from $500 for a broken finger, to about $8.7 million to a surviving individual with third-degree burns over eighty-five percent of her body. Those are the range of the payments. The average payment was $2 million; the median payment was $1.8 million. These two numbers, the average and the median, tell you a lot about how I exercised my discretion under the program.

What did Congress say and not say about this program? First, you have to be eligible. Who is eligible? Somebody who lost a loved one as a result of the 9/11 terrorist attacks or somebody who was physically injured. Pure mental or emotional distress is not compensable. (There would have been seven million people from New York just looking at CNN that would have filed a claim.) There has to be a physical injury,

---

18. Kenneth R. Feinberg served as the Special Master of the federal September 11th Victim Compensation Fund of 2001, Pub. L. No.107–42 tit. IV, 115 Stat. 230, 237–41 (2001); 28 C.F.R. pt. 104 (2004).

but if there was a physical injury in the vicinity of the terrorist attacks—"vicinity" to be worked out by the Special Master—you are eligible. What will you receive in compensation? The statute laid out a four-part formula.

First, the Special Master shall calculate the "economic loss" suffered as a result of the death of the victim or physical injury of the victim. That is simply tort law, a surrogate for what juries in St. Louis do every day. I have to calculate what a victim would have earned over a lifetime. That is not an easy thing to do, especially when families are convinced that the victim would have been a star in any number of chosen professions, but that is the first part of the test. Of course, that is very provocative, because the minute you have economic loss, that is a guarantee that everybody is going to get a different amount of money, and that fuels division among the very people you are trying to help. But that is the law.

Second, the statute says add to economic loss "non-economic loss." That is tort law, too. Pain and suffering and emotional distress are tort concepts replicated in the statute. I made a very provocative decision with regard to non-economic loss—I said everybody will get the same amount. I am not going to get in the business of trying to distinguish somebody's pain and suffering from another's pain and suffering. I am not Solomon—everybody eligible will get $250,000 for the death of the victim and $100,000 for each surviving spouse and dependent. That is the non-economic component.

Third, the statutory formula said to subtract from economic loss plus non-economic loss any collateral sources of income, such as life insurance. The latter is not tort law. It is a social welfare safety net. That is Congress saying the taxpayers should not be subsidizing these families if they have received ten million dollars worth of life insurance, pensions and 401(k)s. So the law required that I deduct from any net award collateral sources of income. What constitutes a collateral source of income? This is a *big* emotional issue.

And Congress * * * added a fourth requirement: the Special Master will exercise his discretion to see that justice is done. Congress delegated to me: "Make sure that this works. Use your discretion to make it work. We do not know what we are getting into, so take it from here." I exercised my discretion, and you all can tell, if you look at the statistics, how I exercised my discretion. I ran all the numbers, and then I brought down the aberrational top numbers which might be ten, twenty, thirty million, and brought up the bottom numbers. I followed Senator Kennedy and Senator Hagel's advice and made sure that fifteen percent of the eligible claimants did not receive eighty-five percent of the taxpayers' money, much to the chagrin of some high-end wage earners who ran the model and could not understand why they did not receive fifteen or twenty million.

We added some very important regulations. The law said you cannot appeal a finding of the Special Master. We read that to mean no *judicial* appeal, but we did have an *administrative* appeal so that families could have an opportunity to come in and be heard. I would listen and adjust the award based on what they said. Never underestimate the importance of due process in these compensation schemes—if you give families an opportunity to be heard, there is a certain degree of psychological closure that comes with the family coming in and meeting me face-to-face. It was a wonderful addition to the program, the administrative appeal.

Now, what was not in the statute? What was left blank in the statute that caused great difficulty in the administration of the program? There is not one phrase in the statute that tells the Special Master who files the claim and who gets the money. Does the first spouse? The second spouse? One sibling? Another sibling? The granddaughter? The parents? The same-sex partner? The fiancée? Who files the claim? Who binds the family and who is awarded the money? This is not an easy issue.

* * *

* * *[W]e worked out most of them using mediation * * *. Where we could not get an agreement, we did the only sensible thing: we looked to state tort law and the state's estate law of the victim's domicile.

* * *

VII. AGGREGATION OF CASES WITHIN A JUDICIAL SYSTEM: EXAMPLES FROM ENGLAND, JAPAN, AND THE UNITED STATES

So far this Chapter primarily has focused on joinder devices that build on a bilateral model and permit the aggregation of claims and parties within a single proceeding. However, sometimes a transaction may give rise to multiple lawsuits by multiple plaintiffs—an industrial explosion, for example, may produce dozens if not hundreds of claims by injured workers or by residents who live near the site of the accident. The fact that litigants typically have options in choosing from among different courts generates the possibility of duplicative, parallel, or overlapping lawsuits being filed that raise similar or even identical questions on behalf of many different claimants. Allowing multiple lawsuits to proceed unquestionably respects the autonomy of individual litigants and has the potential to create reinforcing structures of compensation, deterrence, and accountability. On the other hand, multiple lawsuits also can produce inefficiencies, delay, and other dysfunctions, including a "race to the courthouse" that allows the first victor to exhaust the pool of funds available for compensation. Various procedures and doctrines have developed to deal with the resulting problem. In this section, we survey aggregation techniques in England, Japan, and the United States that permit the consolidation of actions that have been filed in different courts or before different judges. In reviewing these procedures, try to relate their application to what you already have learned about the judge's power to manage a law suit in order to promote efficiency, fairness to the parties, and overall justice.

ENGLAND

Civil Procedure Rules, Part 3—The Court's Case Management Powers (The White Book Service 2006).

The court's general powers of management

3.1—(1) The list of powers in this rule is in addition to any powers given to the court by any other rule or practice direction or by any other enactment or any powers it may otherwise have.

(2) Except where these Rules provide otherwise, the court may—

* * *

(g) consolidate proceedings;

(h) try two or more claims on the same occasion;

* * *

Zuckerman on Civil Procedure: Principles of Practice 508 (2nd ed. 2006).

[Civil Procedure Rules] 3.1(2)(g) gives the court the power to "consolidate proceedings" and CPR 3.1(2)(h) empowers the court to "try two or more claims on the same occasion". Prior to the CPR, [different procedural rules] dealt with consolidation and * * * with the joinder of different parties in one action. All that was needed to consolidate different proceedings was the presence of some common question of law or fact, or that the issues arose out of the same transaction, or that there was some other good reason. Different sets of proceedings could be consolidated even if different claimants and defendants were involved. * * *

Whether the court is considering consolidation or trying different claims on the same occasion, the aim is the same: to avoid wasting party and court resources in a multiplicity of proceedings that involves identical or similar issues and to protect defendants from the cost and vexation of having to defend in separate proceedings against essentially the same allegations. Under the CPR the court has various powers to achieve this aim by trying different claims together or by giving appropriate directions for the manner in which they should be disposed of * * *. It is therefore doubtful whether the distinction between consolidating proceedings and trying various claims together serves any purpose, other than giving rise to technical disputes. The rule maker should therefore consider removing the reference to the arcane process of consolidation. The essence of the matter is that the court will order different claims to be tried together when there is substantial overlap between them or where trying them separately would create a risk of irreconcilable decisions.

JAPAN

The Code of Civil Procedure of Japan.*

(Transfer to avoid delay, etc.)

Article 17—The court of the first instance may, if, though suit comes under its jurisdiction, the court deems it necessary to ensure equitableness between the parties or to avoid delay in the suit in consideration of circumstances such as the domiciles of the parties and witnesses to be examined, and the place where evidence of inspection to be used is situated, transfer the suit in whole or in part upon motion or on its authority.

* * *

Article 152—The court may order restriction, separation or combination of oral argument or cancel such order.

2.   If, in the case where the court has ordered the combination of oral argument for the case in which different parties are involved, a party who had no opportunity to make an examination has applied for examination with regard to the witness who was examined before, the court shall proceed to the examination.

Takaaki Hattori and Dan Fenno Henderson, Civil Procedure in Japan 7.03, note 223 (Yasuhei Taniguchi, Pauline C. Reich, and Hiroto Myake, eds., Rev. 2nd ed. 2004).

If several actions are filed in different courts, the defendant may apply for transfers to the court where one of the actions is pending * * *, and, after the transfer, he may apply for joinder of the oral proceedings.

UNITED STATES

Federal Rule of Civil Procedure 42 Consolidation; Separate Trials.

(a) Consolidation. When actions involving a common question of law or fact are pending before the court, it may order a joint hearing or trial of any or all the matters in issue in the actions; it may order all the actions consolidated; and it may make such orders concerning proceedings therein as may tend to avoid unnecessary costs or delay.

(b) Separate Trials. The court, in furtherance of convenience or to avoid prejudice, or when separate trials will be conducive to expedition and economy, may order a separate trial of any claim, cross-claim, counterclaim, or third-party claim, or of any separate issue of or any number of claims, cross-claims, counterclaims, third-party claims, or issues, always preserving inviolate the right of trial by jury as declared by the Seventh Amendment to the Constitution or as given by a statute of the United States.

---

* Translation in EHS Law Bulletin Series, EHS Vol. II, No. 2300 (2004).

United States Code, 28 U.S.C. § 1407 (2006)—Multidistrict Litigation.

(a) When civil actions involving one or more common questions of fact are pending in different districts, such actions may be transferred to any district for coordinated or consolidated pretrial proceedings. Such transfers shall be made by the judicial panel on multidistrict litigation authorized by this section upon its determination that transfers for such proceedings will be for the convenience of parties and witnesses and will promote the just and efficient conduct of such actions. Each action so transferred shall be remanded by the panel at or before the conclusion of such pretrial proceedings to the district from which it was transferred unless it shall have been previously terminated: Provided, however, That the panel may separate any claim, cross-claim, counter-claim, or third-party claim and remand any of such claims before the remainder of the action is remanded.

(b) Such coordinated or consolidated pretrial proceedings shall be conducted by a judge or judges to whom such actions are assigned by the judicial panel on multidistrict litigation. For this purpose, upon request of the panel, a circuit judge or a district judge may be designated and assigned temporarily for service in the transferee district by the Chief Justice of the United States or the chief judge of the circuit, as may be required, in accordance with the provisions of chapter 13 of this title. * * *

(c) Proceedings for the transfer of an action under this section may be initiated by—

(i) the judicial panel on multidistrict litigation upon its own initiative, or

(ii) motion filed with the panel by a party in any action in which transfer for coordinated or consolidated pretrial proceedings under this section may be appropriate. A copy of such motion shall be filed in the district court in which the moving party's action is pending.

* * *

(f) The panel may prescribe rules for the conduct of its business not inconsistent with Acts of Congress and the Federal Rules of Civil Procedure.

* * *

Judith Resnik, From "Cases" to "Litigation," Law and Contemporary Problems 5, 29–35 (Summer 1991).

Multidistrict Litigation. Another statute of great importance in group litigation these days is section 1407 of Title 28—the provision for multidistrict litigation. I will spend more time talking about multidistrict litigation—"MDL" as it is known in the trade—than the other aggregative techniques described thus far. In part, my interest in MDL stems from its relative absence (until recently) from the academic literature on federal procedure. Further, the history of MDL is relevant to the history of the revision of class actions and to the decision of the Advisory

Committee members *not* to include mass torts under the rubric of class action litigation. The 1966 Advisory Committee note (and the memos circulated among the committee members during 1963 when they were working on Rule 23) make reference to the predecessor of MDL, "the Coordinating Committee on Multiple Litigation in the United States District Courts," which in the 1960s was "charged with developing methods for expediting" cases involving damages (mass accidents as well as antitrust cases seeking damages). The 1966 Advisory Committee note to Rule 23 stated that work by such committees—rather than changes in the federal rules—should be the vehicles for dealing with the burdens that mass accidents placed on federal court caseloads. Moreover, as I suggested above and will detail below, although creation of the MDL panel and the revisions of the class action rule occurred at about the same time (the middle to late 1960s), responses to the two have differed dramatically—and intriguingly.

The background of MDL grows out of the federal judiciary's concern, dating from sometime after World War II, about "similar" and "protracted" cases filed in district courts across the country. In 1949, then Chief Justice Vinson appointed a committee, chaired by Judge E. Barrett Prettyman, called "The Committee to Study Procedure in Anti–Trust and Other Protracted Cases." In 1951, that committee issued a report that the Judicial Conference of the United States adopted. The report described the concern that a "protracted case" "might threaten the judicial process itself," and urged, as a response, that trial judges take control of such cases.

During the 1950s, Chief Justice Warren appointed another committee, once again charged with considering the problems of "protracted cases." That committee, chaired by Judge Alfred Murrah, conducted seminars for federal judges and developed a *Handbook of Recommended Procedures for the Trial of Protracted Cases*. Again, the theme of judicial control emerged; the seminars advocated that "[t]he judge assigned should at the earliest moment take *actual control* of the case and rigorously exercise such *control* throughout the proceedings in such case."

In the early 1960s, the United States government successfully litigated antitrust claims against electrical equipment manufacturers. Thereafter, "more than 1800 separate damage actions were filed in 33 federal district courts." In response, the Judicial Conference authorized the creation of a special subcommittee from its standing Committee on Pre–Trial Procedures and Practices, and, in 1962, Chief Justice Warren appointed Judge Murrah as the chair of that subcommittee, called the "Co–Ordinating Committee for Multiple Litigation of the United States District Courts." This group of nine federal judges supervised nation-wide discovery in these damage antitrust cases. According to staff of the Committee, the nine judges decided to "facilitate communication" among the federal judges before whom the antitrust cases were pending and urged adoption of "uniform" pretrial orders.

In other words, instead of transferring all the pending electrical cases to a single judge (for which no express statutory authorization arguably existed at the time), the Committee attempted to have different judges behave similarly towards cases over which they presided. In the electrical cases, national pretrial hearings were held at which several of the judges assigned to these cases sat together at arguments, conferred, and issued proposed orders that were then sent back to the more than thirty district courts in which the cases were pending. Apparently, some of the procedures were crafted to avoid confronting questions about the authority of judges over each other (as well as over the cases). Again, in the words of the Committee's staff, "[t]he absence of a provision [for consolidation before a single judge] in the statutes or rules ... was recognized at the outset," and efforts were made for "obtaining the voluntary co-operation of the judges concerned." Cooperation of the lawyers was also elicited; a meeting of some eighty plaintiffs' lawyers resulted in the delegation of the logistics of taking depositions to a "steering committee."

Much legal commentary describes the work of the Committee as successful. In March of 1964, the Judicial Conference adopted a resolution to continue to consider "discovery problems arising in multiple litigation with common witnesses and exhibits so as to develop ... general principles and guidelines including any recommendations for statutory change." Thereafter, according to legislative history, the Judicial Conference requested legislation to authorize transfer and consolidation of cases; the Department of Justice and eventually members of the American Bar Association supported the proposal.

In 1968, Congress responded with the multidistrict litigation statute ("MDL"), which authorized a single judge to preside, during the pretrial phase, in the mandatory consolidation of cases pending in federal courts throughout the country. MDL is thus a statutorily-based (rather than rule-based) mechanism for consolidation of lawsuits. MDL is a possibility when "civil actions involving one or more common questions of fact are pending in different districts." The other statutory criteria are that the transfer must be "for the convenience of the parties and witnesses" and must "promote the just and efficient conduct of such actions." Obviously, these criteria enable many categories of cases to be subject to MDL treatment, and MDL records indicate that cases that have been consolidated pursuant to section 1407 include antitrust, air disasters, contracts, common disasters, copyright and patents, employment, and trademark.

Either by motion of the court or of the parties, cases that are candidates for consolidation are sent to "the panel" on MDL. That panel consists of seven circuit and district judges appointed by the Chief Justice of the United States. The panel either decides to authorize the cases for MDL treatment and to designate a judge to handle them or to decline to permit MDL treatment. No direct appeal of that decision is possible; under the statute, "review of any order of the panel" is available only "by extraordinary writ" pursuant to the provisions of the All Writs Act, and "[t]here shall be no appeal or review of an order of the panel denying a motion to transfer for consolidated or coordinated proceedings." After cases have been transferred, subsequently filed cases (called "tag-along actions" that involve "common questions of fact" with cases already transferred) can also be sent to the designated transferee judge. The MDL statute also authorizes the panel to promulgate rules "not inconsistent with Acts of Congress and the Federal Rules of Civil Procedure," and thereby permits nationwide federal procedural rulemaking outside the Rules Enabling Act process.

Under section 1407 [of 28 United States Code], cases in any federal district court can be transferred but are only consolidated "pretrial," for decision of issues such as summary judgment, discovery, and the like. Formally, cases are supposed to be "remanded" to the originating courts at the conclusion of the "pretrial proceedings." However, transferee judges have upon occasion used either the parties' consent or the general change of venue statute to transfer the cases to themselves for "subsequent proceedings"—that is, trial. Further, many cases are disposed of by the transferee judge during the "pretrial" process. As one member of the MDL panel stated in 1977, "[i]n point of fact, slightly less than five percent of the actions transferred by the Panel have been remanded. Most actions are terminated either in the transferee district (often by settlement) or are transferred by the transferee judge to the transferee district or to another district for trial pursuant to sections 1404(a) or 1406 [of 28 United States Code]." Further, several commentators (judges included) have criticized the MDL statute for being too limited; some urge expanding the reach of MDL—to include, officially, the transfer of cases for trial as well as for pretrial proceedings.

Chapter 9

FINALITY AND PRECLUSION

I. INTRODUCTION

Finality is an important value for any system of civil procedure, and this chapter will examine how different legal systems balance the need for bringing litigation to an end with competing concerns of justice and fairness for the individual litigants. As we will see, a legal system's approach to finality often reflects other aspects of its procedural framework. For example, a liberal approach to the joining of claims and parties, as in the United States, yields a relatively strict approach to relitigation and precludes assertion of claims or issues that could have been brought in the original action, whereas a system such as Germany, where filing fees depend on the amount of the claim asserted, takes a more relaxed approach to a second action for a related claim or additional damages.

Almost all judicial systems recognize certain exceptions to the finality principle. For example, most systems have special procedures for setting aside default judgments.[1] Also, judgments rendered by a court without authority over the matter may be subject to collateral challenge in some systems.[2] Finally, judicial systems usually provide for mechanisms to reopen a contested judgment even after all appellate measures have been exhausted if there were serious defects in the proceedings such as injustice, corruption, or fraud. For example, in the federal courts in the United States, Rule 60(b) of the Federal Rules of Civil Procedure provides for a motion for relief from a final judgment for such things as mistake or neglect, newly discovered evidence not previously discoverable, and fraud or misrepresentation. The German Code of Civil Proce-

---

1. In the United States, see Rule 55 of the Federal Rules of Civil Procedure; in Germany, see ZPO §§ 339–342, translated in German Commercial Code and Code of Civil Procedure in English 280–281 (Charles E. Stewart trans., 2001). For a more extensive discussion of the German procedure, see Peter L. Murray and Rolf

Stürner, German Civil Justice 317–322 (2004) (hereinafter, Murray and Stürner).

2. In the United States, collateral attack for lack of subject matter jurisdiction is generally permitted. See Robert C. Casad and Kevin M. Clermont, 250–251 (2001). By contrast, lack of subject matter jurisdiction is not a permissible basis for a collateral

dure (ZPO) § 578 provides for the reopening of a trial concluded by a final judgment through an action for annulment (*nichtigkeitsklage*) (§ 579) or an action for restitution (*restitutionsklage*) (§ 580). The restitution route seems a close counterpart to U.S. Federal Rule 60(b); among the grounds for reopening an earlier judgment are the use of false documents, the making of false statements under oath by the opposing party, the giving of false testimony by a witness or expert, and the emergence of newly discovered evidence. Another basis for reopening a judgment in Germany is a showing of criminal conduct by a party or judge in connection with the judgment if there has been a sentence by a criminal court in that regard. By contrast, the German action for annulment addresses defects in the structural aspects of the proceeding such as incorrect composition of the court, failure of required representation of a party, or lack of impartiality of the judge. Certain defects can be raised only if the party could not have raised them on appeal and in some situations, the party will have to show that the defect actually affected the judgment.[3]

The particular mechanisms described above represent exceptions to a more basic doctrine of finality embraced by almost all judicial systems. That doctrine is *res judicata* or preclusion, and it not only prohibits a challenge to the final judgment of a court but also prevents repeated litigation of matters already brought and determined in a prior litigation. This chapter focuses on the various ways that preclusion is implemented in different judicial systems.

The Latin term *res judicata* (literally translated as "the thing adjudged") is used to refer to the principle that matters adjudicated and resulting in a conclusive judgment should not be relitigated, and the principle is adopted in most judicial systems. It finds expression in two Latin maxims: (1) *Interest rei publicae ut sit finis litium* ("it is in the public interest that there should be an end of litigation") and (2) *Nemo debet bis vexari pro una et eadem causa* ("no one should be proceeded against twice for the same cause").[4] Res judicata has both a positive and negative effect. The positive effect is that the judgment is final and binding between the parties and should be implemented, subject to any available appeal or challenge. The negative effect is that the matter of the judgment cannot be relitigated a second time.

Judicial systems use a variety of terminologies to refer to various aspects of res judicata. In the United States, the term res judicata typically encompasses two related doctrines: claim preclusion and issue preclusion. In England, the terms are cause of action estoppel and issue estoppel. Although similar in nature and ultimately serving the same objective of furthering finality of litigation, claim preclusion (cause of

---

attack in Germany. See Murray and Stürner, supra note 1, 149.

3. For a general discussion of these German procedures for a reopening civil judgment, see Murray and Stürner, supra note 1, at 362–365.

4. See International Law Association (ILA), Committee on International Com-

mercial Arbitration, Interim Report: "*Res judicata*" and Arbitration (Berlin Conference 2004), available at http://www.ila-hq.org/pdf/Int% 20Commercial% 20Arbitration/Report% 202004.pdf (Site last visited Aug. 20, 2007).

action estoppel) and issue preclusion (issue estoppel) have distinct defining characteristics. Claim preclusion forbids the relitigation of the same "claims" in a subsequent proceeding. In the United States, this kind of preclusion covers not only the particular claim or claims that were raised and decided in a first action but also encompasses any and all claims that arose out of the same transaction or series of transactions that comprised the first action and could have been brought as part of that initial action. As we will see, this broad dimension of claim preclusion—claims that *should have been brought*—is not necessarily part of preclusion doctrine in other countries.

In addition, the common law countries, and in particular the United States, also embrace a second aspect of res judicata/preclusion—and that is the doctrine of issue preclusion (referred to as collateral estoppel in the United States and issue estoppel in England). Issue preclusion operates to prevent parties from relitigating specific issues that were actually litigated and decided against them, even when the claims asserted in the second proceeding are different from those raised in the first proceeding. In some modern applications of the doctrine, issue preclusion may be extended to bind a party to a finding made against him even when asserted by someone who was not a party to the first action. Issue preclusion is generally not part of res judicata principles in civil law countries, although we will see that different legal systems often incorporate some elements of the doctrine without precisely identifying it as such.

This Chapter examines how these principles of claim and issue preclusion operate in different countries and highlights some of the differences. As you read through the materials, think about whether there are particular characteristics of a judicial system that explain that system's approach to preclusion. For example, does the scope of preclusion turn on whether the proceedings are party or court driven? Does the availability of access to information during the proceedings impact on how broadly preclusion is defined? Does a system's imposition of burdens on the public, such as the use of juries in the United States, affect how a system might weigh the costs of multiple litigation as against the private interests of the parties who might eschew consolidation? And finally, are there alternative mechanisms within a particular judicial system that offer an adequate substitute to formal preclusion in terms of achieving similar objectives?

As noted above, courts in the United States adopt both claim and issue preclusion to prevent relitigation of matters decided in an initial action. Claim preclusion prevents further litigation of claims that were *or could have been* raised and conclusively adjudicated, where the parties to both proceedings are the same. The doctrine of privity may extend the concept of who is considered a party to the litigation. Issue preclusion bars relitigation of specific issues that were determined in another case, even when a new and different claim—not barred by claim preclusion—is being asserted in the second action. In some cases, issue preclusion may be asserted against a party in an action brought by someone who was not a party to the initial action. In contrast, in civil law countries, claim preclusion is significantly narrower than in the United States—it serves only to prevent relitigation of those claims actually submitted for determination and does not operate in a transactional fashion to bar claims arising out of the same set of facts that were not but could have been raised. Further, the concept of issue preclusion as understood in common law countries is not recognized in most civil law countries.[5] Also, in civil law jurisdictions, preclusion generally extends only to parties to the litigation, and privity concepts tend to be limited and expressly identified in civil and procedural codes.[6] More detailed descriptions as set forth below highlight the approaches to preclusion in a number of different countries.

II. PRECLUSION DOCTRINE AS APPLIED BY NATIONAL COURTS

THE UNITED STATES

Claim preclusion doctrine in the United States is applied so as to further three principal policies: (1) lending credence to the judicial authority of the court or tribunal that rendered the judgment, (2) providing litigants with a sense of closure and security that they will not need to revisit claims that have already been decided, and (3) promoting efficient use of judicial resources. Where a plaintiff does not prevail on a claim asserted, the judgment against that plaintiff is said to act as a "bar"[7] to bringing a second claim. On the other hand, where a plaintiff prevails on a claim but seeks to relitigate the same claim in an attempt to obtain a more favorable remedy, any such claim is regarded as having "merged"[8] with the initial judgment.

The scope of the doctrine of claim preclusion is thus dependent upon the definition of "same claim." The Restatement (Second) of Judgments provides the following, with respect to the dimensions of a claim for purposes of merger or bar:

> § 24. Dimensions Of "Claim" For Purposes Of Merger Or Bar— General Rule Concerning "Splitting"
>
> (1) When a valid and final judgment rendered in an action extinguishes the plaintiff's claim pursuant to the rules of merger or bar

---

5. See Robert C. Casad, Issue Preclusion and Foreign Country Judgments: Whose Law?, 70 Ia. L. Rev. 53 (1984).

6. See Stavros Breoulakis, The Effect of an Arbitral Award and Third Parties in International Arbitration: Res Judicata Revisited, 16 Am. Rev. Int'l Arb. 177, 209 n. 25 (2005) (identifying German Code of Civil Procedure (ZPO) §§ 326–327).

7. The Restatement (Second) of Judgments, § 19 provides, with respect to bar: "A valid and final personal judgment rendered in favor of the defendant bars another action by the plaintiff on the same claim."

8. The Restatement (Second) of Judgments, § 18 provides, with respect to merger that: "(1) The plaintiff cannot thereafter maintain an action on the original claim or any part thereof, although he may be able to maintain an action upon the judgment; and (2) In an action upon the judgment, the defendant cannot avail himself of defenses he might have interposed, or did interpose, in the first action."

(see §§ 18, 19), the claim extinguished includes all rights of the plaintiff to remedies against the defendant with respect to all or any part of the transaction, or series of connected transactions, out of which the action arose.

(2) What factual grouping constitutes a "transaction", and what groupings constitute a "series", are to be determined pragmatically, giving weight to such considerations as whether the facts are related in time, space, origin, or motivation, whether they form a convenient trial unit, and whether their treatment as a unit conforms to the parties' expectations or business understanding or usage.

The Restatement definition of "same claim" represents a quite expansive view of claim preclusion and has been adopted in a majority of the states of the United States; however, some jurisdictions in the United States continue to follow a more restrictive approach. The Restatement position reflects the expanded options that a party has to join claims and arguments in a single proceeding and in effect imposes a rule of compulsory joinder in the first proceeding by requiring parties to join claims that they "could have brought" in the first proceeding or face the risk of forever losing the right to bring those claims. However, the Restatement also offers a number of exceptions[9] to its general rule of claim splitting, such as situations where the parties or the court have agreed that splitting is appropriate, or where the plaintiff was unable to rely on a certain theory or seek a certain remedy due to jurisdictional limitations, or where specific statutory or constitutional schemes or substantive policies in a particular area contemplate multiple actions. The Restatement position also does not impose preclusion where the party against whom preclusion is asserted was a defendant in the first proceeding and was not required by rule to assert a claim as a compulsory counterclaim.[10]

As regards issue preclusion in courts in the United States, the Restatement (Second) of Judgments formulates the definition and requirements as follows:

§ 27.   Issue Preclusion—General Rule

When an issue of fact or law is actually litigated and determined by a valid and final judgment, and the determination is essential to the judgment, the determination is conclusive in a subsequent action between the parties, whether on the same or a different claim.

Note the more rigorous requirements for issue preclusion than for claim preclusion. In addition, there are numerous exceptions to issue preclusion, many of which leave room for broad exercises of discretion by the court.

§ 28.   Exceptions to the General Rule of Issue Preclusion

Although an issue is actually litigated and determined by a valid and final judgment, and the determination is essential to the judgment,

9. See Restatement (Second) of Judgments § 26.

10. See id. § 22.

relitigation of the issue in a subsequent action between the parties is not precluded in the following circumstances:

(1) The party against whom preclusion is sought could not, as a matter of law, have obtained review of the judgment in the initial action; or

(2) The issue is one of law and (a) the two actions involve claims that are substantially unrelated, or (b) a new determination is warranted in order to take account of an intervening change in the applicable legal context or otherwise to avoid inequitable administration of the laws; or

(3) A new determination of the issue is warranted by differences in the quality or extensiveness of the procedures followed in the two courts or by factors relating to the allocation of jurisdiction between them; or

(4) The party against whom preclusion is sought had a significantly heavier burden of persuasion with respect to the issue in the initial action than in the subsequent action; the burden has shifted to his adversary; or the adversary has a significantly heavier burden than he had in the first action; or

(5) There is a clear and convincing need for a new determination of the issue (a) because of the potential adverse impact of the determination on the public interest or the interests of persons not themselves parties in the initial action, (b) because it was not sufficiently foreseeable at the time of the initial action that the issue would arise in the context of a subsequent action, or (c) because the party sought to be precluded, as a result of the conduct of his adversary or other special circumstances, did not have an adequate opportunity or incentive to obtain a full and fair adjudication in the initial action.

One aspect of issue preclusion in the United States that is quite different from doctrines of preclusion elsewhere is its extension to permit a non-party to a prior action to claim the benefit of issue preclusion with respect to determinations made in the prior proceeding—known as non-mutual issue preclusion. The more compelling context for the application of non-mutual issue preclusion is when preclusion is asserted by a party in a defensive posture—that is, where a party in the second action is attempting to use a finding made against a party in the first action to block the assertion of allegations in support of a claim now being made by that party who lost on that issue in litigation against a different party. For example, non-mutual defensive issue preclusion has been used to prevent a second action for alleged patent infringement by a plaintiff patent holder who brought a prior infringement action against a different infringer and lost on the ground that the patent was invalid.[11] Note that the impact of non-mutual issue preclusion

11. Blonder-Tongue Laboratories, Inc. v. University of Illinois Foundation, 402 U.S. 313 (1971).

in this situation is to encourage a party to join all possible parties in the action because the application of preclusion to any common issues will discourage—indeed prevent—seriatim actions against possible defendants. Issue preclusion may also be used offensively by a non-party to the prior action in order to establish a particular fact against an adversary who has lost on the same issue in prior litigation with a different party. For example, if a defendant's negligence with respect to the operation of a motor vehicle is established in an action brought by the driver of another car, the defendant could not relitigate the issue of negligence in an action brought by a passenger in the car. The use of preclusion in this context raises a concern that a person will intentionally refrain from joining or participating in a case in order to "wait and see" what the results of litigation between others will be. If a potential adversary loses, the would-be plaintiff can then sue and take advantage of that finding to help establish his case, but if the adversary wins, the potential plaintiff is not bound by that finding and can evaluate whether or not to bring his own suit. Although the use of non-mutual offensive issue preclusion has been approved by the Supreme Court,[12] both the Supreme Court and the Restatement have indicated that its application will depend upon consideration of a number of factors[13] and will be determined on a case-by-case basis.

Notes and Comments

The United States is in many ways unique with respect to depth and breadth of its application of preclusion principles to prevent further litigation of claims and issues. Contrast the above discussion of the principles as applied in the United States with the discussion of the English approach excerpted below.

ENGLAND

The underlying philosophy of the principle of res judicata as applied in England is similar to that of the United States, but the terminology and scope are slightly different.[14] What in the United States is known as "claim preclusion" is actually two separate doctrines in England. "Merger" or "former recovery" in English law prevents reassertion of the same claim brought by a successful party who now seeks further relief for the same cause, thus preventing a double recovery—a doctrine similar to the "merger" aspect of claim preclusion in the United States. "Cause of action estoppel" prevents assertion of a claim in contradiction of a prior judgment—similar to the concept of "bar" in the United States. (In some accounts, see the Zuckerman excerpt below, "cause of action estoppel" may be used to refer to both merger and bar). "Issue estoppel" precludes contradiction of issues determined in a previous action and corresponds to American issue preclusion. These doctrines

12. Parklane Hosiery Co., Inc. v. Shore, 439 U.S. 322 (1979).

13. See Restatement (Second) of Judgments § 29.

14. For a summary and explanation of the terminology, see Peter Barnett, Res Judicata, Estoppel, and Foreign Judgments 8–11 (2001).

apply only to preclude relitigation of either the same cause or the same issues between the same parties. But an additional doctrine—abuse of process—is used to supplement the doctrines of merger, cause of action estoppel and issue estoppel, and expands what might be viewed as relatively narrow principles of res judicata. "Abuse of process" may be invoked to prevent a party from proceeding on a claim that could have been part of a prior proceeding, or it may be used to prevent parties other than those to the original proceedings from asserting claims or issues previously decided.

Zuckerman on Civil Procedure: Principles of Practice 931–944 (2nd ed. 2006).

Res Judicata and Abuse of Process—Introduction

Rules and principles for avoiding re-litigation—introduction

24.48   The principle of finality demands that a judgment disposing of a dispute should leave no room for further litigation of the same subject matter.* * * However, although this idea is straightforward, its practical manifestations are far from simple, not least because English law employs three different doctrines for implementing it. These doctrines are neither sharply differentiated from each other nor clearly identified by a generally accepted terminology. The first of these is the doctrine of *res judicata*, which implies that once "the res—the thing actually or directly in dispute—has been already adjudicated upon, ... by a competent court, it cannot be litigated again". It means that a decision of a court of competent jurisdiction gives rise to *estoppel per rem judicatam* so that the parties to the proceedings are bound by it and estopped from disputing it in future proceedings. This general doctrine of estoppel per rem judicatum consists of two distinct rules known as *cause of action estoppel* and *issue estoppel*. Cause of action estoppel implies that once a cause of action has been adjudicated, the parties to the proceedings are estopped from asserting or denying (as the case may be) that particular cause in any subsequent proceedings to which they are also parties. Cause of action estoppel is connected with the idea that a cause of action merges with the judgment given in the proceedings, so that no cause is left to pursue thereafter. The related doctrine of issue estoppel holds that parties to legal proceedings are bound by the court's findings on discrete issues that were essential to the final resolution of the proceedings in which the findings were made. Accordingly, if in order to dispose of the dispute the court has determined particular essential issues of fact or law (such as whether an alleged event occurred or the meaning of a contract term), the parties will not be allowed to advance arguments that are inconsistent with those findings in any later proceedings between themselves, even if such later proceedings are concerned with an entirely different cause of action.

* * *

24.50   The doctrine of res judicata is party relative in both its branches. It applies only to attempts to re-litigate the same cause or the same issues between the same parties. It does not impose restrictions on strangers nor does it allow strangers to invoke court findings made in proceedings between others. * * * A party is not able to hold a non-party bound by the results of proceedings in which the non-party could not participate, since this would involve a denial of the right to be heard. * * * There is also a perfectly good reason why in proceedings against strangers a party should be free to dispute findings made against him in earlier proceedings. The effort that a party invests in litigation is normally relative to the context of the dispute, which will include such factors as its value, its importance to the party, and what the party can afford at the time. A person litigating on the small claims track is unlikely to invest anything like the same resources that he would invest if the same issue arose in a high value claim on the multi-track. It would therefore be unjust to automatically hold a party bound by legal findings beyond the immediate context of the particular dispute in which the findings were made.

24.51   It does not, however, follow that from the rule that strangers should not always be free to rely on findings made in proceedings to which they were not parties that it is never just to allow a stranger to rely on such findings. There will be situations where justice demands that even a stranger should be able to prevent a party from challenging a finding made against that party. There may even be circumstances in which it would be justified to hold a stranger bound by court findings that were made in proceedings to which he was not strictly a party. Finally, justice may require that a party should not only be prevented from re-litigating matters that the court has decided but also from litigating issues that the court never decided because these issues should have been placed before the court in the course of some earlier proceedings. Put differently, the public interest in finality of litigation * * * has implications that are considerably wider than the doctrine of res judicata. English law deals with such situations not by means of rules but through the court's inherent jurisdiction to prevent abuse of process. This essentially discretionary jurisdiction may be invoked to prevent litigation of matters that do not fall under cause of action estoppel or issue estoppel, if such litigation would be contrary to the public interest. The abuse of process jurisdiction is not confined by strict rules or categories but is left flexible in order to enable the court to reach the conclusion that justice and public policy dictate in the particular circumstances of the case.

* * *

RES JUDICATA

Cause of action estoppel

* * *

24.65 Cause of action estoppel arises when the cause of action in later proceedings is identical to that prosecuted in earlier proceedings. An identical cause of action cannot be advanced again even in order to claim a new relief which could not have been claimed in the original proceedings. For example, a claimant, who has recovered damages against builders for breach of warranty to erect a sound structure, cannot subsequently seek damages in respect of defects that emerge after the trial as a result of the same breach. The bar to advancing an identical cause of action is absolute. Neither the discovery of new evidence that could not have been known before, nor a change in the law since the first decision, can justify reopening an adjudicated cause of action. The only way of reviving the cause of action is by having the original judgment set aside on grounds of fraud.

Issue Estoppel

The general rule

24.66 Issue estoppel arises from the determination of discrete issues in the course of civil proceedings. A party is not entitled to advance an argument of fact or of law which conflicts with a court determination of the same issue in earlier proceedings between the same parties.* * *

24.67 Issue estoppel can arise only with respect to issues that a court has actually addressed and determined, and only if the issues were essential to the disposition of the cause in question. Two related reasons justify excluding collateral findings (i.e., findings that would not have made a difference to the outcome of the proceedings) from the application of the issue estoppel rule. It would be unfair to hold parties bound by decisions on matters that they were not obliged to litigate and which, therefore, they may have chosen not to prosecute thoroughly. Further, if issue estoppel extended to inessential issues, parties would feel obliged to invest time and effort in pursuing unimportant issues, which could result distracting attention from the crucial issues, in delaying the disposition of the dispute and in increasing costs.

* * *

Circumstances in which earlier findings may be challenged

24.69 Unlike cause of action estoppel, which holds that once adjudicated a cause of action cannot be revived, issue estoppel may be overcome in certain situations. It has been said that the court may allow a party to challenge an earlier finding whenever the injustice of not allowing the matter to be re-litigated outweighs the hardship to the opponent who is made to lose the benefit of the earlier findings. However, the discretion to allow a party to challenge earlier findings is normally exercised only in two types of situation. The first concerns cases where fresh evidence has come to light subsequent to the judgment in which the findings were made, provided that it could not have been obtained at the earlier proceedings and that it clearly and reliably disproves the earlier finding. The second type of situation in which issue estoppel may be overcome consists of cases where there has been a material change in the law since the findings were made. For example, a party may be allowed to raise an issue concerning the construction of a standard rent review clause if the judicial interpretation of the clause has changed, thereby rendering an earlier interpretation plainly wrong.

General res judicata rules

Judgments bind parties and their privies

24.70 Res judicata applies to privies of the original parties as if they had been parties to the litigation. Accordingly, privies are bound by cause of action estoppel and by issue estoppel and may assert it against any other parties or their privies. Broadly speaking, a privy is a successor in title of an original party. According to Spencer Bower and Turner, privies 'include any person who succeeds to the rights or liabilities of the party upon his death or insolvency or who is otherwise identified with his or her estate or interest; but it is essential that he who is later held to be held estopped must have had some kind of interest in the previous litigation or its subject matter'.* * * The concept of privity is sometimes used more widely. It has been held, for example, that a person who had not been a party to the second action would nevertheless be bound by a finding in that action, because of privity in interest between himself and the other defendants, provided that he had been aware of the proceedings and would have been entitled to be joined in them but had decided without explanation not to apply to be so joined. It is suggested, however, that such situations are better dealt with under the abuse of process jurisdiction.

Res judicata only arises from final judgments

24.71 Only decisions that are final and conclusive of the cause pleaded by the claimant give rise to estoppel per rem judicatam. A decision is final in this sense if it conclusively (as distinguished from provisionally) disposes of the matter. It is often said that in order to give rise to res judicata a decision must be on the merits. But this does not imply that the decision must be given after court determination of the disputed issues on the basis of evidence or argument. All that the expression implies is a final decision that disposes of the matter, other than on purely procedural grounds. Hence, a default judgment is final and conclusive for the purpose of cause of action estoppel even if [it] does not result from a consideration of the merits.* * *

24.72 Res judicata does not arise where litigation is brought to an end without any judgment at all. There is no res judicata where an action has been discontinued, withdrawn, struck out for non-conformity with rules or court orders, * * *.

24.73 While a final and conclusive judgment is a condition precedent for cause of action estoppel and issue estoppel, it is not necessarily so in connection with abuse of process estoppel. This latter jurisdiction is broad enough to allow the court to decide that the raising of a particular issue or cause is an abuse of process notwithstanding that it was not determined by a final judgment on the merits.* * *

ABUSE OF PROCESS ESTOPPEL

The nature of the jurisdiction

24.78   The court may use its general inherent jurisdiction to prevent litigation that amounts to abuse of process in order to stop a party from raising an issue which was, or could have been, determined in earlier civil proceedings notwithstanding that it is not caught by the rules of res judicata. This discretionary jurisdiction is used to address two different situations. The first is concerned with cases where a party seeks to raise a cause of action or an issue which, although not raised in earlier proceedings between the same parties, could have been raised in those proceedings. The second situation is concerned with cases where the findings made in earlier proceedings are relied upon by, or against, a person who was not a party to those proceedings. Since the jurisdiction is discretionary the court must consider all the relevant factors and reach a conclusion that is just in the particular circumstances of the case.

Notes and Comments

In the final analysis, it appears that the English and American interpretations and applications of preclusion principles are quite similar. Although the English doctrines of cause of action estoppel and issue estoppel are framed more narrowly, English courts do address many of the same concerns reflected in preclusion doctrine as applied in the United States through the related "abuse of process" doctrine. Does it make a difference whether preclusion principles are understood as those of res judicata or abuse of process? Consider the comments of one critic, Professor Garry Watson,[15] who in the context of issue preclusion prefers the formal approach of non-mutuality to the "abuse of process" rationale adopted by English and Canadian courts:

> * * *[The] desire to prevent duplicative litigation involving one common party is based simply on the fact that the same issue has been previously determined against the common party by an earlier court, and does not turn on any additional factors or behavior requiring the invocation of "abuse of process". What we are seeking to do is to prevent relitigation, in such circumstances, by the application of estoppel arising from an earlier judgment. * * * Attempting to deal with the problem by using the vague concept of "abuse of process" adds nothing, except confusion, and it should not be used given that we already have a doctrine—issue estoppel—specifically designed to deal with the problem. Moreover, replacing "abuse of process" with non-mutual issue estoppel locates the solution within the appropriate doctrinal and policy context. This is

---

15. Garry D. Watson, Issue Estoppel, Abuse of Process and Repetitive Litigation: The Death of Mutuality, in International Perspectives on Civil Justice 179, 215–216 (I.R. Scott, ed., 1990).

important in itself and has the added advantage of exposing us to the experience of United States courts with this doctrine.

Courts have likely been attracted to the discretionary doctrine of "abuse of process" because of the (quite accurate) perception that, in this area, discretion is important to ensure that preclusion does not operate unfairly. But discretion is also an essential part of the doctrine of non-mutual issue estoppel. * * *

Courts should abandon abuse of process, and the requirement of mutuality, in favour of non-mutual preclusion. However, in adopting this approach, particular care must be taken to ensure that its underlying policies, fairness, and judicial efficiency, are fulfilled. In particular, the "option effect" inherent in offensive non-mutual preclusion must be disarmed and this may be done through "second case strategies" designed to force or encourage all claimants to assert their claims in the first action.* * *

GERMANY

In most civil law countries, the principles of res judicata applied in domestic legal proceedings are codified. For example, in Germany, the basic principle is found in ZPO § 322(1) which provides: "Judgments have legal force only to such extent as they decide the demand raised by the complaint or counterclaim."[16] This quite formalistic and narrow principle seems to offer a stark contrast to the approach of the common law in both England and the United States. Not only does this principle of German res judicata seem to exclude any doctrine of issue preclusion or issue estoppel, it appears substantially more restrictive than even the narrow type of claim preclusion accepted in England. German law attempts to draw a distinction between the dispositive portion of the judgment and the underlying conclusions of fact and law, and to extend preclusion only to the former.[17] As we will see in the excerpt below, however, the underlying conclusions of fact and law do play some role in delineating the judgment's binding effects, and the German courts necessarily examine the pleadings and case file to determine what the judgment may entail.

Peter L. Murray and Rolf Stürner, German Civil Justice 355–361 (2004).

F. *Res Adjudicata* Effect of Judgments

A German judgment which is not subject to further appeal (*formelle Rechtskraft*) stands as the conclusive adjudication of the claims submitted for adjudication and can be raised as a defense to any later effort by either party to submit the same claims for adjudication in another proceeding. That judgment must also be followed in any later proceeding

---

16. German Commercial Code and Code of Civil Procedure in English 275 (Charles E. Stewart trans., 2001).

17. See Arthur T. von Mehren and Donald T. Trautman, Recognition of Foreign Adjudications: A Survey and A Suggested Approach, 81 Harv. L. Rev. 1601, 1675 (1968).

in which the same claims constitute a material element of the matter in dispute. The German doctrine of *res adjudicata* (*materielle Rechtskraft*) serves to guarantee certainty in litigation and to preclude repeated litigation of matters already litigated and decided.

1. Kinds of Judgments Entitled to Binding Effect

In general, only judgments (*Urteile*) not subject to further appeal are entitled to *res adjudicata* effect so far as future legal proceedings are concerned.* * *

2. Scope of Res Adjudicata Effect

The scope of *res adjudicata* effect of a civil judgment is defined by the parties to the litigation and the formal claims (*Ansprüche*) which were submitted to the court for decision. The basic rule is that a judgment binds the parties and their successors in interest with respect to the subject matter of the claims actually asserted and decided. As a rule, non-parties are not bound. Nor are the parties themselves bound with respect to actual or potential claims not actually submitted for adjudication.

a. As Defined by Claims for Relief

The binding effect of a judgment is limited to the "subject matter of the controversy" (*Streitgegenstand*) upon which it was issued. The subject matter of the controversy is in turn defined by the actual claims (*Ansprüche*) asserted by the respective parties and explicitly or implicitly decided by the court.[18]

Thus if a plaintiff sought damages for injuries sustained from a defective consumer product, the final judgment issued in the litigation would be *res adjudicata* only to the extent of the claims (*Ansprüche*) at issue. It would not necessarily cover all claims related to the product, or to injuries received from it. If the plaintiff's claim were limited to a claim for personal injury, an adverse judgment on that claim would not preclude the same party from suing the same defendant for property damage sustained in the same event. Binding effect extends only to claims which were actually at issue, not those which could have been raised or which may have arisen out of the same transaction or occurrence. German civil procedure does not recognize the concept of claim preclusion in the broad sense as is the case in common law countries.

So, for example, if a creditor claimed to be owed 30,000 Euro by a debtor, the creditor could file a partial suit (*Teilklage*) for any portion of the total claim. The judgment rendered would be neither preclusive or conclusive on a subsequent suit for a further part of the unpaid balance of the total claim.

By the same token, the legal theory on which the claim was decided is immaterial. The legal grounds (*Entscheidungsgründe*) for a decision

---

18. ZPO § 322(1): "Judgments are capable of binding effect only to the extent that a claim raised by the complaint or a counterclaim has been decided." [footnote 252 in original].

are not entitled to any binding or limiting effect. If the plaintiff sued for personal injuries arising from medical malpractice based on a tort theory, the judgment in that case would bar a claim for breach of contract asserting the same claims for relief, but on a different legal theory. And a court judgment deciding a claim on a different legal theory than that originally suggested by the plaintiff would prevent relitigation of the actual claims adjudicated based on any legal theory.

When the issue of *res adjudicata* is raised, the court is required to examine and compare not only the formal claims for relief, but also the factual content of the current claim with that of the decided case in order to determine whether they are in fact the same claim. A difference in the operative facts can be sufficient to save the second case from dismissal. An example would be a case in which a purchaser of goods paid for them with a check and then stopped payment on the check. An adverse judgment on the seller's claim based on the check would not necessarily bar a second claim, identical in amount, to recover the purchase price of the goods under the sales contract, since the factual bases of the two claims are not the same. The check claim would be based on issuance and delivery of the check while the contract claim would be founded on conclusion and performance of the contract.

As a rule German law does not recognize issue preclusion short of entire claims. Dismissal of a claim for restoration of converted property on the ground that the plaintiff had failed to prove ownership would not prejudice the plaintiff in a later suit for damages based on the same event. By the same token, a judgment for the plaintiff in an action for restoration of converted property, would not preclude the defendant from challenging the plaintiff's title again in a later action for damages to the converted property. Only a final declaratory judgment directly deciding on the ownership will be given *res judicata* effect to preclude a party from litigating this issue in a later action.

When the defendant's response raises matters of set-off and the court enters a judgment determining the set-off, the judgment will be given *res judicata* effect with respect to the claim pleaded as a set-off against the defendant's obligation. This special form of *res judicata* effect may be considered as an exception from the concept of non-recognition of issue preclusion in German civil procedure.

b. *Parties Bound*

A judgment is *res adjudicata* only between the parties to the litigation and those persons claiming by, through or under those parties. Third parties who claim by, through or under parties to the litigation are bound by the judgment and cannot relitigate the matter in controversy.* * *

Because a judgment is only *res judicata* between the parties to litigation and has no issue-preclusive effect, it does not operate as collateral estoppel to prevent a party to the case from relitigating the same issue of law or fact against other parties in other cases. Thus, if a passenger recovers against her driver for negligence in an automobile accident case, that judgment and its underlying finding of the driver's negligence will not bind the driver in a case brought by the driver of the other car, or even by another passenger in his own car.

3. Effect of the Prior Judgment

A prior judgment may prevent a party from raising the same claim in a future proceeding, or may prejudge the decision in a later action. In the first sense the prior judgment is treated as a barrier to the future claim. In the second the prior judgment serves as a prejudgment of a material element of the second action.

If the subject matter of a newly filed complaint is the same as that of a prior case concluded by final judgment, the final judgment in the former case is a "negative pre-requisite to suit" (*negative Prozessvoraussetzung*) in the new case. The prior judgment may be raised by the opposing party. The court is also required to consider on its own motion any prior judgments of which it has knowledge. Once noticed, the prior judgment makes the subsequent unallowable (*unzulässig*) and requires dismissal.

In some cases the prior judgment establishes beyond contest an element of a second claim. For instance, a declaratory judgment of ownership of real estate or personal property may be pled as the legal basis for a complaint between the same parties seeking possession of the real estate or thing or for reimbursement for damage to the premises or thing in question. This does not mean that there is issue preclusion in Germany. Only a final judgment which directly establishes a material element of the second claim will be given this *res adjudicata* effect. * * *

A judgment is binding not only on the party which commenced the case, but also on the defendant. So, for instance, a defendant who was adjudged liable to the plaintiff in a case for damages may not bring his own action against the plaintiff seeking a declaratory judgment of non-liability or any limitation of liability directly inconsistent with the prior judgment.

Notes and Comments

Are there legal and/or cultural explanations for the more restrictive approach to preclusion taken in Germany? Consider the following explanations offered by Arthur von Mehren and Donald Trautman in their extensively-cited 1968 article.[19] They posit that to "accord extensive binding effects to a judgment * * * would be inconsistent with the fundamental philosophy of the entire German proceeding, a philosophy of individualism and liberalism which gives the parties great control over the dimensions and conduct of litigation". Given some of the recent reforms in German Civil Procedure, is that still an accurate characterization of the German legal

19. von Mehren and Trautman, supra note 17, at 1675.

system? *Are there more particular aspects of German civil procedure that help explain Germany's approach to preclusion?* Professors von Mehren and Trautman point out that the German system of setting counsel and court fees on the basis of a percentage of the value actually placed in controversy encourage and necessitate claim-splitting. They argue that rules such as these are an expression of German procedural bias in favor of party control over the dimensions and conduct of litigation.

JAPAN

You will recall that Japan's Code of Civil Procedure was initially modeled after the German Code, but in the post-war period many reforms have been influenced by American procedure.[20] The principal provision of the Japanese Code (CCP Art. 114)[21] provides for res judicata effect only to "matters contained in the formal disposition". This and other provisions of the Japanese Code, excerpted below, are very much like those in the German Code, but commentators have suggested that the courts in Japan have interpreted the provisions to embrace broader concepts of preclusion, including common law issue preclusion.[22]

Japanese Code of Civil Procedure*

Article 114. (*Scope of effect of Res judicata*)

1. A judgment that has become final and binding has the effect of *res judicata* only concerning the matters contained in the formal disposition.

2. An adjudication upon the validity or invalidity of a claim asserted for set-off has the effect of res judicata with respect to the amount pleaded with regard to such set-off.

Article 115. (*Scope of persons bound by final and binding judgment, etc.*)

---

20. See generally Carl F. Goodman, The Rule of Law in Japan 230–267 (2003); Makoto Itoh, Civil Procedure Law, 26 Law in Japan 66–69 (2000); Takeshi Kojima, Japanese Civil Procedure in Comparative Law Perspective, 46 Kan. L. Rev. 687, 693–694 (1998).

21. Prior to the 1996 Code, CCP Art. 199(1).

22. Takaaki Hattori and Dan Fenno Henderson, Civil Procedure in Japan § 7.06[8][d] (claim preclusion); § 7.06[8][b] (1985) (Yasuhei Taniguchi, Pauline C.

Reich and Hiroto Miyake eds., Rev. 2nd ed. 2004) (commenting on the preclusion provisions prior to the reforms effected in the 1996 Code); Robert C. Casad, Issue Preclusion and Foreign Country Judgments: Whose Law?, 70 Ia. L. Rev. 53, 66 (1984) (discussing issue preclusion in Japan).

* Translation by Masatoshi Kasai and Andrew Thorson, and included as end material in Takaaki Hattori and Dan Fenno Henderson, Civil Procedure in Japan (Yasuhei Taniguchi, Pauline C. Reich, and Hiroto Miyake, eds., Rev. 2nd ed. 2004).

1. A judgment which has become final and binding shall be effective against the following persons:

> i. the parties;
>
> ii. in cases where a party became a plaintiff or defendant on behalf of another person, such other person;
>
> iii. successors who succeeded any persons in the preceding two items following the conclusion of oral argument;
>
> iv. persons who, on behalf of any persons in the preceding three items, possess the subject matter of the claim.

* * *

Article 117. (*Suit requesting amendment of final and binding judgment which has ordered compensation by payment on term*)

1. With regard to a final and binding judgment which has ordered compensation of damages which have occurred prior to the conclusion of oral argument by payment on term, in cases where the after-effects of the injury, the wage level, or any other circumstances which had been the basis of the calculation of the damages amount has, subsequent to the conclusion of oral argument, changed considerably, a suit requesting the amendment of such judgment may be filed. However, this shall be limited to payments due on and after the day of the filing of such suit.

The formal provisions relating to res judicata in the 1996 Code are substantially the same as in the earlier Code. One innovation in the new Code is Article 117, which addresses the situation where the effects of the injury or wage level change after the award has been made. Under prior law, although the judgment itself was final and not subject to modification, the plaintiff was permitted to bring a second action for additional damages because res judicata in Japan bars only claims that were actually litigated.[23] The 1996 Code streamlines the law, expressly authorizing the court to give a judgment by installment[24] and permitting either party to return to the court that entered the judgment to seek modification of installments not yet paid based on changed circumstances that affect the calculation of damages.[25]

As for the more general approach to claim and issue preclusion, the 1985 commentary excerpted below continues to reflect the law of preclusion in Japan:

---

23. See Yasuhei Taniguichi, The 1996 Code of Civil Procedure of Japan—A Procedure for the Coming Century?, 45 Am. J. Comp. L. 767, 784 (1997).

24. Id.

25. See Carl F. Goodman, Justice and Civil Procedure in Japan 420 (2004).

Takaaki Hattori and Dan Fenno Henderson, Civil Procedure in Japan 7–86–7–93 (Yasuhei Taniguchi, Pauline C. Reich and Hiroto Miyake, eds., Rev. 2nd ed. 2002).

[8]—Res Judicata (*kihanryoku*)

[a]—Introductory Remarks. Res judicata doctrine serves the purpose of preventing re-litigation of controversies once judicially determined.* * * Res judicata effect attaches to final judgments either on the merits or on procedural issues when they become irrevocable and immune from ordinary means of attack. A judgment becomes irrevocable in this sense when a party's right to attack the judgment expires. The irrevocability of a judgment is sometimes referred to as its formal finality (*keishikiteki kakuteiryoku*), as contrasted with its substantive res judicata effect. * * *

[b]—The Scope of the Res Judicata Doctrine

[i]—*Res Judicata in Respect to Subject Matter.* The Code of Civil Procedure declares that "only the matters contained in the formal adjudication (*shubun*)" are res judicata. This means that the findings contained in the part called "reasons" are not res judicata. This provision is generally construed to mean that the court's holding on the claim (*seikyū*) or cause of action (*soshōbutsu*) becomes res judicata, but that the findings appearing in the reasoning in support of the holding (*i.e.* the premises of the judgment on the claim) do not constitute res judicata. Thus, it is crucially important to determine what is the "claim."

* * *

There is a tendency in doctrinal writings to recognize an effect similar to the collateral estoppel effect of American law. Such decisions as there are supporting this effect are found only at the district and high court levels, and it appears very unlikely, at least at the present, that the Supreme Court would uphold such judgments on appeal.

* * *

[iii]—*Res Judicata in Respect to Persons Affected.* By virtue of its res judicata effect a judgment binds, as a rule, only the parties to the action. This rule is based on the adversary principle. Certain exceptions to this rule are premised on a strong public policy to end controversies, but generally an explicit statutory provision for such an exception is essential.* * *

[d]—The Dimensions of a Claim.

As explained before, because res judicata effect extends only to the same "claim," it is necessary to determine the dimensions of a "claim" or cause of action in order to determine the operative scope of the res judicata doctrine. The traditional and still prevailing scholarly view, also adopted by the courts, relies on the concept of a right or claim under substantive law, and recognizes a separate "claim" for each correlative substantive right involved. Under this view, a plaintiff who has lost an action for tort damages is not barred by res judicata from recovering the same amount in a new action for unjust enrichment, since a claim arising from tort and a claim arising from unjust enrichment are grounded in two different substantive rights. On the other hand, under this view, a plaintiff who has lost an action to declare himself owner of certain real property allegedly acquired by purchase is barred from obtaining another such declaration grounded on inheritance, because in both actions the same substantive right of ownership is in dispute and accordingly the claims in the two actions are identical. An even more subtle example is the case in which the plaintiff has lost his first action to recover possession of property on the ground of ownership (*bukken*), but is not barred from suing to recover the same thing based on a certain contract (*saiken*), the theory being that the alleged contractual right is quite distinct from the alleged property right.

There is a strong movement in scholarly circles to broaden the concept of "claim" and detach it from its present tie to a single substantive right. Under the broader concept, the objective of civil justice is to determine whether the plaintiff is entitled to the relief demanded, and not to determine whether a substantive right is properly identified in the claim for relief. It is argued, therefore, that by itself a substantive right does not constitute a "claim," but is merely the basis for a "claim," and that once a plaintiff is adjudged not entitled to a certain claim, he should be barred from renewing the same demand even when supported by a different substantive right which he could have asserted in the previous action. This view has been accepted by some theorists, but not yet by the courts.

However, it must be remembered that there is little difference in practice, because under the traditional view the plaintiff need not state his claims in terms of a distinct substantive right; he may state only facts which he thinks relevant to support his demand. The court is responsible for determining what substantive right, therefore what "claim," is asserted. If the court finds several rights asserted, then there can be a joinder of claims, any one of which the court is free to choose as the grounds for a final judgment for the plaintiff. To render a judgment against the plaintiff, the court must be satisfied that all claims are ungrounded. In that case, the plaintiff is barred by res judicata from renewing any of the claims joined in the former action. In practice, therefore, when the plaintiff describes a certain transaction in his complaint, the "claims" (substantive rights) arising from the transaction are deemed to have been stated.

[e]—Concluding Remarks.

Although res judicata is a subject which fascinates procedural theorists, its practical role should not be over-emphasized. Only occasionally do the courts dispose of a case on res judicata grounds. On the other hand, even if res judicata does not technically apply, a prior adjudication may have much evidentiary force. At present, the doctrine of res judicata is rather unsettled and subject to constant reconsideration, and there is an increasing awareness that the subject is bound up with the peculiarities of other institutions of civil procedure, such as the party's and court's roles, and skills of counsel in the investigation, preparation, and presentation of cases.

Notes and Comments

One significant observation emerging from the excerpt on preclusion in Japan is the speculation about possible changes to Japanese preclusion law that might be forthcoming. The excerpt above was written prior to the reforms to civil procedure in Japan made by the 1996 Code revision, effective 1998, such as the expansions to document discovery and the role for witness testimony.[26] *Even though the 1996 Code did not alter the formal preclusion rules, are other reforms in the Code—such as the expansion of document discovery and witness testimony—likely to affect the parameters of claim and issue preclusion in Japan in the future?* Writing about the Japanese system prior to any transformation of procedure resulting from the new Code, Professors Ramseyer and Nakazato contended that one reason for the narrow preclusion rules in Japan was that there were fewer economic incentives for a broader rule.[27] They argued that in the United States the expense of impaneling juries and conducting jury trials encourages broad preclusion rules, whereas in Japan because most evidence is presented in documentary form and the parties to case 2 need only refile the papers they submitted in case 1, a broad claim preclusion rule would produce only minor cost-savings in case 2.

FRANCE

In France, as in Germany and Japan, the scope of res judicata is set forth in a code provision. Like Germany, the preclusive effect of a prior judgment is limited to its "dispositive" part and does not extend to "motives".[28] However, from the excerpt below it appears that the preclusive effects of a French judgment may be broader than the formal Code principle suggests.

Richard H. Field, Benjamin Kaplan and Kevin M. Clermont, 2005 Supplement to Materials for a Basic Course in Civil Procedure 11-12 (2005).

French res judicata (*la chose jugée,* or the thing adjudged) is embodied in its *Code civil* article 1351, which appears in the part of the code treating presumptions:

* * *

[The authority of res judicata extends only to what was the subject matter of the judgment. The thing claimed must be the same; the action

26. See id. at 361–363.

27. J. Mark Ramseyer and Minoru Nakazato, Japanese Law, An Economic Approach 144–145 (1999).

28. Casad, Whose Law?, supra note 22, at 63–64 (discussing preclusion in France).

must be based on the same ground; the action must be between the same parties, and brought by and against them in the same capacities.]

That is to say, French res judicata is based upon presumption of correctness: when raised by a party, a prior judgment is presumed to be correct and should not be contradicted in a subsequent suit. A French judgment acquires the authority of res judicata once it is rendered, but a direct attack such as an appeal suspends its res judicata effect. A reversal will deprive a judgment of its res judicata effect, while an affirmance will render stronger the presumptive force of res judicata. The judgment becomes irrebuttable when all means of direct attack have expired.

In general, only issues advanced in contested *conclusions* (the issues that parties must submit as necessary to decision, such as the existence of some right) and definitively decided by the court will have res judicata effect in a subsequent suit. A defendant must advance *conclusions* in the nature of a declaratory counterclaim on necessarily involved issues in order to get res judicata effect on other than the plaintiff's *conclusions*. Consequently, res judicata effect attaches only to the judgment's decretal portion accepting or rejecting the *conclusions* of the parties (*le dispositif*), and not to its briefly stated rationale portion (*les motifs*); however, if the rationale is closely intertwined with the decree, the second court may consult it to determine the scope of res judicata.

* * *

For such preclusion, French law requires three identities between the lawsuits: of the parties, of the object demanded, and of the *cause* * * *

1. Identity of parties requires not physical identity but identity of quality, or legal capacity. Thus, privies represented in the prior suit have the same identities as the parties, but the same person who later sues in a different capacity does not.

2. The second required identity is the identity of the object demanded. This difficult concept means that the suits must involve generally the same juridical right sought as to the same thing. For close but contrary examples, a person who has lost an action in which he claimed title to a building may later sue for a life estate, but a person who has unsuccessfully claimed a debt owing cannot later sue for interest thereon.

3. The last required identity, and probably even more troublesome, is the identity of *cause*. On the one hand, it is generally accepted that this concept of *cause* is broader than the old common-law concept of cause of action, or theory of recovery. *Cause* refers to the ultimate facts and legal principle upon which the action is grounded, such that a loan is a *cause*. On the other hand, all agree that the concept of *cause* is more restrictive than the new common-law transactional view of a claim. For French examples, a party who has unsuccessfully attacked a will for a

defect of form may renew the attack for lack of testamentary capacity, but that party cannot raise different formal defects in successive actions.

If these three identities are present, res judicata attaches, preventing the losing party from asserting new evidence or theories to change the outcome.

Notes and Comments

Commenting on comparisons between common law and civil law jurisdictions, Professor Kevin Clermont makes the following observations:[29]

> Most interestingly, to affect other causes of action as well as other persons, civil-law countries broadly allow an evidential use of prior judgments, rather than expand their preclusive doctrine of res judicata. One could argue that the United States should have relaxed its hearsay rule in order to follow the same evidential route as the civilians, and so have avoided its battles over scope of claim and nonmutuality of estoppel. Following that route in this country would have given to all rulings a persuasive effect similar to the effect that stare decisis gives to legal rulings. However, there are arguments against extending evidential weight to factual findings: that combining a past decision with new evidence is a bit like combining apples and oranges; that our juries especially would have trouble in weighing a past decision; and that the evidential approach lacks res judicata's advantage of avoiding trial altogether. Therefore, the United States has in the main rejected this civilian solution.

Once again, we see that judicial systems have various mechanisms to achieve similar ends—here avoiding contradictory decisions. *Are there advantages to the civil law approach which enables a civil-law court to use the files of the prior proceedings and its contents, including the decision and the findings set forth therein, as evidence in the new action?*[30] *Are there disadvantages to this approach?*

SPAIN

Spain provides an interesting example of a civil-law country's approach to preclusion. Until several years ago, the Spanish law of res judicata (or *"cosa juzgada"*) was very similar to that of France: (1) it was based on a presumption of correctness[31]; (2) it required three identities between the first and second actions in order for the presumption of res judicata to attach—identity of the thing or object in suit (or

---

29. Richard H. Field, Benjamin Kaplan, and Kevin M. Clermont, 2005 Supplement to Materials for a Basic Course in Civil Procedure 12–13 (2005).

30. For a discussion and explanation of the American rule which prevents introduction of such material as "hearsay," see Hiroshi Motomura, Using Judgments as Evidence, 70 Minn. L. Rev. 979 (1986).

31. Codigo Civil, Art. 1251 provided that:

Presumptions established by law can be overcome only by proof to the contrary, except in cases where the law expressly prohibits that.

Against the presumption that the thing adjudged (*cosa juzgada*) is true, only a reversal of the judgment through appeal shall be effective.

"*cosa*"), identity of the cause (or "*causa*"), and identity of the parties[32]; and, (3) it was applied only to the "dispositive" part of the judgment.[33]

In April of 2001, the Spanish legislature repealed the Law of Civil Procedure (*Ley de Enjuiciamento Civil*) of 1881 and those provisions of its Civil Code that defined the parameters of the Spanish law of res judicata. The new law, Ley 1/2000, redefined the function and role of *cosa juzgada* in Spain—extending the preclusive effect of judgments to claims that could have been but were not brought in the first action,[34] as in the United States, and encouraging a more expansive application of the doctrine of issue preclusion. The Preamble to the new law makes clear that the function of the law was to introduce a new practical and theoretical framework for the Spanish law of res judicata:

> In regard to *cosa juzgada* this law, newly rejecting what would be doctrinaire, sets aside concepts of an almost metajuridical nature and, in accordance with the best juridical technique, treats *cosa juzgada* as a legal principle that is essentially procedural in nature, designed to avoid undue repetition of litigation and to achieve by means of the positive binding effect of the matter previously adjudicated, harmony of judgments on the merits in matters prejudicially connected.

> With this perspective, it departs from the idea of the presumption of truth, from the "sanctity of *cosa juzgada*" and from the confusion about the effects of many judgments. It is understood that, except in well justified cases, the requirement of the identity of parties is reaffirmed. In regard to the other elements, the law provides that *cosa juzgada* makes effective the rule of preclusion of allegations of facts and conclusions of law.*

The drafters of Ley 1/2000 thus set forth two of the principal purposes of the new Spanish law of *cosa juzgada*: to reject the traditional view of *cosa juzgada* as a presumption, and to expand the scope of the positive effect of judgments (i.e., to provide for a more expansive doctrine of issue preclusion). The relevant provisions of Ley 1/2000 are set forth and discussed below.

32. Codigo Civil, Art. 1252 provided that:

> In order for the presumption of *cosa juzgada* to take effect in another suit, it is necessary that between the case resolved by the judgment and the one in which the presumption is invoked, there shall exist the most perfect identity between the things (*cosas*), the causes (*causas*), the persons of the litigants and the capacity in which they litigated. * * *

> It is understood that there is identity of parties if the litigants in the second suit are successors in interest or assignees of those who litigated in the prior suit, or are united with them by bonds of solidarity or by those that are established by the indivisibility of obligations of perform-

ance among those that have a right to demand them or the obligation to fulfill them.

33. A Spanish judgment document will contain separate and numbered paragraphs: the antecedents, the proved facts, the principles of law and the judgment. The judgment statement is the *dispositivo*. Robert C. Casad, Issue Preclusion in the Law of Spain: *Cosa Juzgada Positiva*, in Law and Justice in a Multistate World: Essays in Honor of Arthur T. von Mehren 595, 597 n.9 (James A.R. Nafziger and Symeon C. Symeonides eds., 2002) [hereinafter, *Cosa Juzgada*].

34. Ley 1/2000, Article 400.

* Translation by Robert C. Casad in *Cosa Juzgada*, supra note 33, at 603.

Ley 1/2000.*

Article 222. *Cosa Juzgada Material.*

1. The *cosa juzgada* effect of final judgments, whether they be for or against the claimant, will preclude, in accordance with the law, a later action whose object is identical to that which produced the judgment.

2. The *cosa juzgada* effect applies to the claims made in the complaint and in a counterclaim, as well as to the points referred to in sections 1 and 2 of article 408 of this law.

Facts related to the bases for the claims referred to above that occur after the time when further allegations cannot be made in the proceeding in which the claims were formulated will be considered new and distinct facts.

3. *Cosa juzgada* will affect the parties to the action in which the judgment was ordered and their heirs and assigns, as well as persons not litigants who owned the rights represented by legitimate parties in accordance with article 10 of this law.

* * *

4. Matters resolved with force of *cosa juzgada* in a final judgment that puts an end to an action will bind the court in a later action when the matter appears as a logical antecedent of the object of the later action if the litigants in both actions are the same or if the law extends *cosa juzgada* effect to them.

Article 400. *Preclusion of the Allegation of Facts and Legal Grounds.*

1. When what is asked for in the complaint can be based on different facts or on different legal grounds or legal rights, those that are known and invoked at the time the complaint is filed must be alleged in the complaint. It shall not be permissible to reserve their allegation for a later action.

The burden of making the allegations referred to above does not prevent the addition of complementary allegations or allegations of new facts or newly discovered facts allowed by this law to the complaint or answer at a later time.

2. In conformity with the prior section, by operation of *litispendencia* and *cosa juzgada*, the facts and legal grounds alleged in a lawsuit will be considered the same as those alleged in an earlier action if they should have been alleged in that earlier suit.

---

* Translation by Robert C. Casad in *Cosa Juzgada*, supra note 33, at 604.

Robert C. Casad, Issue Preclusion in the Law of Spain: *Cosa Juzgada Positiva*, in Law and Justice in a Multistate World: Essays in Honor of Arthur T. von Mehren 595, 605–607 (James A.R. Nafziger and Symeon C. Symeonides, eds., 2002).

Among the salient features of the new law, one can see the abandonment of the language of the Civil Code requiring the "most perfect identity" of the three factors. Nevertheless, the requirement of identity of object (*cosa*) is retained, and the provision for extending the *cosa juzgada* effects to non-parties in some instances is retained but is somewhat more restrictive than the old law.

With respect to the negative effect of *cosa juzgada*, the new law, in Article 400, does seem to extend the conclusive effect of the judgment to some claims that might have been, but were not pleaded in the first action.

Although the new law contains language that seems to suggest an expansion of the issue preclusion effects of judgments, it is not clear that that will be the result. Article 222(4) refers to the binding effect in a later action of matters previously resolved, but it qualifies that by limiting it to "matters resolved with the force of *cosa juzgada*." Does *cosa juzgada* here refer to *cosa juzgada formal*: only matters resolved in a final judgment have binding effect in later actions? Or does it refer to *cosa juzgada material*: only those matters already established as conclusive under existing case law are binding in later actions?

* * *

My preliminary conclusion is that the new law has not changed the law of issue preclusion dramatically.* * *

For the time being, it appears that a limited law of issue preclusion is a feature of Spanish law—issues of fact and law litigated and decided in one action can have conclusive effect in a later suit between the same parties when there is at least some connection between the objects sought in the first and second suits. The nature of that connection, however, is very indefinite. The fact that the same question is involved in each suit may not be enough to establish that connection so as to preclude relitigation of that question in a later suit, unless one of the litigants makes a specific claim for a declaratory judgment on that point.* * *

Where issue preclusion does apply, it will be binding on certain specified non-parties to the first suit as well as to the original litigants.

Notes and Comments

The excerpt about Spain illustrates that even among civil law jurisdictions the application of preclusion principles is likely to differ. Spain appears to be moving to a more expansive approach to claim preclusion and embraces (as it did to some extent even under the earlier law)[35] a limited type of issue preclusion. Differences in the practice among civil law jurisdictions are sometimes quite nuanced. A recent report of the International Law Association on "Res judicata and Arbitration" attempts to identify some of the differences among the national laws of *res judicata* in European civil law.[36] Describing the scope of the *dispositif* in France, the Report explains that not only is the *dispositif* to be looked to "but also the necessary underlying motivation". In the Netherlands, the Report observes that "those elements of the motivation which have not been repeated in the *dispositif* but nonetheless are intended to contain final decisions on specific points are deemed to constitute *res judicata*." By contrast in Germany, the Report explains that "[o]nly where the *dispositif* of the judgment is not self-explanatory can the underlying key reasons be looked at. The reasoning and the findings may only help to determine the scope of *res judicata*." Italy appears to have expanded its scope of *res judicata* in the case law. As described in the Report: "In Italy, while the legal doctrine holds that *res judicata* effect is limited to the operative part of the judgment, Italian case law has admitted that the *res judicata* effect may include the entire reasoning, and in almost all cases that *res judicata* includes the grounds that constitute the logical and necessary assumptions for the decision itself (the so-called *"giudicat implicito"*)."

General Observations

The examination of principles of res judicata in this Chapter generally reflects a common law/civil law divide. Civil law countries tend to restrict preclusion to the precise determination that is reflected in the judgment, although some flexibility appears to exist in defining what is part of the judgment. In addition, as the excerpt on Germany exemplifies, in some civil law countries multiple actions may be brought on a single claim if a party chooses to sue for only a partial recovery in the first action.

The "civilians' relative caution in dealing with res judicata, and especially with issue preclusion" is arguably not due to any "conscious lack of confidence in their own fact-finding processes."[37] Rather it relates to alternative ways of making use of prior decisions: "the absence of exclusionary rules of evidence enables a civil-law court to send for the file of the prior proceeding and to use its contents, including the decision and the findings recorded therein, as evidence in the new action. Thus the civilians are not

---

35. Casad, *Cosa Juzgada*, supra note 33, at 604–605.

36. See International Law Association (ILA), Committee on International Commercial Arbitration, Interim Report: *"Res judicata"* and Arbitration, supra note 4.

37. Rudolf B. Schlesinger, Hans W. Baade, Peter E. Herzog, and Edward M. Wise, Comparative Law 483-484 (6th ed. 1998).

faced with the hard choice which an American court normally must make in cases of this kind: either to treat the findings made in the prior case as binding (which often leads to harsh results) or completely to disregard those findings, not even admitting them as evidence (which may be unrealistic and wasteful). This all-or-nothing approach of the common law has been criticized by Bentham and others. The civilians, by rejecting or restricting the doctrine of collateral estoppel, while at the same time treating the earlier findings as evidence, in effect, have adopted the intermediate view advocated by these critics."[38]

The ALI/UNIDROIT Principles on Transnational Civil Procedure address both claim and issue preclusion. Principle 28.2 provides: "In applying the rules of claim preclusion, the scope of the claim or claims decided is determined by reference to the claims and defenses in the parties' pleadings, including amendments, and the court's decision and reasoned explanation."[39] Principle 28.3 states: "The concept of issue preclusion, as to an issue of fact or application of law to facts, should be applied only to prevent substantial injustice."[40] *How would you describe the approach taken in the ALI/UNIDROIT Principles?* Consider the observations of one commentator[41] with respect to an earlier version of the Principles:

> The refusal to give preclusive effect to claims that might have been but were not raised is consistent with the general civil law concept of preclusion and is not unique to Japan. It is also consistent with the Code of Civil Procedure's requirement that the court can only decide claims raised by the parties. * * * While considerably narrower than the common law approach to preclusion, the ALI Principle is closer to the civil law rule under which such preclusion may be achieved not through preclusion rules but through use of the civil law concept of good faith and the prohibition against an abuse of rights.

38. Id. at 483–484.

39. ALI/UNIDROIT Principles of Transnational Civil Procedure 47 (2004).

40. Id. at 48.

41. See Goodman, supra note 25, at 420–421.

Chapter 10

ENFORCEMENT OF JUDGMENTS

I. INTRODUCTION

Certain judgments are self-executing and do not require any further action for their enforcement. For example, a declaratory judgment achieves its purpose by establishing the rights of the parties and giving rise to a res judicata effect. Similarly, a constitutive judgment (*Gestaltungsurteil* in Germany, *jugement constitutif* in France), such as a divorce judgment, automatically transforms a substantive legal relationship. A majority of judgments, however, require the defendant to pay money or to do or to refrain from doing certain things, although the language of such a judgment does not necessarily take the imperative form. Such an "ordering judgment" requires further action if the defendant has not complied. Systems for the enforcement of judgments vary greatly country to country and, when compared with other aspects of civil justice, are not well known outside of the jurisdiction. In many countries this is one of the most neglected areas of law. It has invited considerable criticism for being inefficient, overly complex, and out-of-date. Recently, however, there have been reforms effected in some countries.[1]

II. AGENTS RESPONSIBLE FOR EXECUTION

In almost all civil law or common law countries, the enforcement of judgments, commonly called execution, is traditionally carried out by the court and/or a court-related officer, such as a court clerk, sheriff, or bailiff. There are some notable exceptions. In some Scandinavian countries, such as Sweden, Finland, and Iceland, the enforcement of judgment comes under the jurisdiction of an independent governmental agency separate from the court. The Swedish Enforcement Authority is primarily in charge of tax collection under the administration of the tax

---

1. For a summary overview of each of the European countries including common law, civil law, and Scandinavian systems, see Alexander Layton and Hugh Mercer, eds., European Civil Procedure, Vol. 2. (2004). See also Wendy Kennett, Enforcement: General Report, in Procedural Laws in Europe: Towards Harmonisation 81–111 (Marcel Storme, ed., 2003).

agency and, therefore, is said to be more efficient than elsewhere. The Finnish agency is under the ministry of justice.

In the French type of system, the enforcement officer, called *huissier judiciaire,* has a long tradition, having existed since the time of the *Ancien Régime.* Even today, the *huissier judiciaire* is an independent and the sole agency of execution. In the Germanic systems, there is a division of work between the court (judge or a judicial officer called *Rechtspfleger*) and the court-attached enforcement officer (*Gerichtsvollzieher*). The latter, who is a historical descendant of the French *huissier,* is independently responsible only for executions that require the exercise of physical force, such as eviction or seizure and sale of chattels. The judge is in charge of executions that can be processed by a series of orders and that require prudent judgment because of inherent complications, such as seizure and sale of real property, and the seizure of intangibles (e.g., garnishment).

Huissier type enforcement officers are public officials but they do not receive a fixed salary from the state. They earn fees from the petitioner for the execution. The court clerk may also be an independent agency of execution, as in Japan where a recent reform gave the court clerks the power to execute small claims judgments.

Wendy Kennett, Enforcement: General Report, in Procedural Laws in Europe: Towards Harmonization 81, 96–99 (Marcel Storme, ed., 2003).

* * * More significant in practice, however, are differences in the structure of the enforcement process and the regulation of those responsible for enforcement. History, policy objectives, and conceptions of the role of the state combine to produce a veritable kaleidoscope of different enforcement frameworks.

Probably the most notable distinction between systems concerns the extent to which enforcement of civil law debts is entrusted to agents who specialize in that function.

In Belgium, France, Luxembourg, the Netherlands, Scotland, Sweden and Finland there are dedicated enforcement specialists who have a considerable degree of control over enforcement strategy. Such agents are public officers appointed by the state, but work outside the court system. The *huissier de justice* or *gerechtsdeurwaarder* known in Belgium, France, Luxembourg and the Netherlands is a professionally trained lawyer operating within a regulated profession. Although the broad framework of this regulation is provided by parliamentary legislation, the professional body is competent to draw up the detailed professional rules, subject to their approval by the Minister of Justice. Access to the profession is controlled by licenses issued by the Ministry of Justice, although again education and training is provided by the professional body. Serious disciplinary offences are brought before the competent court, but more minor infractions are normally dealt with by the professional body. The typical form of organization is a civil law partnership. Such enforcement agents may undertake a number of functions apart from forced execution. Although the precise range varies from one jurisdiction to another, all undertake pre-litigation debt collecting.

* * *

Typically it is necessary for a creditor to apply to a court for a particular method of enforcement. In that sense the creditor has control over enforcement. But in another sense the creditor lacks control in that he has no direct contact with the debtor and may have little information about the debtor's financial situation. Such "diffuse" systems of enforcement may also employ different personnel for different aspects of enforcement: judges, court administrators and the agents who actually go out to visit the debtor. The activities of these different personnel are not necessarily well coordinated.

Three examples may be helpful to demonstrate the range of possibilities in diffuse systems.

1. In England and Wales, seizure of tangible moveable property is carried out by "bailiffs". There are three principal types of bailiff: sheriffs' officers who are self-employed professionals and have a monopoly in relation to High Court enforcement; County Court bailiffs who are civil servants and undertake enforcement of County Court judgments; and private (certificated) bailiffs who undertake seizure of tangible movable in other contexts—primarily for the recovery of public sector debts. Regulation of these various bailiffs is very limited. Private bailiffs in particular may also undertake a range of other activities, including debt collection and private investigation. Structural factors—notably cost—have resulted in a situation where bailiff action is by far the most common method of enforcement. Other methods of enforcement include attachment of earning, seizure of bank accounts, and registration of a charge against immovable property. Use of these is quite limited—in part because of a lack of the information needed to make each method of enforcement effective. Each involves an application to the court of the relevant type of order. Communication between the creditor, court and debtor will not necessarily—or even usually—involve a bailiff. There is thus a disjunction between the various parts of the enforcement machinery. The enforcement agent who has closest contact with the debtor in his or her home or pace of business—the bailiff—has limited enforcement competences. The agents with a wider range of competences—the creditor's lawyer and the court only operate at arm's length from the debtor. The system of incentives in place—primarily financial incentives—does little to encourage co-operation between these disparate enforcement agents.

2. In Germany there is also a certain structural uncoupling of seizure of tangible movable property. It is undertaken by the *Gerichtsvollzieher* without the need for a specific court order, whereas other methods of enforcement generally require a court order. Nevertheless, the *Gerichtsvollzieher* is much more closely integrated into the overall

system of enforcement than the English bailiff. He or she is a civil servant who is under the supervision of the *Amtsgericht* [district court], but maintains a separate office. Each *Gerichtsvollzieher* is responsible for a designated area of territorial competence. Communication between creditor and *Gerichtsvollzieher* is normally channelled through the court. More importantly, in terms of achieving a co-ordinated enforcement system, the *Gerichtsvollzieher* is responsible for obtaining the debtor's statement of assets. He or she is also involved in the implementation of court orders for all forms of enforcement (in the sense that each order must be served on the debtor and on any relevant third parties). The *Gerichtsvollzieher* maintains computer records for the debtors in his or her area and can obtain a good picture of their circumstances.

Nevertheless the slow progress in computerisation of the courts in Germany means that there is little co-ordination of information about debtors within the courts themselves, which might inform decisions about enforcement orders.

3.   In Spain decisions about enforcement are in principle undertaken by a judge, although certain lower order steps in the procedure may be initiated by a *Secretario Judiciale*. Implementation of enforcement decisions—through seizure of assets and service of documents, is undertaken by civil servants employed within the court.

It is the court that heard a case on the merits that is responsible for enforcement decisions. In practice this means that decisions about enforcement may often need to be implemented outside that court's area of territorial competence—at the domicile of the debtor, or the place where assets are situated. The lines of communication within and between courts are formal and hierarchical leading to considerable delays.

* * *

* * * For some jurisdictions, enforcement is a part of the judicial process and should be retained within the courts. Competition in relation to enforcement is excluded in the same way that competition in the choice of a judge is excluded. For others the link to the judicial system is less intense. Historically the enforcement function has been (or become) detached from the courts and has flourished within a different institutional framework.

Nevertheless, one of the current trends in enforcement is towards privatisation. Employing civil servants as enforcement agents imposes large costs on the state. There are moves in several jurisdictions to privatize the service—or at least to explore the possibility of doing so. Private sector enforcement agents are likely to be introduced in Portugal (adopting a model akin to that of the French or Belgian *huissier de justice*). The idea has been mooted but abandoned in Austria. It has been adopted in Italy for public sector but not private sector enforcement, and it is under consideration as one of several options in Spain. Private sector enforcement is likely to be extended in England, but with accompanying measures to raise standards. Major reforms of enforcement have also taken place in the applicant states, typically involving privatization of the process * * *.

A study of the regulation of enforcement agents in different jurisdictions suggests that privatization can be beneficial, but is also fraught with difficulties. Where an enforcement agent acts for creditor clients, the structure of enforcement—and the incentives offered to enforcement agents—must be such as to ensure that those agents continue to respect the rights of debtors. The conditions which have led to apparently successful private sector enforcement in some jurisdictions (e.g. France, Belgium and the Netherlands) may be difficult to replicate elsewhere. There is anecdotal evidence to suggest that the export of these systems to applicant states has failed to take account of all the conditions necessary to their success.

III. THE CONCEPT OF "EXECUTION TITLE" IN CIVIL LAW

The fact that the enforcement procedure can be separated from the procedure leading up to the rendition of an enforceable judgment led most civil law countries to make the same enforcement procedure available on the basis not only of a court's judgment but also of other instruments which are sufficiently reliable, albeit without res judicata effect. Such instruments, collectively called "execution titles" (*titre éxécutoire, Vollstreckungstitel, titolo executivo,* etc.) include official documents such as notarized deeds, minutes of settlements before the court, and, exceptionally, as in Italy, even a private instrument such as a note or check. The most important execution title is, of course, a final judgment which has res judicata effect, with no possibility of further appeal. However, in many systems, both in civil law and in common law countries, a judgment may be provisionally executable with or without requirement of security and the judgment may be enforced while an appeal is pending. In these systems, the original or appellate court may stay the execution upon request by the debtor.

In the civil law systems, an execution title further requires an execution clause (*formule exécutoire, Vollstreckungsklausel, formula esecutiva,* etc.) to be attached by the court clerk or notary in order to certify the current validity of the execution title. When appropriate, an execution clause can be granted to enable an execution title to be enforced between persons or entities different from the original creditor and debtor (typically, a successor of debtor or creditor).

On the other hand, in the common law countries and Scandinavian countries, there is no generic concept of the execution title. Only a judgment or order of the court can be enforced. Even a settlement made in the court is enforceable only when it is rendered in the form of a judgment. In some civil law countries such a consent judgment may constitute an execution title (for example, the French *jugement d'expédient*). Interestingly, the Scottish law, as a hybrid between civil law and common law, does have executable documents outside of the final judgment. Thus, a promissory note, for example, can be registered in the court and becomes executable. Traditionally in Common Law, the execution was started by issuing of a writ called fieri facias. In the United States, such a writ is sometimes called by its modern name, the execution.

In most systems, the certified execution title and other documents must be served on the debtor in advance of the commencement of execution. There are some variations in this respect: there is no requirement of advance service of judgment in England and Ireland. In Italy, the service of a document called *precetto* (precept) is required in addition to that of execution title in order to warn the debtor. It has the effect of tolling the statute of limitation, and an execution must be commenced within certain period after *precetto* is served. The French system has a similar notice called *commandement*.

A variety of documents, ranging from judicial settlements to arbitral awards, serve as enforceable instruments in civil law countries; by contrast, the court's judgment alone serves this purpose in common law countries. Professor Kerameus suggests that differences of this sort "may offer some indications about that particular State's understanding of the relationship between State authority and enforcement of private debts." K.D. Kerameus, Enforcement in the International Context, in 264 Hague Recueil des Cours: Collected Courses of the Hague Acad. of Int'l L. 179, 229–231 (1997).

EUROPEAN UNION

Wendy Kennett, Enforcement: General Report, in Procedural Laws in Europe: Towards Harmonization 81, 94–95 (Marcel Storme, ed., 2003).

* * * The types of instrument that are subject to enforcement procedures vary from one jurisdiction to another. In particular, where a judge is the key player (at least in theory) within the enforcement procedure a wider range of instruments may be designated as enforceable * * * The justification for this is that the judge can resolve any disputes that may arise during the course of the enforcement procedures. An example is the Danish *friwilligt forlig* (a written acceptance of debt which includes a statement that the document can be used as the basis for enforcement). A creditor can take a *friwilligt forlig* directly to the enforcement court.

Note on the European Union

Until recently, various enforceable instruments made in a member State of the European Union (EU) were not automatically enforceable in other member States. In principle, there is no full faith and credit in the European Union as in the United States. Regulation (EC) No 805/2004 of the European Parliament and the Council of 21 April 2004, created a European Enforcement Order for uncontested claims. The Regulation, effective 25 January 2005, is important also because it is another significant step towards the formation of a common European law of civil procedure. Here are some of the most important provisions of the Regulation (Official Journal of the European Union, 30 April 2004, L143/15):

Art. 1

Subject Matter

The purpose of this Regulation is to create A European Enforcement Order for uncontested claims to permit, by laying down minimum standards, the free circulation of judgments, court settlements and authentic instruments throughout all Member States without any intermediate proceeding needing to be brought in the Member State of enforcement prior to recognition and enforcement.

Art. 2

Scope

1. This regulation shall apply in civil and commercial matters, whatever the nature of the court or tribunal* * *

Art. 5

Abolition of exequatur

A Judgment which has been certified as a European Enforcement Order in the Member State of origin shall be recognized and enforced in the other Member States without the need for a declaration of enforceability and without any possibility of opposing its recognition.

JAPAN

Japanese Civil Execution Act*

Article 22

Compulsory execution shall be effected by virtue of any of the following (hereinafter referred to as "obligation title"):

---

* Translation available in Zentaro Kitagawa, Doing Business in Japan App. 4E (2005).

1.   a final and binding judgment;

2.   a judgment accompanied by a declaration of provisional execution;

3.   a decision against which no appeal other than a *kokoku-*appeal [a special appeal authorized by statute] may be filed (In cases where a decision shall not be effected until it becomes final and binding, this shall apply only when such decision becomes final and binding);

4.   a payment order accompanied by a declaration of provisional execution;

5.   a document drawn up by a notary for a claim the subject matter of which is the payment of a certain amount of money or the delivery of a certain quantity of fungible things or valuable instruments and which includes a statement that the obligor shall be immediately subject to compulsory execution (hereinafter referred to as an "execution document");

6.   a judgment of a foreign court or award accompanied by a judgment concerning execution which has become final and binding;

7.   anything which has the same effect as a final and binding judgment (except the decision referred to in item 3 above).

ITALY

Alexander Layton and Hugh Mercer, eds., European Civil Practice, Vol. 2, 339–340 (2nd ed. 2004).

Most negotiable instruments such as bills of exchange, promissory notes and certain cheques are *titoli esecutivi* and may be executed without the addition of a *formula esecutiva* [indorsement confirming executory character], requiring only service of an *atto di precetto* setting out the contents of the instrument. The *precetto* is a formal demand to comply with an obligation appearing in the *titolo esecutivo* within a period of at least 10 days, with a warning that there will be forced execution in the absence of voluntary compliance. The *precetto* loses its effect if execution is not initiated within 90 days of service.

Other instruments are enforceable if a certified copy, bearing a *formula esecutiva*, is issued by the authority which issued the instrument, but in such cases a copy of the instrument must be served with or before the *atto di precetto*. Instruments of the latter kind must be in respect of an obligation to pay a specific sum of money, and most important among them are public acts executed before a notary. Various instruments may be notarized, and in some cases (such as deeds of gift, or transfers of real property) notarization is mandatory if the instrument is to have effect.

Elisabetta Silverstri, Enforcement of Civil Judgments and Orders in Italy: An Overview, 12 Bond L.R. 183, 184–185 (2000).

According to a well-established doctrine, not every judgment calls for judicial enforcement. Declaratory and constitutive judgments[2] are self-executing, while the relief sought requires the machinery of judicial enforcement when the judgment entered is a condemnatory one and the judgment debtor does not comply with it spontaneously. A final judgment on the merits is enforceable even before it becomes *res judicata*, unless a stay is granted by the court having jurisdiction over the matter.[3]

Besides judgments, several kinds of court orders (such as eviction orders and certain types of interim measures) can be enforced. A few legal instruments—including public deeds, bills of exchange, and promissory notes—are enforceable as well. Judgments, courts orders and public deeds can be enforced only if the judgment creditor obtains from the court clerk or a public notary a special certification authorizing the enforcement. The wording of such a certification is a good example of obsolete and pretentious 'legalese'. It reads: 'It is hereby commanded that any marshal so requested and whoever is entrusted with the duty to do so enforce this instrument, that public prosecutors grant their assistance, and that all police officers aid in the enforcement upon lawful request to do so'.

GERMANY

Alexander Layton and Hugh Mercer, eds., European Civil Practice, Vol. 2, 209 (2nd ed. 2004).

Under German law, certain notarial instruments and court settlements are enforceable by the same means of execution as are available in the case of judgments. In each case it is a condition of its enforceability in Germany that the relevant document, known as a *Titel*, should have been certified by the court as enforceable and should have been served.

---

2. Constitutive judgments "create or change a legal relationship rather than judicially affirm the pre-existing rights and duties of the parties" see Mauro Cappelletti and Joseph M. Perillo, Civil Procedure in Italy 152 (1965).

3. Until 1990, judgments issued by a court of first instance could not be enforced while they were still subject to appeal or the appellate proceeding was pending. However, enforcement could be authorized in exceptional circumstances. Appellate judgments were enforceable immediately, even though their enforcement could be stayed when the aggrieved party launched a further appeal to the Court of cassation (the Italian court of last resort). Nowadays, articles 282 and 283 of the Code of Civil Procedure, both reformed in 1990, provide that judgments rendered by a court of first instance can always be enforced unless the appellate court grants the debtor a stay of enforcement for "serious reasons".

As regards notarial instruments, it is a condition of their enforceability that they should relate to an obligation to pay a fixed sum of money or to deliver certain types of goods, and that the document should record the debtor's consent to immediate execution. They must have been drawn up by a German notary within the scope of this competence and in the prescribed form.

FRANCE

Alexander Layton and Hugh Mercer, eds., European Civil Practice, Vol. 2, 174 (2nd ed. 2004).

French law permits the enforcement of certain authentic instruments (*actes authentiques*) in the same manner as judgments. The principal category of such instruments is notarial acts, which may relate to an obligation to pay money or to any other obligation envisaged by civil law. Some matters must be made the subject of notarial acts, notably contracts for the sale of land and marriage contracts. Other acts (especially wills) are frequently notarized in practice.

The instrument is enforceable if it is endorsed with a *formule exécutoire*. Such an endorsement may be made by the notary who authenticated the instrument, but he will only do so if the person against whom enforcement is to be carried out has signified his consent to the instrument being enforceable. A copy of the instrument will be an authentic copy (a *grosse*) if it bears the notary's seal. It must then be served by the *huissier* in the same way as a judgment, normally by showing the debtor the *grosse* and handing him a copy, before execution can proceed.

IV. ENFORCEMENT OF MONEY CLAIMS AND NON–MONEY CLAIMS COMPARED

A basic distinction must be made between the enforcement of a money claim and a non-money claim. The distinction is derived from the nature of the respective processes of enforcement. The enforcement of money claims basically takes the following three stages under any system: First, the seizure of a specific piece of property from which the debt can be paid; second, conversion of the seized property into cash; and third, satisfaction of the enforcing creditor. Details of each of these stages vary according to the types of property seized and whether other creditors are allowed to receive any of the proceeds. Some comparative details of enforcement of money claims will be discussed below in Section V.

The enforcement of non-money claims has no uniform pattern. The method of enforcement varies according to the kind of claim that is enforced. The eviction of a defendant from a house, for example, can be enforced by the enforcement officer who forcibly ousts the defendant from the house, if necessary, with the help of the police. A claim for removal of a building can be enforced by a court order which authorizes a third party (such as a contractor) to demolish the house, the cost of which can be collected from the defendant as a money claim (substituted execution). This and other claims to require an act or prohibition of an act (the equivalent of injunction) can also be enforced by threatening the obligor with imposition of a monetary penalty. For example, the court orders the obligor to pay to the claimant $1,000 a day until the building is removed. This is the traditional French procedure called *astreinte* and is adopted in all civil law countries with differing names, procedures, and effects. In the common law countries, civil and criminal contempt serves a similar purpose. Even in civil law countries, some systems allow imprisonment to be inflicted on a recalcitrant obligor (German *Zwangshaft*). But, like the common law contempt, such a measure is exceptional in practice.

One noteworthy method adopted by some Germanic systems (such as Austria and Japan as well as Germany) for enforcing an obligation to make a required legal declaration (e.g., a consent agreement, etc.) is to legally deem that such a declaration has been given as soon as a judgment ordering the defendant to give the declaration attains res judicata status. Under this system, there is no actual need for an enforcement procedure. This possibility is frequently utilized in Japan for having a title to real property registered or deleted from the real property registration system. Real property registration can be made only by a joint petition with the Registry. When one of the parties refuses to cooperate, the other party sues for a declaration to be given by the defendant to the Registry. When a judgment ordering such a declaration becomes res judicata, the winning plaintiff alone can apply for the desired registration by proving the other party's declaration by the judgment. The same procedure can be used to enforce an obligation to enter into a contract.

In some countries, a party can seek to enforce a non-money claim through the imposition of financial penalties on the recalcitrant party. Professor Kerameus observes: "And here precisely arises the important question with regard to the recipient of money penalties or fines: should they benefit the enforcing creditor or the State treasury? While French law and some Latin American laws ... opt for the first solution, Central European ... and common law in general follow the second one." K.D. Kerameus, Enforcement in the International Context, in 264 Hague Recueil des Cours Collected Courses of the Hague Acad. of Int'l L. 179, 204–205 (1997).

THE UNITED STATES

Federal Rule of Civil Procedure 69—Execution

(a) In General. Process to enforce a judgment for the payment of money shall be a writ of execution, unless the court directs otherwise. The procedure on execution, in proceedings supplementary to and in aid of a judgment, and in proceedings on and in aid of execution shall be in accordance with the practice and procedure of the state in which the district court is held, existing at the time the remedy is sought, except that any statute of the United States governs to the extent that it is applicable. In aid of the judgment or execution, the judgment creditor or a successor in interest when that interest appears of record, may obtain discovery from any person, including the judgment debtor, in the manner provided in these rules or in the manner provided by the practice of the state in which the district court is held.

GERMANY

Peter L. Murray and Rolf Stürner, German Civil Justice 459–462 (2004).

A. Judgments for Delivery of Possession of Tangible Personal Property or Real Estate

Judgments requiring the judgment debtor to deliver to the judgment creditor possession of tangible personal property are enforced by the court executor, who simply takes possession of the designated item and turns it over to the judgment creditor. The same is true if the creditor is entitled to a designated quantity of fungible property. If the court executor cannot find the property, the debtor can be required to give a disclosure under oath as to its existence and whereabouts. If the property is in the possession of a third party and the latter will not voluntarily turn it over to the court executor, the creditor must levy on the debtor's right to possession of the property * * * and then bring an appropriate action against the third party to secure possession.

Judgments requiring the debtor to surrender possession of real estate are also executed by the court executor, whose assignment is to remove the judgment debtor from property and place the judgment creditor in possession.

B. Judgments for Specific Performance

German substantive and procedural law offers specific performance as a remedy of first resort to vouchsafe for the claimant exactly that to which she is legally entitled without exposing her to the risk that she would not be able to obtain full reimbursement via damages. The manner of execution of judgments for specific performance differs with the various kinds of specific performance that can be compelled by civil judgment. In one class are various kinds of actions * * * and restraints or forbearances. * * * Performance requiring declaration of the actor's will * * * such as property conveyance or apologies, are treated as a separate class.

If the actions required by the judgment are of a kind that can be performed by someone other than the judgment debtor, on motion by the creditor the court will authorize the creditor to have the action performed by a person of the creditor's reasonable choice at the cost of the debtor.

If the action required by the judgment is one that only the debtor can perform, and performance lies within the debtor's power, the court has the power to force the debtor to render actual performance. However the court does not have the power to compel a judgment debtor to perform or create a work of art, or to perform actions when the actions required cooperation of others not under the debtor's control. If the debtor refuses to perform the action as required by the judgment, the court rendering the judgment may append fines and imprisonment as inducements to perform.

ENGLAND

Civil Procedure Rules, Schedule 1, Rules of the Supreme Court Order 45, Rule 3—Enforcement of judgment for possession of land (The White Book Service, 2006).

3.—(1) Subject to the provision of these rules, a judgment or order for the giving of possession of land may be enforced by one or more of the following means, that is to say—

(a) writ of possession;

(b) in a case in which rule 5 applies, an order of committal;

(c) in such a case, writ of sequestration

Rules of the Supreme Court Order 45, Rule 4—Enforcement of judgment for delivery of goods

(1) Subject to the provisions of these rules, a judgment or order for the delivery of any goods which does not give a person against whom the judgment is given or order made the alternative of paying the assessed value of the goods may be enforced by one or more of the following means, that is to say—

(a) writ of delivery to recover the goods without alternative provisions for recovery of the assessed value thereof (hereafter in this rule referred to as a "writ of specific delivery")

(b) in a case in which rule 5 applied, an order of committal;

(c) in such a case, writ of sequestration.

Rules of the Supreme Court Order 45, Rule 5—Enforcement of judgment to do or abstain from doing any act

5.—(1) Where—

(a) a person required by a judgment or order to do an act within a time specified in the judgment or order refuses or neglects to do it within that time or, as the case may be, within that time as extended or abridged under a court order * * *.

(b) a person disobeys a judgment or order requiring him to abstain from doing an act,

then, subject to the provision of these rules, the judgment or order may be enforced by one ore more of the following means, that is to say—

(i) with the permission of the court, a writ of sequestration against the property of that person;

(ii) where that person is a body corporate, with the permission of the court, a writ of sequestration against the property of any director or other officer of the body;

(iii) subject to the provisions of the Debtors Act 1869 and 1878, an order of committal against that person or, where that person is a body corporate, against any such officer.

Zuckerman on Civil Procedure: Principles of Practice 818–819 (2nd ed. 2006).

Contempt of court—English courts have a general jurisdiction of committing persons for contempt of court. The jurisdiction is used for two distinct purposes: first, to enforce obedience to court orders and, second, to safeguard the court's authority and protect the administration of justice from improper interference and abuse.

Committal for contempt is wholly inappropriate for dealing with the great majority of procedural defaults * * *. Committal for contempt provides the courts with a formidable tool for securing compliance with court orders. Contempt proceedings may be used to enforce interim orders, such as interim injunctions, as well as orders made in final judgment, such as permanent injunctions. Failure to comply with an order of the court is enough to give rise to liability for contempt; there is no need to establish a specific intention to disobey the order, provided that the disobedience is more than causal or accidental or unintentional.

ITALY

Alexander Layton and Hugh Mercer, eds., European Civil Practice, Vol. 2, 338–339 (2nd ed. 2004).

Execution for liquidated judgment debts. The normal method for the execution of a judgment ordering the payment of money is by seizure (*pignoramento*) of the judgment debtor's property. Subject to certain restrictions, the judgment creditor may select the property to be seized. The process of execution is carried out by the *ufficiale giudiziario*, a bailiff, who formally identifies and attaches the debtor's goods, leaving them in the custody of the debtor (walking possession) or of a third party and ordering the debtor not to interfere with that custody or sell them. Ultimately, the assets seized may be sold, but only by public judicial auction or other prescribed form of sale. Alternatively, they may be assigned directly to the creditor. Similarly, land may be made the subject of seizure and sale or transfer. Other creditors having title may intervene in the sale.

Execution by delivery or surrender. A judgment for the delivery of specific goods may be executed by the court officer, by seizing the goods and handing them to the judgment creditor. A judgment for the transfer of specific land is executed by the court officer putting the judgment creditor into physical possession of the land and making the necessary changes to the land register.

Execution of mandatory or restraining orders. Such orders are enforced, if the defendant refuses to perform the act required of him, by appointing some other person to perform the act. This can only apply where it is possible for performance of the obligation to be substituted.

Other methods of execution. Garnishee proceedings can also be brought against a third party who owes money to the debtor or who is in possession of the debtor's property. The third party is summoned before the *giudice dell'esecuzione* to declare what sums he owes to the debtor or what property of the debtor he has in his possession. The judge holds a hearing to determine whether the third party has an object or debt owing to the debtor. The garnishee is bound to preserve the money or the property as a judicial custodian, pending disposal of the matter.

Italian law does not employ a system of enforcement by means of periodic penalty payments, nor does it have a system of punishment for contempt of court, though there is a little used criminal offence of failure to comply with the order of "Authority", including a judge.

Elisabetta Silverstri, Enforcement of Civil Judgments and Orders in Italy: An Overview, 12 Bond L.R. 183, 183–191 (2000).

In Italy, enforcement proceedings are cumbersome, long, and highly ineffective. Their major shortcomings are complexity, outdated procedures, and lack of efficient compulsory measures. In spite of the recurring complaint about the odd situation of an enforcement machinery that might have worked well in the last century, but looks like an antique in contemporary society, the rules governing the enforcement of judgments have neither changed substantially since the code of civil procedure went into force in 1942, nor are they likely to be improved in the short run. Therefore, judgment-holders find it very difficult to fulfill their expectations when the debtor fails to comply with the court order voluntarily, and there is often no way to overcome the debtor's obduracy. As a result, many legal rights are doomed to remain ineffective, since the system either provides no adequate remedies, or offers, at the most, an award of damages for the wrong inflicted by the defaulting judgment-obligee. It is clear that money restoration is not suitable for every right, most of all for the so called 'new rights' emerging in sensitive areas of substantive law, such as the ones dealing with the protection of minorities, the environment, consumers, and so on. Still, money restoration turns out to be the only remedy available when the system surrenders to a debtor who refuses to comply with a court order and nurtures the certainty that no coercive instrument will be resorted to in order to bend his will.

* * *

Courts are short of means suitable to bring about the enforcement of non-money judgments and orders compelling (or enjoining) the debtor to do something other than activities whose practical results can be obtained by entrusting a 'substitute' with the task to perform the obligation instead of the debtor. Anybody can build a wall or tear it down when the debtor refuses to do so; this case and very few others of the same kind are the only ones for which the enforcement machinery provided by the code of civil procedure seems to work smoothly. The nature of the so-called surrogate performance and its limits make it unavailable for the enforcement of a variety of non-money remedies that are much more frequent and socially relevant than an order directing the judgment-obligee to dismantle the wall he built on his neighbor's land. In short, there is no way out: either the debtor can be 'bypassed', resorting to somebody else for the fulfillment of his obligation, or the non-money remedy cannot be enforced according to the ordinary procedure.

This being the situation, one would expect the Italian procedural system to be at least well-equipped with appropriate and effective coercive measures aimed at forcing compliance with those non-money remedies unsuited for the mechanics of surrogate performance. On the contrary, no coercive measure is contemplated by the law in force: no *astreintes*, no *Geldstrafen,* let alone contempt of court. What is the judgment-holder supposed to do when he realises that his right cannot be made effective because even a court of justice lacks the legal tools necessary to bend the debtor's will? Unfortunately, not very much. It may be wise of him to seek compensation for the damages suffered, but rarely can a mere award of damages satisfy his expectations. Nobody could reasonably argue, for instance, that the employee who experienced an unfair dismissal, and obtained a judgment ordering his reinstatement, would content himself with an award of damages. In this case, like in many others, there is no 'second best', and money cannot be a substitute for what the creditor is entitled to receive.

* * *

The Italian legislator places an unshakeable confidence in the effectiveness of criminal penalties in bending the will of the reluctant debtor and persuading him to fulfill his obligations spontaneously, most of all when no enforcement process can overcome his defaulting conduct. On the contrary, plenty of evidence shows that the threat of a criminal prosecution does not increase the degree of voluntary compliance with court orders, at least not in Italy, where the debtor can count on the fact that the rules according to which the failure to abide by a civil judgment could generate criminal liability are construed very narrowly. In spite of that, a few recent statutes seal the fate of important non-money remedies by committing their enforcement to the mild coercion exerted by criminal penalties. This is the case, for instance, with some statutes related to labor relations, such as the one on the protection of unfairly dismissed employees, or the ones on affirmative action against discrimination on the grounds of gender or nationality.

FRANCE

Alexander Layton and Hugh Mercer, eds., European Civil Practice, Vol. 2, 174 (2nd ed. 2004).

Non-money judgments are normally enforced by the imposition of a penalty (*astreinte*), which increases periodically until the obligation in question has been performed. The sum finally payable is then usually determined by the court, and the total accumulated sum is often reduced to a more reasonable level than that provided by simple arithmetical calculation. This procedure is also frequently used in the case of money judgments. The court may also order an act required by a non-money judgment to be performed by someone other than the person against whom the judgment was given, and making the latter liable for the costs of such performance.

V. PROCEEDINGS FOR EXECUTION OF MONEY CLAIMS

A. PRELIMINARY REMARKS

The execution of money claims is the most common kind of enforcement but there are significant differences from system to system. The salient features of various systems will first be summarized from a comparative point of view before going into greater detail with respect to specifics.

1. Availability of Discovery of Debtor's Asset

Successful enforcement of monetary claims depends on the availability of assets of the debtor. It is generally difficult for a creditor to locate a debtor's property for seizure by way of execution, as a debtor anticipating a creditor's action tends to hide or dissipate his or her assets. Systems vary respecting the effectiveness of tools for the discovery of assets. Generally speaking, common law systems afford effective discovery by virtue of equitable supplementary proceedings. When the enforcement officer's (sheriff's) initial efforts to find the debtor's assets fail, the debtor will be subpoenaed to disclose under oath the location of assets and past transfers of assets, under the threat of contempt of court. In the federal courts of the United States, discovery in aid of execution is provided for in Fed. R. Civ. Proc. 60, and many state statutes have followed the pattern of the federal rules.

A similar procedure is available in Germany where the debtor can be summoned before the enforcement officer (*Gerichtsvollzieher*) to disclose all kind of the assets under oath. He or she is also required to disclose any transfer of assets made within two years. If disclosure is refused, the debtor is not only subject to a court order of imprisonment (*Haftbefehl*) but notice of this is officially published. (A much milder version of disclosure procedure has recently been adopted in Japan.)

A different and perhaps even more effective approach has been taken by the French system. Originally, French law empowered the *huissier* to search for the debtor's assets, but this effort often proved futile. A new system, which became effective in 1993 provided powerful help. When a *huissier* cannot locate sufficient assets, he may request the *procureur de la République* to inquire into the debtor's residence, his bank accounts, and his employment. The *procureur de la République* is a prestigious public official who not only handles criminal prosecution as prosecutor but also is given a general power as the guardian of the peace and order in the country. The *procureur de la République* can have access to the data base held by the central bank which includes all information of bank accounts in the country with the current address of the account holders. Thus, even the unknown address of the debtor can be retrieved. The German discovery procedure, however, cannot be used when the debtor is not found.

Where the execution is carried out by a public authority which is also in charge of tax collection, as in Sweden, that agency may not only have special powers of investigation but also may already have information about the available assets of a particular debtor.

In many other countries, there are no special means available to locate a debtor's assets. Creditors must somehow locate the assets through their own effort.

2. *Treatment of Competing Creditors*

It is often the case that there are many claimants who wish to collect from the same debtor. Bankruptcy is the institution by which creditors can be satisfied to the extent the total assets of the debtor permit. Where the debtor is not in bankruptcy and particular property is sought to be seized in execution, however, systems vary in the treatment of competing creditors. There are basically two different approaches, namely, the priority approach and the equality approach. The priority approach takes the position that the most diligent creditor should be rewarded by a priority over less diligent creditors. This is the "first come first served" approach in execution. The common law and German law take this approach. This is very straight forward but may result in injustice because the priority may depend on fortuity, not necessarily justifiable diligence, and professional lenders tend to be preferred.

Under the equality approach, all unsecured creditors are treated equally in the distribution of the proceeds of seized property if they participate in an execution proceedings commenced by a creditor. The result is almost like a bankruptcy when the sole property of the debtor has been seized and sold in execution. This is said to be the traditional French approach. The equality approach also has its own problems. If it is pushed forward to its extreme form, the proceedings will become just as cumbersome as a bankruptcy. Moreover, such a system may invite abuse and dilatory tactics. Therefore, many countries which originally adopted the equality approach have modified their system by adding some elements of priority through such devices as limiting the qualification and/or timing for participation by other creditors. In Japan, for example, only creditors with an execution title of their own can participate within a limited period fixed by the court or by the law. French law also limits the participating creditors to those with an execution title.

Italy, too, is now moving in the same direction. In fact, according to art. 499 of the Code of Civil procedure, as amended by the law of May 14, 2005, No. 80, only those creditors whose credit is based on an execution title of their own, creditors who have already obtained a sequestration order on the attached property, and secured creditors may intervene.

3. *Exemptions*

A good balance must be struck between satisfaction of creditors and protection of an individual debtor's life. Although all legal systems provide for the exemption of some assets from seizure, their scope varies considerably. In the United States, this is a matter of state law and some states have an exemption law more favorable to the debtor than others. Thus, the family dwelling house, or "homestead," and some chattels, such as an automobile, are usually exempted. In civil law, exemptions are generally limited to chattels necessary for the debtor's and his family's life or trade and a portion of his or her wages. Only one-fourth of the wages can be attached, for example. Swiss law takes a unique approach to exemptions: it does not give the creditor the power to choose which of the debtor's assets to seize. The execution authority (*Betreibungsamt*) must first look for chattels (movable properties) and then is allowed to seize real property only when the seized movables are not enough to satisfy the claim. This is probably a legacy of the medieval era when land enjoyed a special protection.

4. *Enforcement of Security Rights*

All legal systems provide for some sort of protection for secured creditors, such as the mortgage in common law and the *hypothec (hypothèque, hypothek, ipoteca)* in civil law. When these security rights, broadly called liens in common law, are enforced, a similar procedure to that of execution must ensue, namely, seizure, sale and payment. In many countries, however, this is considered different from the execution. In common law, an action for mortgage foreclosure must be brought in order to forfeit the debtor's right of redemption. In civil law, the enforcement of security rights is generally included in the concept of execution. Some sort of special execution title for that purpose is provided for, depending on the kind of security right. Where the creation of *hypothec* requires a notarized deed, such a deed serves as the execution title (France). It is also possible that a judgment establishing a security right will serve the same purpose (Germany). In Japan, the authenticated certificate of *hypothec* issued by the local real property registry under the administration of Ministry of Justice also serves the same purpose (though such a certificate is not technically considered as an execution title).

B. EXECUTION ON VARIETY OF PROPERTIES

1. *Execution on Chattels*

To execute against a chattel, the enforcement officer seizes unexempted chattels at the premise of the debtor, sells them and delivers the proceeds to the creditor. Even if the property does not belong to the debtor, the purchaser always get a good title as a bona fide purchaser or otherwise in all systems. When other creditors participate under the equality approach and/or a priority creditor exists, the distribution of the proceeds must be made in accordance to the order of priorities. In any event, the execution on chattels has recently lost much of its utility in practice because in the ordinary case there are no valuable chattels available. Execution on chattels tends to function only as a means of putting psychological pressure upon the debtor.

2. *Execution on Claims*

This is a very important kind of execution today because almost all debtors have a bank account and get a regular salary from their employer. The method of seizure is essentially the same everywhere. Some kind of notice of seizure (court order as in Germany or creditor's demand as in France) is served on the debtor's debtor (bank, employer, etc.). This enables the creditor to secure a seized claim for satisfaction of the creditor. The mechanism is rather complex and varies considerably.

In Germany, the court issues either a collection grant (*Uberweisung zur Einziehung*) or a turn-over order (*Uberweisung an Zahlungs Statt zum Nennswert*). The collection grant endows the creditor with the right to collect the attached debt from the debtor's debtor (third debtor). If the third debtor does not pay, the debtor must commence an action against the third debtor in order to obtain an execution title against the latter (collection action). On the other hand, a turn-over order has the effect of making the attached claim the creditor's property so the creditor is deemed paid to the extent of the face value of the attached claim. The turn-over order is simple and effective but the creditor bears the risk of insolvency of the third debtor.

Japanese law adopted this German mechanism but at the same time adopted the equality approach which did not exist in Germany. Thus, a turn-over order was actively used to achieve the same result as the priority approach in spite of the risk of insolvency of the third debtor. If a turn-over order was issued, the attached claim ceased to exist, and, therefore, other creditors could not attach it in order to get a share of distribution. The Japanese equality approach was much curtailed by the new Civil Execution Law of 1979. Now, the creditor is automatically given the right to collect one week after the seizure, and as soon as a complaint in a collection action is served on the third debtor, no other creditors can participate. Nonetheless, because there is still a possibility of other creditors' participation in the mean time, the turn-over order is still commonly sought and is served on the third debtor at the same time as the seizure order. This is especially common when the solvency of the latter is not in question, as when a bank as the third debtor.

In this connection, the new French system presents an interesting solution. The traditional French system in this respect was an attachment-seizure (*saisie-arrêt*) which did not require an execution title and was followed by a declaratory action for establishing the validity of seizure. Moreover, under the equality approach, participation of other creditors could not be prevented. The new law (*décret*) of 1991 (effective since 1993) adopted a very different system. When a notice of seizure (*saisie-attribution*) is served with the help of a *huissier* upon the third debtor, a turn-over effect arises automatically and no other creditors can attach the same claim. Thus, the historical equality approach was abolished and French law now resembles the German and Japanese turn-over order. A significant difference is, however, that under the *saisie-attribution*, the risk of the third debtor's insolvency does not exist. The creditor's claim against the debtor is not thereby extinguished. He now simply has two debtors to satisfy his claim. The 1991 amendment also came to require an execution title to get a *saisie-attribution* but preserved the old system under which *saisie arrêt* is available without an execution title as a means of attachment of wages under the control of the court (*saisie des rémunérations by tribunal d'instance*). The equality approach is also maintained here in order to protect the creditors' rights to the wage claim, which is often the sole assets of the debtor.

In common law, the same kind of procedure is called garnishment, garnishee proceedings, or third party debt order, etc., and the priority approach prevails. Under these procedures, the third debtor (garnishee) is ordered to pay his debt to the judgment creditor. The civil law type of turn-over of debt in lieu of payment does not seem to exist. In some states of the United States, instead of using wage garnishment, the judgment creditor may ask the court to issue an order requiring the defendant debtor to satisfy the judgment in installment payments (New York CPLR § 5226).

3. *Execution on Real Property*

There are two possible methods for collecting a debt out of real property. One is the seizure followed by a sale of the property (forced sale). Under the other method, the creditor is paid from the fruits of the property. Typically, for example, when a rental apartment house is seized, the rents are collected up to the satisfaction of the claim (forced management). These two methods may be employed cumulatively, that is, the property can be managed to collect rents until the sale is achieved because preparation for a judicial sale always requires time. German law provides for both of the methods (*Zwangsversteigerung* and *Zwangsverwaltung*). Japanese law follows. French law does not have a separate forced management system. However, a seizure embraces the fruits from the property. Thus, the debtor landlord loses the right to the rents and the rents are treated as a part of the seized real property (*immobilisation des fruits*).

The judicial sale of real property in most countries must take the form of a public auction in order to realize the highest value possible, either orally or silently by placing a written bid. Systems vary in terms of the right obtained by the purchaser. In some systems, the purchaser gets title subject to all prior encumbrances, i.e., liens and leases. Common law generally takes this approach. Under the Japanese law, the property is sold free of liens but subject to perfected leases. The system allows creditors to realize as much of the proceeds as possible while protecting the lessees. A nicety of it is that if a lease is executed after a lien (typically a *hypothec*) is perfected, the sale is made free of such a lease because it is subordinate to a lien which is extinguished by a judicial sale. If the property does not legally belong to the debtor, the purchaser in most countries will not get the title. In Germany, however, the title of the purchaser is guaranteed because the sovereign gets the original title by a seizure and sells it to the purchaser.

When the property is sold or rents are collected, the process of distribution of proceeds varies according to whether the system takes the priority approach or the equality approach. Under the equality approach in a pure form as existed in Italy, before a 2005 amendment, other creditors with or without an execution title might intervene and be entitled to a pro rata distribution of the proceeds. Prior lien creditors can enjoy a priority, of course. In this respect, a judgment creditor may obtain a judicial *hypothec* (*ipoteca giudiziale*) thereby securing his lien creditor status. Therefore, a judgment creditor can enjoy a special priority over creditors with other kind of execution titles by registering the judgment with real property registry as soon as possible. The same result obtains in France where the *hypothèque judiciaire* is also available. However, the French law now limits the intervention to those creditors with an execution title. Somehow, Japan did not, and still does not, have the concept of judicial *hypothec* and traditionally took the equality approach in its pure form. Thus, a judgment creditor and other creditors with or without an execution title are treated equally in the distribution of proceeds. The law of 1979 limits the intervening creditors to other execution title holders and also allows the court to set a short time period within which an intervention can be made. The only exception is the provisional attachment creditor, who is not an execution title holder but can intervene to secure a future distribution. This exception was included in the 1979 law in order to enable a legitimate creditor without an execution title, such as a recent automobile accident victim, to participate. Such a creditor may obtain a provisional attachment order even after a creditor has commenced an execution and participate in the proceedings by filing his claim. His recovery must be deposited in the official depository pending the final adjudication of his claim through ordinary litigation.

Under the priority approach, as in Germany, the creditor who initiates the proceedings by seizing a property enjoys a priority. But the judicial *hypothec* plays a role also here. A judgment creditor can register a judgment lien (*Zwangshypothek*) with the real property registry (which is the local court of the situs of property) and secure a priority as of the time of registration. Therefore, even if another creditor with a notarized deed, for example, has thereafter started an execution, the judgment creditor is treated as a prior lien creditor. Where there is no judgment lien creditor, a seizure creates a seizure lien (*Phändungspfandrecht*). A second seizure only creates the second seizure lien.

In common law countries, the United States somehow inherited the institution of judgment lien from the continental Europe. Strangely, the idea is not known in English law. In most states of the United States, a judgment lien attaches when a judgment is docketed in the court of situs of the real property. Such a lien can be asserted whenever the property is sold and the proceeds are distributed. Thus, the system works much as the German does. A judgment lien holder who initiates an execution enjoys a priority unless there is a prior lien holder of some kind on the same property. If no judgment creditor is involved, a prior seizure creates a levy lien. A second seizure by another creditor is junior only to the first one. Thus, the system is constructed upon the priority approach.

In English law, there is no judgment lien. Its alternative is the charging order by the court which turns a judgment creditor into a secured creditor. The judgment creditor first get an order *nisi* which freezes the property and, only after objections are cleared, the order *nisi* is made an order absolute. The charge is registered and the charging order is enforced by a sale. The whole process is complex, but the system is based on the priority approach. Other creditors have no possibility to share in the proceeds of the sale except for prior lien holders.

JAPAN

Carl F. Goodman, Justice and Civil Procedure in Japan 388–389 (2004).

Not only do criminal activities hamper the effort to collect on judgments but also there is little effective way to discover the whereabouts of a debtor's assets when the debtor has engaged in activity designed to hide assets from a creditor. Even if property has to be registered and thus there is the possibility of tracing ownership via official registers, there may be difficulty in proceeding against the property. The named register owner is presumed to be the owner and has rights to prevent execution against "its" property. Where movable property (personal property) that does not require registration is involved, it may be even more difficult to locate assets. There is no supplementary proceeding as in the United States.

* * *

The Civil Execution Law nonetheless now contains provisions that permit the bailiff to investigate into the location of certain assets of the debtor. The court has a general authority to examine judgment debtors and in the process may ask about the location of assets.

Japanese Civil Execution Act.*

Article 43 (Method of execution against immovables)

1. Compulsory execution on an immovable (except for fixtures on land for which registration may not be made; hereinafter,

* Translation in Zentaro Kitigawa, Doing Business in Japan App. 4E (2005).

the same exception shall apply throughout this Section) shall be carried out by way of compulsory sale by auction or compulsory administration (hereinafter referred to as "execution against an immovable"). These methods may be used in conjunction with each other.

Article 59 (Extinguishment of right by sale)

1. Preferential rights, rights of pledge with provisions neither to use nor to make a profit and hypothecs on the immovable are extinguished by sale.

2. The acquisition of rights concerning the immovable which cannot be set up against those who have a right which will be extinguished in accordance with the provision of the preceding paragraph, or against an attachment oblige or a provisional attachment oblige, shall lose its effect by the sale.

3. An attachment, execution of provisional attachment, or provisional disposition concerning the immovable which cannot be set up against an attachment obligee, a provisional attachment obligee, or those who have a right which will be extinguished in accordance with the provision of paragraph 1 shall lose its effect by the sale.

4. In cases where a right of retention or right of pledge without provisions prohibiting use or the making of profits and to which the provision of paragraph 2 do not apply, exists on the immovable, the buyer shall be liable for satisfaction of the obligation right secured by such right.

5. * * *.

Article 122 (Commencement of execution concerning movables)

1. Compulsory execution against movables * * * shall be commenced by seizure of the subject matter by the execution officer. * * *

Article 143 (Commencement of execution on an obligation-right)

Compulsory execution on an obligation-right, the subject matter of which is the payment of money or the delivery of a ship or a movable * * * shall be commenced by the issuance of an attachment order by the execution court. * * *

Article 168 (Compulsory execution of delivery of immovable)

1. Compulsory execution of delivery or surrender of an immovable or a ship or the like in which a person dwells shall be carried out by the execution officer dispossessing the obligor of the subject matter and having the obligee take possession thereof.

Article 169 (Compulsory execution of delivery of movables)

1. Compulsory execution of delivery of movables * * * shall be carried out by the execution officer's taking them from the obligor and delivering them to the obligee.

Article 172 (Compulsory execution of obligation-duty to act or forbear from an act)

1. Compulsory execution of an obligation-duty whose subject matter is an act or forbearance from action shall be carried out by the execution court's ordering the obligor to pay a certain amount of money deemed reasonable to secure the performance of the obligation-duty to the obligee, either for delayed period, or immediately if the obligation-duty is not performed within a certain period deemed reasonable.

Article 173 (Fiction of declaration of intention)

1. If a judgment or any other decision ordering an obligor to declare his intention becomes final and binding, or a compromise, acknowledgment or conciliation ordering the obligor to declare his intention is accomplished, the obligor shall be deemed to have declared his intention at the time the said judgment or other decision became final and binding or at the time of accomplishment of the said compromise, acknowledgment or conciliation * * *.

Takaaki Hattori and Dan Fenno Henderson, Civil Procedure in Japan 14–24 (Yasuhei Taniguchi, Pauline C. Reich, and Hiroto Myake, eds., Rev. 2nd ed. 2002).

COMPULSORY MANAGEMENT

Upon receiving an application similar to the one for compulsory sale, the court makes a ruling initiating compulsory management * * *, which, when served, has the effect of a seizure. The court at the same time appoints an administrator, who seeks to produce income from the seized immovable by any appropriate method (e.g., by leasing the house or having land cultivated to produce crops). In case of compulsory management, only creditors with enforceable instruments may demand distribution.

While compulsory management of immovables to enforce monetary payments follows the old law in most respects, the powers of administrator * * * have been classified and strengthened by the [Civil Execution Law]. Also, the execution court is given flexible authority (1) to allow a debtor to remain in his/her seized residence for a time, when alternative housing is unavailable, and (2) to allocate some of the income from the managed property to the debtor to ensure a minimal livelihood.

ENGLAND

Civil Procedure Rules, Part 71—Orders to Obtain Information from Judgment Debtors (The White Book Series 2006)

Order to attend court

71.2—(1) A judgment creditor may apply for an order requiring—

(a) a judgment debtor; or

(b) if a judgment debtor is a company or other corporation, an officer of that body,

to attend court to provide information about—

(i) the judgment debtor's means; or

(ii) any other matter about which information is needed to enforce a judgment or order.

Civil Procedure Rules, Part 70—General Rules about Enforcement of Judgments and Orders (The White Book Service 2006)

Methods of enforcing judgments or orders

70.2—(1) The relevant practice direction sets out methods of enforcing judgments or orders for the payment of money.

(2) A judgment creditor may, except where an enactment, rule or practice direction provides otherwise—

(a) use any method of enforcement which is available; and

(b) use more than one method of enforcement, either at the same time or one after another

Civil Practice Direction, Part 70

1.1   A judgment creditor may enforce a judgment or order for the payment of money by any of the following methods:

(1) a write of *fieri facias* or warrant or execution * * *.

(2) a third party debt order * * *.

(3) a charging order, stop order or stop notice * * *.

(4) in a county court, an attachment of earnings order

(5) the appointment of a receiver * * *.

1.2   In addition the court may make the following orders against a judgment debtor—

(1) an order of committal, but only if permitted by—

(a) a rule; and

(b) the Debtors Acts 1869 and 1878 * * *,

(2) in the High Court, a writ of sequestrations, but only if permitted by RSC Order 45 rule 5.

Civil Procedure Rules, Part 72—Third Party Debt Orders (The White Book Service 2006)

Third party debt order

72.2—(1) Upon the application of a judgment creditor, the court may make an order (a "final third party debt order") requiring a third party to pay to the judgment creditor—

(a) the amount of any debt due or accruing due to the judgment debtor from the third party; or

(b) so much of that debt as is sufficient to satisfy the judgment debt and the judgment creditor's cost of the application

Zuckerman on Civil Procedure: Principles of Practice 822–824, 826, 828–829 (2nd ed. 2006).

Orders to obtain information from judgment debtors

A claimant who has obtained a judgment against the defendant might be wholly ignorant of the defendant's means. He may therefore lack the information necessary for deciding whether it is worth commencing enforcement proceedings, which may be expensive, or the information needed to decide which method of enforcement would be the most appropriate. CPR 71 establishes a procedure for requiring judgment debtors to attend court to provide information that may be needed in order to enforce a judgment or order against him * * *. A person served with such an order must attend court at the time and place specified in the order an must produce at court documents in his control which are described in the order (such as bank statements). He must answer on oath such questions as the court may require * * *. Where the question takes place before a court officer, the judgment creditor or his representative may attend and ask questions. However, if the matter is likely to give rise to difficulty, the court may direct that the hearing should be before a judge ... The judgment creditor or his representative must attend and conduct the questioning if the hearing is before a judge.

* * *

Charging orders

A procedure is provided for enforcing money judgments against the property of judgment debtors * * *. Section 1 of the 1979 Charging Orders Act states that for the purpose of enforcing a judgment or order, which directs a judgment debtor to pay money, the court may make a charging order imposing on such property of the debtor as may be specified in the order a charge for securing the payment of any money due under the judgment or order.

* * *

Stop orders

A stop order prohibits the judgment debtor from dealing with the subject matter of the order while the judgment creditor applies for a charging order over the same.

* * *

Stop notices

A *stop notice* * * * is a notice issued by the court which requires a person not tot take, in relation to securities specified in the notice, any of the steps listed * * * without first giving notice to the person who obtained the notice * * *. A stop notice is intended to prevent dealings in securities, without first giving notice to the person who obtained the order, who may be a judgment creditor.

* * *

Writ of fieri facias or warrant of execution

A money judgment may be enforced by execution on the goods of the judgment creditor. The process consists of authorizing the appropriate court officer to seize sufficient goods of the judgment debtor in order to sell them and use the proceeds to satisfy the judgment debt and the cost of enforcement.

* * *

The appointment of a receiver

Where it proves impossible to obtain the cooperation of a judgment debtor, or of any person ordered by the court to perform a particular act, the court may appoint a receiver to carry out the act as directed by the court. A receiver may be authorized, for instance, to receive rents, profits and moneys receivable in respect of the judgment debtor's interest in certain property, and to apply that income in specified ways, including the payment of a judgment debt.

* * *

A judgment creditor who has discovered * * * that the debtor has valuable liquid assets that are held by others, such as bank deposits, will be interested in obtaining access to such assets. CPR 72 makes provision for such situations, replacing the form garnishee proceedings. It enables a judgment creditor to obtain an order compelling a third party, owing a debt to the judgment debtor, to pay the debt directly to the judgment creditor in satisfaction of the judgment. A third party who pays money to the judgment creditor under such an order is discharged from his debt to the judgment debtor * * *.

GERMANY

Peter L. Murray and Rolf Stürner, German Civil Justice 455–456 (2004).

c. Disclosure under Oath

A judgment creditor can request the court executor to conduct the disclosure of the debtor under oath in order to discover assets or income for the satisfaction of the judgment. Disclosure is in order if the creditor makes a showing that efforts to levy on the assets of the judgment debtor have not resulted in full satisfaction of the judgment or are not likely to do so, that the debtor has refused to permit the court officer to search through his premises, or that the court executor has not found the debtor in his premises in repeated visits after sufficient notice and without excuse.

Upon receipt of a proper request for disclosure, the court executor must notify the debtor and set a time for the disclosure hearing at least 2 weeks but not more than four weeks following receipt of the request. Upon notification by the court executor the judgment debtor is required to provide a written disclosure under oath of all of his tangible and intangible property as well as all claims against third parties. The disclosure must include all transfers of property to a relative or close associate made within two years before the disclosure hearing, and all gifts and transfers of property without full consideration to anyone made within four years of the disclosure hearing.

If the debtor makes a showing that he will pay and discharge the judgment within a time period of not more than six moths, the court executor must delay the disclosure hearing to give him a chance to do so. At the disclosure hearing, the court executor may question the debtor about the disclosure in order to clarify ambiguity and insure completeness. The debtor then swears an affidavit to the accuracy and completeness of his written disclosure as supplemented at the hearing. A debtor can be subject to a repeated disclosure within three years only if the creditor makes a plausible showing that the debtor has acquired new property or income in the interval since the last disclosure.

Astrid Stadler and Wolfgang Hau, The Law of Civil Procedure in Introduction to German Law 365, 381–383 (Matthias Reimann and Joachim Zekoll, eds., 2nd ed. 2005).

1. ATTACHMENT OF THE DEBTOR'S MOVABLE PROPERTY

The attachment of movable property is accomplished by the enforcement officer. Enforcement begins with the attachment of the chattel in question, which means that the debtor can no longer dispose of the chattel. In order to do so, the enforcement officer will take possession of the chattel that must be under the debtor custody or under the custody of a third party willing to give up possession. Since the enforcement officer normally does not examine the status of ownership, attachment of a third party's property which is found in the debtor's custody is effective * * *

Money, negotiable instruments and other valuables will be taken by the execution officer and held in custody. All other things are left in the debtor custody, with an official stamp marking the attachment * * * In order to protect the debtor basis of subsistence, the Code of Civil

Procedure specifies chattels that are exempt from execution. The judicial sale of attached goods occurs by way of public auction. After deduction of costs, the creditor receives the proceeds of the sale while the debtor is entitled to any surplus.

2.   GARNISHMENT OF CLAIMS AND OTHER PROPRIETARY INTERESTS

It may be more acceptable and cheaper for the creditor to initiate garnishment proceedings in which the debtor claims, such as wages and salaries, are subject to execution * * * The creditor must file a petition for enforcement identifying the claim to be garnished. The court will examine the general prerequisites for enforcement but will not inquire whether the claim actually exists or not. If the debtor does not hold a valid claim, the garnishment will be without legal effect. Another prerequisite is that the claim must be susceptible to enforcement. Only claims which are assignable may be attached by garnishment * * * Wages, for example, are exempt from garnishment up to a certain limit in order to grant the debtor the necessities of life.

If all prerequisites are fulfilled, the court will issue a garnishment order identifying the claim and forbidding the garnishee to pay the debtor. The latter will be ordered not to dispose of the claim in any way. The garnishment order becomes effective when served upon the garnishee. In a second step, often taken together with the garnishment order, the court will transfer the garnished claim to the creditor, who then has the right to submit the claim to the garnishee and to file an action if the garnishee does not pay voluntarily * * *.

3.   ENFORCEMENT PROCEEDINGS INVOLVING THE DEBTOR'S IMMOVABLE PROPERTY

The enforcement may be effected by way of public auction in order to liquidate the substance value of the real estate and discharge the creditor claim with the proceeds. The public sale necessitates a court order which will be issued only if the debtor is the actual owner according to the public land register * * * The highest bidder in the auction will be awarded a contract, and legal title in the estate will be transferred to him by judicial act. The proceeds will be distributed among the judgment creditor and other creditors of the debtor whose encumbrances did not survive the public sale.

Another enforcement option is sequestration: upon motion of the creditor, the court will issue an order depriving the debtor of his right and authority to administrate his property. The court will appoint an administrator, and the creditor will receive all income from the real estate * * *

Alexander Layton and Hugh Mercer, eds., European Civil Practice, Vol. 2, 208 (2nd ed. 2004).

If the judgment debtor does not satisfy the judgment voluntarily, the *Gerichtsvollzieher* [bailiff] visits the debtor and demands payment. If the debtor cannot pay, the *Gerichtsvollzieher* will seize property to the required value by attaching official seals to it. If there is insufficient property at the debtor's premises he will be summoned to court for an examination as to his means. Thereafter, other assets may be seized or an attachment of earnings order may be made. Inability to pay will ultimately lead to insolvency. It should be noted that if a company appears to have insufficient assets even to pay for insolvency proceedings, the enforcement procedure is closed forthwith and the company is struck from the register.

The claimant may also obtain, while the judgment is provisionally enforceable, a form of execution whereby the defendant is required to pay the amount of the judgment and costs to the *Gerichtsvollzieher*. In this latter instance, the claimant does not put up security, but the money is not paid over to him until the judgment has become final.

THE UNITED STATES

Federal Rules of Civil Procedure

Rule 64 Seizure of Person or Property

At the commencement of and during the course of an action, all remedies providing for seizure of person or property for the purpose of securing satisfaction of the judgment ultimately to be entered in the action are available under the circumstances and in the manner provided by the law of the state in which the district court is held, existing at the time the remedy is sought, subject to the following qualifications: (1) any existing statute of the United States governs to the extent to which it is applicable; (2) the action in which any of the foregoing remedies is used shall be commenced and prosecuted or, if removed from a state court, shall be prosecuted after removal, pursuant to these rules. The remedies thus available include arrest, attachment, garnishment, replevin, sequestration, and other corresponding or equivalent remedies, however designated and regardless of whether by state procedure the remedy is ancillary to an action or must be obtained by an independent action.

Rule 70 Judgment for Specific Acts; Vesting Title

If a judgment directs a party to execute a conveyance of land or to deliver deeds or other documents or to perform any other specific act and the party fails to comply within the time specified, the court may direct the act to be done at the cost of the disobedient party by some other person appointed by the court and the act when so done has like effect as if done by the party. On application of the party entitled to performance, the clerk shall issue a writ of attachment or sequestration against the property of the disobedient party to compel obedience to the judgment. The court may also in proper cases adjudge the party in contempt. If real or personal property is within the district, the court in lieu of directing a conveyance thereof may enter a judgment divesting the title of any party and vesting it in others and such judgment has the effect of a conveyance executed in due form of law. When any order or judgment is for the delivery of possession, the party in whose favor it is entered is entitled to a writ of execution or assistance upon application to the clerk.

FRANCE

Alexander Layton and Hugh Mercer, eds., European Civil Practice, Vol. 2, 173–174 (2nd ed. 2004).

The execution is carried out by the *huissier* attaching assets of the judgment debtor. A range of different forms of attachment is available, including the seizure and sale of personal goods (*saisi vente*), the charging of land (*saisie immoblilière*) and the attachment of third party debts such as a bank account (*saisie attribution*) or earnings (*saisie des rémunérations*). Exceptionally, attachment of earnings is within the exclusive jurisdiction of the *tribunal d'instances*. A judgment creditor obtains an order from the court which is then passed to the employer for implementation. The judgment debtor may apply to the court by a procedure of *opposition* to amend or set aside the order. There is no procedure whereby a debtor can be examined as to his assets or their whereabouts. However, when a *huissier* cannot manage to locate the debtor or his assets in order to enforce a judgment, he may require the *procureur de la République* to make enquiries about the residence of the debtor, his bank accounts and his employer. A stay of execution may be obtained only on an application in *référé* proceedings to the court of first instance or to the *juge de l'exécution*.

COUR DE CASSATION*

3rd Civil Chamber
Public Hearing on May 26, 1992

No. of appeal: 90–13248
Published in Report

Presiding: M. Senselme
Reporter: M. Mouvrelerur
Advocate General: M. Mourier
Advocates: La SCP Lyon–Caen, Fabiani and Thiriez, La SCP Le Bret and Laugier

REPUBLIC OF FRANCE
IN THE NAME OF THE FRENCH PEOPLE

On the first count (allegation):

* Translation by Yasuhei Taniguchi.

Articles 2093 and 2094 of Civil Code having been seen;

For the reason that the properties of the debtor are the common security of the creditors and that its price is to be distributed pro rata among them unless there is a legitimate basis for preference among them; that the legitimate bases for preference are privileges and hypothecs;

For the reason that, in the framework of the procedure for distribution of the proceeds, after a seizure of an immovable pursued by virtue of a demand (commandement) delivered upon application of SDBO Bank, the appealed appellate judgment (Paris, January 18, 1990), after having found, on the one hand, that the provisional registration of hypothecs taken by the Soci Union de Credit for the building (UCB) were, for the reason of their dates, not valid as against the SDBO, and, on the other hand, that the latter, not having renewed the registration of hypothec of which it was the beneficiary, remained as a simple unsecured creditor and maintained in the distribution of UCB a rank inferior to that of the SDBO, while holding in the stated reasons that the SDBO enjoyed a preferential rank because of earlier publication of its demand for payment;

that, by holding this way, while the seizing unsecured creditor can not by the simple fact of its demand of seizure enjoy a preference in regards to other unsecured creditors of the debtor, the Appellate Court (cour d'appel) violated the above mentioned provisions;

FOR THESE REASONS, and without any room for deciding on the second count:

QUASH AND ANNUL, in respect to its totality, the judgment of January 18, 1990, by the Appellate Court of Paris between the parties: as a result, return the case and the parties to the state where they had been before the said judgment, and in order to do justice, remand them to the Appellate Court of Orleans.

VI. RELIEF FROM EXECUTION

The execution law of every system provides the debtor and third parties with elaborate means of obtaining relief from execution. These means may be based either on procedural or substantive grounds. Because the execution must be carried out according to law, procedural errors must be corrected and appropriate relief provided. Court intervention is available to correct procedural errors in all systems, and a debtor or third party may raise an objection (*Errinerung, opposizione agli atti esecutivi*, etc.) based on such an error. Generally speaking, objections on a procedural ground tend to be abused by the debtor in an attempt to delay the process. Because of the nature of the objection, a summary procedure is appropriate for disposing of it. Thus, a good balance must be struck between the requirement of due process and the need for an efficient execution.

Relief on substantive grounds is necessary because the claim to be enforced may have changed prior to execution. Even with an execution title which has res judicata effect, the claim embodied in it may have ceased to exist at the time of execution, for example, by virtue of a payment since made. The onus to assert and prove such a new development in the substantive relationship between the parties generally rests on the debtor in all systems even where there is no concept of the execution title. Because the matter relates to the determination of a substantive right, a formal law suit is sometimes necessary to serve the purpose. In some civil law systems, a special law-suit is provided for in the law of execution, such as *Vollstreckungsgegenklage* (Germany), *Oppositionsklage* (Austria), *opposizione all'esecuzione*, etc. When these law-suits are commenced, the execution may be stayed upon an application. Common law does not seem to have such a formalistic means for the purpose, but a stay of execution is available from the court in appropriate situation. As mentioned before, when an appeal is pending from a provisionally enforceable judgment of the lower court, the appellate court (or the lower court) may stay the execution.

Another concern is the third party's right. If a third party claims a right (typically, ownership) to the seized property, he should be able to assert his right and prevent the execution. In civil law, such objection must be asserted by way of a special law-suit for that purpose (*Drittwiderspruchsklage* (Germany), *Exszindierungsklage* (Austria), *opposizione del terzo, terceria de dominio o de major derecho*, etc.). A stay of execution is available when such an action is filed. In common law, a similar effect is reached. In English law, an interpleader is the proper procedural means to be employed in case of execution against chattels. American state statutes provide for a similar remedy for the third party in the same situation (e.g., New York CPLR § 5239).

Relief from an unjustifiable execution may be available even after an execution has been completed. If a malicious execution has been completed, the debtor may be able to recover damages through an action for tort. When a lawful execution has been completed with result of a substantively unjust enrichment, an action for recovery of the unjust enrichment can be instituted by the person who suffered the loss. For example, a property of a third party may be seized and sold without knowledge of the third party, who could have had the seizure lifted if he had known of it. When the third party cannot retrieve the property from a bona fide purchaser who has acquired the title through a legitimate procedure, he can recover the loss either from the creditor who is paid unjustifiably from a third party's property or from the debtor who is unjustifiably released from the debt.

GERMANY

Peter L. Murray and Rolf Stürner, German Civil Justice 467 (2004).

There are a number of circumstances under which the court executor or execution court is required to suspend or restrict execution. One is a court decision on an action in arrest of execution or otherwise ordering that the execution be suspended, modified, or delayed either temporarily or permanently, or allowing the execution to go forward only on furnishing of security. Execution must also be suspended if the judgment provides for a stay of execution upon furnishing security for the judgment or depositing sufficient funds to satisfy the judgment in an appropriate escrow account and if the debtor produces official documentary confirmation that these requirements have been satisfied. The court officer may not proceed if the debtor produces an official or private post-judgment document from the judgment creditor acknowledging payment or agreeing to suspension or delay of execution or a receipt from a bank indicating that sufficient funds to pay the judgment have been deposited to the creditor of the judgment creditor or are available to be drawn on by him. If the creditor has already enough security for his claim through a consensual security interest, the debtor can raise objection to execution of the judgment against other property of the debtor.

Astrid Stadler and Wolfgang Hau, The Law of Civil Procedure, in Introduction to German Law 365, 383–384 (Matthias Reimann and Joachim Zekoll, eds. 2nd ed. 2005).

IV.   REMEDIES IN ENFORCEMENT PROCEEDINGS

If the enforcement is unlawful, the party affected has specific remedies that apply only as long as the enforcement proceedings continue, i.e. the enforcement process has been initiated but has not yet been completed. Objections may be raised if the enforcement agency (court, enforcement officers, or land register office) does not comply with the formal requirements of the enforcement proceedings. In this case, the court competent for enforcement matters will examine whether procedural rules were violated.

The debtor may apply for a stay or provisional suspension of enforcement if its continuation would cause undue hardship due to exceptional circumstances. The debtor can also file an action with the trial court to challenge the enforcement of the judgment arguing that there are objections to the creditor claim based on substantive law * * *.

A third party action against enforcement offers a third party the opportunity to prove his rights in the property attached by the court or the enforcement officer. In this action against the creditor, the third party requests that the court declare the enforcement unlawful and suspend execution. As a prerequisite, the third party must have a right that operates as a bar against enforcement (e.g. a property right, security interest, or pledge).

ENGLAND

Alexander Layton and Hugh Mercer, eds., European Civil Practice, Vol. 2, 634 (2nd ed. 2004).

It is for the successful party to decide whether, and if so how, to enforce the judgment. Money judgments are enforceable as soon as they have been drawn up and entered, or otherwise perfected. Judgments must be served on the unsuccessful party solicitor or, if the court so orders, on that party personally. The bringing of an appeal does not suspend the enforceability of a judgment, although the appellant may obtain an order for a stay of execution from the trial judge or from the appellate court. In certain circumstances, notably after six years from the date of the judgments or when any change has taken place in the identity of the parties entitled to or liable to execution, the permission of the court is required for the issue of measure of execution. The methods of enforcement are undergoing changes, but the reform of this area of the law is only partly complete.

Civil Procedure Rules, Rules of the Supreme Court Order 47, Rule 1—Power to stay execution by writ of fieri facias (White Book Service, 2006).

(1) Where a judgment is given or an order made for the payment by any person of money, and the Court is satisfied, on an application made at the time of the judgment or order, or at any time thereafter, by the judgment debtor or other party liable to execution—

> (a) that there are special circumstances which render it inexpedient to enforce the judgment or order; or

> (b) that the application is unable from any cause to pay the money,

Then, notwithstanding anything in rule 2 or 3, the Court may by order stay the execution of the judgment or order a writ of *fieri facias* either absolutely or for such period and subject to such conditions as the Court thinks fit.

Civil Procedure Rules, Part 72.7—Arrangements for debtors in hardship.

(1) If—

> (a) a judgment debtor is an individual;

> (b) he is prevented from withdrawing money from his account with a bank or building society as a result of an interim third party debt order; and

> (c) he or his family is suffering hardship in meeting ordinary living expenses as a result,

the court may, on an application by the judgment debtor, make an order permitting the bank or building society to make a payment or payments out of the account ("a hardship payment order").

ITALY

Alexander Layton and Hugh Mercer, eds., European Civil Practice, Vol. 2, 339 (2nd ed. 2004).

If he wants to challenge the right of the creditor to proceed to execution, the judgment debtor may oppose the *atto di precetto* [a formal command to comply with an executable instrument], by means of a protesting *opposizione all' secuzione.*

If the judgment debtor challenges the formal regularity of the judgment or of the subsequent *atto di precetto*, the opposition is called *opposizione agli atti esecutivi* and must be made within five days from the service on the debtor of the judgment or *atto di precetto*, as the case may be. The decision made in these proceedings, which otherwise follow the normal rule of procedure, is not subject to appeal.

There is considerable dissatisfaction with the enforcement procedure; it proves too often to be long and expensive and to duplicate findings already made by the judge of the merits. Creditors who can afford to wait have a reasonable prospect of achieving full execution. They will have to advance expenses in the process, though these too can be recovered from the debtor. For those without the patience, the defences and delays may prove frustrating.

JAPAN

Japanese Civil Execution Act.*

Article 35 (Action of objection to claim)

1. An obligor who has an objection to the existence or contents of a claim right concerning an obligation title * * * may institute an action of objection to the claim in order to demand a declaration that compulsory execution by virtue of the obligation title shall not be permitted. The same shall apply to cases where the obligor has some objection to the accomplishment of an obligation title other than one created by a court decision.

2. The grounds for objection to a final and binding judgment shall be restricted to those arising after the conclusion of oral argument, and the grounds for objection to a payment order accompanied by a declaration of provisional execution shall be restricted to those arising after service thereof * * *.

* Translation in Zentaro Kitagawa, Doing Business in Japan App. 4E (2005).

Article 36 (Decision of stay of execution concerning an action of objection)

1. In cases where an action of objection to the issuance of an execution clause or an action of objection to a claim has been instituted and the circumstances alleged as grounds for the objection appear reasonable in law and a preliminary showing on the points of fact has been made, the court in which the action has been brought may, upon motion, order a stay of compulsory execution either upon or without security being provided, or order continuation of compulsory execution upon security being provided, or order annulment of a disposition already made upon security being provided until the decision outlines in the next Article, paragraph 1 is rendered in the final judgment. In cases of urgency, the presiding judge may also order such disposition * * *.

Article 39 (Stay of compulsory execution)

1. Compulsory execution must be stayed in cases where any of the following documents are submitted:

 1. exemplification of a decision having executory power which states that the obligation title (except for an execution document) or the declaration of provisional execution shall be annulled, or that the compulsory execution shall not be permitted;

 2. exemplification of a final and binding judgment which declares that the compromise, acknowledgment or conciliation concerning the obligation title is invalid;

 3. exemplification of a record or any other document made by the court clerk which proves that the obligation title referred to in Article 22 items 2 to 4 inclusive has lost its effect by reason of the withdrawal of the suit or other grounds;

 4. exemplification of compromise before the court or conciliation which states that compulsory execution shall not be carried out or that the motion thereof shall be withdrawn;

 5. document which proves that security to avoid compulsory execution has been provided;

 6. exemplification of a decision ordering a stay of compulsory execution or an annulment of the disposition concerning execution;

 7. exemplification of a decision ordering a temporary stay of compulsory execution;

 8. document which states that the obligee has received performance or that he has granted a period of grace for performance after accomplishment of the obligation title.

THE UNITED STATES

Federal Rule of Civil Procedure 62 Stay of Proceedings to Enforce a Judgment

(a) Automatic Stay; Exceptions—Injunctions, Receiverships, and Patent Accountings. Except as stated herein, no execution shall issue upon a judgment nor shall proceedings be taken for its enforcement until the expiration of 10 days after its entry. Unless otherwise ordered by the court, an interlocutory or final judgment in an action for an injunction or in a receivership action, or a judgment or order directing an accounting in an action for infringement of letters patent, shall not be stayed during the period after its entry and until an appeal is taken or during the pendency of an appeal. The provisions of subdivision (c) of this rule govern the suspending, modifying, restoring, or granting of an injunction during the pendency of an appeal.

(b) Stay on Motion for New Trial or for Judgment. In its discretion and on such conditions for the security of the adverse party as are proper, the court may stay the execution of or any proceedings to enforce a judgment pending the disposition of a motion for a new trial or to alter or amend a judgment made pursuant to Rule 59, or of a motion for relief from a judgment or order made pursuant to Rule 60, or of a motion for judgment in accordance with a motion for a directed verdict made pursuant to Rule 50, or of a motion for amendment to the findings or for additional findings made pursuant to Rule 52(b).

(c) Injunction Pending Appeal. When an appeal is taken from an interlocutory or final judgment granting, dissolving, or denying an injunction, the court in its discretion may suspend, modify, restore, or grant an injunction during the pendency of the appeal upon such terms as to bond or otherwise as it considers proper for the security of the rights of the adverse party. * * *

(d) Stay Upon Appeal. When an appeal is taken the appellant by giving a supersedeas bond may obtain a stay subject to the exceptions contained in subdivision (a) of this rule. The bond may be given at or after the time of filing the notice of appeal or of procuring the order allowing the appeal, as the case may be. The stay is effective when the supersedeas bond is approved by the court.

(e) Stay in Favor of the United States or Agency Thereof. When an appeal is taken by the United States or an officer or agency thereof or by direction of any department of the Government of the United States and the operation or enforcement of the judgment is stayed, no bond, obligation, or other security shall be required from the appellant.

(f) Stay According to State Law. In any state in which a judgment is a lien upon the property of the judgment debtor and in which the judgment debtor is entitled to a stay of execution, a judgment debtor is entitled, in the district court held therein, to such stay as would be accorded the judgment debtor had the action been maintained in the courts of that state.

(g) Power of Appellate Court Not Limited. The provisions in this rule do not limit any power of an appellate court or of a judge or justice thereof to stay proceedings during the pendency of an appeal or to suspend, modify, restore, or grant an injunction during the pendency of an appeal or to make any order appropriate to preserve the status quo or the effectiveness of the judgment subsequently to be entered.

VII. CONCLUDING NOTE

As the materials in this Chapter reveal, the civil justice systems described provide a variety of methods for enforcing judgments and the different methods are hardly all equally effective. Consider which of the methods described most appropriately balance the interests of judgment creditors against those of the debtors. Also consider whether and how the differences in enforcement techniques would affect your decision about where to litigate if you had a choice. This question underscores the importance of the next chapter, which addresses the doctrines which limit the parties' power to pick or avoid jurisdictions in which to litigate.

Chapter 11

TRANSNATIONAL LITIGATION

I. INTRODUCTION

This Chapter compares and contrasts the regimes of judicial jurisdiction/forum access and recognition/enforcement of judgments for transborder cases in both civil and common law countries. Transnational litigation is the inevitable result of global commerce and cross-border transactions. Disputes arise that involve parties from different countries and transactions and events that span national borders. The laws and judicial systems of a number of countries may have a role to play in the resolution of that dispute. The choice of forum is one of the most critical aspects of transnational litigation. As we have already seen, judicial systems take different approaches as to how a lawsuit is initiated and financed, how issues are framed, how facts are uncovered, and who the trier of fact may be. The procedure that will control and the broader cultural and judicial philosophy embraced in that system of procedure will be a function of the choice of forum.

We first examine the fundamental principles that justify the exercise of authority over a defendant in a particular case. In some instances, the rules of domestic jurisdiction will also apply in transnational cases. For some countries, regional arrangements (such as the European Regulation on Jurisdiction and the Recognition and Enforcement of Judgments in Civil and Commercial Matters) or international treaties provide specialized standards for the assertion of jurisdiction in certain transnational cases.

The rules of judicial jurisdiction in various countries reflect different values about when it is appropriate to assert authority over a foreign defendant. Some systems, such as the United States, require some type of affiliation by the defendant with the country exercising jurisdiction. In other systems, the interest of the state in providing a convenient forum for its nationals will justify the exercise of authority and in others, litigational convenience based on where events occur and where witnesses will be located will be instrumental in defining the rules of jurisdiction. Often, the rules of jurisdiction will reflect more than a single set of values. As to some bases of jurisdiction, there may be an international consensus about its acceptance—for example, that a defendant can consent to jurisdiction—although there may be differences about how that consent is manifest. Forum access is not only about the formal rules of territorial jurisdiction. In some systems, courts are permitted to consider whether a forum elsewhere is more appropriate and forum access in such situations is also dependent upon the exercise of judicial discretion.

In the transnational setting, rules of judicial jurisdiction cannot be viewed only as a matter of domestic law. If a defendant has assets in the country asserting jurisdiction, a judgment resulting from the court's exercise of jurisdiction will be enforced in that country. But in many instances, the court exercising jurisdiction can do nothing about enforcement of a judgment it renders. Thus, in order to obtain recognition of a judgment in another country, the rules of jurisdiction adopted by the rendering country must be ones that other countries will accept. National laws on recognition and enforcement of judgments will determine the effect to be given to a foreign judgment, unless there is an international or regional convention in force. In the European Union, for example, the European Regulation provides standards for both the assertion of jurisdiction in Member States and the recognition of judgments among those States.

II. FORUM ACCESS: JURISDICTION

Questions of "intra-country" jurisdiction are to some extent outside the scope of the discussion here, which focuses on transnational jurisdiction. At the same time, it is often the case that the rules of domestic jurisdiction also control "international jurisdiction". Consider the following provisions from the German Code of Civil Procedure.

GERMANY

German Code of Civil Procedure.*

§ 12

The court before which a person is generally amenable to suit [hereinafter: "general venue"] shall have jurisdiction for all complaints brought against him or her, unless an exclusive venue shall be established for a complaint.

§ 13

The general venue of a person shall be determined by his or her residence.

§ 17(1)

The general venue of communities, corporate bodies, as well as that of such companies, cooperatives and other associations and

---

* Translation in German Commercial Code and Code of Civil Procedure in English 193–197 (Charles E. Stewart, trans., 2001).

of such trusts, agencies and funds as may be sued as such shall be determined by their seat. Such seat shall be deemed to be, absent a contrary result, the place where management is conducted.

§ 20

In the event that persons shall remain in a location in circumstances the nature of which indicate a long-term sojourn, such persons to include, but not be limited to, household servants, laborers, commercial assistants, students, pupils or apprentices, the court of such location shall have jurisdiction over all complaints at law brought against such persons.

§ 21(1)

In the event that a person maintains, for the operation of a factory, a merchant operation or other commercial operation, an establishment from which business is transacted directly, all complaints against him or her relating to the conduct of business at such establishment may be brought in the court of the place where such establishment is located.* * *

§ 23

That court shall have jurisdiction over complaints because of claims at law against a person with no domestic residence, within the district of which property of the latter or the property claimed in the complaint is located. With regard to claims for payment, the place where the property is deemed to be located shall be the residence of the debtor, and, in the event that there is a pledge for the claim, the place where the property pledged is located.

§ 23a

That court shall have jurisdiction over complaints in support matters against a person with no domestic venue, at which the plaintiff has his or her general domestic venue.

§ 29

(1) The court of the place at which the obligation in dispute is to be performed shall have jurisdiction over disputes arising out of contractual relations or the existence thereof.

(2) An agreement with respect to the place of performance shall confer jurisdiction only in the event that the parties to the contract are merchants, juridical persons of public law or other special public law bodies.

§ 32

The court in the district of which a tort was committed shall have jurisdiction over complaints relating to torts.

Notes and Comments

These provisions determine "venue" ("*Allgemeiner Gerichsstand*") in a purely domestic German case by prescribing the proper district in Germany where the case is to be brought. These same provisions are equally applicable to questions of international jurisdiction when the action is brought against a defendant domiciled in a state outside of the European Union. Thus when § 32 ZPO provides that claims for tort may be brought in the court "in the district of which a tort was committed", in the case of an accident in Frankfurt, the appropriate venue is Frankfurt; in an international case (other than one governed by the EU Regulation on Jurisdiction and Recognition and Enforcement of Judgments), § 32 ZPO establishes jurisdiction in Germany because the tort was committed in Germany. However, when a suit is brought against a defendant domiciled in a Member State of the European Union, the question of jurisdiction is governed by the European Regulation and not by the ZPO.

Contrast the above-excerpted provisions of the ZPO with provisions of the European Regulation on Jurisdiction and the Recognition and Enforcement of Judgments, that are excerpted below. A brief word on this Regulation, often referred to as the "Brussels I" or "European" ("EU") Regulation. The Regulation came into effect on March 1, 2002 and replaced the earlier "European" or "Brussels" Convention on Jurisdiction and the Recognition and Enforcement of Judgments. The Convention, which was entered into in 1968 by the original Common Market countries, covered both rules of jurisdiction and enforcement of judgments. (In 1988, a parallel convention—the Lugano Convention—adopted the jurisdiction and enforcement provisions of the Brussels Convention for the Member States of the larger European Free Trade Association). The Conventions provided jurisdictional rules for Member States in any case in which a defendant was domiciled in a Member State. National rules on jurisdiction were required to give way to the Convention rules, and only the jurisdictional grounds identified in the Convention were considered proper bases of jurisdiction when exercised with respect to a defendant domiciled in a Member State. All other bases of jurisdiction were prohibited, but the Convention also expressly identified rules of jurisdiction in certain Member States that it identified as "exorbitant". They include the nationality of the plaintiff, the presence of property of the defendant, and service on the defendant during his temporary presence in the forum state.

In 1971, a separate Protocol conferred authority upon the European Court of Justice to provide rulings on questions arising under the Brussels Convention, thereby ensuring uniformity of interpretation of the Convention. In March 2002, the Brussels Convention was replaced by EU Regulation 44/2001, which slightly altered a number of provisions in the original Convention. (The use of a "regulation" rather than a revision of the Convention made the provisions directly effective in Member States without the need for ratification by the respective parliaments.)

THE EUROPEAN UNION

Council Regulation (EC) No 44/2001 of 22 December 2000 on jurisdiction and the recognition and enforcement of judgments in civil and commercial matters, O.J. 2001 (L 12), amended by 2002 O.J. (L 225).

CHAPTER II—JURISDICTION

Section 1—General provisions

Article 2

1. Subject to this Regulation persons domiciled in a Member State shall, whatever their nationality, be sued in the courts of that Member State.

2. Persons who are not nationals of the Member State in which they are domiciled shall be governed by the rules of jurisdiction applicable to nationals of that State.

Section 2—Special jurisdiction

Article 5

A person domiciled in a Member State may, in another Member State, be sued:

1. (a) in matters relating to a contract, in the courts for the place of performance of the obligation in question;

(b) for the purpose of this provision and unless otherwise agreed, the place of performance of the obligation in question shall be:

—in the case of the sale of goods, the place in a Member State where, under the contract, the goods were delivered or should have been delivered,

—in the case of the provision of services, the place in a Member State where, under the contract, the services were provided or should have been provided,

(c) if subparagraph (b) does not apply then subparagraph (a) applies;

2. in matters relating to maintenance, in the courts for the place where the maintenance creditor is domiciled or habitually resident or, if the matter is ancillary to proceedings concerning the status of a person, in the court which, according to its own law, has jurisdiction to entertain those proceedings, unless that jurisdiction is based solely on the nationality of one of the parties;

3. in matters relating to tort, delict or quasi-delict, in the courts for the place where the harmful event occurred or may occur;

4. as regards a civil claim for damages or restitution which is based on an act giving rise to criminal proceedings, in the court

seised of those proceedings, to the extent that that court has jurisdiction under its own law to entertain civil proceedings;

5. as regards a dispute arising out of the operations of a branch, agency or other establishment, in the courts for the place in which the branch, agency or other establishment is situated; * * *

Article 6

A person domiciled in a Member State may also be sued:

1. where he is one of a number of defendants, in the courts for the place where any one of them is domiciled, provided the claims are so closely connected that it is expedient to hear and determine them together to avoid the risk of irreconcilable judgments resulting from separate proceedings;

2. as a third party in an action on a warranty or guarantee or in any other third party proceedings, in the court seised of the original proceedings, unless these were instituted solely with the object of removing him from the jurisdiction of the court which would be competent in his case; * * *

Section 3—Jurisdiction in matters relating to insurance

Article 8

In matters relating to insurance, jurisdiction shall be determined by this Section, without prejudice to Article 4 and point 5 of Article 5.

Article 9

1. An insurer domiciled in a Member State may be sued:

    (a) in the courts of the Member State where he is domiciled, or

    (b) in another Member State, in the case of actions brought by the policyholder, the insured or a beneficiary, in the courts for the place where the plaintiff is domiciled,

    (c) if he is a co-insurer, in the courts of a Member State in which proceedings are brought against the leading insurer.

2. An insurer who is not domiciled in a Member State but has a branch, agency or other establishment in one of the Member States shall, in disputes arising out of the operations of the branch, agency or establishment, be deemed to be domiciled in that Member State.

Section 4—Jurisdiction over consumer contracts

Article 15

1. In matters relating to a contract concluded by a person, the consumer, for a purpose which can be regarded as being outside his trade or profession, jurisdiction shall be determined by this

Section, without prejudice to Article 4 and point 5 of Article 5, if:

(a) it is a contract for the sale of goods on instalment credit terms; or

(b) it is a contract for a loan repayable by instalments, or for any other form of credit, made to finance the sale of goods; or

(c) in all other cases, the contract has been concluded with a person who pursues commercial or professional activities in the Member State of the consumer's domicile or, by any means, directs such activities to that Member State or to several States including that Member State, and the contract falls within the scope of such activities.

2. Where a consumer enters into a contract with a party who is not domiciled in the Member State but has a branch, agency or other establishment in one of the Member States, that party shall, in disputes arising out of the operations of the branch, agency or establishment, be deemed to be domiciled in that State.

3. This Section shall not apply to a contract of transport other than a contract which, for an inclusive price, provides for a combination of travel and accommodation.

Article 16

1. A consumer may bring proceedings against the other party to a contract either in the courts of the Member State in which that party is domiciled or in the courts for the place where the consumer is domiciled.

2. Proceedings may be brought against a consumer by the other party to the contract only in the courts of the Member State in which the consumer is domiciled.

3. This Article shall not affect the right to bring a counter-claim in the court in which, in accordance with this Section, the original claim is pending.

Article 17

The provisions of this Section may be departed from only by an agreement:

1. which is entered into after the dispute has arisen; or

2. which allows the consumer to bring proceedings in courts other than those indicated in this Section; or

3. which is entered into by the consumer and the other party to the contract, both of whom are at the time of conclusion of the contract domiciled or habitually resident in the same Member State, and which confers jurisdiction on the courts of that

Member State, provided that such an agreement is not contrary to the law of that Member State.

CHAPTER V

General Provisions

Article 60

1. For the purposes of this Regulation, a company or other legal person or association of natural or legal persons is domiciled at the place where it has its:

     (a) statutory seat, or

     (b) central administration, or

     (c) principal place of business.

* * *

Notes and Comments

What features stand out as the significant differences between a case that is covered by the ZPO as contrasted with the Regulation? It appears that under both German law and the EU Regulation jurisdiction can be asserted by a court in the place where the contract is to be performed and the place where the defendant committed a tortious act or caused the injury resulting from the tortious act. Jurisdiction over a defendant for claims arising out of the activities of its branch can also be asserted in the place where the branch is located under both regimes. But German national law does not provide for international jurisdiction "by joinder". That is, if a claim is asserted against multiple defendants, there must be a basis for jurisdiction against each of them regardless of how closely the claims are related.[1] Nor does German national law allow for jurisdiction based on the domicile of the consumer; and jurisdiction asserted by a maintenance creditor is limited to the place where the creditor is domiciled and does not extend, as the Regulation does, to the habitual residence of the creditor. On the other hand, some bases of jurisdiction pursuant to national law are more expansive than those under the Regulation—for example, jurisdiction on the basis of the presence of defendant's property, which, per the Regulation, cannot be asserted against a domiciliary of a Member State. Also under German national law jurisdiction can be asserted over a defendant on the basis of a defendant's "long-time sojourn" and not merely on the basis of domicile. For an excellent discussion of international jurisdiction in Germany and a comparison of the ZPO and the European Regulation, see Peter L. Murray and Rolf Stürner, German Civil Justice 499–525 (2004).

As we see, Germany has two regimes for international jurisdiction—one that applies when suit is brought against a defendant domiciled in the European Union—and one that applies when the defendant is domiciled elsewhere. Strictly speaking, the European Regulation, which applies to a defendant domiciled in a Member State, would be applicable in a case before a German court involving a plaintiff from Munich and a defendant from

---

1. Peter L. Murray and Rolf Stürner,
German Civil Justice 517 (2004).

Hamburg. However, the Regulation has been construed to apply only to disputes containing an international element, where that element is connected to another Member State.

This "two-regime" feature of German international jurisdiction should be contrasted with that of Italy, which has adopted the European Regulation as its national law and applies the rules of the Regulation to all cases of international jurisdiction.

ITALY

Michele Angelo Lupoi, Italy, International Encyclopaedia of Laws, Civil Procedure, Vol. 2 (P. Lemmens ed., 2002 Supp.).

RULES APPLICABLE IN THE ABSENCE OF A TREATY

136. The rules on Italian international jurisdiction have recently been reformed by the Law No. 218 of 31 May 1995. Most notably, the Italian nationality of the defendant is no longer a general connecting factor as it was before, under Art. 4 CPC [Italian Code of Civil Procedure], even though nationality (and the application of Italian law) still plays an important role in many specific matters.

137. General jurisdiction of Italian courts, whatever the subject matter of the dispute, exists when the defendant is either resident or domiciled in Italy. Domicile of election, however, is no longer a connecting factor. Enterprises and companies can also be sued in Italy if they have a legal representative here. According to Art. 43 CC [Italian Civil Code], a person's residence is the place where he or she habitually demurs, while his or her domicile is the place where her or she has concentrated his or her interests and affairs.

138. As concerns special jurisdiction, within the scope of application of the Brussels Convention of 1968 (now Regulation No. 44/01), Italy has opted to extend the jurisdictional provisions contained in Sec. 2, 3, 4 of Title II of the Convention to disputes against defendants domiciled in a third State.[2] In other words, Italy has effectively harmonized her domestic provisions on jurisdiction to (most) of the European rules in civil and commercial matters, in the true spirit of the common juridical space.

It is a matter of some dispute whether Italian courts could refer preliminary questions to the ECJ concerning the interpretation of the Brussels I rules, in relation to disputes against defendants domiciled in a third State. From the Court point of view, this might prove possible; it is however submitted that this would prove highly inconvenient vis-à-vis the *'extra-communitary'* defendant.

---

2. Art. 3(2) 1. 218/95. [footnote in original].

FRANCE

French Civil Code.*

Article 14

A foreigner, even if not residing in France, may be cited before French courts for the execution of obligations by him contracted in France with a Frenchman; he may be brought before the courts of France for obligations by him in foreign countries towards Frenchmen.

Article 15

A Frenchman may be brought before a court of France for obligations by him contracted in a foreign country, even with a foreigner.

French Code of Civil Procedure.**

Chapter II TERRITORIAL JURISDICTION

Article 42

The court that is territorially competent shall be, subject to any contrary provisions, the one where the defendant lives.

Where there are several defendants, the claimant shall, at his/her choice, apply to the court where one of the defendants lives.

Where the defendant has no known domicile or known residence, the claimant may apply to the court where he/she lives or if he/she lives abroad, to the court of his/her choice.

Article 46

At his/her choice, the claimant may, instead of the court where the defendant resides, bring his/her claim to a different court:

—in contractual matters, before the court within whose jurisdiction the subject matter of the contract was performed or where the performance of the agreed services had been contemplated;

—in tortious matters, before the court within whose jurisdiction the wrongful act was done or where the loss or damage incurred;

—in mixed matters, before the court within whose jurisdiction the property is situated;

—in matters of family maintenance or contribution to the expense of marriage, before the court within whose jurisdiction the creditor resides.

Notes and Comments

Articles 14 and 15 are the two articles in the French Civil Code that expressly deal with the international jurisdiction of French courts. They

---

* Translation in The French Civil Code, Revised Edition (as amended to 1 July 1994) 4 (John H. Crabb, trans., 1995).

** Translation in The French Code of Civil Procedure in English 8–9 (Christian Todd, trans., 2006).

provide a special rule for French nationals in French courts. The term "obligation" here has a broad meaning and is not limited to matters of contract. The rules of domestic jurisdiction found in Articles 42 through 48 of the New Code of Civil Procedure also apply in international cases. Indeed, Article 14 appears to now be a proper basis of jurisdiction only when no other basis of international jurisdiction can be used. For an interesting discussion of Article 14 jurisdiction, see Kevin M. Clermont & John R.B. Palmer, French and American Perspectives Towards International Law and International Institutions: Exorbitant Jurisdiction, 58 Me. L. Rev. 473 (2006).

JAPAN

Unlike in Germany or Italy, in Japan, the courts have not interpreted the Code of Civil Procedure (CCP) to address the adjudicatory authority of courts in international cases, though Japanese domestic jurisdiction provisions have had an important role to play in the development of international jurisdictional standards.

Takaaki Hattori and Dan Fenno Henderson, Civil Procedure in Japan, 4–45–4–50 (Yasuhei Taniguchi, Pauline C. Reich, and Hiroto Miyake, eds., Rev. 2nd ed. 2004).

GENERAL RULES ON INTERNATIONAL JURISDICTION

[a] Leading Case: The 1981 Malaysia Airlines Case

On October 16, 1981, the Supreme Court found a Japanese court competent to handle a wrongful death claim by Japanese heirs of a victim of a Malaysia Airlines crash in Malaysia. The Court based Japanese jurisdiction on Malaysia Airlines' having a place of business in Japan, even though the ticket was bought in Malaysia and the flight began and ended there. The court offered the following general explanation for finding the Japanese court's jurisdiction with regard to civil and commercial matters in the Malaysia Airlines case:

> Generally speaking, adjudicatory authority shall be exercised as an aspect of national sovereignty and its scope in principle is coextensive with national sovereignty.... [I]f a defendant is a foreign corporation which has its head office abroad, it is generally beyond the adjudicatory authority of Japan, unless it is willing to subject itself to the jurisdiction of Japan. However, if a case involves land in Japan or if defendant has a legal connection with Japan, he/she can be, as an exception, subject to the authority of the Japanese courts, whatever his/her nationality is and wherever he/she may be.

> With regard to the limits of these exceptions, we have no statutes expressly prescribing international adjudicatory authority, no treaties to be obeyed and no well-defined rules of international law which are generally recognized. Due to these circumstances, it is

reasonable to decide international jurisdiction in accordance with principles of justice (*jori*) requiring fairness in the treatment of the parties and a speedy and fair adjudication. According to these principles of justice, a defendant is subject to the authority of the Japanese courts when the conditions meet those provisions for internal venue set in the CCP, for example, when the following are in Japan: the defendant's residence (Article 4(1)), the office or place of business in case of a juridical person or any other association (Article 4(3)), the place of performance (Article 5(i)), the location of the defendant's property (Article 5(iv)), the place of the tort (Article 5(9)), and the like.

As stated above, mentioning respect for the "principles of justice" (*jori*), the Malaysia Airlines case seemed to establish a simple rule that the provisions for territorial competence set forth in the CCP were the grounds for permitting the international jurisdiction of Japan, contrary to the previous holdings by the Supreme Court itself with respect to international divorce and the choice of the forum clause in an international contract case. These cases held that the international jurisdiction of Japan should be determined solely in reliance on the principles of justice and the venue provisions of the CCP were mere guidelines for inferring international jurisdiction.

The Malaysia Airlines case did not expressly mention any condition to bring about equitable results, including consideration of the proper international distribution of jurisdiction or comparing the interests and hardship of parties, in applying the above rule. We should note, however, that there were the following special circumstances in this case: both the addresses of the plaintiffs and the defendant's business office were located in Japan; the defendant was a company operating an international airline business and had the economic capacity to proceed in litigation in a foreign country; it was very difficult, if not impossible, for the plaintiffs to file a complaint with the court of the country in which the address of the defendant's principal business office was located; and the issue in the case was how to calculate the damages, etc. Though almost all the commentators agree with the conclusion in the case, the general rule stated in the Supreme Court ruling has resulted in controversy among commentators.

[b]   Case Law After Malaysia Airlines

Since the Malaysia Airlines case, many lower court cases have applied the rule established in Malaysia Airlines, but in doing so, further reviewed whether the results were reasonable on a case-by-case basis, modifying the results if there were "special circumstances" (*tokudan no jijo*) which ran contrary to principles of fairness in the treatment of both parties and a proper and prompt disposition of the controversy. Therefore, practically speaking, even after Malaysia Airlines, the international jurisdiction of Japan has been determined in the following two steps:

(i) whether a Japanese court should exercise jurisdiction is first determined pursuant to the provisions for territorial competence set forth in the CCP; and

(ii) if there are special circumstances which make the conclusion derived from (1) above violative of the principles of justice requiring fairness in the treatment of both parties and a proper and prompt disposition of the controversy, the conclusion will be modified by refusing (or permitting) exercise of jurisdiction.

The Supreme Court later confirmed this test in its judgment of November 11, 1997.[3] In that case, the plaintiff, a Japanese company which imported cars from the defendant, a German company, filed suit in a Japanese court for a pecuniary claim. The plaintiff asserted that the place of performance was Japan and therefore the jurisdiction of the Japanese court should apply in accordance with Article 5 of the pre–1996 CCP (Article 5(1) of the present Code). The Supreme Court followed the Malaysia Airlines case and admitted that jurisdiction could be established on the basis of place of performance, but refused to exercise jurisdiction because: 1) the agreement between the parties was executed in Germany; 2) the purpose of the agreement was to assign to the defendant authority to conduct various transactions in Germany; 3) the agreement on the place of performance of the pecuniary claim of the plaintiff and on the governing law was not clearly agreed upon by the parties; 4) the evidence for the defense was located in Germany.* * *

With respect to the first step established by the Supreme Court, some commentators criticize the reasoning on the ground that courts should consider not only the provisions of domestic law but also the international rules adopted by foreign courts or conventions to which Japan is not a signatory. Furthermore, some commentators point out that some of the territorial competence provisions set forth in the CCP (for example, Article 4(2), Article 5(i)[4]) should be excluded altogether as a basis of international jurisdiction. In fact, some lower courts have typically refused to assume jurisdiction when the jurisdictional basis derives from the latest address of a defendant (Article 4(2)) or the place of performance (Article 5(i)).

Another problematic provision has been Article 7 (partly the same as Article 21 of the pre–1996 CCP), which allows a plaintiff to join several claims against a defendant before the proper court for one of the joined

3. Family Inc. Ltd. v. Shin Miyahara, 51 MINSHU 4055 (Sup. Ct., Nov. 11, 1997) (English version in 41 JAIL 117 (1998)) [footnote 202 in original].

4. Article 4(2) of the CCP (Article 2(2) of the pre–1996 CCP) provides: "The general forum of a person shall be determined by such person's domicile, or by the place of residence when there is no domicile in Japan or the domicile is unknown, or by the last domicile when there is no place of residence in Japan or the place of residence is unknown." Some commentators raise a question about territorial competence based on the "last domicile." Under Article 5(i) of the CCP (Article 5 of the pre–1996 CCP), a suit concerning a property right *may* be brought to a court at the place of performance, thus enabling a claimant to sue in his/her own domicile because the Civil Code makes the domicile of the claimant the place of performance unless otherwise agreed. CC art. 484 [footnote 204 in original].

claims. The courts expanded the application of this provision to the joinder of defendants when the claims against different defendants are "common or arise from the same factual and legal ground." This case law has been incorporated into the new CCP of 1996 (Article 7 *proviso*). Thus, on the basis of this case law or the statutory provision in the new Code, plaintiffs have tried to sue several foreign defendants in a Japanese court when the Japanese jurisdiction against one of the joined defendants is assumed under the ordinary rule stated above.

Under this special venue provision, two situations should be distinguished, namely a simple joinder of claims against a single defendant and a joinder of defendants. As far as purely domestic litigation is concerned, there is no doubt that totally unrelated claims against a defendant can be joined if the venue is found for one of the joined claims. This rule, however, has been held not applicable to international jurisdiction. A Supreme Court judgment of June 8, 2001 held that, in order to establish international jurisdiction deriving from another claim which is raised against the same defendant pursuant to Article 7, a close relationship between the two claims is required.

When several foreign defendants are joined, the interest of joined defendants should be protected more carefully than that of a foreign defendant who can be sued before a Japanese court for one of the joined claims. There the application of the aforementioned Article 7 *proviso* to the international jurisdiction issue needs to be further limited to appropriate cases. Thus, lower courts have held that such a rule should apply only when the result is consistent with the principles of fairness in the treatment of both parties and a proper and prompt disposition of the controversy.

Notes and Comments

For further comparative reading on jurisdictional theory in Japan in relation to U.S. and Continental European approaches, see Akihiro Hironaka, Jurisdictional Theory "Made in Japan": Convergence of U.S. and Continental European Approaches, 37 Vand. J. Transnat'l L. 1317 (2004); Akira Takakuwa, International Jurisdiction in Contract and Tort Cases—Recent Developments in Japanese Case Law, in Intercontinental Cooperation Through Private International Law: Essays in Memory of Peter Nygh 435 (Talia Einhorn and Kurt Siehr, eds., 2004)

ENGLAND

Civil Procedure Rules (The White Book Service 2006).

Service out of the jurisdiction where the permission of the court is required

6.20　In any proceedings to which rule 6.19 does not apply, a claim form may be served out of the jurisdiction with the permission of the court if—

General grounds

(1) a claim is made for a remedy against a person domiciled within the jurisdiction;

(2) a claim is made for an injunction ordering the defendant to do or refrain from doing an act within the jurisdiction;

(3) a claim is made against someone on whom the claim form has been or will be served (otherwise than in reliance on this paragraph) and—

    (a) there is between the claimant and that person a real issue which it is reasonable for the court to try; and

    (b) the claimant wishes to serve the claim form on another person who is a necessary or proper party to that claim;

(3A) a claim is a Part 20 claim and the person to be served is a necessary or proper party to the claim against the Part 20 claimant;

Claims for interim remedies

(4) a claim is made for an interim remedy under section 25(1) of the 1982 Act;

Claims in relation to contracts

(5) a claim is made in respect of a contract where the contract—

    (a) was made within the jurisdiction;

    (b) was made by or through an agent trading or residing within the jurisdiction;

    (c) is governed by English law; or

    (d) contains a term to the effect that the court shall have jurisdiction to determine any claim in respect of the contract;

(6) a claim is made in respect of a breach of contract committed within the jurisdiction;

(7) a claim is made for a declaration that no contract exists where, if the contract was found to exist, it would comply with the conditions set out in paragraph (5);

Claims in tort

(8) a claim is made in tort where—

    (a) damage was sustained within the jurisdiction; or

    (b) the damage sustained resulted from an act committed within the jurisdiction;

Enforcement

(9) a claim is made to enforce any judgment or arbitral award;

Claims about property within the jurisdiction

(10) the whole subject matter of a claim relates to property located within the jurisdiction;

* * *

Notes and Comments

Like Germany, England has two regimes of adjudicatory jurisdiction in transnational cases—the EU Regulation covers actions brought against a defendant domiciled in a Member State and CPR 6.20 provides jurisdictional rules for other defendants. Jurisdiction pursuant to r. 6.20 is essentially discretionary, and application must be made to "serve out". According to 1 Dicey, Morris and Collins, The Conflict of Laws 364–367 (2006):

> Four cardinal points have been emphasised in the decided cases. First, the court ought to be cautious in allowing process to be served on a foreigner out of England. This has frequently been said to be because service out of the jurisdiction is an interference with the sovereignty of other countries, although today all countries exercise a degree of jurisdiction over persons abroad. Secondly, if there is any doubt in the construction of any of the heads of CPR r.6.20, that doubt ought to be resolved in favour of the defendant. Thirdly, since the application for permission is made without notice to the defendant, a full and fair disclosure of all relevant facts ought to be made. Fourthly, the court will refuse permission if the case is within the letter but outside the spirit of the Rule.

* * *

> In exercising its jurisdiction * * * the court will consider, inter alia, whether England is the *forum conveniens*. . . . The claimant must show good reasons why service on a foreign defendant should be permitted, and in considering the question the court must take into account the nature of the dispute, the legal and practical issues involved, such questions as local knowledge, availability of witnesses and their evidence, and expense. * * * To justify the exercise of the discretion, the claimant has to show that England is clearly the appropriate forum for the trial of the action.* * *

> A defendant who wishes to contest the jurisdiction of the court, either on the ground that the case is not within CPR, r.6.20, or that the case is not a proper one for the exercise of the discretion, should acknowledge service of the proceedings, and * * * apply to the court for an order declaring that it has no jurisdiction.

The discretion exercised in a "service out" case is the equivalent of a request for a stay based on *forum non conveniens*, except that the burden is on the plaintiff to demonstrate that England is the appropriate forum in a "service out" case, whereas the burden is on the defendant when a motion to stay on the grounds of *forum non conveniens* is asserted. See Spiliada Maritime Corp. v. Cansulex Ltd., [1987] 1 AC 460; [1986] 3 All E.R. 843

A comprehensive account of civil jurisdiction in England outside of the European Regulation can be found in Chapter 4 of Adrian Briggs and Peter Rees, Civil Jurisdiction and Judgments 289–383 (4th ed. 2005).

THE UNITED STATES

The United States is not a party to any treaty on jurisdiction, such as the EU Regulation, and thus jurisdictional rules in the United States are the product of domestic U.S. law alone. However, because jurisdictional rules for the United States were developed in the context of a federal system, those rules reflect "international" values, such as sovereignty, territoriality and regulatory authority in relation to the respective states of the United States. Indeed, a unique feature of the exercise of judicial jurisdiction in the United States is that standards of jurisdiction are subject to the constitutional limitations of the Due Process Clause of the Constitution. (When jurisdictional authority is based on a state statute or state common law principles, the Due Process Clause of the Fourteenth Amendment is invoked. If a federal jurisdictional statute is involved, the relevant limitation is the Due Process Clause of the Fifth Amendment.)

As a first step, jurisdiction in the United States is generally a matter of state law—either common law or a state statute—and depends upon a defendant's contacts with the forum state. A federal court will not generally have greater territorial reach than the court of the state in which it sits, see Fed. R. Civ. P. 4(k)(1), unless the claim arises under a particular federal statute with nationwide jurisdiction, such as the antitrust and securities acts. There is also a special rule for service and jurisdiction in an international case when a foreign defendant is not subject to jurisdiction in any single state of the United States and the claim arises under federal law. In that situation, the defendant's connection with the United States—so long as it meets the constitutional standard of minimum contacts with the United States—will subject the defendant to suit anywhere in the United States.

Whether by common law or statute, most states provide for jurisdiction with respect to any claim—that is, general jurisdiction—either at the residence or domicile of the defendant or on the basis of defendant's presence in the state if served with process while there. With respect to a corporation or legal entity, its "presence" may be established wherever the defendant is "doing business"—interpreted as having systematic and continuous activities in the forum state. Jurisdiction with respect to a particular claim related to the activity of the defendant—that is, specific jurisdiction—is predicated on the basis of certain acts by the defendant in the forum state or effect in the forum state caused by acts of the defendant elsewhere. With respect to specific jurisdiction, a defendant in a commercial case may be subject to jurisdiction in the forum state for various types of activities. For example, many state statutes authorize the assertion of jurisdiction for claims that arise of out a defendant's "transaction of business within the state". Alternatively, or additionally, statutes may provide for jurisdiction when the claim arises from the defendant's "performance of a contract within the state" or when the claim arises from a defendant's "breaching a contract in this state by failing to perform acts required by the contract to be performed in this state". In tort cases, the nexus with the forum that creates jurisdiction may be acts of the defendant in the forum state or effects there (such as injuries) caused by the defendant. Thus, most state specific-act statutes authorize jurisdiction over a defendant who, in person or through an agent, commits a tortious act or injury within the state. With respect to causing injury within a state, the statutes often require that the defendant carry on other conduct in the state, derive substantial revenue from goods used in the state, or reasonably expect the act to have consequences in the state and derive substantial revenue from interstate or international commerce.

Unlike the statutes in countries like Germany or Italy or England that either do or don't authorize jurisdiction, in the United States, there is a second step to the jurisdictional analysis. A unique feature of the exercise of judicial jurisdiction in the United States is that it is subject to the constitutional limitations of the Due Process Clause of the Constitution. This constitutional restraint applies in both interstate and international cases; and it focuses upon the relationship between the individual defendant and the forum state rather than on the connection between the *dispute and the forum state* that tends to characterize jurisdiction rules in other countries.

Two elements have developed in the judicial case law and comprise this amorphous "due process" standard that is central to jurisdiction jurisprudence in the United States. First, the defendant is required to have "minimum contacts" with the forum state "such that the maintenance of the suit does not offend 'traditional notions of fair play and substantial justice' "—the formulation used in the leading case of International Shoe Co. v. Washington, 326 U.S. 310, 316 (1945). Subsequent case law expanded on the concept of "minimum contacts" to require that the defendant engage in some type of purposeful conduct in the forum state. For example, a defendant who sells goods that cause injury in the forum state will not be held subject to jurisdiction in the state where the injury occurs unless the defendant has exploited the market in the forum state through sale or distribution of the goods. See World–Wide Volkswagen Corp. v. Woodson, 444 U.S. 286 (1980). A second element of "reasonableness" was introduced into the analysis in the leading contemporary Supreme Court case, Asahi Metal Industry Co. v. Superior Court, 480 U.S. 102 (1987), specifically addressing judicial jurisdiction in the international context. The Court there indicated that even where there is a sufficient connection between the defendant and the forum state, other factors, such as the burden imposed on a foreign defendant in defending in the United States, may make the assertion of jurisdiction over the foreign defendant unreasonable. Specifically, the Supreme Court called for a court "to consider the procedural and substantive policies of other nations whose interests are affected" by the assertion of jurisdiction by a court in the United States:

> The procedural and substantive interests of other nations in a state court's assertion of jurisdiction over an alien defendant will differ from case to case. In every case, however, those interests, as well as the Federal interest in Government's foreign relations policies, will

be best served by a careful inquiry into the reasonableness of the assertion of jurisdiction in the particular case, and an unwillingness to find the serious burdens on an alien defendant outweighed by minimal interests on the part of the plaintiff or the forum State.[5]

CANADA

The approach to judicial jurisdiction in Canada has substantial similarities to the approach taken in the United States. Canada, like the United States, is a federal system, but the provincial codes were derived from the jurisdictional provisions in England (now CPR 6.20) which in England were rules for "international" jurisdiction. The Canadian provinces adopted these standards for both inter-provincial and international cases, though recent case law has superimposed a constitutional standard of order and fairness that may play out differently in an international case.

The procedural rules in the provinces with common law systems supplement traditional bases of jurisdiction based on the presence or domicile of the defendant with additional provisions that provide for "service out" of the jurisdiction based on the defendant's activity and the consequences thereof. Strictly speaking, these rules are viewed as creating a "rebuttable presumption of a real and substantial connection of jurisdiction, which is subject to evidence to the contrary". In some provinces, plaintiffs wishing to serve a defendant outside the territory under these rules are required, as in England, to obtain leave of the court that encompasses an element of discretion. More frequently, however, leave is not required when the proceeding falls within the scope of the relevant rule. For example, Rule 17.02 of the Ontario Rules provides that a party may be served outside of Ontario: "in respect of a contract where (i) the contract was made in Ontario, (ii) the contract provides that it is to be governed by or interpreted in accordance with the law of Ontario, (iii) the parties to the contract have agreed that the courts of Ontario are to have jurisdiction over legal proceedings in respect of the contract, or (iv) a breach of the contract has been committed in Ontario, even though the breach was preceded or accompanied by a breach outside Ontario that rendered impossible the performance of the part of the contract that ought to have been performed in Ontario; or in respect of a tort committed in Ontario; or in respect of damage sustained in Ontario arising from a tort, breach of contract, breach of fiduciary duty or breach of confidence, wherever committed."

Traditional bases of jurisdiction, such as presence, domicile, and consent are accepted in Canada. In addition, the Canadian Supreme Court has indicated that the assertion of jurisdiction by a provincial court must have a "real and substantial connection with the parties or the subject matter of the action" and that assertions of jurisdiction must also meet Canadian constitutional standards of order and fairness.[6]

---

5. Asahi, 480 U.S. at 115.

6. See Morguard Investments Ltd. v. De Savoye, [1990] 3 S.C.R. 1077.

Lower courts in Canada are continuing to develop the criteria for the "real and substantial connection" test. The criteria that the common law courts that have not enacted jurisdictional statutes consider are as follows: (1) the connection between the forum and the plaintiff's claim; (2) the connection between the forum and the defendant; (3) unfairness to the defendant in assuming jurisdiction; (4) unfairness to the plaintiff in not assuming jurisdiction; (5) the involvement of other parties to the suit; (6) the court's willingness to recognize and enforce an extra-provincial judgment rendered on the same jurisdictional basis; (7) whether the case is inter-provincial or international in nature; and (8) comity and the standards of jurisdiction, recognition and enforcement prevailing elsewhere.

As is true of jurisdiction jurisprudence in the United States, the relationship between the "real and substantial connection" test and Canadian constitutional principles of order and fairness have given rise to some confusion in Canada. Consider the following excerpt with respect to Rule 17.02(h) and (o) of the Ontario Rules of Civil Procedure. Rule 17.02(h) permits service outside Ontario in respect of "damage sustained in Ontario arising from tort, breach of contract, breach of fiduciary duty or breach of confidence, wherever committed". Rule 17.02(o) permits service outside Ontario "against a person outside Ontario who is a necessary or proper party to a proceeding properly brought against another person served in Ontario."

Janet Walker, Beyond Real and Substantial Connection: The *Muscutt* Quintet, in Annual Review of Civil Litigation 61, 74–77 (Todd Archibald & Michael G. McGowan eds., 2003).

What is the rationale for exercising jurisdiction over a claim based on "damage sustained in" the forum, or for exercising jurisdiction over a person because that person is a "necessary or proper party" to a proceeding over which the court has jurisdiction? The rationale for exercising jurisdiction over damage sustained in the jurisdiction is based on an interest in promoting access to justice. Where a plaintiff is unable to travel to another forum to pursue a claim against a defendant, but the defendant is able to travel to defend the claim, it may be unfair to deprive the plaintiff of access to justice by refusing to exercise jurisdiction over the matter. The rationale for exercising jurisdiction over a person who is a necessary or proper party to a proceeding over which the court has jurisdiction is based on an interest in avoiding a multiplicity of actions with potentially inconsistent results. Indeed, taken in reverse order, it would seem that these two grounds for exercising jurisdiction could well be described as based on the principles of "order" (the avoidance of multiplicity) and "fairness" (access to justice). Accordingly, even though it seems that these two grounds cannot easily be characterized as examples of "real and substantial connections" to the jurisdiction, they seem to serve an important role in making jurisdictional determinations that conform to the principles of order and fairness.

* * *

Does this mean that the real and substantial connection test may not be a comprehensive basis after consent and presence for making jurisdictional determinations in accordance with the principles of order and fairness? Or does this mean that the real and substantial connection test properly comprises the "jurisdiction *simpliciter*" part of the jurisdictional determination, and considerations of access to justice and the avoidance of multiplicity properly comprise the *forum non conveniens* part of the jurisdictional determination?

* * *

Clearly, a consideration of fairness could not be pre-empted in a jurisdictional determination that proceeds in accordance with the constitutional requirements of order and fairness. If the interposition of the real and substantial connection test could pre-empt the consideration of fairness because the test did not encompass considerations of fairness then the test simply cannot be comprehensive of the grounds of jurisdiction prescribed by the principles of order and fairness.

* * *

[I]t may be time to clarify the purpose that the real and substantial connection test can serve and to recognize that the considerations of order and fairness occasionally require the courts to go beyond it in order to promote access to justice and to avoid a multiplicity of proceedings. This view is similar to that taken in some civil law jurisdictions, notably in Québec and Switzerland, where in addition to the various provisions for jurisdiction, there is a special provision permitting the court to exercise jurisdiction as a forum of necessity, or as a forum of last resort. The provision is found in article 3 of the Swiss Private International Law, and in article 3136 of the Québec Civil Code, which states:

> Even though a Québec authority has no jurisdiction to hear a dispute, it may hear it, if the dispute has a sufficient connection with Québec, where proceedings cannot possibly be instituted outside Québec or where the institution of such proceedings outside Québec cannot reasonably be required * * *

[I]t is suggested that it is better * * * to recognize that considerations of access to justice and the avoidance of multiplicity may occasionally warrant the exercise of jurisdiction in order to meet the requirements of the principle of order and fairness even where there is no real and substantial connection.

Notes and Comments

The following observations emerge from a brief look at the jurisdictional provisions in various countries. The regimes in civil law countries have a preference for formal rules and the code provisions on jurisdiction set forth those rules directly without any additional inquiry. By contrast, the United States imposes a constitutional overlay of "minimum contacts" and "reasonableness" against which jurisdiction must be measured; Canada imposes a test of "real and substantial connection" (in Québec, the test would come solely from the Québec Code) and concerns with "order and fairness" also appear to have a constitutional dimension. Although not a matter of constitutional limitation, Japan also seems to impose a standard of reasonableness on assertions of jurisdiction through its consideration of *jori*; and English law also contains some element of discretion in the grant of leave to make "service out" of the jurisdiction.

In most civil law jurisdictions, the rules on judicial jurisdiction tend to be the sole determinative of forum access. By contrast, in common law countries, there may be an additional consideration of whether or not there is a more appropriate forum—the doctrine of *forum non conveniens*, which introduces an additional set of facts for consideration by a court as to whether or not to hear the case. Such discretion is not usually part of the civil law tradition, although there are some exceptions. For example, Section 3135 of the Québec Civil Code provides: "Even though a Québec authority has jurisdiction to hear a dispute, it may exceptionally and on an application by a party, decline jurisdiction if it considers that the authorities of another country are in a better position to decide." Many civil law countries do adopt devices such as *lis pendens* to allocate cases of parallel litigation. Further discussion of *forum non conveniens* and *lis pendens* appear in Section III.

In the United States, the jurisdictional rules offer numerous "connection points" that create the possibility of multiple fora. Although many of the countries whose jurisdictional rules we have reviewed offer rules of "general" jurisdiction, supplemented by rules for "specific" jurisdiction, those provisions combine to identify a very limited number of fora to hear a particular dispute, thus minimizing opportunities for forum shopping. For example, under the EU Regulation, in matters relating to contract, apart from suit in the defendant's domicile, jurisdiction is appropriate only "in the courts for the place of performance of the obligation in question". This reflects one of the objectives of the original Brussels regime—that rules adopted in the context of "special" jurisdiction should point to a single forum. By contrast, in the United States, a defendant is often amenable to specific jurisdiction in a number of places—such as where the contract negotiations occurred, where the contract was performed, and possibly (if there are additional activities) where the contract was entered into—all, of course, subject to the standard of "minimum contacts" and "reasonableness" as interpreted in case law. In this sense, the rules in the United States create broader possibilities for forum shopping.

In almost every country, domicile, habitual residence, or consent of the defendant will provide a basis for jurisdiction. Countries then differ as to what other connections should provide appropriate bases of jurisdiction. In the United States, it is primarily the connection of the forum with the defendant that gives rise to adjudicatory authority. Thus, in the United States, without some type of "purposeful conduct" by the individual defendant, jurisdiction—whether interstate or international—will not meet constitutional requirements. In Canada, the "real and substantial connection" test has been imposed as a limit on jurisdiction, although the focus is not solely on the individual defendant but on the relationship between the claim and the forum more generally. There is also some suggestion that even when there is not a "real and substantial connection between the subject matter of the litigation and the court", the need to promote access to justice or the need to avoid a multiplicity of proceedings might warrant an assertion of jurisdiction. Likewise, a number of civil law countries require connections with the forum, but those connections may include the forum's relationship with the plaintiff or with the defendant or with the events in question. As a result, the jurisdictional reach of U.S. courts often turns out to be more restrictive than that of the courts of other countries. This is particularly true, for example, with respect to jurisdiction on behalf of consumers in the United States, who will generally not be able to sue in their home state unless the defendant has directed activity there, whereas other countries provide that consumers may sue a defendant in the consumer's home state. See, e.g., Article 114(a) of the Swiss Private International Law Statute: "For a consumer's lawsuits based on contracts for which the prerequisites of Article 120 are fulfilled jurisdiction lies, at the option of the consumer, with the Swiss courts: (a) at the domicile of the consumer or his or her habitual residence or (b) at the domicile or, if there is none, at the habitual residence, of the supplier". See also Article 16 of the European Regulation.

However, one major area of jurisdiction where the assertion of jurisdiction by courts in the United States is substantially broader than that of many other countries—particularly civil law countries—is the general "doing business" jurisdiction—that is, where jurisdiction may be asserted on the basis of defendant's substantial activity in the forum state, even when the claim is unrelated to those activities. The underlying rationale for such jurisdiction is that the extensive and continuous activities in the forum state by the defendant—usually a corporate defendant[8]—represent a manifestation of the defendant's presence there—analogous to the physical presence or habitual residence of an individual. Most countries accept the concept of general jurisdiction but identify only a limited number of fora where a defendant may be sued on

---

8. The Supreme Court of the United States has cast some doubt on whether general "doing business" jurisdiction can be applied to individuals. See Burnham v. Suany claim. For individuals, that is likely to be "domicile" or "habitual residence", and with respect to corporations, it may be limited to their statutory seat, see § 17 of the German Code of Civil Procedure, or, as defined in Article 60 of the EU Regulation, the place where it has its statutory seat, or its central administration, or its principal place of business. Section 21 of the German Code as well as Article 5(5) of the EU Regulation subject a foreign defendant to jurisdiction if the defendant has created an "establishment" in the forum state, but under these provisions, the claim has to be directly related to the activities of the branch office or other establishment—an example of specific, not general, jurisdiction. The United States is not alone in treating foreign defendants who have a manifest presence in the forum as if they were locally-based defendants. England asserts jurisdiction over foreign defendants who have an "established place of business".[9] Japan, as in the *Malaysian Airlines* case discussed earlier, permitted a court to assert jurisdiction over a foreign defendant on the basis of a branch office in Japan, even though the suit involved a trip between points in Malaysia. In both cases, however, particular criteria are identified. Case law in the United States defines the "doing business" jurisdiction. But the question of when the level of activity is sufficiently "continuous, ongoing, and pervasive" to satisfy both state and constitutional standards has few clear answers and the resulting standard is an indeterminate one. An additional difficulty with U.S. "doing business" jurisdiction is its broad reach, particularly when the activities of subsidiaries or agents are used to define the presence of the corporation itself. A related concern is the broad forum-shopping opportunities this type of jurisdiction presents in the international context.

As noted earlier, neither the European Regulation nor national rules of Member States of the European Union generally impose the kind of constitutional limitations found in the Due Process Clause of the United States Constitution. But a court in a Member State cannot exercise jurisdiction on any other basis than the grounds set forth in the Regulation in an action against a domiciliary of another Member State. Moreover, Annex I to the Regulation identifies particular grounds of jurisdiction found in the national laws of various Member States that cannot be used and expressly prohibits the exercise of such jurisdiction against a defendant domiciled in another Member State. Included as "exorbitant" bases of jurisdiction are: Article 23 of the German Code of Civil Procedure (jurisdiction based on the presence of property); Articles 14 and 15 of the French Civil Code (jurisdiction based on the nationality of the plaintiff and exclusive jurisdiction in France due to the nationality of the defendant); in the United Kingdom, jurisdiction based on the service of process on the defendant during a temporary presence in the United Kingdom and jurisdiction based on the presence or seizure of the defendant's property situated in the United Kingdom. *Does such an*

perior Court of Cal., 495 U.S. 604, 610 n.1 (1990).

9. See, e.g., South India Shipping Corp. Ltd. v. Export–Import Bank of Korea [1985] 1 W.L.R. 585, 592 (C.A.).

expression of "exorbitance" in an international convention—albeit a regional arrangement—signify an evolving international norm?

A recent attempt at reaching an international consensus about jurisdiction showed how great the differences are. From 1993 until 2001, the Hague Conference on Private International Law conducted negotiations in the hopes of obtaining a world-wide Convention on Jurisdiction and the Recognition of Judgments. But by 2002, it was clear that sharp divisions in legal traditions and cultures about appropriate jurisdictional reach would stand in the way of any successful negotiation. In 2002, the Hague Conference changed course and began negotiations on a more limited Convention—the Hague Convention on Choice of Court Agreements—which was successfully concluded in 2005, although it has not yet been ratified by any country.

The initial interest of the United States in the more comprehensive jurisdiction/judgments Convention was to make a broad range of U.S. judgments enforceable in other countries. As we will see in Section IV on Recognition and Enforcement of Foreign Judgments, the United States is not a party to any bilateral judgments convention, and enforcement of U.S. judgments abroad is often difficult. From the perspective of the Member States of the European Union and the European Free Trade Association, their judgments were enforced among themselves through the Brussels and Lugano Conventions, and also enforced in the United States where foreign judgments are liberally recognized without benefit of treaty and usually without any requirement of reciprocity. Thus, the incentives for the EU and EFTA countries (as well as other countries) to enter into a recognition/enforcement convention with the United States was to obtain from the United States, in exchange for broader enforcement, restrictions on the perceived excesses with respect to U.S. assertions of jurisdiction. Of course, the tensions about the proper scope of jurisdictional rules that came to a head in the Hague negotiations were not only about standards for the exercise of jurisdiction, but were really reflective of other aspects of American procedure discussed in this book: juries, discovery, class actions, contingent fees, and U.S. choice of law rules. In the context of transnational litigation, of course, implementation of those features of U.S. "procedure" is achieved through assertion of judicial jurisdiction in U.S. courts, often over foreign country defendants.

The blueprint for the Hague Jurisdiction and Judgments Convention was a "mixed" Convention, establishing "required", "permitted", and "prohibited" categories of jurisdiction. One of the strongest objections to particular provisions in the Draft Convention came from the United States. The Draft Convention listed as a prohibited ground of jurisdiction "the carrying on of commercial or other activities by the defendant in that State, whether or not through a branch, agency or other establishment of the defendant, except where the dispute is directly related to those activities". Under this provision, courts of a country would not be able to exercise jurisdiction over a claim that arose outside the forum state with respect to a foreign defendant even if that defendant maintained a branch in the forum state or had systematic and continuous activities there. The prohibition was not confined to the situation of recognition of a judgment based on such an assertion of jurisdiction but restricted a forum's direct exercise of jurisdiction even where enforcement of the judgment would take place in the country rendering the judgment. Another concern of the United States involved the need to include some type of "targeting" or "purposeful conduct" to bring jurisdictional grounds into compliance with the U.S. Constitution. The broad scope of the Draft Convention—encompassing intellectual property disputes, consumer contracts, and defamation—highlighted other differences in various legal regimes of jurisdiction, and the implications of e-commerce and the Internet exacerbated those differences in areas where national law was still evolving. For discussions about the breakdown of the Hague negotiations, see Samuel P. Baumgartner, The Proposed Hague Convention on Jurisdiction and Foreign Judgments: Trans–Atlantic Lawmaking for Transnational Litigation (2003); Linda J. Silberman, Comparative Jurisdiction in the International Context: Will the Proposed Hague Judgments Convention Be Stalled?, 52 DePaul L. Rev. 319 (2002); David Bennett, The Hague Convention on Recognition and Enforcement of Foreign Judgments—A failure of characterization, in Intercontinental Cooperation Through Private International Law 19–23 (Talia Einhorn and Kurt Siehr, eds., 2004).

III. FORUM ACCESS: FORUM NON CONVENIENS/LIS PENDENS

Formal rules of jurisdiction may be only the first step in the determination of the proper forum in a transnational case. In many instances, jurisdiction may exist in any one of a number of fora, and each of the parties to the dispute may attempt to initiate litigation. In some situations, the result is parallel litigation; in other cases, the defendant may merely attempt to have an action stayed or dismissed in favor of an alternative forum.

In common law countries, such as England, Canada, Australia, and the United States, *forum non conveniens* operates as an additional mechanism to allocate jurisdiction transnationally. Pursuant to this doctrine, a court which has jurisdiction over a defendant under national law may decline to exercise it on the ground that it is not the appropriate forum for the action because considerations of justice and fairness dictate that the plaintiff litigate in another jurisdiction. The criteria for *forum non conveniens* differ among these various countries, but they have in common an approach where a court will consider a variety of different factors and exercise discretion to determine the appropriate forum. For a more detailed explanation of the differences in the formulations and applications of *forum non conveniens* in different jurisdictions, see Andrew Bell, Forum Shopping and Venue in Transnational Litigation 149–169 (2003); Ronald A. Brand, Comparative Forum Non Conveniens and the Hague Convention on Jurisdiction and Judgments, 37 Tex. Int'l L.J. 467 (2002).

Civil law countries generally resist this type of discretionary approach, and for the most part civil law countries reject the doctrine of *forum non conveniens*. At the same time, the avoidance of a multiplicity of proceedings is an important objective in the civil law, and thus many countries adopt a strict rule of *lis pendens* to avoid parallel proceedings. Article 27 of the EU Regulation is one such example. It provides:

1. Where proceedings involving the same cause of action and between the same parties are brought in the courts of different Member States, any court other than the court first seised shall of its own motion stay its proceedings until such time as the jurisdiction of the court first seised is established.

2. Where the jurisdiction of the court first seised is established, any court other than the court first seised shall decline jurisdiction in favour of that court.

In addition, Article 28 of the Regulation reflects a more flexible standard for a "related" rather than the "same" matter:

1. Where related actions are pending in the courts of different Member States, any court other than the court first seised may stay its proceedings.

2. Where these actions are pending at first instance, any court other than the court first seised may also, on the application of one of the parties, decline jurisdiction if the court first seised has jurisdiction over the actions in question and its law permits the consolidation thereof.

3. For the purposes of this Article, actions are deemed to be related where they are so closely connected that it is expedient to hear and determine them together to avoid the risk of irreconcilable judgments resulting from separate proceedings.

These provisions (Articles 27 and 28) of the European Regulation apply only among Member States of the European Union. However, national laws of a number of countries also include various types of *lis pendens* rules. For example, under the German ZPO § 261(3), when an action has the same subject matter as an action pending elsewhere in Germany, the action must be dismissed on ground of *lis alibi pendens*. Professors Murray and Stürner in German Civil Justice[10] explain how that provision has been applied in cases of transnational jurisdiction:

The same considerations lead to a general willingness of German courts to recognize the defense of *lis alibi pendens* based on pendency in a foreign court, at least where there is a high likelihood that German courts would recognize the judgment of the court in question. As is the case within Germany, the key issues are the identity of the parties and the functional identity of the subject

---

10. Murray and Stürner, *supra* note 1, at 547–548.

matter of the controversy. Of course circumstances requiring denial of recognition of a foreign judgment, such as lack of international jurisdiction, inadequate service of process or *ordre public* may also serve as reasons for refusal to dismiss a German proceeding based on prior pendency of the case abroad. Unless there appears to be a likelihood of recognition of the judgment (*positive Anerkennungsprognose*) the German court need not defer to the foreign proceeding.

The rule in Italy is substantially similar. Article 7 of Law 218/95 [Reform of the Italian System of Private International Law] provides:

> When in a proceeding a plea of lis pendens is brought concerning an action between the same parties having the same object and the same title, the Italian court may stay the proceeding if it deems that the decision of the foreign court may have an effect in the Italian legal system. If the foreign court declines its jurisdiction or the foreign decision is not recognized under Italian law, the Italian court shall continue the proceeding upon the application of the party concerned.[10]

For a comprehensive and comparative treatment of the declination of jurisdiction in various systems, see J.J. Fawcett, Declining Jurisdiction in Private International Law: Reports to the XIVth Congress of the International Academy of Comparative Law (1995).

Notes and Comments

Can you think of advantages in having a strict lis pendens rule instead of the doctrine of forum non conveniens for determining whether or not to decline jurisdiction? Are there disadvantages to having a strict rule of lis pendens, such as that in the EU Regulation?

On the one hand, a *lis pendens* rule offers greater certainty and predictability by requiring a second-filed action to defer to one that was filed previously; such an approach precludes multiplicity of suits, thereby avoiding parallel litigation and its attendant costs. On the other hand, a strict *lis pendens* rule offers the possibility for strategic behavior by litigants. The incentive to be the first to file is increased, encouraging the likelihood of litigation rather than negotiation. Moreover, a party may bring suit in a clearly inappropriate forum—for example, in contravention of an exclusive choice-of-forum clause—and forestall proceedings in the proper forum until the first court has acted.[11] Indeed, a forum with a slow-moving judiciary can as a practical matter eliminate the likelihood that the suit will ever be heard on the merits.[12]

---

10. 35 I.L.M. 760, 766 (1996).

11. See Erich Gasser Gmbh v. MISAT Srl, [2003] ECR I–14693 (interpreting Article 21 of the Brussels Convention—now Article 27 of the EU Regulation—and holding that the second seised court must stay proceedings until the first seised court determines that it has no jurisdiction).

12. One favorite forum choice for this tactic was Italy, where court proceedings moved very slowly. A lawsuit filed in Italy to impede litigation elsewhere came to be known as the "Italian Torpedo". See Trevor C. Hartley, How to Abuse the Law and (Maybe) Come Out on Top: Bad–Faith Proceedings Under the Brussels Jurisdiction and Judgments Convention, in Law and Justice in a Multistate World 73 (James A.R. Nafziger and Symeon C. Symeonides, eds., 2002).

IV. RECOGNITION AND ENFORCEMENT OF FOREIGN JUDGMENTS

The issue of the appropriate forum may be the most essential element of a transnational case. That is particularly true when the plaintiff obtains a judgment against the defendant and the defendant has assets within the jurisdiction. In many cases, however, the defendant will not have assets in the country where the judgment has been obtained, either because the defendant was careful not to place assets there or has by now removed them. In such a situation, it will be necessary for a plaintiff to seek *enforcement of the judgment* in another country. Conversely, if the defendant was successful in the litigation, the defendant will want to avoid a repeat of that litigation in a new forum. Thus, a defendant will want to ensure *recognition of the foreign judgment.*

As we have seen throughout the course of this book, the system of adjudication of a dispute in one country's courts may be substantially different than the system used in another country. Given those differences, it might be asked why one country should recognize or enforce a judgment from a system that is so fundamentally different from its own. Of course, a judgment does reflect the fact that there has been a resolution of the dispute in a formal system of adjudication. The traditional values of *res judicata*—giving repose to the parties and preserving judicial resources—are still relevant when the judgment is a foreign judgment. There is no reason to litigate a matter more than once assuming that the process of adjudication was a fair one. A liberal regime of foreign judgment recognition and enforcement also facilitates the development of international business by encouraging cross-border decisional harmony.

In looking comparatively at transnational recognition and enforcement practice, one finds a basic similarity of frameworks in the national laws of the various countries even though the particular solutions may be slightly different. That is to say, most countries agree that recognition and enforcement of foreign judgments is appropriate, subject to particular limitations. And most agree on the criteria that should be considered in shaping recognition and enforcement practice, even when they come to different resolutions about which of those criteria to adopt. Indeed, even some notable outliers to judgment recognition, such as Sweden and the Netherlands, have carved out judicial exceptions to non-recognition, and in 2004 Belgium changed its *revision au fond* procedure, such that review on the merits is no longer permitted.[13]

In a number of countries, international treaties may also play a role with respect to recognition/enforcement practice in transnational litiga-

---

13. See Belgian Code of International Private Law, article 25, paragraph 2, discussed in Byblos Bank Europe, S.A. v. Sek- erbank Turk Anonym Syrketi, 837 N.Y.S.2d 54 (App.Div. 1st Dep't May 29, 2007).

tion. The most prominent example is the European Regulation (the successor Regulation to the Brussels Convention) not only for required and prohibited bases of judicial jurisdiction but also for recognition and enforcement of judgments. In effect, the enforcement provisions of the Regulation (and the earlier Brussels Convention) operate as the full faith and credit for judgments analogue with respect to judgments within the European Union. Judgments rendered on jurisdictional grounds authorized by the Regulation are entitled to recognition and enforcement in other Member States. Jurisdictional rulings are made by the court that hears the case and renders the judgment. Jurisdictional challenges are not permitted in the State in which enforcement is sought, even with respect to default judgments. Only a very limited number of defenses to recognition and enforcement are available. The relevant provisions of the EU Regulation are set forth below. Consider how they compare to the "national laws" in certain Member States that are also included here.

THE EUROPEAN UNION

Council Regulation (EC) No 44/2001 of 22 December 2000 on jurisdiction and the recognition and enforcement of judgments in civil and commercial matters, O.J. 2001 (L 12), amended by 2002 O.J. (L 225).

CHAPTER III—RECOGNITION AND ENFORCEMENT

Article 32

For the purposes of this Regulation, 'judgment' means any judgment given by a court or tribunal of a Member State, whatever the judgment may be called, including a decree, order, decision or writ of execution, as well as the determination of costs or expenses by an officer of the court.

Section 1

Recognition

Article 33

1.   A judgment given in a Member State shall be recognised in the other Member States without any special procedure being required.

2.   Any interested party who raises the recognition of a judgment as the principal issue in a dispute may, in accordance with the procedures provided for in Sections 2 and 3 of this Chapter, apply for a decision that the judgment be recognised.

3.   If the outcome of proceedings in a court of a Member State depends on the determination of an incidental question of recognition that court shall have jurisdiction over that question.

Article 34

A judgment shall not be recognised:

1.   if such recognition is manifestly contrary to public policy in the Member State in which recognition is sought;

2.   where it was given in default of appearance, if the defendant was not served with the document which instituted the proceedings or with an equivalent document in sufficient time and in such a way as to enable him to arrange for his defence, unless the defendant failed to commence proceedings to challenge the judgment when it was possible for him to do so;

3.   if it is irreconcilable with a judgment given in a dispute between the same parties in the Member State in which recognition is sought;

4.   if it is irreconcilable with an earlier judgment given in another Member State or in a third State involving the same cause of action and between the same parties, provided that the earlier judgment fulfils the conditions necessary for its recognition in the Member State addressed.

Notes and Comments

An interesting point of comparison with the EU Regulation recognition provisions for Member States of the European Union is the U.S. Constitution Article IV "full faith and credit" requirement for the recognition of judgments of states within the United States. See Article IV of the United States Constitution and the implementing statute, 28 U.S.C. § 1738.

In the United States, there is no public-policy exception with respect to enforcement of a sister-state judgment, see Fauntleroy v. Lum, 210 U.S. 230 (1908), whereas Article 34(1) of the EU Regulation allows a Member State to refuse recognition/enforcement of a judgment of another Member State when it is *manifestly* contrary to the public policy of the Member State. In both the U.S. and EU regimes, jurisdiction cannot generally be reviewed in the enforcement/recognition proceeding; but in the United States, lack of jurisdiction may be raised collaterally if the defendant defaulted in lieu of appearing in the first action. No such jurisdictional challenge is permitted under the Regulation. Under Article 26 of the EU Regulation, when the defendant does not enter an appearance, the court is instructed to determine whether or not it has jurisdiction under the Regulation, and subject to limited exceptions, such as insurance or consumer cases, the jurisdiction of the court of origin is not reviewable.

GERMANY

German Code of Civil Procedure.*

§ 328

(1) The recognition of a foreign judgment shall be excluded:

* Translation in German Commercial Code
and Code of Civil Procedure in English 277
(Charles E. Stewart, trans., 2001).

1. In the event that the courts of the state to which the foreign court belongings are not competent according to the German law;

2. In the event that the defendant, who shall have not participated in the proceedings and raises such plea, shall have not been served with the written pleadings initiating the proceedings in the regular way or in a timely manner, so that he or she was not in a position to defend himself;

3. In the event that the judgment is inconsistent with a judgment issued here or with an earlier foreign judgment subject to recognition or in the event that the proceedings on which it is based are inconsistent with an earlier proceeding here which shall have become final;

4. In the event that the recognition of the judgment would give rise to a result that is manifestly incompatible with the basic principles of the German law, including, but not limited to, the circumstances when the recognition would be inconsistent with the constitution;

5. In the event that reciprocity is not assured.

(2) The provision of no. 5 shall not bar the recognition of the judgment in the event that the judgment concerns a claim other than a claim at law and no domestic venue was established pursuant to German law or in the event that it concerns an affiliation matter (§ 640).

Notes and Comments

The German Code provisions set forth the circumstances under which a foreign judgment will *not* be recognized, thereby establishing the conditions for recognition by way of negative implication. Provided the provisions are satisfied, foreign judgments are automatically recognized. There is no mandatory formal proceeding by which a "declaration of recognition" would have to be obtained. A judgment that is recognized in Germany is to be given the same effect as a German judgment—the so-called "theory of equal treatment". Thus, a U.S. judgment would be given whatever preclusive effect a German judgment would be given and not the claim or issue preclusion it might have in the United States.

To be recognized under German law, a foreign judgment must be in civil and commercial matters. Decisions of a criminal, administrative, or tax nature are entitled to recognition and enforcement only if specific laws or regulations so provide. Only "final" judgments are entitled to recognition; judgments that are still subject to an appeal in the rendering state will neither be recognized nor enforced.

As subsection (5) of § 328 ZPO makes clear, a foreign judgment will only be recognized and enforced in Germany if the state of origin recognizes and enforces German judgments—that is, German law imposes a requirement of reciprocity of treatment.[14] The burden to show reciprocity is with the party relying on the foreign judgment—thus, in an action for enforcement, the judgment creditor must show that the courts in the country that rendered the judgment would enforce a German judgment. Because of the difficulty of establishing reciprocity, it has been held sufficient if the rendering state applies conditions to the recognition of foreign judgments that are "in principle comparable" (*im wesentlichen gleichwertig*) to those in Germany. Thus, even though South Africa does not recognize all German bases of international jurisdiction, a South African judgment against a South African defendant was recognized since South Africa recognizes foreign judgments when jurisdiction is based on the defendant's domicile. See Federal Supreme Court, 42 BGHZ 194 (1965), 52 BGHZ 251 (1970). In addition, "partial reciprocity" (*partielle Verbuergun der Gegenseitigkeit*) will also suffice. Thus, for example, even if a country denies recognition and enforcement to German default judgments, other types of judgments will be recognized and enforced if the rendering state recognizes and enforces German judgments of that type.

The two most common defenses to judgment recognition and enforcement are § 328 ZPO (1) lit 1 (jurisdiction of the rendering court) and lit 4 (irreconcilability with fundamental principles of German law). The former excludes recognition of a foreign judgment if the foreign court was not "competent according to the German law". In evaluating the jurisdiction exercised by the rendering court in a transnational dispute, the German court asked to recognize the judgment considers whether the foreign court had jurisdiction "according to German law". The effect is to adopt a "mirror principle"—if Germany would have exercised jurisdiction on the basis of the particular facts, then § 328 ZPO (1) lit 1 is satisfied. Indeed, the foreign court need not have applied the specific ground of jurisdiction relied upon by the foreign court, but rather, it is sufficient if a German court would have found any jurisdictional basis under German law.

Section 328 ZPO (1) lit 4 is the German formulation of "public policy" or "*ordre public*". In Germany the concept has both a procedural and substantive aspect. Irreconcilability on the procedural side would exist if, for example, the foreign judgment results from proceedings that would violate the defendant's right to a fair judicial hearing guaranteed by the German Constitution ("*Grundgesetz*") (Art. 103, section 1 GG) or a right to due process guaranteed by Article 6 of the European Convention on Human Rights. On the substantive side, judgments that violate fundamental principles of the German legal and social system will be denied recognition, but it is consistently stated that differences between German and foreign law or wrongful application of a foreign law will not result in a denial of recognition or enforcement. Although the rhetoric is that the public policy exception should be applied narrowly, counter-examples abound. For example, a German court refused enforcement of a U.S. tort judgment against a German manufacturer based on a jury verdict where the judgment did not contain a written statement of reasons and U.S. law was based on strict liability.[15]

---

14. Germany abolished the reciprocity requirement in family law matters in 1986, and later also abolished it for judgments in non-financial matters if there was no basis for jurisdiction in Germany. See § 328(2) ZPO.

15. Solimene v. B. Grauel & Co., Landgericht Berlin (June 13, 1989).

Often it seems that a German court takes into account the particular nexus with the foreign country when evaluating a policy policy defense. For example, although a $200,000 award for pain and suffering by a court in the United States went well beyond what a German court would grant as damages in a case, the German Federal Supreme Court did not find a violation of German public policy, explaining that the defendant was a dual German–American citizen who committed the acts of sexual abuse giving rise to the proceedings and the judgment in the United States and who had lived his entire life in the United States until he fled to Germany after the events and the proceedings. For more on the recognition and enforcement of foreign judgments in Germany, see Peter L. Murray & Rolf Stürner, German Civil Justice 525–546 (2004).

ITALY

[Reform of the Italian System of Private International Law].*

Article 64

(Recognition of foreign judgements)

1.   A judgement rendered by a foreign authority shall be recognized in Italy without requiring any further proceedings if:

a) the authority rendering the judgement had jurisdiction pursuant to the criteria of jurisdiction in force under Italian law;

b) the defendant was properly served with the document instituting the proceedings pursuant to the law in force in the place where the proceedings were carried out, and the fundamental rights of the defence were complied with;

c) the parties proceeded to the merits pursuant to the law in force in the place where the proceedings were carried out, or default of appearance was pronounced in pursuance of that law;

d) the judgement became final according to the law in force in the place where it was pronounced;

e) the judgement does not conflict with any other final judgement pronounced by an Italian court/authority;

f) no proceedings are pending before an Italian court between the same parties and on the same object, which was initiated before the foreign proceedings;

g) the provisions of the judgement do not conflict with the requirements of public policy (ordre public).

Notes and Comments

In many ways, national law in Italy is similar to that in Germany. However, as is apparent from Article 64, there is no requirement of reciprocity as a condition of recognition or enforcement of a foreign judgment in Italy. For a foreign judgment to be recognized in Italy, the jurisdiction of the

* Translation in 35 I.L.M. 760 (1996).

foreign court must satisfy Italian rules of jurisdiction, which as we have seen earlier, are the jurisdictional bases set forth in the European Regulation. Recall that Italy, unlike most EU countries, applies the jurisdiction rules of the Regulation to all transnational cases. Thus, the provisions in the EU Regulation also provide the bases for the "indirect" jurisdiction of Article 64(1)(a). Because some activity-based jurisdiction on which U.S. judgments are predicated departs from jurisdiction prescribed by the EU Regulation, one might expect resistance to the recognition of certain U.S. judgments. But the Italian courts have proved liberal in interpreting Article 64(1)(a). For example, an Italian court has enforced a U.S. judgment despite the fact that performance of the contract was exclusively in Italy because the judgment concerned not only contractual claims but also tort claims, such as commercial fraud and unfair competition, and the effects of the tort occurred in the United States—a basis of jurisdiction recognized in Italy—and thus enforceable under Article 64. See Semeraro Confezioni Mario Valente–Firenze S.R.l. v. Mario Valente Collezioni Ltd. (Bari Court of Appeal, 11 May 2000).

Article 64(1)(b) introduces a standard of fair procedures but they need not conform to the specifics of Italian procedure; also Article 64(1)(c) indicates that default judgments will be enforced if the foreign rules on default judgments have been followed. Given the specific provision for fair procedures in Article 64(1)(b) the public policy provision in Article 64(1)(g) has been understood to refer to substantive public policy. The Italian Court of Cassation has drawn a distinction between internal Italian public policy and "international" public policy. It has suggested that when the foreign judgment relates only to foreign citizens, recognition should only be refused if there is a violation of "international" public policy; however, in a case involving an Italian citizen, the question becomes a matter of "internal" public policy, requiring less deference to the foreign judgment.

For a more detailed analysis of recognition and enforcement in Italy, see Alessandro Barzaghi, Recognition and Enforcement of United States Judgments in Italy, 18 N.Y. Int'l L. Rev. 61 (2005); Michele Angelo Lupoi, Recognition and Enforcement of Foreign Judgments Outside the Scope of the Brussels and Lugano Conventions: Italy, in 3 Civil Procedure in Europe 347–370 (Gerhard Walter and Samuel P. Baumgartner, eds., 2000).

JAPAN

Code of Civil Procedure of Japan.*

Article 118. *(Effect of foreign court's final and binding judgment)*

---

* Translated by Masatoshi Kasai and Andrew Thorson, and included as end material in Takaaki Hattori and Dan Fenno Henderson, Civil Procedure in Japan (Yasuhei Taniguchi, Pauline C. Reich and Hiroto Miyake eds., Rev. 2nd ed. 2004).

A final and binding judgment of a foreign court shall be valid only upon the fulfillment of all of the following conditions:

i.   the foreign court's jurisdiction is allowed by laws and ordinances or by treaty;

ii.   the defeated defendant has received service (except for service by publication of notice or any similar means) of summons or any other necessary orders to commence procedures or has responded in the action without receiving service thereof;

iii.   the contents of the judgment and the procedures of the litigation are not contrary to the public order or morals of Japan;

iv.   there is reciprocity.

Notes and Comments

Cases interpreting and commentary expounding upon Article 118 shed light on how recognition and enforcement actually operates in Japan. For example, the jurisdictional law referred to in Article 118(i) is a reference to the bases of jurisdiction that are acceptable under Japanese law. The public order/good morals provision of Article 118(iii) is roughly similar to the exception to recognition/enforcement on public policy grounds that we have seen elsewhere. With respect to a U.S. judgment that awarded both compensatory and punitive damages, the Supreme Court of Japan allowed enforcement of the compensatory portion of the award but found the punitive damages part of the award unenforceable. See Northcon I v. Mansei Kogyo Co., 51 Minshu 2573 (July 11, 1997), English translation in 41 Jap. Ann. Int'l L. 104 (1998). In another case, a foreign judgment was held unenforceable as contrary to public order where the judgment was inconsistent with a final and irrevocable judgment rendered by a Japanese court. See Marubeni America Corp. v. Kansai Iron Works, 361 Hanta 127 (Osaka Dist. Ct., Dec. 22, 1977), discussed in Sawaki, Battle of Lawsuits Lis Pendens in International Relations, 23 Jap. Ann. Int'l L. 17 (1979–80). With respect to reciprocity, Japan, like many countries, finds the reciprocity requirement satisfied if the requirements for recognition and enforcement in the foreign country are substantially similar to those in Japan. For further discussion of recognition practice in Japan, see Hideyuki Kobayashi and Yoshimasa Furuta, Products Liability Act and Transnational Litigation in Japan, 34 Tex. Int'l L.J. 93 (1999); Kevin Clermont, A Global Law of Jurisdiction and Judgments: Views from the United States and Japan, 37 Cornell Int'l L.J. 1 (2004).

THE UNITED STATES

Uniform Foreign Money–Judgments Recognition Act (1962), 13 Uniform Laws Annotated (Part II) 39 (2002 ed. and 2006 Supp.).

§ 1. [Definitions].

As used in this Act:

(1) "foreign state" means any governmental unit other than the United States, or any state, district, commonwealth, territory, insular possession thereof, or the Panama Canal Zone, the Trust Territory of the Pacific Islands, or the Ryukyu Islands;

(2) "foreign judgment" means any judgment of a foreign state granting or denying recovery of a sum of money, other than a judgment for taxes, a fine or other penalty, or a judgment for support in matrimonial or family matters.

§ 2. [Applicability].

This Act applies to any foreign judgment that is final and conclusive and enforceable where rendered even though an appeal therefrom is pending or it is subject to appeal.

§ 3. [Recognition and Enforcement].

Except as provided in section 4, a foreign judgment meeting the requirements of section 2 is conclusive between the parties to the extent that it grants or denies recovery of a sum of money. The foreign judgment is enforceable in the same manner as the judgment of a sister state which is entitled to full faith and credit.

§ 4. [Grounds for Non-recognition].

(a) A foreign judgment is not conclusive if

(1) the judgment was rendered under a system which does not provide impartial tribunals or procedures compatible with the requirements of due process of law;

(2) the foreign court did not have personal jurisdiction over the defendant; or

(3) the foreign court did not have jurisdiction over the subject matter.

(b) A foreign judgment need not be recognized if

(1) the defendant in the proceedings in the foreign court did not receive notice of the proceedings in sufficient time to enable him to defend;

(2) the judgment was obtained by fraud;

(3) the [cause of action] [claim for relief] on which the judgment is based is repugnant to the public policy of this state;

(4) the judgment conflicts with another final and conclusive judgment;

(5) the proceeding in the foreign court was contrary to an agreement between the parties under which the dispute in

question was to be settled otherwise than by proceedings in that court; or

(6) in the case of jurisdiction based only on personal service, the foreign court was a seriously inconvenient forum for the trial of the action.

§ 5. [Personal Jurisdiction].

(a) The foreign judgment shall not be refused recognition for lack of personal jurisdiction if

(1) the defendant was served personally in the foreign state;

(2) the defendant voluntarily appeared in the proceedings, other than for the purpose of protecting property seized or threatened with seizure in the proceedings or of contesting the jurisdiction of the court over him;

(3) the defendant prior to the commencement of the proceedings had agreed to submit to the jurisdiction of the foreign court with respect to the subject matter involved;

(4) the defendant was domiciled in the foreign state when the proceedings were instituted, or, being a body corporate had its principal place of business, was incorporated, or had otherwise acquired corporate status, in the foreign state;

(5) the defendant had a business office in the foreign state and the proceedings in the foreign court involved a [cause of action] [claim for relief] arising out of business done by the defendant through that office in the foreign state; or

(6) the defendant operated a motor vehicle or airplane in the foreign state and the proceedings involved a [cause of action] [claim for relief] arising out of such operation.

(b) The courts of this state may recognize other bases of jurisdiction.

Notes and Comments

Because the United States has no bilateral or multinational treaties dealing with recognition or enforcement of foreign judgments, the subject is left completely to "national" law. Curiously, "national" law in this context means the law of the various states of the United States—regardless of whether enforcement is sought in state or federal court. However, the practice on recognition and enforcement of foreign country judgments within the fifty states of the United States is largely uniform. That is party due to the fact that there is a Uniform Act—the Uniform Foreign Money–Judgments Recognition Act (excerpted above)—which has been adopted in 32 states and territories. Also, even in states without the Act, the common law practice on recognition and enforcement embraces similar principles. See Restatement (Third) of the Foreign Relations Law of the United States, §§ 481–483 (1987).

One significant difference among the states is whether reciprocity should be a condition of recognition/enforcement. The official version of the Uniform Act (set forth above) does not include it, but some states, including several that have the Uniform Act, have added a reciprocity requirement as either a mandatory or discretionary basis for refusal of enforcement and recognition.

In general, a judgment must be final and enforceable in the rendering state to be recognized or enforced in a state in the United States, but an appeal does not necessarily prevent finality. Default judgments as well as contested judgments are entitled to recognition.

The Uniform Act distinguishes between mandatory and discretionary refusals to recognize/enforce. The mandatory grounds are (1) failure to provide a system of impartial tribunals compatible with due process and (2) lack of personal or subject matter jurisdiction. The case law is clear that mere differences in procedure—e.g., failure to provide for cross-examination or discovery or juries—do not make the system unfair. In addition, the approach in the United States is to look to systemic unfairness in the system and not to a defect in the particular proceedings. However, there are other discretionary defenses, such the adequacy of notice of the proceeding and fraud, that relate to the particulars of the individual case. Interestingly, a 2005 revision to the Uniform Act added a new discretionary defense to enforcement/recognition that would give greater attention to the particular proceeding resulting in the foreign judgment: it specifics that a judgment need not be recognized or enforced when "the specific proceeding in the foreign court leading to the judgment was not compatible with the require-ments of due process of law"—a move directed to the adequacy of the particular proceedings. But even under this more individualistic or "retail" approach, the provision does not impose a particular set of procedural requirements of U.S. law on foreign courts; rather the procedure undertaken in the foreign court must have been "fair" in a broader international sense.

As for the requisite jurisdictional links, the approach by courts in the United States appears to be quite close to the "mirror principle" approach, adopted in Germany and elsewhere, but it is not always easy to tell. The Uniform Act lists a number of jurisdictional criteria that provide an appro-priate jurisdictional nexus for enforcement of a foreign judgment. An addi-tional provision of the Act states that other bases of jurisdiction may be acceptable; and the case law reveals that most courts in the United States will recognize foreign judgments where the basis of the foreign court's jurisdiction is similar to a jurisdictional ground that would be accepted for direct jurisdiction in the United States.

Other grounds for non-recognition/enforcement are set forth in § 4(b) and are characterized as "discretionary", although once the defense is satisfied, the judgment is almost always refused recognition. A foreign judgment need not be recognized if it resulted from a proceeding where there was inadequate notice, fraud in obtaining the judgment, contravention of a forum selection clause, conflict with another final judgment, or the forum was a seriously inconvenient forum and jurisdiction was based only on personal service, or—the most frequently invoked defense—"the cause of action (or claim for relief) on which the judgment was based was repugnant to the public policy of the state." As in many countries, the public policy exception has generally been interpreted narrowly. One particular feature of the Uniform Act's formulation of "public policy" is its reference to the "cause of action on which the foreign judgment is based". That language led some courts to conclude that as long the *cause of action* is not "repugnant to public policy", the judgment can be recognized and enforced. The 2005 revision to the Uniform Act reformulated this discretionary ground to provide for non-recognition if *either the cause of action or the judgment* itself violates public policy. In other ways, the attitude in the United States to the public-policy defense may also be changing. In certain areas where American values are threatened, the use of the public-policy exception is expanding. Recent cases have invoked the public-policy exception to deny enforcement of defamation judgments obtained in foreign countries after determining that the defamation or other law of those countries was contrary to the "fundamental importance of the free flow of ideas and opinions on matters of public interest and concern" described as "at the heart of the First Amendment."[17]

ENGLAND

There are in fact multiple regimes for recognition and enforcement of foreign judgments in England. With respect to judgments of Member States of the European Union, Article 33 of the EU Regulation provides that the judgment "shall be recognised in the other Member States." With respect to certain other countries, United Kingdom legislation—the Foreign Judgments (Reciprocal Enforcement) Act 1933—provides for registration of a foreign judgment on a reciprocal basis. The United Kingdom is party to a number of bilateral conventions which create the obligation within that legislative framework. As to countries where there is no such obligation, such as the United States, the foreign judgment will be recognized and enforced on the basis of English common law. The following excerpt provides an excellent summary of the common law recognition and enforcement practice:

Adrian Briggs and Peter Rees, Civil Jurisdiction and Judgments 531–532, 546 (4th ed. 2005).

FOREIGN JUDGMENTS AT COMMON LAW: RECOGNITION, AND ENFORCEMENT BY ACTION

General

7.36 * * * For a judgment to be entitled to be *recognised* as *res judicata*, it must be final and conclusive in the court which pro-

---

17. See Telnikoff v. Matusevitch, 347 Md. 561, 602, 702 A.2d 230, 251 (1997) (declining by 2–1 to enforce an English libel judgment obtained by one English resident against another, both of whom were Rus- sian émigrés, where the offending letter and published comments had no connection with the United States), aff'd (table) 159 F.3d 636 (D.C. Cir. 1998).

nounced it, and it must have been given by a court regarded by English law as competent to do so. In order to be *enforceable*, it must be recognised as being final and conclusive upon the merits of the claim, and be for a fixed sum of money. A party opposing recognition of the judgment may rely upon a number of defenses regarded as sufficient by English law. The method of enforcement is to bring an action at common law on the judgment for the debt it creates; and to seek summary judgment on the claim.

In general it is irrelevant that (i) the foreign court had, or did not have, jurisdiction according to its own law: what matters is its having had international jurisdiction according to English private law; or (ii) the foreign court decided the case differently from the way an English court would have done. Once the foreign court has given a judgment which is entitled to recognition under English law, no proceedings may be brought on the underlying cause of action: the foreign judgment itself now constitutes the sole and exclusive basis of claim in the English court* * *

Recognition of judgments *in personam*: the jurisdictional competence of the foreign court

7.37 A judgment *in personam* will be recognized only if it was delivered by a court which, according to English private international law, was competent to do so. This means that it must be either (i) a court within the jurisdiction of which the defendant was present when proceedings were instituted, or (ii) a court to the jurisdiction of which the defendant submitted. Nothing more is required; nothing less will do * * *

Defences to recognition other than lack of jurisdiction

7.46 If the foreign court was not jurisdictionally competent in the eyes of the English common law, its judgment has no effect in England. But if the court was jurisdictionally competent, the defendant will in principle be obliged by English law to accept it as *res judicata*, or the unsuccessful claimant will be bound by the dismissal of his claim, unless he can rely upon one of the defences allowed by English law. They may be formulated as seven, though they do overlap. The first is the judgment was not "final and conclusive" on the issue in respect of which its recognition is sought. The second is if the court gave judgment in breach of a valid and binding arbitration or choice of court clause. This objection can only be relied on by a party who did not agree to the bringing of the proceedings in the foreign court. The third is if the successful party procured judgment in his favour by fraud. The fourth is if the court gave judgment contrary to the rules of natural (or perhaps of substantial) justice. The fifth is if recognition of the judgment would be contrary to English public policy. The sixth is if recognition of the judgment would violate the Human Rights Act 1998. The seventh is if the judgment was in conflict with a prior English judgment * * *

Notes and Comments[17]

As indicated earlier, the framework of recognition/enforcement is similar in the laws of many countries. But interpretations of the codes (in civil law countries) and the case law (in common law jurisdictions) indicate variations in a number of respects, such as: (1) what types of judgments should be entitled to recognition and enforcement; (2) what criteria constitute a fair and impartial proceeding such that recognition and enforcement is appropriate; (3) when is national public policy sufficiently strained to justify a refusal to recognize and enforce a foreign judgment; (4) what jurisdictional links with the rendering forum are sufficient to warrant recognition and enforcement; and (5) is reciprocity of treatment a necessary prerequisite to recognition and enforcement.

International enforcement practice is generally thought to be limited to money judgments. But neither the English Foreign Judgments Act 1933 nor the EU Regulation on Jurisdiction and the Recognition and Enforcement of Judgments in Civil and Commercial Matters excludes non-money judgments from its scope. In the United States, the Uniform Act covers only money judgments, but other types of judgments have frequently been enforced on grounds of comity. In a recent case decided by the Canadian Supreme Court, Pro Swing Inc. v. Elta Golf, Inc., [2006] 2 S.C.R. 612, a unanimous court agreed that the time had come to "revise the traditional common law rule" that recognition and enforcement should be limited to final money judgments, although it declined (4–3) to enforce the particular injunctive order in question.

The quality of procedures is another universally accepted element in recognition practice, although it is implemented in quite different ways in various countries and as a result produces different inquiries in the respective countries. For example, as we have seen, in the United States, the approach is to look to a systemic flaw in the judicial system, whereas the English and Canadian courts appear to subject the particular proceedings in question to the requirement that the proceedings are in compliance with "natural justice". Of course, in the United States, there are other specific defenses to recognition/enforcement relating to adequate notice of the proceedings and the absence of fraud, and these provisions are directed to the proceedings in the individual case. Germany does not appear to have a specific provision phrased in terms of the adequacy of the procedure, but two other provisions of the German Code ensure the fairness of proceedings in the foreign court—§ 328(1) lit 2 (failure to serve the writ in a regular or timely manner) and lit 4 (the result is "manifestly incompatible with the basic principles of German

---

17. These observations are based on remarks prepared by Professor Linda Silberman for her Graveson Lecture, King's College, December 2006. The lecture is entitled "Some Judgments On Judgments: A View from America," and will be formally published in 2007.

law"). The latter limitation includes not only substantive principles but also the procedures under which the foreign judgment was obtained. As a general matter, the laws of most countries do not make the matter of procedure a parochial one and do not impose the specifics of their national procedure in order to meet the standard of "fair procedures".

The residual grant of authority to deny recognition or enforcement to a foreign judgment for public policy/*ordre public* is contained in almost every code or treaty provision concerned with recognition and enforcement of foreign judgments. Interestingly, as noted earlier, the interstate framework within the United States (between states of the United States) does not contain such an exception. The EU Regulation revised the language in the earlier Brussels Convention to now limit public policy to situations "*manifestly* contrary to public policy" in the Member State in which recognition is sought. It is hard to predict what will constitute public policy in any given country, and case interpretation in both civil and common law countries defines its content. One interesting development has been in Italy where the Italian courts have distinguished between "international" public policy which is invoked when the foreign judgment relates only to foreign citizens and "internal" public policy—that requires less deference to the foreign judgment—which applies when an Italian citizen is involved.

Likewise, judicial jurisdiction is generally an integral party of judgment recognition/enforcement practice. As we have seen, within the European Union, the Brussels/Lugano Conventions, and now the EU Regulation, tie jurisdiction and recognition/enforcement together even more closely for purposes of the common internal market. The jurisdictional rules of the EU Regulation provide not only the bases upon which a judgment will be recognized but also the agreed-upon set of rules for the exercise of direct jurisdiction over persons domiciled in Member States. In the absence of such a double convention, however, countries generally identify grounds of "indirect" jurisdiction—i.e. bases of jurisdiction exercised by a foreign court that are acceptable for the purpose of recognizing or enforcing the resulting judgment. As we have seen, a number of countries—such as Germany and Italy—adopt what is characterized as the "mirror principle": that is, if a country permits the exercise of a particular basis of jurisdiction over a foreign defendant by its courts, it will accept a similar assertion of jurisdiction by a foreign court as an appropriate basis of jurisdiction in the recognition/enforcement context. A recent decision by the Canadian Supreme Court, *Beals v. Saldanha* [2003] 3 S.C.R. 416, determined that its "real and substantial connection" test for direct jurisdiction was the appropriate test for indirect jurisdiction in the context of recognition/enforcement of foreign country judgments; the Court had previously applied that test with respect to the recognition and enforcement of inter-provincial judgments. In England, however, the approach is substantially different. The liberal grounds for assertions of direct jurisdiction of English courts under Rule 6.20 of the Civil Practice Rules will *not* suffice as bases on which a foreign court can exercise its jurisdiction for purposes of recognition/enforcement in England; and England accepts only the limited grounds of presence, residence, and various forms of consent or submission as appropriate jurisdictional bases. France is both more liberal in some ways and more restrictive in others. For example, under French law, a foreign court is deemed to have jurisdiction for purposes of recognition/enforcement, if there is a significant relationship between the dispute and the foreign forum, irrespective of the French rules on direct jurisdiction; however, until just recently it was thought that a court in France would not recognize judgments against French nationals as per the exclusive jurisdiction of Article 15 (unless the defendant consented).[18] But in a very recent case, The Cour de Cassation ruled that Article 15 of the French Civil Code does not exclude the jurisdiction of a foreign court so long as the dispute has a significant link to the foreign court and so long as the choice of the foreign forum was not fraudulent.[19]

At one time, in a number of countries the issue of the law applied by the rendering court was a relevant inquiry in determining whether to recognize or enforce a foreign judgment, but choice-of-law review is rarely used today, except in family law or succession cases. Interestingly, in France, a landmark decision of the Cour de Cassation on recognition and enforcement practice identified application of the proper law as one of the conditions that must be satisfied to obtain recognition/enforcement of a foreign judgment.[20] The obligation was not a re-examination of the actual application of law to the merits but rather a check to ensure that the proper law, according to French conflicts principles, was not distorted. Nonetheless, the position of many French commentators today is that choice-of-law review no longer exists in France. By contrast, in Portugal, the issue of applicable law continues to be a serious impediment to recognition.[21]

One of the significant differences to be found among recognition/enforcement practices is the view taken about reciprocity in various countries and in countries that impose the requirement, the method and criteria for establishing reciprocity. Where reciprocity is still a formal requirement, it generally can be satisfied by evidence of recognition practice in the requesting state and often, as in Japan, the conditions are met if the rendering country's requirements for recognition are substantially the same as those in the country asked to enforce the judgment. Specific proof of reciprocity is not necessarily required in certain countries; in Germany, if the leading commentaries list the state of origin as regularly recognizing and enforcing German judgments, the court will not require the judgment creditor to offer proof of reciprocity in the

18. This point is made in Gerhard Walter and Samuel P. Baumgartner, General Report: The Recognition and Enforcement of Judgments Outside the Scope of the Brussels and Lugano Conventions, in 3 Civil Procedure in Europe 23 (Gerhard Walter & Samuel P. Baumgartner eds., 2000).

19. Prieur vs. Montenach, Cass. Civ. 1st Sect., 23 May 2006, discussed in Marina Matousekova, Would French Courts Enforce U.S. Class Action Judgments?, Contratto E–Impresa/Europa 651, 657–659 (2006).

20. Munzer c. dame Munzer, Cass. 1e civ., Jan. 7, 1964.

21. For a discussion of choice of law in recognition practice, see Walter and Baumgartner, supra note 18, at 32–33.

individual case. A few countries, such as Austria, require that the reciprocity requirement be met with a formal guarantee by treaty or ministerial declaration. In the United Kingdom, reciprocity via a treaty is needed to come within the legislation that provides for registration of foreign judgments, but no reciprocity of any kind is necessary to have a foreign judgment enforced or recognized at common law. In Australia, the Foreign Judgments Act 1991 provides a system for establishing reciprocity both affirmatively and negatively. Where a country is found to accord "substantial reciprocity of treatment", a foreign judgment from that country may be registered in Australia as if it were a domestic judgment. Where a country is identified as according less favorable treatment than Australian courts accord to judgments of that country, Australian courts may not enforce judgments from that country. If a country is on neither list, a judgment of that country may be recognized or enforced under the common law, but without the benefit of the registration provisions.

Can you think of ways in which this kind of comparative study of jurisdiction and recognition practices can be useful? Consider this recent effort by the American Law Institute to promulgate a national federal law on the recognition and enforcement of foreign judgments:

ALI, Recognition and Enforcement of Foreign Judgments: Analysis and Proposed Statute 2006.

The Foreign Judgments Recognition and Enforcement Act

§ 1. Scope and Definitions

(a) This Act applies to foreign judgments as herein defined other than:

(i) judgments for divorce, support, maintenance, division of property, custody, adoption, or other judgments rendered in connection with matters of domestic relations;

(ii) judgments rendered in connection with bankruptcy, liquidation, or similar proceedings; and

(iii) foreign arbitral awards or court orders in respect of agreements to arbitrate, except that if judgments of foreign courts confirming or setting aside arbitral awards are sought to be recognized or enforced, they are subject to the criteria for recognition and enforcement set out in the Act.

(b) "Foreign judgment" means any final judgment or final order of the court of a foreign state granting or denying a sum of money, or determining a legal controversy. A judgment or order that is subject to appeal or where an appeal is pending is nonetheless final for purposes of the Act if it is subject to enforcement in the state of origin.

(c) "Foreign state" means any governmental unit outside the United States or outside any territory under control of the United States, including subdivisions of federal states or independent administrative units.

§ 2.   Recognition and Enforcement Generally

(a) Except as provided in subsection (b), a foreign judgment shall be recognized and enforced by courts in the United States in accordance with this Act.

(b) (i) Judgments for taxes, fines, and penalties may be recognized and enforced provided they meet the criteria of this Act, including reciprocity in accordance with § 7, but recognition and enforcement of such judgments is not obligatory.

> (ii) Declaratory judgments and injunctions or comparable orders that meet the criteria of this Act may be entitled to recognition or enforcement under such procedures as the recognizing court deems appropriate.

(c) An action or other proceeding to enforce a judgment shall be brought within 10 years from the time the judgment becomes enforceable in the rendering state, or in the event of an appeal, from the time when the judgment is no longer subject to ordinary forms of review in the state of origin.

§ 3.   Effect of Foreign Judgment in the United States

(a) A foreign judgment that meets the standards set out in this Act is entitled to recognition and enforcement by a court in the United States with respect to the liability or nonliability of a party, and with respect to the damages or other relief, whether monetary or non-monetary, as well as interest and costs, including attorneys' fees, awarded to the prevailing party. If the foreign judgment orders payment in a foreign currency, a court in the United States may order payment in that currency or in United States dollars at the exchange rate prevailing on the date of the judgment granting enforcement.

(b) A foreign judgment rendered in default of appearance of the defendant is entitled to recognition and enforcement, provided that the party seeking recognition satisfies the court in the United States that (i) the rendering court had jurisdiction over the defendant in accordance with the law of the state of origin of the judgment; (ii) the defendant was served with initiating process in accordance with the law of the state of origin; and (iii) the rendering court had jurisdiction over the defendant on a basis not unacceptable in the United States under § 6 of this Act.

(c) If the party resisting recognition or enforcement appears in the proceeding in the United States, that party bears the initial burden of challenging the jurisdiction of the rendering court; if a credible challenge to the jurisdiction of the rendering court is raised, it is up to the party relying on the judgment to establish that the jurisdictional and due-process requirements for enforcement of foreign judgments have been met. If the party resisting recognition or enforcement does not appear in the proceeding in the United States, the party relying on the judgment must make the required showing.

(d) A judgment of dismissal rendered by a foreign court, if otherwise entitled to recognition, shall be treated in the same way as a judgment for the defendant, except

   (i) if the ground for dismissal was lack of jurisdiction of the rendering court;

   (ii) if the ground for dismissal was that the action was time-barred, unless the party seeking to rely on the judgment of dismissal establishes that the claim is extinguished under the law applied to the claim by the rendering court;

   (iii) if the dismissal was based on other grounds not regarded by courts in the United States as constituting dismissal with prejudice, including defective service, failure to pay the required filing fees, failure to post security, failure to join required parties, or similar defects.

§ 4. Claim and Issue Preclusion; Effect of Challenge to Jurisdiction in the Court of Origin

(a) Except as provided in § 3, a foreign judgment that meets the standards set out in this Act shall be given the same preclusive effect by a court in the United States that the judgment would be accorded in the state of origin, unless the rule of preclusion applicable in the state of origin would be manifestly incompatible with a superior interest in the United States in adjudicating or not adjudicating the claim or issue in question. The party seeking to rely on the preclusive effect of a foreign judgment shall have the burden to establish that the claim or issue is precluded.

(b) If the judgment debtor challenged the jurisdiction of the rendering court in the foreign proceeding,

   (i) findings of fact pertinent to the determination of jurisdiction of the rendering court are conclusive in the proceeding in the United States,

   (ii) legal determinations as to the jurisdiction of the rendering court under the law of the state of origin are conclusive in the proceeding in the United States, but the judgment debtor or other party resisting recognition or enforcement may show that such jurisdiction is unacceptable under § 6.

(c) If the judgment debtor has appeared in the foreign action without challenging the jurisdiction of the rendering court, the judgment debtor or other party resisting recognition or enforcement may not challenge the jurisdiction of the rendering court under the law of the state of origin in the proceeding in the United States, but may show that such jurisdiction is unacceptable under § 6.

§ 5.   Nonrecognition of a Foreign Judgment

(a) A foreign judgment shall not be recognized or enforced in a court in the United States if the party resisting recognition or enforcement establishes that:

(i) the judgment was rendered under a system (whether national or local) that does not provide impartial tribunals or procedures compatible with fundamental principles of fairness;

(ii) the judgment was rendered in circumstances that raise substantial and justifiable doubt about the integrity of the rendering court with respect to the judgment in question;

(iii) the judgment was rendered on a basis of jurisdiction over the defendant unacceptable under § 6;

(iv) the judgment was rendered without notice reasonably calculated to inform the defendant of the pendency of the proceeding in a timely manner;

(v) the judgment was obtained by fraud that had the effect of depriving the party resisting recognition or enforcement of adequate opportunity to present its case to the court; or

(vi) the judgment or the claim on which the judgment is based is repugnant to the public policy of the United States, or to the public policy of a particular state of the United States when the relevant legal interest, right, or policy is regulated by state law.

(b) (i) Except as provided in subsections (ii) and (iii), a foreign judgment shall not be recognized or enforced in a court in the United States if the party resisting recognition or enforcement establishes that the judgment resulted from a proceeding undertaken contrary to an agreement under which the dispute was to be determined exclusively in another forum.

(ii) If the party resisting recognition or enforcement participated in the proceeding before the rendering court without raising the defense of the forum-selection agreement, the judgment shall not be denied recognition or enforcement unless it is clear that raising the defense would have been futile.

(iii) If the party resisting recognition or enforcement raised the defense of the forum-selection agreement and the rendering court held that the agreement was inapplicable or invalid, the judgment shall not be denied recognition or enforcement unless the determination of inapplicability or invalidity of the agreement was manifestly unreasonable.

(c) A foreign judgment need not be recognized or enforced in a court in the United States if the party resisting recognition or enforcement establishes that:

(i) the state of origin of the court that issued the foreign judgment did not have jurisdiction to prescribe, or the foreign court was not competent to adjudicate, with respect to the subject matter of the controversy;

(ii) the judgment is irreconcilable with another foreign judgment entitled to recognition or enforcement under the Act and involving the same parties;

(iii) the judgment results from a proceeding initiated after commencement in a court in the United States of a proceeding including the same parties and the same subject matter, and the proceeding in the United States was not stayed or dismissed; or

(iv) the judgment results from a proceeding undertaken with a view to frustrating a claimant's opportunity to have the claim adjudicated in a more appropriate court in the United States, whether by an anti-suit injunction or restraining order, by a declaration of nonliability, or by other means.

(d) The party resisting recognition or enforcement shall have the burden of proof with respect to the defenses set out in subsections (a) and (c). If a defense is raised pursuant to subsection (b) that the judgment was rendered in contravention of a forum-selection agreement, the party seeking recognition or enforcement shall have the burden of establishing the inapplicability or invalidity of the agreement.

§ 6. Bases of Jurisdiction Not Recognized or Enforced

(a) A foreign judgment rendered on any of the following bases of jurisdiction shall not be recognized or enforced in the United States:

(i) except in admiralty and maritime actions, the presence or seizure of property belonging to the defendant in the forum state, when the claim does not assert an interest in or is otherwise unrelated to the property;

(ii) the nationality of the plaintiff;

(iii) the domicile, habitual residence, or place of incorporation of the plaintiff;

(iv) service of process based solely on the transitory presence of the defendant in the forum state, unless no other appropriate forum was reasonably available;

(v) any other basis that is unreasonable or unfair given the nature of the claim and the identity of the parties. A basis of jurisdiction is not unreasonable or unfair solely because it is not an acceptable basis of jurisdiction for courts in the United States.

(b) A foreign judgment based on an assertion of an unacceptable basis of jurisdiction as defined in subsection (a) shall not be denied recognition or enforcement if the factual circumstances would clearly support jurisdiction not inconsistent with subsection (a).

(c) An appearance by the defendant in the rendering court, or an unsuccessful objection to the jurisdiction of the rendering court, does not deprive the defendant of the right to resist recognition or enforcement under this section.

§ 7.   Reciprocal Recognition and Enforcement of Foreign Judgments

(a) A foreign judgment shall not be recognized or enforced in a court in the United States if the court finds that comparable judgments of courts in the United States would not be recognized or enforced in the courts of the state of origin.

(b) A judgment debtor or other person resisting recognition or enforcement of a foreign judgment in accordance with this section shall raise the defense of lack of reciprocity with specificity as an affirmative defense. The party resisting recognition or enforcement shall have the burden to show that there is substantial doubt that the courts of the state of origin would grant recognition or enforcement to comparable judgments of courts in the United States. Such showing may be made through expert testimony, or by judicial notice if the law of the state of origin or decisions of its courts are clear.

(c) In making the determination required under subsections (a) and (b), the court shall, as appropriate, inquire whether the courts of the state of origin deny enforcement to

(i) judgments against nationals of that state in favor of nationals of another state;

(ii) judgments originating in the courts of the United States or of a state of the United States;

(iii) judgments for compensatory damages rendered in actions for personal injury or death;

(iv) judgments for statutory claims;

(v) particular types of judgments rendered by courts in the United States similar to the foreign judgment for which recognition or enforcement is sought;

The court may also take into account other aspects of the recognition practice of courts of the state of origin, including practice with regard to judgments of other states.

(d) Denial by courts of the state of origin of enforcement of judgments for punitive, exemplary, or multiple damages shall not be regarded as denial of reciprocal enforcement of judgments for the purposes of this section if the courts of the state of origin would enforce the compensatory portion of such judgments.

Courts in the United States may enforce a foreign judgment for punitive, exemplary, or multiple damages on the basis of reciprocity.

(e) The Secretary of State is authorized to negotiate agreements with foreign states or groups of states setting forth reciprocal practices concerning recognition and enforcement of judgments rendered in the United States. The existence of such an agreement between a foreign state or group of foreign states and the United States establishes that the requirement of reciprocity has been met as to judgments covered by the agreement. The fact that no such agreement between the state of origin and the United States is in effect, or that the agreement is not applicable with respect to the judgment for which recognition or enforcement is sought, does not of itself establish that the state fails to meet the reciprocity requirement of this section.

§ 8. Jurisdiction of Courts in the United States

(a) The district courts of the United States shall have original jurisdiction, concurrently with the courts of the states, of an action brought to enforce a foreign judgment or to secure a declaration with respect to recognition under this Act, without regard to the citizenship or residence of the parties or the amount in controversy.

(b) Any such action brought in a state court may be removed by any defendant against whom the enforcement or declaration is sought to the United States District Court for the district embracing the place where the action is pending, without regard to the citizenship or residence of the parties or the amount in controversy. A notice of removal shall be filed in accordance with the time limits and procedures of 28 U.S.C. § 1446(b).

The district court may, in its discretion, remand any claim to which the foreign judgment does not apply. In exercising its discretion, the district court shall consider whether the claims involving the foreign judgment are so closely related to the other claims that it would be efficient to hear the entire action.

[(c) Any action brought in a state court in which a foreign judgment asserted to be entitled to recognition or enforcement under the Act is raised as a partial or complete defense, set-off, counterclaim, or otherwise, may be removed to the United States District Court for the district embracing the place where the action is pending, without regard to the citizenship or residence of the parties or the amount in controversy. Any party by or against whom such defense, set-off, counterclaim or other claim is asserted is entitled to remove the action. A notice of removal shall be filed by such party within 30 days after the issue of recognition is raised.

(d) (i) When an action has been removed pursuant to subsection (c), the district court may, prior to determining whether the foreign judgment is entitled to recognition, decide to retain the entire action or, in its discretion, remand to the state court from which the action was removed, any claim with respect to which recognition of a foreign judgment is not invoked. In exercising the discretion to remand pursuant to this subsection, the district court shall consider whether the claims or defenses involving recognition of a foreign judgment are so closely related to other claims or defenses that it would be efficient to retain the entire action.

(ii) After making a determination as to whether the foreign judgment is entitled to recognition, the district court may decide to retain the action, or, in its discretion, remand all or part of the action to the state court from which the action was removed. In exercising the discretion to remand pursuant to this subsection, the district court shall consider the impact of the determination with respect to recognition on the remaining claims and issues in the case, the interests of the parties, and judicial efficiency.

(iii) A remand pursuant to subsections (d)(i) or (d)(ii) shall not be subject to review by appeal or otherwise; however, in a case remanded under subsection (d)(ii), the determination by the district court with respect to recognition of the foreign judgment under this Act shall be subject to immediate appellate review as a final decision.]

§ 9.   Means of Enforcement of Foreign Judgments

(a) (i) Any foreign judgment entitled to recognition and enforcement under this Act may be enforced by means of a civil action, as provided in this section.

(ii) A foreign judgment for a sum of money only, entitled to enforcement under this Act, other than a judgment rendered by default or a judgment subject to appeal, may also be enforced by registration, as provided in § 10.

(b) An action to recognize or enforce a judgment under this Act may be brought in the appropriate state or federal court

(i) where the judgment debtor is subject to personal jurisdiction; or

(ii) where assets belonging to the judgment debtor are situated.

(c) Process in such actions may be served upon the judgment debtor in accordance with applicable state or federal law, including treaties to which the United States is a party.

(d) (i) When a judgment creditor brings more than one action to enforce a foreign judgment in the United States, at least one such action must be brought in the state or federal court for the place where the judgment debtor (if an individual) is domiciled or (if a juridical entity) has its principal establishment in the United States, or where the judgment debtor has substantial assets.

> (ii) If pursuant to paragraph (i) the judgment creditor brings an action where the judgment debtor is domiciled or has its principal establishment, that action is deemed the "main enforcement action," and the court at such place is deemed the "main enforcement court." If the judgment creditor has not brought an action in such place or there is no such place, the judgment creditor shall designate the action at a place where the judgment debtor has substantial assets as the "main enforcement action," and the court at such place is deemed the "main enforcement court."

> (iii) A judgment creditor bringing more than one action pursuant to this section shall inform each court in the United States where such action is brought of all other proceedings relating to the same judgment and shall identify the main enforcement action. Such information shall be supplemented as appropriate.

> (iv) All issues concerning the recognition of a foreign judgment under the Act shall be decided by the main enforcement court, and proceedings relating to the issue of recognition shall be stayed in all other courts in the United States where an action to enforce the judgment may be pending. The decision on recognition shall be binding on all such courts and every other court in the United States.

(e) Any court where an action to enforce is pending may, in appropriate circumstances, require the party resisting enforcement to post security to prevent dissipation of assets.

§ 10. Registration of Foreign Money Judgments in Federal Courts

(a) Except as provided hereafter, a foreign judgment issued by the court of a state that has entered into an agreement with the United States for reciprocal recognition of judgments pursuant to § 7(e) of this Act may be registered in accordance with this section in any United States court for a district in which the judgment debtor has property when the debtor (if an individual) is domiciled in the state or (if a juridical entity) has an establishment in the state. Alternatively, a judgment may be registered in any United States court for a district in which the judgment debtor has substantial assets. A judgment so registered, upon expiration of the 60–day period provided for in subsection (f), or upon denial of a motion to vacate pursuant to subsection (g), shall be a judgment of the district court, and may be enforced in like manner. This section authorizes registration only of money judgments, and does not authorize registration of judgments rendered by confession, in default of appearance or for failure to defend on the merits, or of judgments subject to appeal. A judgment not eligible for registration under this section may not be registered in a state court.

(b) A judgment creditor seeking to register a foreign judgment shall file with the clerk of the registering court (i) a certified copy of the judgment, together with a certified translation into English where necessary; (ii) a statement setting forth the agreement between the state of origin of the judgment and the United States pursuant to § 7(e); (iii) proof that the judgment was rendered within the period prescribed by § 2(c); and (iv) the affidavit prescribed by subsection (c).

An application for registration under this section does not expose the judgment creditor to personal jurisdiction.

(c) The affidavit required by subsection (b) shall set forth (i) grounds for the belief that the judgment debtor is domiciled or has an establishment in the state and has property in the district where the federal court is located, or alternatively, has substantial property in the district where the federal court is located; (ii) that the judgment was not rendered by confession, in default of appearance or for failure to defend on the merits; (iii) that all appeals from the judgment have been exhausted or the time for appeal has expired; (iv) that the judgment has not been satisfied; and (v) that the judgment debtor has insufficient assets in the state of origin of the judgment to satisfy the judgment, or that the judgment debtor has taken steps to conceal assets in the state of origin. The affidavit shall also identify any other court in the United States in which registration or enforcement has been sought. The judgment creditor is under a duty to supplement or correct the affidavit in order to keep the required information current.

(d) Upon receipt of the application for registration and supporting documents, the clerk of the court shall register the foreign judgment in the same manner as a judgment of the court in which it is registered. A judgment so registered shall have the same effect as a judgment of the registering court, including creation of a lien in accordance with state law.

(e) (i) The judgment creditor shall promptly notify the judgment debtor of the registration of the judgment, by first-class mail or other reliable means.

(ii) If the judgment debtor has a registered agent in the United States, notice of the registration shall be given to such agent; if the judgment debtor is a juridical entity with an establishment in the United States, notice shall be given to a managing agent or other responsible person at any such establishment; in other cases, notice shall be given at the last known address or addresses of the judgment debtor, as well as at other addresses of the debtor over the preceding five years known to the creditor, in the United States and elsewhere. The judgment creditor, upon certification under oath, shall furnish to the clerk a list of the addresses to which the notice has been sent and a copy of the notice showing its date.

(iii) The notice shall advise the judgment debtor that a writ of execution may be issued 60 days from the date that notice of the registration is sent to the judgment debtor, unless within that time the judgment debtor files a motion addressed to the court to vacate the registration.

(f) A motion to vacate the registration shall be filed with the clerk of the registering court, with a copy to the judgment creditor, within 60 days of the date that notice of the registration is sent. Unless the court orders otherwise, any lien or other security in place under subsection (d) shall remain in effect, but may not be enforced before the motion to vacate is decided. Notice that a motion to vacate the registration has been filed shall be given by the clerk of the district court where the motion is pending to all other courts in the United States in which registration or enforcement has been sought, and no execution shall issue in any court while the motion to vacate is pending. The court may, in appropriate cases, require a bond or other security to be furnished by the person seeking enforcement.

A motion to vacate does not expose the judgment debtor to personal jurisdiction if such jurisdiction is not otherwise available.

(g) (i) A motion to vacate the registration may be made on the basis that the foreign judgment is not entitled to recognition or enforcement on the ground of any of the defenses set out in this Act.

(ii) A motion to vacate registration of a foreign judgment under this section may also be made on any of the following grounds: that the judgment debtor has no property under the jurisdiction of the registering court available for execution; that the affidavit submitted by the judgment creditor is erroneous; that the judgment has been satisfied; that the judgment has been overturned on appeal; or that an appeal of the judgment is pending in the state of origin.

(h) When a motion to vacate the registration under this section raises a genuine issue with respect to recognition of the foreign judgment under the Act, the court shall vacate the registration and if the judgment creditor chooses to proceed, treat the application as an action to enforce the judgment as under § 9. In such case, the judgment creditor shall have process served upon the defendant in accordance with federal law. If the motion to vacate is granted, the court shall decide whether to continue any lien that may be in effect or to order the judgment debtor to give security under such conditions as may be necessary.

(i) In the case of multiple registrations under this Act, each district court to which a motion to vacate is addressed shall decide issues focused on the property alleged to be situated within the district; for issues concerning recognition under the Act, the proceeding called for by subsection (g) shall be held in the court for the district in a state where the judgment debtor (if an individual) is domiciled or (if a juridical entity) has its principal establishment in the United States, provided that the judgment debtor has property in that district and that an application for registration has been filed in that district. If these conditions are not met, the proceeding called for by subsection (g) shall be held in the district court where the first application for registration was filed. If the judgment creditor brings both an action under § 9 and an application for registration under this section, the proceeding called for by subsection (g) shall be held in the main enforcement court as defined in § 9.

(j) Pending decision on the motion to vacate, no writ of execution may be issued, and no other court shall hear or determine the issue of recognition. If the motion to vacate is granted, all courts before which registration or enforcement has been sought shall be notified, and all liens entered pursuant to subsection (d) shall be discharged, unless the court granting the motion orders the liens to remain in effect pending appeal, or orders security as may be appropriate if the action proceeds under § 9.

§ 11.   Declination of Jurisdiction When Prior Action Is Pending

(a) Except as provided in subsection (b), when an action is brought in a court in the United States and it is shown that a proceeding concerning the same subject matter and including the same or related parties as adversaries has previously been brought and is pending in the courts of a foreign state, the court in the United States shall stay, or when appropriate, dismiss the action, if:

(i) the foreign court has jurisdiction on a basis not unacceptable under § 6; and

(ii) the foreign court is likely to render a timely judgment entitled to recognition under this Act.

(b) A court in the United States may decline to stay or dismiss the action under subsection (a) if the party bringing the action shows

(i) that the jurisdiction of the foreign court was invoked with a view to frustrating the exercise of jurisdiction of the court in the United States, when that court would be the more appropriate forum;

(ii) that the proceedings in the foreign court are vexatious or frivolous; or

(iii) that there are other persuasive reasons for accepting the burdens of parallel litigation.

§ 12.   Provisional Measures in Aid of Foreign Proceedings

(a) A court in the United States may grant provisional relief in support of an order, whether or not it is final, issued by a foreign court

(i) to secure enforcement of a judgment entitled to recognition and enforcement under this Act; or

(ii) to provide security or disclosure of assets in connection with proceedings likely to result in a judgment entitled to recognition and enforcement under this Act.

(b) Before granting provisional relief in support of the order of a foreign court, the court in the United States shall require the applicant to show that the court of origin has determined that the judgment debtor or defendant is likely to dispose of or conceal assets, that the assets within the jurisdiction of the foreign court are or are likely to be insufficient to meet the obligations determined to be owing in the principal action, and that the judgment debtor or defendant has been given notice and a reasonable opportunity to be heard before the court of origin or that it was impossible to give such notice.

(c) In granting provisional relief in accordance with this section,

(i) the court is authorized to make use of such remedies and procedures as are available to it in connection with ordinary proceedings in courts in the United States;

(ii) a federal court may grant an injunction freezing assets of the defendant situated anywhere in the United States.

(d) An order issued pursuant to subsection (c)(i) and notice thereof shall be in accordance with the applicable state statute or rule; an order issued pursuant to subsection (c)(ii) and notice thereof shall be in accordance with the provisions of the Federal Rules of Civil Procedure pertaining to injunctions. Notice of an order issued pursuant to this section shall be given to the judgment debtor or defendant in the foreign action whether or not the judgment debtor or defendant is present in or subject to personal jurisdiction in the United States.

No order pursuant to this section shall be made unless it provides an opportunity for the judgment debtor or defendant within a reasonable time to contest the issuance of the order or to apply for a modification.

(e) The applicant for provisional relief in accordance with this section may be required to give security.

(f) A court in the United States to which application has been made in accordance with this section for provisional relief in aid of an order of a foreign court may, in the interests of justice, communicate directly with the foreign court.

§ 13. Foreign Orders Concerning Litigation in the United States

Orders of a foreign court that may concern or affect litigation in the United States may be taken into account for purposes of determining motions to stay, dismiss, or otherwise regulate related proceedings in the United States.

Notes and Comments

One objective of this proposed ALI statute was to establish uniform federal law for the recognition and enforcement of foreign country judgments. Existing law in the United States, as reflected by the Uniform Act and the Restatement (Third) of Foreign Relations Law, were obvious sources upon which to draw. But in addition, the Reporters were influenced by their study of comparative jurisdiction and recognition practices in designing a number of these provisions. *Can you identify areas where the comparative perspective may have influenced particular provisions of the proposal?* Consider, for example: (1) the types of judgments to be accorded recognition and enforcement under the proposed statute (§§ 1 and 2); (2) the bases of jurisdiction that will lead to a refusal to recognize or enforcement a foreign judgment (§ 6); the approach to reciprocity (§ 7); and the approach to parallel litigation, both directly (§ 11) and for recognition/enforcement purposes (§§ 5(c)(iii) and (iv)).

Chapter 12

HARMONIZATION OF CIVIL PROCEDURE: PROSPECTS AND PERILS

I. INTRODUCTION

The readings in this book reveal many of the ways in which civil litigation differs among nations and yet rests on shared basic principles. In this Chapter we will examine the factors that are leading to cross-border convergence of processes, as well as the concerns that have slowed the process. We begin by asking whether harmonization of procedure is a desirable goal.

According to the great Austrian procedural scholar, Franz Klein, "[T]he squalid, arid, neglected phenomenon of civil procedure is in fact strictly connected with the great intellectual movements of people; and its varied manifestations are among the most important documents of mankind's culture."[1] As one of the "great intellectual movements" of our time is "globalization," by which we mean the increasing irrelevance of national borders to art, business, and technology, it would be surprising if law escaped the influence of that movement. And yet consider more carefully Professor Klein's words. He refers to the "varied manifestations" of procedure. This suggests that "localism" can act as a brake on the momentum of globalization—a reaction to the sometimes numbing effects of global homogenization. As you think back on the preceding readings, do you have the sense that procedural harmonization is an important phenomenon? What direction has it taken? What areas of practice have been or are likely to be affected?

---

1. Mauro Cappelletti, Social and Political Aspects of Civil Procedure—Reforms and Trends in Western and Eastern Europe, 69 Mich. L. Rev. 847, 885–886 (1971).

II. IS HARMONIZATION DESIRABLE?

Geoffrey P. Miller, The Legal–Economic Analysis of Comparative Civil Procedure, 45 Am. J. Comp. L. 905, 916–918 (1997).

III. HARMONIZATION AND UNIFORMITY

Let us turn to the question of harmonization, which is always a central concern for comparativists. Although the goal of harmonization is sometimes treated as a talisman, without substantial consideration of the possible costs and benefits, economic analysis suggests at least a note of caution about the virtues of harmonization.

Harmonization, it should be noted, is not the same thing as efficiency. One can imagine efficient reforms that do not harmonize. If it turns out that a variety of procedural regimes can resolve disputes efficiently, then within a given system, the purpose of reform might be to improve the operation of that system, even if doing so renders the system more unlike, rather than more like, those of its neighbors. One can equally imagine harmonization that does not increase efficiency. Think of a program that enforced a rigid uniformity on procedural systems without regard to the efficiency of the rules being adopted. Such a harmonized system would, as a matter of public policy, be worse than any of the individual systems it replaces.

This does not necessarily mean that harmonization is undesirable from an economic point of view. Indeed, a number of economic arguments counsel in favor of harmonization. Harmonization can break down local bar monopolies by opening up legal practice to persons from outside the jurisdiction. This would appear to be a significant social benefit—and a reason why some elements in the organized bar might oppose harmonization. Harmonization might also reduce transactions costs, since the parties to international legal transactions might have a somewhat better sense of the risks and costs of litigation they face in a harmonized system than they do in a diverse one. This point may be overstated, however, since the parties can specify the jurisdiction and law which they want to govern disputes arising out of their relationship, and so can engage to some extent in "home made" harmonization. Finally harmonization can have some efficiency benefits. The concept of "harmonization" implies that procedural systems will not be reformed wholesale, but rather brought more into line with one another through elimination of quirks. We may assume that, other things equal, idiosyncratic features are likely to be less efficient than features that have gained wider acceptance. If this assumption is correct, then harmonization can offer some benefits in terms of eliminating inefficient rules and replacing them with more efficient ones.

On the other hand, harmonization carries economic costs. One of the most important of such costs is the elimination of human capital which has been built up among the local bar on the operation of a given procedural system. Lawyers must be retrained. Another cost of harmonization is that it removes diversity from the procedural system, and thus reduces the available menu of options that can be looked to as models for procedural reform. Harmonization also limits the options available to contracting parties who may desire to use a particular set of procedures to resolve future disputes. Finally, the process of harmonization will not necessarily generate efficient rules, because it is likely to be carried out by elites selected in a political process, who may not necessarily give a high value to the efficiency of the rules they adopt.

One cannot object on this score to the interesting proposal by Geoffrey C. Harzard and Michele Taruffo for a set of "transnational rules of civil procedure." These rules appear quite well-crafted to serve the end of achieving efficiency in the resolution of international legal disputes. * * *

Note

The "transnational rules of civil procedure" referred to in the preceding passage are the subject of the following excerpt, in which Professor Hazard argues that harmonization is particularly desirable when litigation involves parties from different nations and concerns a commercial dispute. Professor Hazard describes an ambitious project that was the joint effort of the American Law Institute (the "ALI") and the International Institute for the Unification of Private Law ("UNIDROIT"), located in Rome. The goal of the project was to develop a set of rules and principles that could be applied to commercial disputes involving parties from different legal systems. After several years of consultation with legal experts from all over the world, the ALI and UNIDROIT approved the Principles of Transnational Civil Procedure. They were published by Cambridge University Press in French and English under the title Principles of Transnational Procedure (2004). The volume includes extensive commentaries on the principles and is a rich source of learning for any student of procedure. The excerpt that follows, written some years before the project came to fruition, explains the justification for developing transnational harmonization and some of the problems that the efforts faced.

Geoffrey C. Hazard, Jr., International 'Harmonization' of Procedural Law, 76 Texas L. Rev. 1665 (1998).

The human community of the world lives at closer quarters today than in ancient days: international trade is at an all time high and steadily increasing; international investment and monetary flows increase apace; businesses from the developed countries establish themselves all over the globe directly or through subsidiaries; business people travel abroad as a matter of routine; and increasing numbers of ordinary citizens live temporarily or permanently outside of their native countries. As a consequence, there are positive and productive interactions among citizens of different nations in the form of increased commerce and wide possibilities for personal experience and development. There are also inevitable negative interactions, however, including increased social friction, legal controversy, and litigation.

In dealing with these negative consequences, it is recognized that the costs and misery resulting from legal conflict can be mitigated by reducing differences in legal systems, whereby the same or similar "rules of the game" apply no matter where the participants may find themselves. The effort to reduce differences between national legal systems is commonly referred to as "harmonization." Another term, more often used in other countries, is "approximation," meaning that the rules of various legal systems should be reformed in the direction of approximating each other. Most endeavors at harmonization have addressed substantive law, particularly the law governing commercial and financial transactions.

* * *

Harmonization of the law of procedure is avoided, so it appears, on the supposition that national procedural systems are too different and too deeply embedded in local political history and cultural tradition to permit reduction or reconciliation of differences between legal systems. For example, UNIDROIT ("International Institute for the Unification of Private Law"), an institution engaged for more than 70 years in the work of legal harmonization, traditionally has regarded procedural law as beyond its agenda. There are some international conventions dealing with procedural law—notably The Hague Convention on the Taking of Evidence Abroad and European conventions on recognition of judgments—and effort continues on a more general convention on personal jurisdiction and recognition of judgments. The international conventions on procedural law, however, have thus far addressed the front and back ends of procedural law, but not procedure as such. That is, the conventions and draft conventions govern the bases of personal jurisdiction and the mechanics of service of process to commence a lawsuit on one end of the litigation process and recognition of judgments on the other end. The events in between—the formulation of claims, the development of evidence, and the decision procedure—remain matters governed by local national law.

International arbitration often is a substitute for adjudication in national courts. However, the international conventions on arbitration have the same limited scope as the conventions dealing with international litigation in judicial forums. Thus, the international conventions on arbitration specify aspects of commencement in an arbitration proceeding and specify also the recognition to be accorded an arbitration award, but they say little or nothing about the procedure in an international arbitration proceeding.

* * *

Nevertheless, The American Law Institute is now engaged in a project seeking to take the next step in international harmonization of procedural law. The project is entitled "Transnational Rules of Civil Procedure" and is under the direction of Professor Michele Taruffo, of the University of Pavia, Italy, and myself. Our approach has been to draft proposed procedural rules that a country could adopt for adjudication of private international controversies that find their way into the ordinary courts of justice. Perhaps this venture involves fools walking where angels fear to tread. The project is inspired in part by the model of the Federal Rules of Civil Procedure, undertaken over a half century ago in pursuance of the Rules Enabling Act of 1934. The Federal Rules established a single procedure to be employed in courts sitting in forty-eight different semi-sovereign states, each of which had its own procedural law, its own procedural culture, and its own bar. The Federal Rules thereby accomplished what many thoughtful observers thought impossible—a single system of procedure for four dozen different legal communities. If experience with the Federal Rules proves that it has been possible to establish a single procedure for litigation in Louisiana (civil-law system), Virginia (common-law pleading in 1938) and California (code pleading), the ALI project conjectures that a procedure for litigation in transactions across national boundaries is also worth the attempt.

In any event, The American Law Institute, in sponsoring the project for Transnational Rules of Civil Procedure, has assumed that the task of procedural harmonization has to start sometime.

* * *

As Professor Taruffo and I have worked our way into international harmonization of procedural law, we have come to identify fundamental similarities and differences among procedural systems. Obviously, the fundamental differences present the difficulties. It is important, however, not to forget that all modern civil procedural systems have fundamental similarities. These similarities result from the fact that a procedural system must respond to several inherent requirements. Recognition of these requirements makes the task of identifying functional similarities in diverse legal systems easier, and it simultaneously puts the ways in which procedural systems differ from one another into sharper perspective.

The fundamental similarities among procedural systems can be summarized as follows: (1) standards governing assertion of personal and subject matter jurisdiction; (2) specifications for a neutral adjudicator; (3) procedure for notice to defendant; (4) rules for formulation of claims; (5) rules governing development of evidence, particularly evidence beyond that presented by the respective parties through their autonomous efforts; (6) in modern litigation, provisions for expert testimony; (7) rules for deliberation and decision leading to judgment by the tribunal, and in modern systems for appellate review; and (8) rules governing the finality of judgments. The extent of transnational similarity, of course, varies from rule to rule.

Of these, the rules of personal jurisdiction, notice, and recognition of judgments are so similar from one country to another that they have been susceptible to substantial resolution through international conventions. Although the United States is aberrant in having an expansive concept of "long arm" jurisdiction, this difference is one of degree rather than one of kind.

Similarly, with specification of a neutral adjudicator we can begin with the realization that all legal systems have rules to assure that a judge or other adjudicator should be disinterested as between the parties. Accordingly, in transnational litigation reliance generally can be placed on the local rules maintaining that principle. Similarly, an adjudicative system by definition requires a principle of finality. The concept of "final" judgment therefore is also generally recognized, although some legal systems permit reopening a determination more liberally than other systems. The corollary concept of mutual recognition of judgments is also universally accepted.

* * *

The fundamental differences in civil procedural systems are, along one division, differences between the common-law and civil-law systems. Equally significant differences exist, however, among the common-law systems. Here, as in the case of the pleading rules, it is the American system that is aberrant.

* * *

There are many significant differences between common-law and civil-law systems. First, the judge in civil-law systems rather than the advocates in common-law systems, has responsibility for development of the evidence and exposition of the legal concepts that should govern decision. However, there is great variance among civil-law systems in the manner and degree to which this responsibility is exercised, and no doubt variance among the judges in any given system. In general, however, in the civil-law systems the final selection of witnesses to be examined and the examination itself are done by the judge and only indirectly by the advocates, who nominate the witnesses and who may suggest questions that should be asked. Second, civil-law litigation proceeds through a series of short hearing sessions—sometimes less than an hour each—focused on development of evidence. The products of this are then consigned to the case file until an eventual final stage of analysis and decision. In contrast, common-law litigation has one or more preliminary or pretrial stages, and then a trial at which all the evidence is received consecutively, including all "live" testimony. Third, a civil-law final hearing usually takes less time than a common-law trial of a similar case. This is partly due to a difference in the role of judge and advocates, but it also results from the different character of a common-law trial and a civil-law final hearing. Fourth, a civil-law judgment in the court of first instance (i.e., trial court) is generally subject to a more searching re-examination in the court of second instance (i.e., appellate court) than a common-law judgment. Also, re-examination in the civil-law systems extends to facts as well as law. Fifth, a judge in a civil-law system serves his entire professional career as a judge, whereas the judges in common-law systems are almost entirely selected from the ranks of the bar. Thus, civil-law judges lack the experience of having been a lawyer, which may affect their views.

These are important differences, but not worlds of difference. The American common-law system, however, has differences from most other common-law systems that are of equally great if not greater significance. The American system is unique in many respects. First, jury trial is a broadly available right in the American federal courts and, more or less to the same extent, in the state court systems. No other country routinely uses juries in civil cases. Second, the American version of the adversary system generally affords the advocates far greater latitude in the form and style of the case's presentation than in other common-law systems. This is in part because of our use of juries. Third, in the American system, each party, including a winning party, pays his own lawyer and cannot recover that cost from a losing opponent. This rule has been changed by statute for specific types of cases but almost invariably in the direction of allowing recovery of litigation costs only by a successful plaintiff. In most all other countries the winning party, whether plaintiff or defendant, recovers at least a substantial portion of his litigation costs. Fourth, American rules of discovery give wide latitude for exploration of potentially relevant evidence. * * * Thus, discovery of documents requires no prior judicial intervention, as it does in all civil-law systems * * * Fifth, American judges are selected in a variety of ways in which political affiliation plays an important part. In most of the other common-law countries, judges are selected on the basis of professional standards.

* * *

Notes

1. You may have noticed that in the article excerpted Professor Hazard describes the project as an attempt to develop "Transnational Rules of Civil Procedure." As finally adopted, the product was the Principles of Transnational Civil Procedure. According to the Introduction, the focus shifted to the development of "principles" because that approach "appeals to the civil-law mentality." The principles were adopted by the ALI and UNIDROIT, and while a set of model rules based on them is included in the published work, they were not formally adopted but are the "Reporters' model implementation of the Principles, providing greater detail and illustrating concrete fulfillment of the Principles."[2]

2. Consider whether and how the described differences between American procedure and that prevalent elsewhere can be compromised sufficiently to achieve genuine harmonization. Professor Chase has argued that procedural systems are not only influenced by local culture but that they in turn influence the society around them by providing a model of thought, behavior, and social hierarchy. He offers as an example the use of the civil jury in the United States, which, he argues, serves as a model of democratic decision-

2. ALI/UNIDROIT Principles of Transnational Civil Procedure, at 99.

making and as an exemplar of social equality. In this vein, one might object to the abolition of the jury not only if one thought it was useful as a procedural device but also to preserve an important feature of American culture. See Oscar G. Chase, Law, Culture, and Ritual: Disputing Systems in Cross–Cultural Context 47–71, 138–140 (2005).

3. A critical European response to the proposed harmonization approach described by Professor Hazard, above, is offered in the subsequent excerpt from an article by Professors Walter and Baumgartner.

Gerhard Walter and Samuel P. Baumgartner, Utility and Feasibility of Transnational Rules of Civil Procedure: Some German and Swiss Reactions to the Hazard–Taruffo Project, 33 Tex. Int'l L.J. 463 (1998).

I. INTRODUCTION

As Judge Vanderbilt pointed out earlier in this century, "judicial reform is no sport for the short-winded[.]" The difficulties involved in such reform are intensified when combined with an attempt at global harmonization. Organizations such as UNIDROIT and UNCITRAL have attempted harmonization for decades with varying degrees of success. But even they have traditionally refrained from harmonization in the field of procedure where, as the wisdom goes, the law is strongly connected to the cultural and historical heritage of a particular jurisdiction. Thus, in setting out to draft uniform rules of civil procedure for transnational cases that seek both to combine "the best elements in various legal traditions" and to be "culturally neutral," Professors Hazard and Taruffo have not only set high standards for themselves but have also embarked upon an enterprise that seems to face virtually insurmountable barriers.

At the same time, Professors Hazard and Taruffo appear to be in accord with a current trend. In their search for improvements, procedural reformers are increasingly studying the approaches of foreign legal systems. The jurisprudence of international tribunals, particularly that of the European Court of Justice, has shown an increasing trend toward harmonizing specific aspects of civil procedure. Indeed, a private group of experts recently submitted to the European Commission a Draft Directive that seeks to harmonize many areas of European civil procedure, both domestic and transnational.

What, then, are the chances that the Transnational Rules project will beat the odds, both real and perceived, and turn this trend toward procedural harmonization into a valuable and lasting development in transnational litigation? The answer to that question depends heavily upon one's predilections. Thus, we decided to conduct a small survey among Swiss and German proceduralists, both academics and practitioners, to collect their views on the Transnational Rules. The beginning of this survey dates back to early 1996, when Professors Hazard and Taruffo mailed out their first draft of the Transnational Rules and requested the comments of proceduralists in various countries. As one such proceduralist acting as reporter for Switzerland, Professor Walter solicited the written comments of a number of academics and practitioners in his country. In the meantime, Professors Hazard and Taruffo have revised their first draft several times, in some respects, substantially so. We wondered how this latest draft would fare and wanted to expand the base for our inquiry. Thus, we repeated the process in neighboring Germany.

* * *

Although this survey is far from scientific, it provides a better picture than would our own views of the difficulties Professors Hazard and Taruffo are likely to face in these two civil-law jurisdictions and perhaps in other continental European countries as well. The survey also provides the basis for a number of suggestions to improve the project's chances of success.

II. THE RESPONSES

In spite of the relatively small sample, the responses to the surveys were surprisingly similar in their basic thrust. While several of those answering generally supported addressing transnational proceedings involving the United States and Europe, all were highly skeptical about the goal of global harmonization—at least in the current form of the Transnational Rules. Thus, all of those responding expressed their general concerns about the Rules, and some of them did so in a very negative tone. * * * An understanding of these general concerns provides invaluable lessons on how to improve the chances of success for the Transnational Rules project. Therefore, we will consider them in more detail and offer some of our own conclusions below.

III. GENERAL CONCERNS ABOUT THE TRANSNATIONAL RULES

Thirteen of those responding expressed (the others implied) their disbelief that the Transnational Rules could create a harmonized set of rules for transnational proceedings that would be familiar to "all legal traditions" and, thus, could "reduce the uncertainty and anxiety that particularly attend parties obliged to litigate in unfamiliar surroundings." According to these individuals, from a German and Swiss perspective, the major stumbling block was the combination of "elements of adversary procedure * * * [and] judge-centered procedure" in the Rules.

* * *

These changes go to the heart of existing continental European procedure. In order to implement them, it would be necessary to rewrite vast portions of current practice and procedure and to recast the traditional role and understanding of judges, attorneys, and parties. In addition, most lawyers in Germany and Switzerland are hardly familiar with the essential differences between common-law and civil-law litigation, let alone with their implications in everyday practice. While we can imagine insurmountable American opposition to the abolition of the jury trial and the severe limitation of U.S.-style discovery proposed by the Transnational Rules, the essential implications of these aspects of the Rules on the existing judicial process can at least be grasped by American lawyers. The same cannot be assumed of most German and Swiss lawyers regarding the proposed adversarial procedure.

* * *

It is precisely these aspects of adversarial procedure and expanded evidentiary obligations that many in our survey on the Transnational Rules criticized as "too American." And it is these aspects that most of those responding had in mind when expressing their doubts regarding the feasibility of the stated goals of the Transnational Rules. * * *

A. *Harmonized Procedure That Is Fair and Familiar to All?*

Several of those surveyed argued that rather than bringing about a unified, fair procedure reducing "the uncertainty and anxiety" involved in litigating abroad, the adoption of the current form of the Transnational Rules in their respective countries would result in a steep increase in uncertainty and anxiety for all and would cause considerable delay. Their argument is based on the fair assumption that transnational litigation, although increasingly significant, will remain a small portion of a national court's workload for some time to come. Thus, they maintained, courts and attorneys in Germany and Switzerland would continue to use their traditional procedure in most of the cases while forced to cope with the unknown adversarial procedure of the Transnational Rules in others. For although Professors Hazard and Taruffo do seem to hope that, ultimately, the system set out in the Transnational Rules will prevail, they wisely do not purport to harmonize domestic civil procedure. Many of those responding expressed their fear that fundamental uncertainties about how to apply this new system would hamper transnational litigation for a long time, possibly decades. That, in turn, would entail enormous error costs and considerable inefficiency, causing anxiety not only among foreign litigants but also among lawyers and judges who are directly involved in making the Transnational Rules work at home.

Given that Professor Hazard has already likened the Transnational Rules project to the U.S. endeavor, earlier in this century, to introduce unified federal rules of civil procedure, it is tempting to draw a parallel between arguments concerning the Transnational Rules and the arguments of those who opposed the Rules Enabling Act. But one should not forget that, among many essential differences between the two projects, there is a significant difference of degree here. The Federal Rules of Civil Procedure did not and were never meant to break with the historically-grown adversarial procedure of the United States. The current draft of the Transnational Rules, however, does impose the converse break upon traditional continental European procedure.

* * *

The concerns our German and Swiss commentators expressed about overly general procedural rules, however, were not merely about understanding the workings of adversarial procedure but also about defining—ahead of time and as clearly as possible—the duties and rights of those involved in the litigation process. Providing such definition may be hard to do for someone who has witnessed the way in which the simple and flexible Federal Rules of Civil Procedure have accommodated modifications necessary to promote social change. Yet there are countries where social change is achieved primarily through the political process and where the judiciary has been much less trusted given its historical involvement with oppressive regime.

Thus, most of those in our survey who complained that some of the Transnational Rules were too general and, hence, would lead to insurmountable questions of interpretation—including determining which provisions of the current procedural code would still be applicable—also feared that in the occasional case, considerable uncertainty would result during years of adjusting to the Transnational Rules. That, they maintained, would jeopardize the principle of Rechtssicherheit. The principle of Rechtssicherheit, part of the German and Swiss version of the rule of law, requires that the legal consequences of one's actions be reasonably predictable. This principle is taken very seriously in procedural law, to a considerable degree out of a fear of judicial overreaching.

* * *

C. Harmonization

Eleven of those answering our survey expressed more fundamental concerns about harmonizing the procedure applicable to transnational cases through the adoption of the Transnational Rules. They pointed out that existing German and Swiss procedures have continuously evolved over centuries; that these procedures are closely connected to local culture and history; and that replacing them with an entirely different procedural system in one bold stroke would be both unsound and politically unfeasible.

The precise reasoning varied. Some simply did not think that common-law and civil-law systems could be merged into a useful and workable procedure on the drawing board. A similar theme was expressed by those who insisted that a procedural system works as a whole and, thus, cannot import entire segments from another system without disrupting its proper operation. Others pointed out that a procedural system consists not only of procedural rules but also of what the legal community does with these rules, or, as one of our experts called it, the Prozerechtskultur (procedural culture). Some argued that this procedural culture cannot be changed overnight. Others feared that imposing an entirely different procedural system, as the Transnational Rules would do, might release unexpected forces and, thus, lead to changes in that culture that the Rules do not seem to intend.

Professors Hazard and Taruffo appear to be aware of the problems expressed by these individuals. And perhaps some of our experts were too pessimistic about importing foreign elements into a grown procedural system. After all, Professor Watson's work has shown that entire sets of legal rules are often borrowed from foreign societies. Yet, these concerns should be taken very seriously. The rules of practice and procedure are often more interdependent than the rules of private law, and adopting entire elements from foreign procedure may, indeed, have unintended consequences. * * *

The ultimate task of the drafters—as many of those who expressed doubt about the feasibility of harmonization through adoption of the Transnational Rules pointed out—will be to explain to the legal community of a country why discarding their traditional procedural system for the Transnational Rules is more sensible than improving their system through incremental reform. To that end, the argument that the Rules will be limited to a small portion of a country's caseload may not be convincing.

* * *

On the other hand, a number of those responding to our survey did think that the Transnational Rules project could provide an effective forum for a comparative discussion of procedural systems. Through such a discussion, perspective could be gained and a measure of respect for the functioning of other systems developed, particularly between the United States and its continental European counterparts. . . .

One of our experts, however, expressed his belief that trying to tackle the current problems of transnational litigation involving the United States and continental Europe by discussing the Transnational Rules could turn out to be counterproductive. Instead of enabling a more open-minded approach to those problems, he argued that such a discussion could lead to a further deterioration in German–American judicial relations given the impending adoption of some of the much-criticized Americanisms. Such an assessment may appear rather pessimistic. Yet, it should be taken very seriously in countries in which the "judicial conflict" has made people wary about U.S. procedure and in which news reports about the perceived excesses of American practice have helped shape the legal community's views about the U.S. litigation process.

E.   *Transnational Rules and Developments in Europe*

Finally, a few of those responding mentioned that the European countries are currently working toward further integration of transnational procedure in Europe. Harmonization is occurring both through the Brussels and Lugano Conventions, and through new measures intended to simplify judicial cooperation, perhaps through the harmonization of some aspects of the litigation process itself. They argued that because these efforts are all based on traditional continental European procedure, the introduction of the Transnational Rules with their adversarial system into the discussion would severely complicate and unnecessarily burden these efforts.

This and similar reactions to proposed multilateral treaties dealing with aspects of transnational litigation are not uncommon. The Europeans have worked long and hard to find satisfactory solutions to problems specific to transnational litigation through bilateral and multilateral treaties, if only among themselves. The Brussels and Lugano Conventions are the most prominent examples of such treaties. To convince Europeans to embark upon an enterprise of procedural harmonization, the content of which significantly deviates from these efforts, will require special attention.

IV.   CONCLUSION

Transnational litigation raises a host of issues that are not present in purely domestic proceedings. Every country has naturally developed solutions to these issues based on its own procedure. This approach has created many inefficiencies and, at times, outright hostility as evidenced by the perception of a "judicial conflict" between the United States and continental Europe.

The Transnational Rules project offers an important opportunity to engage in much needed cross-systemic education about procedural concepts and philosophies in order to diffuse the conflict and to find more efficient and mutually acceptable approaches. As one of our experts indicated, when such eminent scholars as Professors Hazard and Taruffo speak, people listen. Others have cautioned, however, that it is also important to spend the available resources wisely, particularly now that the American Law Institute has adopted the project.

As some of those responding to our survey observed, the issue of transnational litigation really needs an in-depth comparative dialogue, particularly between the United States and continental Europe. It appears that, in judging a foreign legal system, perception is more important than reality, therefore, the task of such a dialogue should be to bring the former in line with the latter. The critical responses that we have reported in this article should provide some help in carrying out this task.

* * *

Procedural law reform does require time, particularly when conducted on a global level. If those involved in drafting and, ultimately, selling the Transnational Rules to the various countries of the world are willing to take that time, the effort will indeed have a good chance of turning procedural harmonization into a lasting trend.

Notes

1.   As we have noted earlier in this chapter, the Principles of Transnational Procedure were endorsed by the ALI and UNIDROIT and published in 2006. As of this writing, however, they have not been put into effect by the

courts of any nation and remain important primarily as a model for the future.

2. The preceding excerpt by Professors Walter and Baumgartner reveals some of the discomfort that at least some European lawyers feel about the prospect of harmonizing their procedures with those of other systems. In the following selection, Professor Langbein considers the matter from the American point of view and argues that there is much to be gained by adopting some of the civil law processes. In the selection that follows Professor Langbein's, Professor Damaška sounds a cautionary note about the effects of borrowing procedures from a foreign system. These conflicting views should help you to develop your own view of the matter.

John H. Langbein, The German Advantage in Civil Procedure, 52 U. of Chi. L. Rev. 823–825 (1985).

Our lawyer-dominated system of civil procedure has often been criticized both for its incentives to distort evidence and for the expense and complexity of its modes of discovery and trial. The shortcomings inhere in a system that leaves to partisans the work of gathering and producing the factual material upon which adjudication depend.

We have comforted ourselves with the thought that a lawyerless system would be worse. The excesses of American adversary justice would seem to pale by comparison with a literally nonadversarial system—one in which litigants would be remitted to faceless bureaucratic adjudicators and denied the safeguards that flow from lawyerly intermediation.

The German advantage. The main theme of this article is drawn from Continental civil procedure, exemplified for me by the system that I know reasonably well, the West German. My theme is that, by assigning judges rather than lawyers to investigate the facts, the Germans avoid the most troublesome aspects of our practice. * * *

To be sure, since the greater responsibility of the bench for fact-gathering is what distinguishes the Continental tradition, a necessary (and welcome) correlative is that counsel's role in eliciting evidence is greatly restricted. Apart from fact-gathering, however, the lawyers for the parties play major and broadly comparable roles in both the German and American systems. Both are adversary systems of civil procedure. There as here, the lawyers advance partisan positions from first pleadings to final arguments. German litigators suggest legal theories and lines of factual inquiry, they superintend and supplement judicial examination of witnesses, they urge inferences from fact, they discuss and distinguish precedent, they interpret statutes, and they formulate views of the law that further the interests of their clients. I shall urge that German experience shows that we would do better if we were greatly to restrict the adversaries' role in fact-gathering.

Convergence. The concluding theme of this article directs attention to recent trends in American civil procedure. Having developed the view that judicialized fact-gathering has immense advantages over traditional American practice, I point to the growing manifestations of judicial control of fact-gathering in certain strands of federal procedure. The *Manual for Complex Litigation* is infused with notions of judicial management of fact-gathering for the multi-party Big Case, but there has been no natural stopping place, and these techniques have been seeping into the conduct of ordinary litigation in the development that has been called "managerial judging."

In principle, managerial judging is more compatible with the theory of German procedure than with our own. Having now made the great leap from adversary control to judicial control of fact-gathering, we would need to take one further step to achieve real convergence with the German tradition: from judicial control to judicial conduct of the fact-gathering process. In the success of managerial judging, I see telling evidence for the proposition that judicial fact-gathering could work well in a system that preserved much of the rest of what we now have in civil procedure.

I should emphasize, however, that the main concern of this article is not the sprawling Big Case, but the traditional bipolar lawsuit in contract, tort, or entitlement. The Big Case is testing and instructive but quantitatively unimportant. Ordinary litigation is the place to compare and to judge civil procedural systems.

* * *

It is curious that managerial judging took hold so easily in a legal system supposedly governed by the counterprinciple of judicial inactivity. Because managerial judging imposes such major limits on partisan autonomy in fact-gathering, it is in principle irreconcilable with that branch of adversary theory that purports to justify adversary fact-gathering.

Regardless of where managerial judging is headed for the future, it has already routed adversary theory. I take that as further support for the view * * * that adversary theory was misapplied to fact-gathering in the first place. Nothing but inertia and vested interests justify the waste and distortion of adversary fact-gathering. The success of German civil procedure stands as an enduring reproach to those who say that we must continue to suffer adversary tricksters in the proof of fact.

Mirjan Damaška, The Uncertain Fate of Evidentiary Transplants: Anglo–American and Continental Experiments, 45 Am. J. Comp. L. 839–852 (1997).

Whenever new laws are framed it is imperative that they should be consonant with the institutions of the state to which they are destined.

Inspiration for procedural reform is increasingly sought in the legal thesaurus of foreign countries. In their search for new solutions, lawyers are prone to focus almost exclusively on normative aspects of foreign arrangements, trying to ascertain whether they hold promise of advantages over domestic law. But this understandable *déformation professionnelle* is not without its costs: the success of most procedural innovation depends less than lawyers like to think on the excellence of rules. More than in the private law domain, perhaps, the meaning and impact of procedural regulation turn on external conditions—most directly on the institutional context in which justice is administered in a particular country. If imported rules are combined with native ones in disregard of this context, unintended consequences are likely to follow in living law. And while some of these consequences can turn out to be a pleasant surprise, others can be very disappointing.

Those contemplating to combine common law and civil law approaches to factfinding should be especially sensitive to the potential costs of normative shortcuts to procedural reform; institutional differences between the two Western legal families capable of affecting the factfinding style are quite considerable. In criminal procedure, a few good lessons have already been learned about problems that arise when factfinding arrangements from one family are incorporated into the institutional milieu of the other. Here experience has shown how easily an imported evidentiary doctrine, or practice, alters its character in interaction with the new environment. Even textually identical rules acquire a different meaning and produce different consequences in the changed institutional setting. The music of the law changes, so to speak, when the musical instruments and the players are no longer the same.

In civil procedure, the mixing of factfinding arrangements has been urged somewhat less frequently, despite the fact that the contrast between the continental and Anglo–American institutional context is here somewhat reduced: continental civil litigation contains pronounced "adversarial" features. Nevertheless, important differences of procedural ecology remain, and their importance for the success of evidentiary transplants should not be ignored. Among the many factors responsible for the contrast between the Anglo–American and continental factfinding style, three stand out sharply in importance: the different court organization, the varying temporal organization of proceedings, and the unequal allocation of procedural control between the court and the parties. Mainly responsible for the contrast, these three factors are the most likely suspects for imposing constraints on the transplantation of evidentiary arrangements across the two great families of Western procedure.

* * *

What conclusions can be drawn from these remarks? Reducing the disparities of factfinding arrangements in the two Western families of civil procedure may well be desirable, provided, of course, that our world is coming together rather than flying apart in the twilight of this century. The impetus to seek inspiration for reform beyond national borders should also be greeted with understanding and sympathy; since dissatisfaction with existing procedures is so widespread.

Yet reformers beware! The transplantation of fact-finding arrangements between common law and civil law systems would give rise to serious strains in the recipient justice system. The interaction between the contemplated transplant and the new environment must be carefully studied, and the question must always be considered whether the recipient culture is prepared—or can be readied—to live with the wider effects of contemplated reform. As the examples of changes in the proof-taking method demonstrate, these wider effects cannot easily be contained: various elements of fact-finding activity are too closely intertwined. In seeking inspiration for change, it is perhaps natural for lawyers to go browsing in a foreign law boutique. But it is an illusion to think that this is a boutique in which one is always free to purchase some items and reject others. An arrangement stemming from a partial purchase—a legal pastiche—can produce a far less satisfactory factfinding result in practice than under either continental or Anglo–American evidentiary arrangements in their unadulterated form.

III. TREATIES AS INSTRUMENTS OF HARMONIZATION

Harmonization of procedures can result from agreement among nations to use particular processes for particular kinds of disputes or for particular issues. Examples include the Hague Convention on the Taking of Evidence Abroad in Civil or Commercial Matters which establishes procedures by which litigants in one country may seek the aid of a court in another country to obtain evidence located there. Another treaty, the Hague Convention on the Service Abroad of Judicial and Extrajudicial Documents in Civil or Commercial Matters provides for a uniform means of serving such documents as a summons and complaint in a foreign country. As we shall see, these treaties are subject to the interpretation of the national courts that must interpret and apply them.

Société Nationale Industrielle Aérospatiale v. United States District Court for the Southern District of Iowa, 482 U.S. 522 (1987).

Justice STEVENS delivered the opinion of the Court.

The United States, the Republic of France, and 15 other Nations have acceded to the Hague Convention on the Taking of Evidence Abroad in Civil or Commercial Matters, opened for signature, Mar. 18, 1970, 23 U.S.T. 2555, T.I.A.S. No. 7444. This Convention—sometimes referred to as the "Hague Convention" or the "Evidence Convention"—prescribes certain procedures by which a judicial authority in one contracting state may request evidence located in another contracting state. The question presented in this case concerns the extent to which a federal district court must employ the procedures set forth in the

Convention when litigants seek answers to interrogatories, the production of documents, and admissions from a French adversary over whom the court has personal jurisdiction.

I

The two petitioners are corporations owned by the Republic of France. They are engaged in the business of designing, manufacturing, and marketing aircraft. One of their planes, the "Rallye," was allegedly advertised in American aviation publications as "the World's safest and most economical STOL plane." [The term "STOL," an acronym for "short takeoff and landing," "refers to a fixed-wing aircraft that either takes off or lands with only a short horizontal run of the aircraft."]

On August 19, 1980, a Rallye crashed in Iowa, injuring the pilot and a passenger. Dennis Jones, John George, and Rosa George brought separate suits based upon this accident in the United States District Court for the Southern District of Iowa, alleging that petitioners had manufactured and sold a defective plane and that they were guilty of negligence and breach of warranty. Petitioners answered the complaints, apparently without questioning the jurisdiction of the District Court. * * *

Initial discovery was conducted by both sides pursuant to the Federal Rules of Civil Procedure without objection. When plaintiffs served a second request for the production of documents pursuant to Rule 34, a set of interrogatories pursuant to Rule 33, and requests for admission pursuant to Rule 36, however, petitioners filed a motion for a protective order. The motion alleged that because petitioners are "French corporations, and the discovery sought can only be found in a foreign state, namely France," the Hague Convention dictated the exclusive procedures that must be followed for pretrial discovery. In addition, the motion stated that under French penal law, the petitioners could not respond to discovery requests that did not comply with the Convention.*

The Magistrate denied the motion insofar as it related to answering interrogatories, producing documents, and making admissions. After reviewing the relevant cases, the Magistrate explained:

> To permit the Hague Evidence Convention to override the Federal Rules of Civil Procedure would frustrate the courts' interests, which particularly arise in products liability cases, in protecting United States citizens from harmful products and in compensating them for injuries arising from use of such products.

---

* Article 1A of the French "blocking statute," French Penal Code Law No. 80–538, provides:

"Subject to treaties or international agreements and applicable laws and regulations, it is prohibited for any party to request, seek or disclose, in writing, orally or otherwise, economic, commercial, industrial, financial or technical documents or information leading to the constitution of evidence with a view to foreign judicial or administrative proceedings or in connection therewith."

Article 2 provides:

"The parties mentioned in [Article 1A] shall forthwith inform the competent minister if they receive any request concerning such disclosures.

[Footnote in original].

The Magistrate made two responses to petitioners' argument that they could not comply with the discovery requests without violating French penal law. Noting that the law was originally " 'inspired to impede enforcement of United States antitrust laws,' " and that it did not appear to have been strictly enforced in France, he first questioned whether it would be construed to apply to the pretrial discovery requests at issue. Second, he balanced the interests in the "protection of United States citizens from harmful foreign products and compensation for injuries caused by such products" against France's interest in protecting its citizens "from intrusive foreign discovery procedures." The Magistrate concluded that the former interests were stronger, particularly because compliance with the requested discovery will "not have to take place in France" and will not be greatly intrusive or abusive.

* * *

II

In the District Court and the Court of Appeals, petitioners contended that the Hague Evidence Convention "provides the exclusive and mandatory procedures for obtaining documents and information located within the territory of a foreign signatory." 782 F.2d, at 124.* We are satisfied that the Court of Appeals correctly rejected this extreme position. We believe it is foreclosed by the plain language of the Convention. Before discussing the text of the Convention, however, we briefly review its history.

The Hague Conference on Private International Law, an association of sovereign states, has been conducting periodic sessions since 1893. S.Exec. Doc. A, 92d Cong., 2d Sess. p. v (1972) (S.Exec. Doc. A). The United States participated in those sessions as an observer in 1956 and 1960, and as a member beginning in 1964 pursuant to congressional authorization. In that year Congress amended the Judicial Code to grant foreign litigants, without any requirement of reciprocity, special assistance in obtaining evidence in the United States. In 1965 the Hague Conference adopted a Convention on the Service Abroad of Judicial and Extrajudicial Documents in Civil or Commercial Matters (Service Convention), 20 U.S.T. 361, T.I.A.S. No. 6638, to which the Senate gave its advice and consent in 1967. The favorable response to the Service Convention, coupled with the longstanding interest of American lawyers in improving procedures for obtaining evidence abroad, motivated the United States to take the initiative in proposing that an evidence convention be adopted. The Conference organized a special commission to prepare the draft convention, and the draft was approved without a dissenting vote on October 26, 1968. It was signed on behalf of the United States in 1970 and ratified by a unanimous vote of the Senate in

---

* The Republic of France likewise takes the following position in this case:

"The Hague Convention Is the Exclusive Means of Discovery in Transnational Litigation Among the Convention's Signatories Unless the Sovereign on Whose Territory Discovery Is to Occur Chooses Otherwise." Brief for Republic of France as *Amicus Curiae* 4. [Footnote in original].

1972. The Convention's purpose was to establish a system for obtaining evidence located abroad that would be "tolerable" to the state executing the request and would produce evidence "utilizable" in the requesting state. Amram, Explanatory Report on the Convention on the Taking of Evidence Abroad in Civil or Commercial Matters, in S.Exec. Doc. A, p. 11.

* * *

The Convention was fairly summarized in the Secretary of State's letter of submittal to the President:

"The willingness of the Conference to proceed promptly with work on the evidence convention is perhaps attributable in large measure to the difficulties encountered by courts and lawyers in obtaining evidence abroad from countries with markedly different legal systems. Some countries have insisted on the exclusive use of the complicated, dilatory and expensive system of letters rogatory or letters of request. Other countries have refused adequate judicial assistance because of the absence of a treaty or convention regulating the matter. The substantial increase in litigation with foreign aspects arising, in part, from the unparalleled expansion of international trade and travel in recent decades had intensified the need for an effective international agreement to set up a model system to bridge differences between the common law and civil law approaches to the taking of evidence abroad.

"Civil law countries tend to concentrate on *commissions rogatoires,* while common law countries take testimony on notice, by stipulation and through commissions to consuls or commissioners. Letters of request for judicial assistance from courts abroad in securing needed evidence have been the exception, rather than the rule. The civil law technique results normally in a résumé of the evidence, prepared by the executing judge and signed by the witness, while the common law technique results normally in a verbatim transcript of the witness's testimony certified by the reporter.

"Failure by either the requesting state or the state of execution fully to take into account the differences of approach to the taking of evidence abroad under the two systems and the absence of agreed standards applicable to letters of request have frequently caused difficulties for courts and litigants. To minimize such difficulties in the future, the enclosed convention, which consists of a preamble and forty-two articles, is designed to:

"1. Make the employment of letters of request a principal means of obtaining evidence abroad;

"2. Improve the means of securing evidence abroad by increasing the powers of consuls and by introducing in the civil law world, on a limited basis, the concept of the commissioner;

"3. Provide means for securing evidence in the form needed by the court where the action is pending; and

"4. Preserve all more favorable and less restrictive practices arising from internal law, internal rules of procedure and bilateral or multilateral conventions.

"What the convention does is to provide a set of minimum standards with which contracting states agree to comply. Further, through articles 27, 28 and 32, it provides a flexible framework within which any future liberalizing changes in policy and tradition in any country with respect to international judicial cooperation may be translated into effective change in international procedures. At the same time it recognizes and preserves procedures of every country which now or hereafter may provide international cooperation in the taking of evidence on more liberal and less restrictive bases, whether this is effected by supplementary agreements or by municipal law and practice." *Id.,* vi.

III

In arguing their entitlement to a protective order, petitioners correctly assert that both the discovery rules set forth in the Federal Rules of Civil Procedure and the Hague Convention are the law of the United States. This observation, however, does not dispose of the question before us; we must analyze the interaction between these two bodies of federal law. Initially, we note that at least four different interpretations of the relationship between the federal discovery rules and the Hague Convention are possible. Two of these interpretations assume that the Hague Convention by its terms dictates the extent to which it supplants normal discovery rules. First, the Hague Convention might be read as requiring its use to the exclusion of any other discovery procedures whenever evidence located abroad is sought for use in an American court. Second, the Hague Convention might be interpreted to require first, but not exclusive, use of its procedures. Two other interpretations assume that international comity, rather than the obligations created by the treaty, should guide judicial resort to the Hague Convention. Third, then, the Convention might be viewed as establishing a supplemental set of discovery procedures, strictly optional under treaty law, to which concerns of comity nevertheless require first resort by American courts in all cases. Fourth, the treaty may be viewed as an undertaking among sovereigns to facilitate discovery to which an American court should resort when it deems that course of action appropriate, after considering the situations of the parties before it as well as the interests of the concerned foreign state.

* * *

We reject the first two of the possible interpretations as inconsistent with the language and negotiating history of the Hague Convention. The preamble of the Convention specifies its purpose "to facilitate the transmission and execution of Letters of Request" and to "improve mutual judicial co-operation in civil or commercial matters." 23 U.S.T., at 2557, T.I.A.S. No. 7444. The preamble does not speak in mandatory terms which would purport to describe the procedures for all permissible transnational discovery and exclude all other existing practices. The text of the Evidence Convention itself does not modify the law of any contracting state, require any contracting state to use the Convention procedures, either in requesting evidence or in responding to such requests, or compel any contracting state to change its own evidence-gathering procedures.

The Convention contains three chapters. Chapter I, entitled "Letters of Requests," and chapter II, entitled "Taking of Evidence by Diplomatic Officers, Consular Agents and Commissioners," both use permissive rather than mandatory language. Thus, Article 1 provides that a judicial authority in one contracting state "may" forward a letter of request to the competent authority in another contracting state for the purpose of obtaining evidence. Similarly, Articles 15, 16, and 17 provide that diplomatic officers, consular agents, and commissioners "may ... without compulsion," take evidence under certain conditions. The absence of any command that a contracting state must use Convention procedures when they are not needed is conspicuous.

Two of the Articles in chapter III, entitled "General Clauses," buttress our conclusion that the Convention was intended as a permissive supplement, not a pre-emptive replacement, for other means of obtaining evidence located abroad. Article 23 expressly authorizes a contracting state to declare that it will not execute any letter of request in aid of pretrial discovery of documents in a common-law country. Surely, if the Convention had been intended to replace completely the broad discovery powers that the common-law courts in the United States previously exercised over foreign litigants subject to their jurisdiction, it would have been most anomalous for the common-law contracting parties to agree to Article 23, which enables a contracting party to revoke its consent to the treaty's procedures for pretrial discovery. In the absence of explicit textual support, we are unable to accept the hypothesis that the common-law contracting states abjured recourse to all pre-existing discovery procedures at the same time that they accepted the possibility that a contracting party could unilaterally abrogate even the Convention's procedures. Moreover, Article 27 plainly states that the Convention does not prevent a contracting state from using more liberal methods of rendering evidence than those authorized by the Convention. Thus, the text of the Evidence Convention, as well as the history of its proposal and ratification by the United States, unambiguously supports the conclusion that it was intended to establish optional procedures that would facilitate the taking of evidence abroad. See Amram, The Proposed Convention on the Taking of Evidence Abroad, 55 A.B.A.J. 651, 655 (1969); President's Letter of Transmittal, Sen. Exec. Doc. A, p. iii.

An interpretation of the Hague Convention as the exclusive means for obtaining evidence located abroad would effectively subject every American court hearing a case involving a national of a contracting state to the internal laws of that state. Interrogatories and document requests are staples of international commercial litigation, no less than of other suits, yet a rule of exclusivity would subordinate the court's supervision of even the most routine of these pretrial proceedings to the actions or, equally, to the inactions of foreign judicial authorities. As the Court of Appeals for the Fifth Circuit observed in *In re Anschuetz and Co., GmbH,* 754 F.2d 602, 612 (1985), cert. pending, No. 85–98:

> "It seems patently obvious that if the Convention were interpreted as preempting interrogatories and document requests, the Convention would really be much more than an agreement on taking evidence abroad. Instead, the Convention would amount to a major regulation of the overall conduct of litigation between nationals of different signatory states, raising a significant possibility of very serious interference with the jurisdiction of United States courts.

> "While it is conceivable that the United States could enter into a treaty giving other signatories control over litigation instituted and pursued in American courts, a treaty intended to bring about such a curtailment of the rights given to all litigants by the federal rules would surely state its intention clearly and precisely identify crucial terms."

The Hague Convention, however, contains no such plain statement of a pre-emptive intent. We conclude accordingly that the Hague Convention did not deprive the District Court of the jurisdiction it otherwise possessed to order a foreign national party before it to produce evidence physically located within a signatory nation.

IV

While the Hague Convention does not divest the District Court of jurisdiction to order discovery under the Federal Rules of Civil Procedure, the optional character of the Convention procedures sheds light on one aspect of the Court of Appeals' opinion that we consider erroneous. That court concluded that the Convention simply "does not apply" to discovery sought from a foreign litigant that is subject to the jurisdiction of an American court. Plaintiffs argue that this conclusion is supported by two considerations. First, the Federal Rules of Civil Procedure provide ample means for obtaining discovery from parties who are subject to the court's jurisdiction, while before the Convention was ratified it was often extremely difficult, if not impossible, to obtain evidence from nonparty witnesses abroad. Plaintiffs contend that it is appropriate to construe the Convention as applying only in the area in which improvement was badly needed. Second, when a litigant is subject to the jurisdiction of the district court, arguably the evidence it is required to produce is not "abroad" within the meaning of the Convention, even though it is in fact located in a foreign country at the time of the discovery request and even though it will have to be gathered or otherwise prepared abroad.

Nevertheless, the text of the Convention draws no distinction between evidence obtained from third parties and that obtained from the litigants themselves; nor does it purport to draw any sharp line between evidence that is "abroad" and evidence that is within the control of a party subject to the jurisdiction of the requesting court. Thus, it appears clear to us that the optional Convention procedures are available whenever they will facilitate the gathering of evidence by the means authorized in the Convention. Although these procedures are not mandatory, the Hague Convention does "apply" to the production of evidence in a litigant's possession in the sense that it is one method of seeking evidence that a court may elect to employ.

V

Petitioners contend that even if the Hague Convention's procedures are not mandatory, this Court should adopt a rule requiring that American litigants first resort to those procedures before initiating any discovery pursuant to the normal methods of the Federal Rules of Civil Procedure. The Court of Appeals rejected this argument because it was convinced that an American court's order ultimately requiring discovery that a foreign court had refused under Convention procedures would constitute "the greatest insult" to the sovereignty of that tribunal. We disagree with the Court of Appeals' view. It is well known that the scope of American discovery is often significantly broader than is permitted in other jurisdictions, and we are satisfied that foreign tribunals will recognize that the final decision on the evidence to be used in litigation conducted in American courts must be made by those courts. We therefore do not believe that an American court should refuse to make use of Convention procedures because of a concern that it may ultimately find it necessary to order the production of evidence that a foreign tribunal permitted a party to withhold.

Nevertheless, we cannot accept petitioners' invitation to announce a new rule of law that would require first resort to Convention procedures whenever discovery is sought from a foreign litigant. Assuming, without deciding, that we have the lawmaking power to do so, we are convinced that such a general rule would be unwise. In many situations the Letter of Request procedure authorized by the Convention would be unduly time consuming and expensive, as well as less certain to produce needed evidence than direct use of the Federal Rules. A rule of first resort in all cases would therefore be inconsistent with the overriding interest in the "just, speedy, and inexpensive determination" of litigation in our courts. See Fed.Rule Civ.Proc. 1.

Petitioners argue that a rule of first resort is necessary to accord respect to the sovereignty of states in which evidence is located. It is true that the process of obtaining evidence in a civil-law jurisdiction is normally conducted by a judicial officer rather than by private attorneys. Petitioners contend that if performed on French soil, for example, by an unauthorized person, such evidence-gathering might violate the "judicial sovereignty" of the host nation. Because it is only through the Convention that civil-law nations have given their consent to evidence-gathering activities within their borders, petitioners argue, we have a duty to employ those procedures whenever they are available. Brief for Petitioners 27–28. We find that argument unpersuasive. If such a duty were to be inferred from the adoption of the Convention itself, we believe it would have been described in the text of that document. Moreover, the concept of international comity* requires in this context a more particularized analysis of the respective interests of the foreign nation and the requesting nation than petitioners' proposed general rule would generate. We therefore decline to hold as a blanket matter that comity requires resort to Hague Evidence Convention procedures without prior scrutiny in each case of the particular facts, sovereign interests, and likelihood that resort to those procedures will prove effective.**

The American Law Institute has summarized this interplay of blocking statutes and discovery orders: "[W]hen a state has jurisdiction to prescribe and its courts have jurisdiction to adjudicate, adjudication should (subject to generally applicable rules of evidence) take place on the basis of the best information available.... [Blocking] statutes that frustrate this goal need not be given the same deference by courts of the United States as substantive rules of law at variance with the law of the United States." See Restatement, § 437, Reporter's Note 5, pp. 41, 42. "On the other hand, the degree of friction created by discovery requests ... and the differing perceptions of the acceptability of American-style discovery under national and international law, suggest some efforts to moderate the application abroad of U.S. procedural techniques, consistent with the overall principle of reasonableness in the exercise of jurisdiction." *Id.,* at 42.

Some discovery procedures are much more "intrusive" than others. In this case, for example, an interrogatory asking petitioners to identify

---

* Comity refers to the spirit of cooperation in which a domestic tribunal approaches the resolution of cases touching the laws and interests of other sovereign states. This Court referred to the doctrine of comity among nations in *Emory v. Grenough,* 3 Dall. 369, 370, n., 1 L.Ed. 640 (1797) (dismissing appeal from judgment for failure to plead diversity of citizenship, but setting forth an extract from a treatise by Ulrich Huber (1636–1694), a Dutch jurist) * * *. [Footnote in original].

** The French "blocking statute," n. 6, *supra,* does not alter our conclusion. It is well settled that such statutes do not deprive an American court of the power to order a party subject to its jurisdiction to produce evidence even though the act of production may violate that statute. See *Societe Internationale Pour Participations Industrielles et Commerciales, S.A. v. Rogers,* 357 U.S. 197, 204–206, 78 S.Ct. 1087, 1091–1092, 2 L.Ed.2d 1255 (1958). Nor can the enactment of such a statute by a foreign nation require American courts to engraft a rule of first resort onto the Hague Convention, or otherwise to provide the nationals of such a country with a preferred status in our courts. It is clear that American courts are not required to adhere blindly to the directives of such a statute. Indeed, the language of the statute, if taken literally, would appear to represent an extraordinary exercise of legislative jurisdiction by the Republic of France over a United States district judge, forbidding him or her to order any discovery from a party of French nationality, even simple requests for admissions or interrogatories that the party could respond to on the basis of personal knowledge. It would be particularly incongruous to recognize such a preference for corporations that are wholly owned by the enacting nation. Extraterritorial assertions of jurisdiction are not one-sided. While the District Court's discovery orders arguably have some impact in France, the French blocking statute asserts similar authority over acts to take place in this country. The lesson of comity is that neither the discovery order nor the blocking statute can have the same omnipresent effect that it would have in a world of only one sovereign. The blocking statute thus is relevant to the court's particularized comity analysis only to the extent that its terms and its enforcement identify the nature of the sovereign interests in nondisclosure of specific kinds of material. [Footnote in original].

the pilots who flew flight tests in the Rallye before it was certified for flight by the Federal Aviation Administration, or a request to admit that petitioners authorized certain advertising in a particular magazine, is certainly less intrusive than a request to produce all of the "design specifications, line drawings and engineering plans and all engineering change orders and plans and all drawings concerning the leading edge slats for the Rallye type aircraft manufactured by the Defendants." Even if a court might be persuaded that a particular document request was too burdensome or too "intrusive" to be granted in full, with or without an appropriate protective order, it might well refuse to insist upon the use of Convention procedures before requiring responses to simple interrogatories or requests for admissions. The exact line between reasonableness and unreasonableness in each case must be drawn by the trial court, based on its knowledge of the case and of the claims and interests of the parties and the governments whose statutes and policies they invoke.

American courts, in supervising pretrial proceedings, should exercise special vigilance to protect foreign litigants from the danger that unnecessary, or unduly burdensome, discovery may place them in a disadvantageous position. Judicial supervision of discovery should always seek to minimize its costs and inconvenience and to prevent improper uses of discovery requests. When it is necessary to seek evidence abroad, however, the district court must supervise pretrial proceedings particularly closely to prevent discovery abuses. For example, the additional cost of transportation of documents or witnesses to or from foreign locations may increase the danger that discovery may be sought for the improper purpose of motivating settlement, rather than finding relevant and probative evidence. Objections to "abusive" discovery that foreign litigants advance should therefore receive the most careful consideration. In addition, we have long recognized the demands of comity in suits involving foreign states, either as parties or as sovereigns with a coordinate interest in the litigation. See *Hilton v. Guyot,* 159 U.S. 113, 16 S.Ct. 139, 40 L.Ed. 95 (1895). American courts should therefore take care to demonstrate due respect for any special problem confronted by the foreign litigant on account of its nationality or the location of its operations, and for any sovereign interest expressed by a foreign state. We do not articulate specific rules to guide this delicate task of adjudication.

VI

In the case before us, the Magistrate and the Court of Appeals correctly refused to grant the broad protective order that petitioners requested. The Court of Appeals erred, however, in stating that the Evidence Convention does not apply to the pending discovery demands. This holding may be read as indicating that the Convention procedures are not even an option that is open to the District Court. It must be recalled, however, that the Convention's specification of duties in executing states creates corresponding rights in requesting states; holding that the Convention does not apply in this situation would deprive domestic litigants of access to evidence through treaty procedures to which the contracting states have assented. Moreover, such a rule would deny the foreign litigant a full and fair opportunity to demonstrate appropriate reasons for employing Convention procedures in the first instance, for some aspects of the discovery process.

Accordingly, the judgment of the Court of Appeals is vacated, and the case is remanded for further proceedings consistent with this opinion.

It is so ordered.

Justice BLACKMUN, with whom Justice BRENNAN, Justice MARSHALL, and Justice O'CONNOR join, concurring in part and dissenting in part.

Some might well regard the Court's decision in this case as an affront to the nations that have joined the United States in ratifying the Hague Convention on the Taking of Evidence Abroad in Civil or Commercial Matters ... The Court ignores the importance of the Convention by relegating it to an "optional" status, without acknowledging the significant achievement in accommodating divergent interests that the Convention represents. Experience to date indicates that there is a large risk that the case-by-case comity analysis now to be permitted by the Court will be performed inadequately and that the somewhat unfamiliar procedures of the Convention will be invoked infrequently. I fear the Court's decision means that courts will resort unnecessarily to issuing discovery orders under the Federal Rules of Civil Procedure in a raw exercise of their jurisdictional power to the detriment of the United States' national and international interests. The Court's view of this country's international obligations is particularly unfortunate in a world in which regular commercial and legal channels loom ever more crucial.

* * *

Notes

1. What does the preceding case tell us about the prospects for procedural harmonization through international agreement?

2. The Supreme Court of the United States also took a restrictive approach to the Hague Convention on the Service Abroad of Judicial and Extrajudicial Documents in Civil or Commercial Matters, which prescribes a method for serving a summons or other paper on a party in another nation. See Volkswagenwerk Aktiengesellschaft v. Schlunk, 486 U.S. 694 (1988). In that case the Court held that the Service Convention did not apply to an action against Volkswagenwerk Aktiengesellschaft (VWAG), a German corporation sued in a products liability action in an Illinois court. Under Illinois law, it was acceptable to serve VWAG by delivering the summons to its wholly owned subsidiary, Volkswagen of America, Inc (VWoA). The latter had appointed an agent for the service of process in Illinois. VWAG argued that since VWoA would be required to transmit the summons to its parent in Germany, this constituted "service abroad." Thus, it argued the Convention

applied and required service in Germany in accordance with the method it prescribed. Said the Supreme Court:

> We reject this argument. Where service on a domestic agent is valid and complete under both state law and the Due Process Clause, our inquiry ends and the Convention has no further implications. Whatever internal, private communications take place between the agent and a foreign principal are beyond the concerns of this case. The only transmittal to which the Convention applies is a transmittal abroad that is required as a necessary part of service. And, contrary to VWAG's assertion, the Due Process Clause does not require an official transmittal of documents abroad every time there is service on a foreign national. Applying this analysis, we conclude that this case does not present an occasion to transmit a judicial document for service abroad within the meaning of Article 1. Therefore the Hague Service Convention does not apply, and service was proper.[7]

3. Apparently successful harmonization of the bases on which jurisdiction can be exercised has been effected within the European Community by the Brussels Convention on Jurisdiction and the Recognition and Enforcement of Judgments, ratified in 1973. Its terms were later incorporated into the European Council Regulation on Jurisdiction and the Recognition and Enforcement of Judgments in Civil and Commercial Matters, EC No. 44/2001. It has proven more difficult—indeed, impossible so far—to draft a similar treaty that would effect rules of jurisdiction and enforcement acceptable to the United States and its major trading partners. *See* Chapter 11, Transnational Litigation.

IV. CURRENT TRENDS

Nicolò Trocker and Vincenzo Varano, Concluding Remarks, The Reforms of Civil Procedure in Comparative Perspective 243, 244–263 (Nicolò Trocker and Vincenzo Varano, eds., 2005).

[Note: In the following excerpt the authors comment on a series of papers that were initially presented at a conference held in Florence, Italy in 2003 and later published in the book edited by Professors Trocker and Varano in which their remarks appear.]

What are the lessons which can be derived from the worldwide reform movement as described and discussed in this impressive array of national reports? It is the purpose of these notes to try and catch the most important among them in a comparative perspective.

THE CONVERGENCE OF PROCEDURAL SYSTEMS

The first point which comes out from the reports is that the reform movement has brought about an attenuation of the differences, accord-

---

7. Volkswagenwerk Aktiengesellschaft v. Schlunk, 486 U.S. 694, 707–708.

ing to which we were used to classify procedural models. If the common law procedural systems were usually defined as adversarial, based as they were on the predominance of the parties, they are presently placing more and more emphasis on the role and powers of the judge especially as far as the management of procedure is concerned. Adrian Zuckerman has been very clear in underlining that "the modern trend of Anglo–American systems is to adopt judicial control of litigation as the principal instrument for accommodating rule enforcement with the objective of doing justice on the merits". But the role and responsibility of the judge has gone as far as to control also the mode of proceeding to be followed depending on the peculiarities of the dispute, and the taking of evidence. Civil law procedural systems, in turn, which used to be labeled as inquisitorial in an even more arbitrary and simplistic way, not only have made clear their adherence to the principles of parties' initiative, and adversary procedure, but they have also reshaped their character, sometimes adopting institutions typical of the common law such as the cross-examination, other times opening the door to such ideas as that embodied in the mechanisms of discovery, or moving towards a bifurcation of the proceeding clearly based on the pretrial/trial separation experience. All this has been made possible through a sort of dialogue among legislators more and more aware of the need to look at each other, to look at what is happening elsewhere in order to see if it is possible to answer the problems of their societies using critically what is being experimented by other legislators, without necessarily resorting to passive reception or imitation.

Having this dialogue in mind, Frédérique Ferrand has rightly warned us that "the distinction between adversary and inquisitorial should be avoided". Just like any other abstract distinction, it must be avoided because it is useless as an instrument of analysis, and is not suited to understand meaningful aspects of the various procedural systems. The French as well as other procedural systems are rather the result of a compromise between an adversary and an inquisitorial system requiring an efficient cooperation between parties and judge. This is the reason why some scholars define civil proceedings as a "chose des parties et chose du juge".

The second lesson which we can draw from the comparison of different procedural models, is that we should avoid emphasizing categories and notions such as "private" and "public", "liberal" and "authoritarian", when we set to discuss, and find the solutions to, the problems of civil justice. These distinctions are historically dated, they are not representative of deeply felt values, and they do not help us in solving the problems which we have to face, and even less so, in understanding other experiences. Just in order to illustrate this point, we do not think that the English civil procedure reform, strengthening the role of the judge, has moved from a "private" to a "public" model of procedure. We think rather that the reform of 1998 simply reflects the need for a less cumbersome, less theatrical, and less costly model of procedure. ...As to the new role of the judge, it is interesting that the English use expressions such as "case management" and "managerial", which avoid any ideological implication, and belong rather to the business language.

Also the distinction based on the oral or written character of procedure comes out rather blurred from the recent reforms. On the one hand, we note that common law countries, traditionally characterized by a predominantly oral procedure, are moving towards a more written procedure. Suffice here to refer to the new English rules, and some institutions which they fully recognize, such as the pre-action protocols, requiring the parties to engage in meaningful exchange of information in order to see whether the dispute could be solved without proceedings (CPR 26.4 and 31.16), or focus on the issues and the core evidence, or to the exchange of witness statements prior to trial (CPR 32.4). On the other hand, Professor Taniguchi underlines the preponderance of orality in Japanese procedure, and Professor Dìez-Picazo informs us of the striking and apparently successful transformation of Spanish procedure from written to oral in the new code of 2000. * * *

The Main Trends and Policies of the Reform Movement

Let us now turn to the main trends and policies which emerge from the various reports.

The first trend which calls for our attention is quite visible in several reforms. If the goal of civil justice is to guarantee effectively the protection of rights in a reasonable time at a reasonable cost, this goal cannot be pursued through the same model of procedure rigidly conceived as applicable in every case. This goal needs rather flexibility, needs different models of procedure to be adopted depending on the peculiarities of each individual case.

This is the lesson of the recent English reforms which provides for three different "tracks"—the small claim track, the fast track, and the multi track. The choice among them depends on the value and the complexity of the case. In order to prevent, then, that the choice be made in the abstract, the rules require that the judge and the parties meet in a conference at the initial stage of the case, and select the most appropriate track.

Professor Ferrand, in turn, informs us (see esp. nos. 13–19) that a similar path has been followed also by the French NCPC, providing for a short track (*circuit court*), a middle track (*circuit moyen*), and a long track (*circuit long*) depending, once again, on the complexity of the case. It is the president of the Division of the court, at an early meeting with the parties' lawyers, who discusses with them the state of the case, the necessities of the preparation of the case, and consequently the track which should be selected.

* * *

When we turn to the German system, we also realize that the idea of a flexible procedural model has been followed since the reform of 1977, adaptable to the peculiarities of individual controversies. Following

§ 272 of the ZPO, the Court can shape the unfolding of the proceeding since the very beginning, and order that the main hearing, where the case is normally decided, be preceded by the setting of an early first hearing (§ 275)—when the initial review of the claim leads the court to believe that an early meeting of the parties and lawyers might likely lead to a rapid disposition of the case—or by the written preparatory procedure (§ 276) which requires the parties to file and exchange written briefs to set forth contentions, clarify issues respond to contentions of the opposing party or to hints from the court. * * *

The same goal of increasing flexibility has been pursued also by the Austrian reformer of 2002, who has eliminated the so called *erste Tagsatzung*, i.e. the first hearing rigidly and exclusively devoted to the decision of preliminary procedural questions and strengthened the role of the "preparatory hearing" (*vorbereitendeTagsatzung*) where the judge will discuss with the parties the factual and legal aspects of the case and determine together with them the procedural program (*Prozessprogramm*) to be followed.

In contrast with this trend, the Italian reform of 1990–1995 seems to have opted for rigidity, providing for a series of predetermined hearings for every type of controversy (see arts. 180, 183, 184, 189 of the Code of civil procedure), the consequences of which are undeniably disastrous in terms of delay and costs.

* * *

Reality, however, is made of lights, but also of shadows as the English experience with the new CPR is there to demonstrate.

Adrian Zuckerman explains very clearly in his Report the difficulties and the problems met by the English system, traditionally dominated by a desire to give priority to justice on the merits, and now moving towards a new "multi dimensional" strategy seeking to deliver substantive justice but only by the use of no more than proportionate resources and within a reasonable time. On the one hand, there are "cultural" difficulties, such as the hesitation of judges to use their case management powers, and above all to sanction party failure to comply with process requirements–nothing to be surprised of, if we consider how deeply the English reform has affected the previous approach and spirit of civil justice. On the other hand, there are technical difficulties such as those caused by the lack of clear guidelines for the exercise of judicial discretion, which is essential to the idea of case management. A further difficulty comes from the rigid and formalistic interpretation of art. 6 ECHR, which has become part of English law through the Human Rights Act 1998. Some English courts seem in fact to think that sanctioning the parties for non-compliance may amount to a denial of the right to a fair trial, notwithstanding that the Strasbourg Court has always made clear that the abuse or the improper use of procedural guarantees—such as obstructive behaviors and the dilatory use of procedural rights—cannot be protected by the Court in the name of procedural fairness.

THE TREND TOWARDS A BIFURCATED PROCEDURE

Professor Taniguchi, in his excellent report, tells us that "[T]he trend of reform of civil procedure in Japan, both in law and in practice, seems to show a direction toward a bifurcation of pre-trial and trial stages typical to the common law procedure. It must be reminded, however, that it is not because of an absolute necessity as in the common law system which was originally based, and still based largely in the United States, on the tradition of the jury trial". In other words, the trend towards a two stage procedural model directed respectively to the preparation (and possibly the anticipated solution) of the case, and the proof taking and decision, meets a demand for the rationalization of litigation. * * *

It is not surprising, therefore, that other procedural systems have adopted a bifurcated model of procedure. Professor Walter, in his Report, tells us, for instance, that following a series of reforms, the German procedural system has become structurally very similar to the Anglo-American pre-trial/trial bifurcated system, with the activities of the main hearing concentrated into a single event in order to assure immediacy to the proof taking stage, and increase the use of orality. Professor Diez-Picazo, in turn, indicates in his report that also the new *Ley de Enjuiciamento Civil* in force since the beginning of the year 2000, has adopted the two stage model, characterized by a strong emphasis placed on orality, concentration and immediacy. This does not mean that the Spanish legislator has abandoned the civil law area; it does mean, however, that the Spanish procedural system does not have very much in common any longer with other civil law procedural systems such as the Italian system, where lawsuits are determined in a sequence of many relatively minor formal hearings and conferences.

THE PREPARATORY STAGE AND THE ACTIVE ROLE OF THE JUDGE

The preparatory stage is an extremely delicate moment for a procedure which aims at pursuing an adequate level of efficiency without disregarding the procedural guarantees of the parties.

It is not by chance that the debate on the introductory stage is often very lively both in the civil law and the common law legal culture, particularly on one aspect, that pertaining to the role and the powers to be attributed to the parties and the judge. Concepts such as that of "discovery" and that of the "*Aufklärungspflicht*" (the duty of clarification) of the judge have been representative for a long time of the different approach to the introductory stage, and in the end of the fundamental contrast between the civil law and the common law procedural models and their philosophies. According to this characterization, the pretrial stage of the common law procedural model, and in particular the US model, is fully party dominated, with the judge performing an essentially passive role, while the introductory stage of the civil law model, and in particular the German and the Austrian systems, is dominated by the judge, who has a positive responsibility to structure the proceedings and a well defined duty to promote clarification of the issues.

The recent evolution of the common law model, and its consequent moving away from the original conception of the pretrial stage, and in particular the discovery phase, as being completely in the hands of the parties and their lawyers, has modified deeply the structure of the preparatory stage of the procedure by entrusting the judge with significant powers of supervision and initiative. Therefore, we can say that almost everywhere, and not only in continental Europe, the concern over adversarial excesses has led to the demand for an active role to be played by the judge in the preparatory stage, whose function is to effectively and quickly reach to the heart of the litigation through a timely clarification of those issues which are really at stake.

Contrary to this common trend, proposals which are presently being discussed in Italy, though providing for a sharper separation between the preparatory and the proof taking and decision stage, vest the main responsibility of managing the preparatory stage exclusively in the parties and their lawyers, with no interference by the judge until one of the parties considers the case ready for the hearing before her.

* * *

The diffusion of forms of discovery

The European codes of the 19th century strictly adhered to the principle *nemo tenetur edere contra se,* i.e., the principle that no party has to help her opponent in her inquiry into the facts, and did not provide for instruments capable of eliciting from the parties all of the preconstituted items of evidence which might be necessary for the decision of the case. More recently, however, the idea gained ground, gradually and not without difficulty, that if procedure aims at getting as close as possible to the truth concerning the litigated issues, it must rely on techniques through which each party can have access to items of evidence not in her possession.

In France, art. 10 of the Code Civil, as amended in 1972, introduces a general duty of procedural discovery, by providing that "each party must bring her contribution to the administration of justice in view of the ascertainment of truth", and that the party who avoids this duty once she has been legally asked to perform it, without any justification, can be forced to fulfill it through the imposition of an *astreinte*, without prejudice of damages. Art. 11 of the *"dispositions liminaires"* of the new code of civil procedure reaffirms the obligation of the parties to contribute to the proof taking stage, and specifies that it shall be sanctioned, as far as the disclosure of documents is concerned, through the power of the judge to order the payment of an *astreinte*.

The French lead has been followed by the German *Zivilprozessnovelle* of 2002, which has introduced the power of the judge to order parties or third parties to disclose documents in their possession, on the simple basis that they may be useful to the ascertainment of the facts of the case. Commentators do not hesitate to define the new wording of §§ 142 and 144 of the ZPO as one of the most meaningful innovations of the recent reform. Professor Walter writes in his Report that "these newly established obligations to producing documents can—with regard to the German tradition of procedural law—be called close to revolutionary", and underlines their analogies to the pretrial discovery of documents of the (Anglo) American procedural tradition, warning however that the so called fishing expeditions continue to be forbidden in German law.

Also the Dutch Code, following the Procedural Law Reform Act of 2002, has introduced a technique designed to assure the acquisition of documents which the parties cannot produce without the collaboration of the opponents or third parties in their possession (art. 22). If a party does not comply, the judge can draw the conclusions she considers appropriate. The Dutch Reporters add that the reform has also introduced a "decidedly revolutionary * * * general article in which it is stipulated that parties and their representatives are obliged to 'fully and truthfully' supply facts that are relevant for the judge's decision. Here too the sanction: if the stipulation is not met, the judge can draw conclusions he considers appropriate".

The Spanish solution, adopted by the new *Ley de Enjuiciamento Civil*, provides that each party, without resorting to the judge, can ask from the opponent, pending the case, the disclosure of documents in her possession. It is interesting and somewhat original, though it may raise doubts about its effectiveness, since the disclosure procedure is not supported by any sanction for the case of non compliance.

All the instruments we have just talked about, introduced by recent European procedural reforms, have a common character, that of being part of the proof taking stage. In other words, they are aimed at obtaining information useful to the ascertainment of specific facts which have come to be discussed in the proceeding through the preliminary stage. As we have already indicated, they cannot be used before the "thema probandum" has been specified. However, the need to obtain the necessary information cannot be considered only in view of reaching the final decision of the case. In many cases, it would be extremely useful to have those information also when the problem is to decide whether, and eventually against whom, to bring a suit, or whether, and within which limits, to settle the case.

Interestingly enough, comparative research shows important trends in this direction. This is the case of France, where courts have interpreted art. 145 of the NCPC so as to facilitate the securing of documents from an opponent or third parties before, and independently from litigation on the merits, even beyond the requirement of there being a reason to conserve or establish facts upon which a solution of the dispute may depend. In this way, a party will be able to understand whether to initiate a suit and against whom, and whether it may be to look for an extrajudicial settlement of the dispute. These seem to be strikingly similar goals as those pursued by the American pretrial discovery when it is used in view of clarifying the controversy.

Professor Taniguchi, in turn, informs us in his Report that Japan, after having adopted in 1996 "a new device called 'interparty inquiry', which allows a party to ask for relevant information from the adversary, and expanded the scope of the document production order", has introduced an amendment in 2003 "which enables the parties to collect information and evidence from the prospective adversary or from a third party even before instituting an action". Professor Taniguchi further explains that the reason for this amendment is that "it is sometimes necessary to have sufficient information in order to formulate a complaint", in order, in other words, to better define the scope of the controversy and to better prepare it.

The pre-action protocols introduced in England by the new Rules * * * are also of the utmost interest: as we have already mentioned * * *, they are exchanges of information between the prospective parties taking place before the beginning of the proceeding, so as to see whether on their basis a conciliation might be possible. In Italy too, the recent proposal of the Vaccarella Committee goes in an analogous direction, in that it gives the attorneys the possibility of gathering evidentiary information in view of prospective litigation, by asking public agencies to disclose documents, by hearing witnesses and asking written statements from them, by securing statements of facts from public officials. This is a truly preliminary discovery, the value of which is stronger than the mere acquisition of information. In fact, all the material which has been gathered through it can be used freely in the course of the proceeding and can be freely evaluated by the judge, who is also free to decide whether to order the renewal of the preliminary evidentiary activities. ... In other countries, commentators have underlined the danger that techniques of this kind may end up in "fishing expeditions".

In any case, when we deal with such techniques as discovery, allegedly typical of the common law procedural models, we cannot conclude the comparison by saying that the civil law countries do not have any discovery. Within any system of law or justice one must be careful about comparing individual elements of the system without sufficient consideration of the system as a whole. In fact, and by way of example, in our legal systems there are several important provisions of substantive law which create a "right of information", in the context of specific legal relationships.* Such substantive legal rights can be en-

---

* A good example is section 810 of the German Civil Code (*Burgerliches Gesetzbuch*) which contains a general obligation relating to contractual negotiations. According to § 810:

"Whoever has a legal interest in inspecting a document which is in the possession of another person, may demand from the possessor permission to inspect the document, provided that the document was made for his benefit or a legal relationship is documented between himself and another or the document describes negotiations relating to a transaction between

forced judicially, and are functional to gain factual information from private parties or from the administration in order eventually to start a proceeding. In general, we should also remember that our pleadings are *fact pleadings*, the statement of claim must include the precise indication of the subject matter, the legal foundation of the claim, as well as a specific prayer for relief. This means that most of the work has to be done by the lawyers who have to verify before they file the claim whether there are sufficient facts substantiating the claim. This means also that, if and when the lawyers decide to bring the suit and do file the claim, they do not need as much as their common law, and especially American, counterparts to fish for facts and information.

PROCEDURE AND EXTRAJUDICIAL DISPUTE RESOLUTION

We have just seen that several legal systems resort to forms of preliminary discovery also in order to favor an anticipated or extrajudicial resolution of the controversy.

This observation leads us to underline a more general trend towards alternative methods of dispute resolution. There are several reasons for this phenomenon, and they vary from one legal system to the other. However, the most important of them is that the state machinery of civil justice is unable to meet a growing "demand of justice" coming from various people on a variety of often new matters, since formal court proceedings prove often to be inefficient, expensive, uncertain as to their results, and possibly also unsuited to guarantee a satisfactory solution of certain categories of legal disputes.

Professor Epstein's report, for instance, demonstrates how the common law systems pursue the goal of an anticipated or extrajudicial settlement with the greatest coherence and decision.

* * *

If one turns to the civil law tradition, a different cultural perspective prevails, due to the emphasis that those procedural systems traditionally place on the decision by the judge as the normal way of disposing of the controversies. The right to sue is seen as the right to a judge and a decision by the judge. This background explains the uncertainties and ambiguities of European legislators when dealing with ADR issues, and the consequent lack of a coherent policy in this respect. What they tend to do is to require in certain kinds of disputes (for example, labor and

him and another or between either of them and someone who is negotiating between them."

This provision has been held to create a substantive legal obligation to produce, for example, letters, receipts, and insurance policies. See also the decision of the German Federal Court (BGH) of June 4, 1992, in 32 *International Legal Materials* 1327 (1993). In a case of recognition and enforcement of a California judgment awarding punitive damages, the Court argued, among other things, that summoning the defendant to a "pre-trial discovery" does not violate ordre public as defined by § 328 ZPO, and does not preclude an enforcement order. In fact, "[I]t is not just the principles of German procedural law which must be considered . . .; the legal system as a whole, including the duties of disclosure under German substantive law, which could supersede foreign procedural regulations which have a comparable effect, also has to be taken into account". [Footnote in original].

social welfare disputes) participation in a conciliation procedure as a precondition to filing suit or to charge the judge with conciliatory duties. This is the case of Italy, but it is true of other countries as well. Professor Walter, for instance, with regard to Germany, reminds us that a 1999 statute had authorized individual *Länder* to introduce mandatory non judicial conciliation proceedings for small claims before filing a suit, thereby indicating a strong preference for regional solutions, which have the advantage of being close and adequate to local needs. The civil procedure reform of 2002 reemphasizes the role of the judge in case settlements during litigation by establishing that if there has not been a prior formal attempt to reach a settlement before an out of court conciliation board, the court itself has to carry out a settlement hearing unless such a hearing appears to be without prospect of success (§ 278 ZPO). The same perspective has been raised to the level of a general principle of procedure by art. 21 of the French NCPC which states that "entre dans la mission du juge de concilier les parties".

Despite this sort of legislative favor, reality suggests to move beyond the faith in judicial conciliation. On the one hand, in order to perform successfully a conciliatory activity, time, patience and a positive attitude are needed. The task is obviously very difficult for courts which are overloaded and overcrowded. On the other hand, the idea of a conciliation conducted by the judge places the latter in a somewhat ambiguous position, which may induce mistrust and cause the resistance of the parties.

* * *

In our view, experiments with various forms of ADR techniques modeled after the peculiar features and the nature of the cases to be solved, and organized, also from a cultural point of view, in such a way as to allow them to operate fairly and effectively, are to be supported. Judges, on the other hand, should be relieved from the burden of conciliating or mediating between the parties and devote their energies and work to their institutional role of implementation of rights and remedies through adjudication.

Index

References are to Pages

†